THE
TWENTIETH CENTURY
NEW TESTAMENT

A TRANSLATION INTO

MODERN ENGLISH

Made from the Original Greek

(Westcott & Hort's Text)

REVISED EDITION

LONDON

Horace Marshall & Son

AMERICA

The Fleming H. Revell Company

NEW YORK & CHICAGO

1904

PREFACE.

A Translation into Modern English. ENGLISH-SPEAKING people of to-day have not, until quite recently, had the opportunity of reading the Bible in the English of their own time. Though in the course of the last hundred years the Bible has been translated into the vernacular of most countries, the language of our Bible remains the English of three hundred years ago.

This translation of the New Testament is an endeavour to do for the English nation what has been done already for the people of almost all other countries—to enable Englishmen to read the most important part of their Bible in that form of their own language which they themselves use. It had its origin in the recognition of the fact that the English of the Authorized Version (closely followed in that of the Revised Version), though widely valued for its antique charm, is in many passages difficult, or even quite unintelligible to the modern reader. The retention, too, of a form of English no longer in common use is liable to give the impression that the contents of the Bible have little to do with the life of to-day. The Greek used by the New Testament writers was not the Classical Greek of some centuries earlier, but the form of the language spoken in their own day. Moreover the writers represent those whose utterances they record as using the words and phrases of every-day life.

We believe that the New Testament will be better understood by modern readers if presented in a modern form ; and that a translation of it, which presents the original in an exalted literary and antiquated dress, cannot, despite its ' aroma ' and the tender memories that have gathered around it, really make the New Testament for the reader of to-day the living reality that it was to its first readers. In this respect the present translation differs altogether in its aim from that of the Revised Version of 1881. No attempt is made in that Version to translate the original into the language of our own time. Its authors state in their preface :

"We have faithfully adhered to the rule that the alterations to be introduced should be expressed, as far as possible, in the language of the Authorized Version, or of the Versions that preceded it."

Our constant effort, on the contrary, has been to exclude all words and phrases not used in current English. We have, however, followed the modern practice of using an older phraseology in the rendering of poetical passages, and of quotations from the Old Testament, and in the language of prayer.

Neither a Revision nor a Paraphrase. The translation of 1611, known as the "Authorized Version," was the outcome of many successive revisions of the translation completed by Tyndale in 1534, which was, at least to some extent, founded on that completed by Wycliffe about 1380. Further, the last named translation was not made from the original Greek, but from the Latin Version, known as the Vulgate. The present translation is not a revision of any previous one, but is made directly from the Greek. Nor is it a paraphrase. A paraphrase might be useful as a help to the interpretation of the New Testament, but it would not be the New Testament itself. Yet, on the other hand, our work is more than a verbal translation. No purely verbal rendering can ever adequately represent the thoughts conveyed in the idioms of another language. In this translation, not only has every word been carefully weighed, but also the emphasis placed upon every word, and the effort has been made to give the exact force and meaning in idiomatic modern English.

The Greek Text. Since the publication of the Authorized Version of 1611, more than 1,500 manuscripts of the whole or of parts of the New Testament have been discovered or have become accessible, and among them are the three oldest and most important. The Greek text here translated, that of Westcott and Hort, is mainly founded on the oldest manuscripts, and may be said to represent that form of the text of the New Testament which was generally in use in the Church at the end of the Third Century.

Parallel Passages. A large amount of time and care has been expended upon those passages of the gospels which record the same, or similar, events or discourses, in order to show the remarkable similarities, and the no less remarkable divergences, which abound in them. Such passages are common in the first three gospels, while in the fourth they are more numerous than is generally supposed. Dr. Westcott writes :

" The English reader has a right to expect that he will find in the Revision which is placed in his hands a faithful indication of the verbal agreement or difference between the several narratives."

In addition to such help as that referred to by Dr. Westcott, the English reader should now be able, to some extent, to study the origins of the gospels, and to discern their relation to a common source. Great advances have been made in the study of this subject since the issue of the Authorized and even of the Revised Version. There are still, however, minute points where such an indication as that required by Dr. Westcott seems impossible.

Quotations and "Borrowed Phrases." The numerous and important quotations from the Old Testament are in this translation set out in modern form; but minor quotations (*i.e.*, those not specially introduced as quotations) from the Old Testament, the Apocrypha, the Book of Enoch, and other sources, are placed between single inverted commas; while, at the foot of the pages, references are given to some of the vast number of places, in which the writers consciously or unconsciously borrow the phraseology of the Old Testament. This will enable the reader to see how familiar the writers were with the very words and phrases of the Septuagint Version of the Old Testament, and how insensibly it influenced them in describing the events of their own day.

Proper Names. The names of persons and places we have, as a rule, left in the forms with which English readers have been made familiar by the Authorized and Revised Versions, except where a change in the spelling seemed likely to show the correct pronunciation.

Measures, Coins, and Titles. We have attempted to give measures of space and time, the values of coins, and also official titles in their nearest English equivalents.

Bracketed Passages. A few passages, numbering fourteen in all, will be found placed between square brackets. These are judged by Westcott and Hort "not to have originally formed part of the work in which they occur," but to be "stray relics from the Apostolic or sub-Apostolic age." The three most important of these will be found at pages 39 and 210.

Order of the Books. The order, in which the Books and Letters of the New Testament appear in this translation, is due to the desire not to inconvenience a reader, familiar with the old order, more than is necessary, but, at the same time, to make an advance in the direction of such a chronological arrangement, as modern research has rendered possible. Three main divisions have been adopted suggested by the character of the books—Historical Books, Letters, and an Apocalypse; and, in the sub-divisions, the Letters have been grouped under the names of those writers to whom they have been traditionally attributed. Within these sub-divisions the Books and Letters stand in a probable chronological arrangement.

It is certain that our translation will not be acceptable to those who regard any attempt to re-translate the New Testament as undesirable, if not dangerous. It is, nevertheless, hoped that, by this modern translation, the New Testament may become a living reality to many by whom the Authorized Version, with all its acknowledged beauties, is but imperfectly understood or never read.

In this hope, we now commend this translation, which has been undertaken as a labour of love, to the good-will of all English-speaking people, and to the blessing of Almighty God.

THE TRANSLATORS.

September, 1904.

NOTE.

The 'Tentative Edition' of this Translation was issued in three parts between 1898 and 1901. In that Edition we endeavoured to discover what was practicable in a modern translation of the New Testament, before issuing a permanent edition. This Revision of our Translation, rendered necessary by the large demand for our 'Tentative Edition' in every part of the English-speaking world, amounts practically to a careful re-translation made in the light of experience derived from our previous attempts, and of the many valuable criticisms that have been received.

THE ORDER

OF THE

BOOKS AND LETTERS

AS ARRANGED IN THIS TRANSLATION.

CONTENTS.

A.—THE HISTORICAL BOOKS.

I.—THE GOSPELS.

(1). THE SYNOPTICAL GOSPELS.

(a). ACCORDING TO MARK.

A*

ACCORDING TO MARK—*Cont.*

ACCORDING TO MARK—*Cont.*

(b). ACCORDING TO MATTHEW.

xii.   CONTENTS.

ACCORDING TO MATTHEW—*Cont.*

THE WORK IN GALILEE—*Cont.*

ACCORDING TO MATTHEW—*Cont.*

ACCORDING TO MATTHEW—*Cont.*

(c). ACCORDING TO LUKE.

ACCORDING TO LUKE—*Cont.*

ACCORDING TO LUKE—*Cont.*

THE JOURNEY TO JERUSALEM—*Cont.*

(2). A LATER GOSPEL.

ACCORDING TO JOHN.

ACCORDING TO JOHN—*Cont.*

ACCORDING TO JOHN—*Cont.*

II.—THE ACTS OF THE APOSTLES.

ACTS OF APOSTLES.

ACTS OF APOSTLES—*Cont.*

B.—THE LETTERS.

(b). TO THE CORINTHIANS.—I.

(c). TO THE CORINTHIANS.—II.

TO THE CORINTHIANS.—II.—*Cont.*

(*d*). TO THE ROMANS.

(d). TO THE PHILIPPIANS.

(4). A LATE GROUP OF PASTORAL LETTERS.
(a). TO TIMOTHY.—I.

TO HEBREWS—*Cont.*

IV.—THE LETTERS ATTRIBUTED TO ST. PETER.

(*a*). FROM PETER.—I.

THE HISTORICAL BOOKS.

THE GOOD NEWS—
        ACCORDING TO MARK.
        ACCORDING TO MATTHEW.
        ACCORDING TO LUKE.
        ACCORDING TO JOHN.
THE ACTS OF THE APOSTLES.

ACCORDING TO MARK.

'THE GOSPEL ACCORDING TO ST. MARK'.

COMPILED AT AN UNCERTAIN DATE LATER THAN 55 A.D.

THIS gospel contains "the earliest and the simplest picture of the ministry of Jesus," but tells nothing of his birth or early life. It appears to be the work of the John Mark who is mentioned more than once in the New Testament, and to have been compiled from information gathered from the Apostle Peter (whose convert Mark is supposed to have been), as well as from other sources, both written and oral. Of these sources it is plain that the compilers of 'The Gospels according to St. Matthew and St. Luke' also availed themselves, as well as, in all probability, of a draft of this gospel. It is evident from the writer's habit of translating Aramaic words, and using Latin expressions, that his Life of Jesus was intended for readers of the Western World ; a view confirmed by many interesting traditions of the Western Church. From the absence of much of the Teaching of Jesus given in 'The Gospels according to St. Matthew and St. Luke,' it has been inferred that this was not available in a connected form for the compiler of the present gospel.

ACCORDING TO MARK.

The beginning of the Good News about Jesus Christ.   I **1**

I.--THE PREPARATION.

The Baptist and his Message.

It is said in the Prophet Isaiah—   2
' Behold ! I send my Messenger before thy face ;
He shall prepare thy way.'
          ' The voice of one crying aloud in the Wilderness :   3
   " Make ready the way of the Lord,
   Make his paths straight." '

And in fulfilment of this, John the Baptizer appeared in the   4
Wilderness, proclaiming a baptism upon repentance, for the
forgiveness of sins.   The whole of Judaea, as well as all the   5
inhabitants of Jerusalem, went out to him ; and they were
baptized by him in the river Jordan, confessing their sins.
John was clad in clothing of camels' hair, with a belt of leather   6
round his waist, and lived on locusts and wild honey ; and he   7
proclaimed—
   " There is coming after me one more powerful than I, and
I am not fit even to stoop down and unfasten his sandals.   I   8
have baptized you with water, but he will baptize you with
the Holy Spirit."

The Baptism of Jesus.

Now about that time Jesus came from Naza-   9
reth in Galilee, and was baptized by John in the
Jordan.   And just as he was coming up out of   10
the water, he saw the heavens rent apart, and the Spirit, like
a dove, descending upon him, and from the heavens came   11
a voice—
   " Thou art my Son, the Beloved ; in thee I delight."

The Temptation of Jesus.

Immediately afterwards the Spirit drove Jesus   12
out into the Wilderness ; and he was there in the   13
Wilderness forty days, tempted by Satan, and
among the wild beasts, while the angels ministered to him.

[1]Ps. 2. 2.   2-3 Mal. 3. 1 ; Isa. 40. 3.   [6] 2 Kings 1. 8.   [7] Ps. 118. 26.   [11] Ps. 2. 7 ;
Isa. 42. 1.

II.—The Work in Galilee.

Jesus begins his Work.   After John had been committed to prison, Jesus 14
went to Galilee, proclaiming the Good News of
God—

"The time has come, and the Kingdom of God is at hand; 15
repent, and believe the Good News."

The first Disciples.   As Jesus was going along the shore of the 16
Sea of Galilee, he saw Simon and his brother
Andrew casting a net in the Sea, for they were fishermen.

"Come and follow me," Jesus said, "and I will set you to 17
fish for men."

They left their nets at once, and followed him.   Going 18, 19
on a little further, he saw James, Zebediah's son, and his
brother John, who also were in their boat mending the nets.
Jesus at once called them, and they left their father Zebediah 20
in the boat with the crew, and went after him.

Cure of a possessed Man.   And they walked into Capernaum.   On 21
the next Sabbath Jesus went into the Synagogue
and began to teach. The people were amazed 22
at his teaching, for he taught them like one who had authority,
and not like the Teachers of the Law. Now there was in their 23
Synagogue at the time a man under the power of a foul
spirit, who called out:

"What do you want with us, Jesus of Nazareth? Have 24
you come to destroy us? I know who you are—the Holy
One of God!"

But Jesus rebuked the spirit: 25

"Be silent! come out from him."

The foul spirit threw the man into a fit, and with a loud 26
cry came out from him. And they were all so amazed that 27
they kept asking:

"What is this? Strange teaching indeed! He gives his
commands with authority even to the foul spirits, and they
obey him!"

And the fame of Jesus spread at once in all directions, through 28
the whole neighbourhood of Galilee.

Cure of Peter's Mother-in-law and of many others.   As soon as they had come out from the Syna- 29
gogue, they went, with James and John, into
the house of Simon and Andrew. Now Simon's 30
mother-in-law was lying ill with fever, and they
at once told Jesus about her. Jesus went up to her and, 31
grasping her hand, raised her up; the fever left her, and she
began to wait upon them.

In the evening, after sunset, the people brought to Jesus 32

<hr>

15 Dan. 2. 44.   24 Ps. 16. 10.

all who were ill or possessed by demons ; and the whole city 33
was gathered round the door. Jesus cured many who were 34
ill with various diseases, and drove out many demons, and
would not permit them to speak, because they knew him to
be the Christ.

Jesus retires for Prayer. In the morning, long before daylight, Jesus 35
rose and went out, and, going to a lonely spot,
there began to pray. But Simon and his companions has- 36
tened after him ; and, when they found him, they exclaimed : 37
"Every one is looking for you !"
But Jesus said to them : 38
"Let us go somewhere else, into the country towns near,
that I may make my proclamation in them also ; for that was
why I came."
And he went about making his proclamation in their Syna- 39
gogues all through Galilee, and driving out the demons.

Cure of a Leper. One day a leper came to Jesus and, falling on 40
his knees, begged him for help.
"If only you are willing," he said, "you are able to make
me clean."
Moved with compassion, Jesus stretched out his hand and 41
touched him, saying as he did so :
"I am willing ; become clean."
Instantly the leprosy left the man, and he became clean ; and 42, 43
then Jesus, after sternly warning him, immediately sent him
away, and said to him : 44
"Be careful not to say anything to any one ; but go and
show yourself to the Priest, and make the offerings for your
cleansing directed by Moses, as evidence of your cure."
The man, however, went away, and began to speak about it 45
publicly, and to spread the story so widely, that Jesus could
no longer go openly into a town, but stayed outside in lonely
places ; and people came to him from every direction.

Cure of a paralyzed Man. Some days later, when Jesus came back to 1 **2**
Capernaum, the news spread that he was in a
house there ; and so many people collected 2
together, that after a while there was no room for them even
round the door ; and he began to tell them his Message.
And some people came bringing to him a paralyzed man, who 3
was being carried by four bearers. Being, however, unable 4
to get him near to Jesus, owing to the crowd, they removed
the roofing below which Jesus was ; and, when they had made
an opening, they let down the mat on which the paralyzed man
was lying. When Jesus saw their faith, he said to the man : 5
'Child, your sins are forgiven."

44 Lev. 13. 49.

But some of the Teachers of the Law who were sitting there 6
were debating in their minds :

"Why does this man speak like this? He is blaspheming! 7
Who can forgive sins except God?"

Jesus, at once intuitively aware that they were debating with 8
themselves in this way, said to them :

"Why are you debating in your minds about this? Which 9
is easier?—to say to the paralyzed man 'Your sins are forgiven'? or to say 'Get up, and take up your mat, and walk
about'? But that you may know that the Son of Man has 10
power to forgive sins on earth"—here he said to the paralyzed man—"To you I say, Get up, take up your mat, and 11
return to your home."

The man got up, and immediately took up his mat, and went 12
out before them all ; at which they were amazed, and, as they
praised God, they said :

"We have never seen anything like this!"

Call of Levi. Jesus went out again to the Sea; and 13
all the people came to him, and he taught
them.   As he went along, he saw Levi, the son of 14
Alphaeus, sitting in the tax-office, and said to him : "Follow me."
Levi got up and followed him.

And later on he was in his house at table, and a number of 15
tax-gatherers and outcasts took their places at table with Jesus
and his disciples ; for many of them were following him. When 16
the Teachers of the Law belonging to the party of the Pharisees
saw that he was eating in the company of such people, they
said to his disciples :

"He is eating in the company of tax-gatherers and outcasts!"

Hearing this, Jesus said : 17

"It is not those who are in health that need a doctor, but
those who are ill. I did not come to call the religious, but
the outcast."

The Disciples blamed for not observing the Law. Now John's disciples and the Pharisees were 18
keeping a fast, and people came and asked Jesus :
"Why is it that John's disciples and the
disciples of the Pharisees fast, while yours do
not?"

Jesus answered : 19

"Can the bridegroom's friends fast, while the bridegroom
is with them? As long as they have the bridegroom with
them, they cannot fast. But the days will come, when the 20
bridegroom will be parted from them, and they will fast
then—when that day comes. No man ever sews a piece of 21
unshrunk cloth on an old garment ; if he does, the patch tears
away from it—the new from the old—and a worse rent is

¹⁰ Dan. 7. 13.

made. And no man ever puts new wine into old wine-skins; 22
if he does, the wine will burst the skins, and both the wine and
the skins are lost. But new wine is put into fresh skins."

One Sabbath, as Jesus was walking through the corn- 23
fields, his disciples began to pick the ears of wheat as they
went along.

"Look!" the Pharisees said to him, "why are they doing 24
what is not allowed on the Sabbath?"

"Have you never read," answered Jesus, "what David did 25
when he was in want and hungry, he and his companions—
how he went into the House of God, in the time of Abiathar 26
the High Priest, and ate 'the consecrated bread,' which only
the priests are allowed to eat, and gave some to his comrades
as well?"

Then Jesus added: 27

"The Sabbath was made for man, and not man for the
Sabbath; so the Son of Man is lord even of the Sabbath." 28

On another occasion Jesus went into a Syna- 1 **3**
Cure of gogue, where there was a man whose hand was
a Man with withered. And they watched Jesus closely, to 2
a withered see if he would cure the man on the Sabbath, so
Hand.
that they might have a charge to bring against him.

"Stand out in the middle," Jesus said to the man with 3
the withered hand; and to the people he said: 4

"Is it allowable to do good on the Sabbath—or harm? to
save a life, or destroy it?"

As they remained silent, Jesus looked round at them in anger, 5
grieving at the hardness of their hearts, and said to the man:
"Stretch out your hand."

The man stretched it out; and his hand had become
sound. Immediately on leaving the Synagogue, the 6
Pharisees and the Herodians united in laying a plot against
Jesus, to put him to death.

Cures by Then Jesus went away with his disciples to 7
the the Sea, followed by a great number of people
Lake-side. from Galilee. And a great number, hearing of
all that he was doing, came to him from Judaea, from 8
Jerusalem, from Edom, from beyond the Jordan, and from
the country round Tyre and Sidon. So Jesus told his dis- 9
ciples to keep a small boat close by, for fear the crowd should
crush him. For he had cured many of them, and so people 10
kept crowding upon him, that all who were afflicted might
touch him. The foul spirits, too, whenever they caught sight 11
of him, flung themselves down before him, and screamed out:
"You are the Son of God"!

But he repeatedly warned them not to make him known. 12

[26] 1 Sam. 21. 6.   [11] Ps. 2. 7.

The twelve Apostles. And Jesus made his way up the hill, and called 13 those whom he wished; and they went to him. And he appointed twelve—whom he also named 'Apostles'— 14 that they might be with him, and that he might send them out as his Messengers, to preach, and with power to drive 15 out demons. So he appointed the Twelve—Peter (which was 16 the name that Jesus gave to Simon), James, the son of Zebediah, 17 and his brother John (to whom he gave the name of Boanerges, which means the Thunderers), Andrew, Philip, Bartholomew, 18 Matthew, Thomas, James the son of Alphaeus, Thaddaeus, Simon the Zealot, and Judas Iscariot, the man that betrayed 19 him.

Jesus and his Relations. Jesus went into a house; and again a crowd 20 collected, so that they were not able even to eat their food. When his relations heard of it, they 21 went to take charge of him, for they said that he was out of his mind. And the Teachers of the Law, who 22 **Jesus accused of Acting** had come down from Jerusalem, said:
by the Help of Satan. "He has Baal-zebub in him, and he drives the demons out by the help of Baal-zebub, their chief."

So Jesus called them to him, and answered them in parables: 23 "How can Satan drive out Satan? When a kingdom is 24 divided against itself, it cannot last; and when a household is 25 divided against itself, it will not be able to last. So, if Satan 26 is in revolt against himself and is divided, he cannot last— his end has come! No man who has got into a strong man's 27 house can carry off his goods, without first securing him; and not till then will he plunder his house. I tell you that 28 men will be forgiven everything—their sins, and all the slanders that they utter; but whoever slanders the Holy Spirit remains 29 unforgiven to the end; he has to answer for an enduring sin." This was said in reply to the charge that he had a foul spirit 30 in him.

The true Brotherhood. And his mother and his brothers came, and 31 stood outside, and sent to ask him to come to them. There was a crowd sitting round Jesus, and some of 32 them said to him:
"Look, your mother and your brothers are outside, asking for you."
"Who is my mother? and my brothers?" was his reply. 33 Then he looked around on the people sitting in a circle round 34 him, and said:
"Here are my mother and my brothers! Whoever does 35 the will of God is my brother and sister and mother."

Parable of the Sower. Jesus again began to teach by the Sea; and, 1 **4** as an immense crowd was gathering round him, he got into a boat, and sat in it on the Sea, while all

the people were on the shore at the water's edge. Then 2
he taught them many truths in parables ; and in the course
of his teaching he said to them :

" Listen ! The sower went out to sow ; and presently, as he 3, 4
was sowing, some of the seed fell along the path ; and the
birds came, and ate it up.   Some fell on rocky ground, where 5
it had not much soil, and, having no depth of soil, sprang up
at once ; but, when the sun rose, it was scorched, and, having no 6
root, withered away.   Some of the seed fell among brambles ; 7
but the brambles shot up and completely choked it, and it
yielded no return.   Some fell into good soil, and, shooting up 8
and growing, yielded a return, amounting to thirty, sixty, and
even a hundred fold."

And Jesus said : 9
" Let any one who has ears to hear with hear.

Afterwards, when he was alone, his followers and the 10
Twelve asked him about his parables ; and he said : 11
" To you the hidden truth of the Kingdom of God has been
imparted ; but to those who are outside it all teaching takes
the form of parables, that—

' Though they have eyes, they may see without perceiving ; 12
And though they have ears, they may hear without understanding;
Lest some day they should turn and be forgiven.'

You do not know the meaning of this parable !" he went 13
on ; "then how will you understand all the other parables?   The sower sows the Message. The people meant 14, 15
by the seed that falls along the path are these—where the Message
is sown, but, as soon as they have heard it, Satan immediately
comes and carries away the Message that has been sown in
them. So, too, those meant by the seed sown on the rocky 16
places are the people who, when they have heard the Message, at once accept it joyfully ; but, as they have no root, they 17
stand only for a short time ; and so, when trouble or persecution arises on account of the Message, they fall away at once.
Those meant by the seed sown among the brambles are 18
different ; they are the people who hear the Message, but 19
the cares of life, and the glamour of wealth, and cravings
for many other things come in and completely choke the
Message, so that it gives no return. But the people meant 20
by the seed sown on the good ground are those who hear
the Message, and welcome it, and yield a return, thirty,
sixty, and even a hundred fold."

Lesson from   And Jesus said to them : 21
a Lamp.   " Is a lamp brought to be put under the corn-
measure or under the couch, instead of being put on the lamp-
stand ? Nothing is hidden unless it is some day to come to 22
light, nor was anything ever kept hidden but that it should

some day come into the light of day.   Let all who have   23
ears to hear with hear.   Take care what you listen to," said   24
Jesus. "The measure you mete will be meted out to you, and
more will be added for you. For, to those who have, more will   25
be given ; while, from those who have nothing, even what they
have will be taken away."

Parable of the   Jesus also said :   26
Seed growing   "This is what the Kingdom of God is like—
unobserved. like a man who has scattered seed on the ground,
and then sleeps by night and rises by day, while the seed is   27
shooting up and growing—he knows not how. The ground   28
bears the crop of itself—first the blade, then the ear, and then
the full grain in the ear ; but, as soon as the crop is ready,   29
immediately he ' puts in the sickle because harvest has come.' "

Parable   Jesus also said :   30
of the   " To what can we liken the Kingdom of God ?   31
Mustard Seed. or by what can we illustrate it ?   Perhaps by
the growth of a mustard-seed.   This seed, when sown in the
ground, though it is smaller than all other seeds, yet, when   32
sown, shoots up, and becomes larger than any other herb, and
puts out great branches, so that even ' the wild birds can roost
in its shelter.' "

With many such parables Jesus used to speak to the people   33
of his Message, as far as they were able to receive it ; and to   34
them he never used to speak except in parables ; but in
private to his own disciples he explained everything.

Jesus stills   In the evening of the same day, Jesus said to   35
a Storm.   them :
" Let us go across."
So, leaving the crowd behind, they took him with them, just   36
as he was, in the boat ; and there were other boats with him.
A violent squall came on, and the waves kept dashing into the   37
boat, so that the boat was actually filling. Jesus was in the   38
stern asleep upon the cushion; and the disciples roused him
and cried :
" Teacher ! is it nothing to you that we are lost ? "
Jesus rose and rebuked the wind, and said to the sea :   39
" Hush ! Be still ! "
Then the wind dropped, and a great calm followed.
" Why are you so timid ? " he exclaimed.   " Have you   40
no faith yet ? "
But they were struck with great awe, and said to one another :   41
" Who can this be that even the wind and the sea obey
him ? "

Cure of a   And they came to the other side of the Sea—   1   **5**
Madman.   the country of the Gerasenes ; and, as soon as   2
Jesus had got out of the boat, he met a man coming out of

the tombs, who was under the power of a foul spirit, and   3
who made his home in the tombs.   No one had ever been able to
secure him, even with a chain ; for, though he had many times   4
been left secured with fetters and chains, he had snapped the
chains and broken the fetters to pieces, and no one could master
him.   Night and day alike, he was continually shrieking in   5
the tombs and among the hills, and cutting himself with stones.
Catching sight of Jesus from a distance, he ran and bowed to   6
the ground before him, shrieking out in a loud voice :   7

"What do you want with me, Jesus, Son of the Most High
God ? For God's sake do not torment me !"
For Jesus had said :   8

"Come out from the man, you foul spirit."   9
And he asked him : "What is your name ?"

"My name," he said, "is Legion, for there are many of
us ; " and he begged Jesus again and again not to send them   10
away out of that country.   There was a large drove of   11
pigs close by, feeding on the hill-side.   And the spirits begged   12
Jesus :

"Send us into the pigs, that we may take possession of
them."

Jesus gave them leave.   They came out, and entered into   13
the pigs ; and the drove—about two thousand in number—
rushed down the steep slope into the Sea and were drowned in
the Sea.   On this the men who tended them ran away,   14
and carried the news to the town, and to the country round ;
and the people went to see what had happened.   When they   15
came to Jesus, they found the possessed man sitting there,
clothed and in his right mind—the very man who had had the
'Legion' in him—and they were awe-struck.   Then those who   16
had seen it related to them all that had happened to the
possessed man, as well as about the pigs ; upon which they   17
began to beg Jesus to leave their neighbourhood.   As   18
Jesus was getting into the boat, the possessed man begged him
to let him stay with him.   But Jesus refused.   19

"Go back to your home, to your own people," he said, "and
tell them of all that the Lord has done for you, and how he
took pity on you."
So the man went, and began to proclaim in the district of   20
the Ten Towns all that Jesus had done for him ; and every one
was amazed.

The Raising of the Daughter of Jaeirus. By the time Jesus had re-crossed in the boat to   21
the opposite shore, a great number of people had
gathered to meet him, and were standing by the
Sea.   And one of the Presidents of the   22
Synagogue, whose name was Jacirus, came and, as soon as he
saw Jesus, threw himself at his feet with repeated entreaties.   23

"My little daughter," he said, "is at the point of death ; I beg you to come and place your hands on her, that her life may be spared."

So Jesus went with him.   A great number of people   24
                    followed Jesus, and kept pressing round him.
Cure of   Meanwhile a woman who for twelve years had   25
an afflicted   suffered   from   haemorrhage,   and   undergone   26
Woman.
much at the hands of many doctors, (spending all she had
without obtaining any relief, but, on the contrary, growing   27
worse), heard about Jesus, came behind in the crowd, and
touched his cloak.

"If I can only touch his clothes," she said, "I shall get   28
well!"

At once the mischief was stopped, and she felt in herself that   29
she was cured of her complaint.   Jesus at once became   30
aware of the power that had gone out from him, and, turning
round in the crowd, he said :

"Who touched my clothes?"

"You see the people pressing round you," exclaimed his   31
disciples, "and yet you say 'Who touched me?'"

But Jesus looked about to see who had done it.   Then the   32, 33
woman, in fear and trembling, knowing what had happened
to her, came and threw herself down before him, and told him
the whole truth.

"Daughter," he said, "your faith has delivered you.   Go,   34
and peace be with you ; be free from your complaint."

Before he had finished speaking, some people from the   35
house of the President of the Synagogue came and said :

"Your daughter is dead!   Why should you trouble the
Teacher further?"

But Jesus, overhearing what they were saying, said to the   36
President of the Synagogue :

"Do not be afraid ; only have faith."

And he allowed no one to accompany him, except Peter,   37
James, and John, the brother of James.   Presently they   38
reached the President's house, where Jesus saw a scene of
confusion—people weeping and wailing incessantly.

"Why this confusion and weeping?" he said on entering.   39
"The little child is not dead ; she is asleep."

They began to laugh at him ; but he sent them all out, and   40
then, with the child's father and mother and his companions,
went into the room where she was lying.   Taking her hand,   41
Jesus said to her :

"Taleitha, koum!"—which means 'Little girl, I am speaking to you—Rise!'

The little girl stood up at once, and began to walk about ;   42
for she was twelve years old.   And, as soon as they saw it, they
were overwhelmed with amazement ; but Jesus repeatedly   43
cautioned them not to let any one know of it, and told them to
give her something to eat.

Jesus teaches at Nazareth. On leaving that place, Jesus, followed by his disciples, went to his own part of the country. When the Sabbath came, he began to teach in the Synagogue; and the people, as they listened, were deeply impressed.

"Where did he get this?" they said, "and what is this wisdom that has been given him? and these miracles which he is doing? Is not he the carpenter, the son of Mary, and the brother of James, and Joses, and Judas, and Simon? And are not his sisters, too, living here among us?"

This proved a hindrance to their believing in him; on which Jesus said:

"A Prophet is not without honour, except in his own country, and among his own relations, and in his own home."

And he could not work any miracle there, beyond placing his hands upon a few infirm persons, and curing them; and he wondered at the want of faith shown by the people.

The Mission of the twelve Apostles. Jesus went round the villages, one after another, teaching. He called the Twelve to him, and began to send them out as his Messengers, two and two, and gave them authority over foul spirits. He instructed them to take nothing but a staff for the journey —not even bread, or a bag, or pence in their purse; but they were to wear sandals, and not to put on a second coat.

"Whenever you go to stay at a house," he said, "remain there till you leave that place; and if a place does not welcome you, or listen to you, as you go out of it shake off the dust that is on the soles of your feet, as a protest against them."

So they set out, and proclaimed the need of repentance. They drove out many demons, and anointed with oil many who were infirm, and cured them.

The Death of the Baptist. Now King Herod heard of Jesus; for his name had become well known. People were saying— "John the Baptizer must have risen from the dead, and that is why these miraculous powers are active in him." Others again said—"He is Elijah," and others—"He is a Prophet, like one of the great Prophets." But when Herod heard of him, he said—"The man whom I beheaded—John— he must be risen!"

For Herod himself had sent and arrested John, and put him in prison, in chains, to please Herodias, the wife of his brother Philip, because Herod had married her. For John had said to Herod—'You have no right to be living with your brother's wife.' So Herodias was incensed against John, and wanted to put him to death, but was unable to do so, because Herod stood in fear of John, knowing him to be an upright and holy man, and protected him. He had listened to John, but still

remained much perplexed, and yet he found pleasure in listening to him.   A suitable opportunity, however, occurred   21
when Herod, on his birthday, gave a dinner to his high officials, and his generals, and the foremost men in Galilee. And   22
when his daughter—that is, the daughter of Herodias—came
in and danced, she delighted Herod and those who were dining
with him. 'Ask me for whatever you like,' the King said to
the girl, 'and I will give it to you'; and he swore to her that   23
he would give her whatever she asked him—up to half his
kingdom. The girl went out, and said to her mother 'What
must I ask for?' 'The head of John the Baptizer,' answered
her mother. So she went in as quickly as possible to the King,   25
and made her request. 'I want you,' she said, 'to give me
at once, on a dish, the head of John the Baptist.' The King was 26
much distressed ; yet, on account of his oath and of the guests
at his table, he did not like to refuse her.   He immediately   27
despatched one of his bodyguard, with orders to bring John's
head. The man went and beheaded John in the prison, and,   28
bringing his head on a dish, gave it to the girl, and the girl
gave it to her mother. When John's disciples heard of it,   29
they came and took his body away, and laid it in a tomb.

**The
Return of the**
Apostles.
When the Apostles came back to Jesus, they   30
told him all that they had done and all that they
had taught.

"Come by yourselves privately to some lonely spot," he said,   31
"and rest for a while "—for there were so many people coming
and going that they had not time even to eat.   So they   32
set off privately in their boat for a lonely spot.   And many   33
people saw them going, and recognised them, and from all the
towns they flocked together to the place on foot, and got there
before them.   On getting out of the boat, Jesus saw a   34
great crowd, and his heart was moved at the sight of them, because they were 'like sheep without a shepherd'; and he began
to teach them many things.   When it grew   35

**Jesus feeds
five thousand
by the Lake
of Galilee.**
late, his disciples came up to him, and said :
"This is a lonely spot, and it is already late.
Send the people away, so that they may go to   36
the farms and villages around and buy themselves something
to eat."

But Jesus answered : "It is for you to give them something   37
to eat."

"Are we to go and buy twenty pounds' worth of bread,"
they asked, "to give them to eat?"

"How many loaves have you?" he asked ; "go, and see."   38
When they had found out, they told him : "Five, and two
fishes."   Jesus directed them to make all the people take their 39

34 Num. 27. 17.

seats on the green grass, in parties ; and they sat down 40
in groups—in hundreds, and in fifties. Taking the five 41
loaves and the two fishes, Jesus looked up to Heaven, and
said the blessing ; he broke the loaves into pieces, and gave
them to his disciples for them to serve out to the people, and
he divided the two fishes also among them all. Every one 42
had sufficient to eat ; and they picked up enough broken 43
pieces to fill twelve baskets, as well as some of the fish. The 44
men who ate the bread were five thousand in number.

Jesus walks on the Water. Immediately afterwards Jesus made his dis- 45
ciples get into the boat, and cross over in advance,
in the direction of Bethsaida, while he himself was
dismissing the crowd. After he had taken leave of the people, 46
he went away up the hill to pray. When evening fell, the 47
boat was out in the middle of the Sea, and Jesus on the shore
alone. Seeing them labouring at the oars—for the wind was 48
against them—about three hours after midnight Jesus came
towards them, walking on the water, intending to join them.
But, when they saw him walking on the water, they thought 49
it was a ghost, and cried out ; for all of them saw him, and 50
were terrified. But Jesus at once spoke to them.
" Courage ! " he said, " it is I ; do not be afraid ! "
Then he got into the boat with them, and the wind dropped. 51
The disciples were utterly amazed, for they had not under- 52
stood about the loaves, their minds being slow to learn.

Jesus at Gennesaret. When they had crossed over, they landed at 53
Gennesaret, and moored the boat. But they had 54
no sooner left her than the people, recognizing Jesus, hurried 55
over the whole country-side, and began to carry about upon
mats those who were ill, wherever they heard he was. So 56
wherever he went—to villages, or towns, or farms—they would
lay their sick in the market-places, begging him to let them
touch only the tassel of his cloak ; and all who touched
were made well.

The Disciples blamed for neglecting Ceremonies. One day the Pharisees and some of the Teachers 1 **7**
of the Law who had come from Jerusalem gathered
round Jesus. They had noticed that some of his 2
disciples ate their food with their hands 'defiled,'
by which they meant unwashed. (For the Pharisees, and 3
indeed all strict Jews, will not eat without first scrupulously
washing their hands, holding in this to the traditions of their
ancestors. When they come from market, they will not eat 4
without first sprinkling themselves ; and there are many other
customs which they have inherited and hold to, such as the
ceremonial washing of cups, and jugs, and copper pans). So 5
the Pharisees and the Teachers of the Law asked Jesus this
question—

"How is it that your disciples do not follow the traditions
of our ancestors, but eat their food with defiled hands?"
His answer was :   6
"It was well said by Isaiah when he prophesied about you
hypocrites in the words—

> 'This is a people that honour me with their lips,
>   While their hearts are far removed from me
> But vainly do they worship me,   7
>   For they teach but the precepts of men.'

You neglect God's commandments and hold to the traditions   8
of men. Wisely do you set aside God's commandments," he ex- 9
claimed, "to keep your own traditions! For while Moses said 10

> 'Honour thy father and thy mother,'

and

> 'Let him who reviles his father or mother suffer death,

you say 'If a man says to his father or mother "Whatever of   11
mine might have been of service to you is Korban"' (which
means 'Given to God')—why, then you do not allow him to do   12
anything further for his father or mother! In this way you   13
nullify the words of God by your traditions, which you hand
down ; and you do many similar things."
Then Jesus called the people to him again, and said :   14
"Listen to me, all of you, and mark my words. There is   15
nothing external to a man, which by going into him can
'defile' him ; but the things that come out from a man are the
things that defile him."
When Jesus went indoors, away from the crowd, his disciples   17
began questioning him about this saying.
"What, do even you understand so little?" exclaimed Jesus.   18
"Do not you see that there is nothing external to a man, which
by going into a man, can 'defile' him, because it does not pass 19
into his heart, but into his stomach, and is afterwards got rid
of?"—in saying this Jesus pronounced all food 'clean.'
"It is what comes out from a man," he added, "that defiles   20
him, for it is from within, out of the hearts of men, that   21
there come evil thoughts—unchastity, theft, murder, adultery, 22
greed, wickedness, deceit, lewdness, envy, slander, haughti-
ness, folly ; all these wicked things come from within, and do 23
defile a man."

**Cure of a
Syrian Girl
near Tyre.**
On leaving that place, Jesus went to the dis-   24
trict of Tyre and Sidon.   And he went into
a house, and did not wish any one to know it, but
could not escape notice. For a woman, whose little daughter 25
had a foul spirit in her, heard of him immediately, and
came and threw herself at his feet—the woman was a foreigner, 26
a native of Syrian Phoenicia—and she begged him to drive the
demon out of her daughter.

6—7 Isa. 29. 13.   10 Exod. 20. 12 ; 21. 17.

"Let the children be satisfied first," answered Jesus. 27
"For it is not fair to take the children's food, and throw it to
dogs."

"Yes, Master," she replied ; "even the dogs under the table 28
do feed on the children's crumbs."

"For saying that," he answered, "you may go. The 29
demon has gone out of your daughter."

The woman went home, and found the child lying on her bed, 30
and the demon gone.

Cure of a deaf Mute. On returning from the district of Tyre, Jesus 31
went, by way of Sidon, to the Sea of Galilee, across
the district of the Ten Towns.   Some 32
people brought to him a man who was deaf and almost
dumb, and they begged Jesus to place his hand on him.
Jesus took him aside from the crowd quietly, put his fingers 33
into the man's ears, and touched his tongue with saliva.
Then, looking up to Heaven, he sighed, and said to the man : 34
"Ephphatha !" which means 'Be opened.'
The man's ears were opened, the string of his tongue was 35
freed, and he began to talk plainly. Jesus insisted upon their 36
not telling any one ; but the more he insisted, the more per-
severingly they made it known, and a profound impression 37
was made upon the people.

"He has done everything well !" they exclaimed. "He
makes even the deaf hear and the dumb speak !"

Jesus feeds four thousand. About that time, when there was again a great 1 **8**
crowd of people who had nothing to eat, Jesus
called his disciples to him, and said :
"My heart is moved at the sight of all these people, for they 2
have already been with me three days and they have nothing
to eat ; and if I send them away to their homes hungry, they 3
will break down on the way ; and some of them have come a
long distance."

"Where will it be possible," his disciples answered, "to get 4
sufficient bread for these people in this lonely place ? "

"How many loaves have you ? " he asked. 5

"Seven," they answered.

Jesus told the crowd to sit down upon the ground. Then he 6
took the seven loaves, and, after saying the thanksgiving,
broke them, and gave them to his disciples to serve out ; and
they served them out to the crowd. They had also a few 7
small fish ; and, after he had said the blessing, he told the
disciples to serve out these as well. The people had sufficient 8
to eat, and they picked up seven baskets full of the broken
pieces that were left. There were about four thousand people. 9
Then Jesus dismissed them.   Immediately afterwards, 10
getting into the boat with his disciples, Jesus went to the
district of Dalmanutha.

Warning against the Teaching of the Pharisees. Here the Pharisees came out, and began to 11 argue with Jesus, asking him for some sign from the heavens, to test him. Sighing deeply, Jesus 12 said :

"Why does this generation ask for a sign? I tell you, no sign shall be given it."

So he left them to themselves, and, getting into the boat again, 13 went away to the opposite shore.

Now the disciples had forgotten to take any bread with them, 14 one loaf being all that they had in the boat. So Jesus gave 15 them this warning.

"Take care," he said, "beware of the leaven of the Pharisees and the leaven of Herod."

They began talking to one another about their being short of 16 bread. And, noticing this, Jesus said to them : 17

"Why are you talking about your being short of bread? Do not you yet see or understand? Are your minds still so slow of comprehension? 'Though you have eyes, do you not see? 18 and though you have ears, do you not hear?' Do not you remember, when I broke up the five loaves for the five thou- 19 sand, how many baskets of broken pieces you picked up?"

"Twelve," they said.

"And when the seven for the four thousand, how many 20 basketfuls of broken pieces did you pick up?"

"Seven," they said.

"Do not you understand now?" he repeated. 21

Cure of a blind Man at Bethsaida. They came to Bethsaida. There some 22 people brought a blind man to Jesus, and begged him to touch him. Taking the blind man's 23 hand, Jesus led him to the outskirts of the village, and, when he had put saliva on the man's eyes, he placed his hands on him, and asked him : "Do you see anything?" The man looked up, and said : 24

"I see the people, for, as they walk about, they look to me like trees."

Then Jesus again placed his hands on the man's eyes ; and 25 the man saw clearly, his sight was restored, and he saw every- thing with perfect distinctness. Jesus sent him to his home, 26 and said : "Do not go even into the village."

Peter's Confession of The Christ. Afterwards Jesus and his disciples went into the 27 villages round Caesarea Philippi ; and on the way he asked his disciples this question— "Who do people say that I am?"

"John the Baptist," they answered, "but others say Elijah, 28 while others say one of the Prophets."

"But you, he asked, "who do you say that I am?" 29

[18] Jer. 5. 21.

To this Peter replied :

" You are the Christ."

On which Jesus charged them not to say this about him to any one.   30

Jesus foretells his Death. Then he began to teach them that the Son of   31
Man must undergo much suffering, and that he
must be rejected by the Councillors, and the Chief
Priests, and the Teachers of the Law, and be put to death,
and rise again after three days.   This statement he made   32
openly.   But Peter took Jesus aside, and began to rebuke him.
Jesus, however, turning round and seeing his disciples,   33
rebuked Peter.

"Out of my sight, Satan!" he exclaimed.   "For you look
at things, not as God does, but as man does."

A Call to renounce Self. Calling the people and his disciples to him,   34
Jesus said :

" If any man wishes to walk in my steps, let
him renounce self, take up his cross, and follow me.   For   35
whoever wishes to save his life will lose it, and whoever, for
my sake and for the sake of the Good News, will lose his life
shall save it.   What good is it to a man to gain the whole   36
world and forfeit his life ?   For what could a man give that is   37
of equal value with his life ?   Whoever is ashamed of me and of   38
my teaching, in this unfaithful and wicked generation, of him
will the Son of Man be ashamed, when he comes in his
Father's Glory with the holy angels.   I tell you," he added,   1 **9**
"that some of those who are standing here will not know death,
till they have seen the Kingdom of God come in power."

The Transfigura- tion. Six days later, Jesus took with him Peter,   2
James, and John, and led them up a high moun-
tain alone by themselves.   There his appearance
was transformed before their eyes, and his clothes became   3
of a more dazzling white than any bleacher in the world could
make them.   And Elijah appeared to them, in company   4
with Moses ; and they were talking with Jesus.

" Rabbi," said Peter, interposing, " it is good to be here ;   5
let us make three tents, one for you, one for Moses, and one
for Elijah."   For he did not know what to say, because they   6
were much afraid.   Then a cloud came down and enveloped   7
them ; and from the cloud there came a voice—

"This is my Son, the Beloved ; him you must hear."

And suddenly, on looking round, they saw that there was now   8
no one with them but Jesus alone.   As they were going   9
down the mountain-side, Jesus cautioned them not
A Question about Elijah. to relate what they had seen to any one, till after
the Son of Man should have risen again from the
dead.   They seized upon these words and discussed with one   10
another what this ' rising from the dead ' meant.

³¹Hos. 6. 2.   7 Ps. 2. 7 ; Isa. 42. 1.

"How is it," they asked Jesus, "that our Teachers of the 11
Law say that Elijah has to come first?"

"Elijah does indeed come first," answered Jesus, "and re- 12
establish everything; and does not Scripture speak, with regard
to the Son of Man, of his undergoing much suffering and being
utterly despised? But I tell you that Elijah has come, and 13
people have treated him just as they pleased, as Scripture says
of him."

Cure of an epileptic Boy. When they came to the other disciples, they saw 14
a great crowd round them, and some Teachers of
the Law arguing with them. But, as soon as they 15
saw Jesus, all the people, in great astonishment, ran up and
greeted him.

"What are you arguing about with them?" Jesus asked. 16

"Teacher," answered a man in the crowd, "I brought my 17
son to see you, as he has a dumb spirit in him; and, wherever 18
it seizes him, it dashes him down; he foams at the mouth and
grinds his teeth, and he is pining away. I asked your disciples
to drive the spirit out, but they failed."

"O faithless generation!" exclaimed Jesus. "How long 19
must I be with you? how long must I have patience with
you? Bring the boy to me."

They brought him to Jesus; but no sooner did the boy see 20
him than the spirit threw him into convulsions; and he fell
on the ground, and rolled about, foaming at the mouth.

"How long has he been like this?" Jesus asked the boy's 21
father.

"From his childhood," he answered; "and it has often 22
thrown him into fire and into water to put an end to his life;
but, if you can possibly do anything, take pity on us, and
help us!"

"Why say 'possibly'?" Jesus replied. "Everything is 23
possible for one who has faith."

The boy's father immediately cried out: 24

"I have faith; help my want of faith!"

But, when Jesus saw that a crowd was quickly collecting, he 25
rebuked the foul spirit:

"Deaf and dumb spirit, it is I who command you. Come
out from him and never enter him again."

With a loud cry the spirit threw the boy into repeated convul- 26
sions, and then came out from him. The boy looked like a
corpse, so that most of them said that he was dead. But Jesus 27
took his hand, and lifted him; and he stood up. When Jesus 28
had gone indoors, his disciples asked him privately:

"Why could not we drive it out?"

"A spirit of this kind," he said, "can be driven out only by 29
prayer."

[12] Mal. 4. 5—6.

Jesus,
a second time,
foretells
his Death.

Leaving that place, Jesus and his disciples went 30 on their way through Galilee; but he did not wish any one to know it, for he was instructing 31 his disciples, and telling them—

"The Son of Man is being betrayed into the hands of his fellow men, and they will put him to death, but, when he has been put to death, he will rise again after three days." But the disciples did not understand his meaning and were 32 afraid to question him.

Jesus
teaches at
Capernaum.

They came to Capernaum. When Jesus 33 had gone into the house, he asked them: "What were you discussing on the way?"

On
Humility.

But they were silent; for on the way they had 34 been arguing with one another which was the greatest. Sitting down, Jesus called the Twelve and said: 35 "If any one wishes to be first, he must be last of all, and servant of all."

Then Jesus took a little child, and placed it in the middle of 36 them. Folding it in his arms, he said to them:

"Any one who, for the sake of my Name, welcomes even a 37 little child like this is welcoming me, and any one who welcomes me is welcoming not me, but him who sent me as his Messenger."

On
Toleration.

"Teacher," said John, "we saw a man driving 38 out demons by using your name, and we tried to prevent him, because he did not follow us."

"None of you must prevent the man," answered Jesus, 39 "for no one will use my name in working a miracle, and yet find it easy to speak evil of me. He who is not against 40 us is for us. If any one gives you a cup of water be- 41 cause you belong to Christ, I tell you, he shall assuredly not lose

Against
hindering
Others.

his reward. And, if any one puts a snare in 42 the way of one of these lowly ones who believe in me, it would be far better for him if he had been thrown into the sea with a great millstone round his neck. If your hand proves a snare to you, cut it off. 43 It would be better for you to enter the Life maimed, than to have both your hands and go into the Pit, into the inextinguish- able fire. If your foot proves a snare to you, cut it off. It 45 would be better for you to enter the Life lame, than to have both your feet and be thrown into the Pit. If your eye proves 47 a snare to you, tear it out. It would be better for you to enter the Kingdom of God with only one eye, than to have both eyes and be thrown into the Pit, where 'their worm does 48 not die, and the fire is not put out.' For it is by fire that every 49 one will be salted. Salt is good, but, if the salt should 50 lose its saltness, what will you use to season it? You must have salt in yourselves, and live at peace with one another."

[31] Hos. 6. 2. [48] Isa. 66. 24.

III. The Journey to Jerusalem.

A Question about Divorce. On leaving that place, Jesus went into the district of Judaea on the other side of the Jordan. Crowds gathered about him again ; and again, as usual, he began teaching them.   Presently some Pharisees came up and, to test him, asked :

"Has a husband the right to divorce his wife ? "

"What direction did Moses give you ? " replied Jesus.

"Moses," they said, "permitted a man to 'draw up in writing a notice of separation and divorce his wife.'"

"It was owing to the hardness of your hearts," said Jesus, "that Moses gave you this direction ; but, at the beginning of the Creation, God 'made them male and female.'

'For this reason a man shall leave his father and mother, and the man and his wife shall become one ;'

so that they are no longer two, but one.   What God himself, then, has yoked together man must not separate."

When they were indoors, the disciples asked him again about this, and he said :

"Any one who divorces his wife and marries another woman is guilty of adultery against his wife ; and, if the woman divorces her husband and marries another man, she is guilty of adultery."

Jesus blesses little Children. Some of the people were bringing little children to Jesus, for him to touch them ; but the disciples found fault with those who had brought them. When, however, Jesus saw this, he was indignant.

"Let the little children come to me," he said, "do not hinder them ; for it is to the childlike that the Kingdom of God belongs.   I tell you, unless a man receives the Kingdom of God like a child, he will not enter it at all."

Then he folded the children in his arms, and, placing his hands on them, gave them his blessing.

The Responsibilities of Wealth. And, as Jesus was resuming his journey, a man came running up to him, and threw himself on his knees before him.

"Good Teacher," he asked, "what must I do to gain Immortal Life ? "

"Why do you call me good ? " answered Jesus.   "No one is good but God.   You know the commandments—

'Do not kill. Do not commit adultery. Do not steal. Do not say what is false about others. Do not cheat. Honour thy father and thy mother.'"

4 Deut. 24. 1.   6 Gen. 1. 27.   7 Gen. 2. 24.   19 Deut. 5. 17—20.

"Teacher," he replied, "I have observed all these from my childhood." 20

Jesus looked at the man, and his heart went out to him, and he said : 21
"There is still one thing wanting in you ; go and sell all that you have, and give to the poor, and you shall have wealth in Heaven ; then come and follow me."

But the man's face clouded at these words, and he went away distressed, for he had great possessions. 22

Then Jesus looked round, and said to his disciples : 23
"How hard it will be for men of wealth to enter the Kingdom of God !"

The disciples were amazed at his words. But Jesus said again : 24
"My children, how hard a thing it is to enter the Kingdom of God ! It is easier for a camel to get through a needle's eye, than for a rich man to enter the Kingdom of God." 25

"Then who can be saved ? " they exclaimed in the greatest astonishment. 26

Jesus looked at them, and answered : 27
"With men it is impossible, but not with God ; for everything is possible with God."

"But we," began Peter, "we left everything and have followed you.' 28

"I tell you," said Jesus, "there is no one who has left house, or brothers, or sisters, or mother, or father, or children, or land, on my account and on account of the Good News, who will not receive a hundred times as much, even now in the present—houses, and brothers, and sisters, and mothers, and children, and land—though not without persecutions, and, in the age that is coming, Immortal Life. But many who are first now will then be last, and the last will be first." 29 30 31

Jesus, a third time, foretells his Death. One day, when they were on their way, going up to Jerusalem, Jesus was walking in front of the Apostles, who were filled with misgivings ; while those who were following behind were alarmed. Gathering the Twelve round him once more, Jesus began to tell them what was about to happen to him. 32

"Listen ! " he said. "We are going up to Jerusalem ; and there the Son of Man will be betrayed to the Chief Priests and the Teachers of the Law, and they will condemn him to death, and they will give him up to the Gentiles, who will mock him, spit upon him, and scourge him, and put him to death ; and after three days he will rise again." 33 34

[34] Hos. 6. 2.

The Request of James and John. James and John, the two sons of Zebediah, went 35 to Jesus, and said :

"Teacher, we want you to do for us whatever we ask."

"What do you want me to do for you?" he asked. 36

"Grant us this," they answered, "to sit, one on your right, 37 and the other on your left, when you come in glory."

"You do not know what you are asking," Jesus said to 38 them. "Can you drink the cup that I am to drink? or receive the baptism that I am to receive?"

"Yes," they answered, "we can." 39

"You shall indeed drink the cup that I am to drink," Jesus said, "and receive the baptism that I am to receive, but as to 40 a seat at my right or at my left—that is not mine to give, but it is for those for whom it has been prepared."

The Dignity of Service. On hearing of this, the ten others were at first 41 very indignant about James and John. But 42 Jesus called the ten to him, and said :

"Those who are regarded as ruling among the Gentiles lord it over them, as you know, and their great men oppress them. But among you it is not so. No, whoever wants 43 to become great among you must be your servant, and whoever wants to take the first place among you must be 44 the servant of all ; for even the Son of Man came, not to be 45 served, but to serve, and to give his life as a ransom for many."

Cure of blind Bartimaeus. They came to Jericho. When Jesus 46 was going out of the town with his disciples and a large crowd, Bartimaeus, the son of Timaeus, a blind beggar, was sitting by the road-side. Hearing that it 47 was Jesus of Nazareth, he began to call out :

"Jesus, Son of David, take pity on me."

Many of the people kept telling him to be quiet ; but the 48 man continued to call out all the louder :

"Son of David, take pity on me."

Then Jesus stopped. "Call him," he said. 49

So they called the blind man.

"Courage!" they exclaimed. "Get up ; he is calling you."

The man threw off his cloak, sprang up, and came to 50 Jesus.

"What do you want me to do for you?" said Jesus, address- 51 ing him.

"Rabboni," the blind man answered, "I want to recover my sight."

"You may go," Jesus said ; "your faith has delivered you." 52 Immediately he recovered his sight, and began to follow Jesus along the road.

IV.—THE LAST DAYS.

Jesus enters Jerusalem. When they had almost reached Jerusalem, as far 1 **11**
as Bethphage and Bethany, near the Mount of
Olives, Jesus sent on two of his disciples.

"Go to the village facing you," he said ; "and, as soon as 2
you get there, you will find a foal tethered, which no one
has ever ridden ; untie it, and bring it. And, if any one says to 3
you 'Why are you doing that?', say 'The Master wants it,
and will be sure to send it back here at once.'"

The two disciples went, and, finding a foal tethered outside a 4
door in the street, they untied it. Some of the by-standers said 5
to them : "What are you doing, untying the foal?" and the two 6
disciples answered as Jesus had told them ; and they allowed
them to go. Then they brought the foal to Jesus, and, when 7
they had laid their cloaks on it, he seated himself upon it.
Many of the people spread their cloaks on the road, while 8
some strewed boughs which they had cut from the fields ;
and those who led the way, as well as those who followed, 9
kept shouting :

"'God save him !
Blessed is He who comes in the name of the Lord !'
Blessed is the coming Kingdom of our father David !   10
'God save him from on high !'"

Jesus entered Jerusalem, and went into the Temple Courts ; 11
and, after looking round at everything, as it was already late,
he went out to Bethany with the Twelve.

The fruitless Fig Tree. The next day, after they had left Bethany, Jesus 12
became hungry ; and, noticing a fig-tree at a 13
distance in leaf, he went to it to see if by any
chance he could find something on it ; but, on coming up to
it, he found nothing but leaves, for it was not the season for
figs. So, addressing the tree, he exclaimed :   14

"May no man ever again eat of your fruit !"
And his disciples heard what he said.

Jesus in the Temple. They came to Jerusalem.   Jesus went 15
into the Temple Courts, and began to drive out
those who were buying and selling there. He
overturned the tables of the money-changers, and the seats of
the pigeon-dealers, and would not allow any one to carry any- 16
thing across the Temple Courts. Then he began to teach. 17

"Does not Scripture say," he asked,

"'My House shall be called a House of Prayer for all the
nations'?

But you have made it 'a den of robbers.'"

Now the Chief Priests and the Teachers of the Law heard this, 18

9 Ps. 118. 25, 26.   10 Ps. 148. 1.   17 Isa. 56. 7 ; Jer. 7. 11.

and began to look for some way of putting Jesus to death ; for they were afraid of him, since all the people were greatly impressed by his teaching.   As soon as evening fell,   19 Jesus and his disciples went out of the city.

As they passed by early in the morning, they noticed that   20 the fig-tree was withered up from the very roots.   Then Peter   21 recollected what had occurred.

"Look, Rabbi," he exclaimed, "the fig-tree which you doomed is withered up!"

"Have faith in God!" replied Jesus.   "I tell you that if   22, 23 any one should say to this hill ' Be lifted up and hurled into the sea !', without ever a doubt in his mind, but in the faith that what he says will be done, he would find that it would be. And therefore I say to you ' Have faith that whatever you ask   24 for in prayer is already granted you, and you will find that it will be.'   And, whenever you stand up to pray, forgive any   25 grievance that you have against any one, that your Father who is in Heaven also may forgive you your offences."

Jesus and the Chief Priests. They came to Jerusalem again.   While   27 Jesus was walking about in the Temple Courts, the Chief Priests, the Teachers of the Law, and the Councillors came up to him.

"What authority have you to do these things?" they said.   28 "Who gave you the authority to do them?"

"I will put one question to you," said Jesus.   "Answer me   29 that, and then I will tell you what authority I have to act as I do.   It is about John's baptism.   Was it of divine or human   30 origin?   Answer me that."

They began arguing together :   31

"If we say 'divine,' he will say 'Why then did not you believe him?'   Yet can we say 'human'?"——   32 They were afraid of the people, for every one regarded John as undoubtedly a Prophet.   So their answer to Jesus was—"We   33 do not know."

"Then I," replied Jesus, "refuse to tell you what authority I have to do these things."

Parable of the wicked Tenants. And Jesus began to speak to them in parables :   1 **12** "A man once planted a vineyard, put a fence round it, dug a wine-press, built a tower, and then let it out to tenants and went abroad.   At the proper time   2 he sent a servant to the tenants, to receive from them a share of the produce of the vintage ; but they seized him, and beat him,   3 and sent him away empty-handed.   A second time the owner   4 sent a servant to them ; this man, too, the tenants struck on the head, and insulted.   He sent another, but him they killed ;   5 and so with many others—some they beat and some they killed.   He had still one son, who was very dear to him ; and   6 him he sent to them last of all.   'They will respect my son,' he said.   But those tenants said to one another ' Here is 7 the heir!   Come, let us kill him, and his inheritance will be ours.'   So they seized him, and killed him, and threw his 8 body outside the vineyard.   What will the owner of the vine- 9 yard do?   He will come and put the tenants to death, and he will let the vineyard to others.   Have you never 10 read this passage of Scripture?—

'The very stone which the builders despised
   Has now itself become the corner-stone ;
  This corner-stone has come from the Lord,
   And is marvellous in our eyes.'"   11

After this his enemies were eager to arrest him, but they were 12 afraid of the crowd ; for they saw that it was at them that he had aimed the parable.   So they let him alone, and went away.

A Question about Tribute. Afterwards they sent to Jesus some of the 13 Pharisees and of the Herodians, to set a trap for him in the course of conversation.   These men 14 came to him and said :

"Teacher, we know that you are an honest man, and are not afraid of any one, for you pay no regard to a man's position, but teach the Way of God honestly ; are we right in paying taxes to the Emperor, or not?   Should we pay, or 15 should we not pay?"
Knowing their hypocrisy, Jesus said to them :
"Why are you testing me?   Bring me a florin to look at."
And, when they had brought it, he asked :   16
"Whose head and title are these?"
"The Emperor's," they said ; and Jesus replied :   17
"Pay to the Emperor what belongs to the Emperor, and to God what belongs to God."
And they wondered at him.

A Question about the Resurrection. Next came some Sadducees—the men who 18 maintain that there is no resurrection.   Their question was this—

"Teacher, in our Scriptures Moses decreed that, should a 19 man's brother die, leaving a widow but no child, the man should take the widow as his wife, and raise up a family for his brother.   There were once seven brothers ; of whom 20 the eldest took a wife, but died and left no family ; and 21 the second took her, and died without family ; and so did the third.   All the seven died and left no family.   The woman 22 herself died last of all.   At the resurrection whose wife will 23 she be, all seven brothers having had her as their wife?"

10—11 Ps. 118. 22, 23.   19 Deut. 25. 5, 6.

" Is not the reason of your mistake," answered Jesus, "your   24
ignorance of the Scriptures and of the power of God? When   25
men rise from the dead, there is no marrying or being
married ; but they are as angels in Heaven. As to the dead,   26
and the fact that they rise, have you never read in the Book
of Moses, in the passage about the Bush, how God spoke to
him thus—

> ' I am the God of Abraham, and the God of Isaac, and the
> God of Jacob'?

He is not God of dead men, but of living. You are   27
greatly mistaken."

The Great Command- ment.   Then came up one of the Teachers of the Law   28
who had heard their discussions. Knowing that
Jesus had answered them wisely, he asked him
this question :
"What is the first of all the commandments ? "
"The first," answered Jesus, " is—   29

> ' Hear, O Israel ; the Lord our God is the one Lord ; and   30
> thou shalt love the Lord thy God with all thy heart, and with
> all thy soul, and with all thy mind, and with all thy strength.'

The second is this—   31

> ' Thou shalt love thy neighbour as thou dost love thyself.'

There is no commandment greater than these."
"Wisely answered, Teacher !" exclaimed the Teacher of the   32
Law. "It is true, as you say, that ' there is one God,' and
that ' there is no other besides him ' ; and to ' love him with   33
all one's heart, and with all one's understanding, and with
all one's strength,' and to ' love one's neighbour as one loves
oneself' is far beyond all ' burnt-offerings and sacrifices.' "
Seeing that he had answered with discernment, Jesus said to   34
him :
"You are not far from the Kingdom of God."
After that no one ventured to question him further.

Christ the Son of David.   While Jesus was teaching in the Temple   35
Courts, he asked :
"How is it that the Teachers of the Law say
that the Christ is to be David's son? David said himself,   36
speaking under the inspiration of the Holy Spirit—

> ' The Lord said to my lord : " Sit at my right hand,
>   Until I put thy enemies beneath thy feet." '

David himself calls him ' lord,' how comes it, then, that he   37
is to be his son ? "

²⁶ Exod. 3. 2—6.   ^{29—30} Deut. 6. 4, 5.   ³¹ Lev. 19. 18.   ³² Deut. 6. 4, 5.
     ³³ Deut. 4. 39 ; Lev. 19. 18 ; 1 Sam. 15. 22.   ³⁶ Ps. 110. 1.

Warnings against the Teachers of the Law. The mass of the people listened to Jesus with delight. In the course of his teaching, 38 Jesus said :

"See that you are on your guard against the Teachers of the Law, who delight to walk about in long robes, and to be greeted in the streets with respect, and to 39 have the best seats in the Synagogues, and places of honour at dinner. They are the men that rob widows of their homes, 40 and make a pretence of saying long prayers. Their sentence will be all the heavier."

The Widow's Offering. Then Jesus sat down opposite the chests for 41 the Temple offerings, and watched how the people put money into them. Many rich people were putting in large sums; but one poor widow came and put in two 42 farthings, which make a half-penny. On this, calling his 43 disciples to him, Jesus said :

"I tell you that this poor widow has put in more than all the others who were putting money into the chests ; for every 44 one else put in something from what he had to spare, while she, in her need, put in all she had—everything that she had to live on."

Jesus foretells the Destruction of the Temple and the End of the Age. As Jesus was walking out of the Temple 1 **13** Courts, one of his disciples said to him :

"Teacher, look what fine stones and buildings these are !"

"Do you see these great buildings ?" asked 2 Jesus. "Not a single stone will be left here upon another, which shall not be thrown down."

When Jesus had sat down on the Mount of Olives, facing 3 the Temple, Peter, James, John, and Andrew questioned him privately : "Tell us when this will be, and what will be the 4 sign when all this is drawing to its close." Then Jesus began : 5

"See that no one leads you astray. Many will take my 6 name, and come saying 'I am He', and will lead many astray. And, when you hear of wars and rumours of wars, 7 do not be alarmed ; such things must occur ; but the end is not yet. For 'nation will rise against nation, and kingdom 8 against kingdom' ; there will be earthquakes in various places ; there will be famines. This will be but the beginning of the birth-pangs. See to yourselves! They will betray you to courts 9 of law ; and you will be taken to Synagogues and beaten ; and you will be brought up before governors and kings for my sake, that you may bear witness before them. But the 10 Good News must first be proclaimed to every nation. When- 11 ever they betray you and hand you over for trial, do not be anxious beforehand as to what you shall say, but say what-ever is given you at the moment ; for it will not be you who

7 Dan. 2. 28. 8 Isa. 19. 2.

speak, but the Holy Spirit.   Brother will betray brother   12
to death, and the father his child ; and children will turn
against their parents, and cause them to be put to death ; and   13
you will be hated by every one on account of my Name.   Yet
the man that endures to the end shall be saved.   As   14
soon, however, as you see 'the Foul Desecration' standing
where he ought not" (the reader must consider what this
means) "then those of you who are in Judaea must take refuge
in the mountains ; and a man on the house-top must not go   15
down, or go in to get anything out of his house ; nor must   16
one who is on his farm turn back to get his cloak.   And alas   17
for the women that are with child, and for those that are nursing infants in those days !   Pray, too, that this may not occur in   18
winter.   For those days will be a time of distress, the like of   19
which has not occurred from the beginning of God's creation
until now—and never will again.   And, had not the Lord put   20
a limit to those days, not a single soul would escape ; but,
for the sake of God's own chosen People, he did limit
them.   And at that time if any one should say to you   21
'Look, here is the Christ !'   'Look, there he is !', do not
believe it ; for false Christs and false Prophets will arise, and   22
display signs and marvels, to lead astray, were it possible,
even God's People.   But see that you are on your guard !   I   23
have told you all this beforehand.   In those days, after   24
that time of distress, 'the sun will be darkened, the moon
will not give her light, the stars will be falling from the   25
heavens,' and 'the forces that are in the heavens will be
convulsed.'   Then will be seen the 'Son of Man coming in   26
clouds' with great power and glory ; and then he will send   27
the angels, and gather his People from the four winds, from
one end of the world to the other.

The Need   Learn the lesson taught by the fig-tree.   As   28
for   soon as its branches are full of sap, and it is
Watchfulness. bursting into leaf, you know that summer is
near.   And so may you, as soon as you see these things hap-   29
pening, know that he is at your doors.   I tell you that even   30
the present generation will not pass away, until all these
things have taken place.   The heavens and the earth will pass   31
away, but my words will not pass away.   But about   32
'That Day,' or 'The Hour,' no one knows—not even the angels
in Heaven, nor yet the Son—but only the Father.   See   33
that you are on the watch ; for you do not know when the
time will be.   It is like a man going on a journey, who leaves   34
his home, puts his servants in charge—each having his special
duty—and orders the porter to watch.   Therefore watch, for   35
you cannot be sure when the Master of the house is coming—

12 Mic. 7. 6.   14 Dan. 12. 11.   16 Gen. 19. 26.   19 Dan. 12. 1.   22 Deut. 13. 1.
24 Isa. 13. 10.   25 Isa. 34. 4.   26 Dan. 7. 13.   27 Deut. 30. 4 ; Zech. 2. 6 ;
Deut. 28. 64.

whether in the evening, at midnight, at daybreak, or in the   36
morning—lest he should come suddenly and find you asleep.   37
And what I say to you I say to all—Watch!"

The Plot against Jesus.   It was now two days before the Festival of the   1 **14**
Passover and the Unleavened Bread.   The
Chief Priests and the Teachers of the Law were
looking for an opportunity to arrest Jesus by stealth, and
to put him to death; for they said: "Not during the Festival,   2
for fear of a riot."

Jesus anointed by a Woman at Bethany.   When Jesus was still at Bethany, in the house   3
of Simon the leper, while he was at table, a
woman came with an alabaster jar of choice
spikenard perfume of great value.   She broke
the jar, and poured the perfume on his head.   Some of those   4
who were present said to one another indignantly:
"Why has the perfume been wasted like this?   This per-   5
fume could have been sold for more than thirty pounds, and
the money given to the poor."

"Let her alone," said Jesus, as they began to find fault with   6
her, "why are you troubling her?   This is a beautiful deed
that she has done for me.   You always have the poor with you,   7
and whenever you wish you can do good to them; but you
will not always have me.   She has done what she could; she   8
has perfumed my body beforehand for my burial.   And I tell you,   9
wherever, in the whole world, the Good News is proclaimed,
what this woman has done will be told in memory of her."

Judas agrees to betray Jesus.   After this, Judas Iscariot, one of the Twelve,   10
went to the Chief Priests, to betray Jesus to
them.   They were glad to hear what he said,   11
and promised to pay him.   So he looked for a way to betray
Jesus opportunely.

The Passover.   On the first day of the Festival of the Un-   12
leavened Bread, when it was customary to kill
the Passover lambs, his disciples said to Jesus:
"Where do you wish us to go and make preparations for
your eating the Passover?"
Jesus sent forward two of his disciples and said to them: 13
"Go into the city, and there a man carrying a pitcher of water
will meet you; follow him; and, wherever he goes in, say to   14
the owner of the house 'The Teacher says—Where is my
room where I am to eat the Passover with my disciples?' He   15
will himself show you a large upstairs room, set out ready;
and there make preparations for us."
So the disciples set out and went into the city, and found   16
everything just as Jesus had told them; and they prepared
the Passover.

In the evening he went there with the Twelve, and, when   17, 18
they had taken their places and were eating, Jesus said :

" I tell you that one of you is going to betray me—one who
is eating with me."

They were grieved at this, and began to say to him, one after   19
another :

" Can it be I ? "

" It is one of you Twelve," said Jesus, " the one who is   20
dipping his bread beside me into the dish.   True, the Son   21
of Man must go, as Scripture says of him, yet alas for that
man by whom the Son of Man is being betrayed ! For that
man ' it would be better never to have been born ! ' "

The 'Lord's Supper.'   While they were eating, Jesus took some bread,   22
and, after saying the blessing, broke it, and gave
it to them, and said :

" Take it ; this is my body."

Then he took a cup, and, after saying the thanksgiving, gave   23
it to them, and they all drank from it.

" This is my Covenant-blood," he said, " which is poured   24
out on behalf of many.   I tell you that I shall never again   25
drink of the juice of the grape, until that day when I shall
drink it new in the Kingdom of God."

They then sang a hymn, and went out up the Mount of Olives.   26

Peter's Fall foretold.   Presently Jesus said to them :   27
" All of you will fall away ; for Scripture says—

' I will strike down the Shepherd, and the sheep will be
scattered.'

Yet, after I have risen, I shall go before you into Galilee."   28
" Even if every one else falls away," said Peter, " yet I shall   29
not."

" I tell you," answered Jesus, " that you yourself to-day—   30
yes, this very night—before the cock crows twice, will disown
me three times."

But Peter vehemently protested :   31
" Even if I must die with you, I shall never disown you ! "
And they all said the same.

Jesus in Gethsemane.   Presently they came to a garden known as   32
Gethsemane, and Jesus said to his disciples " Sit
down here while I pray."

He took with him Peter, James, and John, and began to show   33
signs of great dismay and deep distress of mind.

" I am sad at heart," he said, " sad even to death ; wait   34
here, and watch."

Going on a little further, he threw himself on the ground, and   35
began to pray that, if it were possible, he might be spared that
hour.   36

[18] Ps 41. 9.   [21] Enoch 38. 2.   [24] Exod. 24. 8.   [27] Zech. 13. 7.

"Abba, Father," he said, "all things are possible to thee; take away this cup from me; yet, not what I will, but what thou willest."

Then he came and found the three Apostles asleep.   37
"Simon," he said to Peter, "are you asleep? Could not you watch for one hour? Watch and pray," he said to them 38 all, "that you may not fall into temptation. True, the spirit is eager, but human nature is weak."
Again he went away, and prayed in the same words; and 39, 40 coming back again he found them asleep, for their eyes were heavy; and they did not know what to say to him. A third 41 time he came, and said to them:
"Sleep on now, and rest yourselves. Enough! My time has come. Hark! the Son of Man is being betrayed into the hands of wicked men. Up, and let us be going. Look! 42 my betrayer is close at hand."

The Arrest of Jesus. And just then, while he was still speaking, 43 Judas, who was one of the Twelve, came up; and with him a crowd of people, with swords and clubs, sent by the Chief Priests, the Teachers of the Law, and the Councillors. Now the betrayer had arranged a 44 signal with them.
"The man whom I kiss," he had said, "will be the one; arrest him and take him away safely."
As soon as Judas came, he went up to Jesus at once, and said: 45 "Rabbi!" and kissed him. Then the men seized Jesus, 46 and arrested him. One of those who were standing by 47 drew his sword, and struck at the High Priest's servant, and cut off his ear. But Jesus interposed, and said to the men: 48
"Have you come out, as if after a robber, with swords and clubs, to take me? I have been among you day after 49 day in the Temple Courts teaching, and yet you did not arrest me; but this is in fulfilment of the Scriptures."
And all the Apostles forsook him, and fled.   One young 50, 51 man did indeed follow him, wrapped only in a linen sheet. They tried to arrest him; but he left the sheet in their hands, 52 and fled naked.

Jesus before the High Priest. Then they took Jesus to the High Priest; and 53 all the Chief Priests, the Councillors, and the Teachers of the Law assembled. Peter, who had 54 followed Jesus at a distance into the court-yard of the High Priest, was sitting there among the police-officers, warming himself at the blaze of the fire. Meanwhile the Chief Priests 55 and the whole of the High Council were trying to get such evidence against Jesus as would warrant his being put to death, but they could not find any; for, though there were many who 56 gave false evidence against him, yet their evidence did not

agree.   Presently some men stood up, and gave this false   57
evidence against him—

"We ourselves heard him say 'I will destroy this Temple   58
made with hands, and in three days build another made
without hands.'"

Yet not even on that point did their evidence agree.   Then   59, 60
the High Priest stood forward, and questioned Jesus.

"Have you no answer to make?" he asked.   "What
is this evidence which these men are giving against
you?"

But Jesus remained silent, and made no answer.   A second   61
time the High Priest questioned him.

"Are you," he asked, "the Christ, the Son of the Blessed
One?"

"I am," replied Jesus, "and you shall all see the Son of   62
Man sitting on the right hand of the Almighty ; and 'coming
in the clouds of heaven'."

At this the High Priest tore his vestments.   63

"Why do we want any more witnesses?" he exclaimed.
"You heard his blasphemy?   What is your verdict?"   64

They all condemned him, declaring that he deserved
death.   Some of those present began to spit at him,   65
and to blindfold his eyes, and strike him, saying, as they did
so, "Now play the Prophet!" and even the police-officers
received him with blows.

Peter disowns   While Peter was in the court-yard down below,   66
Jesus.   one of the High Priest's maidservants came up ;
and, seeing Peter warming himself, she looked closely at him,   67
and exclaimed :

"Why, you were with Jesus, the Nazarene!"

But Peter denied it.   68

"I do not know or understand what you mean," he replied.

Then he went out into the porch ; and there the maidservant,   69
on seeing him, began to say again to the by-standers :

"This is one of them!"

But Peter again denied it.   Soon afterwards the by-standers   70
again said to him :

"You certainly are one of them ; why, you are a Galilean!"

But he began to swear with the most solemn imprecations :   71

"I do not know the man you are speaking about."

At that moment, for the second time, a cock crowed; and Peter   72
remembered the words that Jesus had said to him—' Before a
cock has crowed twice, you will disown me three times'; and,
as he thought of it, he began to weep.

Jesus before   As soon as it was daylight, the Chief Priests,   1   **15**
the Roman   after holding a consultation with the Councillors
Governor.   and Teachers of the Law—that is to say, the

62 Ps. 110. 1 ; Dan. 7. 13.

whole High Council—put Jesus in chains, and took him away, and gave him up to Pilate.

"Are you the King of the Jews?" asked Pilate.   2

"It is true," replied Jesus.

Then the Chief Priests brought a number of charges against   3
him; upon which Pilate questioned Jesus again.   4

"Have you no reply to make?" he asked. "Listen, how many charges they are bringing against you."

But Jesus still made no reply whatever; at which Pilate was   5
astonished.   Now, at the Feast, Pilate used to grant the   6
people the release of any one prisoner whom they might ask
for. A man called Barabbas was in prison, with the rioters   7
who had committed murder during a riot. So, when the crowd   8
went up and began to ask Pilate to follow his usual custom,
he answered: 9

"Do you want me to release the 'King of the Jews' for you?"

For he was aware that it was out of jealousy that the Chief   10
Priests had given Jesus up to him. But the Chief Priests   11
incited the crowd to get Barabbas released instead. Pilate,   12
however, spoke to them again:

"What shall I do then with the man whom you call the
'King of the Jews'?"

Again they shouted: "Crucify him!"   13

"Why, what harm has he done?" Pilate kept saying to them.   14
But they shouted furiously: "Crucify him!"

And Pilate, wishing to satisfy the crowd, released Barabbas   15
to them, and, after scourging Jesus, gave him up to be
crucified.

The soldiers then took Jesus away into the court-yard—that   16
is the Government House—and they called the whole garrison
together. They dressed him in a purple robe, and, having   17
twisted a crown of thorns, put it on him, and then began to   18
salute him.

"Long life to you, King of the Jews!" they said.

And they kept striking him on the head with a rod, spitting   19
at him, and bowing to the ground before him—going down
on their knees; and, when they had left off mocking him, they   20
took off the purple robe, and put his own clothes on him.

**The   And they led Jesus out to crucify him; and   21
Crucifixion** they compelled a passer-by, Simon from Cyrene,
of Jesus. who was on his way in from the country, the
father of Alexander and Rufus, to go with them to carry his
cross. They brought Jesus to the place which was known as   22
Golgotha—a name which means 'Place of a Skull.' There   23
they offered him drugged wine; but Jesus refused it. Then   24
they crucified him, and divided his clothes among them, casting
lots for them, to settle what each should take. It was nine in   25

²³ Ps. 69. 21.   ²⁴ Ps. 22. 18.

the morning when they crucified him.   The words of the   26
charge against him, written up over his head, ran thus—

'THE KING OF THE JEWS.'

And with him they crucified two robbers, one on the right,   27
and the other on the left.   The passers-by railed at   29
him, shaking their heads, as they said :

"Ah ! you who 'destroy the Temple and build one in three
days,' come down from the cross and save yourself !"   30
In the same way the Chief Priests, with the Teachers of the   31
Law, said to one another in mockery :

"He saved others, but he cannot save himself !   Let the   32
Christ, the 'King of Israel,' come down from the cross now,
that we may see it and believe."
Even the men who had been crucified with Jesus reviled
him.

The Death of Jesus.   At midday, a darkness came over the whole   33
country, lasting till three in the afternoon.   And,   34
at three, Jesus called out loudly :

"'Eloi, Eloi, lama sabacthani ?'" which means 'My God,
my God, why hast thou forsaken me ?'
Some of those standing round heard this, and said :   35

"Listen !   He is calling for Elijah !"
And a man ran, and, soaking a sponge in common wine, put   36
it on the end of a rod, and offered it to him to drink, saying
as he did so :

"Wait and let us see if Elijah is coming to take him down."
But Jesus, giving a loud cry, expired.   The Temple   37, 38
curtain was torn in two from top to bottom.   The   39
Roman Officer, who was standing facing Jesus, on seeing the
way in which he expired, exclaimed :

"This man must indeed have been 'God's Son'!"
There were some women also watching from a distance,   40
among them being Mary of Magdala, Mary the mother of
James the Little and of Joseph, and Salome—all of whom   41
used to accompany Jesus when he was in Galilee, and attend
on him—besides many other women who had come up with
him to Jerusalem.

The Burial of Jesus.   The evening had already fallen, when, as it was   42
the Preparation Day—the day before the Sabbath—
Joseph from Ramah, a Councillor of good position, who was   43
himself living in expectation of the Kingdom of God, came and
ventured to go in to see Pilate, and to ask for the body of Jesus.
But Pilate was surprised to hear that he had already died.   So   44
he sent for the Officer, and asked if he were already dead ; and,   45
on learning from the Officer that it was so, he gave the corpse

29 Ps. 22. 7.   34 Ps. 22. 1.   36 Ps. 69. 21.   39 Wisd. of Sol. 2. 18.

to Joseph. Joseph, having bought a linen sheet, took Jesus 46
down, and wound the sheet round him, and laid him in a tomb
which had been cut out of the rock ; and then rolled a stone up
against the entrance of the tomb.   Mary of Magdala 47
and Mary, the mother of Joseph, were watching to see where
he was laid.

V.—THE RISEN LIFE ANNOUNCED.

The Resurrection of Jesus. When the Sabbath was over, Mary of Magdala, 1 **16**
Mary the mother of James, and Salome bought
some spices, so that they might go and anoint
the body of Jesus. And very early on the first day of the week 2
they went to the tomb, after sunrise. They were saying to 3
one another :

"Who will roll away the stone for us from the entrance of
the tomb ? "

But, on looking up, they saw that the stone had already been 4
rolled back ; it was a very large one.   Going into the tomb, 5
they saw a young man sitting on their right, in a white robe,
and they were dismayed.   But he said to them : 6

"Do not be dismayed ; you are looking for Jesus, the
Nazarene, who has been crucified ; he has risen, he is not
here ! Look ! Here is the place where they laid him.   But 7
go, and say to his disciples and to Peter ' He is going before
you into Galilee ; there you will see him, as he told you.' "

They went out, and fled from the tomb, for they were trembling 8
and bewildered ; and they did not say a word to any one, for
they were frightened ;   *   *   *   *   *   *   *

A LATE APPENDIX.

(Inserted in some manuscripts from an ancient source).

[After his rising again, early on the first day of the week, 9
Jesus appeared first of all to Mary of Magdala, from whom he
had driven out seven demons.   She went and told the news to 10
those who had been with him and who were now in sorrow and
tears ; yet even they, when they heard that he was alive and 11
had been seen by her, did not believe it.   Afterwards, 12
altered in appearance, he made himself known to two of
them, as they were walking, on their way into the country.
They also went and told the rest, but they did not believe 13
even them.   Later on, he made himself known to the 14
Eleven themselves as they were at a meal, and reproached
them with their want of faith and their stubbornness, because

they did not believe those who had seen him after he had risen from the dead. Then he said to them : 15

"Go into all the world, and proclaim the Good News to all creation. He who believes and is baptized shall be saved ; 16 but he who refuses to believe will be condemned. More- 17 over these signs shall attend those who believe. In my Name they shall drive out demons; they shall speak with 'tongues'; they shall take up serpents in their hands ; and, if they drink 18 any poison, it shall not hurt them ; they will place their hands on sick people and they shall recover."

So the Lord Jesus, after he had spoken to them, was taken up 19 into Heaven, and sat at the right hand of God. But they set 20 out, and made the proclamation everywhere, the Lord work-ing with them, and confirming the Message by the signs which attended it.]

ANOTHER APPENDIX.

[But all that had been enjoined on them they reported briefly to Peter and his companions. Afterwards Jesus him-self sent out by them, from east to west, the sacred and imperishable proclamation of eternal Salvation.]

19 2 Kings 2. 11 ; Ps. 110. 1

ACCORDING TO MATTHEW.

'THE GOSPEL ACCORDING TO ST. MATTHEW'.

COMPILED AT AN UNCERTAIN DATE LATER THAN 60 A.D.

THIS gospel, in common with the 'The Gospel according to St. Luke,' incorporates the greater part of the record of the ministry of Jesus given in 'The Gospel according to St. Mark.' It is probable that the compiler was able to make use of the same sources as St. Mark had at his disposal, and perhaps even of St. Mark's gospel itself. Beyond this, he was able to add to that record a very important collection of the Sayings of Jesus from some source of which the compiler of 'The Gospel according to St. Luke' was also able to avail himself. The gospel, in its present form, begins with a preface giving an account of the birth of Jesus, and concludes with an appendix giving an account of his resurrection. These are evidently from sources other than those from which the body of the work was derived.

The standpoint of the compiler of this gospel is clearly that of a Jew writing primarily for converts from Judaism, one marked feature being the prominence given to the fulfilment of Jewish prophecy.

ACCORDING TO MATTHEW.

I.—The Birth, Parentage, and Infancy.

A Genealogy of Jesus Christ, a descendant of David and 1 **1**
Abraham.

The
Ancestors of
Jesus.

Abraham was the father of Isaac,   2
Isaac of Jacob,
Jacob of Judah and his brothers,
Judah of Perez and Zerah, whose mother was 3
    Tamar,
Perez of Hezron,
Hezron of Ram,
Ram of Amminadab,   4
Amminadab of Nashon,
Nashon of Salmon,
Salmon of Boaz, whose mother was Rahab,   5
Boaz of Obed, whose mother was Ruth,
Obed of Jesse,
Jesse of David the King.   6

David was the father of Solomon, whose mother
    was Uriah's widow,
Solomon of Rehoboam,   7
Rehoboam of Abijah,
Abijah of Asa,
Asa of Jehoshaphat,   8
Jehoshaphat of Jehoram,
Jehoram of Uzziah,
Uzziah of Jotham,   9
Jotham of Ahaz,
Ahaz of Hezekiah,
Hezekiah of Manasseh,   10
Manasseh of Ammon,

1 Ps. 2. 2.

Ammon of Josiah,
Josiah of Jeconiah and his brothers, at the time 11
    of the Exile to Babylon.

    After the Exile to Babylon— 12
Jeconiah was the father of Shealtiel,
Shealtiel of Zerubbabel,
Zerubbabel of Abiud, 13
Abiud of Eliakim,
Eliakim of Azor,
Azor of Zadok, 14
Zadok of Achim,
Achim of Eliud,
Eliud of Eleazar, 15
Eleazar of Matthan,
Matthan of Jacob,
Jacob of Joseph, the husband of Mary, who 16
    was the mother of Jesus, who is called
    'Christ'.

So the whole number of generations from Abraham to David 17
is fourteen ; from David to the Exile to Babylon fourteen ; and
from the Exile to Babylon to the Christ fourteen.

The Birth of Jesus. The birth of Jesus Christ took place as follows:— 18
His mother Mary was betrothed to Joseph, but,
before the marriage took place, she found herself
to be with child by the power of the Holy Spirit. Her husband, 19
Joseph, was a religious man and, being unwilling to expose
her to contempt, resolved to put an end to their betrothal
privately. He had been dwelling upon this, when an 20
angel of the Lord appeared to him in a dream.

" Joseph, son of David," the angel said, " do not be afraid to
take Mary for your wife, for her child has been conceived by
the power of the Holy Spirit. She shall give birth to a son ; 21
and you shall give him the name Jesus, for it is he who shall
save his people from their sins."

All this happened in fulfilment of these words of the Lord in 22
the Prophet, where he says—

'Behold! the virgin shall be with child and shall give birth to a son, 23
    And they will give him the name Immanuel'

—a word which means 'God is with us.' When Joseph 24
awoke from his sleep, he did as the angel of the Lord had

directed him. He made Mary his wife, but did not live with 25
her as her husband until after the birth of her son; and to this
son he gave the name Jesus.

The Visit of the Astrologers. After the birth of Jesus at Bethlehem in Judaea, 1 **2**
in the reign of King Herod, some Astrologers
from the East arrived in Jerusalem, asking: 2
"Where is the new-born King of the Jews? for we saw his
star in the east, and have come to do homage to him."
When King Herod heard of this, he was much troubled, and 3
so, too, was all Jerusalem. He called together all the Chief 4
Priests and Teachers of the Law in the nation, and questioned
them as to where the Christ was to be born.
"At Bethlehem in Judaea," was their answer; "for it is said 5
in the Prophet—

 'And thou, Bethlehem in Judah's land, 6
 Art in no way least among the chief cities of Judah;
 For out of thee will come a Chieftain—
 One who will shepherd my people Israel.'"

Then Herod secretly sent for the Astrologers, and ascertained 7
from them the date of the appearance of the star; and, sending 8
them to Bethlehem, he said: "Go and make careful inquiries
about the child, and, as soon as you have found him, bring me
word, that I, too, may go and do homage to him."
The Astrologers heard what the King had to say, and then 9
continued their journey. And the star which they had seen in
the east led them on, until it reached, and stood over, the
place where the child was. At the sight of the star they 10
were filled with joy. Entering the house, they saw the child 11
with his mother Mary, and fell at his feet and did homage
to him. Then they unpacked their treasures, and offered to
the child presents of gold, frankincense, and myrrh. But 12
afterwards, having been warned in a dream not to go back
to Herod, they returned to their own country by another road.

The Flight into Egypt. After they had left, an angel of the Lord 13
appeared to Joseph in a dream, and said:
"Awake, take the child and his mother, and seek refuge in
Egypt; and stay there until I bid you return, for Herod is
about to search for the child, to put him to death."
Joseph awoke, and, taking the child and his mother by 14
night, went into Egypt, and there he stayed until Herod's 15
death; in fulfilment of these words of the Lord in the Prophet,
where he says—

 'Out of Egypt I called my Son.'

When Herod found that he had been trifled with by the 16
Astrologers, he was very angry. He sent and put to death all

6 Mic. 5. 2. 15 Hos. 11. 1.

the boys in Bethlehem and the whole of that neighbourhood, who were two years old or under, guided by the date which he had ascertained from the Astrologers.   Then were ful- 17
filled these words spoken in the Prophet Jeremiah, where he says—

> 'A voice was heard in Ramah,   18
>   Weeping and much lamentation ;
> Rachel, weeping for her children,
>   Refused all comfort because they were not.'

But, on the death of Herod, an angel of the Lord appeared 19
in a dream to Joseph in Egypt, and said :
"Awake, take the child and his mother, and go into the 20
Land of Israel, for those who sought to take the child's life are
dead."
And he awoke, and, taking the child and his mother, went into 21
the Land of Israel. But, hearing that Archelaus had succeeded 22
his father Herod as King of Judaea, he was afraid to go back
there ; and, having been warned in a dream, he went into the
part of the country called Galilee. And there he settled in the 23
town of Nazareth, in fulfilment of these words in the Prophets—
'He will be called a Nazarene.'

II.—The Preparation.

The Baptist   About that time John the Baptist first appeared, 1 **3**
and his   proclaiming in the Wilderness of Judaea :
Message.   "Repent, for the Kingdom of Heaven is at 2
hand."
This is he who was spoken of in the Prophet Isaiah, where 3
he says—

> 'The voice of one crying aloud in the Wilderness :
> "Make ready the way of the Lord,
>   Make his paths straight."'

John wore clothing made of camels' hair, with a belt of 4
leather round his waist, and his food was locusts and wild
honey.   At that time Jerusalem, and all Judaea, as 5
well as the whole district of the Jordan, went out to him and 6
were baptized by him in the river Jordan, confessing their sins.
When, however, John saw many of the Pharisees and 7
Sadducees coming to receive his baptism, he said to them :
"You brood of vipers ! Who has prompted you to seek
refuge from the coming judgement ? Let your life, then, 8

18 Jer. 31. 15.   20 Exod. 4. 19.   2 Dan. 2. 44.   3 Isa. 40. 3.   4 2 Kings 1. 8.

prove your repentance; and do not think that you can say   9
among yourselves 'Abraham is our ancestor,' for I tell you
that out of these very stones God is able to raise descendants
for Abraham! Already the axe is lying at the root of the   10
trees. Therefore every tree that fails to bear good fruit will
be cut down and thrown into the fire. I, indeed, baptize you   11
with water to teach repentance; but He who is Coming after
me is more powerful than I, and I am not fit even to carry his
sandals. He will baptize you with the Holy Spirit and with
fire. His winnowing-fan is in his hand, and he will clear his   12
threshing-floor, and store his grain in the barn, but the chaff
he will burn with inextinguishable fire."

The Baptism of Jesus. Then Jesus came from Galilee to the Jordan,   13
to John, to be baptized by him. But John tried   14
to prevent him.

"It is I," he said, "who need to be baptized by you; why
then do you come to me?"

"Let it be so for the present," Jesus answered, "since   15
it is fitting for us thus to satisfy every claim of religion."
Upon this, John consented. After the baptism of Jesus, and   16
just as he came up from the water, the heavens opened, and he
saw the Spirit of God descending, like a dove, and alighting
upon him, and from the heavens there came a voice which   17
said:

"This is my Son, the Beloved, in whom I delight."

The Temptation of Jesus. Then Jesus was led up into the Wilderness by the   1 **4.**
Spirit to be tempted by the Devil. And, after he   2
had fasted for forty days and forty nights, he
became hungry.   And the Tempter came to him, and   3
said:

"If you are God's Son, tell these stones to become loaves of
bread."

But Jesus answered: "Scripture says—   4

'It is not on bread alone that man is to live, but on every
word that comes from the mouth of God.'"

Then the Devil took him to the Holy City, and, placing him on   5
the parapet of the temple, said to him: 6

"If you are God's Son, throw yourself down, for Scripture
says—

'He will give his angels commands about thee,
And on their hands they will upbear thee,
    Lest ever thou should'st strike thy foot against a stone.'"

"Scripture also says," answered Jesus,   7

"'Thou shalt not tempt the Lord thy God.'"

---

11 Ps. 118. 26.   17 Ps. 2. 7; Isa. 42. 1.   3 Ps. 2. 7.   4 Deut. 8. 3.   6 Ps. 91. 11—12.
7 Deut. 6. 16.

The third time, the Devil took Jesus to a very high moun-   8
tain, and, showing him all the kingdoms of the world and their
splendour, said to him :   9
    " All these I will give you, if you will fall at my feet and
do homage to me."
Then Jesus said to him :   10
    " Begone, Satan ! for Scripture says—

     ' Thou shalt do homage to the Lord thy God, and worship
him only.' "

Then the Devil left him alone, and angels came and min-   11
istered to him.

III.—The Work in Galilee.

Jesus settles at Capernaum.   When Jesus heard that John had been com-   12
mitted to prison, he retired to Galilee. After-   13
wards, leaving Nazareth, he went and settled at
Capernaum, which is by the side of the Sea, within the borders
of Zebulun and Naphtali ; in fulfilment of these words in the   14
Prophet Isaiah—

   ' The land of Zebulun and the land of Naphtali,   15
     The land of the Road by the Sea, and beyond the Jordan,
       With Galilee of the Gentiles—
     The people who were dwelling in darkness   16
       Have seen a great Light,
     And, for those who were dwelling in the shadow-land of Death,
       A Light has risen ! '

Jesus begins his Work.   At that time Jesus began to proclaim—   17
    " Repent, for the Kingdom of Heaven is at
hand."

The first Disciples.   As Jesus was walking along the shore of the   18
Sea of Galilee, he saw two brothers—Simon,
also known as Peter, and his brother Andrew—casting a net
into the Sea ; for they were fishermen.
    " Come and follow me," Jesus said, "and I will set you to   19
fish for men."
The two men left their nets at once and followed him.   Going   20, 21
further on, he saw two other men who were also brothers,
James, Zebediah's son, and his brother John, in their boat
with their father, mending their nets. Jesus called them,

[10] Deut. 6. 13.   [15—16] Isa. 9. 1—2.

and they at once left their boat and their father, and followed 22
him.

Jesus preaches in Galilee. And Jesus went all through Galilee, teaching 23 in their Synagogues, proclaiming the Good News of the Kingdom, and curing every kind of disease and every kind of sickness among the people; and his fame spread all through Syria. They brought 24 to him all who were ill with any form of disease, or who were suffering pain—-any who were either possessed by demons, or were lunatic, or paralyzed ; and he cured them. And he 25 was followed by large crowds from Galilee, the district of the Ten Towns, Jerusalem, Judaea, and from beyond the Jordan.

'THE SERMON ON THE MOUNT.' On seeing the crowds of people, Jesus went up 1 5 the hill ; and, when he had taken his seat, his disciples came up to him ; and he began to teach 2 them as follows :

The Happy. "Blessed are the poor in spirit, for theirs is the 3 Kingdom of Heaven.

Blessed are the mourners, for they shall be comforted. 4

Blessed are the gentle, for they shall inherit the earth. 5

Blessed are those who hunger and thirst for righteousness, for 6 they shall be satisfied.

Blessed are the merciful, for they shall find mercy. 7

Blessed are the pure in heart, for they shall see God. 8

Blessed are the peacemakers, for they shall be called Sons of 9 God.

Blessed are those who have been persecuted in the cause of 10 righteousness, for theirs is the Kingdom of Heaven.

Blessed are you when people taunt you, and persecute you, 11 and say everything evil about you—untruly, and on my account. Be glad and rejoice, because your reward in Heaven 12 will be great ; for so men persecuted the Prophets who lived before you.

A real Disciple of Jesus. It is you who are the Salt of the earth ; but, if 13 the salt should lose its strength, what will you use to restore its saltness? It is no longer good for anything, but is thrown away, and trampled underfoot. It is you who are the Light of the world. A town that stands 14

Lesson from a Lamp. on a hill cannot be hidden. Men do not light 15 a lamp and put it under the corn-measure, but on the lamp-stand, where it gives light to every one in the house. Let your light so shine before the eyes of your fellow- 16 men, that, seeing your good actions, they may praise your Father who is in Heaven.

The old Law and the new— Do not think that I have come to do away with 17 the Law or the Prophets ; I have not come to do away with them, but to complete them. For I tell you, 18

[3] Isa. 61. 1, [4] Isa. 61. 2. [5] Ps. 37. 11. [8] Ps. 24. 4.

until the heavens and the earth disappear, not even the smallest letter, nor one stroke of a letter, shall disappear from the Law until all is done. Whoever, therefore, breaks one of these 19 commandments, even the least of them, and teaches others to do so, will be the least-esteemed in the Kingdom of Heaven ; but whoever keeps them, and teaches others to do so, will be esteemed great in the Kingdom of Heaven. Indeed I tell you 20 that, unless your religion is above that of the Teachers of the Law, and Pharisees, you will never enter the Kingdom of Heaven.

on Anger,   You have heard that to our ancestors it was 21 said—

'Thou shalt not commit murder,'

and

'Whoever commits murder shall be liable to answer for it to the Court.'

I, however, say to you that any one who cherishes anger against 22 his brother shall be liable to answer for it to the Court ; and whoever pours contempt upon his brother shall be liable to answer for it to the High Council, while whoever calls down curses upon him shall be liable to answer for it in the fiery Pit. Therefore, when presenting your gift at the altar, if 23 even there you remember that your brother has some grievance against you, leave your gift there, before the altar, go and 24 be reconciled to your brother first, then come and present your gift. Be ready to make friends with your opponent, even 25 when you meet him on your way to the court ; for fear that he should hand you over to the judge, and the judge to his officer, and you should be thrown into prison. I tell you, you will 26 not come out until you have paid the last penny.

on Impurity,   You have heard that it was said— 27

'Thou shalt not commit adultery.'

I, however, say to you that any one who looks at a woman with 28 an impure intention has already committed adultery with her in his heart. If your right eye is a snare to you, take it out and 29 throw it away. It would be best for you to lose one part of your body, and not to have the whole of it thrown into the Pit. And, if your right hand is a snare to you, cut it off and throw 30 it away. It would be best for you to lose one part of your body, and not to have the whole of it go down to the Pit.

on Divorce,   It was also said— 31

'Let any one who divorces his wife serve her with a notice of separation.'

I, however, say to you that any one who divorces his wife, 32 except on the ground of her unchastity, leads to her

21 Exod. 20. 13 ; Enoch 27. 2 ; 90. 26, 27.   27 Exod. 20. 14.   31 Deut. 24. 3.

committing adultery; while any one who marries her after her
divorce is guilty of adultery.

on Oaths,   Again, you have heard that to our ancestors it   33
was said—

' Thou shalt not break an oath, but thou shalt keep thine
oaths as a debt due to the Lord.'

I, however, say to you that you must not swear at all, either   34
by Heaven, since that is God's throne, or by the earth, since   35
that is his footstool, or by Jerusalem, since that is the city of
the Great King. Nor should you swear by your head, since you   36
cannot make a single hair either white or black. Let your   37
words be simply ' Yes' or ' No'; anything beyond this
comes from what is wrong.

on Revenge,   You have heard that it was said—   38

' An eye for an eye and a tooth for a tooth.

I, however, say to you that you must not resist wrong; but,   39
if any one strikes you on the right cheek, turn the other to
him also; and, when any one wants to go to law with you,   40
to take your coat, let him have your cloak as well; and, if   41
any one compels you to go one mile, go two miles with him.
Give to him who asks of you; and, from him who wants to   42
borrow from you, do not turn away.

on Love.   You have heard that it was said—   43

' Thou shalt love thy neighbour and hate thy
enemy.'

I, however, say to you—Love your enemies, and pray for those   44
who persecute you, that you may become Sons of your Father   45
who is in Heaven; for he causes his sun to rise upon bad
and good alike, and sends rain upon the righteous and upon
the unrighteous. For, if you love only those who love you, what   46
reward will you have? Even the tax-gatherers do this! And,   47
if you show courtesy to your brothers only, what are you doing
more than others? Even the Gentiles do this! You,   48
then, must become perfect—as your heavenly Father is perfect.

About Giving.   Take care not to perform your religious duties   1 **6**
in public in order to be seen by others; if you do,
your Father who is in Heaven has no reward for you.

Therefore, when you do acts of charity, do not have a   2
trumpet blown in front of you, as hypocrites do in the Synagogues and in the streets, that they may be praised by others.
There, I tell you, is their reward! But, when you do acts of   3
charity, do not let your left hand know what your right hand
is doing, so that your charity may be secret; and your Father,   4
who sees what is in secret, will recompense you.

33 Num. 30. 2; Deut. 23. 21.   34 Isa. 66. 1.   35 Ps. 48. 2.   38 Exod. 21. 24.
43 Lev. 19. 18.   48 Deut. 18. 13.

About Praying. And, when you pray, you are not to behave as 5 hypocrites do. They like to pray standing in the Synagogues and at the corners of the streets, that they may be seen by men. There, I tell you, is their reward ! But, when 6 one of you prays, let him go into his own room, shut the door, and pray to his Father who dwells in secret ; and his Father, who sees what is secret, will recompense him.   When 7 praying, do not repeat the same words over and over again, as is done by the Gentiles, who think that by using many words they will obtain a hearing. Do not imitate them ; for God, your 8 Father, knows what you need before you ask him.   You, 9 therefore, should pray thus—

The 'Lord's Prayer.'
'Our Father, who art in Heaven,
May thy name be held holy,
thy Kingdom come,   10
thy will be done—
on earth, as in Heaven.

Give us to-day   11
the bread that we shall need ;

And forgive us our wrong-doings,   12
as we have forgiven those who have
wronged us ;

And take us not into temptation,   13
but deliver us from Evil.'

For, if you forgive others their offences, your heavenly Father 14 will forgive you also ; but, if you do not forgive others their 15 offences, not even your Father will forgive your offences.

About Fasting. And, when you fast, do not put on gloomy looks, 16 as hypocrites do who disfigure their faces that they may be seen by men to be fasting. That, I tell you, is their reward ! But, when one of you fasts, let him anoint his 17 head and wash his face, that he may not be seen by men to be 18 fasting, but by his Father who dwells in secret ; and his Father, who sees what is secret, will recompense him.

The true Treasure. Do not store up treasures for yourselves on 19 earth, where moth and rust destroy, and where thieves break in and steal. But store up treasures for yourselves 20 in Heaven, where neither moth nor rust destroys, and where thieves do not break in or steal. For where your treasure is, 21 there will your heart be also.   The lamp of the body is 22 **Light and Darkness.** the eye. If your eye is unclouded, your whole body will be lit up ; but, if your eye is diseased, your 23 whole body will be darkened. And, if the inner light is darkness, how intense must that darkness be !   No one can serve 24 **True Service.** two masters, for either he will hate one and love the other, or else he will attach himself to one and despise the other. You cannot serve both God and Money.

6 Isa. 26, 20 ; 2 Kings 4. 33.

The Cares of Life. That is why I say to you, Do not be anxious 25 about your life here—what you can get to eat or drink; nor yet about your body—what you can get to wear. Is not life more than food, and the body than its clothing? Look at the wild birds—they neither sow, nor 26 reap, nor gather into barns; and yet your heavenly Father feeds them! And are not you more precious than they? But which of you, by being anxious, can prolong 27 his life a single moment? And why be anxious about 28 clothing? Study the wild lilies, and how they grow. They neither toil nor spin; yet I tell you that even Solomon in 29 all his splendour was not robed like one of these. If God 30 so clothes even the grass of the field, which is living to-day and to-morrow will be thrown into the oven, will not he much more clothe you, O men of little faith? Do not then ask 31 anxiously 'What can we get to eat?' or 'What can we get to drink?' or 'What can we get to wear?' All these are the 32 things for which the nations are seeking, and your heavenly Father knows that you need them all. But first seek his 33 Kingdom and the righteousness that he requires, and then all these things shall be added for you. Therefore do not be 34 anxious about to-morrow, for to-morrow will bring its own anxieties. Every day has trouble enough of its own.

On Judging Others. Do not judge, that you may not be judged. 1 **7** For, just as you judge others, you will yourselves 2 be judged, and the measure that you mete will be meted out to you. And why do you look at the straw in 3 your brother's eye, while you pay no attention at all to the beam in yours? How will you say to your brother 'Let me 4 take out the straw from your eye,' when all the time there is a beam in your own? Hypocrite! Take out the beam from 5 your own eye first, and then you will see clearly how to take out the straw from your brother's. Do not give what 6 is sacred to dogs; nor yet throw your pearls before pigs, lest they should trample them under their feet, and then turn and attack you.

Encouragement to Prayer. Ask, and your prayer shall 7 be granted; search, and you shall find; knock, and the door shall be opened to you. For 8 he that asks receives, he that searches finds, and to him that knocks the door shall be opened. Who 9 among you, when his son asks him for a loaf, will give him a stone, or when he asks for a fish, will give him a 10 snake? If you, then, wicked though you are, know 11 how to give good gifts to your children, how much more will your Father who is in Heaven give what is good to those that ask him! Do to others what- 12 **The Golden Rule.** ever you would wish them to do to you; for that is the teaching of both the Law and the Prophets.

The two Roads. Go in by the small gate. Broad and spacious 13 is the road that leads to destruction, and those that go in by it are many ; for small is the gate, and narrow 14 the road, that leads to Life, and those that find it are few.

True and false Teachers. Beware of false Teachers—men who come to 15 you in the guise of sheep, but at heart they are ravenous wolves. By the fruit of their lives you 16 will know them. Do people gather grapes from thorn-bushes, or figs from thistles ? So, too, every sound tree 17 bears good fruit, while a worthless tree bears bad fruit. A 18 sound tree cannot produce bad fruit, nor can a worthless tree bear good fruit. Every tree that fails to bear good fruit 19 is cut down and thrown into the fire. Hence it is by the 20 fruit of their lives that you will know such men. Not 21 every one who says to me ' Master! Master!' will enter the Kingdom of Heaven, but only he who does the will of my Father who is in Heaven. On ' That Day ' many will say to 22 me ' Master, Master, was not it in your name that we taught, and in your name that we drove out demons, and in your name that we did many miracles ?' And then I shall say to 23 them plainly ' I never knew you. Go from my presence, you who live in sin.'

The two Foundations. Every one, therefore, that listens to this teaching 24 of mine and acts upon it may be compared to a prudent man, who built his house upon the rock. The rain 25 poured down, the rivers rose, the winds blew and beat upon that house, but it did not fall, for its foundations were upon the rock. And every one that listens to this teaching of 26 mine and does not act upon it may be compared to a foolish man, who built his house on the sand. The rain poured down, 27 the rivers rose, the winds blew and struck against that house, and it fell ; and great was its downfall."

By the time that Jesus had finished speaking, the crowd was 28 filled with amazement at his teaching. For he taught them like 29 one who had authority, and not like their Teachers of the Law.

Cure of a Leper. When Jesus had come down from the hill, great 1　**8** crowds followed him. And he saw a leper 2 who came up, and bowed to the ground before him, and said :
" Master, if only you are willing, you are able to make me clean."
Stretching out his hand, Jesus touched him, saying as he did 3 so :
" I am willing ; become clean."

22 Isa. 2. 11.　28 Ps. 6. 8.

Instantly he was made clean from his leprosy; and then Jesus   4
said to him:

"Be careful not to say a word to any one, but go and show
yourself to the Priest, and offer the gift directed by Moses,
as evidence of your cure."

Cure of   After Jesus had entered Capernaum, a Captain   5
an Officer's in the Roman army came up to him, entreating
Servant.   his help.

"Sir," he said, "my manservant is lying ill at my house   6
with a stroke of paralysis, and is suffering terribly."

"I will come and cure him," answered Jesus.   7

"Sir," the Captain went on, "I am unworthy to receive you   8
under my roof; but only speak, and my manservant will be
cured.   For I myself am a man under the orders of others,   9
with soldiers under me; and, if I say to one of them 'Go,' he
goes, and to another 'Come,' he comes, and to my slave 'Do
this,' he does it."

Jesus was surprised to hear this, and said to those who were   10
following him:

"Never, I tell you, in any Israelite have I met with such
faith as this! Yes, and many will come in from East and West   11
and take their places beside Abraham, Isaac, and Jacob, in
the Kingdom of Heaven; while the heirs to the Kingdom will   12
be 'banished into the darkness' outside; there, there will
be weeping and grinding of teeth."

Then Jesus said to the Captain: 13

"Go now, and it shall be according to your faith."

And the man was cured that very hour.

When Jesus went into Peter's house, he saw   14
Cure   Peter's mother-in-law prostrated with fever. On   15
of Peter's
Mother-in-Law his taking her hand, the fever left her, and she
and of many   rose and began to wait upon him.
others.
              In the evening the people brought to Jesus many   16
who were possessed by demons; and he drove out the spirits
with a word, and cured all who were ill, in fulfilment of these 17
words in the Prophet Isaiah—

'He took our infirmities on himself, and bore the burden of
our diseases.'

Tests of   Seeing a crowd round him, Jesus gave orders   18
Sincerity.   to go across.

And a Teacher of the Law came up to him, and said: 19

"Teacher, I will follow you wherever you go."

"Foxes have holes," answered Jesus, "and wild birds their   20
roosting-places, but the Son of Man has nowhere to lay his
head."

"Master," said another, who was a disciple, "let me first go   21
and bury my father."

4 Lev. 13. 49.   11 Mal. 1. 11.   12 Enoch 10. 4.   17 Isa. 53. 4.   20 Dan. 7. 13.

But Jesus answered :   22
     " Follow me, and leave the dead to bury their dead."

Jesus stills a Storm.   Then he got into the boat, followed by his dis-   23
ciples.   Suddenly so great a storm came on upon   24
the Sea, that the waves broke right over the boat.   But Jesus
was asleep ; and the disciples came and roused him.   25

     " Master," they cried, " save us ; we are lost ! "

     "Why are you so timid ? " he said.   "O men of little   26
faith ! "

Then Jesus rose and rebuked the winds and the sea, and a
great calm followed.   The men were amazed, and   27
exclaimed :

     " What kind of man is this, that even the winds and the sea
obey him ! "

Cure of two Madmen.   And on getting to the other side—the country   28
of the Gadarenes—Jesus met two men who were
possessed by demons, coming out of the tombs.   They were
so violent that no one was able to pass that way.   Suddenly   29
they shrieked out :

     " What do you want with us, Son of God ?   Have you come
here to torment us before our time ? "

A long way off, there was a drove of many pigs, feeding ; and   30, 31
the foul spirits began begging Jesus :

     " If you drive us out, send us into the drove of pigs."

     " Go," he said.   32

The spirits came out, and entered the pigs ; and the whole
drove rushed down the steep slope into the Sea, and died in
the water.   At this the men who tended them ran   33
away and went to the town, carrying the news of all that had
occurred, and of what had happened to the possessed men.
At the news the whole town went out to meet Jesus, and, when   34
they saw him, they entreated him to go away from their
neighbourhood.

Cure of a paralyzed Man.   Afterwards Jesus got into a boat, and, crossing   **1 9**
over, came to his own city.   And there   2
some people brought to him a paralyzed man on
a bed.   When Jesus saw their faith, he said to the man :

     " Courage, Child ! your sins are forgiven."

Then some of the Teachers of the Law said to themselves :   3
     " This man is blaspheming ! "

Knowing their thoughts, Jesus exclaimed :   4

     " Why do you cherish such wicked thoughts ?   Which, I ask,   5
is the easier ?—to say ' Your sins are forgiven ' ? or to say ' Get
up, and walk about ' ?   But, that you may know that the Son   6
of Man has power on earth to forgive sins "—then he said to the
paralyzed man—" Get up, take up your bed, and return to your
home."   The man got up and went to his home.   When   7, 8
the crowd saw this, they were awe-struck, and praised God for
giving such power to men.

Call of Matthew.   As Jesus went along, he saw a man, called 9
Matthew, sitting in the tax-office, and said to him:

"Follow me."

Matthew got up and followed him.

Jesus blamed for his Companions.   And, later on, when he was at table in the 10
house, a number of tax-gatherers and outcasts came in and took their places at table with Jesus and his disciples. When the Pharisees saw this, they 11
said to his disciples:

"Why does your Teacher eat in the company of tax-gatherers and outcasts?"

On hearing this, Jesus said: 12

"It is not those who are in health that need a doctor, but those who are ill. Go and learn what this means— 13

'I desire mercy, and not sacrifice';

for I did not come to call the religious, but the outcast."

The Disciples blamed for not Fasting.   Then John's disciples came to Jesus, and asked: 14
"Why do we and the Pharisees fast while your disciples do not?"

Jesus answered: 15

"Can the bridegroom's friends mourn as long as the bridegroom is with them? But the days will come, when the bridegroom will be parted from them, and they will fast then. No 16
man ever puts a piece of unshrunk cloth on an old garment; for such a patch tears away from the garment, and a worse rent is made. Nor do people put new wine into old wine- 17
skins; for, if they do, the skins burst, and the wine runs out, and the skins are lost; but they put new wine into fresh skins, and so both are preserved."

The Raising of the Daughter of Jaeirus.   While Jesus was saying this, a President of a 18
Synagogue came up and bowed to the ground before him.

"My daughter," he said, "has just died; but come and place your hand on her, and she will be restored to life."

So Jesus rose and followed him, and his disciples went 19
also.   But meanwhile a woman, who had been suffer- 20
Cure of an afflicted Woman.   ing from haemorrhage for twelve years, came up behind and touched the tassel of his cloak.

"If I only touch his cloak," she said to herself, 21
"I shall get well."

Turning and seeing her, Jesus said: 22

"Courage, Daughter! your faith has delivered you." And the woman was delivered from her malady from that very hour.   When Jesus reached the President's house, seeing 23

[13] Hos. 6. 6.   [20] Num. 15. 38.

the flute-players, and a number of people all in confusion, he said:
"Go away, the little girl is not dead ; she is asleep."   24
They began to laugh at him ; but, when the people had been   25
sent out, Jesus went in, and took the little girl's hand, and she
rose.   The report of this spread through all that   26
part of the country.

Cure of two blind Men.   As Jesus was passing on from there, he was   27
followed by two blind men, who kept calling out :
"Take pity on us, Son of David !"
When he had gone indoors, the blind men came up to him ;   28
and Jesus asked them :
"Do you believe that I am able to do this ? "
"Yes, Master !" they answered.
Upon that he touched their eyes, and said :   29
"It shall be according to your faith."
Then their eyes were opened.   Jesus sternly cautioned   30
them.   "See that no one knows of it," he said.   But the men   31
went out, and spread the news about him through all that part
of the country.

Cure of a dumb Man.   Just as they were going out, some people   32
brought up to Jesus a dumb man who was
possessed by a demon ; and, as soon as the demon had been   33
driven out, the dumb man spoke.   The people were astonished
at this, and exclaimed :
"Nothing like this has ever been seen in Israel !"
But the Pharisees said :   34
"He drives out the demons by the help of the chief of
the demons."

The Need for Workers.   Jesus went round all the towns and the vil-   35
lages, teaching in their Synagogues, proclaiming
the Good News of the Kingdom, and curing every
kind of disease and every kind of sickness.
But, when he saw the crowds, his heart was moved with com-   36
passion for them, because they were distressed and harassed,
'like sheep without a shepherd ' ; and he said to his disciples :   37
"The harvest is abundant, but the labourers are few.
Therefore pray to the Owner of the harvest to send labourers   38
to gather in his harvest."

The twelve Apostles.   Calling his twelve Disciples to him, Jesus gave   1   **10**
them authority over foul spirits, so that they
could drive them out, as well as the power of curing every
kind of disease and every kind of sickness.
The names of the twelve Apostles are these :   2
First Simon, also known as Peter, and his brother Andrew ;
James the son of Zebediah, and his brother John ;
Philip and Bartholomew ;   3

Thomas, and Matthew the tax-gatherer ;
James the son of Alphaeus, and Thaddaeus ;
Simon the Zealot, and Judas Iscariot—the Apostle who   4
betrayed him.

The Mission of the twelve Apostles.   These twelve Jesus sent out as his Messengers,   5
after giving them these instructions—

" Do not go to the Gentiles, nor enter any Samaritan town,
but make your way rather to the lost sheep of Israel. And on   6, 7
your way proclaim that the Kingdom of Heaven is at hand.
Cure the sick, raise the dead, make the lepers clean, drive   8
out demons. You have received free of cost, give free of
cost.   Do not provide yourselves with gold, or silver,   9
or pence in your purses ; not even with a bag for the journey,   10
or a change of clothes, or sandals, or even a staff ; for the
worker is worth his food. Whatever town or village you   11
visit, find out who is worthy in that place, and remain
there till you leave. As you enter the house, greet it. Then,   12, 1?
if the house is worthy, let your blessing rest upon it, but,
if it is unworthy, let your blessing return upon yourselves.
If no one welcomes you, or listens to what you say, as you   14
leave that house or that town, shake off its dust from your
feet. I tell you, the doom of the land of Sodom and Gomorrah   15
will be more bearable in the ' Day of Judgement ' than the
doom of that town.

Remember, I am sending you out as my Messengers like sheep   16
among wolves. So be as wise as serpents, and as blameless as   17
doves. Be on your guard against your fellow men, for they
will betray you to courts of law, and scourge you in their Synagogues ; and you will be brought before governors and kings   18
for my sake, that you may witness for me before them and the
nations. Whenever they betray you, do not be anxious as to how   19
you shall speak or what you shall say, for what you shall say
will be given you at the moment ; for it will not be you who   20
speak, but the Spirit of your Father that speaks within you.
Brother will betray brother to death, and the father his child ;   21
and children will turn against their parents, and cause them
to be put to death ; and you will be hated by every one on   22
account of my Name. Yet the man that endures to the end shall
be saved. But, when they persecute you in one town, escape to   23
the next ; for, I tell you, you will not have come to the end of
the towns of Israel before the Son of Man comes.   A   24
scholar is not above his teacher, nor a servant above his
master. It is enough for a scholar to be treated like his   25
teacher, and a servant like his master. If the head of the
house has been called Baal-zebub, how much more the members of his household ! Do not, therefore, be afraid of them.   26
There is nothing concealed which will not be revealed, nor

[15] Enoch 10. 6.   [21] Mic. 7. 6.

anything hidden which will not become known. What I tell 27
you in the dark, say again in the light ; and what is whispered
in your ear, proclaim upon the housetops. And do not be 28
afraid of those who kill the body, but are unable to kill the
soul ; rather be afraid of him who is able to destroy both
soul and body in the Pit. Are not two sparrows sold for a half- 29
penny ? Yet not one of them will fall to the ground without
your Father's knowledge. While as for you, the very hairs of 30
your head are all numbered. Do not, therefore, be afraid ; you 31
are of more value than many sparrows. Every one, 32
therefore, who shall acknowledge me before his fellow men, I,
too, will acknowledge before my Father who is in Heaven ;
but, if any one disowns me before his fellow men, I, too, will 33
disown him before my Father who is in Heaven.

The Cost of Christ's Service. Do not imagine that I have come to bring 34
peace upon the earth. I have come to bring, not
peace, but the sword. For I have come to set— 35

'a man against his father, and a daughter against her
mother, and a daughter-in-law against her mother-in-law. A 36
man's enemies will be the members of his own household.'

He who loves father or mother more than me is not worthy 37
of me ; and he who loves son or daughter more than me is
not worthy of me. And the man who does not take his cross 38
and follow in my steps is not worthy of me. He who has 39
found his life will lose it, while he who, for my sake, has lost
his life shall find it.

He who welcomes you is welcoming me ; and he who 40
welcomes me is welcoming him who sent me as his Messenger.
He who welcomes a Prophet, because he is a Prophet, shall 41
receive a Prophet's reward ; and he who welcomes a good
man, because he is a good man, shall receive a good man's
reward. And, if any one gives but a cup of cold water to one 42
of these lowly ones because he is a disciple, I tell you that he
shall assuredly not lose his reward."

After Jesus had finished giving directions to his twelve 1 **11**
Disciples, he left that place in order to teach and preach in
their towns.

The Baptist's Message to Jesus. Now John had heard in prison what the Christ 2
was doing, and he sent a message by his disciples 3
and asked—

"Are you 'The Coming One,' or are we to look for some
one else ?"

35—36 Mic. 7. 6. 3 Ps. 118. 26.

The answer of Jesus to the question was—　　4

"Go and report to John what you hear and see—The blind　5
recover their sight and the lame walk, the lepers are made
clean and the deaf hear, the dead, too, are raised to life, and
the Good News is told to the poor.　And blessed is the man　6
who finds no hindrance in me."

The Testimony of Jesus to the Baptist.　　While these men were going back, Jesus began　7
to say to the crowds with reference to John :
"What did you go out into the Wilderness to look　8
at?　A reed waving in the wind?　If not, what
did you go out to see?　A man richly dressed?　Why, those
who wear rich things are to be found in the courts of kings !
What, then, did you go for?　To see a Prophet?　Yes, I tell　9
you, and far more than a Prophet.　This is the man of whom　10
Scripture says—

'Behold, I am myself sending my Messenger before thy face,
And he shall prepare thy way before thee.'

I tell you, no one born of a woman has yet appeared who is　11
greater than John the Baptist ; and yet the lowliest in the
Kingdom of Heaven is greater than he.　From the time of　12
John the Baptist to this very hour, the Kingdom of Heaven
has been taken by force, and men using force have been
seizing it.　For the teaching of all the Prophets and of the　13
Law continued till the time of John ; and—if you are ready to　14
accept it—John is himself the Elijah who was destined to
come.　　Let him who has ears hear.　　But to　15, 16
what shall I compare the present generation ?　It is like
little children sitting in the market-places and calling out to　17
their playmates—

'We have played the flute for you, but you have not danced ;
We have wailed, but you have not mourned.'

For, when John came, neither eating nor drinking, men said　18
'He has a demon in him' ; and now that the Son of Man has　19
come, eating and drinking, they are saying 'Here is a glutton
and a wine-drinker, a friend of tax-gatherers and outcasts !'
And yet Wisdom is vindicated by her actions."

The Doom of the Towns of Galilee.　　Then Jesus began to reproach the towns in　20
which most of his miracles had been done, be-
cause they had not repented :

"Alas for you, Chorazin !　Alas for you, Bethsaida !　For, if　21
the miracles which were done in you had been done in Tyre
and Sidon, they would have repented long ago in sackcloth and
ashes.　Yet, I tell you, the doom of Tyre and Sidon will be more　22
bearable in the 'Day of Judgement' than yours.　　And　23
you, Capernaum !　Will you 'exalt yourself to Heaven'?
'You shall go down to the Place of Death.'　For, if the miracles

---

⁵ Isa. 61. 1.　¹⁰ Mal. 3. 1.　²³ Isa. 14. 13—15.

which have been done in you had been done in Sodom, it
would have been standing to this day. Yet, I tell you, the   24
doom of Sodom will be more bearable in the ' Day of Judgement ' than yours."

**The
Child-like
Mind.**

At that same time Jesus uttered the words :   25
"I thank thee, Father, Lord of
Heaven and earth, that, though thou
hast hidden these things from the
wise and learned, thou hast revealed
them to the child-like ! Yes, Father,   26
I thank thee that this has seemed
good to thee.

Everything has been committed to me by my Father ; nor   27
does any one fully know the Son, except the Father, or fully
know the Father, except the Son and those to whom the Son

**Jesus
invites the
Weary.**

may choose to reveal him.   Come to me,   28
all you who toil and are burdened, and I will
give you rest! Take my yoke upon you, and   29
learn from me, for I am gentle and lowly-minded, and ' you
shall find rest for your souls '; for my yoke is easy, and my   30
burden is light."

**The Disciples
blamed for
not observing
the Law.**

About the same time Jesus walked through the   1   **12**
corn-fields one Sabbath.   His disciples were
hungry, and began to pick some ears of wheat
and eat them. But, when the Pharisees saw this,   2
they said :
" Look ! your disciples are doing what it is not allowable to
do on a Sabbath ! "
" Have not you read," replied Jesus, " what David did, when   3
he and his companions were hungry—how he went into the   4
House of God, and how they ate the consecrated bread, though
it was not allowable for him or his companions to eat it, but
only for the priests ? And have not you read in the Law that,   5
on the Sabbath, the priests in the Temple break the Sabbath
and yet are not guilty? Here, however, I tell you, there is   6
something greater than the Temple ! And had you learnt the   7
meaning of the words—

' I desire mercy, and not sacrifice,'

you would not have condemned those who are not guilty.
For the Son of Man is lord of the Sabbath."   8

**Cure of
a Man with
a withered
Hand.**

Passing on, Jesus went into their Synagogue,   9
and there he saw a man with a withered hand.   10
Some people asked Jesus whether it was allowable
to work a cure on the Sabbath—so that they might
have a charge to bring against him. But Jesus said to them :   11

24 Enoch 10. 6.   29 Jer. 6. 16.   4 1 Sam. 21. 6.   7 Hos. 6. 6.

"Which of you, if he had only one sheep, and that sheep fell into a pit on the Sabbath, would not lay hold of it and pull it out? And how much more precious a man is than a sheep! Therefore it is allowable to do good on the Sabbath." Then he said to the man.   12

"Stretch out your hand."   13
The man stretched it out; and it had become as sound as the other.   On coming out, the Pharisees plotted against Jesus, to put him to death.   14

Jesus, however, became aware of it, and went away from that place.   A number of people followed him, and he cured them all; but he warned them not to make him known, in fulfilment of these words in the Prophet Isaiah—   15 16 17

'Behold! the Servant of my Choice,   18
    My Beloved, in whom my heart delights!
I will breathe my spirit upon him,
    And he shall announce a time of judgement to the Gentiles.
He shall not contend, nor cry aloud,   19
    Neither shall any one hear his voice in the streets;
A bruised reed he will not break,   20
And a smouldering wick he will not quench,
    Till he has brought the judgement to a victorious issue,
    And on his name shall the Gentiles rest their hopes.'   21

Cure of a blind and dumb Man. Then some people brought to Jesus a possessed man, who was blind and dumb; and he cured him, so that the man who had been dumb both talked and saw.   At this all the people were astounded.   22 23
"Is it possible that this is the son of David?" they exclaimed. But the Pharisees heard of it and said: 24
Jesus accused of Acting by the Help of Satan. "He drives out demons only by the help of Baal-zebub the chief of the demons." Jesus, however, was aware of what was passing in their minds, and said to them: 25
"Any kingdom divided against itself becomes a desolation, and any town or household divided against itself will not last. So, if Satan drives Satan out, he must be divided against himself; and how, then, can his kingdom last? And, if it is by Baal-zebub's help that I drive out demons, by whose help is it that your own sons drive them out? Therefore they shall themselves be your judges. But, if it is by the help of the Spirit of God that I drive out demons, then the Kingdom of God must already be upon you. How, again, can any one get into a strong man's house and carry off his goods, without first securing him? And not till then will he plunder his house. He who is not with me is against me, and he who does not help me to gather is scattering.   Therefore, I tell you, men will be forgiven every sin and slander; but   26 27 28 29 30 31

18 Isa. 41. 8; 42. 1.   19—21 Isa. 42. 2—4.

slander against the Holy Spirit will not be forgiven. Whoever 32
speaks against the Son of Man will be forgiven, but whoever
speaks against the Holy Spirit will not be forgiven, either
in the present age, or in the age to come.

Words a Test of Character. You must assume either that both tree and fruit 33
are good, or that both tree and fruit are worthless;
since it is by its fruit that a tree is known. You 34
brood of vipers! how can you, evil as you are, say anything
good? For what fills the heart will rise to the lips. A good 35
man, from his good stores, produces good things; while an
evil man, from his evil stores, produces evil things. I 36
tell you that for every careless thing that men say, they must
answer on the 'Day of Judgement.' For it is by your words 37
that you will be acquitted, and by your words that you will be
condemned."

Warning against seeking Signs. At this point, some Teachers of the Law and 38
Pharisees interposed.
"Teacher," they said, "we want to see some
sign from you."

"It is a wicked and unfaithful generation," answered Jesus, 39
"that is asking for a sign, and no sign shall be given it except
the sign of the Prophet Jonah. For, just as 'Jonah was inside 40
the sea-monster three days and three nights,' so shall the Son of
Man be three days and three nights in the heart of the earth.
At the Judgement, the men of Nineveh will stand up with this 41
generation, and will condemn it, because they repented at
Jonah's proclamation; and here is more than a Jonah! At 42
the Judgement the Queen of the South will rise up with the
present generation, and will condemn it, because she came
from the very ends of the earth to listen to the wisdom of
Solomon; and here is more than a Solomon!

Danger of imperfect Reformation. No sooner does a foul spirit leave a man, 43
than it passes through places where there is no
water, in search of rest, and does not find it.
Then it says 'I will go back to the home which I left'; but, 44
on coming there, it finds it unoccupied, and swept, and put in
order. Then it goes and brings with it seven other spirits more 45
wicked than itself, and they go in, and make their home there;
and the last state of that man proves to be worse than the
first.   So, too, will it be with this wicked generation."

The true Brotherhood. While he was still speaking to the crowds, his 46
mother and brothers were standing outside, asking
to speak to him. Some one told him this, and Jesus replied : 47,
"Who is my mother? and who are my brothers?"
Then, stretching out his hand towards his disciples, he said : 49

40 Jon. i. 17.   42 1 Kings 10. 2—4.

"Here are my mother and my brothers! For any one who 50
does the will of my Father who is in Heaven is my brother
and sister and mother."

Parable   That same day, when Jesus had left the house   1 **13**
of the Sower. and was sitting by the Sea, such great crowds   2
gathered round him, that he got into a boat, and sat in it,
while all the people stood upon the beach.   Then he told them   3
many truths in parables.

"The sower," he began, "went out to sow ; and, as he was   4
sowing, some seed fell along the path, and the birds came
and ate it up.   Some fell on rocky places, where it had not   5
much soil, and, having no depth of soil, sprang up at once.
As soon as the sun had risen, it was scorched, and, having no   6
root, withered away.   Some, again, fell into the brambles ;   7
but the brambles shot up and choked it.   Some, however, fell   8
on good soil, and yielded a return, sometimes one hundred,
sometimes sixty, sometimes thirty fold.   Let him who   9
has ears hear."

Afterwards his disciples came to him, and said :   10
"Why do you speak to them in parables ? "

"To you," answered Jesus, "the knowledge of the hidden   11
truths of the Kingdom of Heaven has been imparted, but not to
those.   For, to all who have, more will be given, and they shall   12
have abundance ; but, from all who have nothing, even what
they have will be taken away.   That is why I speak to them   13
in parables, because, though they have eyes, they do not see,
and though they have ears, they do not hear or understand.
And in them is being fulfilled that prophecy of Isaiah which   14
says—

'You will hear with your ears without ever understanding,
    And, though you have eyes, you will see without ever perceiv-
        ing,
For the mind of this nation has grown dense,   15
    And their ears are dull of hearing,
        Their eyes also have they closed ;
        Lest some day they should perceive with their eyes,
    And with their ears they should hear,
And in their mind they should understand, and should turn—
        And I should heal them.'

But blessed are your eyes, for they see, and your ears, for they   16
hear ; for I tell you that many Prophets and good men have   17
longed for the sight of the things which you are seeing, yet
never saw them, and to hear the things which you are hearing,
yet never heard them.

Listen, then, yourselves to the parable of the Sower.   When   18, 19
any one hears the Message of the Kingdom without under-

14—15 Isa. 6. 9—10.

D

standing it, the Evil One comes and snatches away what has been sown in his mind. This is the man meant by the seed which was sown along the path. By the seed which was 20 sown on rocky places is meant the man who hears the Message, and at once accepts it joyfully; but, as he has no root, he 21 stands for only a short time; and, when trouble or persecution arises on account of the Message, he falls away at once. By the seed which was sown among the brambles is meant 22 the man who hears the Message, but the cares of life and the glamour of wealth completely choke the Message, so that it gives no return. But by the seed which was sown on the 23 good ground is meant the man who hears the Message and understands it, and really yields a return, sometimes one hundred, sometimes sixty, sometimes thirty fold."

Parable of the Tares. Another parable which Jesus told them was 24 this—

"The Kingdom of Heaven is compared to a man who sowed good seed in his field. But, while every one was asleep, 25 his enemy came and sowed tares among the wheat, and then went away. So, when the blades of corn shot up, and came 26 into ear, the tares made their appearance also. On this the 27 owner's servants came to him, and said 'Was not it good seed that you sowed in your field? Where, then, do the tares in it come from?'

'An enemy has done this,' was his answer. 28

'Do you wish us, then,' they asked, 'to go and gather them together?'

'No,' said he, 'for fear that, while you are gathering the 29 tares, you should root up the wheat as well. Let both grow 30 side by side till harvest; and then I shall say to the reapers, Gather the tares together first, and tie them in bundles for burning; but bring all the wheat into my barn.'"

Parable of the Mustard Seed. Another parable which he told them was this— 31 "The Kingdom of Heaven is like a mustard-seed, which a man took and sowed in his field. This seed is smaller than all other seeds but, when it has 32 grown up, it is larger than the herbs and becomes a tree, so that 'the wild birds come and roost in its branches.'"

Parable of the Leaven. This was another parable which Jesus related— 33 "The Kingdom of Heaven is like some yeast which a woman took and covered up in three pecks of flour, until the whole had risen."

Of all this Jesus spoke to the crowd in parables; indeed to 34 them he used never to speak at all except in parables, in fulfil- 35 ment of these words in the Prophet—

'I will speak to them in parables;
I will utter things kept secret since the foundation of the world.'

³² Dan. 4. 12.   ³⁵ Ps. 78. 2.

Parable of the Tares explained. Then Jesus left the crowd, and went into the 36 house.   Presently his disciples came to him, and said :

"Explain to us the parable of the tares in the field."

And he answered : "The sower of the good seed is the Son of 37 Man.   The field is the world.   By the good seed is meant the 38 People of the Kingdom.   The tares are the wicked, and the 39 enemy who sowed them is the Devil.   The harvest-time is the close of the age, and the reapers are angels.   And, just 40 as the tares are gathered and burnt, so it will be at the close of the age.   The Son of Man will send his angels, and they will 41 gather from his kingdom all that hinders and those who live in sin, and 'will throw them into the fiery furnace,' where 42 there will be weeping and grinding of teeth.

Then shall the righteous shine, like the sun, in the Kingdom 43 of their Father.   Let him who has ears hear.

Parable of the Treasure. The Kingdom of Heaven is like a treasure hid- 44 den in a field, which a man found and hid again, and then, in his delight, went and sold everything that he had, and bought that field.

Parable of the Pearl. Again, the Kingdom of Heaven is like a mer- 45 chant in search of choice pearls.   Finding one of 46 great value, he went and sold everything that he had, and bought it.

Parable of the Net. Or again, the Kingdom of Heaven is like a net 47 which was cast into the sea, and caught fish of all kinds.   When it was full, they hauled it up on the beach, 48 and sat down and sorted the good fish into baskets, but threw the worthless ones away.   So will it be at the close of the age. 49 The angels will go out and separate the wicked from the righteous, and 'will throw them into the fiery furnace,' where 50 there will be weeping and grinding of teeth.

New and old Truths. Have you understood all this ? " Jesus asked. 51 "Yes," they answered.

Then he added : 52

" So every Teacher of the Law, who has received instruction about the Kingdom of Heaven, is like a householder who pro- duces from his stores things both new and old."

Jesus teaches at Nazareth. When Jesus had finished these parables, he 53 withdrew from that place.   Going to his own part 54 of the country, he taught the people in their Synagogue in such a manner that they were deeply impressed.

"Where did he get this wisdom ? " they said, "and the miracles ?   Is not he the carpenter's son ?   Is not his mother 55 called Mary, and his brothers James, and Joseph, and Simon, and Judas ?   And his sisters, too—are not they all living 56 among us ?   Where, then did he get all this ?"

[41] Enoch 54. 6.   [43] Dan. 12. 3.   [49] Enoch 54. 6.

These things proved a hindrance to their believing in him ; 57
whereupon Jesus said :

"A Prophet is not without honour, except in his own country
and in his own house."

And he did not work many miracles there, because of their 58
want of faith.

The Death of At that time Prince Herod heard of the fame of 1 **14**
the Baptist. Jesus, and said to his attendants : 2

"This must be John the Baptist ; he must be risen from
the dead, and that is why these miraculous powers are active
in him."

For Herod had arrested John, put him in chains, and shut 3
him up in prison, to please Herodias, the wife of Herod's
brother Philip. For John had said to him 'You have no right 4
to be living with her.' Yet, though Herod wanted to put him 5
to death, he was afraid of the people, because they looked on
John as a Prophet. But, when Herod's birthday came, the 6
daughter of Herodias danced before his guests, and so pleased
Herod, that he promised with an oath to give her whatever 7
she asked. Prompted by her mother, the girl said 'Give me 8
here, on a dish, the head of John the Baptist.' The king was 9
distressed at this ; yet, on account of his oath and of the guests at
his table, he ordered it to be given her. He sent and beheaded 10
John in the prison ; and his head was brought on a dish and given 11
to the girl, and she took it to her mother. Then John's 12
disciples came, and took the body away, and buried it ; and
went and told Jesus.

Jesus feeds When Jesus heard of it, he retired privately in a 13
five thousand boat to a lonely spot. The people, however, heard
by the Lake of his going, and followed him in crowds from the
of Galilee. towns on foot. On getting out of the 14
boat, Jesus saw a great crowd, and his heart was moved at the
sight of them ; and he cured all the sick among them. In 15
the evening the disciples came up to him, and said :

"This is a lonely spot, and the day is now far advanced ;
send the crowds away, that they may go to the villages, and
buy themselves food."

But Jesus said : "They need not go away, it is for you to 16
give them something to eat."

"We have nothing here," they said, "except five loaves and 17
two fishes."

"Bring them here to me," was his reply. 18

Jesus ordered the people to take their seats on the grass ; and, 19
taking the five loaves and the two fishes, he looked up to
Heaven, and said the blessing, and, after he had broken the
loaves, gave them to his disciples ; and they gave them to the
crowds. Every one had sufficient to eat, and they picked up 20

enough of the broken pieces that were left to fill twelve
baskets.   The men who ate were about five thousand in   21
number, without counting women and children.

Jesus   Immediately afterwards Jesus made the disci-   22
walks on the ples get into a boat and cross over in advance of
Water.   him, while he dismissed the crowds.   After dis-   23
missing the crowds, he went up the hill by himself to pray ;
and, when evening fell, he was there alone.   The   24
boat was by this time some miles from shore, labouring in the
waves, for the wind was against her.   Three hours   25
after midnight, however, Jesus came towards the disciples,
walking on the water.   But, when they saw him walking on   26
the water, they were terrified.

" It is a ghost," they exclaimed, and cried out for fear.   But
Jesus at once spoke to them.   27

"Courage !" he said, "It is I ; do not be afraid !"

" Master," Peter exclaimed, "if it is you, tell me to come to   28
you on the water."

And Jesus said : "Come."   29
So Peter got down from the boat, and walked on the water,
and went towards Jesus ; but, when he felt the wind, he was   30
frightened, and, beginning to sink, cried out :

" Master ! Save me !"
Instantly Jesus stretched out his hand, and caught hold of him.   31
"O man of little faith !" he said, "Why did you falter ?"
When they had got into the boat, the wind dropped.   But   32, 33
the men in the boat threw themselves on their faces before
him, and said :

"You are indeed God's Son."

Jesus at   When they had crossed over, they landed at   34
Gennesaret. Gennesaret.   But the people of that place, recog-   35
nizing Jesus, sent out to the whole country round, and brought
to him all who were ill, begging him merely to let them touch   36
the tassel of his cloak ; and all who touched were made
perfectly well.

Then some Pharisees and Teachers of the Law   1 **15**
The Disciples came to Jesus, and said :
blamed
for neglecting   "How is it that your disciples break the tra-   2
Ceremonies. ditions of our ancestors ?   For they do not wash
their hands when they eat food."
His reply was :   3
" How is it that you on your side break God's commandments
out of respect for your own traditions ?   For God said—   4

' Honour thy father and mother,'
and
        ' Let him who reviles his father or mother suffer death,'

        [4] Exod. 20. 12 ; Exod. 21. 17.

but you say 'Whenever any one says to his father or mother   5
"Whatever of mine might have been of service to you is 'Given
to God,'" he is in no way bound to honour his father.' In this   6
way you have nullified the words of God on account of your
traditions. Hypocrites! It was well said by Isaiah when he   7
prophesied about you—

     'This is a people that honour me with their lips,   8
        While their hearts are far removed from me;
      But vainly do they worship me,   9
        For they teach but the precepts of men.'"

Then Jesus called the people to him, and said: 10
"Listen, and mark my words. It is not what enters a   11
man's mouth that 'defiles' him, but what comes out from his
mouth—that does defile him!"
On this his disciples came up to him, and said: 12
"Do you know that the Pharisees were shocked on hearing
what you said?"
"Every plant," Jesus replied, "that my heavenly Father has   13
not planted will be rooted up. Let them be; they are but   14
blind guides; and, if one blind man guides another, both of
them will fall into a ditch."
Upon this, Peter said to Jesus: 15
"Explain this saying to us."
"What, do even you understand nothing yet?" Jesus ex-   16
claimed. "Do not you see that whatever goes into the mouth   17
passes into the stomach, and is afterwards expelled? But the   18
things that come out from the mouth proceed from the heart,
and it is these that defile a man. For out of the heart proceed   19
evil thoughts—murder, adultery, unchastity, theft, perjury,
slander. These are the things that defile a man; but eating   20
with unwashed hands does not defile a man."

Cure of a Syrian Girl near Tyre.   On going away from that place, Jesus retired to   21
the country round Tyre and Sidon. There,   22
a Canaanite woman of that district came out
and began calling to Jesus:
"Take pity on me, Master, Son of David; my daughter is
grievously possessed by a demon."
But Jesus did not answer her a word; and his disciples came   23
up and begged him to send her away.
"She keeps calling out after us," they said.
"I was not sent," replied Jesus, "to any one except the lost   24
sheep of Israel."
But the woman came, and, bowing to the ground before him,   25
said:
"Master, help me

8—9 Isa. 29. 13.

"It is not fair," replied Jesus, "to take the children's food   26
and throw it to dogs."

"Yes, Master," she said, "for even dogs do feed on the scraps   27
that fall from their owners' table."

"Your faith is great," was his reply to the woman ; "it shall   28
be as you wish !"

And her daughter was cured that very hour.

Jesus cures many Persons.   On leaving that place, Jesus went to the shore   29
of the Sea of Galilee ; and then went up the hill,
and sat down.   Great crowds of people came   30
to him, bringing with them those who were lame, crippled,
blind, or dumb, and many others.   They put them down at
his feet, and he cured them ; and the crowd were astonished,   31
when they saw the dumb talking, the cripples made sound,
the lame walking about, and the blind with their sight
restored ; and they praised the God of Israel.

Jesus feeds four thousand.   Afterwards Jesus called his disciples to him,   32
and said :

"My heart is moved at the sight of all these people, for
they have already been with me three days and they have
nothing to eat ; and I am unwilling to send them away
hungry, for fear that they should break down on the way."

"Where can we," his disciples asked, "in a lonely place find   33
enough bread for such a crowd as this ? "

"How many loaves have you ? " said Jesus.   34

"Seven," they answered, " and a few small fish."

Telling the crowd to sit down on the ground, Jesus took the   35, 36
seven loaves and the fish, and, after saying the thanksgiving,
broke them, and gave them to the disciples ; and the disciples
gave them to the crowds.   Every one had sufficient to eat, and   37
they picked up seven baskets full of the broken pieces left.   The   38
men who ate were four thousand in number, without counting
women and children.   Then, after dismissing the   39
crowds, Jesus got into the boat, and went to the neighbourhood of Magadan.

Signs of the Times.   Here the Pharisees and Sadducees came up,   1 **16**
and, to test Jesus, requested him to show them
some sign from the heavens.   But Jesus answered :   2

[" In the evening you say 'It will be fine weather, for the
sky is as red as fire.'   But in the morning you say 'To-day it   3
will be stormy, for the sky is as red as fire and threatening.'
You learn to read the sky ; yet you are unable to read the signs
of the times !]   A wicked and unfaithful generation   4
is asking for a sign, but no sign shall be given it except
the sign of Jonah."

So he left them and went away.

Warning against the Teaching of the Pharisees. Now the disciples had crossed to the opposite 5 shore, and had forgotten to take any bread. Presently Jesus said to them : 6 "Take care and be on your guard against the leaven of the Pharisees and Sadducees."

But the disciples began talking among themselves about their 7 having brought no bread. On noticing this, Jesus said : 8 "Why are you talking among yourselves about your being short of bread, O men of little faith ? Do not you yet see, nor 9 remember the five loaves for the five thousand, and how many baskets you took away ? Nor yet the seven loaves for the four 10 thousand, and how many basketfuls you took away ? How 11 is it that you do not see that I was not speaking about bread ? Be on your guard against the leaven of the Pharisees and Sadducees."

Then they understood that he had told them to be on their 12 guard, not against the leaven of bread, but against the teaching of the Pharisees and Sadducees.

Peter's Confession of the Christ. On coming into the neighbourhood of Caesarea 13 Philippi, Jesus asked his disciples this question— "Who do people say that the Son of Man is?" "Some say John the Baptist," they answered, 14 "others, however, say that he is Elijah, while others again say Jeremiah, or one of the Prophets."

"But you," he said, "who do you say that I am ? " 15 And to this Simon Peter answered : "You are the Christ, 16 the Son of the Living God."

"Blessed are you, Simon, Son of Jonah," Jesus replied. 17 "For no human being has revealed this to you, but my Father who is in Heaven. Yes, and I say to you, Your 18 name is 'Peter'—a Rock, and on this rock I will build my Church, and the Powers of the Place of Death shall not prevail over it. I will give you the keys of the Kingdom of Heaven. 19 Whatever you forbid on earth will be held in Heaven to be forbidden, and whatever you allow on earth will be held in Heaven to be allowed."

Then he charged his disciples not to tell any one that he 20 was the Christ.

Jesus foretells his Death. At that time Jesus Christ began to explain to 21 his disciples that he must go to Jerusalem, and undergo much suffering at the hands of the Councillors, and Chief Priests, and Teachers of the Law, and be put to death, and rise on the third day. But Peter took Jesus 22 aside, and began to rebuke him.

18 Job 38. 17.   19 Isa. 22. 22.   21 Hos. 6. 2.

"Master," he said, "please God that shall never be your fate!"

Jesus, however, turning to Peter, said :   23

"Out of my way, Satan! You are a hindrance to me; for you look at things, not as God does, but as man does."

A Call to renounce Self. Then Jesus said to his disciples :   24 " If any man wishes to walk in my steps, let him renounce self, and take up his cross, and follow me. For whoever wishes to save his life will lose it, and who-   25 ever, for my sake, loses his life shall find it. What good   26 will it do a man to gain the whole world, if he forfeits his life? or what will a man give that is of equal value with his life? For the Son of Man is to come in his Father's Glory, with his   27 angels, and then he ' will give to every man what his actions deserve.' I tell you, some of those who are standing here will   28 not know death till they have seen the Son of Man coming into his Kingdom."

The Transfigura- tion. Six days later, Jesus took with him Peter, and   1 **17** the brothers James and John, and led them up a high mountain alone. There his appearance   2 was transformed before their eyes; his face shone like the sun, and his clothes became as white as the light. And all   3 at once Moses and Elijah appeared to them, talking with Jesus.

"Master," exclaimed Peter, interposing, "it is good to be   4 here ; if you wish, I will make three tents here, one for you, one for Moses, and one for Elijah."

While he was still speaking, a bright cloud enveloped them,   5 and there was a voice from the cloud which said—

"This is my Son, the Beloved, in whom I delight ; him you must hear."

The disciples, on hearing this, fell on their faces, greatly   6 afraid. But Jesus came and touched them, saying as he   7 did so :

"Rise up, and do not be afraid."

When they raised their eyes, they saw no one but Jesus   8 himself alone.   As they were going down the moun-   9 tain side, Jesus gave them this warning—"Do not speak of this vision to any one, until the Son of Man has risen from the dead."

A Question about Elijah. "How is it," his disciples asked, "that our   10 Teachers of the Law say that Elijah has to come first ?"

"Elijah indeed does come," Jesus replied, "and will restore   11 everything ; and I tell you that Elijah has already come, and   12 people have not recognized him, but have treated him just as

27 Ps. 62. 12.   5 Ps. 2. 7 ; Isa. 42. 1.   11 Mal. 4. 5.

D *

they pleased. In the same way, too, the Son of Man is destined to undergo suffering at men's hands."

Then the disciples understood that it was of John the Baptist 13 that he had spoken to them.

Cure of an epileptic Boy. When they came to the crowd, a man came up 14 to Jesus, and, kneeling down before him, said : "Master, take pity on my son, for he is 15 epileptic and suffers terribly ; indeed, he often falls into the fire and into the water ; I brought him to your disciples, but they 16 could not cure him."

The Power of Faith. "O faithless and perverse generation !" Jesus 17 exclaimed, "how long must I be among you? how long must I have patience with you ? Bring the boy here to me."

Then Jesus rebuked the demon, and it came out of the boy ; 18 and he was cured from that very hour.   Afterwards the 19 disciples came up to Jesus, and asked him privately : "Why was it that we could not drive it out ?"

"Because you have so little faith," he answered ; "for, I 20 tell you, if your faith were only like a mustard-seed, you could say to this mountain 'Move from this place to that !' and it would be moved ; and nothing would be impossible to you."

Jesus, a second time, foretells his Death. While Jesus and his disciples were together in 22 Galilee, he said to them : "The Son of Man is destined to be betrayed into the hands of his fellow-men, and they will put 23 him to death, but on the third day he will rise."

And the disciples were greatly distressed.

A Question about the Temple-rate. After they had reached Capernaum, the collec- 24 tors of the Temple-rate came up to Peter, and said :

"Does not your Master pay the Temple-rate ?"

"Yes," answered Peter. 25

But, on going into the house, before he could speak, Jesus said :

"What do you think, Simon ? From whom do earthly kings take taxes or tribute ? From their sons, or from others ?"

"From others," answered Peter. 26

"Well then," continued Jesus, "their sons go free. Still, 27 that we may not shock them, go and throw a line into the Sea ; take the first fish that rises, open its mouth, and you

17 Deut. 32. 5.   23 Hos. 6. 2.

will find in it a piece of money. Take that, and give it to the collectors for both of us."

On Humility. On the same occasion the disciples came to 1 **18**
Jesus, and asked him :
"Who is really the greatest in the Kingdom of Heaven?"
Jesus called a little child to him, and placed it in the middle of 2
them, and then said : 3
"I tell you, unless you change and become like little children, you will not enter the Kingdom of Heaven at all.
Therefore, any one who will humble himself like this child— 4
that man shall be the greatest in the Kingdom of Heaven. And 5
any one who, for the sake of my Name, welcomes even one
little child like this, is welcoming me. But, if any one puts a 6
Against hindering Others. snare in the way of one of these lowly ones who
believe in me, it would be best for him to be sunk
in the depths of the sea with a great millstone
hung round his neck. Alas for the world because of 7
such snares ! There cannot but be snares ; yet alas for the
man who is answerable for the snare !
If your hand or your foot is a snare to you, cut it off, and 8
throw it away. It would be better for you to enter the Life
maimed or lame, than to have both hands, or both feet, and
be thrown into the aeonian fire. If your eye is a snare to you, 9
take it out, and throw it away. It would be better for you to
enter the Life with only one eye, than to have both eyes and
be thrown into the fiery Pit.
Beware of despising one of these lowly ones, for in Heaven, 10
I tell you, their angels always see the face of my Father
who is in Heaven. What think you? If a man owns a 12
Parable of the lost Sheep. hundred sheep, and one of them strays, will he
not leave the ninety-nine on the hills, and go and
search for the one that is straying? And, if he 13
succeeds in finding it, I tell you that he rejoices more over that
one sheep than over the ninety-nine which did not stray. So, 14
too, it is the will of my Father who is in Heaven that not one
of these lowly ones should be lost.
On dealing with Wrong-doers. If your Brother does wrong, go to him and 15
convince him of his fault when you and he are
alone. If he listens to you, you have won your
Brother. But, if he does not listen to you, take with you one 16
or two others, so that 'on the evidence of two or three
witnesses, every word may be put beyond dispute.' If he 17
refuses to listen to them, speak to the Church ; and, if he also
refuses to listen to the Church, treat him as you would a
Gentile or a tax-gatherer.
I tell you, all that you forbid on earth will be held in 18
Heaven to be forbidden, and all that you allow on earth will

¹⁶ Deut. 19. 15.

be held in Heaven to be allowed.   Again, I tell you 19
that, if but two of you on earth agree as to what
they shall pray for, whatever it be, it will be
granted them by my Father who is in Heaven.
For where two or three have come together in my Name, I 20
am present with them."

Encouragement to united Prayer.

Then Peter came up, and said to Jesus : 21
"Master, how often am I to forgive my Brother
when he wrongs me? As many as seven
times?"

Parable of the unforgiving Servant.

But Jesus answered : 22
"Not seven times, but 'seventy times seven.' And there- 23
fore the Kingdom of Heaven may be compared to a king who
wished to settle accounts with his servants. When he had begun 24
to do so, one of them was brought to him who owed him six
million pounds ; and, as he could not pay, his master ordered 25
him to be sold towards the payment of the debt, together with his
wife, and his children, and everything that he had. Thereupon 26
the servant threw himself down on the ground before him and
said 'Have patience with me, and I will pay you all.' The 27
master was moved with compassion ; and he let him go, and
forgave him the debt. But, on going out, that same servant 28
came upon one of his fellow-servants who owed him ten
pounds. Seizing him by the throat, he said 'Pay what you owe
me.' Thereupon his fellow-servant threw himself on the 29
ground, and begged for mercy. 'Have patience with me,' he
said, 'and I will pay you.' But the other would not, but went 30
and put him in prison till he should pay his debt. When his 31
fellow-servants saw what had happened, they were greatly
distressed, and went to their master and laid the whole
matter before him. Upon that the master sent for the servant, 32
and said to him 'You wicked servant! When you begged
me for mercy, I forgave you the whole of that debt. Ought 33
not you, also, to have shown mercy to your fellow-servant, just
as I showed mercy to you?' Then his master, in anger, 34
handed him over to the gaolers, until he should pay the whole
of his debt.   So, also, will my heavenly Father do to you, 35
unless each one of you forgives his Brother from his heart."

IV.—THE JOURNEY TO JERUSALEM.

At the conclusion of this teaching, Jesus with- 1
drew from Galilee, and went into that district of
Judaea which is on the other side of the Jordan.
Great crowds followed him, and he cured them there. 2

A Question about Divorce.

22 Gen. 4. 24.

Presently some Pharisees came up to him, and, to test him, 3
said : "Has a man the right to divorce his wife for every
cause ? "

"Have not you read," replied Jesus, "that at the beginning 4
the Creator 'made them male and female,' and said— 5

'For this reason a man shall leave his father and mother,
and be united to his wife, and the man and his wife shall
become one'?

So that they are no longer two, but one.   What God himself, 6
then, has yoked together man must not separate."

"Why, then," they said, "did Moses direct that a man should 7
'serve his wife with a notice of separation and divorce her'?"

"Moses, owing to the hardness of your hearts," answered 8
Jesus, "permitted you to divorce your wives, but that was
not so at the beginning.   But I tell you that any one who 9
divorces his wife, except on the ground of her unchastity, and
marries another woman, is guilty of adultery."

"If that," said the disciples, "is the position of a man with 10
regard to his wife, it is better not to marry."

"It is not every one," replied Jesus, "who can accept this 11
teaching, but only those who have been enabled to do so.
Some men, it is true, have from birth been disabled for 12
marriage, while others have been disabled by their fellow men,
and others again have disabled themselves for the sake of the
Kingdom of Heaven.   Let him accept it who can."

Jesus blesses little Children.   Then some little children were brought to Jesus, 13
for him to place his hands on them, and pray ;
but the disciples found fault with those who had
brought them.   Jesus, however, said : 14
"Let the little children come to me, and do not hinder
them, for it is to the childlike that the Kingdom of Heaven
belongs."

So he placed his hands on them, and then went on his way. 15

The Responsibilities of Wealth.   And a man came up to Jesus, and said : 16
"Teacher, what good thing must I do to obtain
Immortal Life ? "

"Why ask me about goodness?" answered Jesus.   "There 17
is but One who is good.   If you want to enter the Life, keep
the commandments."

"What commandments ? " asked the man. 18

"These," answered Jesus :—

"'Thou shalt not kill.   Thou shalt not commit adultery.
Thou shalt not steal.   Thou shalt not say what is false about
others.   Honour thy father and thy mother.' 19
And
'Thou shalt love thy neighbour as thou dost thyself."

4 Gen. 1. 27.   5 Gen. 2. 24.   7 Deut. 24. 1.   18—19 Exod. 20. 12—17 ; Lev. 19. 18.

"I have observed all these," said the young man. "What 20
is still wanting in me?"

"If you wish to be perfect," answered Jesus, "go and sell 21
your property, and give to the poor, and you shall have wealth
in Heaven; then come and follow me."

On hearing these words, the young man went away distressed, 22
for he had great possessions.

At this, Jesus said to his disciples: 23

"I tell you that a rich man will find it hard to enter the
Kingdom of Heaven! I say again, it is easier for a camel to 24
get through a needle's eye than for a rich man to enter the
Kingdom of Heaven!"

On hearing this, the disciples exclaimed in great astonishment: 25
"Who then can possibly be saved?"

But Jesus looked at them, and said: 26

"With men this is impossible, but with God everything is
possible."

Then Peter turned and said to Jesus:

"But we—we left everything, and followed you; what, 27
then, shall we have?"

"I tell you," answered Jesus, "that at the New Creation, 28
'when the Son of Man takes his seat on his throne of glory,'
you who followed me shall be seated upon twelve thrones, as
judges of the twelve tribes of Israel. Every one who has left 29
houses, or brothers, or sisters, or father, or mother, or children,
or land, on account of my Name, will receive many times as
much, and will 'gain Immortal Life.'   But many who 30
are first now will then be last, and those who are last will be
first.   For the Kingdom of Heaven is like an em- 1 **20**
ployer who went out in the early morning to hire

Parable of the Labourers in the Vineyard. labourers for his vineyard. He agreed with the 2
labourers to pay them two shillings a day, and
sent them into his vineyard. On going out 3
again, about nine o'clock, he saw some others
standing in the market-place, doing nothing. 'You also may 4
go into my vineyard,' he said, 'and I will pay you what is
fair.' So the men went. Going out again about mid-day and 5
about three o'clock, he did as before. When he went out about 6
five, he found some other men standing there, and said to
them 'Why have you been standing here all day long, doing
nothing?'

'Because no one has hired us,' they answered. 7

'You also may go into my vineyard,' he said.

In the evening the owner of the vineyard said to his steward 8
'Call the labourers, and pay them their wages, beginning with
the last, and ending with the first.' Now when those who 9
had been hired about five o'clock went up, they received two
shillings each. So, when the first went up, they thought 10

²⁸ Enoch 62. 3; 108. 12.   ²⁹ Enoch 40. 9.

that they would receive more, but they also received two
shillings each; on which they began to grumble at their   11
employer.

'These last,' they said, 'have done only one hour's work,   12
and yet you have put them on the same footing with us, who
have borne the brunt of the day's work, and the heat.'

'My friend,' was his reply to one of them, 'I am not treat-   13
ing you unfairly.   Did not you agree with me for two shillings?
Take what belongs to you, and go.   I choose to give to this   14
last man the same as to you.   Have not I the right to do as I   15
choose with what is mine?   Are you envious because I am
liberal?'   So those who are last will be first, and the   16
first last."

When Jesus was on the point of going up to   17
Jesus, Jerusalem, he gathered the twelve disciples round
a third time,
foretells him by themselves, and said to them as they were
his Death. on their way :

"Listen! We are going up to Jerusalem; and there the Son   18
of Man will be betrayed to the Chief Priests and Teachers of
the Law, and they will condemn him to death, and give him   19
up to the Gentiles for them to mock, and to scourge, and to
crucify; and on the third day he will rise."

Then the mother of Zebediah's sons came to   20
The Request him with her sons, bowing to the ground, and
of the Mother
of James begging a favour.
and John. "What is it that you want?" he asked.   21

"I want you to say," she replied, "that in your Kingdom
these two sons of mine may sit, one on your right, and the
other on your left."

"You do not know what you are asking," was Jesus' answer.   22
"Can you drink the cup that I am to drink?"

"Yes," they exclaimed, "we can."

"You shall indeed drink my cup," he said, "but as to   23
a seat at my right and at my left—that is not mine to give, but
it is for those for whom it has been prepared by my Father."

On hearing of this, the ten others were very indignant about   24
the two brothers.   Jesus, however, called the ten to him, and   25
said :

The Dignity "The rulers of the Gentiles lord it over them
of Service. as you know, and their great men oppress them.
Among you it is not so.   No, whoever wants to become great   26, 27
among you must be your servant, and whoever wants to take
the first place among you, must be your slave; just as the   28

Son of Man came, not to be served, but to serve, and to give
his life as a ransom for many."

**Cure of
two blind
Men.**   As they were going out of Jericho, a great   29
crowd followed him.   Two blind men who were   30
sitting by the road-side, hearing that Jesus was
passing, called out :
"Take pity on us, Master, Son of David !"
The crowd told them to be quiet ; but the men only called out   31
the louder :
"Take pity on us, Master, Son of David !"
Then Jesus stopped and called them.   32
"What do you want me to do for you ?" he said.
"Master," they replied, "we want our eyes to be opened."   33
So Jesus, moved with compassion, touched their eyes, and   34
immediately they recovered their sight, and followed him.

V.—THE LAST DAYS.

**Jesus enters
Jerusalem.**   When they had almost reached Jerusalem,   1   **21**
having come as far as Bethphage, on the Mount
of Olives, Jesus sent on two disciples.
"Go to the village facing you," he said, "and you will   2
immediately find an ass tethered, with a foal by her side ;
untie her, and lead her here for me.   And, if any one says   3
anything to you, you are to say this—'The Master wants
them' ; and he will send them at once."
This happened in fulfilment of these words in the Prophet—   4

'Say to the daughter of Zion—   5
"Behold, thy King is coming to thee,
Gentle, and riding on an ass,
And on the foal of a beast of burden."'

So the disciples went and did as Jesus had directed them.   6
They led the ass and the foal back, and, when they had put   7
their cloaks on them, he seated himself upon them.   The   8
immense crowd of people spread their cloaks in the road,
while some cut branches off the trees, and spread them on the
road.   The crowds that led the way, as well as those that   9
followed behind, kept shouting :

"God save the Son of David !
Blessed is He who comes in the name of the Lord !
God save him from on high !"

When he had entered Jerusalem, the whole city was stirred,   10
and asked—"Who is this ?", to which the crowd replied—   11
"This is the Prophet Jesus from Nazareth in Galilee."

5 Isa. 62. 11 ; Zech. 9. 9.   9 Ps. 118. 25—26 ; Ps. 148. 1.

Jesus in the Temple. Jesus went into the Temple Courts, and drove 12
out all those who were buying and selling there.
He overturned the tables of the money-changers,
and the seats of the pigeon-dealers, and said to them : 13
" Scripture says—

' My House shall be called a House of Prayer';

but you are making it ' a den of robbers. ' "
While he was still in the Temple Courts, some **blind** and some 14
lame people came up to him, and he cured them.   But, 15
when the Chief Priests and the Teachers of the Law saw the
wonderful things that Jesus did, and the boys who were calling
out in the Temple Courts " God save the Son of David !", they
were indignant, and said to him : 16

" Do you hear what these boys are saying ? "

"Yes," answered Jesus; " but did you never read the words—

' Out of the mouths of babes and sucklings thou hast called
forth perfect praise '? "

Then he left them, and went out of the city to Bethany, and 17
spent the night there.

The fruitless Fig Tree. The next morning, in returning to the city, Jesus 18
became hungry ; and, noticing a solitary fig tree 19
by the road-side, he went up to it, but found
nothing on it but leaves. So he said to it :
" Never again shall fruit be gathered off you."
And suddenly the fig tree withered up. When the disciples 20
saw this, they exclaimed in astonishment :
" How suddenly the fig tree withered up ! "
" I tell you," replied Jesus, " if you have faith, without 21
ever a doubt, you will do not only what has been done to the
fig tree, but, even if you should say to this hill ' Be lifted up
and hurled into the sea !', it would be done. And what- 22
ever you ask for in your prayers will, if you have faith, be
granted you."

Jesus and the Chief Priests. After Jesus had come into the Temple Courts, 23
the Chief Priests and the Councillors of the Nation
came up to him as he was teaching, and said :
" What authority have you to do these things ?   Who gave
you this authority ? "
" I, too," said Jesus in reply, " will ask you one question ; if 24
you will give me an answer to it, then I, also, will tell you
what authority I have to act as I do. It is about John's 25
baptism. What was its origin ? divine or human ? "
But they began arguing among themselves :
" If we say ' divine,' he will say to us ' Why then did not you

believe him?" But if we say 'human,' we are afraid of the   26
people, for every one regards John as a Prophet."

So the answer they gave Jesus was—"We do not know."   27

"Then I," he said, "refuse to tell you what authority I have
to do these things.   What do you think of this? There   28
Parable was a man who had two sons. He went to the
of the elder and said 'Go and work in the vineyard
two Sons. to-day, my son.'

'Yes, sir,' he answered ; but he did not go.   Then the father   29, 30
went to the second son, and said the same.   'I will not,' he
answered ; but afterwards he was sorry and went.   Which   31
of the two sons did as his father wished?"

"The second," they said.

"I tell you," added Jesus, "that tax-gatherers and prostitutes are going into the Kingdom of God before you.   For   32
when John came to you, walking in the path of righteousness,
you did not believe him, but tax-gatherers and prostitutes
did ; and yet you, though you saw this, even then were not
sorry, nor did you believe him.

Parable   Listen to another parable.   A man, who   33
of the wicked was an employer, once planted a vineyard, put a
Tenants. fence round it, dug a winepress in it, built a
tower, and then let it out to tenants and went abroad.   When   34
the time for the vintage drew near, he sent his servants to the
tenants, to receive his share of the produce.   But the tenants   35
seized his servants, beat one, killed another, and stoned a
third.   A second time the owner sent some servants, a larger   36
number than before, and the tenants treated them in the same
way.   As a last resource he sent his son to them.   'They will   37
respect my son,' he said.   But the tenants, on seeing his son,   38
said to each other 'Here is the heir !   Come, let us kill
him, and get his inheritance.'   So they seized him, and threw   39
him outside the vineyard, and killed him.   Now, when the   40
owner of the vineyard comes, what will he do to those
tenants ?"

"Miserable wretches !" they exclaimed, "he will put them
to a miserable death, and he will let out the vineyard to other   41
tenants, who will pay him his share of the produce at the
proper times."

Then Jesus added : "Have you never read in the Scriptures?—   42

'The very stone which the builders despised—
    Has now itself become the corner-stone ;
This corner-stone has come from the Lord,
    And is marvellous in our eyes.'

And that, I tell you, is why the Kingdom of God will be   43
taken from you, and given to a nation that does produce

        ³³ Isa. 5. 1—2.   ⁴² Ps. 118, 22,

the fruit of the Kingdom.   Yes, and he who falls on   44
this stone will be dashed to pieces, while any one on whom it
falls—it will scatter him as dust."

After listening to these parables, the Chief Priests and the   45
Pharisees saw that it was about them that he was speaking;
yet, although eager to arrest him, they were afraid of the   46
crowds, who regarded him as a Prophet.

Once more Jesus spoke to them in parables.   1   **22**

"The Kingdom of Heaven," he said, "may be   2
Parable compared to a king who gave a banquet in
of the honour of his son's wedding.   He sent his   3
Marriage servants to call those who had been invited to the
Feast. banquet, but they were unwilling to come.   A second time he   4
sent some servants, with orders to say to those who had been
invited 'I have prepared my breakfast, my cattle and fat
beasts are killed and everything is ready; come to the banquet.'
They, however, took no notice, but went off, one to his farm,   5
another to his business ; while the rest, seizing his servants,   6
ill-treated them and killed them.   The king, in anger, sent   7
his troops, put those murderers to death, and set their city on
fire.   Then he said to his servants 'The banquet is pre-   8
pared, but those who were invited were not worthy.   So   9
go to the cross-roads, and invite every one you find to the
banquet.'   The servants went out into the roads and collected   10
all the people whom they found, whether bad or good ; and
the bridal-hall was filled with guests.   But, when the king went   11
in to see his guests, he noticed there a man who had not put
on a wedding-robe.   So he said to him 'My friend, how is it   12
that you came in here without a wedding-robe?'   The man was
speechless.   Then the king said to the attendants 'Tie him   13
hand and foot, and 'put him out into the darkness' outside,
where there will be weeping and grinding of teeth.'   For   14
many are called, but few chosen."

A Question Then the Pharisees went away and conferred   15
about together as to how they might lay a snare for
Tribute. Jesus in the course of conversation.   They sent   16
their disciples, with the Herodians, to say to him :

"Teacher, we know that you are an honest man, and that
you teach the Way of God honestly, and are not afraid of any
one ; for you pay no regard to a man's position.   Tell us,   17
then, what you think.   Are we right in paying taxes to the
Emperor, or not?"

Perceiving their malice, Jesus answered :   18

"Why are you testing me, you hypocrites?   Show me the   19
coin with which the tax is paid."

And, when they had brought him a florin, he asked :   20
"Whose head and title are these?"

13 Enoch 10. 4.

"The Emperor's," they answered: on which he said to   21
them :

"Then pay to the Emperor what belongs to the Emperor,
and to God what belongs to God."

They wondered at his answer, and left him alone and went   22
away.

A Question about the Resurrection. That same day some Sadducees came up to   23
Jesus, maintaining that there is no resurrection.
Their question was this :—

"Teacher, Moses said—   24

'Should a man die without children, the man's brother shall
become the husband of the widow, and raise a family for his
brother.'

Now we had living among us seven brothers ; of whom the   25
eldest married and died, and, as he had no family, left his wife
for his brother.   The same thing happened to the second and   26
the third brothers, and indeed to all the seven.   The woman   27
herself died last of all.   At the resurrection, then, whose   28
wife will she be out of the seven, all of them having had her ? "

"Your mistake," replied Jesus, "is due to your ignorance of   29
the Scriptures, and of the power of God.   For at the resur-   30
rection there is no marrying or being married, but all who rise
are as angels in Heaven.   As to the resurrection of the dead,   31
have you not read these words of God—

'I am the God of Abraham, and the God of Isaac, and the   32
God of Jacob'?

He is not the God of dead men, but of living."

The crowds, who had been listening to him, were greatly   33
struck with his teaching.

The Great Commandment. When the Pharisees heard that Jesus had   34
silenced the Sadducees, they collected together.
Then one of them, a Student of the Law, to test   35
him, asked this question—

"Teacher, what is the great commandment in the Law ? "   36
His answer was :   37

"'Thou shalt love the Lord thy God with all thy heart, and
with all thy soul, and with all thy mind.'

This is the great first commandment.   The second, which   38, 39
is like it, is this—

'Thou shalt love thy neighbour as thou dost thyself.'

On these two commandments hang all the Law and the   40
Prophets."

24 Deut. 25. 5.   32 Exod. 3. 6.   37 Deut. 6. 5.   39 Lev. 19. 18.

Christ the Son of David. Before the Pharisees separated, Jesus put this 41 question to them— 42 "What do you think about the Christ? Whose son is he?"

"David's," they said.

"How is it, then," Jesus replied, "that David, speaking 43 under inspiration, calls him 'lord,' in the passage—

'The Lord said to my lord: "Sit at my right hand, 44
Until I put thy enemies beneath thy feet"'?

Since, then, David calls him 'lord,' how is he David's son?" 45
No one could say a word in answer; nor did any one after 46 that day venture to question him further.

Then Jesus, speaking to the crowds and to his disciples, 1 **23** said: 2

Warnings against the Teachers of the Law. "The Teachers of the Law and the Pharisees now occupy the chair of Moses. Therefore 3 practise and lay to heart everything that they tell you, but do not follow their example, for they preach but do not practise. While they make up heavy loads 4 and pile them on other men's shoulders, they decline, themselves, to lift a finger to move them. All their actions are 5 done to attract attention. They widen their phylacteries, and increase the size of their tassels, and like to have the place 6 of honour at dinner, and the best seats in the Synagogues, and 7 to be greeted in the markets with respect, and to be called 'Rabbi' by everybody. But do not you allow yourselves to be 8 called 'Rabbi,' for you have only one Teacher, and you yourselves are all Brothers. And do not call any one on the earth 9 your 'Father,' for you have only one Father, the heavenly Father. Nor must you allow yourselves to be called 'Leaders,' 10 for you have only one Leader, the Christ. The man who would 11 be the greatest among you must be your servant. Who- 12 ever shall exalt himself will be humbled, and whoever shall humble himself will be exalted.

Jesus denounces the Pharisees. But alas for you, Teachers of the Law and 14 Pharisees, hypocrites that you are! You turn the key of the Kingdom of Heaven in men's faces. For you do not go in yourselves, nor yet allow those who try to go in to do so. Alas for you, Teachers of the Law 15 and Pharisees, hypocrites that you are! You scour land and sea to make a single convert, and, when he is gained, you make him twice as deserving of the Pit as you are yourselves. Alas for you, you blind guides! You 16 say 'If any one swears by the Temple, his oath counts for nothing; but, if any one swears by the gold of the Temple, his

44 Ps. 110. 1.

oath is binding on him'! Fools that you are and blind! 17
Which is the more important? the gold? or the Temple
which has given sacredness to the gold? You say, too, 18
'If any one swears by the altar, his oath counts for nothing,
but, if any one swears by the offering placed on it, his oath
is binding on him'! Blind indeed! Which is the more 19
important? the offering? or the altar which gives sacredness to the offering? Therefore a man, swearing by the 20
altar, swears by it and by all that is on it, and a man, 21
swearing by the Temple, swears by it and by him who
dwells in it, while a man, swearing by Heaven, swears by 22
the throne of God, and by him who sits upon it.   Alas 23
for you, Teachers of the Law and Pharisees, hypocrites that
you are! You pay tithes on mint, fennel, and carraway-seed,
and have neglected the weightier matters of the Law—justice,
mercy, and good faith. These last you ought to have put
into practice, without neglecting the first. You blind guides, 24
to strain out a gnat and to swallow a camel!   Alas for 25
you, Teachers of the Law and Pharisees, hypocrites that you
are! You clean the outside of the cup and of the dish, but
inside they are filled with the results of greed and self-
indulgence. You blind Pharisee! First clean the inside of 26
the cup and the dish, so that the outside may become clean
as well.   Alas for you, Teachers of the Law and 27
Pharisees, hypocrites that you are! You are like white-washed
tombs, which indeed look fair outside, while inside they
are filled with dead men's bones and all kinds of filth. It 28
is the same with you. Outwardly, and to others, you have
the look of religious men, but inwardly you are full of hypocrisy and sin.   Alas for you, Teachers of the Law and 29
Pharisees, hypocrites that you are! You build the tombs
of the Prophets, and decorate the monuments of religious
men, and say 'Had we been living in the days of our ances- 30
tors, we should have taken no part in their murder of the
Prophets!' By doing this you are furnishing evidence against 31
yourselves that you are true children of the men who murdered
the Prophets. Fill up the measure of your ancestors' guilt. 32
You serpents and brood of vipers! How can you escape being 33
sentenced to the Pit? That is why I send you Prophets, wise 34
men, and Teachers of the Law, some of whom you will crucify
and kill, and some of whom you will scourge in your Synagogues, and persecute from town to town; in order that upon 35
your heads may fall every drop of innocent 'blood spilt on earth,'
from the blood of innocent Abel down to that of Zechariah,
Barachiah's son, whom you murdered between the Temple
Jesus laments and the altar. All this, I tell you, will come home 36
the fate to the present generation.
of Jerusalem. Jerusalem! Jerusalem! she who slays the 37

[35] Enoch 9. 1.

Prophets and stones the messengers sent to her——Oh, how often have I wished to gather your children round me, as a hen gathers her brood under her wings, and you would not come! Verily, your House is left to you desolate! For nevermore, I tell you, shall you see me, until you say— 38 39

'Blessed is He who comes in the Name of the Lord!'"

Jesus foretells the Destruction of the Temple and the End of the Age. Leaving the Temple Courts, Jesus was walking away, when his disciples came up to draw his attention to the Temple buildings. 1 **24**

"Do you see all these things?" was his answer. "I tell you, not a single stone will be left here upon another, which will not be thrown down." 2

So, while Jesus was sitting on the Mount of Olives, his disciples came up to him privately and said: "Tell us when this will be, and what will be the sign of your Coming, and of the close of the age." 3

Jesus replied to them as follows: 4

"See that no one leads you astray; for many will take my name, and come saying 'I am the Christ,' and will lead many astray. And you will hear of wars and rumours of wars; take care not to be alarmed, for such things must occur; but the end is not yet here. For 'nation will rise against nation and kingdom against kingdom,' and there will be famines and earthquakes in various places. All this, however, will be but the beginning of the birth-pangs! When that time comes, they will give you up to persecution, and will put you to death, and you will be hated by all nations on account of my Name. And then many will fall away, and will betray one another, and hate one another. Many false Prophets, also, will appear and lead many astray; and, owing to the increase of wickedness, the love of most will grow cold. Yet the man that endures to the end shall be saved. And this Good News of the Kingdom shall be proclaimed throughout the world as a witness to all nations; and then will come the end. As soon, then, as you see 'the Foul Desecration', mentioned by the Prophet Daniel, standing in the Holy Place," (the reader must consider what this means) "then those of you who are in Judaea must take refuge in the mountains; and a man on the house-top must not go down to get the things that are in his house; nor must one who is on his farm turn back to get his cloak. And alas for the women that are with child, and for those that are nursing infants in those days! Pray, too, that your flight 5 6 7 8 9 10 11 12 13 14 15 16 17 18 19 20

---

38 Jer. 22. 5. 39 Ps. 118. 26. 6 Dan. 2. 28. 7 Isa. 19. 2. 10 Isa. 8. 15.
15 Dan. 12. 11; 8. 11.

may not take place in winter, nor on a Sabbath ; for that will 21
be 'a time of great distress, the like of which has not occurred
from the beginning of the world down to the present time '—
no, nor ever will again. And, had not those days been limited, 22
not a single soul would escape ; but for the sake of 'God's
People' a limit will be put to them.   And, at that time, if 23
any one should say to you 'Look! here is the Christ!' or 'Here
he is!', do not believe it ; for false Christs and false Prophets will 24
arise, and will display great signs and marvels, so that, were
it possible, even God's People would be led astray. Remember, 25
I have told you beforehand. Therefore, if people say to you 26
'He is in the Wilderness!', do not go out there ; or 'He is in an
inner room!', do not believe it ; for, just as lightning will start 27
from the east and flash across to the west, so will it be with
the Coming of the Son of Man. Wherever a dead body lies, 28
'there will the vultures flock.'   Immediately after the 29
distress of those days, 'the sun will be darkened, the moon
will not give her light, the stars will fall from the heavens,'
and 'the forces of the heavens will be convulsed.' Then will 30
appear the sign of the Son of Man in the heavens ; and all the
peoples of the earth will mourn, when they see the 'Son of
Man coming on the clouds of the heavens,' with power and
great glory ; and he will send his angels, with a great trumpet, 31
and they will gather his People round him from the four winds,
from one end of heaven to the other.

The Need   Learn the lesson taught by the fig tree. As 32
for   soon as its branches are full of sap, and it is
Watchfulness. bursting into leaf, you know that summer is
near. And so may you, as soon as you see all these things, 33
know that he is at your doors. I tell you, that even the pre- 34
sent generation will not pass away, till all these things
have taken place. The heavens and the earth will pass 35
away, but my words shall never pass away.   But about 36
that Day and Hour, no one knows—not even the angels of
Heaven, nor yet the Son—but only the Father himself. For, 37
just as in the days of Noah, so will it be at the Coming of the
Son of Man. In those days before the flood they went on 38
eating and drinking, marrying and being married, up to the
very day on which Noah entered the ark, taking no notice till 39
the flood came and swept them one and all away ; and so will
it be at the Coming of the Son of Man. At that time, of 40
two men on a farm one will be taken and one left ; of two 41
women grinding with the hand-mill one will be taken and one
left. Therefore watch ; for you cannot be sure on what day 42
your Master is coming. But this you do know, that, had the 43
owner of the house known at what time of night the thief

21 Dan. 12. 1.   22 Enoch 1. 1.   24 Deut. 13. 1.   28 Isa. 34. 15.   29 Dan. 12. 1 ;
Isa. 13. 10 ; 34. 4.   30—31 Zech. 12. 12 ; Dan. 7. 13 ; Isa. 27. 13 ; Zech. 2. 6
Deut. 30. 4 ; 28. 64.   38—39 Gen. 7. 7.

was coming, he would have been on the watch, and would not have allowed his house to be broken into. Therefore, do you also prepare, since it is just when you are least expecting him that the Son of Man will come.   Who, then, is 44

that trustworthy, careful servant, who has been placed 45

Parable of the good and bad Servants. by his master over his household, to give them their food at the proper time? Happy will that servant be whom his master, when he comes 46

home, shall find doing this. I tell you that his master will put 47

him in charge of the whole of his property. But, should he 48

be a bad servant, and say to himself 'My master is a long time in coming,' and begin to beat his fellow-servants, and 49

eat and drink with drunkards, that servant's master will come 50

on a day when he does not expect him, and at an hour of 51

which he is unaware, and will flog him severely, and assign him his place among the hypocrites, where there will be weeping and grinding of teeth.

Parable of the ten Bridesmaids Then the Kingdom of Heaven will be like ten 1 **25**

bridesmaids who took their lamps and went out to meet the bridegroom. Five of them were 2

foolish, and five were prudent. The foolish ones took their 3

lamps, but took no oil with them; while the prudent ones, 4

besides taking their lamps, took oil in their jars. As the 5

bridegroom was late in coming, they all became drowsy, and slept. But at midnight a shout was raised—'The Bride- 6

groom is coming! Come out to meet him!' Then all the 7

bridesmaids awoke and trimmed their lamps. And the foolish 8

ones said to the prudent 'Give us some of your oil; our lamps are going out.' But the prudent ones answered 'No, for 9

fear that there will not be enough for you and for us. Go instead to those who sell it, and buy for yourselves.' But 10

while they were on their way to buy it, the bridegroom came; and the bridesmaids who were ready went in with him to the banquet, and the door was shut. Afterwards the other brides- 11

maids came. 'Sir, Sir,' they said, 'open the door to us!' But the bridegroom answered 'I tell you, I do not know 12

you.'   Therefore watch, since you know neither the 13

Day nor the Hour.

Parable of the Talents. For it is as though a man, going on his travels, 14

called his servants, and gave his property into their charge. He gave three thousand pounds 15

to one, twelve hundred to another, and six hundred to a third, in proportion to the ability of each. Then he set out on 16

his travels. The man who had received the three thousand pounds went at once and traded with it, and made another three thousand. So, too, the man who had received the 17

twelve hundred pounds made another twelve hundred. But 18

the man who had received the six hundred went and dug a hole in the ground, and hid his master's money. After a long 19

time the master of those servants returned, and settled accounts
with them.   The man who had received the three thousand   20
pounds came up and brought three thousand more.   ' Sir,' he
said, 'you entrusted me with three thousand pounds ; look,
I have made another three thousand !'

'Well done, good, trustworthy servant !' said his master.   21
' You have been trustworthy with a small sum ; now I will place
a large one in your hands ; come and share your master's joy !'
Then the one who had received the twelve hundred pounds   22
came up and said ' Sir, you entrusted me with twelve hundred pounds ; look, I have made another twelve hundred !'

'Well done, good, trustworthy servant !' said his master.   23
'You have been trustworthy with a small sum ; now I will
place a large one in your hands ; come and share your
master's joy !'

The man who had received the six hundred pounds came up,   24
too, and said ' Sir, I knew that you were a hard man ; you reap
where you have not sown, and gather up where you have not
winnowed ; and, in my fear, I went and hid your money in   25
the ground ; look, here is what belongs to you !'

'You lazy, worthless servant !' was his Master's reply.   26
'You knew that I reap where I have not sown, and gather
up where I have not winnowed ?   Then you ought to have   27
placed my money in the hands of bankers, and I, on my
return, should have received my money, with interest.   There-   28
fore,' he continued, ' take away from him the six hundred
pounds, and give it to the one who has the six thousand.   For,   29
to him who has, more will be given, and he shall have abundance ; but, as for him who has nothing, even what he has
will be taken away from him.   As for the useless servant, ' put   30
him out into the darkness ' outside, where there will be weeping
and grinding of teeth.'

The Great   When the Son of Man has come in his glory   31
Judgement. and all the angels with him, then he ' will take
his seat on his throne of glory ' ; and all the nations will be   32
gathered before him, and he will separate the people—just as
a shepherd separates sheep from goats—placing the sheep on   33
his right hand, and the goats on his left.   Then the King will   34
say to those on his right ' Come, you who are blessed by my
Father, enter upon possession of the Kingdom prepared for
you ever since the beginning of the world.   For, when I was   35
hungry, you gave me food ; when I was thirsty, you gave me
drink ; when I was a stranger, you took me to your homes ;
when I was naked, you clothed me ; when I fell ill, you visited   36
me ; and when I was in prison, you came to me.'

Then the Righteous will answer ' Lord, when did we see you   37
hungry, and feed you ? or thirsty, and give you drink ?   When   38
did we see you a stranger, and take you to our homes ? or

[30] Enoch 10. 4.   [31] Zech. 14. 5 ; Enoch 62. 5.

naked, and clothe you? When did we see you ill, or in 39
prison, and come to you?'

And the King will reply 'I tell you, as often as you did it 40
to one of these my Brothers, however lowly, you did it to me.'

Then he will say to those on his left 'Go from my presence, 41
accursed, into the 'aeonian fire which has been prepared for the
Devil and his angels.' For, when I was hungry, you gave me 42
no food; when I was thirsty, you gave me no drink; when I 43
was a stranger, you did not take me to your homes; when I
was naked, you did not clothe me; and, when I was ill and in
prison, you did not visit me.'

Then they, in their turn, will answer 'Lord, when did we see 44
you hungry, or thirsty, or a stranger, or naked, or ill, or in
prison, and did not supply your wants?'

And then he will reply 'I tell you, as often as you failed to 45
do it to one of these, however lowly, you failed to do it to me.'

And these last will go away 'into aeonian punishment,' but 46
the righteous 'into aeonian life.'"

The Plot against Jesus. When Jesus had finished all this teaching, he 1 **26**
said to his disciples:
"You know that in two days' time the Festival 2
of the Passover will be here; and that the Son of Man is to be
given up to be crucified."

Then the Chief Priests and the Councillors of the Nation met 3
in the house of the High Priest, who was called Caiaphas, and 4
plotted together to arrest Jesus by stealth and put him to
death; but they said: "Not during the Festival, for fear of 5
causing a riot."

Jesus anointed by a Woman at Bethany. After Jesus had reached Bethany, and while he 6
was in the house of Simon the leper, a woman 7
came up to him with an alabaster jar of very costly
perfume, and poured the perfume upon his head as
he was at table. The disciples were indignant at seeing this. 8

"What is this waste for?" they exclaimed. "It could 9
have been sold for a large sum, and the money given to poor
people."

"Why are you troubling the woman?" Jesus said, when 10
he noticed it. "For this is a beautiful deed that she has
done to me. You always have the poor with you, but you 11
will not always have me. In pouring this perfume on my 12
body, she has done it for my burying. I tell you, wher- 13
ever, in the whole world, this Good News is proclaimed, what
this woman has done will be told in memory of her."

⁴¹ Enoch 54. 1, 5.   ⁴⁶ Dan. 12. 2.

Judas agrees
to betray
Jesus. It was then that one of the Twelve, named 14
Judas Iscariot, made his way to the Chief Priests,
and said "What are you willing to give me, if I 15
betray Jesus to you?" The Priests 'weighed him out thirty
pieces of silver' as payment. So from that time Judas looked 16
for an opportunity to betray Jesus.

**The
Passover.** On the first day of the Festival of the Unleavened 17
Bread, the disciples came up to Jesus, and said :
"Where do you wish us to make preparations for you to eat
the Passover?"

"Go into the city to a certain man," he answered, "and 18
say to him 'The Teacher says—My time is near. I will keep
the Passover with my disciples at your house.'"

The disciples did as Jesus directed them, and prepared the 19
Passover.

In the evening Jesus took his place with the twelve 20
disciples, and, while they were eating, he said : 21

"I tell you that one of you will betray me."

In great grief they began to say to him, one by one : 22
"Can it be I, Master?"

"The one who dipped his bread beside me in the dish," 23
replied Jesus, "is the one who will betray me. True, the Son 24
of Man must go, as Scripture says of him, yet alas for that man
by whom the Son of Man is being betrayed ! For that man 'it
would be better never to have been born !'"

And Judas, who was betraying him, turned to him and said : 25
"Can it be I, Rabbi?"

"It is," answered Jesus.

**The 'Lord's
Supper.'** While they were eating, Jesus took some bread, 26
and, after saying the blessing, broke it and, as he
gave it to his disciples, said :

"Take it and eat it ; this is my body."

Then he took a cup, and, after saying the thanksgiving, gave 27
it to them, with the words :

"Drink from it, all of you ; for this is my Covenant-blood, 28
which is poured out for many for the forgiveness of sins. And 29
I tell you that I shall never, after this, drink of this juice of the
grape, until that day when I shall drink it new with you in the
Kingdom of my Father."

**Peter's Fall
foretold.** They then sang a hymn, and went out to 30
the Mount of Olives.

Then Jesus said to them : 31
"Even you will all fall away from me to-night. Scripture
says—

  'I will strike down the shepherd, and the sheep of the flock
  will be scattered.'

15 Zech. 11. 12.   24 Enoch 38. 2.   23 Exod. 24. 8.   31 Zech. 13. 7.

But, after I have risen, I shall go before you into Galilee." 32

"If every one else falls away from you," Peter answered, "I 33
shall never fall away!"

"I tell you," replied Jesus, "that this very night, before the 34
cock crows, you will disown me three times!"

"Even if I must die with you," Peter exclaimed, "I shall 35
never disown you!"

All the disciples spoke in the same way.

Jesus in Gethsemane. Then Jesus came with them to a garden called 36
Gethsemane, and he said to his disciples:

"Sit down here while I go and pray yonder."

Taking with him Peter and the two sons of Zebediah, he 37
began to show signs of sadness and deep distress of mind.

"I am sad at heart," he said, "sad even to death; wait 38
here, and watch with me."

Going on a little further, he threw himself on his face in 39
prayer.

"My Father," he said, "if it is possible, let me be spared
this cup; only, not as I will, but as thou willest."

Then he came to his disciples, and found them asleep. 40

"What!" he said to Peter, "could none of you watch with
me for one hour? Watch and pray, that you may not fall into 41
temptation. True, the spirit is eager, but human nature is
weak."

Again, a second time, he went away, and prayed. 42

"My Father," he said, "if I cannot be spared this cup, but
must drink it, thy will be done!"

And coming back again he found them asleep, for their eyes 43
were heavy. So he left them, and went away again, and 44
prayed a third time, again saying the same words.

Then he came to the disciples, and said: 45

"Sleep on now, and rest yourselves. Hark! my time is
close at hand, and the Son of Man is being betrayed into the
hands of wicked men. Up, and let us be going. Look! my 46
betrayer is close at hand."

The Arrest of Jesus. And, while he was still speaking, Judas, who 47
was one of the Twelve, came in sight; and with
him was a great crowd of people, with swords
and clubs, sent from the Chief Priests and Councillors of
the Nation. Now the betrayer had arranged a signal with 48
them.

"The man whom I kiss," he had said, "will be the one;
arrest him."

So he went up to Jesus at once, and exclaimed: "Welcome, 49
Rabbi!" and kissed him; on which Jesus said to him: 50

"Friend, do what you have come for."

Thereupon the men went up, seized Jesus, and arrested him.

[38] Ps. 42. 5.

Suddenly one of those who were with Jesus stretched out his 51
hand, and drew his sword, and striking the High Priest's
servant, cut off his ear.

"Sheathe your sword," Jesus said, "for all who draw the 52
sword will be put to the sword. Do you think that I cannot ask 53
my Father for help, when he would at once send to my aid more
than twelve legions of angels? But in that case how would 54
the Scriptures be fulfilled, which say that this must be?"
Jesus at the same time said to the crowds: 55

"Have you come out, as if after a robber, with swords and
clubs, to take me? I have sat teaching day after day in the
Temple Courts, and yet you did not arrest me."
The whole of this occurred in fulfilment of the Prophetic Scrip- 56
tures.

Then the disciples all forsook him and fled.

Jesus   Those who had arrested Jesus took him to 57
before the   Caiaphas, the High Priest, where the Teachers
High Priest. of the Law and the Councillors had assembled.
Peter followed him at a distance as far as the court-yard of the 58
High Priest, and went in and sat down among the police-
officers, to see the end. Meanwhile the Chief Priests and the 59
whole of the High Council were trying to get such false evidence
against Jesus, as would warrant putting him to death, but they 60
did not find any, although many came forward with false
evidence. Later on, however, two men came forward and 61
said:

"This man said 'I am able to destroy the Temple of God,
and to build it in three days.'"
Then the High Priest stood up, and said to Jesus: 62

"Have you no answer? What is this evidence which these
men are giving against you?"
But Jesus remained silent. On this the High Priest said to 63
him:

"I adjure you, by the Living God, to tell us whether you
are the Christ, the Son of God."

"It is true,' Jesus answered; "moreover I tell you all 64
that hereafter you shall 'see the Son of Man sitting on the
right hand of the Almighty, and coming on the clouds of the
heavens.'"
Then the High Priest tore his robes. 65

"This is blasphemy!" he exclaimed. "Why do we want
any more witnesses? You have just heard his blasphemy!
What is your decision?" 66
They answered:

"He deserves death."
Then they spat in his face, and struck him, while others dealt 67
blows at him, saying as they did so: 68

64 Ps. 110. 1; Dan. 7. 13.

"Now play the Prophet for us, you Christ! Who was it that struck you?"

Peter disowns Jesus. Peter, meanwhile, was sitting outside in the 69 court-yard; and a maidservant came up to him, and exclaimed:

"Why, you were with Jesus the Galilean!"

But Peter denied it before them all. 70

"I do not know what you mean," he replied.

When he had gone out into the gateway, another maid saw 71 him, and said to those who were there:

"This man was with Jesus of Nazareth!"

Again he denied it with an oath: 72

"I do not know the man!"

But soon afterwards those who were standing by came up and 73 said to Peter:

"You also are certainly one of them; why, your very way of speaking proves it!"

Then Peter began to swear, with most solemn imprecations: 74

"I do not know the man."

At that moment a cock crowed; and Peter remembered the 75 words which Jesus had said—'Before a cock has crowed, you will disown me three times'; and he went outside, and wept bitterly.

The End of Judas. At daybreak all the Chief Priests and the Coun- 1 **27** cillors of the Nation consulted together against Jesus, to bring about his death. They put him in chains and led 2 him away, and gave him up to the Roman Governor, Pilate.

Then Judas, who betrayed him, seeing that Jesus was con- 3 demned, repented of what he had done, and returned the thirty pieces of silver to the Chief Priests and Councillors.

"I did wrong in betraying a good man to his death," he 4 said.

"What has that to do with us?" they replied. "You must see to that yourself."

Judas flung down the pieces of silver in the Temple, and left; 5 and went away and hanged himself. The Chief Priests 6 took the pieces of silver, but they said:

"We must not put them into the Temple treasury, because they are blood-money."

So, after consultation, they bought with them the 'Potter's 7 Field' for a burial-ground for foreigners; and that is why that 8 field is called the 'Field of Blood' to this very day. Then 9 it was that these words spoken by the Prophet Jeremiah were fulfilled—

'They took the thirty pieces of silver, the price of him who was valued, whom some of the people of Israel valued, and 10 gave them for the Potter's field, as the Lord commanded me.'

9–10 Zech. ii. 13.

Jesus before the Roman Governor. Meanwhile Jesus was brought before the Roman 11 Governor.

"Are you the King of the Jews?" asked the Governor.

"It is true," answered Jesus.

While charges were being brought against him by the Chief 12 Priests and Councillors, Jesus made no reply. Then Pilate 13 said to him:

"Do not you hear how many accusations they are making against you?"

Yet Jesus made no reply—not even a single word; at which 14 the Governor was greatly astonished.   Now, at the 15 Feast, the Governor was accustomed to grant the people the release of any one prisoner whom they might choose. At that 16 time they had a notorious prisoner called Barabbas. So, when 17 the people had collected, Pilate said to them:

"Which do you wish me to release for you? Barabbas? or Jesus who is called 'Christ'?"

For he knew that it was out of jealousy that they had given 18 Jesus up to him.   While he was still on the Bench, 19 his wife sent this message to him—

"Do not have anything to do with that good man, for I have been very unhappy to-day in a dream on account of him."

But the Chief Priests and the Councillors persuaded the crowds 20 to ask for Barabbas, and to kill Jesus. The Governor, how- 21 ever, said to them:

"Which of these two do you wish me to release for you?"

"Barabbas," they answered.

"What then," Pilate asked, "shall I do with Jesus who 22 is called 'Christ'?"

"Let him be crucified," they all replied.

"Why, what harm has he done?" he asked. 23

But they kept shouting furiously: "Let him be crucified!"

When Pilate saw that his efforts were unavailing, but that, on 24 the contrary, a riot was beginning, he took some water, and washed his hands in the sight of the crowd, saying as he did so:

"I am not answerable for this bloodshed; you must see to it yourselves."

And all the people answered: 25

"His blood be on our heads and on our children's!"

Then Pilate released Barabbas to them; but Jesus he scourged, 26 and gave him up to be crucified.

The Crucifixion of Jesus. After that, the Governor's soldiers took Jesus with 27 them into the Government House, and gathered the whole garrison round him. They stripped 28 him, and put on him a red military cloak, and, having twisted 29 some thorns into a crown, put it on his head, and a rod in his right hand, and then, going down on their knees before him, they mocked him.

"Long life to you, King of the Jews!" they said.

They spat at him and, taking the rod, kept striking him on the head; and, when they had left off mocking him, they took off the military cloak, and put his own clothes on him, and led him away to be crucified. 30 31

As they were on their way out, they came upon a man from Cyrene of the name of Simon; and they compelled him to go with them to carry the cross. On reaching a place named Golgotha (a place named from its likeness to a skull), they gave him some wine to drink which had been mixed with gall; but, after tasting it, Jesus refused to drink it. When they had crucified him, they divided his clothes among them by casting lots. Then they sat down, and kept watch over him there. Above his head they fixed the accusation against him written out— 32 33 34 35 36 37

'THIS IS JESUS THE KING OF THE JEWS.'

At the same time two robbers were crucified with him, one on the right, the other on the left. The passers-by railed at him, shaking their heads as they said: 38 39 40

"You who 'destroy the Temple and build one in three days,' save yourself! If you are God's Son, come down from the cross!"

In the same way the Chief Priests, with the Teachers of the Law and Councillors, said in mockery: 41

"He saved others, but he cannot save himself! He is the 'King of Israel'! Let him come down from the cross now, and we will believe in him. He has trusted in God; if God wants him, let him deliver him now; for he said 'I am God's Son.'" Even the robbers, who were crucified with him, reviled him in the same way. 42 43 44

The Death of Jesus. After mid-day a darkness came over all the country, lasting till three in the afternoon. And about three Jesus called out loudly: 45 46

"Eloi, Eloi, lema sabacthani"—that is to say, 'O my God, my God, why hast thou forsaken me?'

Some of those standing by heard this, and said: 47

"The man is calling for Elijah!"

One of them immediately ran and took a sponge, and, filling it with common wine, put it on the end of a rod, and offered it to him to drink. But the rest said: 48

"Wait and let us see if Elijah is coming to save him." 49

[However another man took a spear, and pierced his side; and water and blood flowed from it.] But Jesus, uttering another loud cry, gave up his spirit. Suddenly the 50 51

---

[34] Ps. 69. 21.　[35] Ps. 22. 18.　[39] Ps. 22. 7.　[43] Ps. 22. 8.　[46] Ps. 22. 1.
[48] Ps. 69. 21.

E

Temple curtain was torn in two from top to bottom, the earth shook, the rocks were torn asunder, the tombs opened, and 52 the bodies of many of God's People who had fallen asleep rose, and they, leaving their tombs, went, after the resurrec- 53 tion of Jesus, into the Holy City, and appeared to many people.   The Roman Captain, and the men with him 54 who were watching Jesus, on seeing the earthquake and all that was happening, became greatly frightened and exclaimed:

"This must indeed have been God's Son!"

There were many women there, watching from a distance, 55 who had accompanied Jesus from Galilee and had been at- tending on him.   Among them were Mary of Magdala, Mary 56 the mother of James and Joseph, and the mother of Zebediah's sons.

The Burial of Jesus.   When evening had fallen, there came a rich 57 man belonging to Ramah, named Joseph, who had himself become a disciple of Jesus.   He went to see Pilate, 58 and asked for the body of Jesus; upon which Pilate ordered it to be given him.   So Joseph took the body, and wrapped it in 59 a clean linen sheet, and laid it in his newly-made tomb which 60 he had cut in the rock; and, before he left, he rolled a great stone against the entrance of the tomb.   Mary of 61 Magdala and the other Mary remained behind, sitting in front of the grave.

The next day—that is, the day following the Preparation- 62 Day—the Chief Priests and Pharisees came in a body to Pilate, and said: 63

"Sir, we remember that, during his lifetime, that impostor said 'I shall rise after three days.'   So order the tomb to be 64 made secure till the third day.   Otherwise his disciples may come and steal him, and then say to the people 'He has risen from the dead,' when the latest imposture will be worse than the first."

"You may have a guard," was Pilate's reply; "go and 65 make the tomb as secure as you can."

So they went and made the tomb secure, by sealing the stone, 66 in presence of the guard.

VI.—THE RISEN LIFE.

The Resurrection of Jesus.   After the Sabbath, as the first day of the week 1 began to dawn, Mary of Magdala and the other Mary had gone to look at the grave, when sud- 2 denly a great earthquake occurred.   For an angel of the Lord descended from Heaven, and came and rolled away the stone, and seated himself upon it.   His appearance was as 3

54 Wisd. of Sol. 2. 18.

dazzling as lightning, and his clothing was as white as snow; and, in their terror of him, the men on guard trembled violently and became like dead men. But the angel, addressing the women, said: 4 5

"You need not be afraid. I know that it is Jesus, who was crucified, for whom you are looking. He is not here; for he has risen, as he said he would. Come, and see the place where he was lying; and then go quickly and say to his disciples 'He has risen from the dead, and is going before you into Galilee; there you will see him.' Remember, I have told you." 6 7

On this they left the tomb quickly, in awe and great joy, and ran to tell the news to the disciples. Suddenly Jesus met them. 8

"Welcome!" he said. 9

The women went up to him, and clasped his feet, bowing to the ground before him. Then Jesus said to them:

"Do not be afraid; go and tell my brothers to set out for Galilee, and they shall see me there." 10

While they were still on their way, some of the guard came into the city, and reported to the Chief Priests everything that had happened. So they and the Councillors met and, after holding a consultation, gave a large sum of money to the soldiers, and told them to say that his disciples came in the night, and stole him while they were asleep; "and should this matter come before the Governor," they added, "we will satisfy him, and see that you have nothing to fear." 11 12 13 14

So the soldiers took the money, and did as they were instructed.   And this story has been current among the Jews from that day to this. 15

Jesus appears to the Apostles. The eleven disciples went to Galilee, to the mountain where Jesus told them to meet him; and, when they saw him, they bowed to the ground before him; although some felt doubtful. 16 17

Then Jesus came up, and spoke to them thus: 18

"All authority in heaven and on the earth has been given to me. Therefore go and make disciples of all the nations, baptizing them into the Faith of the Father, the Son, and the Holy Spirit, and teaching them to lay to heart all the commands that I have given you; and, remember, I myself am with you every day until the close of the age." 19 20

[18] Enoch 62. 6.

ACCORDING TO LUKE.

'THE GOSPEL ACCORDING TO ST. LUKE'.

COMPILED AT AN UNCERTAIN DATE LATER THAN 60 A.D.

The compiler of this gospel was probably the Luke who also compiled the 'Acts of the Apostles' and appears in that book as a companion of St. Paul. That apostle's influence may apparently be traced in the selection of many of the incidents and parables that are peculiar to this record of the Life and Teaching of Jesus.

In addition to the record of the ministry given in 'The Gospel according to St. Mark' (which appears to rest largely on information derived from the Apostle Peter, and the greater part of which is embodied here), this gospel contains much of the teaching of Jesus which is also recorded in 'The Gospel according to St. Matthew,' as well as a quantity of additional and very important matter. The sources from which this matter was drawn cannot yet be identified with certainty; but the compiler evidently aimed at presenting a more complete picture of the Life of Jesus than had hitherto been attempted. His standpoint appears to be that of a converted Gentile, writing for his fellow-converts.

There is nothing to show where this gospel was compiled, though it was probably outside Palestine. It is not clear that it was originally drawn up in its present form; nor can its date be fixed with any certainty. Its compiler is evidently at times translating from the Aramaic language, and at other times writing, with greater ease, of events of which he had learnt from Greek sources. Apparently he was not himself an eye-witness of the Life that he records. The tradition that he was a doctor by profession is to some extent supported by the internal evidence of this gospel.

ACCORDING TO LUKE.

DEDICATION.

To his Excellency, Theophilus.   1   **1**

Many attempts have been already made to draw up an account of those events which have reached their conclusion among us, just as they were reported to us by those who from the beginning 2 *were eye-witnesses, and afterwards became bearers of the Message. And, therefore, I also, since I have investigated all* 3 *these events with great care from their very beginning, have resolved to write a connected history of them for you, in order* 4 *that you may be able to satisfy yourself of the accuracy of the story which you have heard from the lips of others.*

I.—THE BIRTH, PARENTAGE, INFANCY, AND BOYHOOD.

The Birth of the Baptist foretold.   In the reign of Herod, King of Judaea, there 5 was a priest named Zechariah, who belonged to the Division called after Abijah. His wife, whose name was Elizabeth, was also a descendant of Aaron. They were both righteous people, who lived blameless 6 lives, guiding their steps by all the commandments and ordinances of the Lord. But they had no child, Elizabeth 7 being barren ; and both of them were advanced in years.

One day, when Zechariah was officiating as priest before 8 God, during the turn of his Division, it fell to him by lot, in 9 accordance with the practice among the priests, to go into the Temple of the Lord and burn incense ; and, as it was the Hour 10 of Incense, the people were all praying outside. And an 11 angel of the Lord appeared to him, standing on the right of the Altar of Incense. Zechariah was startled at the sight and 12 was awe-struck. But the angel said to him : 13

" Do not be afraid, Zechariah ; your prayer has been heard, and your wife Elizabeth shall bear you a son, whom you shall

call by the name John.　He shall be to you a joy and a　14
delight ; and many shall rejoice over his birth.　For he shall　15
be great in the sight of the Lord ; he shall not drink any wine
or strong drink, and he shall be filled with the Holy Spirit
from the very hour of his birth, and shall reconcile many of the　16
Israelites to the Lord their God.　He shall go before him in the　17
spirit and with the power of Elijah, 'to reconcile fathers to their
children' and the disobedient to the wisdom of the righteous,
and so make ready for the Lord a people prepared for him."

" How can I be sure of this ? " Zechariah asked the angel.　18
" For I am an old man and my wife is advanced in years."

" I am Gabriel," the angel answered, " who stand in the　19
presence of God, and I have been sent to speak to you and to
bring you this good news.　And now you shall be silent and　20
unable to speak until the day when this takes place, because
you did not believe what I said, though my words will be
fulfilled in due course."

Meanwhile the people were watching for Zechariah, wonder-　21
ing at his remaining so long in the Temple.　When he came　22
out, he was unable to speak to them, and they perceived that he
had seen a vision there.　But Zechariah kept making signs to
them, and remained dumb.　　　　　And, as soon as his term　23
of service was finished, he returned home.

After this his wife, Elizabeth, expecting to become a mother,　24
lived in seclusion for five months.

" This is what the Lord has done for me," she said, " now　25
that he has deigned to take away the reproach under which I
have been living."

**The Birth
of Jesus
foretold.**
Six months later the angel Gabriel was sent　26
from God to a town in Galilee called Nazareth,
to a maiden there who was betrothed to a man　27
named Joseph, a descendant of David.　Her name was Mary.
Gabriel came into her presence and said :　　　　　　　　　28

" Hail, you who have been highly favoured !　The Lord is
with you."

Mary was much disturbed at his words, and was wondering to　29
herself what such a greeting could mean, when the angel　30
spoke again :

" Do not be afraid, Mary, for you have found favour with God.
And now, you shall be with child and give birth to a son,　31
and you shall give him the name Jesus.　The child shall be　32
great and shall be called ' Son of the Most High,' and the
Lord God will give him the throne of his ancestor David, and
he shall reign over the descendants of Jacob for ever ; and to　33
his kingdom there shall be no end."

" How can this be ? " Mary asked the angel.　" For I have　34
no husband."

[15] Num. 6. 3.　[17] Mal. 4. 5—6.　[32] Isa. 9. 7.

"The Holy Spirit shall descend upon you," answered the **35** angel, "and the Power of the Most High shall overshadow you ; and therefore the child will be called 'holy,' and 'Son of God.' And Elizabeth, your cousin, is herself also expecting a **36** son in her old age ; and it is now the sixth month with her, though she is called barren ; for no promise from God shall **37** fail to be fulfilled."

"I am the servant of the Lord," exclaimed Mary; "let it be **38** with me as you have said."
Then the angel left her.

Mary's Visit to Elizabeth. Soon after this Mary set out, and made her **39** way quickly into the hill-country, to a town in Judah ; and there she went into Zechariah's house and greeted **40** Elizabeth. When Elizabeth heard Mary's greeting, the child **41** moved within her, and Elizabeth herself was filled with the Holy Spirit, and cried aloud : **42**

"Blessed are you among women, and blessed is your unborn child ! But how have I this honour, that the mother of my **43** Lord should come to me? For, as soon as your greeting **44** reached my ears, the child moved within me with delight ! Happy indeed is she who believed that the promise which she **45** received from the Lord would be fulfilled."
And Mary said : **46**

"My soul exalts the Lord,
  My spirit delights in God my Saviour ; **47**
For he has remembered his servant in her lowliness ; **48**
  And from this hour all ages will count me happy !

Great things has the Almighty done for me ; **49**
  And holy is his name.
From age to age his mercy rests **50**
  On those who reverence him.

Mighty are the deeds of his arm ; **51**
  He scatters the proud with their own devices,
He casts down princes from their thrones, and the lowly he **52**
  uplifts,
    The hungry he loads with gifts, and the rich he sends empty **53**
    away.

He has stretched out his hand to his servant Israel, **54**
  Ever mindful of his mercy
(As he promised to our forefathers) **55**
  For Abraham and his race for ever."

Mary stayed with Elizabeth about three months, and then **56** returned to her home.

[35] Exod. 13. 12 ; Ps. 2. 7. [37] Gen. 18. 14. [46] Ps. 104. 1. [47] 1 Sam. 2. 1 ; Ps. 95. 1 (Septuagint). [48] 1 Sam. 1. 11 ; Mal. 3. 12. [49] Ps. 126. 3 ; 111. 9. [50] Ps. 103. 17. [51] Ps. 89. 10 ; Job 5. 13. [52] Job 12. 18—19 ; 5. 11 ; Enoch 46. 5. [53] Ps. 107. 9 ; 34. 10 (Septuagint). [54] Isa. 41. 8—9 ; Ps. 98. 3. [55] Mic. 7. 20 ; Gen. 13. 17.

E*

The Birth and Circumcision of the Baptist. When Elizabeth's time came, she gave birth to 57 a son; and her neighbours and relations, hearing 58 of the great goodness of the Lord to her, came to share her joy.   A week later they met to circumcise 59 the child, and were about to call him 'Zechariah' after his father, when his mother interposed : 60

"No, he is to be called John."

"You have no relation of that name!" they exclaimed ; and 61, 62 they made signs to the child's father, to find out what he wished the child to be called.   Asking for a writing-tablet, he 63 wrote the words—'His name is John.'   Every one was surprised ; and immediately Zechariah recovered his voice and the 64 use of his tongue, and began to bless God.   All their 65 neighbours were awe-struck at this ; and throughout the hill-country of Judaea the whole story was much talked about ; and all who heard it kept it in mind, asking one another— 66 "What can this child be destined to become ?"   For the Power of the Lord was with him.

Then his father Zechariah was filled with the Holy Spirit, 67 and, speaking under inspiration, said :

" Blessed is the Lord, the God of Israel, 68
    Who has visited his people and wrought their deliverance,
And has raised up for us the Strength of our Salvation 69
    In the House of his servant David—

As he promised by the lips of his holy Prophets of old— 70
    Salvation from our enemies and from the hands of all that 71
    hate us,
Showing mercy to our forefathers, 72
    And mindful of his sacred Covenant.

This was the oath which he swore to our forefather Abraham— 73
    That we should be rescued from the hands of our enemies, 74
And should serve him without fear in holiness and righteousness, 75
    In his presence all our days.

And thou, Child, shalt be called Prophet of the Most High, 76
    For thou shalt go before the Lord to make ready his way,
To give to his people the knowledge of salvation 77
    In the forgiveness of their sins,

Through the tender mercy of our God, 78
    Whereby the Dawn will break on us from Heaven,
To give light to those who dwell in darkness and the shadow of 79
    death,
    And guide our feet into the Way of Peace."

The child grew and became strong in spirit ; and he lived in 80 the Wilds till the time came for his appearance before Israel.

63 Ps. 41. 13 ; Exod. 3. 16 ; Ps. 111. 9.   69 Ps. 18. 2 ; 89. 24, 20.   71 Ps. 106. 10. 72 Mic. 7. 20 ; Ps. 105. 8 ; Dan. 11. 28.   73 Mic. 7. 20.   76 Mal. 3. 1.   78 Zech. 6. 12. (Septuagint).   79 Isa. 9. 2 ; Ps. 107. 10 ; Isa. 59. 8.

The Birth and Circumcision of Jesus. About that time an edict was issued by the Emperor Augustus that a census should be taken of the whole Empire. (This was the first census taken while Quirinius was Governor of Syria). And every one went to his own town to be registered. Among others Joseph went up from the town of Nazareth in Galilee to Bethlehem, the town of David, in Judaea—because he belonged to the family and house of David—to be registered with Mary, his betrothed wife, who was about to become a mother. While they were there her time came, and she gave birth to her first child, a son. And because there was no room for them in the inn, she swathed him round and laid him in a manger.

In that same country-side were shepherds out in the open fields, watching their flocks that night, when an angel of the Lord suddenly stood by them, and the Glory of the Lord shone around them ; and they were seized with fear. "Have no fear," the angel said. "For I bring you good news of a great joy in store for all the nation. This day there has been born to you, in the town of David, a Saviour, who is Christ and Lord. And this shall be the sign for you. You will find the infant swathed, and lying in a manger." Then suddenly there appeared with the angel a multitude of the heavenly Host, praising God, and singing—

"Glory to God on high,
And on earth peace among men in whom he finds pleasure."

Now, when the angels had left them and gone back to Heaven, the shepherds said to one another :

"Let us go at once to Bethlehem, and see this thing that has happened, of which the Lord has told us."

So they went quickly, and found Mary and Joseph, and the infant lying in a manger ; and, when they saw it, they told of all that had been said to them about this child. All who heard the shepherds were astonished at their story, while Mary treasured up all that they said, and dwelt upon it in her thoughts. And the shepherds went back, giving glory and praise to God for all that they had heard and seen, as it had been told them.

Eight days after the birth of the child, when it was time to circumcise him, he received the name Jesus—the name given him by the angel before his conception.

The Presentation of Jesus in the Temple. When the period of purification of mother and child, enjoined by the Law of Moses, came to an end, his parents took the child up to Jerusalem to present him to the Lord, in compliance with the Law of the Lord that 'every first-born male shall be

11 Ps. 2. 2.   22 Lev. 12. 6.   23 Exod. 13. 2.

dedicated to the Lord,' and also to offer the sacrifice enjoined   24
in the Law of the Lord—'a pair of turtle-doves or two young
pigeons.'

There was at that time in Jerusalem a man named Simeon,   25
a righteous and devout man, who lived in constant expectation of the Consolation of Israel, and under the guidance of the
Holy Spirit.   It had been revealed to him by the Holy Spirit   26
that he should not die until he had seen the Lord's Christ.
Moved by the Spirit, Simeon came into the Temple Courts,   27
and, when the parents brought in the child Jesus, to do for
him what was customary under the Law, Simeon himself   28
took the child in his arms, and blessed God, and said :

" Now, Lord, thou wilt let thy servant go,   29
    According to thy word, in peace,
For my eyes have seen the Salvation   30
    Which thou hast prepared in the sight of all nations—   31
A Light to bring light to the Gentiles,   32
    And to be the Glory of thy people Israel."

While the child's father and mother were wondering at what   33
was said about him, Simeon gave them his blessing, and said   34
to Mary, the child's mother :
" This child is appointed to be the cause of the fall and rise
of many in Israel, and to be a sign much spoken against—
yes, the sword will pierce your own heart—and so the thoughts   35
in many minds will be disclosed."

There was also a Prophetess named Hannah, a daughter of   36
Phanuel and of the tribe of Asher.   She was far advanced in
years, having lived with her husband for seven years after
marriage, and then a widow, till she had reached the age of   37
eighty-four.   She never left the Temple Courts, but, fasting and
praying, worshipped God night and day.   At that moment   38
she came up, and began publicly to thank God and to speak
about the child to all who were looking for the deliverance of
Jerusalem.

The Boyhood   When the child's parents had done everything   39
of   enjoined by the Law of the Lord, they returned
Jesus.   to Galilee to their own town of Nazareth.

The child grew and became strong and wise, and the bless-   40
ing of God was upon him.

Every year the child's parents used to go to Jerusalem at the   41
Passover Festival.   When Jesus was twelve years old,   42
they went according to custom to Jerusalem, and had finished   43
their visit ; but, when they started to return, the boy Jesus remained behind in Jerusalem, without their knowing it.   Think-   44
ing that he was with their fellow-travellers, they went one day's

journey before searching for him among their relations and
acquaintances; and then, as they did not find him, they returned   45
to Jerusalem, searching everywhere for him.   It was not till the   46
third day that they found him in the Temple Courts, sitting
among the Teachers, now listening to them, now asking them
questions.   All who listened to him marvelled at his intelligence   47
and his answers.   His parents were amazed when they saw   48
him, and his mother said to him :

" My child, why have you treated us like this ?   Your father
and I have been searching for you in great distress."

"What made you search for me?" he answered.   "Did   49
not you know that I must be in my Father's House ?"
His parents did not understand what he meant.   However he   50, 51
went down with them to Nazareth, and submitted himself to
their control; and his mother treasured all that was said in
her heart.

And Jesus grew in wisdom as he grew in years, and   52
'gained the blessing of God and men.'

II.—THE PREPARATION.

The Baptist   In the fifteenth year of the reign of the Emperor   1 **3**
and his   Tiberius, when Pontius Pilate was Governor of
Message.   Judaea, Herod Ruler of Galilee, his brother Philip
Ruler of the territory comprising Ituraea and Trachonitis, and
Lysanias Ruler of Abilene, and when Annas and Caiaphas   2
were High Priests, a Command from God came to John, the son
of Zechariah, while he was in the Wilderness.   And John went   3
through the whole district of the Jordan, proclaiming a baptism
upon repentance, for the forgiveness of sins.   This was in ful-   4
filment of what is said in the writings of the Prophet Isaiah—

' The voice of one crying aloud in the Wilderness :
" Make ready the way of the Lord,
    Make his paths straight.
Every chasm shall be filled,
    Every mountain and hill shall be levelled,
The winding ways shall be straightened,   5
    The rough roads made smooth,
        And all mankind shall see the Salvation of God."'   6

And John said to the crowds that went to be baptized by   7
him :

" You brood of vipers ! who has prompted you to seek refuge
from the coming judgement ?   Let your lives, then, prove your   8

⁵² 1 Sam. 2. 26.   4—6 Isa. 40. 3—5.

repentance ; and do not begin to say among yourselves 'Abraham is our ancestor,' for I tell you that out of these very stones God is able to raise descendants for Abraham ! Already, 9 indeed, the axe is lying at the root of the trees. Therefore every tree that fails to bear good fruit will be cut down and thrown into the fire."

"What are we to do then ? " the people asked. 10

" Let the man who has two coats," answered John, "share 11 with him who has none ; and the man who has food do the same."

Even tax-gatherers came to be baptized, and said to John : 12 " Teacher, what are we to do ? "

" Do not collect more than you have authority to demand," 13 John answered. And when some soldiers on active service 14 asked "And we—what are we to do ? ", he said :

" Never use violence, or exact anything by false accusation ; and be content with your pay."

Then, while the people were in suspense, and were all 15 debating with themselves whether John could be the Christ, John, addressing them all, said : 16

" I, indeed, baptize you with water ; but there is coming one more powerful than I, and I am not fit even to unfasten his sandals. He will baptize you with the Holy Spirit and with fire. His winnowing-fan is in his hand, that he may clear his 17 threshing-floor, and store the grain in his barn, but the chaff he will burn with inextinguishable fire."

And so with many different exhortations John told his Good 18 News to the people. But Prince Herod, being rebuked by 19 John respecting Herodias, the wife of Herod's brother, and for all the evil things that he had done, crowned them all by 20 shutting John up in prison.

The Baptism of Jesus. Now after the baptism of all the people, and 21 when Jesus had been baptized and was still pray- ing, the heavens opened, and the Holy Spirit 22 descended, in a visible form, like a dove, upon him, and from the heavens came a voice—

" Thou art my Son, the Beloved ; in thee I delight."

The Ancestors of Jesus. When beginning his work, Jesus was about 23 thirty years old. He was regarded as the son of Joseph, whose ancestors were—

Eli		Amos		Joseph
Mattith	24	Nahum		Josheh
Levi		Azaliah		Johanan	27
Melchiah		Nogah		Rhesa
Janna		Mattith	26	Zerubbabel
Joseph		Mattithiah		Shealtiel
Mattithiah	25	Shimei		Neriah

[16] Ps. 118, 26. [22] Ps. 2. 7 ; Isa. 42. 1.

Melchiah	28	Nathan		Reu	
Addi		David		Peleg	
Cosam		Jesse	32	Eber	
Elmodam		Obed		Shelah	
Er		Boaz		Kenan	36
Joshua	29	Salah		Arpachshad	
Eliezer		Nahshon		Shem	
Joram		Amminadab	33	Noah	
Mattith		Arni		Lamech	
Levi		Hezron		Methuselah	37
Simeon	30	Perez		Enoch	
Judah		Judah		Jared	
Joseph		Jacob	34	Mahalalel	
Jonam		Isaac		Kenan	
Eliakim		Abraham		Enosh	38
Meleah	31	Terah		Seth and	
Menan		Nahor		Adam the son of	
Mattithiah		Serug	35	GOD.	

The Temptation of Jesus. On returning from the Jordan, full of the Holy Spirit, Jesus was led by the power of the Spirit through the Wilderness for forty days, tempted by the Devil. All that time he ate nothing; and, when it was over, he became hungry. So the Devil said to him: "If you are God's Son, tell this stone to become a loaf of bread."

And Jesus answered him: "Scripture says—

'It is not on bread alone that man is to live.'"

And the Devil led Jesus up, and, showing him in a single moment all the kingdoms of the earth, said to him: "I will give you all this power, and the splendour of them; for it has been given into my hands and I give it to whom I wish. If you, therefore, will do homage before me, it shall all be yours."

And Jesus answered him: "Scripture says—

'Thou shalt do homage to the Lord thy God, and worship him only.'"

The Devil next led him into Jerusalem, and, placing him on the parapet of the Temple, said: "If you are God's Son throw yourself down from here, for Scripture says—

'He will give his angels commands about thee, to guard thee safely,'

and

'On their hands they will upbear thee, Lest ever thou shouldst strike thy foot against a stone.'"

But Jesus answered him : " It is said—   12

    ' Thou shalt not tempt the Lord thy God.' "

When he had tried every kind of temptation, the Devil left   13
Jesus, till another opportunity.

III.—The Work in Galilee.

Jesus begins   Moved by the power of the Spirit, Jesus returned   14
his Work.   to Galilee.   Reports about him spread through all
that neighbourhood ; and he began to teach in their Syna-   15
gogues, and was honoured by every one.

            Coming to Nazareth, where he had been brought   16
Jesus   up, Jesus, as was his custom, went on the
teaches at
Nazareth.   Sabbath into the Synagogue, and stood up to
read the Scriptures.   The book given him was that of the   17
Prophet Isaiah ; and Jesus opened the book and found the
place where it says—

    ' The Spirit of the Lord is upon me,   18
For he has consecrated me to bring Good News to the poor,
He has sent me to proclaim release to captives and restoration
      of sight to the blind,
    To set the oppressed at liberty,
      To proclaim the accepted year of the Lord.'   19

Then, closing the book and returning it to the attendant, he   20
sat down.   The eyes of all in the Synagogue were fixed upon
him, and Jesus began :   21
    "This very day this passage has been fulfilled in your
hearing."
All who were present spoke well of him, and were astonished   22
at the beautiful words that fell from his lips.
    " Is not he Joseph's son ? " they asked.
    "Doubtless," said Jesus, "you will remind me of the saying—   23
' Doctor, cure yourself ;' and you will say ' Do here in your
own country all that we have heard has been done at Capernaum.'   I tell you," he continued, " that no Prophet is accept-   24
able in his own country.   There were, doubtless, many widows   25
in Israel in Elijah's days, when the heavens were closed for
three years and six months, and a severe famine prevailed
throughout the country ; and yet it was not to one of them that   26
Elijah was sent, but to a widow at Zarephath in Sidonia.
And there were many lepers in Israel in the time of the   27

   [12] Deut. 6, 16. [18—19] Isa. 61. 1—2, [26] 1 Kings 17. 9.

Prophet Elisha, yet it was not one of them who was made clean, but Naaman the Syrian."

All the people in the Synagogue, as they listened to this, 28 became enraged. Starting up, they drove Jesus out of the 29 town, and led him to the brow of the hill on which their town stood, intending to hurl him down. But he passed through 30 the middle of the crowd and went on his way.

Cure of a possessed Man. Then Jesus went down to Capernaum, a city 31 in Galilee. On the Sabbath he taught the people. They were amazed at his teaching, 32 because his words were spoken with authority. In the Syna- 33 gogue there was a man with the spirit of a foul demon in him, who called out loudly :

"Stop! What do you want with us, Jesus of Nazareth? 34 Have you come to destroy us? I know who you are—the Holy One of God!"

But Jesus rebuked the demon. 35

"Be silent! Come out from him," he said.

The demon flung the man down in the middle of the people, and then came out from him, without causing him further harm. And they were all lost in amazement, and kept saying 36 to one another :

"What words are these? For he gives his commands to the foul spirits with a marvellous authority, and they come out." And rumours about Jesus travelled through every place in the 37 neighbourhood.

Cure of Peter's Mother-in-law and of many others. On leaving the Synagogue, Jesus went into 38 Simon's house. Now Simon's mother-in-law was suffering from a severe attack of fever, and they asked Jesus to cure her. Bending over her, he 39 rebuked the fever; the fever left her, and she immediately got up and began to wait upon them.

At sunset, all who had friends suffering from various 40 diseases took them to Jesus; and he placed his hands upon every one of them and cured them. And even demons came 41 out from many people, screaming 'You are the Son of God.' Jesus rebuked them, and would not allow them to speak, because they knew that he was the Christ.

Jesus retires to a lonely Place. At daybreak, Jesus went out and walked to a 42 lonely spot. But crowds of people began to look for him; and they came to where he was and tried to detain him and prevent his leaving them. Jesus, 43 however, said to them :

"I must take the Good News of the Kingdom of God to the other towns also, for that was why I was sent."

And he continued to make his proclamation in the Synagogues 44 of Judaea.

34 Ps. 16, 10.

The great Catch of Fish. Once, when the people were pressing round Jesus as they listened to God's Message, he happened to be standing by the shore of the Lake of Gennesaret, and saw two boats close to the shore. The fishermen had gone away from them and were washing the nets. So, getting into one of the boats, which belonged to Simon, Jesus asked him to push off a little way from the shore, and then sat down and taught the people from the boat. When he had finished speaking, he said to Simon :

"Push off into deep water, and all throw out your nets for a haul."

"We have been hard at work all night, Sir," answered Simon, "and have not caught anything, but, at your bidding, I will throw out the nets."

They did so, and enclosed such a great shoal of fish that their nets began to break. So they signalled to their partners in the other boat to come and help them ; and they came and filled both the boats so full of fish that they were almost sinking. When Simon Peter saw this, he threw himself down at Jesus' knees, exclaiming :

"Master, leave me, for I am a sinful man !"

For he and all who were with him were lost in amazement at the haul of fish which they had made ; and so, too, were James and John, Zebediah's sons, who were Simon's partners.

"Do not be afraid," Jesus said to Simon ; "from to-day you shall catch men."

And, when they had brought their boats to shore, they left everything, and followed him.

Cure of a Leper. On one occasion Jesus was staying in a town, when he saw a man who was covered with leprosy. When the leper saw Jesus, he threw himself on his face and implored his help :

"Master, if only you are willing, you are able to make me clean."

Stretching out his hand, Jesus touched him, saying as he did so :

"I am willing ; become clean."

Instantly the leprosy left the man ; and then Jesus impressed upon him that he was not to say a word to any one, "but," he added, "set out and show yourself to the Priest, and make the offerings for your cleansing, in the manner directed by Moses, as evidence of your cure." However, the story about Jesus spread all the more, and great crowds came together to listen to him, and to be cured of their illnesses ; but Jesus used to withdraw to lonely places and pray.

14 Lev. 13. 49.

Cure of a paralyzed Man. On one of those days, when Jesus was teaching, 17 some Pharisees and Doctors of the Law were sitting near by. (They had come from all the villages in Galilee and Judaea, and from Jerusalem ; and the power of the Lord was upon Jesus, so that he could work cures.) And there some men brought on a bed a man who 18 was paralyzed. They tried to get him in and lay him before Jesus ; but, finding no way of getting him in, owing to the 19 crowd, they went up on the roof and lowered him through the tiles, with his pallet, into the middle of the people and in front of Jesus. When he saw their faith, Jesus said : 20

" Friend, your sins have been forgiven you."

The Teachers of the Law and the Pharisees began debating 21 about this.

"Who is this man who speaks so blasphemously ? " they asked. " Who can forgive sins except God ? "

When Jesus became aware of the way in which they were 22 debating, he turned to them and exclaimed :

"What are you debating with yourselves ? Which is the 23 easier ?—to say ' Your sins have been forgiven you ' ? or to say ' Get up, and walk about ' ? But that you may know that 24 the Son of Man has power on earth to forgive sins—" here he spoke to the paralyzed man—"To you I say, Get up, and take up your pallet, and go to your home."

Instantly the man stood up before their eyes, took up what 25 he had been lying on, and went to his home, praising God. The people, one and all, were lost in amazement, 26 and praised God ; and in great awe they said :

" We have seen marvellous things to-day ! "

Call of Levi. After this, Jesus went out ; and he noticed a 27 tax-gatherer, named Levi, sitting in the tax-office, and said to him : " Follow me."

Levi left everything and got up and followed him. And 28, 29 **Jesus blamed for his Companions.** Levi gave a great entertainment at his house, in honour of Jesus ; and a large number of tax-gatherers and others were at table with them. The Pharisees and the Teachers of the Law belonging to their 30 party complained of this to the disciples of Jesus.

" Why do you eat and drink with tax-gatherers and out-casts ? "

In answer Jesus said : 31

" It is not those who are well that need a doctor, but those who are ill. I have not come to call the religious, but the 32 outcast, to repent."

The Disciples blamed for not observing the Law. " John's disciples," they said to Jesus, " often 33 fast and say prayers, and so do the disciples of the Pharisees, while yours are eating and drinking ! "

24 Dan. 7. 13.

But Jesus answered them : 34

"Can you make the bridegroom's friends fast while the bridegroom is with them ? But the days will come—a time 35 when the bridegroom will be parted from them ; and they will fast then, when those days come."

Then, as an illustration, Jesus said to them : 36

"No man ever tears a piece from a new garment and puts it upon an old one ; for, if he does, he will not only tear the new garment, but the piece from the new one will not match the old. And no man puts new wine into old wine-skins ; for, if 37 he does, the new wine will burst the skins, and the wine itself will run out, and the skins be lost. But new wine 38 must be put into fresh skins. No man after drinking 39 old wine wishes for new. 'No,' he says, 'the old is excellent.'"

One Sabbath Jesus was walking through cornfields, and 1 **6** his disciples were picking the ears of wheat, and rubbing them in their hands, and eating them.

"Why are you doing what it is not allowable to do on the 2 Sabbath ? " asked some of the Pharisees.

Jesus' answer was : 3

"Have not you read even of what David did, when he was hungry, he and his companions—that he went into the House 4 of God, and took the consecrated bread and ate it, and gave some to his companions, though only the priests are allowed to eat it? "

Then Jesus added : 5

"The Son of Man is .ord even of the Sabbath."

Cure of   On another Sabbath Jesus went into the Syna- 6
a Man with gogue and taught ; and there was a man there
a withered whose right hand was withered. The Teachers of 7
Hand.   the Law and the Pharisees watched Jesus closely,
to see if he would work cures on the Sabbath, so that they
might find a charge to bring against him. Jesus, however, 8
knew what was in their minds, and said to the man whose
hand was withered :

"Stand up and come out into the middle."

The man stood up ; and Jesus said to them : 9

"I ask you, is it allowable to do good on the Sabbath—or
harm ? to save a life, or let it perish ? "

Then, looking round at them all, he said to the man : 10

"Stretch out your hand."

The man did so ; and his hand had become sound. But 11
the Teachers of the Law and the Pharisees were goaded to
madness, and consulted together what they could do to
Jesus.

⁴ 1 Sam. 21. 6.

The twelve Apostles. Now about that time, Jesus went out, up the hill, 12 to pray, and spent the whole night in prayer to God. When day came, he summoned his disciples, and 13 chose twelve of them, whom he also named 'Apostles.' They were Simon (whom Jesus also named Peter), and his brother 14 Andrew, James, John, Philip, Bartholomew, Matthew, 15 Thomas, James son of Alphaeus, Simon known as the Zealot, Judas son of James, and Judas Iscariot, who proved a traitor. 16 Afterwards Jesus came down the hill with them and took 17 his stand on a level place. With him were a large crowd of his disciples, and great numbers of people from the whole of Judaea, Jerusalem, and the coast district of Tyre and Sidon, who had come to hear him and to be restored to health. Those, 18 too, who were troubled with foul spirits were cured; and 19 every one in the crowd was trying to touch him, because a power went out from him which restored them all. Then, 20

THE 'SERMON ON THE MOUNT.' raising his eyes and looking at his disciples, Jesus spoke as follows:

The Happy. "Blessed are you who are poor, for yours is the Kingdom of God.

Blessed are you who hunger now, for you shall be 21 satisfied.

Blessed are you who weep now, for you shall laugh.

Blessed are you when men hate you, and when they expel you 22 from among them, and taunt you, and reject your Name as an evil thing—on account of the Son of Man. Then indeed you 23 may be glad and dance for joy, for be sure that your reward in Heaven will be great; for that is what their ancestors did to the Prophets.

The Unhappy. But 'alas for you who are rich,' for you have 24 had your comforts in full.

Alas for you who are sated now, for you will hunger. 25

Alas for you who laugh now, for you will mourn and weep.

Alas for you when all men speak well of you; for this is what 26 their ancestors did to the false Prophets.

The New Law— on Love, But to you who hear I say—Love your enemies, 27 show kindness to those who hate you, bless those 28 who curse you, pray for those who insult you.

on Revenge. When a man gives one of you a blow on the cheek, offer the 29 other cheek as well; and, when any one takes away your cloak, do not keep back your coat either. Give to every one who asks of you; and, when 30 any one takes away what is yours, do not demand its return.

The Golden Rule. Do to others as you wish them to do to you. If 31, 32 you love only those who love you, what thanks will be due to you? Why, even the outcast love those who love them! For, if you show kindness only to those who show 33

kindness to you, what thanks will be due to you? Even
the outcast do that! If you lend only to those from whom   34
you expect to get something, what thanks will be due to you?
Even the outcast lend to the outcast in the hope of getting as much in return! But love your enemies, and   35
show them kindness, and lend to them, never despairing.
Then your reward shall be great, and you shall be Sons of
the Most High, for he is kind to the thankless and the
bad.   Learn to be merciful—even as your Father is   36
On   merciful. Do not judge, and you will not be   37
Judging   judged; do not condemn, and you will not be con-
Others.   demned. Forgive, and you will be forgiven. Give,
and others will give to you. A generous measure, pressed and
shaken down, and running over, will they pour into your lap;   38
for the measure that you mete will be meted out to you in
return."

Then, speaking in parables, Jesus said: 39
"Can one blind man guide another? Will they not both fall
into a ditch? A scholar is not above his teacher; yet every   40
finished scholar shall be like his teacher.   And why do   41
you look at the straw in your brother's eye, while you pay
no attention at all to the beam in your own? How can you   42
say to your brother 'Brother, let me take out the straw in
your eye,' while you yourself do not see the beam in your own?
Hypocrite! Take out the beam from your own eye first, and
then you will see clearly how to take out the straw in your
brother's.   There is no such thing as a good tree bear-   43
True and false ing worthless fruit, or, on the other hand, a worth-
Teachers. less tree bearing good fruit. For every tree is   44
known by its own fruit. People do not gather figs off thorn
bushes, nor pick a bunch of grapes off a bramble. A good   45
man, from the good stores of his heart, brings out what is good;
while a bad man, from his bad stores, brings out what is bad.
For what fills a man's heart will rise to his lips.   Why   46
The two   do you call me 'Master! Master!' and yet fail to
Foundations. do what I tell you? Every one who comes to me   47
and listens to my teaching and acts upon it—I will show you
to whom he may be compared. He may be compared to a man   48
building a house, who dug, and went deep, and laid the
foundation upon the rock. Then, when a flood came,
the river swept down upon that house, but had no power to
shake it, because it had been built well. But those who have   49
listened and not acted upon what they have heard may be
compared to a man who built a house on the ground without
any foundation. The river swept down upon it, and the
house immediately collapsed; and great was the crash that
followed."

When Jesus had brought to a conclusion all that he then had   1   **7**
to say to the people, he entered Capernaum.

Cure of an Officer's Servant. A Captain in the Roman army had a slave 2 whom he valued, and who was seriously ill— almost at the point of death. And, hearing about 3 Jesus, he sent some Jewish Councillors to him, with the request that he would come and save his slave's life. When 4 they found Jesus, they earnestly implored him to do so.

" He is a man who deserves that you should show him this favour," they said, " for he is devoted to our nation, and him- 5 self built our Synagogue for us."

So Jesus went with them. But, when he was no great distance 6 from the house, the Captain sent some friends with the message—

" Do not trouble yourself, Sir ; for I am unworthy to receive you under my roof. That was why I did not even venture to 7 come to you myself ; but speak, and let my manservant be cured. For I myself am a man under the orders of others, with 8 soldiers under me ; and if I say to one of them ' Go,' he goes, and to another ' Come,' he comes, and to my slave ' Do this,' he does it."

Jesus was surprised to hear these words from him ; and, turn- 9 ing to the crowd which was following him, he said :

" I tell you, nowhere in Israel have I met with such faith as this ! "

And, when the messengers returned to the house, they found 10 the slave recovered.

Raising of a Widow's Son. Shortly after, Jesus went to a town called Nain, 11 his disciples and a great crowd going with him. Just as he approached the gate of the town, there was a dead 12 man being carried out for burial—an only son, and his mother was a widow. A large number of the people of the town were with her. When he saw her, the Master was moved 13 with compassion for her, and he said to her : " Do not weep." Then he went up and touched the bier, and the bearers 14 stopped ; and Jesus said :

" Young man, I am speaking to you—Rise ! "

The dead man sat up and began to talk, and Jesus restored 15 him to his mother. Every one was awe-struck and 16 began praising God.

" A great Prophet has arisen among us," they said ; "and God has visited his people."

And this story about Jesus spread all through Judaea, and in 17 the neighbouring countries as well.

The Baptist's Message to Jesus. All these events were reported to John by his 18 disciples. So he summoned two of them, and 19 sent them to the Master to ask—

" Are you ' The Coming One,' or are we to look for some one else ? "

When these men found Jesus, they said :   20
  "John the Baptist has sent us to you to ask—'Are you 'The
Coming One,' or are we to look for somebody else ?'"
At that very time Jesus had cured many people of diseases,   21
afflictions, and wicked spirits, and had given many blind people
their sight.   So his answer to the question was :   22
  "Go and report to John what you have witnessed and heard
—the blind recover their sight, the lame walk, the lepers are
made clean, and the deaf hear, the dead are raised to life, the
Good News is told to the poor.   And blessed is the man who   23
finds no hindrance in me."

The Testimony of Jesus to the Baptist.   When John's messengers had left, Jesus,   24
speaking to the crowds, began to say with
reference to John :
  "What did you go out into the Wilderness to   25
look at ?   A reed waving in the wind ?   If not, what did you go
out to see ?   A man dressed in rich clothing ?   Why, those
who are accustomed to fine clothes and luxury live in royal
palaces.   What then did you go to see ?   A Prophet ?   Yes, I   26
tell you, and far more than a Prophet.   This is the very man   27
of whom Scripture says—

  ' Behold, I am sending my Messenger before thy face,
    And he shall prepare thy way before thee.'

There is, I tell you, no one born of a woman who is greater   28
than John ; and yet the lowliest in the Kingdom of God is
greater than he."
(All the people, when they heard this, and even the tax-   29
gatherers, having accepted John's baptism, acknowledged the
justice of God.   But the Pharisees and the Students of the
Law, having rejected John's baptism, frustrated God's purpose   30
in regard to them.)
  "To what then," Jesus continued, "shall I compare the   31
people of the present generation ?   What are they like ?   They   32
are like some little children who are sitting in the market-
place and calling out to one another—
  ' We have played the flute for you, but you have not danced ;
    We have wailed, but you have not wept !'
For now that John the Baptist has come, not eating bread or   33
drinking wine, you are saying 'He has a demon in him';
and now that the Son of Man has come, eating and drinking,   34
you are saying ' Here is a glutton and a wine-drinker, a friend
of tax-gatherers and outcasts.'   And yet Wisdom is vindicated   35
by all her children."

Jesus anointed by a Woman.   One of the Pharisees asked Jesus to dine with   36
him, so Jesus went to his house and took his
place at table.   Just then a woman, who   37

²² Isa. 61. 1.   ²⁷ Mal. 3. 1.

was an outcast in the town, having ascertained that Jesus was
at table in the Pharisee's house, brought an alabaster jar of perfume, and placed herself behind Jesus, near his feet, weeping.   38
Then she began to make his feet wet with her tears, and she
dried them with the hair of her head, repeatedly ki sing his
feet and anointing them with the perfume.   When the
Pharisee who had invited Jesus saw this, he said to himself :   39
  "Had this man been 'The Prophet,' he would have known
who, and what sort of woman, this is who is touching him, and
that she is an outcast."
But, addressing him, Jesus said :   40
  "Simon, I have something to say to you."
  "Pray do so, Teacher," Simon answered ; and Jesus began :
  'There were two people who were in debt to a money-lender ;   41
one owed fifty pounds, and the other five.   As they were   42
unable to pay, he forgave them both.   Which of them, do you
think, will love him the more ? "
  "I suppose," answered Simon, "it will be the man to whom   43
he forgave the greater debt."
  "You are right," said Jesus, and then, turning to the woman,   44
he said to Simon :
  "Do you see this woman ? I came into your house—you gave
me no water for my feet, but she has made my feet wet with
tears and dried them with her hair.   You did not give me one   45
kiss, but she, from the moment I came in, has not ceased
to kiss my feet.   You did not anoint even my head with oil,   46
but she has anointed my feet with perfume.   And for this,   47
I tell you, her sins, many as they are, have been pardoned,
because she has loved greatly ; but one who has little
pardoned him, loves but little."
Then he said to the woman : "Your sins have been pardoned."   48
On this, those at table began to say to one another :   49
  "Who is this man who even pardons sins ? "
But Jesus said to the woman :   50
  "Your faith has delivered you ; go, and peace be with you."

Women who ministered to Jesus.   Shortly afterwards, Jesus went on a journey   1   **8**
through the towns and villages, proclaiming the
Good News of the Kingdom of God.   With him
went the Twelve, as well as some women who had been cured   2
of wicked spirits and of infirmities.   They were Mary, known
as Mary of Magdala (from whom seven demons had been
expelled), and Joanna (the wife of Herod's steward, Chuza),   3
and Susannah, and many others—all of whom ministered to
Jesus and his Apostles out of their means.

Parable of the Sower.   Once, when a great crowd was collecting, and,   4
when the people of town after town were flocking
to Jesus, he spoke to them in the form of a parable :
  "The sower went out to sow his seed ; and, as he was sowing,   5

some of the seed fell along the path and was trodden upon ;
and the wild birds ate it up.   Other seed fell upon rock,   6
and, as soon as it began to grow, having no moisture,
withered away.   Other seed fell in the middle of brambles,   7
but the brambles grew up with it and choked it entirely.
Other seed fell into rich soil, and grew, and gave a hundred-   8
fold return."

After saying this, Jesus cried aloud :
    "Let him who has ears to hear with hear."

    His disciples asked Jesus the meaning of this parable.   9
    "To you," he said, "the knowledge of the hidden truths of the   10
Kingdom of God has been imparted, but to others in parables
only, that 'though they have eyes they may not see, and
though they have ears, they may not understand.'   This is
the parable—   11

The seed is God's Message.   By the seed which fell along the   12
path are meant those who hear the Message ; but then comes
the Devil and carries away the Message from their minds, to
prevent their believing it and being saved.

By the seed which fell upon the rock are meant those who, as   13
soon as they hear the Message, welcome it joyfully ; but they
have no root, and believe it only for a time, and, when the time
of temptation comes, they draw back.

By that which fell among the brambles are meant those who   14
hear the Message, but who, as they go on their way, are completely choked by this world's cares and wealth and pleasures,
and bring nothing to perfection.

But by that in the good ground are meant those who, having   15
heard the Message, keep it in the good, rich soil of their
hearts, and patiently yield a return.

Lesson from   No man sets light to a lamp and then covers it   16
a Lamp.   with a bowl or puts it underneath a couch, but he
puts it on a lamp-stand, so that anyone who comes in may see
the light.   Nothing is hidden which will not be brought into   17
the light of day, nor ever kept hidden which will not some day
become known and come into the light of day.   Take   18
care, then, how you listen.   For, to all those who have, more
will be given ; while, from all those who have nothing, even
what they seem to have will be taken away."

The true   Presently Jesus' mother and brothers came   19
Brotherhood. where he was, but they were not able to join him
on account of the crowd.   So word was brought to him—   20
'Your mother and your brothers are standing outside, wanting
to see you.'

His reply, spoken to them all, was :   21
    " My mother and my brothers are those who listen to God's
teaching and do what it bids."

Jesus stills a Storm. One day about that time, Jesus got into a boat 22 with his disciples and said to them : "Let us go across the lake." So they put off. While they were sailing, 23 Jesus fell asleep. A squall swept down upon the lake, and their boat was filling and they were in danger. So the 24 disciples came and roused him.

"Sir, Sir," they cried, "we are lost!"

Jesus rose and rebuked the wind and the rushing waves, and they fell, and a calm followed.

"Where is your faith?" he exclaimed. 25

But in great awe and amazement they said to one another :

"Who can this be, that he commands even the winds and the waves, and they obey him?"

Cure of a Madman. And they reached the country of the Gerasenes, 26 which is on the opposite side to Galilee; and, on 27 getting ashore, Jesus met a man, who had demons in him, coming out of the town. For a long time this man had worn no clothing, and he had not lived in a house, but in the tombs. Catching sight of Jesus, he shrieked out and threw himself 28 down before him, and in a loud voice exclaimed :

"What do you want with me, Jesus, Son of the Most High God? I beseech you not to torment me."

For Jesus was commanding the foul spirit to come out from 29 the man. On many occasions it had seized him, and, even when secured with chains and fetters, and watched, he would break through anything that bound him, and be driven by the demon into the Wilds.

"What is your name?" Jesus asked. 30

"Legion," he answered (for many demons had taken pos- session of him) ; and the demons begged Jesus not to order 31 them away into the bottomless pit.   There was a drove 32 of many pigs close by feeding upon the hill-side; and the demons begged Jesus to give them leave to enter into them. Jesus gave them leave. They came out from the man and took 33 possession of the pigs; and the drove rushed down the steep slope into the lake and were drowned.   When the men 34 who tended them saw what had happened, they ran away, and carried the news to the town, and to the country round. The 35 people went out to see what had happened, and, when they came to Jesus, they found the man from whom the demons had gone out, sitting, clothed and in his right mind, at Jesus' feet ; and they were awe-struck. Those who had seen it told them how 36 the possessed man had been delivered ; upon which all the 37 people in the neighbourhood of the Gerasenes asked Jesus to leave them, for they were terrified. Jesus got into a boat and returned. The man from whom the demons had gone out 38 begged Jesus to let him be with him ; but Jesus sent him away.

"Go back to your home," he said, "and relate the story of 39 all that God has done for you."

So the man went through the whole town and proclaimed, as he went, all that Jesus had done for him.

The Raising of the Daughter of Jaeirus. On his return, Jesus was welcomed by the people; 40 for every one was looking out for him.　　　And 41 a man named Jaeirus, who was a President of the Synagogue, came to Jesus, and threw himself at Jesus' feet, with entreaties that he would come to his house, because his only daughter, who was about 42 twelve years old, was dying.

Cure of an afflicted Woman. As Jesus was going, the people were pressing closely round him. And a woman, who had suffered from 43 haemorrhage for twelve years, and whom no one could cure, came up behind and touched the tassel of his cloak. Instantly 44 the haemorrhage ceased.

"Who was it that touched me?" Jesus asked; and, 45 while every one was denying having done so, Peter exclaimed:

"Why, Sir, the people are crowding round you and pressing upon you!"

"Somebody touched me," said Jesus; "for I felt that power 46 had gone out from me."

Then the woman, when she saw that she was discovered, came 47 forward trembling, and threw herself down before him; and, in presence of all the people, she told him her reason for touching him, and that she had been cured instantly.

"Daughter," he said, "your faith has delivered you. Go, 48 and peace be with you."

Before he had finished speaking, some one came from the 49 house of the President of the Synagogue and said:

"Your daughter is dead! Do not trouble the Teacher further."

But Jesus, hearing this, spoke to the President: 50

"Do not be afraid; only have faith, and she shall yet be delivered."

When he reached the house, he did not allow any one to go in 51 with him, except Peter, John, and James, and the child's father and mother. And every one was weeping and mourning for 52 her.

"Do not weep," Jesus said, "she is not dead; she is asleep." They began to laugh at him, for they knew that she was 53 dead. But, taking her by the hand, Jesus said in a loud 54 voice:

"Child, rise!"

The child's spirit returned to her, and she instantly stood up; 55 and Jesus ordered them to give her something to eat. Her 56 parents were amazed, but Jesus impressed on them that they were not to tell any one what had happened.

44 Num. 15. 38.

The Mission of the twelve Apostles. Jesus called the Twelve together, and gave them power and authority over all demons, as well as to cure diseases. He sent them out as his Messengers, to proclaim the Kingdom of God, and to work cures.

"Do not," he said to them, "take anything for your journey ; not even a staff, or a bag, or bread, or any silver, or a change of clothes with you. Whatever house you go to stay in, remain there, and leave from that place. If people do not welcome you, as you leave that town, shake even the dust off your feet, as a protest against them."

Then they set out and went from village to village, telling the Good News and curing people everywhere.

Herod and the Baptist. Prince Herod heard of all that was happening, and was perplexed, because it was said by some that John must be risen from the dead. Some again said that Elijah had appeared, and others that one of the old Prophets had risen again. But Herod himself said :

"John I beheaded ; but who is this of whom I hear such things ? "

And he endeavoured to see him.

The Return of the Apostles. When the Apostles returned, they related to Jesus all that they had done. Then Jesus retired privately to a town called Bethsaida, taking the Apostles with him. But the people recognized him and followed him in crowds ; and Jesus welcomed them and spoke to them about the Kingdom of God, while he cured those who were in need of help. The day was drawing to a close, when the Twelve came up to him, and said :

Jesus feeds five thousand by the Lake of Galilee. "Send the crowd away, so that they may make their way to the villages and farms round about, and find themselves lodgings and provisions, for we are in a lonely spot here."

But Jesus said : "It is for you to give them something to eat."

"We have not more than five loaves and two fishes," they answered ; "unless indeed we are to go and buy food for all these people."

(For the men among them were about five thousand.)

"Get them seated in companies," was his reply, "about fifty in each."

This they did, and got all the people seated. Taking the five loaves and the two fishes, Jesus looked up to Heaven and said the blessing over them. Then he broke them in pieces, and gave them to his disciples to set before the people. Every one had sufficient to eat, and what was left of the broken pieces was picked up—twelve baskets.

Peter's Confession of The Christ. Afterwards, when Jesus was alone, praying, 18 his disciples joined him, and he asked them this question—

"Who do the people say that I am?"

"John the Baptist," was their answer; "others, however, 19 say that you are Elijah, while others say that one of the old Prophets has risen again."

"But you," he went on, "who do you say that I am?" 20 And to this Peter answered:

"The Christ of God."

Jesus, however, strictly charged them not to say this to any 21 one; he told them that the Son of Man must 22 **Jesus foretells his Death.** undergo much suffering, and be rejected by the Councillors, and Chief Priests, and Teachers of the Law, and be put to death, and rise on the third **A Call to renounce Self.** day.   And to all present he said: 23 "If any man wishes to walk in my steps, let him renounce self, and take up his cross daily, and follow me. For whoever wishes to save his life will lose it, 24 and whoever, for my sake, loses his life—that man shall save it. What good does it do a man if, when he has gained the 25 whole world, he has lost or forfeited himself? Whoever is 26 ashamed of me and of my teaching, the Son of Man will be ashamed of him, when he comes in his Glory and the Glory of the Father and of the holy angels.   Indeed, I tell you, 27 some who are standing before me will not know death, till they have seen the Kingdom of God."

The Transfigura- tion. About eight days after speaking these words, 28 Jesus went up the mountain to pray, taking with him Peter, John, and James. As he was pray- 29 ing, the aspect of his face was changed, and his clothing became of a glittering whiteness. And all at once two men 30 were talking with Jesus; they were Moses and Elijah, who 31 appeared in a glorified state, and spoke of his departure, which was destined to take place at Jerusalem. Peter and his 32 companions had been overpowered by sleep but, suddenly becoming wide awake, they saw Jesus glorified and the two men who were standing beside him. And, as Moses and 33 Elijah were passing away from Jesus, Peter exclaimed:

"Sir, it is good to be here; let us make three tents, one for you, and one for Moses, and one for Elijah."

He did not know what he was saying; and, while he was 34 speaking, a cloud came down and enveloped them; and they were afraid, as they passed into the cloud; and from the cloud 35 came a voice which said—

²² Hos. 6. 2.   ³⁵ Ps. 2. 7; Isa. 42. 1; Enoch 40. 5.

"This is my Son, the Chosen One; him you must hear."

And, as the voice ceased, Jesus was found alone. The 36 Apostles kept silence, and told no one about any of the things that they had seen.

Cure of an epileptic Boy. The next day, when they had come down from 37 the mountain, a great crowd met Jesus. And 38 just then a man in the crowd shouted out :

"Teacher, I entreat you to look at my son, for he is my only child ; all at once a spirit will seize him, suddenly shriek out, 39 and throw him into convulsions till he foams, and will leave him only when he is utterly exhausted. I entreated your 40 disciples to drive the spirit out, but they could not."

"O faithless and perverse generation !" Jesus exclaimed ; 41 "how long must I be with you and have patience with you ? Lead your son here."

While the boy was coming up to Jesus, the demon dashed him 42 down and threw him into convulsions. But Jesus rebuked the foul spirit, and cured the boy, and gave him back to his father. And all present were struck with awe at the 43 majesty of God.

Jesus a second time foretells his Death. In the midst of the general astonishment at all that Jesus was doing, he said to his disciples : "Listen carefully to my words. For the Son 44 of Man is destined to be betrayed into the hands of his fellow men."

But the disciples did not understand the meaning of this ; 45 it had been concealed from them so that they did not see it, and they were afraid to question him as to what he meant.

On Humility. A discussion arose among the disciples as 46 to which of them was the greatest ; and Jesus, 47 knowing of the discussion that was occupying their thoughts, took hold of a little child, and placed it beside him, and then 48 said to them :

"Any one who, for the sake of my Name, welcomes even this little child is welcoming me ; and any one who welcomes me is welcoming him who sent me as his Messenger. For whoever is lowliest among you all—that man is great."

On Toleration. Thereupon John said : "Sir, we saw a man driving out demons by 49 using your name, and we tried to prevent him, because he does not follow you with us."

"None of you must prevent him," Jesus said to John ; 50 "he who is not against you is for you."

41 Deut. 32. 5.

IV.—The Journey to Jerusalem.

As the days before his being taken up to Heaven were 51
growing few, Jesus set his face resolutely in the direction of
Jerusalem; and he sent on messengers in advance.   On 52
their way, they went into a Samaritan village to make preparations for him, but the people there did not welcome him, 53
because his face was set in the direction of Jerusalem. When 54
James and John saw this, they said:

"Master, do you wish us to call for fire to come down from
the heavens and consume them?"

But Jesus turned and rebuked them. And they made their 55, 56
way to another village.

Tests of Sincerity.   And, while they were on their way, a man said 57
to Jesus:

"I will follow you wherever you go."

"Foxes have holes," he replied, "and wild birds their roost- 58
ing-places, but the Son of Man has nowhere to lay his head."
To another man Jesus said: "Follow me." 59

"Let me first go and bury my father," said the man.

But Jesus said: 60

"Leave the dead to bury their dead; but go yourself and
carry far and wide the news of the Kingdom of God."

"Master," said another, "I will follow you; but first let me 61
say good-bye to my family."

But Jesus answered: 62

"No one who looks back, after putting his hand to the
plough, is fitted for the Kingdom of God."

The Mission of the Seventy.   After this, the Master appointed seventy-two 1 **10**
other disciples, and sent them on as his
Messengers, two and two, in advance, to every
town and place that he was himself intending to visit.

"The harvest," he said, "is abundant, but the labourers are 2
few.   Therefore pray to the Owner of the harvest to send
labourers to gather in his harvest.   Now, go.   Remember, I 3
am sending you out as my Messengers like lambs among
wolves.   Do not take a purse with you, or a bag, or sandals; 4
and do not stop to greet any one on your journey.   Whatever 5
house you go to stay at, begin by praying for a blessing
on it.   Then, if any one there is deserving of a blessing, 6
your blessing will rest upon him; but if not, it will come
back upon yourselves.   Remain at that same house, and 7
eat and drink whatever they offer you; for the worker is worth
his wages.   Do not keep changing from one house to another.
Whatever town you visit, if the people welcome you, eat 8
what is set before you; cure the sick there, and tell people 9

[54] 2 Kings i. 10.

'The Kingdom of God is close at hand.' But, whatever town 10
you go to visit, if the people do not welcome you, go out
into its streets and say 'We wipe off the very dust of your 11
town which has clung to our feet ; still, be assured that the
Kingdom of God is close at hand.' I tell you that the 12
doom of Sodom will be more bearable on 'That Day' than
the doom of that town.   Alas for you, Chorazin ! Alas 13

The Doom of for you, Bethsaida ! For, if the miracles which
the Towns of have been done in you had been done in Tyre
Galilee.   and Sidon, they would have sat in sackcloth
and ashes and repented long ago. Yet the doom of Tyre 14
and Sidon will be more bearable at the Judgement than
yours.   And you, Capernaum ! Will you 'exalt your- 15
self to Heaven'?   'You shall go down to the Place of
Death.'   He who listens to you is listening to me, 16
and he who rejects you is rejecting me ; while he who rejects
me is rejecting him who sent me as his Messenger."

          When the seventy-two returned, they exclaimed 17
The Return of joyfully : "Master, even the demons submit to
the Seventy.   us when we use your name." And Jesus replied : 18
" I have had visions of Satan, fallen, like lightning from the
heavens.   Remember, I have given you the power to ' trample 19
upon serpents and scorpions,' and to meet all the strength of
the Enemy.   Nothing shall ever harm you in any way. Yet 20
do not rejoice in the fact that the spirits submit to you, but
rejoice that your names have been enrolled in Heaven."

The Child-like   At that same time, moved to exultation by the 21
Mind.   Holy Spirit, Jesus said :
          " I thank thee, Father, Lord of Heaven and
          earth, that, though thou hast hidden these
          things from the wise and learned, thou hast
          revealed them to the childlike ! Yes, Father,
          I thank thee that this has seemed good to
          thee.

Everything has been committed to me by my Father ; nor 22
does any one know who the Son is, except the Father, or
who the Father is, except the Son and those to whom the
Son may choose to reveal him."

Then, turning to his disciples, Jesus said to them alone : 23
" Blessed are the eyes that see what you are seeing ; for, I tell 24
you, many Prophets and Kings wished for the sight of the
things which you are seeing, yet never saw them, and to hear
the things which you are hearing, yet never heard them."

The Great   Just then a Student of the Law came forward 25
Command- to test Jesus further.
ment.   "Teacher," he said, "what must I do if I am
to 'gain Immortal Life'?"

12 Isa. 2. 11.   15 Isa. 14. 13, 15.   19 Ps. 91. 13.   25 Enoch 40. 9.

"What is said in the Law?" answered Jesus.   "What do   26
you read there?"
His reply was—   27

   "'Thou shalt love the Lord thy God with all thy heart, and
   with all thy soul, and with all thy strength, and with all thy
   mind; and thy neighbour as thou dost thyself.'"

"You have answered right," said Jesus; "do that, and you   28
shall live."
But the man, wanting to justify himself, said to Jesus: "And   29
who is my neighbour?"   To which Jesus replied: 30

The Good   "A man was once going down from Jerusalem
Samaritan.   to Jericho when he fell into the hands of robbers,
who stripped him of everything, and beat him, and went away
leaving him half dead.   As it chanced, a priest was going down   31
by that road.   He saw the man, but passed by on the opposite
side.   A Levite, too, did the same; he came up to the spot,   32
but, when he saw the man, passed by on the opposite side.
But a Samaritan, travelling that way, came upon the man, and,   33
when he saw him, he was moved with compassion.   He went   34
to him and bound up his wounds, dressing them with oil and
wine, and then put him on his own mule, and brought him to
an inn, and took care of him.   The next day he took out   35
four shillings and gave them to the inn-keeper.   'Take
care of him,' he said, 'and whatever more you may spend
I will myself repay you on my way back.'   Now which,   36
do you think, of these three men," asked Jesus, "proved
himself a neighbour to the man who fell into the robbers'
hands?"

"The one that took pity on him," was the answer; on which   37
Jesus said:
"Go and do the same yourself."

The   As they continued their journey, Jesus came   38
Sisters of   to a village, where a woman named Martha
Bethany.   welcomed him to her house.   She had a sister   39
called Mary, who seated herself at the Master's feet, and
listened to his teaching; but Martha was distracted by the   40
many preparations that she was making.   So she went up to
Jesus and said:
"Master, do you approve of my sister's leaving me to make
preparations alone?   Tell her to help me."
"Martha, Martha," replied the Master, "you are anxious and   41
trouble yourself about many things; but only a few are   42
necessary, or rather one.   Mary has chosen the good part,
and it shall not be taken away from her."

The 'Lord's Prayer.' One day Jesus was at a certain place praying, 1 **11**
and, when he had finished, one of his disciples
said to him :

" Master, teach us to pray, as John taught his disciples."

" When you pray," Jesus answered, " say— 2
' Father, May thy name be held holy, thy
Kingdom come. Give us each day the bread 3
that we shall need ; And forgive us our sins, 4
for we ourselves forgive every one who wrongs
us ; And take us not into temptation.'"

Persistence in Prayer. Jesus also said to them : 5
" Suppose that one of you who has a friend
were to go to him in the middle of the night and
say ' Friend, lend me three loaves, for a friend of mine has 6
arrived at my house after a journey, and I have nothing to
offer him ' ; and suppose that the other should answer from 7
inside ' Do not trouble me ; the door is already fastened, and my
children and I are in bed ; I cannot get up and give you
anything' ; I tell you that, even though he will not get up and 8
give him anything because he is a friend, yet because of
his persistence he will rouse himself and give him what he
wants. And so I say to you—Ask, and your prayer 9

Encouragement to Prayer. shall be granted : search, and you shall find ;
knock, and the door shall be opened to you.
For he that asks receives, he that searches 10
finds, and to him that knocks the door shall be opened. What 11
father among you, if his son asks him for a fish, will give
him a snake instead, or, if he asks for an egg, will give him 12
a scorpion ? If you, then, naturally wicked though you 13
are, know how to give good gifts to your children, how much
more will the Father in Heaven give the Holy Spirit to those
that ask him ! "

Cure of a dumb Man. Once Jesus was driving out a dumb demon, 14
and, when the demon had gone out, the dumb
man spoke. The people were amazed at this ; but some 15
of them said : " He drives out demons by the help of Baal-zebub,

Jesus accused of Acting by the Help of Satan. the chief of the demons " ; while others, to test 16
him, asked him for some sign from the heavens.
Jesus himself, however, was aware of what they 17
were thinking, and said to them :

" Any kingdom wholly divided against itself becomes a
desolation ; and a divided house falls. So, too, if Satan is 18
wholly divided against himself, how can his kingdom last ?
Yet you say that I drive out demons by the help of Baal-
zebub. But, if it is by Baal-zebub's help that I drive out 19
demons, by whose help is it that your own sons drive them
out? Therefore they shall themselves be your judges. But, if 20
it is by the hand of God that I drive out demons, then the

Kingdom of God must already be upon you.   When a strong   21
man is keeping guard, fully armed, over his own mansion, his
property is in safety ; but, when one still stronger has attacked   22
and overpowered him, he takes away all the weapons on which
the other had relied, and divides his spoil.   He who is not   23
with me is against me, and he who does not help me to
Danger of gather is scattering.   No sooner does a   24
imperfect foul spirit leave a man, than it passes through
Reformation. places where there is no water, in search of rest ;
and finding none, it says 'I will go back to the home which I
left'; but, on coming there, it finds it unoccupied, swept,   25
and put in order.   Then it goes and brings with it seven   26
other spirits more wicked than itself, and they go in, and
make their home there ; and the last state of that man proves
to be worse than the first."

As Jesus was saying this, a woman in the crowd, raising her   27
voice, exclaimed :

"Happy was the mother who bore you and nursed you ! "
But Jesus replied :   28

"Rather, happy are those who listen to God's Message and
keep it."

Warning   As the crowds increased, Jesus began to   29
against   speak :
seeking Signs.   "This generation is a wicked generation.   It
is asking a sign, but no sign shall be given it except the sign
of Jonah.   For, as Jonah became a sign to the people of   30
Nineveh, so shall the Son of Man be to this generation.   At   31
the Judgement the Queen of the South will rise up with the
men of this generation, and will condemn them, because she
came from the very ends of the earth to listen to the wisdom
of Solomon ; and here is more than a Solomon !   At the Judge-   32
ment the men of Nineveh will stand up with this generation,
and will condemn it, because they repented at Jonah's proclamation ; and here is more than a Jonah !   No one sets   33
Lesson   light to a lamp, and then puts it in the cellar or
from a Lamp. under the corn-measure, but he puts it on the
lamp-stand, so that any one who comes in may see the
Light and light.   The lamp of the body is your eye.   34
Darkness. When your eye is unclouded, your whole body,
also, is lit up ; but, as soon as your eye is diseased, your body,
also, is darkened.   Take care, therefore, that the inner Light   35
is not darkness.   If, then, your whole body is lit up, and no   36
corner of it darkened, the whole will be lit up, just as when a
lamp gives you light by its brilliance."

Jesus   As Jesus finished speaking, a Pharisee asked   37
denounces him to breakfast with him, and Jesus went in and
the Pharisees. took his place at table.   The Pharisee noticed, to   38

his astonishment, that Jesus omitted the ceremonial washing before breakfast. But the Master said to him :

"You Pharisees do, it is true, clean the outside of the cup and of the plate, but inside you yourselves are filled with greed and wickedness. Fools ! did not the maker of the outside make the inside too ? Only give away what is in them in charity, and at once you have the whole clean. But alas for you Pharisees ! You pay tithes on mint, rue, and herbs of all kinds, and pass over justice and love to God. These last you ought to have put into practice without neglecting the first. Alas for you Pharisees ! You delight to have the front seat in the Synagogues, and to be greeted in the markets with respect. Alas for you ! You are like unsuspected graves, over which men walk unawares."

Here one of the Students of the Law interrupted him by saying :

"Teacher, when you say this, you are insulting us also."

But Jesus went on :

"Alas for you, too, you Students of the Law ! You load men with loads that are too heavy to carry, but do not, yourselves, touch them with one of your fingers. Alas for you ! You build the monuments of the Prophets whom your ancestors killed. You are actually witnesses to your ancestors' acts and show your approval of them, because, while they killed the Prophets, you build tombs for them. That is why the Wisdom of God said—" I will send to them Prophets and Apostles, some of whom they will persecute and kill, in order that the 'blood' of all the prophets 'that has been spilt' since the creation of the world may be exacted from this generation— from the blood of Abel down to the blood of Zechariah, who was slain between the altar and the House of God." Yes, I tell you, it will be exacted from this generation. Alas for you Students of the Law ! You have taken away the key of the door of Knowledge. You have not gone in yourselves and you have hindered those who try to go in."

A Plot against Jesus. When Jesus left the house, the Teachers of the Law and the Pharisees began to press him hard and question him closely upon many subjects, laying traps for him, so as to seize upon anything that he might say.

Warnings and Encouragements. Meanwhile the people had gathered in thousands, so that they trod upon one another, when Jesus, addressing himself to his disciples, began by saying to them :

"Be on your guard against the leaven—that is, the hypocrisy—of the Pharisees. There is nothing, however covered up, which will not be uncovered, nor anything kept secret which will not become known. Hence all that you have said in the dark will be heard in the light, and what you have

39
40
41
42

43

44

45

46

47

48

49

50

51

52

53

54

1 12

2

3

50 Enoch 9. 1.

spoken in the ear, within closed doors, will be proclaimed upon the housetops.   To you who are my friends I 4 say, Do not be afraid of those who kill the body, but after that can do no more. I will show you of whom you should be 5 afraid. Be afraid of him who, after killing you, has the power to fling you into the Pit. Yes, I say, be afraid of him. Are 6 not five sparrows sold for a penny ? Yet not one of them has escaped God's notice. No, the very hairs of your head are all 7 numbered. Do not be afraid ; you are of more value than many sparrows.   Every one, I tell you, who shall acknow- 8 ledge me before his fellow men, the Son of Man, also, will acknowledge before God's angels ; but he, who disowns me 9 before his fellow men, will be altogether disowned before God's angels.   Every one who shall say anything against the 10 Son of Man will be forgiven, but for him who slanders the Holy Spirit there will be no forgiveness.   Whenever they 11 take you before the Synagogue Courts or the magistrates or other authorities, do not be anxious as to how you will defend yourselves, or what your defence will be, or what you will say ; for the Holy Spirit will show you at the moment what you 12 ought to say."

Instances of Covetousness.   "Teacher," a man in the crowd said to Jesus, 13 "tell my brother to share the property with me." But Jesus said to him : 14
"Man, who made me a judge or an arbiter between you ?"
And then he added : 15
"Take care to keep yourselves free from every form of covetousness ; for even in the height of his prosperity a man's true Life does not depend on what he has."
Then Jesus told them this parable— 16
"There was once a rich man whose land was very fertile ; and he began to ask himself 'What shall I do, for I have 17 nowhere to store my crops? This is what I will do,' he said ; 18 'I will pull down my barns and build larger ones, and store all my grain and my goods in them ; and I will say to myself, 19 Now you have plenty of good things put by for many years ; take your ease, eat, drink, and enjoy yourself.' But God 20 said to the man 'Fool! This very night your life is being demanded ; and as for all that you have prepared—who will have it ?'
So it is with those who lay by wealth for themselves and are 21 not rich to the glory of God."

The Cares of Life.   And Jesus said to his disciples : 22
"That is why I say to you, Do not be anxious about the life here—what you can get to eat ; nor yet about your body—what you can get to wear. For life is more than 23 food, and the body than its clothes. Think of the ravens— 24 they neither sow nor reap ; they have neither storehouse nor

barn ; and yet God feeds them ! And how much more precious
are you than birds ! But which of you, by being anxious,   25
can prolong his life a moment ? And, if you cannot do even   26
the smallest thing, why be anxious about other things ? Think   27
of the lilies, and how they grow. They neither toil nor spin ;
yet, I tell you, even Solomon in all his splendour was not robed
like one of these. If, even in the field, God so clothes the grass   28
which is living to-day and to-morrow will be thrown into the
oven, how much more will he clothe you, O men of little faith !
And you—do not be always seeking what you can get to eat   29
or what you can get to drink ; and do not waver. These are the   30
things for which all the nations of the world are seeking, and
your Father knows that you need them. No, seek his Kingdom,   31
and these things shall be added for you. So do not be afraid,   32
my little flock, for your Father has been pleased to give you
the Kingdom.   Sell what belongs to you, and give in   33

**The true
Treasure.** charity. Make yourselves purses that will not
wear out—an inexhaustible treasure in Heaven,
where no thief comes near, or moth works ruin. For where your   34
treasure is, there also will your heart be.   Make your-   35
selves ready, with your lamps alight ; and be like   36

Watchfulness. men who are waiting for their Master's return from
his wedding, so that, when he comes and knocks, they may
open the door for him at once. Happy are those servants whom,   37
on his return, the Master will find watching. I tell you that
he will make himself ready, and bid them take their places at
table, and will come and wait upon them. Whether it is late   38
at night, or in the early morning that he comes, if he finds
all as it should be, then happy are they. This you do know,   39
that, had the owner of the house known at what time the
thief was coming, he would have been on the watch, and would
not have let his house be broken into. Do you also prepare,   40
for when you are least expecting him the Son of Man will
come."

**Parable of the
good and bad
Servants.** "Master," said Peter, "are you telling this   41
parable with reference to us or to every one ?"
"Who, then," replied the Master, "is that   42
trustworthy steward, the careful man, who will be placed
by his master over his establishment, to give them their rations
at the proper time ? Happy will that servant be whom his   43
master, when he comes home, shall find doing this. His   44
master, I tell you, will put him in charge of the whole of
his property. But should that servant say to himself 'My   45
master is a long time coming,' and begin to beat the menservants and the maidservants, and to eat and drink and get
drunk, that servant's master will come on a day when   46
he does not expect him, and at an hour of which he is unaware, and will flog him severely and assign him his place
among the untrustworthy. The servant who knows his   47

master's wishes and yet does not prepare and act accordingly will receive many lashes ; while one who does not know his master's wishes, but acts so as to deserve a flogging, will receive but few. From every one to whom much has been given much will be expected, and from the man to whom much has been entrusted the more will be demanded. 48

The Cost of Christ's Service. I came to cast fire upon the earth ; and what more can I wish, if it is already kindled? There is a baptism that I must undergo, and how great is my distress until it is over! Do you think that I am here to give peace on earth? No, I tell you, but to cause division. For from this time, if there are five people in a house, they will be divided, three against two, and two against three. 49 50 51 52

'Father will be opposed to son and son to father, mother to daughter and daughter to mother, mother-in-law to her daughter-in-law and daughter-in-law to her mother-in-law.'" 53

Signs of the Times. And to the people Jesus said : "When you see a cloud rising in the west, you say at once 'There is a storm coming,' and come it does. And when you see that the wind is in the south, you say 'It will be burning hot,' and so it proves. Hypocrites! You know how to judge of the earth and the sky ; how is it, then, that you cannot judge of this time? Why do not you yourselves decide what is right? 54 55 56 57 58

The Settlement of Disputes. When, for instance, you are going with your opponent before a magistrate, on your way to the court do your best to be quit of him ; for fear that he should drag you before the judge, when the judge will hand you over to the bailiff of the court, and the bailiff throw you into prison. You will not, I tell you, come out until you have paid the very last farthing." 59

The Meaning of Calamities. Just at that time some people had come to tell Jesus about the Galilaeans, whose blood Pilate had mingled with the blood of their sacrifices. **13** 1

"Do you suppose," replied Jesus, "that, because these Galilaeans have suffered in this way, they were worse sinners than any other Galilaeans? No, I tell you ; but, unless you repent, you will all perish as they did. Or those eighteen men at Siloam on whom the tower fell, killing them all, do you suppose that they were worse offenders than any other inhabitants of Jerusalem? No, I tell you ; but, unless you repent, you will all perish in the same manner." And Jesus told them this parable— 2 3 4 5 6

The barren Fig Tree. "A man, who had a fig tree growing in his vineyard, came to look for fruit on it, but could not find any. So he said to his gardener 'Three years now I have come to look for fruit on this fig tree, 7 without finding any! Cut it down. Why should it rob the soil?'

'Leave it this one year more, Sir,' the man answered, 'till 8
I have dug round it and manured it. Then, if it bears in 9
future, well and good ; but if not, you can have it cut down.'"

A Woman   Jesus was teaching on a Sabbath in one of 10
healed on the the Synagogues, and he saw before him a woman 11
Sabbath. who for eighteen years had suffered from weakness, owing to her having an evil spirit in her. She was bent double, and was wholly unable to raise herself. When 12
Jesus saw her, he called him to him, and said :

"Woman, you are released from your weakness."

He placed his hands on her, and she was instantly made 13
straight, and began to praise God. But the President of the 14
Synagogue, indignant that Jesus had worked the cure on the Sabbath, interposed and said to the people :

"There are six days on which work ought to be done ; come to be cured on one of those, and not on the Sabbath."

"You hypocrites !" the Master answered him. "Does not 15
every one of you let his ox or his ass loose from its manger, and take it out to drink, on the Sabbath ? But this woman, a 16
daughter of Abraham, who has been kept in bondage by Satan for now eighteen years, ought not she to have been released from her bondage on the Sabbath ? "

As he said this, his opponents all felt ashamed ; but all the 17
people rejoiced to see all the wonderful things that he was doing.

So Jesus said :
                                                                 18
Parable   "What is the Kingdom of God like? and to
of the   what can I liken it? It is like a mustard-seed 19
Mustard Seed. which a man took and put in his garden. The seed grew and became a tree, and 'the wild birds roosted in its branches.'"

And again Jesus said :
                                                                 20
Parable   "To what can I liken the Kingdom of God ?
of the   It is like some yeast which a woman took and 21
Leaven.   covered in three pecks of flour, until the whole had risen."

The narrow   Jesus went through towns and villages, teach- 22
Door.   ing as he went, and making his way towards
Jerusalem.

"Master," some one asked, "are there but few in the path 23
of Salvation ? "

And Jesus answered :

"Strive to go in by the small door. Many, I tell you, will 24
seek to go in, but they will not be able when once the 25

¹⁹ Dan. 4. 12.

F*

master of the house has got up and shut the door, while you begin to say, as you stand outside and knock, 'Sir, open the door for us.' His answer will be—'I do not know where you come from.' Then you will begin to say 'We have eaten and 26 drunk in your presence, and you have taught in our streets,' and his reply will be—'I do not know where you come from. 27 Leave my presence, all you who are living in wickedness.'

There, there will be weeping and grinding of teeth, when you 28 see Abraham, Isaac, and Jacob, and all the Prophets, in the Kingdom of God, while you yourselves are being driven out- side. People will come from East and West, and from North 29 and South, and take their places at the banquet in the Kingdom of God. There are some who are last now who 30 will then be first, and some who are first now who will then be last!"

A Message to Herod Antipas. Just then some Pharisees came up to Jesus and 31 said : "Go away and leave this place, for Herod wants to kill you."

But Jesus answered : 32 "Go and say to that fox 'Look you, I am driving out demons and shall be completing cures to-day and to-morrow, and on the third day I shall have done.' But to-day and to-morrow 33 and the day after I must go on my way, because it cannot be that a Prophet should meet his end outside Jerusalem. Jerusalem! Jerusalem! she who slays the Prophets and stones 34 the messengers sent to her—Oh, how often have I **Jesus laments the Fate of Jerusalem.** wished to gather your children round me, as a hen takes her brood under her wings, and you would not come! Verily your House is left to you desolate! 35 and never, I tell you, shall you see me, until you say—

'Blessed is He who comes in the name of the Lord.'"

Cure of a dropsical Man. On one occasion, as Jesus was going, on a 1 Sabbath, into the house of one of the leading Pharisees to dine, they were watching him closely. There he saw before him a man who was suffering from 2 dropsy.

"Is it allowable," said Jesus, addressing the Students of the 3 Law and the Pharisees, "to work a cure on the Sabbath, or is it not?"

They remained silent. Jesus took hold of the man and 4 cured him, and sent him away. And he said to them : 5 "Which of you, finding that his son or his ox has fallen into a well, will not immediately pull him out on the Sabbath Day?"

27 Ps. 6. 8.   29 Mal. 1. 11.   35 Jer. 22. 5; Ps. 118. 26.

And they could not make any answer to that.   6

Observing that the guests were choosing the   7
best places for themselves, Jesus told them this
parable—

"When you are invited by any one to a wedding banquet, do   8
not seat yourself in the best place, for fear that some one of
higher rank should have been invited by your host; and he who   9
invited you both will come and say to you 'Make room for this
man,' and then you will begin in confusion to take the lowest
place. No, when you are invited, go and take the lowest   10
place, so that, when he who has invited you comes, he may
say to you 'Friend, come higher up'; and then you will be
honoured in the eyes of all your fellow-guests. For every one   11
who exalts himself will be humbled, and he who humbles
himself will be exalted."

Then Jesus went on to say to the man who had invited   12
him:

"When you give a breakfast or a dinner, do not ask your
friends, or your brothers, or your relations, or rich neighbours,
for fear that they should invite you in return, and so you should
be repaid. No, when you entertain, invite the poor, the   13
crippled, the lame, the blind; and then you will be happy   14
indeed, since they cannot recompense you; for you shall be
recompensed at the resurrection of the good."

One of the guests heard what he said and ex-   15
claimed:
"Happy will he be who shall eat bread in the
Kingdom of God!"

But Jesus said to him: 16

"A man was once giving a great dinner. He invited many
people, and sent his servant, when it was time for the dinner, to   17
say to those who had been invited 'Come, for everything is now
ready.' They all with one accord began to ask to be excused.   18
The first man said to the servant 'I have bought a field and
am obliged to go and look at it. I must ask you to consider
me excused.' The next said 'I have bought five pairs of   19
bullocks, and I am on my way to try them. I must ask
you to consider me excused'; while the next said 'I am just   20
married, and for that reason I am unable to come.' On   21
his return the servant told his master all these answers.
Then in anger the owner of the house said to his servant
'Go out at once into the streets and alleys of the town, and
bring in here the poor, and the crippled, and the blind, and the
lame.' Presently the servant said 'Sir, your order has been   22
carried out, and still there is room.'

'Go out,' the master said, 'into the roads and hedgerows,   23
and make people come in, so that my house may be filled;
for I tell you all that not one of those men who were invited   24
will taste my dinner.'"

The Cost of Self-denial. One day, when great crowds of people were walking with Jesus, he turned and said to them: " If any man comes to me and does not hate his father, and mother, and wife, and children, and brothers, and sisters, yes and his very life, he can be no disciple of mine. Whoever does not carry his own cross, and walk in my steps, can be no disciple of mine. Why, which of you, when he wants to build a tower, does not first sit down and reckon the cost, to see if he has enough to complete it?—for fear that, if he has laid the foundation and is not able to finish it, every one who sees it should begin to laugh at him, and say 'Here is a man who began to build and was not able to finish!' Or what king, when he is setting out to fight another king, does not first sit down and consider if with ten thousand men he is able to meet one who is coming against him with twenty thousand? And if he cannot, then, while the other is still at a distance, he sends envoys and asks for terms of peace. And so with every one of you who does **A real Disciple of Jesus.** not bid farewell to all he has—he cannot be a disciple of mine. Yes, salt is good; but, if the salt itself should lose its strength, what shall be used to season it? It is not fit either for the land or for the manure heap. Men throw it away. Let him who has ears to hear with hear !"

The tax-gatherers and the outcasts were all drawing near to Jesus to listen to him ; but the Pharisees and the Teachers of the Law found fault.

"This man always welcomes outcasts, and takes meals with them !" they complained. So Jesus told them this parable—

Parable of the lost Sheep. " What man among you who has a hundred sheep, and has lost one of them, does not leave the ninety-nine out in the open country, and go after the lost sheep till he finds it? And, when he has found it, he puts it on his shoulders rejoicing ; and, on reaching home, he calls his friends and his neighbours together, and says 'Come and rejoice with me, for I have found my sheep which was lost.' So, I tell you, there will be more rejoicing in Heaven over one outcast that repents, than over ninety-nine religious men, who have no need to repent. Or again, what **Parable of the lost Coin.** woman who has ten silver coins, if she loses one of them, does not light a lamp, and sweep the house, and search carefully until she finds it? And, when she has found it, she calls her friends and neighbours together, and says 'Come and rejoice with me, for I have found the coin which I lost.' So, I tell you, there is rejoicing in the presence of God's angels over one outcast that repents."

Then Jesus continued :   11

Parable of the lost Son "A man had two sons; and the younger of 12
them said to his father 'Father, give me my share
of the inheritance.' So the father divided the
property between them. A few days later the younger son got 13
together all that he had, and went away into a distant land; and
there he squandered his inheritance by leading a dissolute life.
After he had spent all that he had, there was a severe famine 14
through all that country, and he began to be in actual want.
So he went and engaged himself to one of the people of that 15
country, who sent him into his fields to tend pigs. He even 16
longed to satisfy his hunger with the bean-pods on which the
pigs were feeding; and no one gave him anything. But, 17
when he came to himself, he said 'How many of my father's
hired servants have more bread than they can eat, while
here am I starving to death! I will get up and go to my 18
father, and say to him "Father, I sinned against Heaven
and against you; I am no longer fit to be called your son; 19
make me one of your hired servants."'   And he got 20
up and went to his father. But, while he was still a long way
off, his father saw him and was deeply moved; he ran and
threw his arms round his neck and kissed him. 'Father,' 21
the son said, 'I sinned against Heaven and against you;
I am no longer fit to be called your son; make me one of
your hired servants.'
But the father turned to his servants and said 'Be quick and 22
fetch a robe—the very best—and put it on him; give him
a ring for his finger and sandals for his feet; and bring the 23
fattened calf and kill it, and let us eat and make merry; for here 24
is my son who was dead, and is alive again, was lost, and is
found.'   So they began making merry. Meanwhile the 25
elder son was out in the fields; but, on coming home, when
he got near the house, he heard music and dancing, and he 26
called one of the servants and asked what it all meant.
'Your brother has come back,' the servant told him, 'and 27
your father has killed the fattened calf, because he has him
back safe and sound.'
This made him angry, and he would not go in. But his father 28
came out and begged him to do so. 'No,' he said to his father, 29
'look at all the years I have been serving you, without ever
once disobeying you, and yet you have never given me even a
kid, so that I might have a merry-making with my friends.
But, no sooner has this son of yours come, who has eaten up 30
your property in the company of prostitutes, than you have
killed the fattened calf for him.'
'Child,' the father answered, 'you are always with me, 31
and everything that I have is yours. We could but make merry 32
and rejoice, for here is your brother who was dead, and is
alive; who was lost, and is found.'"

Parable of the dishonest Steward.

Jesus said to his disciples : 1

"There was a rich man who had a steward ; and this steward was maliciously accused to him of wasting his estate. So the master called him 2 and said 'What is this that I hear about you ? Give in your accounts, for you cannot act as steward any longer.'

'What am I to do,' the steward asked himself, 'now that my 3 master is taking the steward's place away from me ? I have not strength to dig, and I am ashamed to beg. I know what 4 I will do, so that, as soon as I am turned out of my stewardship, people may welcome me into their homes.' One by one he 5 called up his master's debtors. 'How much do you owe my master ?' he asked of the first. 'Four hundred and forty 6 gallons of oil,' answered the man. 'Here is your agreement,' he said ; 'sit down at once and make it two hundred and twenty. And you,' the steward said to the next, 'how much 7 do you owe ?' 'Seventy quarters of wheat,' he replied. 'Here is your agreement,' the steward said ; 'make it fifty-six.' His 8 master complimented this dishonest steward on the shrewdness of his action. And indeed men of the world are shrewder in dealing with their fellow-men than those who have the Light. And I say to you 'Win friends for yourselves 9 with your dishonest money,' so that, when it comes to an end, there may be a welcome for you into the Eternal Home. He who is trustworthy in the smallest matter is trustworthy 10 in a great one also ; and he who is dishonest in the smallest matter is dishonest in a great one also. So, if you have proved 11 untrustworthy with the 'dishonest money,' who will trust you with the true ? And, if you have proved untrustworthy with 12 what does not belong to us, who will give you what is really our own ? No servant can 13 serve two masters, for, either he will hate one and love the other, or else he will attach himself to one and despise the other. You cannot serve both God and Money."

True Service.

Jesus rebukes the Pharisees.

All this was said within hearing of the 14 Pharisees, who were lovers of money, and they began to sneer at Jesus.

"You," said Jesus, "are the men who justify themselves 15 before the world, but God can read your hearts ; and what is highly esteemed among men may be an abomination in the sight of God. The Law and the Prophets sufficed until 16 the time of John. Since then the Good News of the Kingdom of God has been told, and everybody has been forcing his way into it. It would be easier for the heavens and the 17 earth to disappear than for one stroke of a letter in the Law to be lost. Every one who divorces his wife and marries 18 another woman is an adulterer, and the man who marries a divorced woman is an adulterer.

8 Enoch 108. 11.   9 Enoch 63. 10.   11 Enoch 63. 10.

**Parable of
the rich Man
and Lazarus.** There was once a rich man, who dressed in 19
purple robes and fine linen, and feasted every day
in great splendour. Near his gateway there had 20
been laid a beggar named Lazarus, who was covered with sores,
and who longed to satisfy his hunger with what fell from the 21
rich man's table. Even the very dogs came and licked his
sores. After a time the beggar died, and was taken by the 22
angels to be with Abraham. The rich man also died and was
buried. In the Place of Death he looked up in his torment, 23
and saw Abraham at a distance and Lazarus at his side. So he 24
called out 'Pity me, Father Abraham, and send Lazarus to dip
the tip of his finger in water and cool my tongue, for I am
suffering agony in this flame.'

'Child,' answered Abraham, 'remember that you in 25
your lifetime received what you thought desirable, just as
Lazarus received what was not desirable ; but now he has his
consolation here, while you are suffering agony. And not 26
only that, but between you and us there lies a great chasm, so
that those who wish to pass from here to you cannot, nor can
they cross from there to us.'

'Then, Father,' he said, 'I beg you to send Lazarus to my 27
father's house—for I have five brothers—to warn them, so that 28
they may not come to this place of torture also.'

'They have the writings of Moses and the Prophets,' replied 29
Abraham ; 'let them listen to them.'

'But, Father Abraham,' he urged, 'if some one from the 30
dead were to go to them, they would repent.'

'If they do not listen to Moses and the Prophets,' answered 31
Abraham, 'they will not be persuaded, even if some one were
to rise from the dead.' "

**Against
hindering
Others.** Jesus said to his disciples : 1 **17**
"It is inevitable that there should be snares ;
yet alas for him who is answerable for them ! It 2
would be good for him if he had been flung into the sea with
a mill-stone round his neck, rather than that he should prove a
snare to even one of these lowly ones. Be on your guard ! If 3
**On dealing
with
Wrong-doers.** your brother does wrong, reprove him ; but, if he
repents, forgive him. Even if he wrongs you 4
seven times a day, but turns to you every time
and says 'I am sorry,' you must forgive him."

**The Power
of Faith.** "Give us more faith," said the Apostles to the 5
Master ; but the Master said : 6
"If your faith were only like a mustard-seed, you could say
to this mulberry tree 'Be up-rooted and planted in the sea,' and
it would obey you.

Duty. Which of you, if he had a servant ploughing, 7
or tending the sheep, would say to him, when he
came in from the fields, 'Come at once and take your place

at table,' instead of saying ' Prepare my dinner, and then make 8
yourself ready and wait on me while I am eating and drinking,
and after that you shall eat and drink yourself'? Does he feel 9
grateful to his servant for doing what he is told? And so with 10
you—when you have done all that you have been told, still
say ' We are but useless servants ; we have done no more than
we ought to have done.'"

**Jesus
heals ten
Lepers.** On the way to Jerusalem Jesus passed between 11
Samaria and Galilee.   As he was entering 12
a village, ten lepers met him.   Standing still,
some distance off, they called out loudly :   13
  " Jesus ! Sir ! pity us !"
When Jesus saw them, he said :   14
  " Go and show yourselves to the priests."
And, as they were on their way, they were made clean.   One of 15
them, finding he was cured, came back, praising God loudly,
and threw himself on his face at Jesus' feet, thanking him for 16
what he had done ; and this man was a Samaritan.
  " Were not all the ten made clean?" exclaimed Jesus. 17
" But the nine—where are they ? Were there none to come 18
back and praise God except this foreigner ? Get up," he said to 19
him, "and go on your way. Your faith has delivered you."

**The Coming
of the
Kingdom.** Being once asked by the Pharisees when the 20
Kingdom of God was to come, Jesus answered :
  "The Kingdom of God does not come in a way
that admits of observation, nor will people say ' Look, here 21
it is !' or ' There it is!'; for the Kingdom of God is within
you !   The day will come," he said to his disciples, 22
" when you will long to see but one of the days of the Son of
Man, and will not see it. People will say to you ' There he 23
is !' or ' Here he is !' Do not go and follow them. For, just 24
as lightning will lighten and flare from one side of the
heavens to the other, so will it be with the Son of Man. But 25
first he must undergo much suffering, and he must be
rejected by the present generation. As it was in the days 26
of Noah, so will it be again in the days of the Son of Man.
They were eating and drinking and marrying and being 27
married, up to the very day on which Noah entered the ark,
and then the flood came and destroyed them all. So, too, in 28
the days of Lot. People were eating, drinking, buying,
selling, planting, building ; but, on the very day on which Lot 29
came out of Sodom, it rained fire and sulphur from the skies
and destroyed them all. It will be the same on the day 30
on which the Son of Man reveals himself. On that day, if a 31
man is on his house-top and his goods in the house, he must
not go down to get them ; nor again must one who is on the

<hr>

[14] Lev. 13. 49.   [27] Gen. 7. 7.   [29—31] Gen. 19. 24, 26.

farm turn back.   Remember Lot's wife.   Whoever is eager to   32, 33
get the most out of his life will lose it ; but whoever will lose it
shall preserve it.   On that night, I tell you, of two men upon   34
the same bed, one will be taken and the other left ; of two women   35
grinding together, one will be taken and the other left."

"Where will it be, Master ? " interposed the disciples.   37

"Where there is a body," said Jesus, " 'there will the
vultures flock.' "

Parable of the corrupt Judge. Jesus told his disciples a parable to show them   1 **18**
that they should always pray and never despair.
"There was," he said, "in a certain town a   2
judge, who had no fear of God nor regard for man.   In the   3
same town there was a widow who went to him again and
again, and said 'Grant me justice against my opponent.'
For a time the judge refused, but afterwards he said to   4
himself ' Although I am without fear of God or regard for man,
yet, as this widow is so troublesome, I will grant her justice,   5
to stop her from plaguing me with her endless visits.' "
Then the Master added :   6

" Listen to what this iniquitous judge says ! And God—will   7
not he see that his own People, who cry to him night and
day, have justice done them—though he holds his hand ?   He   8
will, I tell you, have justice done them, and that soon ! Yet,
when the Son of Man comes, will he find faith on the earth ? "

Another time, speaking to people who were satisfied that   9
they were religious, and who regarded every one else with
scorn, Jesus told this parable—

Parable of the Pharisee and the Tax-gatherer. " Two men went up into the Temple Courts to   10
pray.   One was a Pharisee and the other a tax-
gatherer.   The Pharisee stood forward and began   11
praying to himself in this way—
'O God, I thank thee that I am not like other men—thieves,
rogues, adulterers—or even like this tax-gatherer.   I fast   12
twice a week, and give a tenth of everything I get to God.'
Meanwhile the tax-gatherer stood at a distance, not ventur-   13
ing even ' to raise his eyes to Heaven '; but he kept striking
his breast and saying ' O God, have mercy on me, a sinner.'
This man, I tell you, went home pardoned, rather than the   14
other ; for every one who exalts himself will be humbled, while
every one who humbles himself shall be exalted."

Jesus blesses little Children. Some of the people were bringing even their   15
babies to Jesus, for him to touch them ; but, when
the disciples saw it, they began to find fault with
those who had brought them.   Jesus, however, called the little   16
children to him.

³⁷ Isa. 34. 15.   ⁷ Enoch 47. 1, 2.   ¹³ Enoch 13. 5.

"Let the little children come to me," he said, "and do not hinder them ; for it is to the childlike that the Kingdom of God belongs. I tell you, unless a man receives the Kingdom 17 of God like a child, he will not enter it at all."

The Responsibilities of Wealth. And one of the Presidents asked Jesus this 18 question—

"Good Teacher, what must I do if I am to gain Immortal Life?"

"Why do you call me good?" answered Jesus. "No one 19 is good but God. You know the commandments— 20

'Do not commit adultery, Do not kill, Do not steal, Do not say what is false about others, Honour thy father and thy mother.'"

"I have observed all these," he replied, "from childhood." 21 Hearing this, Jesus said to him : 22 "There is one thing still lacking in you ; sell every thing that you have, and distribute to the poor, and you shall have wealth in Heaven ; then come and follow me."

But the man became greatly distressed on hearing this, for he 23 was extremely rich.   Seeing this, Jesus said to his 24 disciples :

"How hard it is for men of wealth to enter the Kingdom of God ! It is easier, indeed, for a camel to get through a 25 needle's eye than for a rich man to enter the Kingdom of God !"

"Then who can be saved?" asked those who heard this. 26 But Jesus said : 27 "What is impossible with men is possible with God."

"But we," said Peter, "we left what belonged to us and 28 followed you."

"I tell you," he answered, "that there is no one who has left 29 house, or wife, or brothers, or parents, or children, on account of the Kingdom of God, who will not receive many times as much 30 in the present, and in the age that is coming Immortal Life."

Jesus, a third time, foretells his Death. Gathering the Twelve round him, Jesus said to 31 them :

"Listen ! We are going up to Jerusalem ; and there everything that is written in the Prophets will be done to the Son of Man. For he will be given up 32 to the Gentiles, mocked, insulted and spat upon ; they will 33 scourge him, and then put him to death ; and on the third day he will rise again."

The Apostles did not comprehend any of this ; his meaning 34 was unintelligible to them, and they did not understand what he was saying.

[20] Exod. 20. 12—16. [33] Hos. 6. 2.

**Cure of
a blind
Man.** As Jesus was getting near Jericho, a blind man 35
was sitting by the road-side, begging. Hearing 36
a crowd going by, the man asked what was the
matter ; and, when people told him that Jesus of Nazareth was 37
passing, he shouted out : 38

"Jesus, Son of David, take pity on me ! "

Those who were in front kept telling him to be quiet, but he 39
continued to call out the louder :

"Son of David, take pity on me ! "

Then Jesus stopped and ordered the man to be brought to him. 40
And, when he had come close up to him, Jesus asked him :

"What do you want me to do for you ? " 41

"Master," he said, " I want to recover my sight."

And Jesus said : " Recover your sight, your faith has delivered 42
you."

Instantly he recovered his sight, and began to follow Jesus, 43
praising God.   And all the people, on seeing it, gave
glory to God.

**Zacchaeus
the
Tax-gatherer.** Jesus entered Jericho and made his way through 1 **19**
the town.   There was a man there, known 2
by the name of Zacchaeus, who was a commis-
sioner of taxes and a rich man. He tried to see what Jesus
was like ; but, being short, he was unable to do so because 3
of the crowd. So he ran on ahead and climbed up into a 4
mulberry tree, to see Jesus, for he knew that he must pass
that way. When Jesus came to the place, he looked up and 5
said to him :

"Zacchaeus, be quick and come down, for I must stop at
your house to-day."

So Zacchaeus got down quickly, and joyfully welcomed him. 6
On seeing this, every one began to complain : 7

" He has gone to stay with a man who is an outcast."

But Zacchaeus stood forward and said to the Master : 8

" Listen, Master ! I will give half my property to the poor,
and, if I have defrauded any one of anything, I will give
him back four times as much."

" Salvation has come to this house to-day," answered Jesus, 9
" for even this man is a son of Abraham. The Son of Man 10
has come to ' search for those who are lost ' and to save them."

**Parable
of the
Pounds.** As the people were listening to this, Jesus went 11
on to tell them a parable. He did so because he
was near Jerusalem, and because they thought
that the Kingdom of God was going to be proclaimed at
once. He said : 12

" A nobleman once went to a distant country to receive his
appointment to a Kingdom and then return. He called ten 13

[10] Ezek. 34. 16.

of his servants and gave them ten pounds each, and told
them to trade with them during his absence. But his subjects 14
hated him and sent envoys after him to say 'We will not
have this man as our King.'   On his return, after 15
having been appointed King, he directed that the servants to
whom he had given his money should be summoned, so that
he might learn what amount of trade they had done. The first 16
came up, and said 'Sir, your ten pounds have made a hundred.'

'Well done, good servant!' exclaimed the master. 'As you 17
have proved trustworthy in a very small matter, I appoint you
governor over ten towns.' When the second came, he said 18
'Your ten pounds, Sir, have produced fifty.' So the master 19
said to him 'And you I appoint over five towns.' Another 20
servant also came and said 'Sir, here are your ten pounds; I
have kept them put away in a handkerchief. For I was afraid 21
of you, because you are a stern man. You take what you
have not planted, and reap what you have not sown.' The 22
master answered 'Out of your own mouth I judge you, you
worthless servant. You knew that I am a stern man, that I
take what I have not planted, and reap what I have not sown?
Then why did not you put my money into a bank? And I, on 23
my return, could have claimed it with interest. Take away 24
from him the ten pounds,' he said to those standing by, 'and
give them to the one who has the hundred.'

'But, Sir,' they interposed, 'he has a hundred pounds 25
already!'

'I tell you,' he answered, 'that, to him who has, more will 26
be given, but, from him who has nothing, even what he
has will be taken away.   But as for my enemies, 27
these men who would not have me as their King, bring them
here and put them to death in my presence.'"

After saying this, Jesus went on in front, going up to 28
Jerusalem.

V.—THE LAST DAYS.

Jesus enters It was when Jesus had almost reached Beth- 29
Jerusalem. phage and Bethany, near the Mount of Olives,
that he sent on two of the disciples.

"Go to the village facing us," he said, "and, when you get 30
there, you will find a foal tethered, which no one has yet
ridden; untie it and lead it here. And, if anybody asks 31
you 'Why are you untying it?,' you are to say this—'The
Master wants it.'"

So the two who were sent went and found it as Jesus had 32
told them. While they were untying the foal, the owners 33
asked them—"Why are you untying the foal?" And the two 34
disciples answered—"The Master wants it."

Then they led it back to Jesus, and threw their cloaks on the 35
foal and put Jesus upon it. As he went along, the people kept 36
spreading their cloaks in the road. When he had almost 37
reached the place where the road led down the Mount of
Olives, every one of the many disciples began in their joy to
praise God loudly for all the miracles that they had seen :

> " Blessed is He who comes— 38
>   Our King—in the name of the Lord !
> Peace in Heaven,
>   And glory on high."

Some of the Pharisees in the crowd said to him : 39
   "Teacher, reprove your disciples."
But Jesus answered : 40
   " I tell you that if these men are silent, the very stones will
call out."
   When he drew near, on seeing the city, he wept over it, and 41
said : 42
   " Would that you had known, while yet there was time—
even you—the things that make for peace ! But now they
have been hidden from your sight. For a time is coming upon 43
you when your enemies will surround you with earthworks,
and encircle you, and hem you in on all sides ; they will 44
trample you down and your children within you, and they will
not leave in you one stone upon another, because you did not
know ' the time of your visitation.' "

Jesus in the Temple. Jesus went into the Temple Courts and began 45
to drive out those who were selling, saying as he 46
did so :
   " Scripture says—' My House shall be a House of Prayer ' ;
but you have made it ' a den of robbers.' "

Jesus continued to teach each day in the Temple Courts ; 47
but the Chief Priests and Teachers of the Law were eager to
take his life, and so also were the leading men. Yet they 48
could not see what to do, for the people all hung upon his
words.

Jesus and the Chief Priests. On one of these days, when Jesus was teaching 1 **20**
the people in the Temple Courts and telling the
Good News, the Chief Priests and the Teachers of
the Law, joined by the Councillors, confronted him, and ad- 2
dressing him, said :
   " Tell us what authority you have to do these things.
Who is it that has given you this authority ? "
   " I, too," said Jesus in reply, " will ask you one question. 3

---

38 Ps. 118. 25, 26 ; Zech. 9. 9. 41 Ps. 137. 9. 46 Isa. 56. 7 ; Jer. 7. 11.

Give me an answer to it. It is about John's baptism—was it   4
of divine or of human origin?"
But they began arguing together :   5
  "If we say 'divine,' he will say 'Why did not you believe
him?' But, if we say 'human,' the people will all stone us,   6
for they are persuaded that John was a Prophet."
So they answered that they did not know its origin.   7
  "Then I," said Jesus, "refuse to tell you what authority I   8
have to do these things."

Parable of the wicked Tenants.   But Jesus began to tell the people this parable—   9
"A man once planted a vineyard, and then let
it out to tenants, and went abroad for a long while.
At the proper time he sent a servant to the tenants, that they   10
should give him a share of the produce of the vineyard. The
tenants, however, beat him and sent him away empty-handed.
The owner afterwards sent another servant ; but the tenants   11
beat and insulted this man too, and sent him away empty-
handed. He sent a third ; but they wounded this man also,   12
and threw him outside. 'What shall I do?' said the owner of   13
the vineyard. 'I will send my son, who is very dear to me.
Perhaps they will respect him.' But, on seeing him, the tenants   14
consulted with one another. 'Here is the heir!' they said.
'Let us kill him, and then the inheritance will become
ours.' So they threw him outside the vineyard and killed him.   15
Now what will the owner of the vineyard do to them ? He will   16
come and put those tenants to death, and will let the vineyard
to others."

  "Heaven forbid !" they exclaimed when they heard it. But   17
Jesus looked at them and said :

  "What then is the meaning of this passage?—

    'The very stone which the builders despised
    Has now itself become the corner-stone.'

Every one who falls on that stone will be dashed to pieces, while   18
any one on whom it falls—it will scatter him as dust."
  After this the Teachers of the Law and the Chief Priests were   19
eager to lay hands on Jesus then and there, but they were
afraid of the people ; for they saw that it was at them that he

A Question about Tribute.   had aimed this parable. Having watched   20
their opportunity, they afterwards sent some
spies, who pretended to be good men, to catch
Jesus in the course of conversation, and so enable them to
give him up to the Governor's jurisdiction and authority.
These men asked Jesus a question. They said :   21
  "Teacher, we know that you are right in what you say and
teach, and that you do not take any account of a man's position, but teach the Way of God honestly ; are we right in   22
paying tribute to the Emperor or not?"

            9 Isa. 5. 1.   17 Ps. 118. 22.

Seeing through their deceitfulness, Jesus said to them : 23
" Show me a florin. Whose head and title are on it ? " 24
" The Emperor's," they said ; and Jesus replied : 25
" Well then, pay to the Emperor what belongs to the
Emperor, and to God what belongs to God."
They could not lay hold of this answer before the people ; 26
and, in their wonder at his reply, they held their tongues.

**A Question
about the
Resurrection.** Presently there came up some Sadducees, who 27
maintain that there is no resurrection. Their
question was this—
" Teacher, Moses laid down for us in his writings that— 28

' Should a man's married brother die, and should he be
childless, the man should take the widow as his wife, and
raise up a family for his brother.'

Well, there were once seven brothers ; of whom the eldest, 29
after taking a wife, died childless. The second and third 30
brothers both took her as their wife ; and so, too, did all seven 31
—dying without children. The woman herself was the last 32
to die. About the woman, then—at the resurrection, whose 33
wife is she to be, all seven brothers having had her as their
wife ? "
" The men and women of this world," said Jesus, " marry 34
and are given in marriage ; but, for those who are thought 35
worthy to attain to that other world and the resurrection
from the dead, there is no marrying or being married, nor 36
indeed can they die again, for they are like angels and, having
shared in the resurrection, they are God's Sons. As to the 37
fact that the dead rise, even Moses indicated that, in the
passage about the Bush, when he calls the Lord—

' The God of Abraham, and the God of Isaac, and the God
of Jacob.'

Now he is not God of dead men, but of living. For in his 38
sight all are alive."
" Well said, Teacher ! " exclaimed some of the Teachers of 39
the Law, for they did not venture to question him any 40
further.

**Christ
the Son of
David.** But Jesus said to them : 41
" How is it that people say that the Christ is
to be David's son ? For David, in the Book of 42
Psalms, says himself—

' The Lord said to my lord : " Sit at my right hand,
Until I put thy enemies as a stool for thy feet." ' 43

David, then, calls him ' lord,' so how is he David's son ? " 44

²⁸ Deut. 25. 5—6.   ³⁷ Exod. 3. 2—6.   ³⁸ 4 Macc. 16. 25.   ⁴²—⁴³ Ps. 110. 1.

Warnings against the Teachers of the Law. While all the people were listening, Jesus said 45 to the disciples :

" Be on your guard against the Teachers of the 46 Law, who delight to walk about in long robes, and like to be greeted in the streets with respect, and to have the best seats in the Synagogues, and places of honour at dinner. These are the men who rob widows of their houses, 47 and make a pretence of saying long prayers. Their sentence will be all the heavier."

The Widow's Offering. Looking up, Jesus saw the rich people putting 1 **21** their gifts into the chests for the Temple offerings. He saw, too, a widow in poor circumstances putting 2 two farthings into them. On this he said : 3

" I tell you that this poor widow has put in more than all the others ; for every one else here put in something from what 4 he had to spare, while she, in her need, has put in all she had to live upon."

Jesus foretells the Destruction of the Temple and the End of the Age. When some of them spoke about the Temple 5 being decorated with beautiful stones and offerings, Jesus said :

" As for these things that you are looking 6 at, a time is coming when not one stone will be left upon another here, which will not be thrown down."

So the disciples questioned Jesus : " But, Teacher, 7 when will this be ? and what sign will there be when this is near ? "

And Jesus said : 8

" See that you are not led astray ; for many will take my name, and come saying ' I am He,' and ' The time is close at hand.' Do not follow them. And, when you hear of wars 9 and disturbances, do not be terrified, for these things must occur first ; but the end will not be at once."

Then he said to them : 10

" ' Nation will rise against nation and kingdom against kingdom,' and there will be great earthquakes, and plagues 11 and famines in various places, and there will be terrible appearances and signs in the heavens. Before all this, they will 12 lay hands on you and persecute you, and they will betray you to Synagogues and put you in prison, when you will be brought before kings and governors for the sake of my Name. Then 13 will be your opportunity of witnessing for me. Make up your 14 minds, therefore, not to prepare your defence ; for I will myself 15 give you words, and a wisdom which all your opponents together will be unable to resist or defy. You will be betrayed 16 even by your parents and brothers and relations and friends,

---

5 Dan. 2. 28.   10 Isa. 19. 2.

and they will cause some of you to be put to death, and you 17
will be hated by every one on account of my Name. Yet 18
not a single hair of your heads shall be lost! By your 19
endurance you shall win yourselves Life.   As soon, 20
however, as you see Jerusalem surrounded by armed camps,
then you may know that the hour of her desecration is
at hand. Then those of you who are in Judaea must take 21
refuge in the mountains, those who are in Jerusalem must
leave at once, and those who are in the country places must
not go into it. For these are to be the Days of Vengeance, 22
when all that Scripture says will be fulfilled. Alas for the 23
women that are with child, and for those that are nursing
infants in those days! For there will be great suffering in the
land, and anger against this people. They will fall by the edge 24
of the sword, and will be taken prisoners to every land, and
'Jerusalem will be under the heel of the Gentiles,' until their
day is over—as it shall be. There will be signs, too, in the 25
sun and moon and stars, and on the earth despair among the
nations, in their dismay at the roar of the sea and the surge.
Men's hearts will fail them through dread of what is coming 26
upon the world; for 'the forces of the heavens will be convulsed.' Then will be seen the 'Son of Man coming in a cloud' 27
with power and great glory.   And, when these things 28
begin to occur, look upwards and lift your heads, for your
deliverance will be at hand."

The Need ......Then he taught them a lesson thus— 29
for ......"Look at the fig tree and all the other trees. As 30
Watchfulness. soon as they shoot, you know, as you look
at them, without being told, that summer is near. And so 31
may you, as soon as you see these things happening,
know that the Kingdom of God is near. I tell you that even 32
the present generation will not pass away till all has taken
place. The heavens and the earth will pass away, but my 33
words will never pass away.   Be on your guard lest 34
your minds should ever be dulled by debauches or drunkenness or the anxieties of life, and lest 'That Day' should come
suddenly upon you, like a snare. For come it will upon all 35
who are living upon the face of the whole earth. Be on the 36
watch at all times, and pray that you may have strength to
escape all that is destined to happen, and to stand in the
presence of the Son of Man."

During the days, Jesus continued to teach in the Temple 37
Courts, but he went out and spent the nights on the hill called
the 'Mount of Olives.' And all the people would get up early 38
in the morning and come to listen to him in the Temple
Courts.

[22] Hos. 9. 7. [24] Zech. 12. 3 (Septuagint). [25] Ps. 65. 7. [26] Isa. 34. 4.
[27] Dan. 7. 13; Jer. 7. 13. [28] Enoch 51. 2. [34-36] Isa. 24. 17.

The Plot against Jesus. The Feast of the Unleavened Bread, known as 1 the Passover, was near. The Chief Priests 2 and the Teachers of the Law were looking for an opportunity of destroying Jesus, for they were afraid of the people.

Judas agrees to betray Jesus. Now Satan took possession of Judas, who was 3 known as Iscariot, and who belonged to the Twelve; and he went and discussed with the Chief 4 Priests and Officers in charge at the Temple the best way of betraying Jesus to them. They were glad of this, and 5 agreed to pay him. So Judas assented, and looked for an 6 opportunity to betray Jesus to them, in the absence of a crowd.

The Passover. When the day of the Festival of the Unleavened 7 Bread came, on which the Passover lambs had to be killed, Jesus sent forward Peter and John, saying to them : 8 " Go and make preparations for our eating the Passover."

" Where do you wish us to make preparations ? " they 9 asked.

" Listen," he answered, " when you have got into the city, a 10 man carrying a pitcher of water will meet you; follow him into whatever house he enters; and you shall say to the owner of the 11 house ' The Teacher says to you—Where is the room where I am to eat the Passover with my disciples ? ' The man will 12 show you a large upstairs room, set out ; there make preparations."

So Peter and John went on, and found everything just as Jesus 13 had told them, and they prepared the Passover.

When the time came, Jesus took his place at table, and the 14 Apostles with him.

" I have most earnestly wished," he said, " to eat this Pass- 15 over with you before I suffer. For I tell you that I shall not 16 eat it again, until it has had its fulfilment in the Kingdom of God."

Then, on receiving a cup, after saying the thanksgiving, he 17 said :

" Take this and share it among you. For I tell you that I 18 shall not, after to-day, drink of the juice of the grape, till the Kingdom of God has come."

The ' Lord's Supper.' Then Jesus took some bread, and, after saying 19 the thanksgiving, broke it and gave to them, with the words :

" This is my body, [which is now to be given on your behalf. Do this in memory of me."

And in the same way with the cup, after supper, saying : 20

" This cup is the New Covenant made by my blood which is being poured out on your behalf.] Yet see ! the hand of the 21 man that is betraying me is beside me upon the table ! True, 22

²⁰ Exod. 24. 8.

the Son of Man is passing, by the way ordained for him, yet alas for that man by whom he is being betrayed!"

Then they began questioning one another which of them it 23 could be that was going to do this.

The Dignity of Service. And a dispute arose among them as to which 24 of them was to be regarded as the greatest. Jesus, 25 however, said:

"The kings of the Gentiles lord it over them, and their oppressors are styled 'Benefactors.' But with you it must 26 not be so. No, let the greatest among you become like the youngest, and him who leads like him who serves. Which is 27 the greater—the master at the table or his servant? Is not it the master at the table? Yet I myself am among you as one who serves. You are the men who 28 have stood by me in my trials; and, just as my Father 29 has assigned me a Kingdom, I assign you places, so that 30 you may eat and drink at my table in my Kingdom, and be seated upon twelve thrones as judges of the twelve tribes of

Peter's Fall foretold. Israel. Simon! Simon! listen. Satan 31 demanded leave to sift you all like wheat, but 32 I prayed for you, Simon, that your faith should not fail. And you, when you have returned to me, are to strengthen your Brothers."

"Master," said Peter, "with you I am ready to go both to 33 prison and to death."

"I tell you, Peter," replied Jesus, "the cock will not crow 34 to-day till you have disowned all knowledge of me three times."

The End at Hand. Then he said to them all: 35 "When I sent you out as my Messengers, without either purse, or bag, or sandals, were you in need of anything?"

"No; nothing," they answered.

"Now, however," he said, "he who has a purse must take 36 it and his bag as well; and he who has not must sell his cloak and buy a sword. For, I tell you, that passage of Scripture 37 must be fulfilled in me, which says—

'He was counted among the godless';

indeed, all that refers to me is finding its fulfilment."

"Master," they exclaimed, "look, here are two swords!" 38 "Enough!" said Jesus.

Jesus on the Mount of Olives. Jesus then went out, and made his way as usual 39 to the Mount of Olives, followed by his disciples. And, when he reached the spot, he said 40 to them:

"Pray that you may not fall into temptation."

37 Isa. 53. 12.

Then he withdrew about a stone's throw, and knelt down and   41
began to pray.

"Father," he said, "if it is thy pleasure, spare me this cup;   42
only, not my will but thine be done."

[Presently there appeared to him an angel from Heaven, who   43
strengthened him. And, as his anguish became intense, he   44
prayed still more earnestly, while his sweat was like great
drops of blood falling on the ground.] Then he rose from   45
praying, and came to the disciples and found them sleeping
for sorrow.

"Why are you asleep?" he asked them. "Rise and pray,   46
that you may not fall into temptation."

The   While he was still speaking, a crowd ap-   47
Arrest of peared in sight, led by the man called Judas,
Jesus.   who was one of the Twelve. Judas approached
Jesus, to kiss him; on which Jesus said to him :   48

"Judas, is it by a kiss that you betray the Son of Man?"

But when those who were round Jesus saw what was going to   49
happen, they exclaimed :

"Master, shall we use our swords?"

And one of them struck the High Priest's servant and cut off   50
his right ear; on which Jesus said : "Let me at least do this";   51
and, touching his ear, he healed the wound. Then, turning to   52
the Chief Priests and Officers in charge at the Temple and
Councillors, who had come for him, he said :

"Have you come out, as if after a robber, with swords and
clubs? When I was with you day after day in the Temple   53
Courts, you did not lay hands on me; but now your time has
come, and the power of Darkness."

Jesus   Those who had taken Jesus prisoner took him   54
before the away into the house of the High Priest. Peter fol-
High Priest. lowed at a distance. But, when they had lit a fire in   55
the centre of the court-yard and had all sat down there, Peter
seated himself in the middle of them. Presently a maidservant   56
Peter disowns saw him sitting near the blaze of the fire. Fixing
Jesus.   her eyes on him, she said :

"Why, this man was one of his companions!"

But Peter denied it.

"I do not know him," he replied.   57

A little while afterwards some one else—a man—saw him and   58
said :

"Why, you are one of them!"

"No," Peter said, "I am not."

About an hour later another man declared positively :   59

"This man also was certainly with him. Why, he is a
Galilaean!"

But Peter said : "I do not know what you are speaking   60
about."

Instantly, while he was still speaking, a cock crowed. And the 61
Master turned and looked at Peter; and Peter remembered
the words that the Master had said to him—" Before a cock has
crowed to-day, you will disown me three times"; and he went 62
outside and wept bitterly.

The men that held Jesus kept making sport of him and 63
beating him. They blindfolded him and then questioned 64
him.

"Now play the Prophet," they said; "who was it that
struck you?"

And they heaped many other insults on him.   65

Jesus before the Chief Priests. At daybreak the National Council met—both 66
the Chief Priests and the Teachers of the Law—
and took Jesus before their High Council.

"If you are the Christ," they said, "tell us so."   67

"If I tell you," replied Jesus, "you will not believe me;
and, if I question you, you will not answer. But from this 68, 69
hour 'the Son of Man will be seated on the right hand of God
Almighty.'"

"Are you, then, the Son of God?" they all asked.   70
"It is true," answered Jesus, "I am."

At this they exclaimed: 71
"Why do we want any more evidence? We have heard it
ourselves from his own lips!"

Jesus before the Roman Governor. Then they all rose in a body and led Jesus 1 **23**
before Pilate. And they began to accuse him: 2
"This is a man whom we found misleading our
people, preventing them from paying taxes to the Emperor, and
giving out that he himself is 'Christ, a King.'"

"Are you the King of the Jews?" Pilate asked him.   3
"It is true," replied Jesus.

But Pilate, turning to the Chief Priests and the people, said: 4
"I do not see anything to find fault with in this man."

But they insisted: 5
"He is stirring up the people by his teaching all through
Judaea; he began with Galilee and has now come here."

Hearing this, Pilate asked if the man was a Galilaean; and, 6, 7
having satisfied himself that Jesus came under Herod's jurisdiction, he sent him to Herod, who also was at Jerusalem at the

Jesus before Herod. time. When Herod saw Jesus, he was ex- 8
ceedingly pleased, for he had been wanting to see
him for a long time, having heard a great deal about him; and
he was hoping to see some sign given by him. So he questioned 9
him at some length, but Jesus made no reply. Meanwhile the 10
Chief Priests and the Teachers of the Law stood by and
vehemently accused him. And Herod, with his soldiers, treated 11
Jesus with scorn; he mocked him by throwing a gorgeous robe

69 Ps. 110. 1; Dan. 7. 13.

round him, and then sent him back to Pilate.   And 12
Herod and Pilate became friends that very day, for before
that there had been ill-will between them.

So Pilate summoned the Chief Priests, and the 13
Jesus again before the Roman Governor. leading men, and the people, and said to them : 14
"You brought this man before me charged with
misleading the people ; and yet, for my part,
though I examined him before you, I did not find this man
to blame for any of the things of which you accuse him ; nor 15
did Herod either ; for he has sent him back to us. And,
as a fact, he has not done anything deserving death ; so 16
I shall have him scourged, and then release him."
But they began to shout as one man : 18
"Kill this fellow, but release Barabbas for us."
(Barabbas was a man who had been put in prison for a riot 19
that had broken out in the city and for murder.) Pilate, how- 20
ever, wanting to release Jesus, called to them again ; but they 21
kept calling out :
"Crucify, crucify him !"
"Why, what harm has this man done ? " Pilate said to them 22
for the third time. "I have found nothing in him for which
he could be condemned to death. So I will have him scourged,
and then release him."
But they persisted in loudly demanding his crucifixion ; and 23
their clamour gained the day. Pilate decided that their 24
demand should be granted. He released the man who had 25
been put in prison for riot and murder, as they demanded, and
gave Jesus up to be dealt with as they pleased.

The Crucifixion of Jesus. And, as they were leading Jesus away, they 26
laid hold of Simon from Cyrene, who was on his
way in from the country, and they put the cross
on his shoulders, for him to carry it behind Jesus.   There 27
was a great crowd of people following him, many being women
who were beating their breasts and wailing for him. So Jesus 28
turned and said to them :
"Women of Jerusalem, do not weep for me, but weep for
yourselves and for your children. A time, I tell you, is coming, 29
when it will be said—'Happy are the women who are barren,
and those who have never borne children or nursed them !'
At that time people will begin to say to the mountains 'Fall 30
on us,' and to the hills 'Cover us.' If what you see is done 31
while the tree is green, what will happen when it is dry ? "
There were two others also, criminals, led out to be executed 32
with Jesus.
When they had reached the place called 'The Skull,' there 33
they crucified Jesus and the criminals, one on the right, and
one on the left.

[30] Hos. 10. 8. [31] Ezek. 20. 47.

[Then Jesus said :
" Father, forgive them ; they do not know what they are
doing."]   34

His clothes they divided among them by casting lots.   Mean-   35
while the people stood looking on.   Even the leading men said
with a sneer :
" He saved others, let him save himself, if he is God's Christ,
his Chosen One."

The soldiers, too, came up in mockery, bringing him common   36
wine, and saying as they did so :   37
" If you are the King of the Jews, save yourself."

Above him were the words—   38

'THIS IS THE KING OF THE JEWS.'

The penitent Robber.   One of the criminals who were hanging beside   39
Jesus railed at him.   " Are not you the Christ ? Save yourself and us,"
he said.

But the other rebuked him.   40
" Have not you," he said, "any fear of God, now that you
are under the same sentence ?   And we justly so, for we are   41
only reaping our deserts, but this man has not done anything
wrong.   Jesus," he went on, " do not forget me when you have   42
come to your Kingdom."

And Jesus answered :   43
" I tell you, this very day you shall be with me in Paradise."

The Death of Jesus.   It was nearly mid-day, when a darkness came   44
over the whole country, lasting till three in the
afternoon, the sun being eclipsed ; and the Temple curtain was   45
torn down the middle.   Then Jesus, with a loud cry, said :   46
" Father, into thy hands I commit my spirit."

And with these words he expired.   The Roman Captain,   47
on seeing what had happened, praised God, exclaiming :
" This must have been a good man ! "

All the people who had collected to see the sight watched what   48
occurred, and then went home beating their breasts.   All   49
the friends of Jesus had been standing at a distance, with the
women who accompanied him from Galilee, watching all this.

The Burial of Jesus.   Now there was a man of the name of Joseph,   50
who was a member of the Council, and who bore a
good and upright character.   (This man had not assented to   51
the decision and action of the Council.)   He belonged to
Ramah, a town in Judaea, and lived in expectation of the
Kingdom of God.   He now went to see Pilate, and asked for   52
the body of Jesus ; and, when he had taken it down, he wrapped   53
it in a linen sheet, and laid him in a tomb cut out of stone,

³⁴ Ps. 22. 18.   ³⁵ Ps. 22. 7 ; Enoch 40. 5.   ³⁵ Ps. 69. 21.   ⁴⁶ Ps. 31. 5.
⁴⁷ Wisd. of Sol. 2. 18.   ⁴⁹ Ps. 38. 11.

in which no one had yet been buried.   It was the Pre- 54
paration Day, and just before the Sabbath began.   The 55
women who had accompanied Jesus from Galilee followed, and
saw the tomb and how the body of Jesus was laid, and then 56
went home, and prepared spices and perfumes.

VI.—THE RISEN LIFE.

The Resurrection of Jesus.
During the Sabbath they rested, as directed by
the commandment. But very early on the first 1 **24**
day of the week they went to the tomb, taking
with them the spices that they had prepared.   They found that 2
the stone had been rolled away from the tomb ; and, on going 3
into it, they could not find the body [of the Lord Jesus].   While 4
they were at a loss to account for this, all at once two men
stood beside them, in dazzling clothing.   But, when in their 5
fear the women bowed their faces to the ground, the men said
to them :

"Why are you looking among the dead for him who is
living ? [He is not here ; but he has risen.]   Remember how 6
he spoke to you before he left Galilee—how he said that the 7
Son of Man must be betrayed into the hands of wicked men,
and be crucified, and rise again on the third day."
Then they remembered the words of Jesus, and, on returning 8, 9
from the tomb, they told all this to the Eleven and to all the
rest.   There were Mary of Magdala, and Joanna, and Mary, 10
the mother of James.   The other women, too, spoke about this
to the Apostles.   What they said seemed to the Apostles mere 11
nonsense, and they did not believe them.

[But Peter got up and ran to the tomb.   Stooping down he 12
saw nothing but the linen wrappings, and he went away,
wondering to himself at what had taken place.]

Jesus appears on the road to Emmaus.
It happened that very day that two of the disci- 13
ples were going to a village called Emmaus,
which was about seven miles from Jerusalem,
talking together, as they went, about all that had just taken 14
place.   While they were talking about these things and 15
discussing them, Jesus himself came up and went on their
way with them ; but their eyes were blinded so that they 16
could not recognize him.

"What is this that you are saying to each other as you walk 17
along ?" Jesus asked.
They stopped, with sad looks on their faces, and then one of 18
them, whose name was Cleopas, said to Jesus :

"Are you staying by yourself at Jerusalem, that you have
not heard of the things that have happened there within the
last few days ?"

"What things do you mean?" asked Jesus. 19

"Why, about Jesus of Nazareth," they answered, "who, in the eyes of God and all the people, was a Prophet, whose power was felt in both his words and actions; and how the 20 Chief Priests and our leading men gave him up to be sentenced to death, and afterwards crucified him. But we 21 were hoping that he was the Destined Deliverer of Israel; yes, and besides all this, it is now three days since these things occurred. And what is more, some of the women among 22 us have greatly astonished us. They went to the tomb at daybreak and, not finding the body of Jesus there, came and 23 told us that they had seen a vision of angels who told them that he was alive. So some of our number went to the tomb 24 and found everything just as the women had said; but they did not see Jesus."

Then Jesus said to them: 25

"O foolish men, slow to accept all that the Prophets have said! Was not the Christ bound to undergo this suffering 26 before entering upon his Glory?"

Then, beginning with Moses and all the Prophets, he explained 27 to them all through the Scriptures the passages that referred to himself. When they got near the village to which 28 they were walking, Jesus appeared to be going further; but 29 they pressed him not to do so.

"Stay with us," they said, "for it is getting towards evening, and the sun is already low."

So Jesus went in to stay with them. After he had 30 taken his place at table with them, he took the bread and said the blessing, and broke it, and gave it to them. Then their eyes were opened and they recognized him; but he 31 disappeared from their sight.

"How our hearts glowed," the disciples said to each other, 32 "while he was talking to us on the road, and when he explained the Scriptures to us!"

Then they immediately got up and returned to Jerusalem, 33 where they found the Eleven and their companions all together, who told them that the Master had really risen, and had 34 appeared to Simon. So they also related what had happened 35 during their walk, and how they had recognized Jesus at the Breaking of the Bread.

Jesus appears to the Apostles. While they were still talking about these things, 36 Jesus himself stood among them, [and said "Peace be with you."] In their terror and alarm 37 they thought they saw a spirit, but Jesus said to them: 38

"Why are you so startled? and why do doubts arise in your minds? Look at my hands and my feet, and you will 39 know that it is I. Feel me, and look at me, for a spirit has not flesh and bones, as you see that I have."

[After saying this he showed them his hands and his feet.] 40

While they were still unable to believe it all for very joy, 41
and were wondering if it were true, Jesus said to them :
    " Have you anything here to eat ? "
They handed him a piece of broiled fish, and he took it and 42, 43
ate it before their eyes.
    " This is what I told you," he said, " when I was still with 44
you—that everything that had been written about me in
the Law of Moses, the Prophets, and the Psalms, must be
fulfilled."
Then he enabled them to understand the meaning of the 45
Scriptures, saying to them :   46
    " Scripture says that the Christ should suffer, and that
he should rise again from the dead on the third day, and that 47
repentance for forgiveness of sins should be proclaimed on his
authority to all the nations—beginning at Jerusalem. You 48
yourselves are to be witnesses to all this. And now I am my- 49
self about to send upon you that which my Father has
promised. But you must remain in the city until you have
been invested with power from above."

**Jesus
ascends to
Heaven.**   After this, Jesus led them out as far as Bethany, 50
and there raised his hands and blessed them. As 51
he was in the act of blessing them, he left them
[and was carried up into Heaven.]   They [bowed to the ground 52
before him and] returned to Jerusalem full of joy; and they 53
were constantly in the Temple Courts, blessing God.

[51] 2 Kings 2. 11.

ACCORDING TO JOHN.

'THE GOSPEL ACCORDING TO ST. JOHN'.

WRITTEN AT EPHESUS AT AN UNCERTAIN DATE LATER THAN 80 A.D.

THIS gospel appears to embody the doctrine concerning Christ which was accepted in the Ephesian Church in Asia Minor by the end of the First Century. It was not authoritatively attributed to the Apostle John till towards the end of the Second Century after Christ; but it may safely be ascribed, if not to St. John himself, to some writer brought up in the Church of Ephesus, over which that Apostle so long presided.

The writer apparently proposed to himself to illustrate the spirit of the 'Gospel of Love' by such incidents in the life of Jesus as best suited his purpose ; at the same time correcting previous gospels, and making such additions to them, as his information enabled him to do. There is no attempt at a regular connected narrative ; and the writer allows himself such freedom in commenting upon the teaching of Jesus, that it is not always easy to tell where that teaching ends and the writer's comment begins.

It is to the great struggle between Light and Darkness, Death and Life—words much in use and much debated in the current philosophy of Ephesus—that the writer devotes his attention, rather than to the external incidents of a story which has already been told, and which is plainly viewed by him from a greater distance of time than is the case with the compilers of the three other gospels.

ACCORDING TO JOHN.

INTRODUCTION.

In the Beginning the Word was ;
And the Word was with God ;
And the Word was God.   **1**

He was in the Beginning with God ;   2
Through him all things came into being,
And nothing came into being apart from him.   3
That which came into being in him was Life ;
And the Life was the Light of Man ;   4
And the Light shines in the darkness,
And the darkness never overpowered it.   5

There appeared a man sent from God, whose name was John ;   6
He came as a witness—to bear witness to the Light,   7
That through him all men might believe.
He was not the Light,   8
But he came to bear witness to the Light.

That was the True Light which enlightens every man coming   9
     into the world.
He was in the world ;   10
And through him the world came into being—
Yet the world did not know him.

He came to his own—   11
Yet his own did not receive him.
But to all who did receive him he gave power to become   12
     Children of God—
To those who believe in his Name.
For not to natural conception, nor to human instincts, nor to   13
     will of man did they owe the new Life,
But to God.

[1] Gen. i. 1 ; Ps. 33. 6.   [3] Wisd. of Sol. 9. 1.   [4] Ps. 36. 9.

And the Word became Man, and dwelt among us,   14
(We saw his glory—the glory of the Only Son sent from the
     Father),
Full of love and truth.
(John bears witness to him; he cried aloud—for it was he   15
     who spoke—
"'He who is Coming' after me is now before me,
For he was ever First");
Out of his fulness we have all received some gift,   16
Gift after gift of love;
For the Law was given through Moses,   17
Love and truth came through Jesus Christ.
No man has ever yet seen God;   18
God the Only Son, who is ever with the Father—
He has revealed him.

I.—The Preparation.

The Testimony of the Baptist to Jesus.
When the Jews sent some Priests and Levites   19
to John from Jerusalem, to ask—"Who are
you?", his statement was this: he confessed   20
and did not deny it, he confessed—"I am not
the Christ."

"What then?" they asked. "Are you Elijah?"   21
"No," he said, "I am not."
"Are you 'the Prophet'?"
He answered "No."

"Who then are you?" they continued; "tell us, that we   22
may have some answer to give to those who have sent us.
What do you say about yourself?"
"I," he answered, "am—   23

     'The voice of one crying aloud in the Wilderness—
"Straighten the way of the Lord"',

as the Prophet Isaiah said."
These men had been sent from the Pharisees; and their next   24, 25
question was:
"Why then do you baptize, if you are not the Christ, nor
Elijah, nor yet 'the Prophet'?"
John's answer was—"I baptize with water, but among you   26
stands one whom you do not know; he is coming after me,   27
yet I am not worthy even to unfasten his sandal."
All this took place at Bethany, across the Jordan, where John   28
was then baptizing.
The next day John saw Jesus coming towards him, and   29
exclaimed:
"Here is the Lamb of God, who is to take away the sin of

---

[14] Lev. 26. 11.   [15] Ps. 118. 26.   [17] Ps. 2. 2.   [21] Mal. 4. 5; Deut. 18. 15.
   [23] Isa. 40. 3.   [25] Deut. 18. 15.   [29] Isa. 53. 7, 12.

the world! It was of him that I spoke when I said 'After me 30
there is coming a man who is now before me, for he was
ever First.' I myself did not know him, but, that he may be 31
made known to Israel, I have come, baptizing with water."
John also made this statement—   32

"I have seen the Spirit descending as a dove out of the
heavens, and it remained upon him. I myself did not know 33
him, but he who sent me to baptize with water, he said to me
'He upon whom you see the Spirit descending, and remaining upon him—he it is who baptizes with the Holy Spirit.'
This I have seen myself, and I have declared my belief that he 34
is the Son of God."

The first Disciples of Jesus. The next day, when John was standing 35
with two of his disciples, he looked at Jesus as 36
he passed and exclaimed :
"There is the Lamb of God !"
The two disciples heard him say this, and followed Jesus. 37
But Jesus turned round, and saw them following.   38
"What are you looking for ? " he asked.
"Rabbi," they answered (or, as we should say, "Teacher"),
"where are you staying ? "
"Come, and you shall see," he replied.   39
So they went, and saw where he was staying, and spent
that day with him. It was then about four in the afternoon.   One of the two, who heard what John said and 40
followed Jesus, was Andrew, Simon Peter's brother. He first 41
found his own brother Simon, and said to him : " We have
found the Messiah ! " (a word which means ' Christ,' or ' Consecrated '.) Then he brought him to Jesus. Fixing his eyes 42
on him, Jesus said :
"You are Simon, the son of John ; you shall be called
Kephas " (which means ' Peter,' or ' Rock ').
The following day Jesus decided to leave for Galilee. He 43
found Philip, and said to him : " Follow me."
Philip was from Bethsaida, and a fellow-townsman of Andrew 44
and Peter. He found Nathanael and said to him :   45
"We have found him of whom Moses wrote in the Law,
and of whom the Prophets also wrote—Jesus of Nazareth,
Joseph's son ! "
"Can anything good come out of Nazareth ? " asked 46
Nathanael.
"Come and see," replied Philip.
When Jesus saw Nathanael coming towards him, he said : 47
"Here is a true Israelite, in whom there is no deceit !"
"How do you know me ? " asked Nathanael.   48
"Even before Philip called you," replied Jesus, " when you
were under the fig tree, I saw you."

34 Ps. 2, 7.   47 Gen. 27. 35.

"Rabbi," Nathanael exclaimed, "you are the Son of God,   49
you are King of Israel!"

"Do you believe in me," asked Jesus, "because I told you   50
that I saw you under the fig tree? You shall see greater
things than those! In truth I tell you," he added, "you shall   51
all see Heaven open, and 'the angels of God ascending and
descending' upon the Son of Man."

II.—The Work in Judaea, Galilee, and Samaria.

Jesus at a Wedding at Cana.   Two days after this there was a wedding at   1 **2**
Cana in Galilee, and Jesus' mother was there.
Jesus himself, too, with his disciples, was   2
invited to the wedding. And, when the wine ran short, his   3
mother said to him: "They have no wine left."

"What do you want with me?" answered Jesus. "My   4
time has not come yet."
His mother said to the servants: "Do whatever he tells you."   5
There were standing there six stone water-jars, in accordance   6
with the Jewish rule of 'purification,' each holding twenty or
thirty gallons.
Jesus said to the servants: "Fill the water-jars with water;"   7
and, when they had filled them to the brim, he added: 8
"Now take some out, and carry it to the Master of the Feast."
The servants did so. And, when the Master of the Feast had   9
tasted the water which had now become wine, not knowing
where it had come from—although the servants who had taken
out the water knew—he called the bridegroom and said to him: 10
"Every one puts good wine on the table first, and
inferior wine afterwards, when his guests have drunk freely;
but you have kept back the good wine till now!"
This, the first sign of his mission, Jesus gave at Cana in   11
Galilee, and by it revealed his glory; and his disciples
believed in him.

Jesus at Capernaum.   After this, Jesus went down to Capernaum—   12
he, his mother, his brothers, and his disciples;
but they stayed there only a few days.

Jesus at the Temple in Jerusalem.   Then, as the Jewish Passover was near, Jesus   13
went up to Jerusalem. In the Temple Courts he   14
found people who were selling bullocks, sheep,
and pigeons, and the money-changers at their counters. So   15
he made a whip of cords, and drove them all out of the Temple

49 Ps. 2. 6.   51 Gen. 28. 12; Dan. 7. 13.

Courts, and the sheep and bullocks as well; he scattered the money of the money-changers, and overturned their tables, and said to the pigeon-dealers :   16

"Take these things away. Do not turn my Father's House into a market-house."

His disciples remembered that Scripture said—   17

'Zeal for thy House will consume me.'

Upon this the Jews asked Jesus :   18

"What sign are you going to show us, since you act in this way?"

"Destroy this temple," was his answer, "and I will raise it in three days."   19

"This Temple," replied the Jews, "has been forty-six years in building, and are you going to 'raise it in three days'?" But Jesus was speaking of his body as a temple.   After- 21, 22 wards, when he had risen from the dead, his disciples remembered that he had said this ; and they believed the passage of Scripture, and the words which Jesus had spoken.   20

While Jesus was in Jerusalem, during the Passover Festival,   23 many came to trust in him, when they saw the signs of his mission that he was giving.   But Jesus did not trust himself   24 to them, since he could read every heart, and because he did   25 not need that others should tell him what men were ; for he could of himself read what was in men.

The Visit of Nicodemus to Jesus. Now there was a Pharisee named Nicodemus,   1 who was a leading man among the Jews.   This   2 man came to Jesus by night, and said to him :   **3**

"Rabbi, we know that you are a Teacher come from God ; for no one could give such signs as you are giving, unless God were with him."

"In truth I tell you," exclaimed Jesus, "unless a man is   3 reborn, he cannot see the Kingdom of God."

"How can a man," asked Nicodemus, "be born when he is   4 old ? Can he be born a second time?"

"In truth I tell you," answered Jesus, "unless a man owes   5 his birth to Water and Spirit, he cannot enter the Kingdom of God.   All that owes its birth to human nature is human,   6 and all that owes its birth to the Spirit is spiritual.   Do not   7 wonder at my telling you that you all need to be reborn. The wind blows where it wills, and you can hear the sound of   8 it, but you do not know whence it comes, or where it goes ; it is the same with every one that owes his birth to the Spirit."

"How can that be?" asked Nicodemus.   9

"What! You a teacher of Israel," exclaimed Jesus, "and   10

yet do not understand this ! In truth I tell you that we speak 11
of what we know, and state what we have seen ; and yet you do
not accept our statements. If, when I tell you earthly things, 12
you do not believe me, how will you believe me when I tell you
of heavenly things ? No one has ascended to Heaven, except 13
him who descended from Heaven—the Son of Man himself.
And, as Moses lifted up the serpent in the desert, so must the 14
Son of Man be lifted up ; that every one who believes in him 15
may have Immortal Life."

For God so loved the world, that he gave his only Son, that 16
every one who believes in him may not be lost, but have
Immortal Life. For God did not send his Son into the world 17
to condemn the world, but that the world might be saved
through him. He who believes in him escapes condemnation, 18
while he who does not believe in him is already condemned,
because he has not believed in the only Son of God. The 19
ground of his condemnation is this, that though the Light
has come into the world, men preferred the darkness to the
Light, because their actions were wicked. For he who lives 20
an evil life hates the light, and will not come to it, for fear
that his actions should be exposed ; but he who acts up to the 21
truth comes to the light, that his actions may be shown to have
been done in dependence upon God.

After this, Jesus went with his disciples into the 22
The Baptist's Testimony to Jesus in Judaea. country parts of Judaea ; and there he stayed with
them, and baptized. John, also, was baptizing 23
at Aenon near Salim, because there were many
streams there ; and people were constantly coming and being
baptized. (For John had not yet been imprisoned). Now 24, 25
a discussion arose between some of John's disciples and a Jew
on the subject of 'purification ;' and the disciples came to 26
John and said :

"Rabbi, the man who was with you on the other side of the
Jordan, and to whom you have yourself borne testimony—he,
also, is baptizing, and everybody is going to him,"
John's answer was— 27

"A man can gain nothing but what is given him from
Heaven. You are yourselves witnesses that I said 'I am 28
not the Christ,' but 'I have been sent before him as a
Messenger.' It is the bridegroom who has the bride ; but the 29
bridegroom's friend, who stands by and listens to him, is
filled with joy when he hears the bridegroom's voice. This
joy I have felt to the full. He must become greater, and 30
I less."

He who comes from above is above all others ; but a child 31
of earth is earthly, and his teaching is earthly, too. He who

13 Prov. 30. 4.

comes from Heaven is above all others. He states what he 32
has seen and what he heard, and yet no one accepts his statement. They who did accept his statement attested the fact 33
that God is true. For he whom God sent as his Messenger 34
gives us God's own teaching, for God does not limit the gift
of the Spirit. The Father loves his Son, and has put every- 35
thing in his hands. He who believes in the Son has Immortal 36
Life, while he who rejects the Son will not even see that Life,
but remains under 'God's displeasure.'

Jesus and the Woman of Samaria. Now, when the Master heard that the Pharisees 1 **4**
had been told that he was making and baptizing
more disciples than John (though it was not 2
Jesus himself, but his disciples, who baptized), he left Judaea, 3
and set out again for Galilee. He had to pass through 4
Samaria, and, on his way, he came to a Samaritan town called 5
Shechem, near the plot of land that Jacob gave to his son
Joseph. Jacob's Spring was there, and Jesus, being tired after 6
his journey, sat down beside the spring, just as he was. It
was then about mid-day. A woman of Samaria came to draw 7
water; and Jesus said to her—"Give me some to drink," for 8
his disciples had gone into the town to buy food.

"How is it," replied the Samaritan woman, "that you who 9
are a Jew ask for water from a Samaritan woman like me?"
(For Jews do not associate with Samaritans).

"If you knew of the gift of God," replied Jesus, "and who 10
it is that is saying to you 'Give me some water,' you would have
asked him, and he would have given you 'living water'."

"You have no bucket, Sir, and the well is deep," she said; 11
"where did you get that 'living water?' Surely you are 12
not greater than our ancestor Jacob who gave us the well,
and used to drink from it himself, and his sons, and his
cattle!"

"All who drink of this water," replied Jesus, "will be 13
thirsty again; but whoever once drinks of the water that I 14
will give him shall never thirst any more; but the water that
I will give him shall become a spring welling up within him—
a source of Immortal Life."

"Give me this water, Sir," said the woman, "so that I 15
may not be thirsty, nor have to come all the way here to
draw water."

"Go and call your husband," said Jesus, "and then come 16
back."

"I have no husband," answered the woman. 17

"You are right in saying 'I have no husband,'" replied
Jesus, "for you have had five husbands, and the man 18
with whom you are now living is not your husband; in saying
that, you have spoken the truth."

36 Ps. 78. 31.   5 Gen. 48. 22 (Septuagint Version).   10 Enoch 17. 4.   14 Jer. 2. 13.

"I see, Sir, that you are a Prophet!" exclaimed the woman. 19
"It was on this mountain that our ancestors worshipped; 20
and yet you Jews say that the proper place for worship is in
Jerusalem."

"Believe me," replied Jesus, "a time is coming when it 21
will be neither on this mountain nor in Jerusalem that you
will worship the Father. You Samaritans do not know what 22
you worship; we know what we worship, for Salvation comes
from the Jews. But a time is coming, indeed it is already 23
here, when the true worshippers will worship the Father
spiritually and truly; for such are the worshippers that the
Father desires. God is Spirit; and those who worship him 24
must worship spiritually and truly."

"I know," answered the woman, "that the Messiah, who 25
is called the Christ, is coming; when once he has come, he
will tell us everything."

"I am he," Jesus said to her, "I who am speaking to you." 26

At this moment his disciples came up, and were surprised 27
to find him talking with a woman; but none of them asked
'What do you want?' or 'Why are you talking with her?'
So the woman, leaving her pitcher, went back to the town, 28
and said to the people:

"Come and see someone who has told me everything that 29
I have done. Can he be the Christ?"

And the people left the town and went to see Jesus. 30

Meanwhile the disciples kept saying to him: 31

"Take something to eat, Rabbi."

"I have food to eat," he answered, "of which you know 32
nothing."

"Can any one have brought him anything to eat?" the 33
disciples said to one another.

"My food," replied Jesus, "is to do the will of him who 34
sent me, and to complete his work. Do not you say that it 35
still wants four months to harvest? Why, look up, and see
how white the fields are for harvest! Already the reaper is 36
receiving wages and gathering in sheaves for Immortal Life,
so that sower and reaper rejoice together. For here the 37
proverb holds good—'One sows, another reaps.' I have 38
sent you to reap that on which you have spent no labour;
others have laboured, and you have entered upon the results of
their labour."

Many from that town came to believe in Jesus—Samaritans 39
though they were—on account of the woman's statement—
'He has told me everything that I have done.' And, when 40
these Samaritans had come to Jesus, they begged him to stay
with them, and he stayed there two days. But far more came 41
to believe in him on account of what he said himself, and 42
they said to the woman:

"It is no longer because of what you say that we believe in

him, for we have heard him ourselves and know that he really is the Saviour of the world."

Jesus cures an Officer's Son in Galilee. After these two days Jesus went on to Galilee ; 43 for he himself declared that 'a Prophet is not 44 honoured in his own country.' When he entered 45 Galilee, the Galilaeans welcomed him, for they had seen all that he did at Jerusalem during the Festival, at which they also had been present.

So Jesus came again to Cana in Galilee, where he had turned 46 the water into wine.   Now there was one of the King's officers whose son was lying ill at Capernaum. When this 47 man heard that Jesus had returned from Judaea to Galilee, he went to him, and begged him to come down and cure his son ; for he was at the point of death.   Jesus answered : 48

" Unless you all see signs and wonders, you will not believe."

" Sir," said the officer, " come down before my child dies." 49 And Jesus answered : " Go, your son is living."   The man 50 believed what Jesus said to him, and went ; and, while he was 51 on his way down, his servants met him, and told him that his child was living.   So he asked them at what time the boy 52 began to get better.

" It was yesterday, about one o'clock," they said, " that the fever left him."

By this the father knew that it was at the very time when 53 Jesus had said to him ' Your son is living '; and he himself, with all his household, believed in Jesus.   This was 54 the second occasion on which Jesus gave a sign of his mission on coming from Judaea to Galilee.

Jesus cures a Cripple in Jerusalem on the Sabbath. Sometime after this there was a Jewish Festival ; 1 and Jesus went up to Jerusalem.   There is 2 in Jerusalem, near the Sheep-gate, a Bath with five colonnades round it.   It is called in Hebrew ' Bethesda.'   In these colonnades a large number of afflicted 3 people were lying—blind, lame, and crippled.   One man who 5 was there had been afflicted for thirty-eight years.   Jesus saw 6 the man lying there, and, finding that he had been in this state a long time, said to him :

" Do you wish to be cured ? "

" I have no one, Sir," the afflicted man answered, " to put 7 me into the Bath when there is a troubling of the water, and, while I am getting to it, some one else steps down before me."

" Stand up,"said Jesus, "take up your mat, and walk about." 8 The man was cured immediately, and took up his mat and 9 began to walk about.

Now it was the Sabbath.   So the Jews said to the man who   10
had been cured :

"This is the Sabbath ; you must not carry your mat."

"The man who cured me," he answered, " said to me 'Take   11
up your mat and walk about.'"

"Who was it," they asked, "that said to you ' Take up your   12
mat and walk about'?"

But the man who had been restored did not know who it   13
was ; for Jesus had moved away, because there was a crowd
there.   Afterwards Jesus found the man in the Temple   14
Courts, and said to him :

"You are cured now ; do not sin again, for fear that something worse may befall you."

The man went away, and told the Jews that it was Jesus who   15
had cured him.   And that was why the Jews began to perse-   16
cute Jesus—because he did things of this kind on the Sabbath.
But Jesus replied :   17

Jesus defends his Action "My Father works to this very hour, and I work also."

and explains his Mission. This made the Jews all the more eager to kill him,   18
because not only was he doing away with the
Sabbath, but he actually called God his own Father—putting
himself on an equality with God.   So Jesus made this   19
further reply :

"In truth I tell you, the Son can do nothing of himself ; he
does only what he sees the Father doing ; whatever the Father
does, the Son does also.   For the Father loves his Son, and   20
shows him everything that he is doing ; and he will show
him still greater things—so that you will be filled with wonder.
For, just as the Father raises the dead and gives them Life, so   21
also the Son gives Life to whom he pleases.   The Father him-   22
self does not judge any man, but has ' entrusted the work of
judging entirely to his Son,' so that all men may honour the   23
Son, just as they honour the Father.   He who does not honour
the Son fails to honour the Father who sent him.   In   24
truth I tell you that he who listens to my Message and believes
him who sent me, has Immortal Life, and does not come under
condemnation, but has already passed out of Death into Life.
In truth I tell you that a time is coming, indeed it is already   25
here, when the Dead will listen to the voice of the Son of God,
and when those who listen will live.   For, just as the Father   26
has inherent Life within him, so also he has granted to the Son
to have inherent Life within him ; and, because he is Son of   27
Man, he has also given him authority to act as judge.   Do not   28
wonder at this ; for the time is coming when all who are in
their graves will hear his voice, and will come out—those   29
who have done good rising to Life, and those who have lived
evil lives rising for condemnation.   I can do nothing   30

22—27 Enoch 69. 27.

of myself; I judge as I am taught; and the judgement that I give is just, because my aim is not to do my own will, but the will of him who sent me.

If I bear testimony to myself, my testimony is not trust-   31
worthy; it is another who bears testimony to me, and I know   32
that the testimony which he bears to me is trustworthy.   You   33
have yourselves sent to John, and he has testified to the Truth.
But the testimony which I receive is not from man; I am say-   34
ing this for your Salvation.   He was the 'Lamp that was   35
burning' and shining, and you were ready to rejoice, for a
time, in his light.   But the testimony which I have is of   36
greater weight than John's; for the work that the Father has
given me to carry out—the work that I am doing—is in itself
proof that the Father has sent me as his Messenger.   The   37
Father who has sent me has himself borne testimony to me.
You have neither listened to his voice, nor seen his form; and   38
you have not taken his Message home to your hearts, because
you do not believe him whom he sent as his Messenger.   You   39
search the Scriptures, because you think that you find in them
Immortal Life; and, though it is those very Scriptures that
bear testimony to me, you refuse to come to me to have   40
Life.   I do not receive honour from men, but I know   41, 42
this of you, that you have not the love of God in your hearts.   I   43
have come in my Father's name, and you do not receive me; if
another comes in his own name, you will receive him.   How   44
can you believe in me, when you receive honour from one
another and do not desire the honour which comes from the
only God?   Do not think that I shall accuse you to the   45
Father; your accuser is Moses, on whom you have been
resting your hopes.   For, had you believed Moses, you would   46
have believed me, for it was of me that Moses wrote; but, if   47
you do not believe his writings, how will you believe my
teaching?"

Jesus feeds   After this, Jesus crossed the Sea of Galilee—   1   6
five thousand   otherwise called the Lake of Tiberias.   A great   2
by the Lake   crowd of people, however, followed him, because
of Galilee.   they saw the signs of his mission in his work
among those who were afflicted.   Jesus went up the hill,   3
and sat down there with his disciples.   It was near the time   4
of the Jewish Festival of the Passover.   Looking up, and   5
noticing that a great crowd was coming towards him, Jesus
said to Philip:

"Where are we to buy bread for these people to eat?"
He said this to test him, for he himself knew what he meant   6
to do.

³⁵ Ecclesiasticus 48. 1.

"Twenty pounds' worth of bread," answered Philip, "would not be enough for each of them to have a little."

"There is a boy here," said Andrew, another of his disciples, Simon Peter's brother, "who has five barley loaves and two fishes; but what is that for so many?" 8 9

"Make the people sit down," said Jesus. 10
It was a grassy spot; so the men, who numbered about five thousand, sat down, and then Jesus took the loaves, and, after saying the thanksgiving, distributed them to those who were sitting down; and the same with the fish, giving the people as much as they wanted. When they were satisfied, Jesus said to his disciples: 11 12

"Collect the broken pieces that are left, so that nothing may be wasted."
The disciples did so, and filled twelve baskets with the pieces of the five barley loaves, which were left after all had eaten. 13

When the people saw the signs which Jesus gave, they said: 14
"This is certainly 'the Prophet who was to come' into the world."
But Jesus, having discovered that they were intending to come and carry him off to make him King, retired again up the hill, quite alone. 15

Jesus walks on the Water. When evening fell, his disciples went down to the Sea, and, getting into a boat, began to cross to Capernaum. By this time darkness had set in, and Jesus had not yet come back to them; the Sea, too, was getting rough, for a strong wind was blowing. When they had rowed three or four miles, they caught sight of him walking on the water and approaching the boat, and they were frightened. But Jesus said to them: 16 17 18 19 20
"It is I; do not be afraid!"
And after this they were glad to take him into the boat; and the boat at once arrived off the shore, for which they had been making. 21

Jesus teaches at Capernaum. The Bread of Life. The people who remained on the further side of the Sea had seen that only one boat had been there, and that Jesus had not got into it with his disciples, but that they had left without him. Some boats, however, had come from Tiberias, from near the spot where they had eaten the bread after the Master had said the thanksgiving. So, on the next day, when the people saw that Jesus was not there, or his disciples either, they themselves got into the boats, and went to Capernaum to look for him. And, when they found him on the other side of the Sea, they said: 22 23 24 25
"When did you get here, Rabbi?"

14 Deut. 18. 15; Ps. 118. 26.

"In truth I tell you," answered Jesus, "it is not on account 26
of the signs which you saw that you are looking for me, but
because you had the bread to eat and were satisfied. Work, 27
not for the food that perishes, but for the food that lasts
for Immortal Life, which the Son of Man will give you;
for upon him the Father—God himself—has set the seal of
his approval."

"How," they asked, "are we to do the work that God 28
would have us do?"

"The work that God would have you do," answered Jesus, 29
"is to believe in him whom God sent as his Messenger."

"What sign, then," they asked, "are you giving, which we 30
may see, and so believe you? What is the work that you are
doing? Our ancestors had the manna to eat in the desert; as 31
Scripture says—

'He gave them bread from Heaven to eat.'"

"In truth I tell you," replied Jesus, "Moses did not give 32
you the Bread from Heaven, but my Father does give you the
true Bread from Heaven; for the Bread that God gives is that 33
which comes down from Heaven, and gives Life to the world."

"Master," they exclaimed, "give us that Bread always!" 34

"I am the Life-giving Bread," Jesus said to them; "he 35
that comes to me shall never be hungry, and he that believes
in me shall never thirst again. But, as I have said already, 36
you have seen me, and yet you do not believe in me.   All 37
those whom the Father gives me will come to me; and no one
who comes to me will I ever turn away. For I have come down 38
from Heaven, to do, not my own will, but the will of him who
sent me; and his will is this—that I should not lose one of all 39
those whom he has given me, but should raise them up at the
Last Day. For it is the will of my Father that every one who 40
sees the Son, and believes in him, should have Immortal Life;
and I myself will raise him up at the Last Day."

Upon this the Jews began murmuring against Jesus for 41
saying—'I am the Bread which came down from Heaven.'

"Is not this Jesus, Joseph's son," they asked, "whose father 42
and mother we know? How is it that he now says that he
has come down from Heaven?"

"Do not murmur among yourselves," said Jesus in reply. 43
"No one can come to me, unless the Father who sent me 44
draws him to me; and I will raise him up at the Last Day.
It is said in the Prophets— 45

'And they shall all be taught by God.'

Every one who is taught by the Father and learns from him
comes to me. Not that any one has seen the Father, except him 46

31 Exod. 16. 4, 15.   45 Isa. 54. 13.

who is from God—he has seen the Father. In truth I tell you,   47
he who believes in me has Immortal Life. I am the Life-giving   48
Bread. Your ancestors ate the manna in the desert, and   49
yet died. The Bread that comes down from Heaven is such   50
that whoever eats of it will never die. I am the Living Bread   51
that has come down from Heaven. If any one eats of this
Bread, he will live for ever ; and the Bread that I shall give is
my flesh, which I will give for the Life of the world."

Upon this the Jews began disputing with one another :   52
" How is it possible for this man to give us his flesh to
eat ? "

" In truth I tell you," answered Jesus, " unless you eat the   53
flesh of the Son of Man, and drink his blood, you have not
Life within you. He who takes my flesh for his food, and   54
drinks my blood, has Immortal Life ; and I will raise him up
at the Last Day. For my flesh is true food, and my blood true   55
drink. He who takes my flesh for his food, and drinks my   56
blood, remains united to me, and I to him. As the Living   57
Father sent me as his Messenger, and as I live because
the Father lives, so he who takes me for his food shall live
because I live. That is the Bread which has come down from   58
Heaven—not such as your ancestors ate, and yet died ; he
who takes this Bread for his food shall live for ever."

All this Jesus said in a Synagogue, when he was teaching in   59
Capernaum.

On hearing it, many of his disciples said :   60
" This is harsh doctrine ! Who can bear to listen to it ? "
But Jesus, aware that his disciples were murmuring about it,   61
said to them :

" Is this a hindrance to you? What, then, if you should see   62
the Son of Man ascending where he was before ? It is the   63
Spirit that gives Life ; mere flesh is of no avail. In the teaching that I have been giving you there is Spirit and there is
Life. Yet there are some of you who do not believe in me."   64
For Jesus knew from the first who they were that did not
believe in him, and who it was that would betray him ; and he   65
added :

" This is why I told you that no one can come to me, unless
enabled by the Father."

After this many of his disciples drew back, and did not go   66
about with him any longer.   So Jesus said to the   67
Twelve :

" Do you also wish to leave me ? "
But Simon Peter answered : " Master, to whom shall we   68
go ? Immortal Life is in your teaching ; and we have learnt   69
to believe and to know that you are the Holy One of God."

" Did not I myself choose you to be the Twelve ? " replied   70
Jesus ; " and yet, even of you, one is playing the ' Devil's ' part."

69 Ps. 16. 10.   70 Esther 7. 4.

he meant Judas, the son of Simon Iscariot, who was about to   71
betray him, though he was one of the Twelve.

7

Jesus and his Brothers. After this, Jesus went about in Galilee, for he   1
would not do so in Judaea, because the Jews   2
were eager to put him to death.   When the
Jewish Festival of Tabernacles was near, his brothers said to   3
him:
    "Leave this part of the country, and go into Judaea, so
that your disciples, as well as we, may see the work that you
are doing.   For no one does a thing privately, if he is seeking   4
to be widely known.   Since you do these things, you should
shew yourself publicly to the world."
For even his brothers did not believe in him.   5
    "My time," answered Jesus, "is not come yet, but your   6
time is always here.   The world cannot hate you, but it does   7
hate me, because I testify that its ways are evil.   Go yourselves   8
up to the Festival; I am not going to this Festival yet, because
my time has not yet come."
After telling them this, he stayed on in Galilee.   9
    But, when his brothers had gone up to the Festival, Jesus   10
also went up—not publicly, but privately.   The Jews were   11
looking for him at the Festival and asking 'Where is he?'; and   12
there were many whispers about him among the people, some
saying 'He is a good man;' others: 'No! he is leading
the people astray.'
No one, however, spoke freely about him, for fear of the Jews.   13

Jesus teaches at the Festival of Tabernacles in Jerusalem. About the middle of the Festival week, Jesus   14
went up into the Temple Courts, and began
teaching.   The Jews were astonished.   15
    "How has this man got his learning," they
asked, "when he has never studied?"
So, in reply, Jesus said: 16
    "My teaching is not my own; it is his who sent me.   If   17
any one has the will to do God's will, he will find out whether
my teaching is from God, or whether I speak on my own
authority.   The man who speaks on his own authority seeks   18
honour for himself; but the man who seeks the honour of him
that sent him is sincere, and there is nothing false in him.
Was not it Moses who gave you the Law?   Yet not one of you   19
obeys it!   Why are you seeking to put me to death?"
    "You must be possessed by a demon!" the people exclaimed.   20
"Who is seeking to put you to death?"
    "There was one thing I did," replied Jesus, "at which you   21
are all still wondering.   But that is why Moses has instituted   22

circumcision among you—not, indeed, that it began with him, but with our ancestors—and that is why you circumcise even on a Sabbath. When a man receives circumcision on a Sabbath to prevent the Law of Moses from being broken, how can you be angry with me for making a man sound and well on a Sabbath? Do not judge by appearances; judge justly." 23 24

At this some of the people of Jerusalem exclaimed: 25

" Is not this the man that they are seeking to put to death? Yet here he is, speaking out boldly, and they say nothing to him! Is it possible that our leading men have really discovered that he is the Christ? Yet we know where this man is from; but, when the Christ comes, no one will be able to tell where he is from." 26 27

Therefore, Jesus, as he was teaching in the Temple Courts, raised his voice and said: 28

" Yes; you know me, and you know where I am from. Yet I have not come on my own authority, but he who sent me may be trusted; and him you do not know. I do know him, for it is from him that I have come, and he sent me as his Messenger." 29

So they sought to arrest him; but no one touched him, for his time was not come yet. Many of the people, however, believed in him. 30 31

" When the Christ comes," they said, " will he give more signs of his mission than this man has given?"

The Pharisees heard the people whispering about him in this way, and so the Chief Priests and the Pharisees sent officers to arrest him; on which Jesus said: 32 33

" I shall be with you but a little longer, and then I am going to him who sent me. You will look for me, and you will not find me; and you will not be able to come where I shall be." 34

" Where is this man going," the Jews asked one another, " that we shall not find him? Will he go to our countrymen abroad, and teach foreigners? What does he mean by saying 'You will look for me, and you will not find me; and you will not be able to come where I shall be'?" 35 36

The 'Living Water.' On the last and greatest day of the Festival, Jesus, who was standing by, exclaimed: 37

" If any one thirsts, let him come to me, and drink. He who believes in me——As Scripture says, Out of his heart shall flow rivers of 'Living Water.'" 38

(By this he meant the Spirit, which those who had believed in him were to receive; for the Spirit had not yet come, because Jesus had not yet been exalted.) Some of the people, when they heard these words, said: 39 40

" This is certainly 'the Prophet'!"; others said: "This is the Christ!"; but some asked: 41

" What! does the Christ come from Galilee? Is not it said 42

38 Jer. 2. 13; Enoch 17, 4.　40 Deut. 18. 15.　41 Ps. 2. 2.　42 Ps. 89. 3–4; Mic. 5. 2.

in Scripture that it is of the race of David, and from Bethlehem, the village to which David belonged, that the Christ is to come?"

So there was a sharp division among the people on account of Jesus. Some of them wanted to arrest him, and yet no one touched him. 43 44

When the officers returned to the Chief Priests and Pharisees, they were asked: 45

"Why have you not brought him?"

"No man ever spoke as he speaks!" they answered. 46

"What! have you been led astray too?" the Pharisees replied. "Have any of our leading men believed in him, or any of the Pharisees? As for these people who do not know the Law—they are cursed!" 47 48 49

But one of their number, Nicodemus, who before this had been to see Jesus, said to them: 50

"Does our Law pass judgement on a man without first giving him a hearing, and finding out what he has been doing?" 51

"Are you also from Galilee?" they retorted. "Search, and you will find that no Prophet is to arise in Galilee!" 52

The 'Light of the World.' Jesus again addressed the people. "I am the Light of the World," he said. He who follows me shall not walk in darkness, but shall have the Light of Life." *12 **8**

"You are bearing testimony to yourself!" exclaimed the Pharisees, "your testimony is not trustworthy." 13

"Even if I bear testimony to myself," answered Jesus, "my testimony is trustworthy; for I know where I came from, and where I am going; but you do not know where I come from, nor where I am going. You judge by appearances; I judge no one. Yet, even if I were to judge, my judgement would be trustworthy; because I am not alone, but the Father who sent me is with me. Why, in your own Law it is said that the testimony of two persons is trustworthy. I, who bear testimony to myself, am one, and the Father who sent me also bears testimony to me." 14 15 16 17 18

"Where is your father, then?" they asked. 19

"You know neither me nor my Father," replied Jesus. "If you had known me, you would have also known my Father."

These statements Jesus made in the Treasury, while teaching in the Temple Courts. Yet no one arrested him, for his time had not then come. 20

Jesus defends his Mission and Authority. Jesus again spoke to the people. "I am going away," he said, "and you will look for me, but you will die in your sin; you cannot come where I am going." 21

17 Deut. 17. 6.   * (See page 210).

"Is he going to kill himself," the Jews exclaimed, "that he says—'You cannot go where I am going'?" 22

"You," added Jesus, "are from below, I am from above; 23 you are of this present world, I am not; and so I told you that 24 you would die in your sins, for, unless you believe that I am what I am, you will die in your sins."

"Who are you?" they asked. 25

"Why ask exactly what I have been telling you?" said Jesus. "I have still much that concerns you to speak of and 26 to pass judgement on; yet he who sent me may be trusted, and I speak to the world only of the things which I have heard from him."

They did not understand that he meant the Father. So Jesus 27, 28 added:

"When you have lifted up the Son of Man, then you will understand that I am what I am, and that I do nothing of myself, but that I say just what the Father has taught me. Moreover, he who sent me is with me; he has not left me 29 alone; for I always do what pleases him."

While he was speaking in this way, many came to believe in 30 him.

So Jesus went on to say to those Jews who had believed him: 31 "If you remain constant to my Message, you are truly my disciples; and you shall find out the Truth, and the Truth will 32 set you free."

"We are descendants of Abraham," was their answer, "and 33 have never yet been in slavery to any one. What do you mean by saying 'you will be set free'?"

"In truth I tell you," replied Jesus, "every one who sins is a 34 slave to sin. And a slave does not remain in the home always; 35 but a son remains always. If, then, the Son sets you free, you 36 will be free indeed! I know that you are descendants of 37 Abraham; yet you are seeking to put me to death, because my Message finds no place in your hearts. I tell you what I 38 have myself seen in the presence of my Father; and you, in the same way, do what you have learnt from your father."

"Our father is Abraham," was their answer. 39

"If you are Abraham's children," replied Jesus, "do what Abraham did. But, as it is, you are seeking to put me to 40 death—a man who has told you the Truth as he heard it from God. Abraham did not act in that way. You are doing what 41 your own father does."

"We are not bastards," they said, "we have one Father— God himself."

"If God were your Father," Jesus replied, "you would have 42 loved me, for I came out from God, and now am here; and I have not come of myself, but he sent me as his Messenger. How is it that you do not understand what I say? It is because 43 you cannot bear to listen to my Message. As for you, you are 44 children of your father the Devil, and you are determined to do what your father loves to do. He was a murderer from the first, and did not stand by the truth, because there is no truth in him. Whenever he lies, he does what is natural to him; because he is a liar, and the father of lying. But, as for me, 45 it is because I speak the truth to you that you do not believe me. Which of you can convict me of sin? Why then do not 46 you believe me, if I am speaking truth? He who comes from 47 God listens to God's teaching; the reason why you do not listen is because you do not come from God."

"Are not we right, after all," replied the Jews, "in saying 48 that you are a Samaritan, and are possessed by a demon?"

"I am not possessed by a demon," Jesus answered, "but 49 I am showing reverence for my Father; and yet you have no reverence for me. Not that I am seeking honour for 50 myself; there is one who is seeking my honour, and he decides. In truth I tell you, if any one lays my 51 Message to heart, he will never really die."

"Now we are sure that you are possessed by a demon," the 52 Jews replied. "Abraham died, and so did the Prophets; and yet you say 'If any one lays my Message to heart, he will never know death.' Are you greater than our ancestor Abraham, 53 who died? And the Prophets died too. Whom do you make yourself out to be?"

"If I do honour to myself," answered Jesus, "such honour 54 counts for nothing. It is my Father who does me honour— and you say that he is your God; and yet you have not learnt 55 to know him; but I know him; and, if I were to say that I do not know him, I should be a liar like you; but I do know him, and I lay his Message to heart. Your ancestor Abraham rejoiced 56 that he would see my day; and he did see it, and was glad."

"You are not fifty years old yet," the Jews exclaimed, "and 57 have you seen Abraham?"

"In truth I tell you," replied Jesus, "before Abraham 58 existed I was."

At this they took up stones to throw at him; but Jesus hid him- 59 self, and left the Temple Courts.

Jesus cures a Man born blind. As Jesus passed by, he saw a man who had 1 **9** been blind from his birth.

"Rabbi," asked his disciples, "who was it that 2 sinned, this man or his parents, that he was born blind?"

"Neither the man nor the parents," replied Jesus; "but he 3 was born blind that the work of God should be made plain in him. We must do the work of him who sent me, while it is 4 day; night is coming, when no one can work. As long as I 5 am in the world, I am the Light of the world."

Saying this, Jesus spat on the ground, made clay with the 6 saliva, and put it on the man's eyes.

"Go," he said, "and wash your eyes in the Bath of Siloam"   7
(a word which means 'Messenger'). So the man went and
washed his eyes, and returned able to see.

Upon this his neighbours, and those who had formerly   8
known him by sight as a beggar, exclaimed :

"Is not this the man who used to sit and beg?"

"Yes," some said, "it is"; while others said : "No, but he   9
is like him."

The man himself said : "I am he."

"How did you get your sight, then?" they asked.   10

"The man whom they call Jesus," he answered, "made   11
clay, and anointed my eyes, and said to me 'Go to Siloam and
wash your eyes.' So I went and washed my eyes, and gained
my sight."

"Where is he?" they asked.   12

"I do not know," he answered.

They took the man, who had been blind, to the Pharisees.   13
Now it was a Sabbath when Jesus made the clay and gave   14
him his sight. So the Pharisees also questioned the man as   15
to how he had gained his sight.

"He put clay on my eyes," he answered, "and I washed
them, and I can see."

"The man cannot be from God," said some of the Pharisees,   16
"for he does not keep the Sabbath."

"How is it possible," retorted others, "for a bad man to give
signs like this?"

So there was a difference of opinion among them, and they   17
again questioned the man :

"What do you yourself say about him, for it is to you that he
has given sight?"

"He is a Prophet," the man replied.

The Jews, however, refused to believe that he had been   18
blind and had gained his sight, until they had called his parents
and questioned them.

"Is this your son," they asked, "who you say was born   19
blind? If so, how is it that he can see now?"

"We know that this is our son," answered the parents,   20
"and that he was born blind ; but how it is that he can see   21
now we do not know ; nor do we know who it was that gave
him his sight. Ask him—he is old enough—he will tell you
about himself."

His parents spoke in this way because they were afraid of the   22
Jews ; for the Jews had already agreed that, if any one should
acknowledge Jesus as the Christ, he should be expelled from
their synagogues. This was why his parents said 'He is old   23
enough ; ask him.'   So the Jews again called the man   24
who had been blind, and said to him :

"Give God the praise ; we know that this is a bad man."

"I know nothing about his being a bad man," he replied ;   25 "one thing I do know, that although I was blind, now I can see."

"What did he do to you?" they asked. "How did he give you your sight?" 26

"I told you just now," he answered, "and you did not listen. Why do you want to hear it again? Surely you also do not want to become his disciples?" 27

"You are his disciple," they retorted scornfully; "but we are disciples of Moses. We know that God spoke to Moses; but, as for this man, we do not know where he comes from." 28 29

"Well," the man replied, "this is very strange; you do not know where he comes from, and yet he has given me my sight! We know that God never listens to bad men, but, when a man is god-fearing and does God's will, God listens to him. Since the world began, such a thing was never heard of as any one's giving sight to a person born blind. If this man had not been from God, he could not have done anything at all." 30 31 32 33

"You," they retorted, "were born totally depraved; and are you trying to teach us?" 34
So they expelled him.

Jesus heard of their having put him out; and, when he had found the man, he asked: 35

"Do you believe in the Son of Man?"

"Tell me who he is, Sir," he replied, "so that I may believe in him." 36

"Not only have you seen him," said Jesus; "but it is he who is now speaking to you." 37

"Then, Sir, I do believe," said the man, bowing to the ground before him; and Jesus added: 38 39

"It was to put men to the test that I came into this world, in order that those that cannot see should see, and that those that can see should become blind."

Hearing this, some of the Pharisees who were with him said: 40
"Then are we blind too?"

"If you had been blind," replied Jesus, "you would have had no sin to answer for; but, as it is, you say 'We can see,' and so your sin remains. 41

The 'Good Shepherd.' In truth I tell you, whoever does not go into the sheepfold through the door, but climbs up at some other place, that man is a thief and a robber; but the man who goes in through the door is shepherd to the sheep. For him the watchman opens the door; and the sheep listen to his voice; and he calls his own sheep by name, and leads them out. When he has brought them all out, he walks in front of them, and his sheep follow him, because they know his voice. They will not follow a stranger, but will run away from him; because they do not know a stranger's voice." 1 **10** 2 3 4 5

This was the allegory that Jesus told them, but they did not understand of what he was speaking. 6

So he continued :   7

"In truth I tell you, I am the Door for the sheep.   All who   8
came before me were thieves and robbers ; but the sheep did not
listen to them.   I am the Door ; he who goes in through me will   9
be safe, and he will go in and out and find pasture.   The thief   10
comes only to steal, to kill, and to destroy ; I have come that they
may have Life, and may have it in greater fulness.   I   11
am the Good Shepherd.   The Good Shepherd lays down his
life for his sheep.   The hired man who is not a shepherd, and   12
who does not own the sheep, when he sees a wolf coming,
leaves them and runs away ; then the wolf seizes them, and
scatters the flock.   He does this because he is only a hired   13
man and does not care about the sheep.   I am the Good   14
Shepherd ;   and I know my sheep, and my sheep know
me—just as the Father knows me and I know the Father—   15
and I lay down my life for the sheep.   I have other sheep   16
besides, which do not belong to this fold ; I must lead them
also, and they will listen to my voice ; and they shall become
one flock under 'one Shepherd.'   This is why the Father loves   17
me, because I lay down my life—to receive it again.   No   18
one took it from me, but I lay it down of myself.   I have
authority to lay it down, and I have authority to receive it
again.   This is the command which I received from my
Father."

In consequence of these words a difference of opinion again   19
arose among the Jews.   Many of them said : "He is possessed   20
by a demon and is mad ; why do you listen to him ?"   Others   21
said : "This is not the teaching of one who is possessed by a
demon.   Can a demon give sight to the blind ?"

Jesus at the   Soon after this the Festival of the Re-dedication   22
Re-dedication was held at Jerusalem.   It was winter ; and Jesus   23
Festival.   was walking in the Temple Courts, in the Colon-
nade of Solomon, when the Jews gathered round him, and said :   24

"How long are you going to keep us in suspense ?   If you
are the Christ, tell us so frankly."

"I have told you so," replied Jesus, "and you do not believe   25
me.   The work that I am doing in my Father's name bears
testimony to me.   But you do not believe me, because you are   26
not of my flock.   My sheep listen to my voice ; I know them,   27
and they follow me ; and I give them Immortal Life, and they   28
shall not be lost ; nor shall any one snatch them out of my hands.
What my Father has entrusted to me is more than all else ;   29
and no one can snatch anything out of the Father's hands.
The Father and I are one."   30

The Jews again brought stones to throw at him ; and seeing   31
this, Jesus said :   32

[8] Ps. 118. 26.   [16] Ezek. 34. 23.   [22] 1 Macc. 4. 59.

" I have done before your eyes many good actions, inspired by the Father ; for which of them would you stone me ? "

" It is not for any good action that we would stone you," answered the Jews, " but for blasphemy ; and because you, who are only a man, make yourself out to be God." 33

" Are there not," replied Jesus, " these words in your Law— 34

'I said "Ye are gods"'?

If those to whom God's words were addressed were said to be 'gods'—and Scripture cannot be set aside—do you say of one whom the Father has consecrated and sent as his Messenger to the world 'You are blaspheming,' because I said 'I am God's Son'? If I am not doing the work that my Father is doing, do not believe me ; but, if I am doing it, even though you do not believe me, believe what that work shows ; so that you may understand, and understand more and more clearly, that the Father is in union with me, and I with the Father." 35 36 37 38

Upon this the Jews again sought to arrest him ; but he escaped their hands. 39

Jesus retires beyond the Jordan. Then Jesus again crossed the Jordan to the place where John used to baptize at first, and stayed there some time, during which many people came to see him. 40 41

" John gave no sign of his mission," they said ; " but everything that he said about this man was true."

And many learnt to believe in Jesus there. 42

11

Jesus raises Lazarus to Life at Bethany. Now a man named Lazarus, of Bethany, was lying ill ; he belonged to the same village as Mary and her sister Martha. This Mary, whose brother Lazarus was ill, was the Mary who anointed the Master with perfume, and wiped his feet with her hair. The sisters, therefore, sent this message to Jesus —' Master, your friend is ill' ; and, when Jesus heard it, he said : 1 2 3 4

' This illness is not to end in death, but is to redound to the honour of God, in order that the Son of God may be honoured through it."

Jesus loved Martha and her sister, and Lazarus. Yet, when he heard of the illness of Lazarus, he still stayed two days in the place where he was. Then, after that, he said to his disciples : 5, 6 7

" Let us go to Judaea again."

" Rabbi," they replied, " the Jews were but just now seeking to stone you ; and are you going there again ? " 8

" Are not there twelve hours in the day ? " answered Jesus. " If a man walks about in the day-time, he does not stumble, 9

because he can see the light of the sun ; but, if he walks about   10
at night, he stumbles, because he has not the light."

And, when he had said this, he added :   11

"Our friend Lazarus has fallen asleep ; but I am going that
I may wake him."

"If he has fallen asleep, Master, he will get well," said the   12
disciples.

But Jesus meant that he was dead ; they, however, supposed   13
that he was speaking of natural sleep.   Then he said to them   14
plainly :

"Lazarus is dead ; and I am glad for your sakes that I was   15
not there, so that you may learn to believe in me.   But let us
go to him."

At this, Thomas, who was called 'The Twin,' said to his   16
fellow-disciples :

"Let us go too, so that we may die with him."

When Jesus reached the place, he found that Lazarus had   17
been four days in the tomb already.   Bethany being only about   18
two miles from Jerusalem, a number of the Jews had come   19
there to condole with Martha and Mary on their brother's
death.   When Martha heard that Jesus was coming, she went   20
to meet him ; but Mary sat quietly at home.

"Master," Martha said to Jesus, "if you had been here, my   21
brother would not have died.   Even now, I know that God   22
will grant you whatever you ask him."

"Your brother shall rise to life," said Jesus.   23

"I know that he will," replied Martha, "in the resurrection   24
at the Last Day."

"I am the Resurrection and the Life," said Jesus.   "He   25
that believes in me shall live, though he die ; and he who   26
lives and believes in me shall never die.   Do you believe
this ? '

"Yes Master," she answered ; "I have learnt to believe   27
that you are the Christ, the Son of God, 'who was to come'
into the world."

After saying this, Martha went and called her sister Mary,   28
and whispered :

"The Teacher is here, and is asking for you."

As soon as Mary heard that, she got up quickly, and went to   29
meet him.   Jesus had not then come into the village, but was   30
still at the place where Martha had met him.   So the Jews, who   31
were in the house with Mary, condoling with her, when they
saw her get up quickly and go out, followed her, thinking that
she was going to the tomb to weep there.   When Mary came   32
where Jesus was and saw him, she threw herself at his feet.

"Master," she exclaimed, "if you had been here, my
brother would not have died !"

When Jesus saw her weeping, and the Jews who had come   3.

²⁷ Ps. 118, 26.

with her weeping also, he groaned deeply, and was greatly distressed.

"Where have you buried him?" he asked. 34

"Come and see, Master," they answered.

Jesus burst into tears. 35

"How he must have loved him!" the Jews exclaimed; 36
but some of them said: 37

"Could not this man, who gave sight to the blind man, have also prevented Lazarus from dying?"

Again groaning inwardly, Jesus came to the tomb. It was 38
a cave, and a stone lay against the mouth of it.

"Move the stone away," said Jesus. 39

"Master," said Martha, the sister of the dead man, "by this time the smell must be offensive, for this is the fourth day since his death."

"Did not I tell you," replied Jesus, "that, if you would 40
believe in me, you should see the glory of God?"

So they moved the stone away; and Jesus, with uplifted eyes, 41
said:

> "Father, I thank thee that thou hast heard
> my prayer; I knew that thou always hearest 42
> me; but I say this for the sake of the people
> standing near, so that they may believe that
> thou hast sent me as thy Messenger."

Then, after saying this, Jesus called in a loud voice: 43
"Lazarus! come out!"

The dead man came out, wrapped hand and foot in a winding- 44
sheet; his face, too, had been wrapped in a cloth.

"Set him free," said Jesus, "and let him go."

In consequence of this, many of the Jews, who had come to 45
visit Mary and had seen what Jesus did, learnt to believe in
him. Some of them, however, went to the Pharisees, and 46
told them what he had done.

The Chief Priests plot the Death of Jesus. Upon this the Chief Priests and the Pharisees 47
called a meeting of the High Council, and said:
"What are we to do, now that this man is
giving so many signs? If we let him alone as we 48
are doing, every one will believe in him; and the Romans will
come and will take from us both our City and our Nationality."

One of them, however, Caiaphas, who was High Priest 49
that year, said to them:

"You are utterly mistaken. You do not consider that it 50
is better for you that one man should die for the people, rather
than that the whole nation should be destroyed."

Now he did not say this of his own accord; but, as High Priest 51

---

48 Dan. 11, 30 (Septuagint Version).

that year, he prophesied that Jesus was to die for the nation—
and not for the nation only, but also that he might unite
in one body the Children of God now scattered far and   52
wide.   So from that day they plotted to put Jesus to   53
death.

Jesus retires to Ephraim. In consequence of this, Jesus did not go about   54
publicly among the Jews any more, but left that
neighbourhood, and went into the country bor-
dering on the Wilderness, to a town called Ephraim, where
he stayed with his disciples.   But the Jewish Festival   55
of the Passover was near ; and many people had gone up
from the country to Jerusalem, for their ' purification,' before
the Festival began.   So they looked for Jesus there, and said   56
to one another, as they stood in the Temple Courts :

"What do you think ?   Do you think he will come to the
Festival ? "

The Chief Priests and the Pharisees had already issued orders   57
that, if any one learnt where Jesus was, he should give information, so that they might arrest him.

III.—The Last Days.

Jesus anointed by Mary at Bethany. Six days before the Passover Jesus came to   1
Bethany, where Lazarus, whom he had raised
from the dead, was living.   There a supper was   2
given in his honour, at which Martha waited,
while Lazarus was one of those present at the table.   So Mary   3
took a pound of choice spikenard perfume of great value, and
anointed the feet of Jesus with it, and then wiped them with
her hair.   The whole house was filled with the scent of the
perfume.   One of the disciples, Judas Iscariot, who was about   4
to betray Jesus, asked :

"Why was not this perfume sold for thirty pounds, and the   5
money given to poor people ? "

He said this, not because he cared for the poor, but because   6
he was a thief, and, being in charge of the purse, used to take
what was put in it.

"Let her alone," said Jesus, "that she may keep it   7
till the day when my body is being prepared for burial.   The   8
poor you always have with you, but you will not always have
me."

Now great numbers of the Jews found out that Jesus was at   9
Bethany ; and they came there, not solely on his account, but
also to see Lazarus, whom he had raised from the dead.   The   10
Chief Priests, however, plotted to put Lazarus, as well as Jesus,
to death, because it was owing to him that many of the Jews   11
had left them, and were becoming believers in Jesus.

**Jesus publicly
enters
Jerusalem for
the Last Time.** On the following day great numbers of people 12
who had come to the Festival, hearing that Jesus
was on his way to Jerusalem, took palm-branches, 13
and went out to meet him, shouting as they went:

> "'God save Him!
> Blessed is He who Comes in the name of the Lord'—
> The King of Israel!'"

Having found a young ass, Jesus seated himself on it, in 14
accordance with the passage of Scripture—

> 'Fear not, Daughter of Zion; 15
> Behold, thy King is coming to thee,
> Sitting on the foal of an ass.'

His disciples did not understand all this at first; but, when 16
Jesus had been exalted, then they remembered that these
things had been said of him in Scripture, and that they had
done these things for him.   Meanwhile the people who 17
were with him, when he called Lazarus out of the tomb and
raised him from the dead, were telling what they had seen.
This, indeed, was why the crowd met him—because people had 18
heard that he had given this sign of his mission.   So the 19
Pharisees said to one another:
"You see that you are gaining nothing!   Why, all the world
has run after him!"

**Jesus closes
his public
Ministry.** Among those who were going up to worship at 20
the Festival were some Greeks, who went to 21
Philip of Bethsaida in Galilee, and said:
"Sir, we wish to see Jesus."
Philip went and told Andrew, and then together they went 22
and told Jesus.   This was his reply— 23
"The time has come for the Son of Man to be exalted.   In 24
truth I tell you, unless a grain of wheat falls into the ground
and dies, it remains solitary; but, if it dies, it becomes fruitful.
He who loves his life loses it; while he who hates his 25
life in the present world shall preserve it for Immortal
Life.   If a man is ready to serve me, let him follow me; and 26
where I am, t ere my servant shall be also.   If a man is ready to
serve me, my Father will honour him.   Now I am distressed 27
at heart and what can I say?   Father, bring me safe through
this hour—yet it was for this very reason that I came to this
hour—Father, honour thine own name." 28
At this there came a voice from Heaven, which said:
"I have already honoured it, and I will honour it again."
The crowd of bystanders, who heard the sound, said that 29
it was thundering.
Others said: "An angel has been speaking to him."

"It was not for my sake that the voice came," said Jesus, 30
"but for yours. Now this world is on its trial. Now the Spirit 31
that is ruling this world shall be driven out; and I, when 32
I am lifted up from the earth, shall draw all men to myself."
By these words he indicated what death he was destined to die. 33

"We," replied the people, "have learnt from the Law that 34
the 'Christ is to remain for ever'; how is it, then, that you
say that the Son of Man must be 'lifted up'? Who is this
'Son of Man'?"

"Only a little while longer," answered Jesus, "will 35
you have the Light among you. Travel on while you have
the Light, so that darkness may not overtake you; he
who travels in the darkness does not know where he is going.
While you still have the Light, believe in the Light, that you 36
may be 'Sons of Light.'"

After he had said this, Jesus went away, and hid himself from
them.   But, though Jesus had given so many signs of 37
his mission before their eyes, they still did not believe in him,
in fulfilment of the words of the Prophet Isaiah, where he 38
says—

    'Lord, who has believed our teaching?
    And to whom has the might of the Lord been revealed?

The reason why they were unable to believe is given by Isaiah 39
elsewhere, in these words—

    'He has blinded their eyes, and blunted their mind, 40
    So that they should not see with their eyes, and perceive with
      their mind, and turn—
        And I should heal them.'

Isaiah said this, because he saw Christ's glory; and it was of 41
him that he spoke.   Yet for all this, even among the 42
leading men there were many who came to believe in Jesus;
but, on account of the Pharisees, they did not acknowledge it,
for fear that they should be expelled from their Synagogues; for 43
they valued honour from men more than honour from God.

But Jesus had proclaimed: 44
"He who believes in me believes, not in me, but in him who
sent me; and he who sees me sees him who sent me. I have 45, 4
come as a Light into the world, that no one who believes in me
should remain in the darkness. When any one hears my teach- 47
ing and pays no heed to it, I am not his judge; for I came not
to judge the world, but to save the world. He who rejects me, 48
and disregards my teaching, has a judge already—the very
Message which I have delivered will itself be his judge at
the Last Day. For I have not delivered it on my own 49
authority; but the Father, who sent me, has himself given
me his command as to what I should say, and what message

---

³⁴ Isa. 9. 7 (Aramaic Version). ³⁶ Enoch 108. 11. ³⁸ Isa. 53. 1. ⁴⁰ Isa. 6. 10.
⁴¹ Isa. 6. 1—3.

I should deliver. And I know that Immortal Life lies in keep- 50
ing his command. Therefore, whatever I say, I say only what
the Father has taught me."

Jesus washes the Disciples' Feet. Before the Passover Festival began, Jesus knew 1 **13**
that the time had come for him to leave the world
and go to the Father. He had loved those who
were his own in the world, and he loved them to the
last. The Devil had already put the thought of betray- 2
ing Jesus into the mind of Judas Iscariot, the son of Simon;
and at supper, Jesus—although knowing that the Father had 3
put everything into his hands, and that he had come from God,
and was to return to God—rose from his place, and, taking 4
off his upper garments, tied a towel round his waist. He 5
then poured some water into the basin, and began to wash
the disciples' feet, and to wipe them with the towel which
was tied round him. When he came to Simon Peter, Peter 6
said:

"You, Master! Are you going to wash my feet?"

"You do not understand now what I am doing," replied 7
Jesus, "but you will learn by and by."

"You shall never wash my feet!" exclaimed Peter. 8

"Unless I wash you," answered Jesus, "you have nothing
in common with me."

"Then, Master, not my feet only," exclaimed Simon Peter, 9
"but also my hands and my head."

"He who has bathed," replied Jesus, "has no need to 10
wash, unless it be his feet, but is altogether clean; and
you," he said to the disciples, "are clean, yet not all of
you." For he knew who was going to betray him, and that 11
was why he said 'You are not all clean.' When he 12
had washed their feet, and had put on his upper garments and
taken his place, he spoke to them again.

"Do you understand what I have been doing to you?" he
asked. "You yourselves call me 'the Teacher' and 'the 13
Master', and you are right, for I am both. If I, then—'the 14
Master' and 'the Teacher'—have washed your feet, you also
ought to wash one another's feet; for I have given you an 15
example, so that you may do just as I have done to you. In 16
truth I tell you, a servant is not greater than his master, nor
yet a messenger than the man who sends him. Now that you 17
know these things, happy are you if you do them. I am not 18
speaking about all of you. I know whom I have chosen; but
this is in fulfilment of the words of Scripture—

'He that is eating my bread has lifted his heel against me.'

18 Ps. 41. 9.

H

For the future I shall tell you of things before they take place,   19
so that, when they take place, you may believe that I am what
I am.   In truth I tell you, he who receives any one that I   20
send receives me ; and he who receives me receives him who
sent me."

Jesus points out the Betrayer.   After saying this, Jesus was much troubled,   21
and said solemnly :
"In truth I tell you that it is one of you who
will betray me."

The disciples looked at one another, wondering whom he   22
meant.   Next to Jesus, in the place on his right hand, was   23
one of his disciples, whom he loved.   So Simon Peter made   24
signs to that disciple, and whispered :
"Tell me who it is that he means."

Being in this position, that disciple leant back on Jesus'   25
shoulder, and asked him :
"Who is it, Master ?"

"It is the one," answered Jesus, "to whom I shall give a   26
piece of bread after dipping it in the dish."

And, when Jesus had dipped the bread, he took it and gave
it to Judas, the son of Simon Iscariot : and it was then, after   27
he had received it, that Satan took possession of him.   So
Jesus said to him :
"Do at once what you are going to do."

But no one at table understood why he said this to Judas.   Some   28, 29
thought that, as Judas kept the purse, Jesus meant that he was
to buy some things needed for the Festival, or to give something to the poor.   After taking the piece of bread, Judas   30
went out immediately ; and it was night.

Jesus teaches his Disciples privately.

The New Commandment.

When Judas had gone out, Jesus said :   31
"Now the Son of Man has been exalted, and
God has been exalted through him ; and God will   32
exalt him with himself—yes, he will exalt him
forthwith.   My children, I am to be with   33
you but a little while longer.   You will look for
me ; and what I said to the Jews—'You cannot come where
I am going '—I now say to you.   I give you a new command-   34
ment—Love one another ; love one another as I have loved
you.   It is by this that every one will recognize you as my   35
disciples—by your loving one another."

"Where are you going, Master ?" asked Peter.   36

"I am going where you cannot now follow me," answered
Jesus, "but you shall follow me later."

"Why cannot I follow you now, Master ?" asked Peter.   "I   37
will lay down my life for you."

"Will you lay down your life for me ?" replied Jesus.   "In   38
truth I tell you, the cock will not crow till you have disowned
me three times.

The Way. Do not let your hearts be troubled. Believe in [1] God ; believe also in me. In my Father's Home [2] there are many dwellings. If it had not been so, I should have told you, for I am going to prepare a place for you. And, [3] since I go and prepare a place for you, I shall return and take you to be with me, so that you may be where I am ; and [4] you know the way to the place where I am going."

"We do not know where you are going, Master," said [5] Thomas ; "so how can we know the way ?"

Jesus answered : "I am the Way, and the Truth, and the Life ; [6] no one ever comes to the Father except through me. If you [7] had recognized me, you would have known my Father also ; for the future you will recognize him, indeed you have already seen him."

"Master, show us the Father," said Philip, "and we shall [8] be satisfied."

"Have I been all this time among you," said Jesus, "and [9] yet you, Philip, have not recognized me ? He who has seen me has seen the Father, how can you say, then, 'Show us the Father'? Do not you believe that I am in union with [10] the Father, and the Father with me ? In giving you my teaching I am not speaking on my own authority ; but the Father himself, always in union with me, does his own work. Believe [11] me," he said to them all, "when I say that I am in union with the Father and the Father with me, or else believe me on account of the work itself. In truth I tell you, [12] he who believes in me will himself do the work that I am doing ; and he will do greater work still, because I am going to the Father. Whatever you ask, in my Name, [13] I will do, that the Father may be honoured in the Son. If [14] you ask anything, in my Name, I will do it.

The Helper. If you love me, you will lay my commands to [15] heart, and I will ask the Father, and he will give [16] you another Helper, to be with you always—the Spirit of [17] Truth. The world cannot receive this Spirit, because it does not see him or recognize him, but you recognize him, because he is always with you, and is within you. I will not [18] leave you bereaved ; I will come to you. In a little while the [19] world will see me no more, but you will still see me ; because I am living, you will be living also. At that time you will [20] recognize that I am in union with the Father, and you with me, and I with you. It is he who has my commands and [21] lays them to heart that loves me ; and he who loves me will be loved by my Father, and I will love him, and will reveal myself to him."

"What has happened, Master," said Judas (not Judas [22] Iscariot), "that you are going to reveal yourself to us, and not to the world ?"

"Whoever loves me," Jesus answered, "will lay my Message 23
to heart; and my Father will love him, and we will come to
him and make our dwelling with him.   He who does not 24
love me will not lay my Message to heart; and the Message
to which you are listening is not my own, but that of the
Father who sent me.

I have told you all this while still with you, but the Helper 25, 26
—the Holy Spirit whom the Father will send in my Name—
he will teach you all things, and will recall to your minds all
that I have said to you.   Peace be with you! My own 27
peace I give you. I do not give to you as the world gives.
Do not let your hearts be troubled, or dismayed.   You heard 28
me say that I was going away and would return to you.   Had
you loved me, you would have been glad that I was going to the
Father, because the Father is greater than I.   And this I have 29
told you now before it happens, that, when it does happen, you
may still believe in me.   I shall not talk with you much more, 30
for the Spirit that is ruling the world is coming.   He has
nothing in common with me; but he is coming that the world 31
may see that I love the Father, and that I do as the Father
commanded me.   Come, let us be going.

The Vine and the Branches.   I am the True Vine, and my Father is the Vine- 1 **15**
grower.   Any unfruitful branch in me he takes 2
away, and he cleanses every fruitful branch, that
it may bear more fruit.   You are already clean because of the 3
Message that I have given you. Remain united to me, and I will 4
remain united to you. As a branch cannot bear fruit by itself,
unless it remains united to the vine; no more can you, unless
you remain united to me. I am the Vine, you are the branches. 5
He that remains united to me, while I remain united to him
—he bears fruit plentifully; for you can do nothing apart
from me.   If any one does not remain united to me, 6
he is thrown away, as a branch would be, and withers up.
Such branches are collected and thrown into the fire, and are
burnt.   If you remain united to me, and my teaching remains 7
in your hearts, ask whatever you wish, and it shall be yours.
It is by your bearing fruit plentifully, and so showing your- 8
selves my disciples, that my Father is honoured.   As the 9
Father has loved me, so have I loved you; remain in my love.
If you lay my commands to heart, you will remain in my love; 10
just as I have laid the Father's commands to heart and
remain in his love.   I have told you all this so that my 11
own joy may be yours, and that your joy may be complete.
This is my command—Love one another, as I have loved 12
you. No one can give greater proof of love than by laying 13
down his life for his friends. And you are my friends, if you 14
do what I command you.   I no longer call you 'servants,' 15
because a servant does not know what his master is doing;

but I have given you the name of 'friends,' because I made known to you everything that I learnt from my Father. It was not you who chose me, but I who chose you, and I appointed you to go and bear fruit—fruit that should remain, so that the Father might grant you whatever you ask in my Name. **16**

The World and the Spirit of Truth. I am giving you these commands that you may love one another. **17** If the world hates **18** you, you know that it has first hated me. If you **19** belonged to the world, the world would love its own. Because you do not belong to the world, but I have chosen you out of the world—that is why the world hates you. Remember **20** what I said to you—'A servant is not greater than his master.' If they have persecuted me, they will also persecute you ; if they have laid my Message to heart, they will lay yours to heart also. But they will do all this to you, because you believe in my **21** Name, for they do not know him who sent me. If I **22** had not come and spoken to them, they would have had no sin to answer for ; but as it is, they have no excuse for their sin. He who hates me hates my Father also. If I had not done **23, 24** among them such work as no one else ever did, they would have had no sin to answer for ; but, as it is, they have both seen and hated both me and my Father. And so is fulfilled **25** what is said in their Law—

'They hated me without cause.'

But, when the Helper comes, whom I will send to you from the **26** Father—the Spirit of Truth, who comes from the Father—he will bear testimony to me ; yes, and you also are to bear **27** testimony, because you have been with me from the first.

I have spoken to you in this way so that you may not falter. **1** **16** They will expel you from their Synagogues ; indeed the time **2** is coming when any one who kills you will think that he is making an offering to God. They will do this, because they **3** have not learnt to know the Father, or even me. But I have **4** spoken to you of these things that, when the time for them comes, you may remember that I told you about them myself. I did not tell you all this at first, because I was with you. But **5** now I am to return to him who sent me ; and yet not one of you asks me—'Where are you going ? ', although your hearts **6** are full of sorrow at all that I have been saying to you. Yet I **7** am only telling you the truth ; it is for your good that I should go away. For otherwise the Helper will never come to you, but, if I leave you, I will send him to you. And he, **8** when he comes, will bring conviction to the world as to Sin, and as to Righteousness, and as to Judgement ; as to Sin, for **9** men do not believe in me ; as to Righteousness, for I am **10**

going to the Father, and you will see me no longer ; as to   11
Judgement, for the Spirit that is ruling this world has been
condemned.   I have still much to say to you, but you   12
cannot bear it now.   Yet when he—the Spirit of Truth—   13
comes, he will guide you into all Truth ; for he will not
speak on his own authority, but he will speak of all that
he hears ; and he will tell you of the things that are to come.
He will honour me ; because he will take of what is mine,   14
and will tell it to you.   Everything that the Father has is   15
mine ; that is why I said that he takes of what is mine, and
will tell it to you.

Words of Farewell.   In a little while you will no longer see me ; and   16
then in a little while you will see me indeed."
At this some of his disciples said to one another :   17
"What does he mean by saying to us 'In a little while you
will not see me, and then in a little while you will see me
indeed'; and by saying 'Because I am going to the Father'?
What does he mean by 'In a little while'?" they said ;   18
"we do not know what he is speaking about."
Jesus saw that they were wanting to ask him a question, and   19
said :
"Are you trying to find out from one another what I meant
by saying 'In a little while you will not see me ; and then in
a little while you will see me indeed'?   In truth I tell you   20
that you will weep and mourn, but the world will rejoice ; you
will suffer pain, but your pain shall turn to joy.   A woman   21
in labour is in pain because her time has come ; but no sooner is
the child born, than she forgets her trouble in her joy that
a man has been born into the world.   You, in the same   22
way, are sorry now ; but I shall see you again, and your
hearts will rejoice, and no one will rob you of your joy.   And   23
at that time you will not ask me anything ; in truth I
tell you, if you ask the Father for anything, he will grant it
to you in my Name.   So far you have not asked for anything,   24
in my Name ; ask, and you will receive, so that your joy may
be complete.
I have spoken to you of all this in figures ; a time is   25
coming, however, when I shall not speak any longer to you
in figures, but shall tell you about the Father plainly.   You   26
will ask, at that time, in my Name ; and I do not say that I
will intercede with the Father for you ; for the Father himself   27
loves you, because you have loved me, and have believed that
I came from the Father.   I came out from the Father, and   28
have come into the world ; and now I am to leave the world,
and go to the Father."
"At last," exclaimed the disciples, "you are using plain   29
words and not speaking in figures at all.   Now we are sure   30
that you know everything, and need not wait for any one to

22 Isa. 66. 14.

question you. This makes us believe that you did come from God."

"Do you believe that already?" Jesus answered. "Listen! a time is coming—indeed it has already come—when you are to be scattered, each going his own way, and to leave me alone; and yet I am not alone, because the Father is with me. I have spoken to you in this way, so that in me you may find peace. In the world you will find trouble; yet, take courage! I have conquered the world." 31, 32

33

The Prayer of Jesus. After saying this, Jesus raised his eyes heavenwards, and said: 1 **17**

"Father, the hour has come; honour thy Son, that thy Son may honour thee; even as thou gavest him power over all mankind, that he should give Immortal Life to all those whom thou hast given him. And the Immortal Life is this—to know thee the one true God, and Jesus Christ whom thou hast sent as thy Messenger. I have honoured thee on earth by completing the work which thou hast given me to do; and now do thou honour me, Father, at thy own side, with the honour which I had at thy side before the world began. 2

3

4

5

I have revealed thee to those whom thou gavest me from the world; they were thy own, and thou gavest them to me; and they have laid thy Message to heart. They recognize now that everything that thou gavest me was from thee; for I have given them the teaching which thou gavest me, and they received it, and clearly understood that I came from thee, and they believed that thou hast sent me as thy Messenger. I intercede for them; I am not interceding for the world, but for those whom thou hast given me, for they are thy own—all that is mine is thine, and all that is thine is mine —and I am honoured in them. Now I am to be in this world no longer, but they are still to be in the world, and I am to come to thee. Holy Father, keep them by that revelation of thy Name which thou hast given me, that they may be one, as we are. Whilst I was with them, I kept them by that revelation, and I have guarded them; and not one of them has been lost, except that lost soul—in fulfilment of Scripture. But now I am to come 6

7

8

9

10

11

12

13

to thee; and I am speaking thus, while still in the world, that they may have my own joy, in all its fulness, in their hearts.   I have given them thy Message; and the world hated them, because they do not belong to the world, even as I do not belong to the world.   I do not ask thee to take them out of the world, but to keep them from Evil.   They do not belong to the world, even as I do not belong to the world.   Consecrate them by the Truth; thy Message is Truth.   Just as thou hast sent me as thy Messenger to the world, so I send them as my Messengers to the world.   And it is for their sakes that I am consecrating myself, so that they also may be truly consecrated.

But it is not only for them that I am interceding, but also for those who believe in me through their Message, that they all may be one—that as thou, Father, art in union with me and I with thee, so they also may be in union with us—and so the world may believe that thou hast sent me as thy Messenger.   I have given them the honour which thou hast given me, that they may be one as we are one—I in union with them and thou with me—that so they may be perfected in their union, and thus the world may know that thou hast sent me as thy Messenger, and that thou hast loved them as thou hast loved me.   Father, my desire for all those whom thou hast given me is that they may be with me where I am, so that they may see the honour which thou hast given me; for thou didst love me before the beginning of the world.   O righteous Father, though the world did not know thee, I knew thee; and these men knew that thou hast sent me as thy Messenger.   I have made thee known to them, and will do so still; that the love that thou hast had for me may be in their hearts, and that I may be in them also."

Jesus in Gethsemane. When Jesus had said this, he went out with his disciples and crossed the brook Kedron to a place where there was a garden, into which he and his disciples went.   The place was well known to Judas, the betrayer, for Jesus and his disciples had often met there.   So Judas, who had obtained the soldiers of the Roman garrison,

and some police-officers from the Chief Priests and the
Pharisees, came there with lanterns, torches, and weapons.
Jesus, aware of all that was coming upon him, went to meet   4
them, and said to them :

"For whom are you looking ? "

"Jesus of Nazareth," was their answer.

"I am he," said Jesus.   5

(Judas, the betrayer, was also standing with them.)

When Jesus said ' I am he,' they drew back and fell to the   6
ground.   So he again asked for whom they were looking, and   7
they answered : "Jesus of Nazareth."

"I have already told you that I am he," replied Jesus, " so, 8
if it is for me that you are looking, let these men go."

This was in fulfilment of his words—'Of those whom thou   9
hast given me I have not lost one.'

At this, Simon Peter, who had a sword with him, drew it,   10
and struck the High Priest's servant, and cut off his right
ear.   The servant's name was Malchus.   But Jesus said to   11
Peter :

"Sheathe your sword.   Shall I not drink the cup which the
Father has given me ? "

The Arrest of Jesus.   So the soldiers of the garrison, with their Com-   12
manding Officer and the Jewish police, arrested
Jesus and bound him, and took him first of   13
all to Annas.   Annas was the father-in-law of
Caiaphas, who was High Priest that year.   It was Caiaphas   14
who had counselled the Jews, that it was best that one man
should die for the people.

Peter disowns Jesus.   Meanwhile Simon Peter followed Jesus, and   15
so did another disciple.   That disciple, being
well-known to the High Priest, went with Jesus
into the High Priest's court-yard, while Peter stood outside   16
by the door.   Presently the other disciple—the one well-known
to the High Priest—went out and spoke to the portress, and
brought Peter in.   So the maidservant said to Peter :   17

"Are not you also one of this man's disciples ? "

"No, I am not," he said.

The servants and police-officers were standing round a char-   18
coal fire (which they had made because it was cold), and were
warming themselves.   Peter, too, was with them, standing and
warming himself.

Jesus before the High Priest.   The High Priest questioned Jesus about his   19
disciples and about his teaching.

"For my part," answered Jesus, "I have   20
spoken to all the world openly.   I always taught in some
Synagogue, or in the Temple Courts, places where all the
Jews assemble, and I never spoke of anything in secret.   Why   21
question me ?   Question those who have listened to me as

to what I have spoken about to them.   They must know what
I said."

When Jesus said this, one of the police-officers, who was   22
standing near, gave him a blow with his hand.

"Do you answer the High Priest like that?" he exclaimed.

"If I said anything wrong, give evidence about it," replied   23
Jesus ; "but if not, why do you strike me?"

Annas sent him bound to Caiaphas the High Priest.   24

Meanwhile Simon Peter was standing there, warming him-   25
self ; so they said to him :

"Are not you also one of his disciples?"

Peter denied it.

"No, I am not," he said.

One of the High Priest's servants, a relation of the man whose   26
ear Peter had cut off, exclaimed :

"Did not I myself see you with him in the garden?"

Peter again denied it ; and at that moment a cock crowed.   27

Jesus before the Roman Governor.   From Caiaphas they took Jesus to the Govern-   28
ment House. It was early in the morning. But
they did not enter the Government House them-
selves, lest they should become 'defiled,' and so be unable to eat
the Passover.   Therefore Pilate came outside to speak to them.   29

"What charge do you bring against this man?" he asked.

"If he had not been a criminal, we should not have given   30
him up to you," they answered.

"Take him yourselves," said Pilate, "and try him by your   31
own Law."

"We have no power to put any one to death," the Jews   32
replied—in fulfilment of what Jesus had said when indicating
the death that he was destined to die.

After that, Pilate went into the Government House again,   33
and calling Jesus up, asked him :

"Are you the King of the Jews?"

"Do you ask me that yourself?" replied Jesus, "or did   34
others say it to you about me?"

"Do you take me for a Jew?" was Pilate's answer.   "It is   35
your own nation and the Chief Priests who have given you
up to me. What have you done?"

"My kingly power," replied Jesus, "is not due to this   36
world. If it had been so, my servants would be doing their
utmost to prevent my being given up to the Jews ; but my
kingly power is not from the world."

"So you are a King after all!" exclaimed Pilate.   37

"Yes, it is true I am a King," answered Jesus. "I was
born for this, I have come into the world for this—to bear
testimony to the Truth. Every one who is on the side of
Truth listens to my voice."

"What is Truth?" exclaimed Pilate.   38

After saying this, he went out to the Jews again, and said :
"For my part, I find nothing with which he can be charged.
It is, however, the custom for me to grant you the release of   39
one man at the Passover Festival.   Do you wish for the
release of the King of the Jews ? "

"No, not this man," they shouted again, "but Barabbas !"   40
This Barabbas was a robber.

After that, Pilate had Jesus scourged.   The soldiers made a   1, 2 **19**
crown with some thorns and put it on his head and threw a
purple robe round him.   They kept coming up to him and   3
saying : " Long live the King of the Jews ! " and they gave him
blow after blow with their hands.   Pilate again came   4
outside, and said to the people :

"Look ! I am bringing him out to you, so that you may
know that I find nothing with which he can be charged."
Then Jesus came outside, wearing the crown of thorns and   5
the purple robe ; and Pilate said to them :

"Here is the man ! "
When the Chief Priests and the police-officers saw him, they   6
shouted :

"Crucify him ! Crucify him ! "

"Take him yourselves and crucify him," said Pilate.   "For
my part, I find nothing with which he can be charged."

"But we," replied the Jews, "have a Law, under which he   7
deserves death for making himself out to be the Son of
God."

When Pilate heard what they said, he became still more   8
alarmed ; and, going into the Government House again, he   9
said to Jesus :

"Where do you come from ? "
But Jesus made no reply.   So Pilate said to him :   10

"Do you refuse to speak to me ? Do not you know that
I have power to release you, and have power to crucify
you ? "

"You would have no power over me at all," answered Jesus,   11
"if it had not been given you from above ; and, therefore, the
man who betrayed me to you is guilty of the greater sin."
This made Pilate anxious to release him ; but the Jews   12
shouted :

"If you release that man, you are no friend of the Emperor !
Any one who makes himself out to be a King is setting himself against the Emperor ! "

On hearing what they said, Pilate brought Jesus out, and   13
took his seat upon the Bench at a place called 'The Stone
Pavement'—in Hebrew 'Gabbatha.'   It was the Passover   14
Preparation Day, and about noon.   Then he said to the
Jews :

"Here is your King ! "

At that the people shouted :   15
 " Kill him ! Kill him ! Crucify him ! "
 " What ! shall I crucify your King ? " exclaimed Pilate.
 " We have no King but the Emperor," replied the Chief
Priests ; whereupon Pilate gave Jesus up to them to be   16
crucified.

               So they took Jesus ; and he went out, carrying   17
The   his cross himself, to the place which is named from
Crucifixion a skull, or, in Hebrew, Golgotha.   There they   18
of Jesus.   crucified him, and two others with him—one on
each side, and Jesus between them.   Pilate also had these   19
words written and put up over the cross—

'JESUS OF NAZARETH, THE KING OF THE JEWS.'

These words were read by many of the Jews, because the   20
place where Jesus was crucified was near the city ; and they
were written in Hebrew, Latin, and Greek.   The Jewish   21
Chief Priests said to Pilate :
 " Do not write ' The King of the Jews ', but write what the
man said—' I am King of the Jews.' "   But Pilate answered :   22
 " What I have written, I have written."

When the soldiers had crucified Jesus, they took his clothes   23
and divided them into four shares—a share for each soldier—
and they took the coat also.   The coat had no seam, being
woven in one piece from top to bottom.   So they said to one   24
another :
 " Do not let us tear it, but let us cast lots for it, to see who
shall have it."   This was in fulfilment of the words of Scripture—
       ' They shared my clothes among them,
        And over my clothing they cast lots.'

That was what the soldiers did.   Meanwhile near the cross   25
of Jesus were standing his mother and his mother's sister, as
well as Mary the wife of Clopas and Mary of Magdala.
When Jesus saw his mother, and the disciple whom he loved,   26
standing near, he said to his mother :
 " There is your son."
Then he said to that disciple :   27
 " There is your mother."
And from that very hour the disciple took her to live in his house.

               Afterwards, knowing that everything was now   28
The Death finished, Jesus said, in fulfilment of the words of
of Jesus.   Scripture :
 " I am thirsty."
There was a bowl standing there full of common wine ; so   29

they put a sponge soaked in the wine on the end of a hyssop-stalk, and held it up to his mouth. When Jesus had received 30
the wine, he exclaimed :

" All is finished ! "

Then, bowing his head, he resigned his spirit to God.

It was the Preparation Day, and so, to prevent the bodies 31
from remaining on the crosses during the Sabbath (for that
Sabbath was a great day), the Jews asked Pilate to have the
legs broken and the bodies removed. Accordingly the soldiers 32
came and broke the legs of the first man, and then those of
the other who had been crucified with Jesus ; but, on coming 33
to him, when they saw that he was already dead, they did
not break his legs. One of the soldiers, however, pierced his 34
side with a spear, and blood and water immediately flowed
from it. This is the statement of one who actually saw it— 35
and his statement may be relied upon, and he knows that he
is speaking the truth—and it is given in order that you also
may be convinced. For all this took place in fulfilment of 36
the words of Scripture—

' Not one of its bones shall be broken.'

And there is another passage which says— 37

' They will look upon him whom they pierced.'

After this, Joseph of Ramah, a disciple of Jesus— 38
The Burial of Jesus. but a secret one, owing to his fear of the Jews—
begged Pilate's permission to remove the body of
Jesus. Pilate gave him leave ; so Joseph went
and removed the body. Nicodemus, too—the man who had 39
formerly visited Jesus by night—came with a roll of myrrh and
aloes, weighing nearly a hundred pounds. They took the body 40
of Jesus, and wound it in linen with the spices, according to the
Jewish mode of burial. At the place where Jesus had been 41
crucified there was a garden, and in the garden a newly-made
tomb in which no one had ever been laid. And so, because of 42
its being the Preparation Day, and as the tomb was close at
hand, they laid Jesus there.

IV.—THE RISEN LIFE.

On the first day of the week, early in the morn- 1 **20**
The Resurrection of Jesus. ing, while it was still dark, Mary of Magdala
went to the tomb, and saw that the stone had
been removed. So she came running to Simon 2
Peter, and to that other disciple who was Jesus' friend, and
said to them :

" They have taken away the Master out of the tomb, and we
do not know where they have laid him ! "

[36] Exod. 12. 46. [37] Zech. 12. 10.

Upon this, Peter started off with that other disciple, and   3
they went to the tomb. The two began running together;   4
but the other disciple ran faster than Peter, and reached the
tomb first.   Stooping down, he saw the linen wrappings lying   5
there, but did not go in.   Presently Simon Peter came   6
following behind him, and went into the tomb; and he
looked at the linen wrappings lying there, and the cloth which   7
had been upon Jesus' head, not lying with the wrappings, but
rolled up on one side, separately.   Then the other disciple,   8
who had reached the tomb first, went inside too, and he saw
for himself and was convinced.   For they did not then under-   9
stand the passage of Scripture which says that Jesus must
rise again from the dead.   The disciples then returned to their   10
companions.

Jesus   Meanwhile Mary was standing close outside the   11
appears to tomb, weeping.   Still weeping, she leant forward
Mary.   into the tomb, and perceived two angels clothed   12
in white sitting there, where the body of Jesus had been lying,
one where the head and the other where the feet had been.

"Why are you weeping?" asked the angels.   13

"They have taken my Master away," she answered, "and
I do not know where they have laid him."
After saying this, she turned round, and looked at Jesus stand-   14
ing there, but she did not know that it was Jesus.

"Why are you weeping?   Whom are you seeking?" he   15
asked.
Supposing him to be the gardener, Mary answered :
"If it was you, Sir, who carried him away, tell me where
you have laid him, and I will take him away myself."

"Mary!" said Jesus.   16
She turned round, and exclaimed in Hebrew :
"Rabboni!" (or, as we should say, 'Teacher').

"Do not hold me," Jesus said; "for I have not yet ascended   17
to the Father.   But go to my Brothers, and tell them that I am
ascending to him who is my Father and their Father, my God
and their God."
Mary of Magdala went and told the disciples that she had   18
seen the Master, and that he had said this to her.

Jesus   In the evening of the same day—the first day   19
appears to of the week—after the doors of the room, in
the Apostles. which the disciples were, had been shut for fear
of the Jews, Jesus came and stood among them and said :
"Peace be with you"; after which he showed them his hands   20
and his side.   The disciples were filled with joy when they
saw the Master.   Again Jesus said to them : "Peace be with   21
you.   As the Father has sent me as his Messenger, so I am
sending you."
After saying this, he breathed on them, and said :   22

"Receive the Holy Spirit; if you remit any one's sins, they 23 have been remitted; and, if you retain them, they have been retained."

Jesus appears to Thomas. But Thomas, one of the Twelve, called 'The 24 Twin,' was not with them when Jesus came; so 25 the rest of the disciples said to him: "We have seen the Master!"

"Unless I see the marks of the nails in his hands," he exclaimed, "and put my finger into the marks, and put my hand into his side, I will not believe it."

A week later the disciples were again in the house, and 26 Thomas with them. After the doors had been shut, Jesus came and stood among them, and said: "Peace be with you." Then he said to Thomas: 27

"Place your finger here, and look at my hands; and place your hand here, and put it into my side; and do not refuse to believe, but believe."

And Thomas exclaimed: 28

"My Master, and my God!"

"Is it because you have seen me that you have believed?" 29 said Jesus. "Blessed are they who have not seen, and yet have believed!"

The Object of this Gospel. There were many other signs of his mission 30 that Jesus gave in presence of the disciples, which are not recorded in this book; but these have 31 been recorded that you may believe that Jesus is the Christ, the Son of God—and that, through your belief in his Name, you may have Life.

•

A later Appearance of Jesus. Later on, Jesus showed himself again to the 1 **21** disciples by the Sea of Tiberias. It was in this 2 way:—Simon Peter, Thomas, who was called 'The Twin,' Nathanael of Cana in Galilee, Zebediah's sons, and two other disciples of Jesus, were together, when Simon 3 Peter said: "I am going fishing."

"We will come with you," said the others.

They went out and got into the boat, but caught nothing that night. Just as day was breaking, Jesus came and stood on 4 the beach; but the disciples did not know that it was he.

"My children," he said, "have you anything to eat?" 5

"No," they answered.

"Cast your net to the right of the boat," he said, "and you 6 will find fish."

So they cast the net, and now they could not haul it in on

account of the quantity of fish.　Upon this the disciple whom　7
Jesus loved said to Peter :

"It is the Master !"

When Simon Peter heard that it was the Master, he fastened
his coat round him (for he had taken it off), and threw himself into the Sea.　But the rest of the disciples came in the　8
boat (for they were only about a hundred yards from shore),
dragging the net full of fish.　　　　　When they had come　9
ashore, they found a charcoal fire ready, with some fish
already on it, and some bread as well.

"Bring some of the fish which you have just caught," said　10
Jesus.　So Simon Peter got into the boat and hauled the net　11
ashore full of large fish, a hundred and fifty-three of them ;
and yet, although there were so many, the net had not been
torn.

And Jesus said to them : "Come and breakfast."　　　12

Not one of the disciples ventured to ask him who he was,
knowing that it was the Master.　Jesus went and took the　13
bread and gave it to them, and the fish too.　　　This was　14
the third time that Jesus showed himself to the disciples after
he had risen from the dead.

**Jesus'
Last Words
to Peter.**　　　When breakfast was over, Jesus said to Simon　15
Peter :
　　"Simon, son of John, do you love me more
than the others ? "

"Yes, Master," he answered, "you know that I am your
friend."

"Feed my lambs," said Jesus.

Then, a second time, Jesus asked :　　　　　　　　　16
　　"Simon, son of John, do you love me ? "

"Yes, Master," he answered, "you know that I am your
friend."

"Tend my sheep," said Jesus.

The third time, Jesus said to him :　　　　　　　　17
　　"Simon, son of John, are you my friend ? "

Peter was hurt at his third question being 'Are you my
friend ? '; and exclaimed :

"Master, you know everything !　You can tell that I am
your friend."

"Feed my sheep," said Jesus.　"In truth I tell you," he　18
continued, "when you were young, you used to put on your
own girdle, and walk wherever you wished ; but, when you
have grown old, you will have to stretch out your hands,
while some one else puts on your girdle, and takes you
where you do not wish."

Jesus said this to show the death by which Peter was to　19
honour God, and then he added : "Follow me."

Peter turned round, and saw the disciple whom Jesus loved　20 following—the one who at the supper leant back on the Master's shoulder, and asked him who it was that would betray him. Seeing him, Peter said to Jesus: 21

"Master, what about this man?"

"If it is my will that he should wait till I come," 22
answered Jesus, "what has that to do with you? Follow me yourself."

So the report spread among the Brethren that that dis- 23
ciple was not to die; yet Jesus did not say that he was not to die, but said "If it is my will that he should wait till I come, what has that to do with you?"

Conclusion. It is this disciple who states these things, and 24
who recorded them; and we know that his statement is true.

There are many other things which Jesus did; but, if every 25
one of them were to be recorded in detail, I suppose that even the world itself would not hold the books that would be written.

A Passage about an Adulteress.

(Inserted in some manuscripts from an ancient source, and found either after John 7. 53, or after Luke 21. 38.)

[And every one went home except Jesus, who went to the Mount of Olives.   But he went again into the Temple Courts early in the morning, and all the people came to him ; and he sat down and taught them.   Presently, however, the Teachers of the Law and the Pharisees brought a woman who had been caught in adultery, and placed her in the middle of the Court, and said to Jesus :

"Teacher, this woman was found in the very act of adultery. Now Moses, in the Law, commanded us to stone[1] such women to death ; what do you say ? "

They said this to test him, in order to have a charge to bring against him.   But Jesus stooped down, and wrote on the ground with his finger.   However, as they continued asking him, he raised himself, and said :

"Let the man among you who has never done wrong throw the first stone at her."

And again he stooped down, and wrote on the ground.   When they heard that, they went out one by one, beginning with the eldest ; and Jesus was left alone with the woman in the middle of the Court.   Raising himself, Jesus said to her :

"Woman, where are they ?   Did no one condemn you ? "

"No one, Sir," she answered.

"Neither do I condemn you," said Jesus ; "go, and do not sin again."]

[1] Deut. 22. 24.

THE ACTS OF THE APOSTLES.

THE ACTS OF THE APOSTLES.

COMPILED AT ROME AT AN UNCERTAIN DATE LATER THAN 64 A.D.

THIS Book contains an account of the principal events in the first years of the Church's history after the Ascension of Jesus into Heaven. These events group themselves round the names of St. Peter and St. Paul; and in this Book the first twelve chapters relate mainly St. Peter's work among Jews, and the last sixteen St. Paul's work among people of other nations. The history ends with the imprisonment of the latter in Rome.

There is strong support for the view that St. Luke was the author or compiler of the Book, and (from the use of the pronoun "we" in several sections) that he took part in many of the events related.

THE ACTS OF THE APOSTLES.

I.—The Church and The Jews.

Doings of the Apostles Peter and John.

Introduction. The first account which I drew up, Theophilus, dealt with all that Jesus did and taught from the very first, down to that day on which he was taken up to Heaven, after he had, by the help of the Holy Spirit, given instructions to the Apostles whom he had chosen. With abundant proofs, he showed himself to them, still living, after his death; appearing to them from time to time during forty days, and speaking of all that related to the Kingdom of God. And once, when he had gathered them together, he charged them not to leave Jerusalem, but to wait there for the fulfilment of the Father's promise—"that promise," he said, "of which you have heard me speak; for, while John baptized with water, you shall be baptized with the Holy Spirit before many days have passed."

Ascension of Jesus. So, when the Apostles had met together, they asked Jesus this question—

"Master, is this the time when you intend to re-establish the Kingdom for Israel?"

His answer was:

"It is not for you to know times or hours, for the Father has reserved these for his own decision; but you shall receive power, when the Holy Spirit shall have descended upon you, and shall be witnesses for me not only in Jerusalem, but throughout Judaea and Samaria, and to the ends of the earth."

No sooner had Jesus said this than he was caught up before their eyes, and a cloud received him from their sight. While they were still gazing up into the heavens, as he went, suddenly two men, clothed in white, stood beside them, and said:

"Men of Galilee, why are you standing here looking up into the heavens? This very Jesus, who has been taken from you

---

[3] Dan. 2. 44.

into the heavens, will come in the very way in which you have seen him go into the heavens."

The Apostles in Jerusalem. Then the Apostles returned to Jerusalem from the hill called Olivet, which is about three quarters of a mile from the city. 12

When they reached Jerusalem, they went to the upstairs room, where they were staying. There were there Peter, John, James, and Andrew, Philip and Thomas, Bartholomew and Matthew, James the son of Alphaeus, Simon the Zealot, and Judas the son of James. They all united in devoting themselves to Prayer, and so did some women, and Mary, the mother of Jesus, and his brothers. 13 14

Appointment of Matthias. About this time, at a meeting of the Brethren, when there were about a hundred and twenty present, Peter rose to speak. 15

"Brothers," he said, "it was necessary that the prediction of Scripture should be fulfilled, which the Holy Spirit made by the lips of David about Judas, who acted as guide to the men that arrested Jesus, for he was one of our number and had his part allotted him in this work of ours." 16 17

(This man had bought a piece of land with the price of his treachery ; and, falling heavily, his body had burst open, and all his bowels protruded.   This became known to every one living in Jerusalem, so that the field came to be called, in their language, 'Akeldama,' which means the 'Field of Blood.') 18 19

"For in the Book of Psalms," Peter continued, "it is said— 20

' Let his dwelling become desolate,
     And let no one live in it ' ;

and also—

' His office let another take.'

Therefore, from among the men who have been with us all the time that Jesus, our Master, went in and out among us— from his baptism by John down to that day on which he was taken from us—some one must be found to join us as a witness of his resurrection." 21 22

So they put forward two men, Joseph called Barsabas, whose other name was Justus, and Matthias ; and they offered this prayer— 23 24

"O Lord, who readest all hearts, show which of these two men thou hast chosen to take the place in this apostolic work, which Judas has abandoned, to go to his proper place." 25

Then they drew lots between them ; and, the lot having fallen   26
on Matthias, he was added to the number of the eleven
Apostles.

The Gift of the Holy Spirit. In the course of the Festival at the close of the   1
Harvest the disciples had all met together, when   2
suddenly there came from the heavens a noise
like that of a strong wind rushing by ; it filled the whole house
in which they were sitting.   Then there appeared tongues of   3
what seemed to be flame, separating, so that one settled on
each of them ; and they were all filled with the Holy Spirit,   4
and began to speak with strange 'tongues' as the Spirit
prompted their utterances.

Now there were then staying in Jerusalem religious Jews   5
from every country in the world ; and, when this sound was   6
heard, numbers of people collected, in the greatest excitement,
because each of them heard the disciples speaking in his own
language.   They were utterly amazed, and kept asking in   7
astonishment :

"What ! Are not all these men who are speaking Gali-
leans ? Then how is it that we each of us hear them in our   8
own native language ?   Some of us are Parthians, some   9
Medes, some Elamites ; and some of us live in Mesopotamia,
in Judaea and Cappadocia, in Pontus and Roman Asia, in   10
Phrygia and Pamphylia, in Egypt and the districts of Libya
adjoining Cyrene ; some of us are visitors from Rome, either
Jews by birth or converts, and some are Cretans and Ara-   11
bians—yet we all alike hear them speaking in our own tongues
of the great things that God has done."
They were all utterly amazed and bewildered.   12
"What does it mean ? " they asked one another.
But there were some who said with a sneer : "They have had   13
too much new wine."

Peter's Address. Then Peter, surrounded by the eleven other   14
Apostles, stood up, and, raising his voice, ad-
dressed the crowd.

"Men of Judaea," he began, "and all you who are staying
in Jerusalem, let me tell you what this means.   Mark well
my words.   These men are not drunk, as you suppose; for it is   15
only now nine in the morning ! No ! This is what is spoken   16
of in the prophet Joel—

'It shall come about in the last days,' God says,   17
'That I will pour out my Spirit on all mankind ;
Your sons and your daughters shall become Prophets,
Your young men shall see visions,
And your old men dream dreams ;

17 Joel 2. 28.

Yes, even on the slaves—for they are mine—both men and   18
     women,
I will in those days pour out my Spirit,
     And they shall become Prophets ;
And I will show wonders in the heavens above,   19
And signs on the earth below—
     Blood and fire and mist of smoke ;
The sun shall become darkness,   20
And the moon blood-red,
     Before the Day of the Lord comes—that great and awful
          day.
          Then shall every one who invokes the Name of the Lord 21
          be saved.'

Men of Israel, listen to what I am saying.   Jesus of Nazareth, 22
a man whose mission from God to you was proved by miracles,
wonders, and signs, which God showed among you through
him, as you know full well—he, I say, in accordance with   23
God's definite plan and with his previous knowledge, was
betrayed, and you, by the hands of lawless men, nailed him
to a cross and put him to death.   But God released him from   24
the pangs of death and raised him to life, it being impossible
for death to retain its hold upon him.   Indeed it was to him   25
that David was referring when he said—

'I have had the Lord ever before my eyes,
     For he stands at my right hand, that I should not be disquieted.
Therefore my heart was cheered, and my tongue told its delight ; 26
     Yes, even my body, too, will rest in hope ;
For thou wilt not abandon my soul to the Place of Death,   27
     Nor surrender me, thy holy one, to undergo corruption.
Thou hast shown me the path to life,   28
     Thou wilt fill me with gladness in thy presence.'

Brothers, I can speak to you the more confidently about the   29
Patriarch David, because he is dead and buried, and his tomb
is here among us to this very day.   David, then, Prophet as   30
he was, knowing that God 'had solemnly sworn to him to set
one of his descendants upon his throne,' looked into the future, 31
and referred to the resurrection of the Christ when he said
that 'he had not been abandoned to the Place of Death, nor
had his body undergone corruption.'   It was this Jesus,   32
whom God raised to life ; and of that we are ourselves all
witnesses.   And now that he has been exalted to the right   33
hand of God, and has received from the Father the promised
gift of the Holy Spirit, he has begun to pour out that gift, as
you yourselves now see and hear.   It was not David who   34
went up into Heaven ; for he himself says—

'The Lord said to my master : " Sit on my right hand,
     Till I put thy enemies as a footstool under thy feet." '   35

18—21 Joel 2. 29—32.   25—28 Ps. 16. 8—11.   30 Ps. 132. 11.   34—35 Ps. 110. 1.

So let the whole nation of Israel know beyond all doubt, that   36
God has made him both Lord and Christ—this very Jesus
whom you crucified."

When the people heard this, they were conscience-smitten,   37
and said to Peter and the rest of the Apostles :

"Brothers, what can we do ?"

"Repent," answered Peter, "and be baptized every one   38
of you in the Faith of Jesus Christ for the forgiveness of
your sins ; and then you will receive the gift of the Holy
Spirit. For the promise is for you and for your children, and   39
also for all those now far away, who may be called by the
Lord our God."

With many other words Peter enforced his teaching, while   40
the burden of his exhortations was—"Save yourselves from
the perverse spirit of this age."   So those who accepted   41
his teaching were baptized, and about three thousand people
joined the disciples on that day alone.   They devoted them-   42
selves to the teaching of the Apostles and to the Common
Life of the Church, to the Breaking of the Bread and to the
Prayers.

Early Days of the Christian Society. A deep impression was made upon every one,   43
and many wonders and signs were done at the
hands of the Apostles.   All who became believers   44
in Christ held everything for the common use ;
they sold their property and their goods, and shared the pro-   45
ceeds among them all, according to their individual needs.
Every day they devoted themselves to meeting together in the   46
Temple Courts, and to the Breaking of Bread at their homes,
while they partook of their food in simple-hearted gladness,
praising God, and winning the good-will of all the people.   47
And the Lord daily added to their company those who were
in the path of Salvation.

Cure of a lame Beggar. One day, as Peter and John were going up into   1 **3**
the Temple Courts for the three o'clock Prayers,
a man, who had been lame from his birth, was   2
being carried by. This man used to be set down every day at
the gate of the Temple called 'the Beautiful Gate,' to beg of
those who went in.   Seeing Peter and John on the point of   3
entering, he asked them to give him something.   Peter fixed   4
his eyes on him, and so did John, and then Peter said : "Look
at us."

The man was all attention, expecting to get something from   5
them ; but Peter added :   6

"I have no gold or silver, but I give you what I have.   In
the Name of Jesus Christ of Nazareth I bid you walk."

Grasping the lame man by the right hand, Peter lifted him up.   7

³⁹ Dan. 9. 7; Joel 2. 32.

Instantly the man's feet and ankles became strong, and, leaping   8
up, he stood and began to walk about, and then went with them
into the Temple Courts, walking, and leaping, and praising
God. All the people saw him walking about and praising   9
God ; and, when they recognized him as the man who used to   10
sit begging at the Beautiful Gate of the Temple, they were
utterly astonished and amazed at what had happened to him.

While the man still clung to Peter and John, the people all   11
quickly gathered round them in the Colonnade named after
Solomon, in the greatest astonishment. On seeing this, Peter   12
said to the people :

Peter's Address in the Temple. "Men of Israel, why are you surprised at this?
and why do you stare at us, as though we, by
any power or piety of our own, had enabled this
man to walk? The God of Abraham, Isaac, and Jacob, the   13
God of our ancestors, has done honour to his Servant Jesus—
him whom you gave up and disowned before Pilate, when
he had decided to set him free. You, I say, disowned the   14
Holy and Righteous One, and asked for the release of a
murderer ! The very Guide to Life you put to death ! But   15
God raised him from the dead—and of that we are ourselves
witnesses. And it is by faith in the Name of Jesus, that this   16
man, whom you all see and know, has—by his Name—been
made strong. Yes, it is the faith inspired by Jesus that has
made this complete cure of the man, before the eyes of you
all. And yet, my Brothers, I know that you acted as you did   17
from ignorance, and your rulers also. But it was in this way   18
that God fulfilled all that he had long ago foretold, as to the
sufferings of his Christ, by the lips of all the Prophets. There-   19
fore, repent and turn, that your sins may be wiped away ; so
that happier times may come from the Lord himself, and that   20
he may send you, in Jesus, your long-appointed Christ. But   21
Heaven must be his home, until the days of the Universal
Restoration, of which God has spoken by the lips of his holy
Prophets from the very first. Moses himself said—   22

'The Lord your God will raise up from among your brothers
a Prophet, as he raised me. To him you will listen whenever he speaks to you And it shall be that should any one   23
among the people not listen to that Prophet, he will be utterly
destroyed.'

Yes, and all the Prophets from Samuel onwards, and all their   24
successors who had a message to deliver, told of these days.
You yourselves are the heirs of the Prophets, and heirs, too, of   25
the Covenant which God made with your ancestors, when he
said to Abraham—

'In your descendants will all the nations of the earth be
blessed.'

[13] Exod. 3. 15; Isa. 52. 13.   [14] Enoch 38. 2.   [21] Mal. 4. 6.   [22-23] Deut. 18. 15—19;
Lev. 23. 29.   [25] Gen. 12. 3.

For you, first, God raised up his Servant, and sent him to bless 26
you, by turning each one of you from his wicked ways."

Peter and John before the Council. While Peter and John were still speaking to 1 **4**
the people, the Chief Priests, with the Officer in
charge at the Temple and the Sadducees, came
up to them, much annoyed because they were teaching the 2
people, and because, through Jesus, they were preaching the
resurrection from the dead. They arrested the Apostles and, 3
as it was already evening, had them placed in custody till the
next day. Many, however, of those who had heard the Apostles' 4
Message became believers in Christ, the number of the men
alone amounting to about five thousand.

The next day, a meeting of the leading men, the Councillors, 5
and the Teachers of the Law was held in Jerusalem. There 6
were present Annas the High Priest, Caiaphas, John, Alexander, and all who were of High-Priestly rank. They had 7
Peter and John brought before them, and questioned them.

" By what power," they asked, " or in whose name have
men like you done this thing ? "
On this, Peter, filled with the Holy Spirit, spoke as follows : 8
" Leaders of the people and Councillors, since we are on 9
our trial to-day for a kind act done to a helpless man, and
are asked in what way the man here before you has been
cured, let me tell you all and all the people of Israel, that 10
it is by the Name of Jesus Christ of Nazareth, whom you
crucified and whom God raised from the dead—it is, I say,
by his Name that this man stands here before you lame no
longer. Jesus is ' the stone which, scorned by you the 11
builders, has yet become the corner stone.' And Salvation 12
is in him alone ; for there is no other Name in the whole
world, given to men, to which we must look for our Salvation."
When the Council saw how boldly Peter and John spoke, and 13
found that they were uneducated men of humble station, they
were surprised, and realized that they had been companions of
Jesus. But, when they looked at the man who had been healed, 14
standing there with them, they had nothing to say. So they 15
ordered them out of court, and then began consulting together.

" What are we to do to these men?" they asked one another. 16
" That a remarkable sign has been given through them is
obvious to every one living in Jerusalem, and we cannot deny
it. But, to prevent this thing from spreading further among 17
the people, let us warn them not to speak in this Name any
more to any one whatever."
So they called the Apostles in, and ordered them not to 18
speak or teach in the Name of Jesus. But Peter and John 19
replied :

¹¹ Ps. 118. 21—22.   ¹² Enoch 4. 2.

"Whether it is right, in the sight of God, to listen to you
rather than to him—judge for yourselves, for we cannot help
speaking of what we have seen and heard." 20

However, after further warnings, the Council set them at 21
liberty, not seeing any safe way of punishing them, because
of the people, for they were all praising God for what had
occurred; for the man who was the subject of this miracu- 22
lous cure was more than forty years old.

After they had been set at liberty, the Apostles went to their 23
friends and told them what the Chief Priests and the Councillors
had said to them. All who heard their story, moved by a 24
common impulse, raised their voices to God in prayer:

"O Sovereign Lord, it is thou who hast
'made the heavens, the earth, the sea, and
everything that is in them,' and who, by the 25
lips of our ancestor, thy servant David, who
spoke under the influence of the Holy Spirit,
hast said—

'Why did the nations rage,
And the peoples form vain designs?
The kings of the earth set their array, 26
And its rulers gathered together,
Against the Lord and against his Christ.'

There have indeed gathered together in this 27
city against thy holy Servant Jesus, whom
thou hast consecrated the Christ, not Herod
and Pontius Pilate only, but the nations and
the people of Israel besides—yet only to do 28
what thou, by thy power and of thy own will,
didst long ago destine to be done. Now, 29
therefore, O Lord, mark their threats, and
enable thy servants, with all fearlessness, to
tell thy Message, while thou stretchest out 30
thy hand to heal, and causest signs and wonders to take place through the Name of thy
holy Servant Jesus."

When their prayer was ended, the place in which they were 31
assembled was shaken; and they were all filled with the
Holy Spirit, and began to tell God's Message fearlessly.

The Common Fund. The whole body of those who had become 32
believers in Christ were of one heart and mind.
Not one of them claimed any of his goods as his

24 Exod. 20. 11. 25—26 Ps. 2. 1.

own, but everything was held for the common use.   The   33
Apostles continued with great power to bear their testimony
to the resurrection of the Lord Jesus, and God's blessing
rested upon them all abundantly.   Nor was there any one   34
in need among them, for all who were owners of land or
houses sold them, and brought the proceeds of the sales and
laid them at the Apostles' feet ; and then every one received   35
a share in proportion to his wants.   A Levite of   36
Cyprian birth, named Joseph, (who had received from the
Apostles the additional name of ' Barnabas '—which means
' The Consoler,') sold a farm that belonged to him, and brought   37
the money and laid it at the Apostles' feet.

Punishment of   There was, however, a man named Ananias,   1 **5**
Ananias and   who, with his wife Sapphira, sold some property,
Sapphira.   and, with her connivance, kept back some of the   2
proceeds.   He brought only a part and laid it at the Apostles'
feet.

" Ananias," Peter exclaimed, " how is it that Satan has so   3
taken possession of your heart that you have lied to the Holy
Spirit, and kept back a part of the money paid for the land ?
While it was unsold, was not it your own ? and after it was   4
sold, was not the money at your own disposal ? How did
you come to think of such a thing ? You have lied, not to
men, but to God ! "

As Ananias heard these words, he fell down and expired ; and   5
every one who heard of it was appalled.   The young men got   6
up, and, winding the body in a sheet, carried it out and buried it.

After an interval of about three hours his wife came in, not   7
knowing what had happened.

" Is it true," Peter asked, addressing her, " that you sold   8
your land for such a sum ? "

" Yes," she answered, " we did."

Then Peter said : " How did you come to agree to provoke   9
the Spirit of the Lord ? Listen ! The foot-steps of those who
have buried your husband are at the door ; and they will
carry you out too."

Instantly Sapphira fell down at Peter's feet and expired.   On   10
coming in, the young men found her dead ; so they carried her
out and buried her by her husband's side.   The whole   11
Church and all who heard of these events were appalled.

Miracles done   Many signs and wonders continued to occur   12
by the   among the people, through the instrumentality
Apostles.   of the Apostles, whose custom it was to meet all
together in the Colonnade of Solomon ; but of the rest no one   13
ventured to join them.   On the other hand, the people were
full of their praise, and still larger numbers, both of men and   14

women, as they became believers in the Lord, were added to
their number.   The consequence was that people would bring   15
out their sick even into the streets, and lay them on mattresses
and mats, in the hope that, as Peter came by, at least his
shadow might fall on some one of them.   Besides this, the   16
inhabitants of the towns round Jerusalem flocked into the city,
bringing with them their sick and those who were troubled by
foul spirits ; and they were cured every one.

At this the High Priest was roused to action,   17
Peter and and he and all his supporters (who formed the
John again
before   party of the Sadducees), moved by jealousy,
the Council. arrested the Apostles, and had them placed in   18
custody.   An angel of the Lord, however, opened the 19
prison doors at night and led them out.

"Go," he said, "and stand in the Temple Courts, and tell   20
the people the whole Message of this new Life."

When they heard this, they went at daybreak into the Temple 21
Courts, and began to teach.   The High Priest and his
party, on their arrival, summoned the High Council, including
all the leading men among the Israelites, and sent to the gaol
to fetch the Apostles.   But, when the officers got there, they 22
did not find them in the prison ; so they returned and reported that, while they had found the gaol barred securely   23
and the guards posted at the doors, yet, on opening them,
they had not found any one inside.   When the Officer in   24
charge at the Temple and the Chief Priests heard their story,
they were perplexed about the Apostles and as to what all this
would lead to.   Presently, however, some one came and   25
told them, that the men whom they had put in prison were actually standing in the Temple Courts, teaching the people.   On 26
this, the Officer went with his men and fetched the Apostles—
without using violence, for they were afraid of being stoned
by the people—and then brought them before the Council.   27
The High Priest demanded an explanation from them.

"We gave you strict orders," he said, "not to teach in this   28
Name.   Yet you have actually flooded Jerusalem with your
teaching, and you want to make us responsible for the death
of this man."

To this Peter and the Apostles replied :   29

"We must obey God rather than men.   The God of our   30
ancestors raised Jesus, whom you put to death by hanging
him on a cross.   It is this Jesus whom God has exalted to   31
his right hand, to be a Guide and a Saviour, to give Israel
repentance and forgiveness of sins.   And we are witnesses to   32
the truth of this, and so is the Holy Spirit—the gift of God to
those who obey him."

The members of the Council became frantic with rage on hearing 33

30 Deut. 21. 22.

this, and were for putting the Apostles to death. But 34
Gamaliel, a Pharisee, who was a Doctor of the Law and
who was held in universal respect, rose in the Council, and
directed that the men should be taken out of court for a little
while. He then said : 35
"Men of Israel, take care as to what you intend to do with
these men. For not long ago Theudas appeared, professing 36
to be somebody, and was joined by a body of some four hundred men. But he was killed ; and all his followers scattered
and dwindled away. After him, Judas the Galilean appeared 37
at the time of the census, and induced people to follow him ;
yet he, too, perished and all his followers were dispersed. And, 38
in this present case, my advice to you is not to interfere with
these men, but to let them alone, for, if their designs and
their work are merely of human origin, they will come to an
end ; but, if they are of divine origin, you will be powerless to 39
put an end to them—or else you may find yourselves fighting
against God !"
The Council followed his advice, and, calling the Apostles in, 40
had them flogged, and then, after cautioning them not to speak
in the Name of Jesus, set them free. But the Apostles 41
left the Council, rejoicing that they had been thought worthy
to suffer disgrace for that Name ; and never for a single day, 42
either in the Temple Courts or in private houses, did they
cease to teach, or to tell the Good News of Jesus, the Christ.

Appointment of 'The Seven.' About this time, when the number of the disci- 1 **6**
ples was constantly increasing, complaints were
made by the Jews of foreign birth against the
native Jews, that their widows were being overlooked in the
daily distribution. The Twelve, therefore, called together the 2
general body of the disciples and said to them :
"It is not well for us to see to the distribution at the tables
and neglect God's Message. Therefore, Brothers, look for 3
seven men of reputation among yourselves, wise and spiri-
tually-minded men, and we will appoint them to attend to
this matter ; while we, for our part, will devote ourselves to 4
Prayer, and to the delivery of the Message."
This proposal was unanimously agreed to ; and the disciples 5
chose Stephen—a man full of faith and of the Holy Spirit—and
Philip, Prochorus, Nicanor, Timon, Parmenas, and Nicholas
of Antioch, a former convert to Judaism ; and they brought 6
these men to the Apostles, who, after praying, placed their
hands on them.

So God's Message spread, and the number of the disciples 7

continued to increase rapidly in Jerusalem, and a large body
of the priests accepted the Faith.

Stephen's Ministry and Trial. Meanwhile Stephen, divinely helped and streng- 8
thened, was showing great wonders and signs
among the people.   But some members 9
of the Synagogue known as that of Libertines, Cyrenians,
Alexandrians, and Visitors from Cilicia and Roman Asia, were
roused to action and began disputing with Stephen; yet they 10
were quite unable to withstand the wisdom and the inspiration with which he spoke. Then they induced some men to 11
assert that they had heard Stephen saying blasphemous things
against Moses, and against God; and they stirred up the 12
people, as well as the Councillors and the Teachers of the
Law, and set upon Stephen, and arrested him, and brought
him before the High Council. There they produced witnesses 13
who gave false evidence.

"This man," they said, "is incessantly saying things
against this Holy Place and the Law; indeed, we have heard 14
him declare that this Jesus of Nazareth will destroy this Place,
and change the customs handed down to us by Moses."
The eyes of all the members of the Council were riveted upon 15
Stephen, and they saw his face looking like the face of an
angel.

Stephen's Defence. Then the High Priest asked: "Is this true?" 1 **7**
And, upon that, Stephen spoke as follows: 2
"Brothers and Fathers, hear what I have to say.   God,
who manifests himself in the Glory, appeared to our ancestor Abraham, when he was in Mesopotamia, and before
he settled in Haran, and said to him—'Leave your country 3
and your kindred, and come into the country that I will show
you.' On this, Abraham left the country of the Chaldaeans 4
and settled in Haran; and from there, after his father's death,
God caused him to migrate into this very country, in which
you are now living. God did not at that time give him any 5
part of it, not even a foot of ground. But he promised to
'give him possession of it and his descendants after him,'
though at that time he had no child. God's words were 6
these—'Abraham's descendants shall live in a foreign country,
where they will be enslaved and ill-treated for four hundred
years. But I myself will judge the nation, to which they will 7
be enslaved,' God said, 'and after that they shall leave the
country and worship me in this place.' Then God made with 8
Abraham the Covenant of Circumcision; and under it Abraham
became the father of Isaac, and circumcised him when he was
eight days old; and Isaac became the father of Jacob; and

---

[2] Ps. 29. 3.   [3] Gen. 12. 1.   [5] Deut. 2. 5; Gen. 17. 8.   [6—7] Gen. 15. 13—14.
[7] Exod. 3. 12.   [8] Gen. 7. 10; 21. 4.

Jacob of the Twelve Patriarchs.   The Patriarchs, out 9
of jealousy, sold Joseph into slavery in Egypt; but God was
with him, and delivered him out of all his troubles, and 10
enabled him to win favour and show wisdom before Pharaoh,
King of Egypt, who appointed him Governor of Egypt and of
his whole household.   Then a famine spread over the whole 11
of Egypt and Canaan, causing great distress, and our ancestors
could find no food.   Hearing, however, that there was corn 12
in Egypt, Jacob sent our ancestors there on their first visit. In 13
the course of their second visit, Joseph revealed himself to his
brothers, and his family became known to Pharaoh.   Then 14
Joseph sent an urgent invitation to his father Jacob and to
his relations, seventy-five persons in all; and so Jacob went 15
down into Egypt.   There he died, and our ancestors also, and 16
their bodies were removed to Shechem, and laid in the tomb
which Abraham had bought for a sum of money from the
sons of Hamor in Shechem.   As the time drew near 17
for the fulfilment of the promise which God had made to
Abraham, the people increased largely in numbers in Egypt,
until a new king, who knew nothing of Joseph, came to the 18
throne.   This king acted deceitfully towards our race and 19
ill-treated our ancestors, making them abandon their own
infants, so that they should not be reared.   It was just at this 20
time that Moses was born.   He was an exceedingly beautiful
child, and for three months was brought up in his own father's
house; and, when he was abandoned, the daughter of Pharaoh 21
found him and brought him up as her own son.   So Moses 22
was educated in all the learning of the Egyptians, and proved
his ability both by his words and actions.   When he 23
was in his fortieth year, he resolved to visit his brother
Israelites; and, seeing an Israelite ill-treated, he defended 24
him, and avenged the man, who was being wronged, by
striking down the Egyptian.   He thought his brothers 25
would understand that God was using him to save them;
but they failed to do so.   The next day he again appeared 26
upon the scene, when some of them were fighting, and
tried to make peace between them.   'Men,' he said, 'you
are brothers; how is it that you are ill-treating one another?'
But the man who was ill-treating his fellow workman 27
pushed Moses aside saying—'Who made you a ruler and
judge over us?   Do you mean to make away with me as you 28
did yesterday with that Egyptian?'   At these words Moses 29
took to flight, and became an exile in Midian; and there he
had two sons born to him.   Forty years had passed 30
when there appeared to him, in the Desert of Mount Sinai, an
angel in a flame of fire in a bush.   When Moses saw it, he was 31

9 Gen. 37. 11, 28.   10 Gen. 39. 21; 41. 37. 40, 43, 55; Ps. 105. 21.   11—12 Gen. 42. 1.
13 Gen. 45. 1.   14—15 Gen. 46. 27; Exod. 1. 6.   16 Joshua 24. 32; Gen. 50. 13.
17—19 Exod. 1. 7—17.   20—29 Exod. 2. 2—15.   30 Exod. 3. 1—10,

astonished at the vision ; but on his going nearer to look at it
more closely, the voice of the Lord was heard to say—'I am   32
the God of your ancestors, the God of Abraham, Isaac, and
Jacob.' Moses trembled, and did not dare to look.   Then   33
the Lord said to him—'Take your sandals off your feet, for the
spot where you are standing is holy ground.   I have seen the   34
oppression of my people who are in Egypt, and heard their
groans, and I have come down to deliver them.   Come now
and I will send you into Egypt.'   This same Moses,   35
whom they had disowned with the words—'Who made you a
ruler and a judge ?' was the very man whom God sent to be
both a ruler and a deliverer, under the guidance of the angel
that had appeared to him in the bush.   He it was who led them 36
out, after he had shown wonders and signs in Egypt, in the
Red Sea, and in the Desert during forty years.   This was the   37
Moses who said to the people of Israel—'God will raise up for
you, from among your brothers, a Prophet, as he raised up me.'
He, too, it was who was present at the assembly in the Desert,   38
with the angel who talked to him on Mount Sinai, and with
our ancestors, and who received living truths to impart to you.
Yet our ancestors refused him obedience ; more than that,   39
they rejected him, and in their hearts turned back to Egypt,
while they said to Aaron—'Make us Gods who will lead the   40
way for us, since, as for this Moses who has brought us out of
Egypt, we do not know what has become of him.'   That was   41
the time when they made the Calf and offered sacrifice to their
idol, and held festivities in honour of their own handiwork !
So God turned from them and left them to the worship of the   42
Starry Host, as is written in the Book of the Prophets—

   ' Did you offer victims and sacrifices to me, O House of Israel,
      All those forty years in the Desert ?
   You took with you the tabernacle of Moloch   43
   And the Star of the god Rephan—
      The images which you had made to worship.
      Therefore I will exile you beyond Babylon.'

   Our ancestors had the Tabernacle of Revelation in the   44
Desert, constructed, just as he who spoke to Moses had directed
him to make it, after the model which he had seen.   This   45
Tabernacle, which was handed down to them, was brought
into this country by our ancestors who accompanied Joshua
(at the conquest of the nations that God drove out before their
advance), and remained here until the time of David.   David   46
found favour with God, and prayed that he might find a
dwelling for the God of Jacob.   But it was Solomon who   47

31—34 Exod. 3. 1—10.   35 Exod. 2. 14.   33 Exod. 7. 3; 15. 4; Num. 14. 33.
37 Deut. 18. 15.   39 Num. 14. 3.   40—41 Exod. 32. 1—8.   42—43 Jer. 8. 2;
Amos, 5. 25—27.   44 Exod. 27. 21; Exod. 25. 1, 40.   45 Deut. 4. 38.
46 Ps. 132. 5.

built a House for God. Yet it is not in buildings made by   48
hands that the Most High dwells. As the Prophet says—

> ' The heavens are a throne for me,   49
>   And the earth a stool for my feet.
> What manner of House will you build me, saith the Lord,
>   Or what place is there where I may rest?
>   Was it not my hand that made all these things?'   50

O ! stubborn race, heathen in heart and ears, you are for   51
ever resisting the Holy Spirit ; your ancestors did it, and you
are doing it still. Which of the Prophets escaped persecution   52
at their hands? They killed those who foretold the coming
of the Righteous One ; of whom you, in your turn, have now
become the betrayers and murderers—you who received the   53
Law as transmitted by angels and yet failed to keep it."

Stephen's Martyrdom. As they listened to this, the Council grew fran-   54
tic with rage, and gnashed their teeth at Stephen.
He, filled as he was with the Holy Spirit, fixed his eyes in-   55
tently on the heavens, and saw the Glory of God and Jesus
standing at God's right hand.

"Look," he exclaimed, "I see Heaven open and the Son   56
of Man standing at God's right hand ! "
At this, with a loud shout, they stopped their ears and all   57
rushed upon him, forced him outside the city, and began to   58
stone him, the witnesses laying their clothes at the feet of a
young man named Saul. And they stoned Stephen, while he   59
cried to the Lord : "Lord Jesus ! receive my spirit ! "
Falling on his knees, he called out loudly :   60

"Lord ! do not charge them with this sin ; " and with these
words he fell asleep.
Saul approved of his being put to death.   1   **8**

The First Persecution. On that very day a great persecution broke out
against the Church which was in Jerusalem ; and
its members, with the exception of the Apostles, were all
scattered over the districts of Judaea and Samaria. Some   2
religious men buried Stephen, with loud lamentations for him.
But Saul began to devastate the Church ; he entered house   3
after house, dragged out men and women alike, and threw
them into prison.

Philip's Ministry in Samaria. Now those who were scattered in different   4
directions went from place to place proclaiming
the Good News. Philip went down to the city of   5
Samaria, and there began to preach the Christ. The people,   6
one and all, listened attentively to what Philip told them,
when they heard of, and saw, the miracles which he was

working. For there were many instances of people with foul 7 spirits, where the spirits, with loud screams, came out of them; and many who were paralyzed or lame were cured, so 8 that there was great rejoicing throughout that city.

There was staying in the city a man named Simon, who 9 had been practising magic there and mystifying the Samaritan people, giving himself out to be some great Being. Every 10 one, high and low, paid attention to him. 'This man,' they used to say, 'must be that Power of God which men call "The Great Power."' And they paid attention to him because 11 they had for a long time been mystified by his magic arts. However, when they came to believe Philip, as he told them 12 the Good News about the Kingdom of God and the Name of Jesus Christ, they were baptized, both men and women. Even 13 Simon believed, and after his baptism attached himself to Philip, and was in his turn mystified at seeing signs and great miracles constantly occurring.

Peter and John at Samaria. When the Apostles at Jerusalem heard that the 14 Samaritans had welcomed God's Message, they sent Peter and John to them; and they, on their 15 arrival, prayed that the Samaritans might receive the Holy Spirit. (As yet the Spirit had not descended upon 16 any of them; they had only been baptized into the Faith of the Lord Jesus). Then Peter and John placed their hands on 17 them, and they received the Holy Spirit. When Simon 18 saw that it was through the placing of the Apostles' hands on them that the Spirit was given, he brought them a sum of money and said:

"Give me also this power of yours, so that, if I place my 19 hands upon any one, he may receive the Holy Spirit."

"A curse upon you and upon your money," Peter ex- 20 claimed, "for thinking that God's free gift can be bought with gold! You have no share or part in our Message, for your 21 'heart is not right with God.' Therefore repent of this 22 wickedness of yours, and pray to the Lord, that, if possible, you may be forgiven for such a thought; for I see that 23 you have fallen into the 'bitterness of envy' and the 'fetters of sin.'"

"Pray to the Lord for me, all of you," Simon answered, 24 "so that none of the things you have spoken of may befall me."

Peter and John, having borne their testimony and delivered 25 the Lord's Message, returned to Jerusalem, telling the Good News, as they went, in many Samaritan villages.

Philip and the Abyssinian. Meanwhile an angel of the Lord had said to 26 Philip: "Set out on a journey southwards, along the

21 Ps. 78. 37.　23 Deut. 29. 18; Isa. 58. 6.

road that runs down from Jerusalem to Gaza." (It is now deserted).

So Philip set out on a journey; and on his way he came upon 27 an official of high rank, in the service of Candace, Queen of the Abyssinians. He was her Treasurer, and had been to Jerusalem to worship, and was now on his way home, sitting 28 in his carriage and reading the Prophet Isaiah. The Spirit 29 said to Philip:

"Go up to the carriage yonder and keep close to it."

So Philip ran up, and he heard the Abyssinian reading the 30 Prophet Isaiah.

"Do you understand what you are reading?" he asked.

"How can I," the other answered, "unless some one will 31 explain it to me?" and he invited Philip to get up and sit by his side. The passage of Scripture which he was reading 32 was this—

'Like a sheep, he was led away to slaughter,
    And as a lamb is dumb in the hands of its shearer,
    So he refrains from opening his lips.
In his lowly condition justice was denied him. 33
Who will tell the story of his generation?
    For his life is cut off from earth.'

"Now," said the Treasurer, addressing Philip, "tell 34 me, of whom is the Prophet speaking? Of himself, or of some one else?"

Then Philip began, and, taking this passage as his text, told 35 him the Good News about Jesus. Presently, as they were 36 going along the road, they came to some water, and the Treasurer exclaimed:

"Look! here is water; what is to prevent my being baptized?"

So he ordered the carriage to stop, and they went down into 38 the water—both Philip and the Treasurer—and Philip baptized him. But, when they came up out of the water, the Spirit of 39 the Lord caught Philip away, and the Treasurer saw no more of him; for he continued his journey with a joyful heart. But 40 Philip was found at Ashdod, and, as he went on his way, he told the Good News in all the towns through which he passed, till he came to Caesarea.

Saul's Conversion. Meanwhile Saul, still breathing murderous 1 **9** threats against the disciples of the Lord, went to the High Priest, and asked him to give him letters to the 2 Jewish congregations at Damascus, authorizing him, if he found there any supporters of the Cause, whether men or women, to have them put in chains and brought to Jerusalem.

32—33 Isa. 53. 7, 8.

While on his journey, as he was nearing Damascus, sud- 3
denly a light from the heavens flashed around him. He fell 4
to the ground and heard a voice saying to him—"Saul, Saul,
why are you persecuting me?"

"Who are you, Lord?" he asked. 5

"I am Jesus, whom you are persecuting," the voice answered; "yet stand up and go into the city, and you will be 6
told what you must do."

The men travelling with Saul were meanwhile standing 7
speechless; they heard the sound of the voice, but saw no one.
When Saul got up from the ground, though his eyes were 8
open, he could see nothing. So his men led him by the
hand, and brought him into Damascus; and for three days 9
he was unable to see, and took nothing either to eat or to
drink.

Saul at Damascus. Now there was at Damascus a disciple named 10
Ananias, to whom, in a vision, the Lord said:
"Ananias."

"Yes, Lord," he answered.

"Go at once," said the Lord, "to the 'Straight Street', and 11
ask at Judas's house for a man named Saul, from Tarsus. He
is at this moment praying, and he has seen, in a vision, a man 12
named Ananias coming in and placing his hands on him, so
that he may recover his sight."

"Lord," exclaimed Ananias, "I have heard from many 13
people about this man—how much harm he has done at
Jerusalem to your People there. And, here, too, he holds 14
authority from the Chief Priests to put in chains all those who
invoke your Name."

But the Lord said to him: "Go, for this man is my chosen 15
instrument to uphold my Name before the Gentiles and their
kings, and the people of Israel. I will myself show him all 16
that he has to suffer for my Name."

So Ananias went, entered the house, and, placing his hands 17
on Saul, said:

"Saul, my Brother, I have been sent by the Lord—by Jesus,
who appeared to you on your way here—so that you may
recover your sight and be filled with the Holy Spirit."

Instantly it seemed as if a film fell from Saul's eyes, and his 18
sight was restored. Then he got up and was baptized, and, 19
after he had taken food, he felt his strength return.

Saul stayed for some days with the disciples who were at
Damascus, and at once began in the Synagogues to pro- 20
claim Jesus as the Son of God. All who heard him were 21
amazed.

"Is not this," they asked, "the man who worked havoc in
Jerusalem among those that invoke this Name, and who had

also come here for the express purpose of having such persons put in chains and taken before the Chief Priests?"

Saul's influence, however, kept steadily increasing, and he 22 confounded the Jews who lived in Damascus by the proofs that he gave that Jesus was the Christ.

After some time the Jews laid a plot to kill Saul, but it 23 became known to him. They even watched the gates day 24 and night, to kill him; but his disciples let him down by 25 night through an opening in the wall, lowering him in a basket.

Saul at Jerusalem and Tarsus. On his arrival in Jerusalem, Saul attempted to 26 join the disciples, but they were all afraid of him, as they did not believe that he was really a disciple. Barnabas, however, taking him by the hand, brought 27 him to the Apostles, and told them the whole story of how Saul on his journey had seen the Lord, and how the Lord had talked to him, and how in Damascus he had spoken out fearlessly in the Name of Jesus. After that, Saul remained in 28 Jerusalem, in close intercourse with the Apostles; and he 29 spoke fearlessly in the Name of the Lord, talking and arguing with the Jews of foreign birth, who, however, made attempts to kill him. But, when the Brethren found this out, 30 they took him down to Caesarea, and sent him on his way to Tarsus.

And so it came about that the Church, throughout Judaea, 31 Galilee, and Samaria, enjoyed peace and became firmly established; and, ordering its life by reverence for the Lord and the help of the Holy Spirit, it increased in numbers.

Peter's Miracles at Lydda and Jaffa. Peter, while travelling from place to place 32 throughout the country, went down to visit the People of Christ living at Lydda. There he found 33 a man named Aeneas, who had been bed-ridden for eight years with paralysis.

"Aeneas," Peter said to him, "Jesus Christ cures you. Get 34 up, and make your bed."

Aeneas got up at once; and all the inhabitants of Lydda and 35 of the Plain of Sharon saw him, and came over to the Lord's side.

At Jaffa there lived a disciple whose name was Tabitha, 36 which is in Greek 'Dorcas'—a Gazelle. Her life was spent in doing kind and charitable actions. Just at that time she 37 was taken ill, and died; and they had washed her body and laid it out in an upstairs room. Jaffa was near Lydda, 38

and the disciples, having heard that Peter was at Lydda, sent
two men with the request that he would come on to them without delay.　Peter returned with them at once.　On his arrival, 39
he was taken upstairs, and all the widows came round him in
tears, showing the coats and other clothing which Dorcas had
made while she was among them.　But Peter sent everybody 40
out of the room, and knelt down and prayed.　Then, turning
to the body, he said :

"Tabitha ! stand up."

She opened her eyes, and, seeing Peter, sat up.　Giving her 41
his hand, Peter raised her up, and, calling in the widows and
others of Christ's People, presented her to them alive.　This 42
became known all through Jaffa, and numbers of people came
to believe in the Lord.　　　　And Peter stayed some days 43
at Jaffa with a tanner named Simon.

10

Peter
and
Cornelius.
There was then in Caesarea a man named 1
Cornelius, a Captain in the regiment known
as the 'Italian Regiment,' a religious man and 2
one who reverenced God, with all his household.　He was
liberal in his charities to the people, and prayed to God constantly.　One afternoon, about three o'clock, he distinctly saw 3
in a vision an angel from God come to him, and call him
by name.　Cornelius fixed his eyes on him and, in great alarm, 4
said : "What is it, Lord ?"

"Your prayers and your charities," the angel answered,
"have been an acceptable offering to God.　And now, send 5
messengers to Jaffa and fetch a man called Simon, who is also
known as Peter.　He is lodging with a tanner named Simon, 6
who has a house near the sea."

When the angel, who had spoken to him, had gone, Cornelius 7
called two menservants and a religious soldier, who was one
of his constant attendants, and, after telling them the whole 8
story, sent them to Jaffa.

On the next day, while these men were on their way, just 9
as they were nearing the town, Peter went up on the house-
top about mid-day to pray.　He became hungry and wanted 10
something to eat; but, while it was being prepared, he fell into
a trance, and saw that the heavens were open, and that some- 11
thing like a great sail was descending, let down by its four
corners towards the earth.　In it were all kinds of quadrupeds, 12
reptiles, and birds.　Then he was aware of a voice which said 13
—"Stand up, Peter, kill something, and eat."

"No, Lord, I cannot," answered Peter, "for I have never 14
eaten anything 'defiled' and 'unclean'."

Again he was aware of a voice which said—"What God 15
has pronounced 'clean', do not regard as 'defiled'."

4 Enoch 99. 3.

This happened three times, and then suddenly it was all 16
taken up into the heavens.

While Peter was still perplexed as to the meaning of the 17
vision that he had seen, the men sent by Cornelius, having
enquired the way to Simon's house, came up to the gate, and 18
called out and asked if the Simon, who was also known as
Peter, was lodging there.   Peter was still pondering 19
over the vision, when the Spirit said to him :

"There are two men looking for you at this moment. Go 20
down at once and do not hesitate to go with them, for I have
sent them."

Peter went down to the men and said : 21

"I am the man for whom you are looking. What is your
reason for coming?"

The men replied : 22

"Our captain, Cornelius, a pious man who reverences God
and is well spoken of by the whole Jewish nation, has been
instructed by a holy angel to send for you to his house, and
to listen to what you have to say."

Upon this Peter invited them in and entertained them. 23

The next day he lost no time in setting out with them,
accompanied by some of the Brethren from Jaffa ; and the 24
day following he entered Caesarea. Cornelius was expecting
them, and had invited his relations and intimate friends to
meet them. So, when Peter entered the city, Cornelius 25
met him, and, throwing himself at Peter's feet, bowed to the
ground. Peter, however, lifted him up, saying as he did so : 26

"Stand up, I am only a man like yourself."

Talking with him as he went, Peter entered the house, where 27
he found a large gathering of people, to whom he said : 28

"You are doubtless aware that it is forbidden for a Jew to
be intimate with a foreigner, or even to enter his house ;
and yet God has shown me that I ought not to call any
man 'defiled' or 'unclean.' That was why I came, when I 29
was sent for, without raising any objection. And now I ask
your reason for sending for me."

"Just three days ago this very hour," Cornelius said, "I 30
was in my house, saying the Afternoon Prayers, when a
man in dazzling clothing suddenly stood before me. 'Cornelius,' 31
he said, 'your prayer has been heard, and your charities have
been accepted, by God. Therefore send to Jaffa, and invite 32
the Simon, who is also known as Peter, to come here. He is
lodging in the house of Simon the tanner, near the sea.'
Accordingly I sent to you at once, and you have been so good 33
as to come. And now we are all here in the presence of God,
to listen to all that you have been instructed by the Lord to say."

Then Peter began. 34

"I see, beyond all doubt," he said, "that 'God does not

34 Deut. 10. 17.

I*

show partiality,' but that in every nation he who reverences **35**
him and does what is right is acceptable to him. God has **36**
sent his Message to the Israelites and told them, through
Jesus Christ, the Good News of peace—and Jesus is Lord of
all ! You yourselves know the story which spread through all **37**
Judaea, how, beginning from Galilee, after the baptism which
John proclaimed—the story, I mean, of Jesus of Nazareth, **38**
and how God consecrated him his Christ by enduing him with
the Holy Spirit and with power ; and how he went about
doing good and curing all who were under the power of the
Devil, because God was with him. We are ourselves, too, **39**
witnesses to all that he did in Judaea and in Jerusalem ; yet
they put him to death by hanging him on a cross ! This Jesus **40**
God raised on the third day, and enabled him to appear, not **41**
indeed to every one, but to witnesses chosen beforehand by
God—to us, who ate and drank with him after his resurrection from the dead. Further, God charged us to proclaim to **42**
the people, and solemnly affirm, that it is Jesus who has been
appointed by God Judge of the living and the dead. To him **43**
it is that all the Prophets bear witness, when they say that
every one who believes in him receives through his Name
forgiveness of sins."

First Before Peter had finished saying these words, **44**
Conversion the Holy Spirit fell on all who were listening to
of Gentiles. the Message. Those converts from Judaism, **45**
who had come with Peter, were amazed that the gift of the
Holy Spirit had been bestowed even upon the Gentiles ; for **46**
they heard them speaking with 'tongues' and extolling God.
At this Peter asked :

"Can any one refuse the water for the baptism of these **47**
people, now that they have received the Holy Spirit as we did
ourselves ? "

And he directed that they should be baptized in the Faith of **48**
Jesus Christ ; after which they asked him to stay there a
few days longer.

Peter's The Apostles and the Brethren throughout **1   11**
Defence of Judaea heard that even the Gentiles had wel-
his Action. comed God's Message.   But, when Peter **2**
went up to Jerusalem, those who were converts from Judaism
began to attack him on the ground that he had visited people **3**
who were not circumcised, and had taken meals with them.
So Peter began to relate the facts to them as they had oc- **4**
curred.

"I was in the town of Jaffa," he said, "and was praying ; **5**
and, while in a trance, I saw a vision. There was something
like a great sail descending, let down by its four corners out
of the heavens ; and it came right down to me. Looking **6**

³⁶ Ps. 147. 18—19; Isa. 52. 7. ³⁸ Isa. 61. 1. ³⁹ Deut. 21. 22.

intently at it, I began to distinguish quadrupeds, wild beasts, reptiles, and birds ; and I also heard a voice saying to me—'Stand up, Peter, kill something and eat.' 'No, Lord, I cannot,' I answered, 'for nothing defiled' or 'unclean' has ever passed my lips.' Then a second time there came a voice from the heavens. "What God has pronounced 'clean '," it said, "you must not call 'defiled '." This happened three times, and then all was drawn up again into the heavens. At that moment three men, who had been sent from Caesarea to see me, came up to the house in which we were. The Spirit told me to go with them without hesitation. These six Brothers also went with me. And, when we came into the man's house, he told us how he had seen the angel standing in his house, and how the angel had said to him—'Send to Jaffa and fetch the Simon, who is also known as Peter; for he will tell you truths, which will prove the means of Salvation to you and all your household.' I had but just begun to speak," continued Peter, "when the Holy Spirit fell on them, exactly as on us at the first ; and I recalled the saying of the Master—'John baptized with water, but you shall be baptized with the Holy Spirit.' Since then, God had given them the very same gift as he gave us when we became believers in Jesus Christ the Master—who was I that I could thwart God ? "

On hearing this statement, they said no more, but broke out into praise of God. "So even to the Gentiles," they exclaimed, "God has granted the repentance which leads to Life !"

'Christians' at Antioch. Now those who had been scattered in different directions, in consequence of the persecution that followed upon the death of Stephen, went as far as Phoenicia, Cyprus, and Antioch, telling the Message—but only to Jews. Some of them, however, who were men of Cyprus and Cyrene, on coming to Antioch, addressed themselves also to the Jews of foreign birth, telling them the Good News about the Lord Jesus. The power of the Lord was with them, so that a great number who had learnt to believe came over to the Lord's side. The news about them reached the ears of the Church at Jerusalem, and they sent Barnabas to Antioch. On coming there he saw to his great joy these tokens of the loving-kindness of God, and encouraged them all to make up their minds to be faithful to the Lord—for Barnabas was a good man and full of the Holy Spirit and of faith—and a large number of people took their stand on the Lord's side. Afterwards Barnabas left for Tarsus to look for Saul ; and, when he had found him, he brought him to

¹⁸ Wisd. of Sol. 12. 10.

Antioch. And so it came about that, for a whole year, they attended the meetings of the Church there, and taught a large number of people ; and it was in Antioch that the disciples were first called ' Christians.'

Errand of Barnabas and Saul to Judaea. During this time, some Prophets came to Antioch from Jerusalem. One of them, named Agabus, came forward and, under the influence of the Spirit, foretold a great famine that was to spread over all the world—a famine which occurred in the reign of Claudius. So the disciples, without exception, determined, in proportion to their means, to send something to help the Brethren living in Judaea. And this they did, sending it to the Officers of the Church by the hands of Barnabas and Saul. 27 28 29 30

Persecution of the Church by Herod Agrippa I. It was at that time that King Herod began to illtreat some of the members of the Church. He had James, the brother of John, beheaded ; and, when he saw that the Jews were pleased with this, he proceeded to arrest Peter also. (This was during the Festival of the Unleavened Bread.) After seizing Peter, Herod put him in prison, and entrusted him to the keeping of four Guards of four soldiers each, intending, after the Passover, to bring him up before the people. So Peter was kept in prison, but meanwhile the prayers of the Church were being earnestly offered to God on his behalf. Just when Herod was intending to bring him before the people, on that very night Peter was asleep between two soldiers, chained to them both, while there were sentries in front of the door, guarding the prison. Suddenly an angel of the Lord stood by him, and a light shone in the cell. The angel struck Peter on the side, and roused him with the words : " Get up quickly." 1 **12** 2 3 4 5 6 7

The chains dropped from his wrists, and then the angel said : " Put on your girdle and sandals." 8

When Peter had done so, the angel added : " Throw your cloak round you and follow me."

Peter followed him out, not knowing that what was happening under the angel's guidance was real, but thinking that he was seeing a vision. Passing the first Guard, and then the second, they came to the iron gate leading into the city, which opened to them of itself ; and, when they had passed through that, and had walked along one street, all at once the angel left him. Then Peter came to himself and said : 9 10 11

" Now I know beyond all doubt that the Lord has sent his angel, and has rescued me from Herod's hands and from all that the Jewish people have been expecting."

As soon as he realized what had happened, he went to the 12
house of Mary, the mother of John who was also known as
Mark, where a number of people were gathered together,
praying. On his knocking at the door in the gate, a maid- 13
servant, named Rhoda, came to answer it. She recognized 14
Peter's voice, but in her joy left the gate unopened, and
ran in, and told them that Peter was standing outside.

"You are mad!" they exclaimed. 15
But, when she persisted that it was so, they said :
"It must be his spirit!"
Meanwhile Peter went on knocking, and, when they opened 16
the gate and saw him, they were amazed. Peter signed to 17
them with his hand to be silent, and then told them how the
Lord had brought him out of the prison, adding :
"Tell James and the Brethren all this."
Then he left the house, and went away to another place.   In 18
the morning there was a great stir among the soldiers—
what could have become of Peter! And, when Herod had 19
made further search for him and failed to find him, he closely
questioned the Guard, and ordered them away to execution.
Then he went down from Judaea to stay at Caesarea.

Herod's Death. It happened that Herod was deeply offended 20
with the people of Tyre and Sidon, but they went
in a body to him, and, having succeeded in winning over
Blastus, the Chamberlain, they begged Herod for a reconciliation, because their country was dependent on the King's
for its food-supply. On an appointed day Herod, wearing his 21
state-robes, seated himself on his throne, and delivered an
oration. The people kept shouting : "It is the voice of God, 22
and not of a man!"
Instantly an angel of the Lord struck him, because he did not 23
give God the glory ; and he was attacked with worms, and died.

Meanwhile the Lord's Message kept extending, and spread- 24
ing far and wide.

When Barnabas and Saul had carried out their mission, 25
they returned to Jerusalem, and took with them John, who
was also known as Mark.

II.—THE CHURCH AND THE GENTILES.

Doings of the Apostle Paul.

PAUL'S FIRST MISSIONARY JOURNEY. Among the members of the Church at Antioch 1
there were several Prophets and Teachers—·
Barnabas, Simeon who was known by the name
The Start from Antioch. of 'Black', Lucius of Cyrene, Manaen, foster-
brother of Prince Herod, and Saul.   While 2

they were engaged in the worship of the Lord and were fasting, the Holy Spirit said :

"Set apart for me Barnabas and Saul, for the work to which I have called them."

Accordingly, after fasting and prayer, they placed their hands on them and dismissed them.   3

Paul and Barnabas at Cyprus. Barnabas and Saul, sent on this mission, as they were, by the Holy Spirit, went down to Seleucia, and from there sailed to Cyprus. On reaching Salamis, they began to tell the Message of God in the Jewish Synagogues ; and they had John with them as an assistant.   4 5

After passing through the whole island, they reached Paphos, where they found an astrologer who pretended to be a Prophet —a Jew by birth, whose name was Barjoshua. He was at the court of the Governor, Sergius Paulus, a man of intelligence, who sent for Barnabas and Saul and asked to be told God's Message. But Elymas, the astrologer (for that is the meaning of the word), opposed them, eager to divert the Governor's attention from the Faith. However, Saul (who is the same as Paul), full of the Holy Spirit, fixed his eyes on him and said :   6 7 8 9 10

"You incarnation of deceit and all fraud ! You son of the Devil ! You opponent of all that is good ! Will you never cease to divert 'the straight paths of the Lord'? Listen ! The hand of the Lord is upon you even now, and you will be blind for a time and unable to see the sun."   11

Immediately a mist and darkness fell upon him, and he went feeling about for some one to guide him. When the Governor saw what had happened, he became a believer in Christ, being greatly impressed by the teaching about the Lord.   12

Paul and Barnabas at Pisidian Antioch. After this, Paul and his companions set sail from Paphos and went to Perga in Pamphylia, where John left them and returned to Jerusalem. The others went on from Perga and arrived at Antioch in Pisidia. There they went into the Synagogue on the Sabbath and took their seats. After the reading of the Law and the Prophets, the Presidents of the Synagogue sent them this message—"Brothers, if you have any helpful words to address to the people, now is the time to speak."   13 14 15

So Paul rose and, motioning with his hand, spoke as follows :   16

"Men of Israel and all here who reverence God, hear what I have to say.   The God of this people Israel chose our ancestors, and during their stay in Egypt increased the prosperity of the people, and then 'with uplifted arm brought them out from that land.' For about forty years 'he bore with   17 18

[19] Hos. 14. 9.   [17] Exod. 6. 6.   [18] Deut. 1. 31.

them in the Desert'; then, after destroying seven heathen   19
nations in Canaan, he allotted their land to this people—for
about four hundred and fifty years. In later times he gave   20
them Judges, of whom the Prophet Samuel was the last. And,   21
when they demanded a king, God gave them Saul the son of
Kish, a man of the tribe of Benjamin, who reigned for forty
years. After removing him, he raised David to the throne,   22
and bore this testimony to him—'In David, the son of Jesse,
I have found a man after my own heart, who will carry
out all my purposes.' It was from this man's descendants   23
that God, in accordance with his promise, gave Israel a
Saviour—Jesus; John having first proclaimed, before the   24
appearance of Jesus, a baptism upon repentance for all the
people of Israel. As John was drawing towards the end of   25
his career, he said 'What do you suppose that I am? I am
not the Christ. But there is "One Coming" after me, whose
very sandal I am not worthy to untie.'   Brothers,   26
descendants of Abraham, and all those among you who reverence God, it was to us that the Message of this Salvation
was sent. The people of Jerusalem and their leading men,   27
failing to recognize Jesus, and not understanding the utterances of the Prophets that are read every Sabbath, fulfilled
them by condemning him. They found no ground at all   28
for putting him to death, and yet demanded his execution
from Pilate; and, after carrying out everything written   29
about him, they took Jesus down from the cross, and laid
him in a tomb. But God raised him from the dead; and   30, 31
he appeared for many days to those who had gone up with
him from Galilee to Jerusalem, and who are now witnesses
for him to the people. We also have good news to tell you,   32
about the promise made to our ancestors—that our children   33
have had this promise completely fulfilled to them by God,
by his raising Jesus. That is just what is said in the second
Psalm—

'Thou art my Son; this day I have become thy Father.'

As to his raising Jesus from the dead, never again to return   34
to corruption, this is what is said—

'I will give to you the sacred promises made to David;'

and, therefore, in another Psalm it is said—   35

'Thou wilt not give up thy Holy One to undergo corruption.'

David, after obediently doing God's will in his own time, 'fell   36
asleep and was laid by the side of his ancestors', and did
undergo corruption; but Jesus, whom God raised from the   37
dead, did not undergo corruption.   I would, therefore,   38

---

[19] Deut. 7. 1; Joshua 14. 1.   [22] Ps. 89. 20; 1 Sam. 13. 14.   [25] Ps. 118. 26.
[33] Ps. 2. 7.   [34] Isa. 55. 3.   [35] Ps. 16. 10.   [36] 1 Kings 2. 10.

have you know, Brothers, that through Jesus forgiveness of
sins is being proclaimed to you, and that, in union with him,   39
every one who believes in him is absolved from every sin from
which under the Law of Moses you could not be absolved.
Beware, therefore, that what is said in the Prophets does not   40
come true of you—

'Look, you despisers, and wonder, and perish;   41
  For I am doing a deed in your days—
    A deed which, though told you in full, you will never believe'."

As Paul and Barnabas were leaving the Synagogue, the   42
people begged for a repetition of this teaching on the next
Sabbath. After the congregation had dispersed, many of the   43
Jews, and of the converts who joined in their worship, followed
Paul and Barnabas, who talked with them and urged them to
continue to rely upon the loving-kindness of God.

On the following Sabbath, almost all the city gathered to   44
hear God's Message. But the sight of the crowds of people   45
filled the minds of the Jews with jealousy, and they kept con-
tradicting Paul's statements in violent language. Then Paul   46
and Barnabas spoke out fearlessly, and said:

"It was necessary that the Message of God should be told
to you first; but, since you reject it and reckon yourselves not
worthy of the Immortal Life—we turn to the Gentiles! For   47
this is the Lord's command to us—

'I have destined thee for a Light to the Gentiles,
  A means of Salvation to the ends of the earth'."

On hearing this, the Gentiles were glad and extolled God's   48
Message; and all those who had been enrolled for Immortal
Life became believers in Christ; and the Lord's Message was   49
carried throughout that district. But the Jews incited the   50
women of position who worshipped with them, and the
leading men of the town, and started a persecution against
Paul and Barnabas, and drove them out of their neighbourhood. They, however, shook the dust off their feet in protest,   51
and went to Iconium, leaving the disciples full of joy and of   52
the Holy Spirit.

Paul and Barnabas at Iconium. The same thing occurred in Iconium, where   1   **14**
Paul and Barnabas went into the Jewish Syna-
gogue, and spoke in such a way that a great
number of both Jews and Greeks believed in Christ. But the   2
Jews who refused to believe stirred up the Gentiles, and
poisoned their minds against the Brethren. Therefore Paul   3
and Barnabas spent a long time there, and spoke out fearlessly, relying upon the Lord, who confirmed the Message of
his Love by permitting signs and wonders to take place at

41 Hab. 1. 5.   47 Isa. 49. 6.

their hands. But the townspeople were divided, some siding 4
with the Jews, some with the Apostles; and, when there was 5
an attempt on the part of both Gentiles and Jews, with their
leading men, to resort to violence and to stone them, the 6
Apostles heard of it, and took refuge in Lystra and Derbe,
towns in Lycaonia, and in the district round, and there they 7
continued to tell the Good News.

Paul and Barnabas at Lystra. In the streets of Lystra there used to sit a 8
man who had no power in his feet; he had been
lame from his birth, and had never walked. This 9
man was listening to Paul speaking, when Paul, fixing his
eyes on him, and seeing that he had the faith to be healed,
said loudly: " Stand upright on your feet." 10
The man leaped up, and began walking about, and the 11
crowd, seeing what Paul had done, called out in the
Lycaonian language:
"The Gods have made themselves like men and have come
down to us."
So they called Barnabas ' Zeus,' and Paul ' Hermes,' because 12
he took the lead in speaking; and the priest of Zeus- 13
beyond-the-Walls, accompanied by the crowd, brought bullocks and garlands to the gates, with the intention of offering
sacrifices. But, when the Apostles Barnabas and Paul 14
heard of it, they tore their clothes and rushed out into the
crowd.
" Friends, why are you doing this?" they shouted. "We 15
are only men like yourselves, and we have come with the
Good News that you should turn away from these follies to a
living God, ' who made the heavens, the earth, the sea, and
everything that is in them.' In bygone times he permitted all 16
the nations to go their own ways. Yet he has not failed to 17
give you, in the good he does, some revelation of himself—
sending you from Heaven rain and fruitful seasons, and
gladdening your hearts with plenty and good cheer."
Even with this appeal they could hardly restrain the people 18
from offering sacrifice to them.
Presently, however, there came some Jews from Antioch 19
and Iconium who, after they had won over the people, stoned
Paul, and dragged him out of the town, thinking him to be
dead. But, when the disciples had gathered round him, he got 20
up and went back into the town; the next day he went with
Barnabas to Derbe. After telling the Good 21
News throughout that town, and making a
number of converts, they returned to Lystra,
Iconium, and Antioch, reassuring the minds of 22
the disciples, urging them to remain true to the
Faith, and showing that it is only through many troubles that
we can enter the Kingdom of God. They also appointed Officers 23

Paul and Barnabas return to Pisidian Antioch.

15 Ps. 146. 5—6.

for them in every Church, and, after prayer and fasting,
commended them to the Lord in whom they had learnt to
believe. Paul and Barnabas then went through Pisidia, and   24
came into Pamphylia, and, after telling the Message at Perga, 25
                   went down to Attaleia. From there they sailed to 26
Paul and   Antioch—the place where they had been com-
Barnabas   mitted to the gracious care of God for the work
again
at Syrian   which they had now finished.   After their 27
Antioch.   arrival, they gathered the Church together, and
gave an account of all that God had helped them to do, and
especially how he had opened to the Gentiles the door of
faith ; and at Antioch they stayed with the disciples for a   28
considerable time.

The Council   But certain persons came down from Judaea,   1 **15**
at   and began to teach the Brethren that, unless
Jerusalem.   they were circumcised, in accordance with the
custom enjoined by Moses, they could not be saved. This   2
gave rise to a serious dispute, and much discussion, between
Paul and Barnabas and these men, and it was therefore settled
that Paul and Barnabas and others of their number should go
up to Jerusalem, to consult the Apostles and Officers of the
Church about the matter under discussion.

The Church, therefore, sent them on their journey, and they   3
made their way through Phoenicia and Samaria, telling the
story of the conversion of the Gentiles, to the great joy of all
the Brethren. On their arrival at Jerusalem, they were   4
welcomed by the Church, as well as by the Apostles and the
Officers, and gave an account of all that God had helped them
to do.   Some of the Pharisees' party, however, who   5
had become believers in Christ, came forward and declared
that they were bound to circumcise converts and to direct them
to observe the Law of Moses.

The Apostles and the Officers of the Church held a meeting   6
to consider this question.   After much discussion, Peter 7
rose and said :
"You, my Brothers, know well that long ago God singled
me out—that through my lips the Gentiles should hear the
Message of the Good News, and become believers in Christ.
Now God, who reads all hearts, declared his acceptance   8
of the Gentiles, by giving them the Holy Spirit, just as
he did to us. He made no distinction between them and   9
us, when he purified their hearts by their faith. Why,   10
then, do you now provoke God, by putting on the necks of
these disciples a yoke which neither our ancestors nor we were

able to bear? No, it is through the loving-kindness of the   11
Lord Jesus that we, just as they do, believe that we have been
saved."

Every voice in the assembly was hushed, as they listened   12
to Barnabas and Paul, while they gave an account of all the
signs and wonders which God had shown among the Gentiles
through them.   After they had finished speaking, James   13
addressed the Council.

"Brothers," he began, "hear what I have to say. Simon   14
has described the manner in which God first visited the
Gentiles, in order to take from among them a people to bear
his Name. And that is in harmony with the words of the   15
Prophets, where they say—

'"After this I will return;   16
And I will rebuild the House of David which has fallen—
Its very ruins I will rebuild,
    And will set it up once more;
That so the rest of mankind may earnestly seek the Lord—   17
Even all the Gentiles on whom my Name has been bestowed,"
    Says the Lord, as he does these things, foreknown from of old.'   18

In my judgement, therefore, we should not add to the   19
difficulties of those Gentiles who are turning to God, but we   20
should write to them to abstain from food that has been
polluted by being sacrificed to idols, from impurity, from eating the flesh of strangled animals, and from blood. For in   21
every town, for generations past, there have been those who
preach Moses, read as he is in the Synagogues every Sabbath."

It was then decided by the Apostles and the Officers, with the   22
assent of the whole Church, to choose some of their number,
and send them to Antioch with Paul and Barnabas. Those
chosen were Judas (called Barsabas) and Silas, who were
leading men among the Brethren. They were bearers of the   23
following letter—

' The Apostles, and the Brothers who are the Officers
of the Church, send their greetings to the Brethren of
Gentile birth in Antioch, Syria, and Cilicia.

As we had heard that some of our number had upset   24
you by their assertions, and unsettled your minds—
without instructions from us—we met and decided to   25
choose certain men and send them to you with our
dear brothers Barnabas and Paul, who have sacrificed   26
themselves for the Name of our Lord, Jesus Christ.
We are accordingly sending Judas and Silas, and   27
they will tell you by word of mouth what we are now
writing. We have, therefore, decided, under the   28
guidance of the Holy Spirit, to lay no further burden

upon you beyond these necessary conditions—that you 29
abstain from food offered to idols, from blood, from
eating the flesh of strangled animals, and from
impurity.   If you guard yourselves against such
things, it will be well with you.   Farewell.'

So the bearers of this letter were sent on their way, and 30
went down to Antioch.   There they called a meeting of all the
Brethren, and delivered the letter, the reading of which caused 31
great rejoicing by its encouraging contents.   Judas and Silas, 32
who were themselves Prophets, further encouraged the
Brethren by many an address, and strengthened their faith.
After some stay, they were dismissed with kind farewells from 33
the Brethren, and returned to those who had sent them.

Paul and Barnabas, however, remained in Antioch, where 35
they taught and, with the help of many others, told the Good
News of the Lord's Message.

Some time after this, Paul said to Barnabas : 36

PAUL'S SECOND MISSIONARY JOURNEY.   " Let us go back, and visit the Brethren in every town in which we have told the Lord's Message, and see how they are prospering."

Paul separates from Barnabas.   Barnabas wished to take with them John, 37 whose other name was Mark; but Paul felt 38 that they ought not to take with them the man who had deserted them in Pamphylia, and
had not gone on with them to their work.   This caused such 39
unpleasant feeling between them that they parted, Barnabas
taking Mark and sailing for Cyprus, while Paul chose Silas 40
for his companion and, after he had been committed by the
Brethren to the gracious care of the Lord, started on his
journey and went through Syria and Cilicia, strengthening the 41
Churches in the Faith.

Paul joined by Timothy at Lystra.   Among other places Paul went to Derbe 1 **1** and Lystra.   At the latter place they found a disciple, named Timothy, whose mother was a
Jewess who had become a believer in Christ, while his father
was a Greek, and who was well spoken of by the Brethren in 2
Lystra and Iconium.   Wishing to take this man with him on 3
his journey, Paul caused him to be circumcised on account of
the Jews in that neighbourhood, for they all knew that his
father had been a Greek.   As they travelled from town 4
to town, they gave the Brethren the decisions which had been
reached by the Apostles and Officers of the Church at Jerusalem,
for them to observe.

So the Churches grew stronger in the Faith, and increased 5
in numbers from day to day.

Paul determines to cross to Macedonia. They next went through the Phrygian district 6 of Galatia, but were restrained by the Holy Spirit from delivering the Message in Roman Asia. When they reached the borders of Mysia, they 7 attempted to go into Bithynia, but the Spirit of Jesus did not permit them. Passing through Mysia, they went down to 8 Troas ; and there one night Paul saw a vision. A Macedonian 9 was standing and appealing to him—'Come over to Macedonia and help us.' So, immediately after Paul had seen the 10 vision, we looked for an opportunity to cross over to Macedonia, concluding that God had summoned us to tell the Good News to the people there.

Paul at Philippi. Accordingly we set sail from Troas, and ran 11 before the wind to Samothrace, reaching Neapolis the next day. From there we made our way to Philippi, 12 which is the principal city of that part of Macedonia, and also a Roman Settlement.

In that city we spent several days. On the Sabbath we 13 went outside the gate to the river-side, where we supposed there would be a Place of Prayer ; and we sat down and talked to the women who were gathered there. Among 14 them was a woman, named Lydia, belonging to Thyatira, a dealer in purple cloth, who was accustomed to join in the worship of God. The Lord touched this woman's heart, so that she gave attention to the Message delivered by Paul, and, 15 when she and her household had been baptized, she urged us to become her guests.

"Since you have shown your conviction," she said, "that I really am a believer in the Lord, come and stay in my house." And she insisted on our doing so.

One day, as we were on our way to the Place of Prayer, we 16 were met by a girl possessed by a divining spirit, who made large profits for her masters by fortune-telling. This girl 17 followed Paul and the rest of us, calling out :

"These men are servants of the most high God, and they are bringing you news of a way to Salvation."

She had been doing this for several days, when Paul, much 18 vexed, turned and said to the spirit within her :

"In the Name of Jesus Christ I command you to leave her." That very moment the spirit left her. When her 19 masters saw that there was no hope of further profit from her, they seized Paul and Silas, dragged them into the public square to the authorities, and took them before the Magistrates. 20

"These men are causing a great disturbance in our town," they complained ; "they are Jews, and they are teaching 21 customs which it is not right for us, as Romans, to sanction or adopt."

On this the mob rose as one man against them, and the 22

Magistrates stripped them of their clothing and ordered them
to be beaten with rods. After beating them severely, the   23
Magistrates put them in prison, with orders to the Governor
of the Gaol to keep them in safe custody. On receiving so   24
strict an order, the Governor put them into the inner cell, and
secured their feet in the stocks.   About midnight, while   25
Paul and Silas were praying and singing hymns to God, and
while the prisoners were listening to them, suddenly there was   26
an earthquake of such violence that the Gaol was shaken to its
foundations; all the doors flew open, and all the prisoners'
chains were loosened. Roused from his sleep, and seeing the   27
prison doors open, the Governor drew his sword intending to
kill himself, in the belief that the prisoners had escaped. But   28
Paul called out loudly :

" Do not harm yourself ; we are all here."

Calling for a light, the Governor rushed in, and flung himself   29
trembling at the feet of Paul and Silas. Then he led them   30
out, and said :

"What must I do to be saved ? "

" Believe in Jesus, our Lord," they replied, "and you shall   31
be saved, you and your household too."

Then they spoke to him of God's Message, and to all his   32
household as well. And that very hour of the night he took   33
them and washed their wounds, and he himself and every one
belonging to him were baptized without delay. Afterwards he   34
took them up to his house and set before them something to eat,
rejoicing that he, with all his household, had come to believe
in God.   In the morning the Magistrates sent the   35
police with an order for the men to be discharged. The   36
Governor of the Gaol told Paul of his instructions.

" The Magistrates have sent an order for your discharge,"
he said, "so you had better leave the place at once and go
quietly away."

But Paul's answer to them was :   37

" They have flogged us in public without trial, though we
are Roman citizens, and they have put us in prison, and now
they are for sending us out secretly ! No, indeed ! Let them
come and take us out themselves."

The police reported his words to the Magistrates, who, on   38
hearing that Paul and Silas were Roman citizens, were
alarmed, and went to the prison, and did their best to con-   39
ciliate them. Then they took them out, and begged them to
leave the city. When Paul and Silas left the prison, they went   40
to Lydia's house, and, after they had seen the Brethren, and
encouraged them, they left the place.

Paul at   After passing through Amphipolis and Apol-   1
Thessalonica. lonia, Paul and Silas came to Thessalonica.
Here the Jews had a Synagogue ; and, following his usual   2

custom, Paul joined them, and for three Sabbaths addressed them, drawing his arguments from the Scriptures. He laid before them and explained that the Christ must undergo suffering and rise from the dead ; and "It is this man," he declared, "who is the Christ—this Jesus about whom I am telling you." 3

Some of the people were convinced, and threw in their lot with Paul and Silas, as did also a large body of Greeks who were accustomed to join in the Jewish services, and a great number of women belonging to the leading families. But the Jews, becoming jealous, engaged some worthless fellows from the streets, and, getting a mob together, kept the city in an uproar. They attacked Jason's house, with the intention of bringing Paul and Silas before the Popular Assembly ; and, not finding them there, they proceeded to drag Jason and some of the Brethren before the City Magistrates, shouting out : 4 5 6

"These men, who have turned the world upside down, have now come here, and have been harboured by Jason ! They are all defying the decrees of the Emperor. They say that some one else is king—a man called Jesus !" 7

On hearing this, the people and the City Magistrates were much concerned ; and, before letting them go, they took bail from Jason and the others. 8 9

Paul at Beroea That very night the Brethren sent Paul and Silas off to Beroea ; and on reaching that place, they went to the Jewish Synagogue. These Jews of Beroea were better disposed than those in Thessalonica, for they welcomed the Message with great readiness, and daily examined the Scriptures to see if what was said was true. As a consequence, many of them became believers in Christ, besides a considerable number of Greek women of position, and of men also. But, when the Jews of Thessalonica found out that God's Message had been delivered by Paul at Beroea, they came there too, exciting and disturbing the minds of the people. Immediately upon that, the Brethren sent Paul off on his way to the sea coast, but both Silas and Timothy stayed behind in Beroea. The friends who escorted Paul took him as far as Athens, and, after receiving a message for Silas and Timothy to join him as quickly as possible, they started on their return. 10 11 12 13 14 15

Paul at Athens. While Paul was waiting for them at Athens, his heart was stirred at seeing the whole city full of idols. So he argued in the Synagogue with the Jews and with those who joined in their worship, as well as daily in the public Square with those who happened to be there. Among others, some Epicurean and Stoic Philosophers joined issue with him. Some would ask "What is this prater 16 17 18

wanting to make out?", while others would say "He seems
to be a Preacher of foreign Deities." (This was because he
was telling the Good News about Jesus and the Resurrection). So they laid hold of him and took him to the Court of   19
Areopagus.

"May we hear," they asked, "what new teaching this is
which you are giving? For you are bringing some strange   20
things to our notice, and we should like to know what they
mean."

(All Athenians and the foreigners staying in the city found no   21
time for anything else but telling, or listening to, the last new
thing.) So Paul took his stand in the middle of the Court,   22
and said—

"Men of Athens, on every hand I see signs of your being
very devout. For as I was going about, looking at your   23
sacred shrines, I came upon an altar with this inscription—
'To an Unknown God.' What, therefore, you worship in
ignorance, that I am now proclaiming to you. The God   24
who made the world and all things that are in it—he, Lord
as he is of Heaven and Earth, does not dwell in Temples
made by hands, nor yet do human hands minister to his   25
wants, as though he needed anything, since he himself gives,
to all, life, and breath, and all things. He made all races of   26
men from one stock, and caused them to settle on all parts of
the earth's surface—fixing a time for their rise and fall, and
the limits of their settlements—that they might search for God,   27
if by any means they might feel their way to him and find him.
And yet he is not really far from any one of us; for in him   28
we live and move and are. To use the words of some of your
own poets—

'His offspring, too, are we.'

Therefore, as the offspring of God, we must not think that   29
the Deity has any resemblance to anything made of gold, or
silver, or stone—a work of human art and imagination.
True, God looked with indulgence on the days of men's ignor-   30
ance, but now he is announcing to every one everywhere the
need for repentance, because he has fixed a day on which he   31
intends to 'judge the world with justice,' by a man whom he
has appointed—and of this he has given all men a pledge by
raising this man from the dead."

On hearing of a resurrection of the dead, some began jeering,   32
but others said that they would hear what he had to say about
that another time. And so Paul left the Court. There were,   33,
however, some men who joined him, and became believers in
Christ. Among them were Dionysius, a member of the Court
of Areopagus, a woman named Damaris, and several others.

24 Ps. 146. 5—6.   25 Isa. 42. 5.   26 Gen. 9. 19.   28 Aratus 5.   31 Ps. 9. 8;
Enoch 41. 9.

Paul at Corinth. On leaving Athens, Paul next went to Corinth. 1
There he met a Jew of the name of Aquila, a 2
native of Pontus, who, with his wife Priscilla,
had lately come from Italy, in consequence of the order which
had been issued by the Emperor Claudius for all Jews to leave
Rome. Paul paid them a visit, and, since their trade was the 3
same as his, he stayed and worked with them—their trade
was tent-making. Every Sabbath Paul gave addresses in the 4
Synagogue, trying to convince both Jews and Greeks.

But, when Silas and Timothy had come down from Mace- 5
donia, Paul devoted himself entirely to delivering the
Message, earnestly maintaining before the Jews that Jesus
was the Christ. However, as they set themselves against him 6
and became abusive, Paul shook his clothes in protest and said
to them :

"Your blood be on your own heads. My conscience is
clear. From this time forward I shall go to the Gentiles."
So he left, and went to the house of a certain Titius Justus, who 7
had been accustomed to join in the worship of God, and whose
house was next door to the Synagogue. Crispus, the 8
President of the Synagogue, came to believe in the Lord, and
so did all his household ; and many of the Corinthians, as
they listened to Paul, became believers in Christ and were
baptized.   One night the Lord said to Paul, in a 9
vision :

"Have no fear, but continue to speak, and refuse to be
silenced ; for I am with you, and no one shall do you harm, 10
for I have many People in this city."
So he settled there for a year and a half, and taught God's 11
Message among the people.

While Gallio was governor of Greece, the Jews made a 12
combined attack on Paul, and brought him before the Governor's Bench, charging him with persuading people to worship 13
God in a way forbidden by the Law. Just as Paul was on the 14
point of speaking, Gallio said to the Jews :

"Jews, if this were a case of misdemeanour or some
serious crime, there would be some reason for my listening
patiently to you ; but, since it is a dispute about words, and 15
names, and your own Law, you must see to it yourselves. I
do not choose to be a judge in such matters."
Saying this, he drove them back from the Bench. Then 16, 17
they all set upon Sosthenes, the President of the Synagogue,
and beat him in front of the Bench, but Gallio did not trouble
himself about any of these things.

Paul's Return. Paul remained there some time after this, and 18
then took leave of the Brethren, and sailed to
Syria with Priscilla and Aquila, but not before his head had
been shaved at Cenchreae, because he was under a vow.

9—10 Isa. 43. 5.

They put into Ephesus, and there Paul, leaving his com-   19
panions, went into the Synagogue and addressed the Jews.
When they asked him to prolong his stay, he declined, saying   20
however, as he took his leave, "I will come back again to   21
you, please God," and then set sail from Ephesus. On reach-   22
ing Caesarea, he went up to Jerusalem and exchanged
greetings with the Church, and then went down to Antioch.

PAUL'S THIRD   After making some stay in Antioch, he set out   23
MISSIONARY on a tour through the Phrygian district of Galatia,
JOURNEY. strengthening the faith of all the disciples as he
Tour in went.
Galatia.

Meanwhile there had come to Ephesus an   24
Apollos.   Alexandrian Jew, named Apollos, an eloquent
man, who was well-versed in the Scriptures. He had been   25
well-instructed in the Cause of the Lord, and with burning
zeal he spoke of, and taught carefully, the facts about Jesus,
though he knew of no baptism but John's. This man began   26
to speak out fearlessly in the Synagogue; and, when Priscilla
and Aquila heard him, they took him home and explained the
Cause of God to him more carefully still. When he wanted to   27
cross to Greece, the Brethren furthered his plans, and wrote
to the disciples there to welcome him. On his arrival he
proved of great assistance to those who had, through the
loving-kindness of God, become believers in Christ, for he   28
vigorously confuted the Jews, publicly proving by the
Scriptures that Jesus was the Christ.

Paul   While Apollos was at Corinth, Paul passed   1 **19**
at Ephesus. through the inland districts of Roman Asia, and
went to Ephesus. There he found some disciples, of whom he   2
asked:
"Did you, when you became believers in Christ, receive the
Holy Spirit?"
"No," they answered, "we did not even hear that there
was a Holy Spirit."
"What then was your baptism?" Paul asked.   3
"John's baptism," was their answer.
"John's baptism was a baptism upon repentance," rejoined   4
Paul, "and John told the people (speaking of the 'One
Coming' after him) that they should believe in him—that is in
Jesus."
On hearing this, they were baptized into the Faith of the Lord   5
Jesus, and, after Paul had placed his hands on them, the Holy   6
Spirit descended upon them, and they began to speak with
'tongues' and to preach. There were about twelve of them   7
in all.
Paul went to the Synagogue there, and for three months   8
spoke out fearlessly, giving addresses and trying to convince

4 Ps. 118. 26.

his hearers, about the kingdom of God.   Some of them, how- 9
ever, hardened their hearts and refused to believe, denouncing
the Cause before the people.   So Paul left them and withdrew
his disciples, and gave daily addresses in the lecture-hall of
Tyrannus.   This went on for two years, so that all who lived in 10
Roman Asia, Jews and Greeks alike, heard'the Lord's Message.

God did miracles of no ordinary kind by Paul's hands ; so 11
that people would carry home to the sick handkerchiefs or 12
aprons that had touched his body, and their diseases would
leave them and the wicked spirits go out of them.   An 13
attempt was made by some itinerant Jews, who were
exorcists, to use the Name of the Lord Jesus over those who
had wicked spirits in them.

"I adjure you," they would say, "by the Jesus, whom Paul
preaches."

The seven sons of Sceva, a Jewish Chief Priest, were doing 14
this ; but the wicked spirit answered them :   15
"Jesus I acknowledge, and Paul I know, but you—who are
you?"

Then the man, in whom this wicked spirit was, sprang upon 16
them, mastered both of them, and so completely overpowered
them, that they fled out of the house, stripped of their clothes,
and wounded.   This incident came to the knowledge of all 17
the Jews and Greeks living at Ephesus ; they were all awe-
struck, and the Name of the Lord Jesus was held in the
highest honour.   Many, too, of those who had become 18
believers in Christ came with a full confession of their
practices ; while a number of people, who had practised 19
magic, collected their books and burnt them publicly ; and on
reckoning up the price of these, they found it amounted to
five thousand pounds.   So irresistibly did the Lord's 20
Message spread and prevail.

Paul plans to visit Jerusalem and Rome.   Sometime after these events Paul resolved to 21
go through Macedonia and Greece, and then
make his way to Jerusalem.   "And after I have
been there," he said, "I must visit Rome also."

So he sent to Macedonia two of his helpers, Timothy and Erastus, 22
while he himself stayed for some time longer in Roman Asia.

The Riot at Ephesus.   Just about that time a great disturbance arose 23
about the Cause. A silversmith named Demetrius, 24
who made silver models of the shrine of Artemis,
and so gave a great deal of work to the artisans, got these 25
men together, as well as the workmen engaged in similar
occupations, and said :

"Men, you know that our prosperity depends upon this

work, and you see and hear that not only at Ephesus, but 26
in almost the whole of Roman Asia, this Paul has convinced
and won over great numbers of people, by his assertion that
those Gods which are made by hands are not Gods at all.
So that not only is this business of ours likely to fall into dis- 27
credit, but there is the further danger that the Temple of
the great Goddess Artemis will be thought nothing of, and
that she herself will be deprived of her splendour—though all
Roman Asia and the whole world worship her."

When they heard this, the men were greatly enraged, and 28
began shouting—" Great is Artemis of the Ephesians !" The 29
commotion spread through the whole city, and the people
rushed together into the amphitheatre, dragging with them
Gaius and Aristarchus, two Macedonians who were Paul's
travelling companions. Paul wished to go into the amphi- 30
theatre and face the people, but the disciples would not let
him, while some of the chief religious officials of the province, 31
who were friendly to him, sent repeated entreaties to him not
to trust himself inside. Meanwhile some were shouting one 32
thing and some another, for the Assembly was all in confusion, most of those present not even knowing why they had
met. But some of the crowd prompted Alexander, whom the 33
Jews had pushed to the front, and he waved his hand to show
that he wanted to speak in their defence to the people. How- 34
ever, when they recognised him as a Jew, one cry broke from
them all, and they continued shouting for two hours—" Great
is Artemis of the Ephesians !"

When the Recorder had succeeded in quieting the crowd, he 35
said :

" Men of Ephesus, who is there, I ask you, who needs to be
told that this city of Ephesus is the Warden of the Temple of
the great Artemis, and of the statue which fell down from
Zeus ? As these are undeniable facts, you ought to keep 36
calm and do nothing rash ; for you have brought these men 37
here, though they are neither robbers of Temples nor blasphe-
mers of our Goddess. If, however, Demetrius and the 38
artisans who are acting with him have a charge to make
against any one, there are Court Days and there are Magistrates ; let both parties take legal proceedings. But if you 39
want anything more, it will have to be settled in the regular
Assembly. For I tell you that we are in danger of being pro- 40
ceeded against for to-day's riot, there being nothing to account
for it ; and in that case we shall be at a loss to give any reason
for this disorderly gathering."

With these words he dismissed the Assembly. 41

**Paul again in
Greece and
Macedonia.** When the uproar had ceased, Paul sent for the 1
disciples, and, with encouraging words, bade them
goodbye, and started on his journey to Macedonia.

After going through those districts and speaking many 2
encouraging words to the disciples, he went into Greece,
where he stayed three months. He was about to sail to 3
Syria, when he learnt that a plot had been laid against
him by the Jews ; so he decided to return by way of Macedonia. He was accompanied by Sopater the son of Pyrrhus, 4
of Beroea, Aristarchus and Secundus from Thessalonica,
Gaius of Derbe, and Timothy, as well as by Tychicus
and Trophimus of Roman Asia. These men went to 5
Paul Troas and waited for us there ; while we our- 6
at Troas. selves sailed from Philippi after the Passover,
and joined them five days later at Troas, where we stayed
for a week.

On the first day of the week, when we had met for the 7
Breaking of Bread, Paul, who was intending to leave the
next day, began to address those who were present, and
prolonged his address till midnight. There were a good 8
many lamps in the upstairs room, where we had met ; and a 9
young man named Eutychus, sitting at the window, was
gradually overcome with great drowsiness, as Paul continued
his address. At last, quite overpowered by his drowsiness, he
fell from the third storey to the ground, and was picked up
for dead. But Paul went down, threw himself upon him, and 10
put his arms round him.

" Do not be alarmed," he said, " he is still alive."
Then he went upstairs ; and, after breaking and partaking of 11
the Bread, he talked with them at great length till daybreak,
and then left. Meanwhile they had taken the lad away alive, 12
and were greatly comforted.

Paul We started first, went on board ship, and 13
at Miletus. sailed for Assos, intending to take Paul on
board there. This was by his own arrangement, as he intended to go by land himself. So, when he met us at Assos, 14
we took him on board and went on to Mitylene. The day 15
after we had sailed from there, we arrived off Chios, touched
at Samos the following day, and the next day reached
Miletus ; for Paul had decided to sail past Ephesus, so as to 16
avoid spending much time in Roman Asia. He was making
haste to reach Jerusalem, if possible, by the Festival at the
close of the Harvest.

From Miletus, however, he sent to Ephesus and invited the 17
Officers of the Church to meet him ; and, when they came, he 18
spoke to them as follows :

" You know well the life that I always led among you from
the very first day that I set foot in Roman Asia, serving the 19
Lord, as I did, in all humility, amid the tears and trials which
fell to my lot through the plots of the Jews. I never shrank 20
from telling you anything that could be helpful to you, or from

teaching you both in public and in private. I earnestly pointed 21
both Jews and Greeks to the repentance that leads to God,
and to faith in Jesus, our Lord. And now, under spiritual 22
constraint, I am here on my way to Jerusalem, not knowing
what will happen to me there, except that in town after town 23
the Holy Spirit plainly declares to me that imprisonment and
troubles await me. But I count my life of no value to myself, 24
if only I may complete the course marked out for me, and
the task that was allotted me by the Lord Jesus—which was
to declare the Good News of the Love of God. And now, I 25
tell you, I know that none of you will ever see my face
again—you among whom I have gone about proclaiming
the Kingdom. Therefore I declare to you this day, that my 26
conscience is clear in regard to the fate of any of you, for I 27
have not shrunk from announcing the whole purpose of God
regarding you. Be watchful over yourselves, and over the 28
whole flock, of which the Holy Spirit has placed you in
charge, to shepherd the Church of God, which he won for
himself at the cost of his life. I know that, after my de- 29
parture, merciless wolves will get in among you, who will not
spare the flock ; and from among yourselves, too, men will 30
arise, who will teach perversions of truth, so as to draw away
the disciples after them. Therefore, be on your guard, re- 31
membering how for three years, night and day, I never ceased,
even with tears, to warn each one of you. And now I 32
commend you to the Lord and to the Message of his Love—a
Message which has the power to build up your characters, and
to give you your place among all those who have become
Christ's People. I have never coveted any one's gold or silver 33
or clothing. You, yourselves, know that these hands of mine 34
provided not only for my own wants, but for my companions
also. I left nothing undone to show you that, labouring as I 35
laboured, you ought to help the weak, and to remember the
words of the Lord Jesus, how he said himself—'It is more
blessed to give than to receive.'"
When Paul had finished speaking, he knelt down and prayed 36
with them all. All were in tears ; and throwing their 37
arms round Paul's neck, they kissed him again and again,
grieving most of all over what he had said—that they would 38
never see his face again. Then they escorted him to the
ship.

Paul   When we had torn ourselves away and had 1 21
at Tyre.   set sail, we ran before the wind to Cos ; the next
day we came to Rhodes, and from there to Patara, where we 2
found a ship crossing to Phoenicia, and went on board and
set sail. After sighting Cyprus and leaving it on the left, we 3
sailed to Syria, and put into Tyre, where the ship was to

discharge her cargo. There we found the disciples and stayed a week with them. Speaking under the influence of the Spirit, they warned Paul not to set foot in Jerusalem. However, when we had come to the end of our visit, we went on our way, all the disciples with their wives and children escorting us out of the city. We knelt down on the beach, and prayed, and then said good-bye to one another; after which we went on board, and they returned home.

Paul at Caesarea. After we had made the run from Tyre, we landed at Ptolemais, and exchanged greetings with the Brethren there, and spent a day with them. The next day we left, and reached Caesarea, where we went to the house of Philip, the Missionary, who was one of 'the Seven,' and stayed with him. He had four unmarried daughters, who had the gift of prophecy. During our visit, which lasted several days, a Prophet, named Agabus, came down from Judaea. He came to see us, and, taking Paul's girdle, and binding his own feet and hands with it, said:

"This is what the Holy Spirit says—'The man to whom this girdle belongs will be bound like this at Jerusalem by the Jews, and they will give him up to the Gentiles'."
When we heard that, we and the people of the place began to entreat Paul not to go up to Jerusalem. It was then that Paul made the reply:

"Why are you weeping and breaking my heart like this? For my part, I am ready not only to be bound, but even to suffer death at Jerusalem for the Name of the Lord Jesus." So, as he would not be persuaded, we said no more to him, only adding—"The Lord's will be done."

Paul arrives at Jerusalem. At the end of our visit, we made our preparations, and started on our way up to Jerusalem. Some of the disciples from Caesarea went with us, and brought Mnason with them, a Cypriot disciple of long standing, with whom we were to stay. On our arrival at Jerusalem, the Brethren there gave us a hearty welcome; and the next day Paul went with us to see James, and all the Officers of the Church were present. After greeting them, Paul related in detail all that God had done among the Gentiles through his efforts; and, when they had heard it, they began praising God, and said to Paul:

"You see, Brother, that the Jews who have become believers in Christ may be numbered by tens of thousands, and they are all naturally earnest in upholding the Jewish Law. Now they have heard it said about you, that you teach all Jews in foreign countries to forsake Moses, for you tell them not to circumcise their children or even to observe Jewish customs. Well now,

as they are certain to hear of your arrival, do what we are 23
going to suggest. We have four men here, who have of their
own accord put themselves under a vow. Join these men, 24
share their purification, and bear their expenses, so that they
may shave their heads ; and then all will see that there is no
truth in what they have been told about you, but that, on the
contrary, you yourself rule your life in obedience to the Jewish
Law. As to the Gentiles who have become believers in Christ, 25
we have sent our decision that they should avoid food offered
to idols, and blood, and the flesh of strangled animals, and
impurity."

On this, Paul joined the men, and the next day shared their 26
purification, and went into the Temple, and gave notice of the
expiration of the period of purification when the usual offering
should have been made on behalf of each of them.

Paul's Arrest. But, just as the seven days were drawing to a 27
close, the Jews from Roman Asia caught sight of
Paul in the Temple, and caused great excitement among all
the people present, by seizing Paul and shouting : 28

" Men of Israel ! help ! This is the man who teaches every
one everywhere against our People, our Law, and this Place ;
and, what is more, he has actually brought Greeks into the
Temple and defiled this sacred place."

(For they had previously seen Trophimus the Ephesian in Paul's 29
company in the city, and were under the belief that Paul had
taken him into the Temple.) The whole city was stirred, 30
and the people quickly collected, seized Paul, and dragged
him out of the Temple, when the doors were immediately
shut. They were bent upon killing him, when it was 31
reported to the Officer commanding the garrison, that all
Jerusalem was in commotion. He instantly got together 32
some officers and men, and charged down upon the crowd,
who, when they saw the Commanding Officer and his men,
stopped beating Paul. Then he went up to Paul, arrested him, 33
ordered him to be doubly chained, and proceeded to inquire
who he was, and what he had been doing. Some of the crowd 34
said one thing, and some another; and, as he could get no definite reply on account of the uproar, he ordered Paul to be taken
into the barracks. When Paul reached the steps, he was 35
actually being carried by the soldiers, owing to the violence of
the mob ; for the people were following in a mass, shouting 36
out : " Kill him ! "

Just as he was about to be taken into the Fort, Paul said to 37
the Commanding Officer :

" May I speak to you ? "

" Do you know Greek ? " asked the Commanding Officer.

" Are not you, then, the Egyptian who some time ago raised 38

26 Num. 6. 5.

an insurrection and led the four thousand Bandits out into the
Wilderness?"

"No," said Paul, "I am a Jew of Tarsus in Cilicia, a citizen   39
of a city of some note; and I beg you to give me permission
to speak to the people."

The Commanding Officer gave his permission, and Paul, stand-   40
ing on the steps, made signs with his hand to the people, and,
when comparative silence had been obtained, he spoke to them
in Hebrew, as follows:

Paul's
Defence to
the People of
Jerusalem.

"Brothers and Fathers, listen to the defence   1   **22**
which I am about to make."
When they heard that he was speaking to them   2
in Hebrew, they were still more quiet; and Paul
went on:

"I am a Jew, a native of Tarsus in Cilicia, but I was brought   3
up in this city under the teaching of Gamaliel, and educated
in accordance with the strict system of our ancestral Law.   I
was as zealous in God's service as any of you who are here to-
day.   In my persecution of this Cause I did not stop even at   4
the taking of life.   I put in chains, and imprisoned, men and
women alike—and to that the High Priest himself and all the   5
Council can testify.   For I had letters of introduction from
them to our fellow Jews at Damascus, and I was on my way
to that place, to bring those whom I might find there
prisoners to Jerusalem for punishment.   While I was   6
still on my way, just as I was getting close to Damascus,
about mid-day, suddenly there flashed from the heavens a
great light all round me.   I fell to the ground, and heard a   7
voice saying to me 'Saul, Saul, why are you persecuting me?'
'Who are you, Lord?' I replied.   Then the voice said 'I am   8
Jesus of Nazareth whom you are persecuting.'   The men with   9
me saw the light, but did not hear the speaker's voice.   Then   10
I said 'What am I to do, Lord?'   'Get up and go into
Damascus,' the Lord said to me, 'and there you shall be
told all that you have been appointed to do.'   In consequence   11
of that dazzling light I could not see, but my companions led
me by the hand, till I reached Damascus.   There a man named   12
Ananias, a strict observer of our Law, well spoken of by all the
Jewish inhabitants, came to see me.   Standing close to me, he   13
said 'Saul, my Brother, recover your sight.'   And then and
there I recovered my sight and looked up at him.   Then he   14
said 'The God of our ancestors has appointed you to learn his
will, and to see the Righteous One, and to hear words from his
lips; for you shall be a witness for him to all the world of what   15
you have just seen and heard.   And now why wait any longer?   16
Be baptized at once, wash away your sins, and invoke his
Name.   After my return to Jerusalem, while I was   17
praying one day in the Temple, I fell into a trance, and saw   18
Jesus saying to me 'Make haste and leave Jerusalem at once,

because they will not accept your testimony about me.' 'Lord,' 19
I answered, 'these people know that I used to imprison and
scourge, in Synagogue after Synagogue, those who believed in
you; and, when the blood of your martyr, Stephen, was being 20
shed, I was myself standing by, approving of his death, and
took charge of the clothes of those who were murdering him.
But Jesus said to me 'Go; for I will send you to the Gentiles 21
far away'."

Paul's Claim as a Roman Citizen. Up to this point the people had been listening 22
to Paul, but at these words they called out:
" Kill him ! A fellow like this ought not to have
been allowed to live !"

As they were shouting, tearing off their clothes, and throwing 23
dust in the air, the Commanding Officer ordered Paul to be 24
taken into the Fort, and directed that he should be examined
under the lash, that he might find out the reason for their
outcry against him.   But just as they had tied him up to be 25
scourged, Paul said to the Captain standing near:
" Is it legal for you to scourge a Roman citizen, uncon-
victed ? "
On hearing this, the Captain went and reported it to the Com- 26
manding Officer.
" Do you know what you are doing ? " he said.   " This man
is a Roman citizen."
So the Commanding Officer went up to Paul and said : 27
" Tell me, are you a Roman citizen ? "
" Yes," replied Paul.
" I had to pay a heavy price for my position as citizen," said 28
the Officer.
" I am one by birth," rejoined Paul.
The men who were to have examined Paul immediately drew 29
back, and the Officer, finding that Paul was a Roman citizen,
was alarmed at having put him in chains.

Paul before the High Council of the Jews. On the next day the Commanding Officer, wish- 30
ing to find out the real reason why Paul was de-
nounced by the Jews, had his chains taken off,
and directed the Chief Priests and the whole of the
High Council to assemble, and then took Paul down and
brought him before them.   Paul fixed his eyes upon the 1
Council, and began:
" Brothers, for my part, I have always ordered my life
before God, with a clear conscience, up to this very day."
At this, the High Priest Ananias ordered the men standing 2
near to strike him on the mouth; whereupon Paul turned to 3
him and said:
" God will strike you, you white-washed wall ! Are you
sitting there to try me in accordance with law, and yet, in
defiance of law, order me to be struck ? "

The people standing near said to Paul :   4
  " Do you know that you are insulting God's High Priest ? "
  " I did not know, Brothers, that it was the High Priest,"   5
said Paul, " for Scripture says—

    ' Of the Ruler of thy People thou shalt speak no ill '."

Noticing that some of those present were Sadducees and others   6
Pharisees, Paul called out in the Council :
  " Brothers, I am a Pharisee and a son of Pharisees. It is
on the question of hope for the dead and of their resurrection
that I am on my trial."
As soon as he said this, a dispute arose between the Pharisees   7
and the Sadducees ; and there was a sharp division of opinion
among those present. (For Sadducees say there is no such   8
thing as a resurrection, and that there is neither angel nor
spirit, while Pharisees believe in both.) So a great uproar   9
ensued, and some of the Teachers of the Law belonging to
the Pharisees' party stood up and hotly protested :
  " We find nothing whatever wrong in this man. Suppose a
spirit did speak to him, or an angel——"
The dispute was becoming so violent, that the Commanding   10
Officer, fearing that Paul would be torn in pieces between
them, ordered the Guard to go down and rescue him from
them, and take him into the Fort.
  That night the Lord came and stood by Paul, and said :   11
  " Courage ! You have borne witness for me in Jerusalem
and you must bear witness in Rome also."

The Plot   In the morning the Jews combined together,   12
against Paul. and took an oath that they would not eat or drink
till they had killed Paul. There were more than forty in the   13
plot ; and they went to the Chief Priests and the Councillors,   14
and said :
  " We have taken a solemn oath not to touch food till we have
killed Paul. So we want you now, with the consent of the   15
Council, to suggest to the Commanding Officer that he should
bring Paul down before you, as though you intended to go
more fully into his case ; but, before he comes here, we will be
ready to make away with him."
However, the son of Paul's sister, hearing of the plot, went to   16
the Fort, and on being admitted, told Paul about it. Paul   17
called one of the Captains of the garrison and asked him to
take the lad to the Commanding Officer, as he had something
to tell him. The Captain went with the lad to the Command-   18
ing Officer, and said :
  " The prisoner Paul called me and asked me to bring this lad
to you, as he has something to tell you."
The Commanding Officer took the lad by the hand, and, step-   19
ping aside, asked what it was he had to tell him.

<hr>

⁵ Exod. 22. 28.

"The Jews have agreed," answered the lad, "to ask you to 20
bring Paul down before the Council to-morrow, on the plea of
your making further inquiry into his case. But do not let them 21
persuade you, for more than forty of them are lying in wait for
him, who have taken an oath that they will not eat or drink,
till they have made away with him; and they are at this very
moment in readiness, counting upon your promise."

The Commanding Officer then dismissed the lad, cautioning 22
him not to mention to anybody that he had given him that
information.   Then he called two Captains, and ordered 23

Paul sent to Caesarea. them to have two hundred men ready to go to
Caesarea, as well as seventy troopers and two
hundred lancers, by nine o'clock that night, and 24
to have horses ready for Paul to ride, so that they might take
him safely to Felix, the Governor. To him he wrote a letter, 25
somewhat as follows—

'Claudius Lysias sends his compliments to His Ex- 26
cellency Felix the Governor.   The man whom 27
I send with this had been seized by the Jews, and was
on the point of being killed by them, when I came upon
them with the force under my command, and rescued
him, as I learnt that he was a Roman citizen. Wish- 28
ing to ascertain exactly the ground of the charges they
made against him, I brought him before their Council,
when I found that their charges were connected with 29
questions of their own Law, and that there was nothing alleged involving either death or imprisonment.
Having, however, information of a plot against the 30
man, which was about to be put into execution, I am
sending him to you at once, and I have also directed
his accusers to prosecute him before you.'

The soldiers, in accordance with their orders, took charge 31
of Paul and conducted him by night to Antipatris; and on the 32
next day, leaving the troopers to go on with him, they returned to
the Fort. On arriving at Caesarea, the troopers delivered the 33
letter to the Governor, and brought Paul before him. As soon 34
as Felix had read the letter, he enquired to what province Paul
belonged, and, learning that he came from Cilicia, he said:

"I will hear all you have to say as soon as your accusers 35
have arrived."

And he ordered Paul to be kept under guard in Herod's
Government House.

Paul before Felix. Five days afterwards the High Priest Ananias 1   **2**
came down with some of the Councillors and a
barrister named Tertullus. They laid an information with
the Governor against Paul; and, when the hearing came on, 2
Tertullus began his speech for the prosecution.

"We owe it to your Excellency," he said, "that we are 3

enjoying profound peace, and we owe it to your foresight that this nation is constantly securing reforms—advantages which we very gratefully accept at all times and places. But—not to be tedious—I beg you, with your accustomed fairness, to listen to a brief statement of our case. We have found this man a public pest; he is one who stirs up disputes among the Jews all the world over, and is a ringleader of the Nazarene heretics. He even attempted to desecrate the Temple itself, but we caught him; and you will be able, by examining him on all these points, to satisfy yourself as to the charges which we are bringing against him."

The Jews also joined in the attack and bore out his statements. On a sign from the Governor, Paul made this reply:

"Knowing, as I do, for how many years you have acted as Judge to this nation, it is with confidence that I undertake my own defence. For you can easily ascertain that it is not more than twelve days ago that I went up to worship at Jerusalem, where my prosecutors never found me holding discussions with any one, or causing a crowd to collect—either in the Temple, or in the Synagogues, or about the city; and they cannot establish the charges which they are now making against me. This, however, I do acknowledge to you, that it is as a believer in the Cause which they call heretical, that I worship the God of my ancestors. At the same time, I believe everything that is in accordance with the Law and that is written in the Prophets; and I have a hope that rests in God—a hope which they also cherish—that there will one day be a resurrection of good and bad alike. This being so, I strive at all times to keep my conscience clear before both God and man. After some years' absence I had come to bring charitable gifts to my nation, and to make offerings; and it was while engaged in this that they found me in the Temple, after completing a period of purification, but not with any crowd or disorder. There were, however, some Jews from Roman Asia who ought to have been here before you, and to have made any charge that they may have against me—Or else let my opponents here say what they found wrong in me when I was before the Council, except as to the one sentence that I shouted out as I stood among them—'It is about the resurrection of the dead that I am on my trial before you to-day'."

Felix, however, adjourned the case—though he had a fairly accurate knowledge of all that concerned the Cause—with the promise:

"When Lysias, the Commanding Officer, comes down, I will give my decision in your case."

So he gave orders to the Captain in charge of Paul to keep him in custody, but to relax the regulations, and not to prevent any of his personal friends from attending to his wants.

Some days later Felix came with his wife Drusilla, who was 24
herself a Jewess, and, sending for Paul, listened to what he
had to say about faith in Christ Jesus. But, while Paul 25
was speaking at length about righteousness, self-control, and
the coming judgement, Felix became terrified, and interrupted
him—

"Go for the present, but, when I find an opportunity, I will
send for you again."
He was hoping, too, for a bribe from Paul, and so he used 26
to send for him frequently and talk with him.

But, after the lapse of two years, Felix was succeeded by 27
Porcius Festus ; and, wishing to gain popularity with the Jews,
he left Paul a prisoner.

Paul before Festus. Three days after Festus had entered upon 1
his Province, he left Caesarea and went up to
Jerusalem. There the Chief Priests and the 2
leading men among the Jews laid an information before him
against Paul, and asked a favour of him, to Paul's injury— 3
to have Paul brought to Jerusalem. All the while they
were plotting to make away with him on the road. But Festus 4
answered that Paul was in prison at Caesarea, and that he
himself would be leaving for that place shortly.

"So let the influential men among you," he said, "go down 5
with me, and, if there is anything amiss in the man, charge him
formally with it."

After staying among them some eight or ten days, Festus 6
went down to Caesarea. The next day he took his seat on the
Bench, and ordered Paul to be brought before him. On Paul's 7
appearance, the Jews who had come down from Jerusalem surrounded him, and made many serious charges, which they failed
to establish. Paul's answer to the charge was—'I have 8
not committed any offence against the Jewish Law, or the
Temple, or the Emperor.' But, as Festus wished to gain 9
popularity with the Jews, he interrupted Paul with the question :

"Are you willing to go up to Jerusalem and be tried on
these charges before me there ? "

"No," replied Paul, "I am standing at the Emperor's Bar, 10
where I ought to be tried. I have not wronged the Jews, as
you yourself are well aware. If, however, I am breaking 11
the law and have committed any offence deserving death, I
do not ask to escape the penalty ; but, if there is nothing in
the accusations of these people, no one has the power to give
me up to them. I appeal to the Emperor."
Upon that, Festus, after conferring with his Council, answered : 12
"You have appealed to the Emperor ; to the Emperor you
shall go."

Paul before Herod Agrippa II. Some days later King Agrippa and Bernice came . 13 down to Caesarea, and paid a visit of congratulation to Festus ; and, as they were staying there 14 for several days, Festus laid Paul's case before the King.

"There is a man here," he said, "left a prisoner by Felix, about whom, when I came to Jerusalem, the Jewish Chief Priests 15 and the Councillors laid an information, demanding judgement against him. My answer to them was, that it was not the 16 practice of Romans to give up any man to his accusers till the accused had met them face to face, and had also had an opportunity of answering the charges brought against him. So they 17 met here, and without loss of time I took my seat on the Bench the very next day, and ordered the man to be brought before me. But, when his accusers came forward, they brought 18 no charge of wrong-doing such as I had expected ; but I found 19 that there were certain questions in dispute between them about their own religion, and about some dead man called Jesus, whom Paul declared to be alive. And, as I was at a loss 20 how to enquire into questions of this kind, I asked Paul if he were willing to go up to Jerusalem, and there be put upon his trial. Paul, however, appealed to have his case reserved 21 for the consideration of his August Majesty, so I ordered him to be detained in custody, until I could send him to the Emperor."

"I should like to hear this man myself," Agrippa said to 22 Festus.

"You shall hear him to-morrow," Festus answered.

So the next day, when Agrippa and Bernice had come in full 23 state and had entered the Audience Chamber, with the superior officers and the principal people of the city, by the order of Festus Paul was brought before them. Then Festus said : 24

"King Agrippa, and all here present, you see before you the man about whom the whole Jewish people have applied to me, both at Jerusalem and here, loudly asserting that he ought not to be allowed to live. I found, however, that he had not done 25 anything deserving death ; so, as he had himself appealed to his August Majesty, I decided to send him. But I have noth- 26 ing definite to write about him to my Imperial Master ; and for that reason I have brought him before you all, and especially before you, King Agrippa, that, after examining him, I may have something to write. For it seems to me absurd to send 27 a prisoner, without at the same time stating the charges made against him."

Turning to Paul, Agrippa said : 1 **26**

"You are at liberty to speak for yourself."

Then Paul stretched out his hand and began his defence.

"I have been congratulating myself, King Agrippa," he 2 said, "that it is before you that I have to make my defence to-day, with regard to all the charges brought against me by Jews, especially as you are so well-versed in all the customs 3

and questions of the Jewish world. I beg you therefore to
give me a patient hearing.　　My life, then, from youth　4
upwards, was passed, from the very first, among my own
nation, and in Jerusalem, and is within the knowledge of
all Jews ; and they have always known—if they choose to give　5
evidence—that, in accordance with the very strictest form of
our religion, I lived a true Pharisee.　Even now, it is because　6
of my hope in the promise given by God to our ancestors that
I stand here on my trial—a promise which our Twelve Tribes,　7
by earnest service night and day, hope to see fulfilled.　It is
for this hope, your Majesty, that I am accused—and by Jews
themselves !　Why do you all hold it incredible that God　8
should raise the dead ?　　I myself, it is true, once　9
thought it my duty to oppose in every way the Name of
Jesus of Nazareth ; and I actually did so at Jerusalem.　10
Acting on the authority of the Chief Priests, I myself threw
many of the People of Christ into prison, and, when it was proposed to put them to death, I gave my vote for it.　Time after　11
time, in every Synagogue, I tried by punishments to force
them to blaspheme.　So frantic was I against them, that I
pursued them even to towns beyond our borders.　It　12
was while I was travelling to Damascus on an errand of this
kind, entrusted with full powers by the Chief Priests, that at　13
mid-day, your Majesty, I saw right in my path, coming from
the heavens, a light brighter than the glare of the sun, which
shone all round me and those travelling with me.　We all fell　14
to the ground, and then I heard a voice saying to me in
Hebrew—'Saul, Saul, why are you persecuting me ?　By
kicking against the goad you are punishing yourself.'　'Who　15
are you, Lord ?' I asked.　And the Lord said : 'I am Jesus,
whom you are persecuting ; but get up and stand upright ;　16
for I have appeared to you in order to appoint you a servant
and a witness of those revelations of me which you have
already had, and of those in which I shall yet appear to you,
since I am choosing you out from your own people and from　17
the Gentiles, to whom I now send you, to open their eyes, and　18
to turn them from darkness to light, and from the power of
Satan to God ; so that they may receive pardon for their sins,
and a place among those who have become God's People, by
faith in me.'　　After that, King Agrippa, I did not fail to　19
obey the heavenly vision ; on the contrary, first to those at　20
Damascus and Jerusalem, and then through the whole of
Judaea, and to the Gentiles as well, I began to preach repentance and conversion to God, and a life befitting that repentance.
This is why the Jews seized me in the Temple, and made　21
attempts upon my life.　However I have received help from　22
God to this very day, and so stand here, and bear my
testimony to high and low alike—without adding a word to

16 Ezek. 2. 1.　17.1 Chron. 16. 35.　17—18 Isa. 42. 7, 16 ; Deut. 33. 3, 4.

what the Prophets, as well as Moses, declared should happen —that the Christ must suffer, and that, by rising from the dead, he was destined to be the first to bring news of Light, not only to our nation, but also to the Gentiles." 23

While Paul was making this defence, Festus called out loudly : 24

"You are mad, Paul; your great learning is driving you mad."

"I am not mad, your Excellency," he replied ; "on the contrary, the statements that I am making are true and sober. 25 Indeed, the King knows about these matters, so I speak 26 before him without constraint. I am sure that there is nothing whatever of what I have been telling him that has escaped his attention ; for all this has not been done in a corner. King Agrippa, do you believe the Prophets ? I know 27 you do."

But Agrippa said to Paul : 28

"You are soon trying to make a Christian of me ! "

"Whether it is soon or late," answered Paul, "I would to 29 God that not only you, but all who are listening to me, might to-day become just what I am myself—except for these chains ! "

Then the King rose, with the Governor and Bernice and 30 those who had been sitting with them, and, after retiring, dis- 31 cussed the case among themselves.

"There is nothing," they said, "deserving death or im- prisonment in this man's conduct " ; and, speaking to Festus, 32 Agrippa added :

"The man might have been discharged, if he had not appealed to the Emperor."

Paul's Voyage to Rome. As it was decided that we were to sail to Italy, 1 **27** Paul and some other prisoners were put in charge of a Captain of the Augustan Guard, named Julius. We went on board a ship from Adramyttium, which was on 2 the point of sailing to the ports along the coast of Roman Asia, and put to sea. Aristarchus, a Macedonian from Thessalonica, went with us. The next day we put into Sidon, where Julius 3 treated Paul in a friendly manner, and allowed him to go to see his friends and receive their hospitality. Putting to sea 4 again, we sailed under the lee of Cyprus, because the wind was against us ; and, after crossing the sea of Cilicia and Pamphylia, 5 we reached Myra in Lycia. There the Roman Officer 6 found an Alexandrian ship on her way to Italy, and put us on board of her. For several days our progress was slow, and it 7 was only with difficulty that we arrived off Cnidus. As the wind was still unfavourable when we came off Cape Salmone,

K*

we sailed under the lee of Crete, and with difficulty, by keeping 8 close in shore, we reached a place called ' Fair Havens,' near which was the town of Lasea.

This had taken a considerable time, and sailing was already 9 dangerous, for the Fast was already over ; and so Paul gave this warning.

" My friends," he said, " I see that this voyage will be 10 attended with injury and much damage, not only to the cargo and the ship, but to our own lives also."

The Roman Officer, however, was more influenced by the cap- 11 tain and the owner than by what was said by Paul. And, as the 12 harbour was not a suitable one to winter in, the majority were in favour of continuing the voyage, in the hope of being able to reach Phoenix, and winter there. Phoenix was a Cretan harbour, open to the north-east and south-east. So, 13 when a light wind sprang up from the south, thinking that they had found their opportunity, they weighed anchor and kept along the coast of Crete, close in shore. But shortly 14 afterwards a hurricane came down on us off the land— a north-easter, as it is called. The ship was caught by it 15 and was unable to keep her head to the wind, so we had to give way and let her drive before it. Running under the lee 16 of a small island called Cauda, we only just managed to secure the ship's boat, and, after hoisting it on board, the men frapped 17 the ship. But, afraid of being driven on to the Syrtis Sands, they lowered the yard, and then drifted. So violently were we 18 tossed about by the storm, that the next day they began throw- ing the cargo overboard, and, on the following day, threw out 19 the ship's tackle with their own hands. As neither sun nor 20 stars were visible for several days, and, as the gale still con- tinued severe, all hope of our being saved was at last aban- doned. It was then, when they had gone a long time 21 without food, that Paul came forward, and said :

" My friends, you should have listened to me, and not have sailed from Crete and so incurred this injury and damage. Yet, even as things are, I urge you not to lose courage, for 22 there will not be a single life lost among you—only the ship. For last night an angel of the God to whom I 23 belong, and whom I serve, stood by me, and said—' Have 24 no fear, Paul ; you must appear before the Emperor, and God himself has given you the lives of all your fellow- voyagers.' Therefore, courage, my friends ! for I believe God, 25 that everything will happen exactly as I have been told. We 26 shall, however, have to be driven on some island."

It was now the fourteenth night of the storm, and we were 27 drifting about in the Adriatic Sea, when, about midnight, the sailors began to suspect that they were drawing near land. So they took soundings, and found twenty fathoms of water. 28 After waiting a little, they took soundings again, and found

fifteen fathoms. Then, as they were afraid of our being driven 29
upon some rocky coast, they let go four anchors from the stern,
and longed for daylight.   The sailors wanted to leave 30
the ship, and had lowered the boat, on pretence of running
out anchors from the bows, when Paul said to the Roman 31
Officer and his men :

" Unless the sailors remain on board, you cannot be saved."
Upon that the soldiers cut the ropes which held the boat, and 32
let her drift away.   In the interval before daybreak 33
Paul kept urging them all to take something to eat.

" It is a fortnight to-day," he said, " that, owing to your
anxiety, you have gone without food, taking nothing.   So 34
I urge you to take something to eat ; your safety depends
upon it, for not one of you will lose even a hair of his head."
With these words he took some bread, and, after saying the 35
thanksgiving to God before them all, broke it in pieces, and
began to eat ; and the men all felt cheered and had something to 36
eat themselves. There were about seventy-six of us on board, 37
all told. After satisfying their hunger, they further lightened 38
the ship by throwing the grain into the sea.   When 39
Paul is daylight came, they could not make out what
shipwrecked. land it was, but, observing a creek in which there
was a beach, they consulted as to whether they could run the
ship safely into it.   Then they cast off, and abandoned the 40
anchors, and at the same time unlashed the gear of the steer-
ing oars, hoisted the foresail to the wind, and made for the
beach.   They got, however, into a kind of channel, and 41
there ran the ship aground.   The bows stuck fast and could
not be moved, while the stern began breaking up under the
strain.   The advice of the soldiers was that the prisoners 42
should be killed, for fear that any of them should swim
away and make their escape.   But the Roman Officer, anxious 43
to save Paul, prevented their carrying out their intention, and
ordered that those who could swim should be the first to
jump into the sea and try to reach the shore ; and that the 44
rest should follow, some on planks, and others on different
pieces of the ship.   In these various ways every one managed
to get safely ashore.

Paul When we were all safe, we found that the 1 **28**
at Malta. island was called Malta.   The natives showed us 2
marked kindness, for they lit a fire and took us all under shelter,
because it had come on to rain and was cold.   Paul had 3
gathered a quantity of dry sticks and laid them on the fire,
when a viper, driven out by the heat, fastened on his hand.
When the natives saw the creature hanging from his hand, 4
they said to one another :

" Evidently this man is a murderer, for, though he has been
saved from the sea, Justice has not allowed him to live."

However, Paul shook the creature off into the fire and took no   5
harm.   The natives were expecting inflammation to set in, or   6
that he would suddenly fall dead ; but, after waiting for a long
time, and seeing that there was nothing amiss with him, they
changed their minds and said that he was a God.

In that neighbourhood there was an estate belonging to the   7
Governor of the island, whose name was Publius.   He took
us up to his house, and for three days entertained us most
courteously.   It happened that the father of Publius was ly-   8
ing ill of fever and dysentery.   So Paul went to see him ; and,
after praying, he placed his hands on him and cured him.
After this, all the people in the island who had any illness came   9
to Paul, and were cured.   They also presented us with many   10
gifts, and when we set sail they put supplies of necessaries on
board.

Paul's Voyage   After three months, we set sail in a ship that   11
to Rome   had wintered in the island.   She was an Alexan-
continued.   drian vessel, and had the Twin Sons of Zeus for
her figure-head.   We put in at Syracuse and stayed there three   12
days, and from there we worked to windward and so got to   13
Rhegium.   A day later a south wind sprang up and took us to
Puteoli in two days.   There we found some of the Brethren,   14
and were urged to stay a week with them ; after which we
went on to Rome.   The Brethren there had heard about us,   15
and came out as far as the Market of Appius and the Three
Taverns to meet us.   At sight of them Paul thanked God and
was much cheered.

On our reaching Rome, Paul was allowed to live by himself,   16
except for the soldier who was in charge of him.

Paul   Three days after our arrival, Paul invited the   17
at Rome.   leading Jews to meet him ; and, when they came,
he spoke to them as follows :

"Brothers, although I had done nothing hostile to the interests of our nation or to our ancestral customs, yet I was sent
from Jerusalem as a prisoner, and handed over to the Romans.
The Romans, when they had examined me, were ready to   18
release me, because there was nothing in my conduct deserving death.   But, as the Jews opposed my release, I was com-   19
pelled to appeal to the Emperor—not, indeed, that I had any
charge to make against my own nation.   This, then, is my   20
reason for urging you to come to see me and talk with me ;
because it is for the sake of the Hope of Israel that I am here
in chains."

"We," was their reply, " have not had any letter about you   21
from Judaea, nor have any of our fellow-Jews come and
reported or said anything bad about you.   But we shall be   22

glad to hear from you what your views are, for, with regard to this sect, we are well aware that it is spoken against on all sides."

They then fixed a day with him, and came to the place 23 where he was staying, in even larger numbers, when Paul proceeded to lay the subject before them. He bore his testimony to the Kingdom of God, and tried to convince them about Jesus, by arguments drawn from the Law of Moses and from the Prophets—speaking from morning till evening.   Some were inclined to accept what he said ; 24 others, however, rejected it.   So, as they disagreed among 25 themselves, they began to disperse, Paul adding only—

" True, indeed, was the declaration made by the Holy Spirit, through the Prophet Isaiah to your ancestors—

'Go to this nation and say— 26
  "You will hear with your ears without ever understanding,
    And, though you have eyes, you will see without ever
      perceiving."
  For the mind of this nation has grown dense, 27
    And their ears are dull of hearing,
      Their eyes also have they closed ;
      Lest some day they should see with their eyes,
    And with their ears they should hear,
  And in their mind they should understand, and should turn—
    And I should heal them.'

Understand, then, that this Salvation of God was sent for the 28 Gentiles ; and they will listen."

For two whole years Paul stayed in a house which he rented 30 for himself, welcoming all who came to see him, proclaiming 31 the Kingdom of God, and teaching about the Lord Jesus Christ, with perfect fearlessness, unmolested.

26—27 Isa. 6. 9—10.   28 Ps. 67. 2.

THE LETTERS.

THE LETTER OF JAMES.

THE LETTERS OF PAUL—

        TO THE THESSALONIANS I. AND II.
        TO THE GALATIANS.
        TO THE CORINTHIANS I. AND II.
        TO THE ROMANS.
        TO THE COLOSSIANS.
        TO PHILEMON.
        TO THE EPHESIANS.
        TO THE PHILIPPIANS.
        TO TIMOTHY I. AND II.
        TO TITUS.

THE LETTER TO HEBREWS.

THE LETTERS OF PETER I. AND II.

THE LETTER OF JUDE.

THE LETTERS OF JOHN I., II., AND III.

THE LETTER OF JAMES.

FROM JAMES.

ST. JAMES'S LETTER TO CHRISTIANS OF JEWISH ORIGIN.

WRITTEN PROBABLY AT JERUSALEM AFTER 44 A.D.

THIS Letter is believed to have been written by the James who was known to the Early Church as 'James the Just.' He was not an Apostle, but was one of the brothers of Jesus, and presided over the Church at Jerusalem, in which position he came into contact with large numbers both of Jews and Christians (Acts 12. 17; 15. 13). The Letter is addressed to converts from Judaism, and speaks, in strong condemnation, of vices which prevailed in the corrupt society of Jerusalem, and into which the recent converts to Christianity were, to some extent, relapsing. There are indications in the Letter that some, at all events, of those for whom it was intended had been passing through days of persecution—possibly the persecution by Herod Agrippa I., 44 A.D. (Acts 12. 1), in which the Apostle James was martyred. The writer of this Letter met with a similar fate in 63 A.D.

FROM

JAMES.

I.—Greeting.

JAMES, a Servant of God and of the Lord Jesus Christ, greets
The Twelve Tribes that are living abroad. **1**

II.—Advice upon Various Subjects.

Trials. My Brothers, whatever may be the temptations that beset you from time to time, always regard them as a reason for rejoicing, knowing, as you do, that the testing of your faith develops endurance. And let endurance do its work perfectly, so that you may be altogether perfect, and in no respect deficient.

Lack of Wisdom. If one of you is deficient in wisdom, let him ask wisdom from the God who gives freely to every one without reproaches, and it will be given to him. But let him ask with confidence, never doubting ; for the man who doubts is like a wave of the sea driven hither and thither at the mercy of the wind—such a man must not expect that he will receive anything from the Lord, vacillating as he is, irresolute at every turn. Let a Brother in humble circumstances be proud of his exalted position, but a rich Brother of **Wealth and Poverty.** his humiliation ; for the rich man will pass away 'like the flower of the grass.' As the sun rises, and the hot wind blows, 'the grass withers, its flower fades,' and all its beauty is gone. So is it with the rich man. In the midst of his pursuits he will come to an untimely end.

Temptation. Blessed is the man who remains firm under temptation, for, when he has stood the test, he will receive the crown of Life, which the Lord has promised to those who love him. Let no one say, when he is tempted, "It is God who is tempting me !" For God, who cannot be

2
3
4
5
6
7
8
9
10
11
12
13

10—11 Isa. 40. 6—7. 12 Dan. 12. 12.

tempted to do wrong, does not himself tempt any one. A 14
man is in every case tempted by his own passions—allured
and enticed by them. Then Passion conceives and gives 15
birth to Sin, and Sin, on reaching maturity, brings forth
Death. 　　　Do not be deceived, my dear Brothers. Every 16, 17
good thing given us, and every perfect gift, is from above, and
comes down to us from the Maker of the Lights in the heavens,
who is himself never subject to change or to eclipse. Because 18
he so willed, he gave us Life, through the Message of the
Truth, so that we should be, as it were, an earnest of still
further creations.

**True
Religion.** 　　Mark this, my dear Brothers :—Let every one 19
be quick to listen, slow to speak, and slow to get
angry ; for the anger of man does not forward the 20
righteous purpose of God. Therefore, have done with all 21
filthiness and whatever wickedness still remains, and in a
humble spirit receive that Message which has been planted in
your hearts and is able to save your souls. 　　Put that 22
Message into practice, and do not merely listen to it—deceiving
yourselves. For, when any one listens to it and does not 23
practice it, he is like a man looking at his own face in a mirror.
He looks at himself, then goes on his way, and immediately 24
forgets what he is like. 　But he who looks carefully into the 25
perfect Law, the Law of Freedom, and continues to do so, not
listening to it and then forgetting it, but putting it into practice—that man will be blessed in what he does. 　　　When 26
a man appears to be religious, yet does not bridle his tongue,
but imposes upon his own conscience, that man's religious
observances are valueless. That religious observance which 27
is pure and spotless in the eyes of God our Father is this—
to visit orphans and widows in their trouble, and to keep oneself uncontaminated by the world.

III.—WARNING UPON VARIOUS SUBJECTS.

**On the
Treatment
of the
Poor.** 　　My Brothers, are you really trying to combine 1 **2**
faith in Jesus Christ, our glorified Lord, with the
worship of rank ? Suppose a man should enter 2
your Synagogue, with gold rings and in grand
clothes, and suppose a poor man should come in also, in
shabby clothes, and you are deferential to the man who is 3
wearing grand clothes, and say—"There is a good seat for
you here," but to the poor man—"You must stand ; or sit
down there by my footstool," is not that to make distinc- 4
tions among yourselves, and to show yourselves prejudiced
judges ? 　　　Listen, my dear Brothers. Has not God 5
chosen those who are poor in the things of this world to be rich

through their faith, and to possess the Kingdom which he has
promised to those who love him? But you—you insult the 6
poor man! Is not it the rich who oppress you? Is not it they
who drag you into law-courts? Is not it they who malign that 7
honourable Name which has been bestowed upon you? Yet, if 8
you keep the royal law which runs—'Thou shalt love thy neighbour as thou dost thyself,' you are doing right; but, if you 9
worship rank, you commit a sin, and stand convicted by that
same law of being offenders against it.   For a man who 10
has laid the Law, as a whole, to heart, but has failed in one
particular, is liable for breaking all its provisions. He who said 11
'Thou shalt not commit adultery' also said 'Thou shalt not
murder.' If, then, you commit murder but not adultery, you
are still an offender against the Law. Therefore, speak and 12
act as men who are to be judged by the 'Law of Freedom.'
For there will be justice without mercy for him who has not 13
acted mercifully. Mercy triumphs over Justice.

My Brothers, what is the good of a man's saying 14
On 'Faith that he has faith, if he does not prove it by actions?
and Can such faith save him? Suppose some Brother 15
Works.' or Sister should be in want of clothes and of daily
bread, and one of you were to say to them—" Go, and peace 16
be with you; find warmth and food for yourselves," and yet you
were not to give them the necessaries of life, what good would
it be to them? In just the same way faith, if not followed by 17
actions, is, by itself, a lifeless thing. Some one, indeed, may 18
say—"You are a man of faith, and I am a man of action."
"Then show me your faith," I reply, "apart from any actions,
and I will show you my faith by my actions." It is a part of 19
your Faith, is it not, that there is one God? Good; yet even
the demons have that faith, and tremble at the thought. Now 20
do you really want to understand, you foolish man, how it is
that faith without actions leads to nothing? Look at our 21
ancestor, Abraham. Was not it the result of his actions that he
was pronounced righteous after he had offered his son, Isaac,
on the altar? You see how, in his case, faith and actions 22
went together; that his faith was perfected as the result of his
actions; and that in this way the words of Scripture came 23
true—"Abraham believed God, and that was regarded by God
as righteousness," and "He was called the friend of God."
You see, then, that it is as the result of his actions that a man is 24
pronounced righteous, and not of his faith only. Was not it 25
the same with the prostitute, Rahab? Was not it as the result
of her actions that she was pronounced righteous, after she
had welcomed the messengers and hastened them away by a
different road? Exactly as a body is dead without a spirit, 26
so faith is dead without actions.

---

[8] Lev. 19. 18.   [11] Exod. 20. 13—14; Deut. 5. 17—18.   [21] Gen. 22. 2, 9.
[23] Gen. 15. 6; Isa. 41. 8.

On
the Control
of the
Tongue.

I do not want many of you, my Brothers, to become teachers, knowing, as you do, that we who teach shall be judged by a more severe standard than others. We often make mistakes, every one of us. Any one who does not make mistakes in speaking is indeed a perfect man, able to bridle his whole body as well. When we put bits into horses' mouths, to make them obey us, we control the rest of their bodies also. Again, think of ships. Large as they are, and even when driven by fierce winds, they are controlled by a very small rudder and steered in whatever direction the man at the helm may determine. So is it with the tongue. Small as it is, it is a great boaster. Think how tiny a spark may set the largest forest ablaze ! And the tongue is like a spark. Among the members of our body it proves itself a very world of mischief ; it contaminates the whole body ; it sets the wheels of life on fire, and is itself set on fire by the flames of the Pit. For while all sorts of beasts and birds, and of reptiles and creatures in the sea, are tame-able, and actually have been tamed by man, no human being can tame the tongue. It is a restless plague ! It is charged with deadly poison ! With it we bless our Lord and Father, and with it we curse men who are made 'in God's likeness.' From the very same mouth come blessings and curses ! My Brothers, it is not right that this should be so. Does a spring give both good and bad water from the same source ? Can a fig tree, my Brothers, bear olives ? or a vine bear figs ? No, nor can a brackish well give good water.

Against
false
Wisdom.

Who among you claims to be wise and intelli-gent ? Let him show that his actions are the out-come of a good life lived in the humility of true wisdom. But, while you harbour envy and bitterness and a spirit of rivalry in your hearts, do not boast or lie to the detriment of the Truth. That is not the wisdom which comes from above ; no, it is earthly, animal, devilish. For, where envy and rivalry exist, there you will also find disorder and all kinds of base actions. But the wisdom from above is, before every thing else, pure ; then peace-loving, gentle, open to conviction, rich in compassion and good deeds, and free from partiality and insincerity. And righteousness, its fruit, is sown in peace by those who work for peace.

Against
Party-Strife.

What is the cause of the fighting and quarrel-ling that goes on among you ? Is not it to be found in the desires which are always at war within you ? You crave, yet do not obtain. You murder and rage, yet cannot gain your end. You quarrel and fight. You do not obtain, because you do not ask. You ask, yet do not receive, because you ask for a wrong purpose—to spend what

9 Gen. 1. 26.

you get upon your pleasures.   Unfaithful people !   Do not   4
you know that to be friends with the world means to be at
enmity with God ?   Therefore whoever chooses to be friends
with the world makes himself an enemy to God.   Do you sup-   5
pose there is no meaning in the passage of Scripture which
asks—'Is envy to result from the longings of the Spirit which
God has implanted within you ?'   No ; the gift that God gives   6
is for a nobler end ; and that is why it is said—'God is opposed
to the haughty, but gives help to the humble.'   There-   7
fore submit to God ; but resist the Devil, and he will flee from
you.   Draw near to God, and he will draw near to you.   Make   8
your hands clean, you sinners ; and your hearts pure, you
vacillating men !   Grieve, mourn, and lament !   Let your   9
laughter be turned to mourning, and your happiness to gloom !
Humble yourselves before the Lord, and he will exalt you.   10

Do not disparage one another, Brothers.   He who dis-   11
parages his Brother, or passes judgement on his Brother, dis-
parages the Law and passes judgement on the Law.   But, if
you pass judgement on the Law, you are not obeying it, but
judging it.   There is only one Lawgiver and Judge—he who   12
has the power both to save and to destroy.   But who are you
that pass judgement on your neighbour ?

**Against
Presumption.** Listen to me, you who say 'To-day or to-morrow   13
we will go to such and such a town, spend a year
there, and trade, and make money,' and yet you do   14
not know what your life will be like to-morrow !   For you are
but a mist appearing for a little while and then disappearing.
You ought, rather, to say 'If the Lord wills, we shall live and   15
do this or that.'   But, as it is, you are constantly boasting   16
presumptuously !   All such boasting is wicked.   He, then, who   17
knows what is right but fails to do it—that is sin in him.

**Against
Oppression.** Listen to me, you rich men, weep and wail for   1   **5**
the miseries that are coming upon you !   Your   2
riches have wasted away, and your clothes have
become moth-eaten.   Your gold and silver are rusted ; and   3
the rust on them shall be evidence against you, and shall eat
into your very flesh.   It was fire, so to speak, that you stored
up for yourselves in these last days.   I tell you, the wages of   4
the labourers who mowed your fields, which you have been
fraudulently keeping back, are crying out against you, and the
outcries of your reapers have reached the ears of the Lord of
Hosts !   You have lived on earth a life of extravagance and   5
luxury ; you have indulged your fancies in a time of bloodshed.
You have condemned, you have murdered, the Righteous One !   6
Must not God be opposed to you ?

¹ Prov. 3. 34.   ³ Prov. 16. 27.   ⁴ Deut. 24, 15, 17 ; Mal. 3. 5 ; Isa. 5. 9.   ⁵ Jer. 12. 3.

IV.—Concluding Exhortations.

Christian Patience. Be patient, then, Brothers, till the Coming of 7 the Lord. Even the farmer has to wait for the precious fruit of the earth, watching over it patiently, till it has had the spring and summer rains. And 8 you must be patient also, and not be discouraged; for the Lord's Coming is near. Do not make complaints against one 9 another, Brothers, or judgement will be passed upon you. The Judge is already standing at the door! Brothers, as an 10 example of the patient endurance of suffering, take the Prophets who spoke in the name of the Lord. We count those 11 who displayed such endurance blessed! You have heard, too, of Job's endurance, and have seen what the Lord's purpose was, for 'the Lord is full of pity and compassion.'

Against Oaths. Above all things, my Brothers, never take an 12 oath, either by heaven, or by earth, or by anything else. With you let 'Yes' suffice for yes, and 'No' for no, so that you may escape condemnation.

The Power of Prayer. If any one of you is in trouble, let him pray; 13 if any one is happy, let him sing hymns If 14 any one of you is ill, let him send for the Officers of the Church, and let them pray over him, after anointing him with oil in the name of the Lord. The 15 prayer offered in faith will save the man who is sick, and the Lord will raise him from his bed; and if he has committed sins, he will be forgiven. Therefore, confess your sins to one 16 another and pray for one another, that you may be cured. Great is the power of a good man's fervent prayer. Elijah was 17 only a man like ourselves, but, when he prayed fervently that it might not rain, no rain fell upon the land for three years and a half. And, when he prayed again, the clouds brought rain, 18 and the land bore crops. My Brothers, should one of 19 **The Blessedness of Saving a Soul.** you be led astray from the Truth, and some one bring him back again, be sure that he who brings 20 a sinner back from his mistaken ways will save that man's soul from Death, and throw a veil over countless sins.

7 Deut. 11. 14.   11 Dan. 12. 12; Ps. 103. 8.   20 Prov. 10. 12.

THE LETTERS OF PAUL.

TO THE THESSALONIANS.

I.

ST. PAUL'S FIRST LETTER TO THE THESSALONIANS.

WRITTEN PROBABLY DURING HIS STAY AT CORINTH, IN THE COURSE OF HIS SECOND MISSIONARY JOURNEY, ABOUT 52 A.D.

THESSALONICA, now the Turkish town of Salonica, was an important seaport in Macedonia, on the great highway by which trade travelled between Europe and Roman Asia. Attracted, probably, by its large Jewish population, and by its admirable position as a centre for the diffusion of his Message, the Apostle Paul visited the town in the course of his second missionary journey (Acts 17), preaching in the Synagogue, and working at his trade as a tent-maker (I. Thess. 2. 9; II. Thess. 3. 8). At first he gained many converts, but after a short time his unbelieving countrymen succeeded in arousing a strong opposition against him and his companions. This was carried so far that a mob collected and attacked the house in which they were staying, and Paul and Silas barely escaped with their lives. Leaving Thessalonica, they went on to Beroea, and from there to Athens and Corinth. But while the Apostle was at Athens, news reached him that the little Christian community, from which he had thus been compelled to part, was itself suffering persecution. On hearing this, the keen interest which he felt in their welfare made him eager to return to them (2. 18). But, this proving at the time impossible, he sent Timothy to them, to obtain further information, and to comfort and encourage them amidst their sufferings (3. 2). Upon Timothy's return to Corinth, with good news of the faith and love shown by the Thessalonian converts, the Apostle wrote this Letter.

TO THE
THESSALONIANS.
I.

I.—INTRODUCTION.

To the Thessalonian Church in union with God 1
Greeting. the Father and the Lord Jesus Christ,
FROM Paul, Silas, and Timothy.
May God bless you and give you peace.

II.—THE APOSTLE AND HIS CONVERTS.

We always mention you in our prayers and thank God 2
for you all; recalling continually before our God and Father 3
the efforts that have resulted from your faith,
His Thank- the toil prompted by your love, and the patient
fulness for endurance sustained by your hope in our Lord
their Faith, Jesus Christ. Brothers, whom God loves, we 4
and its know that he has chosen you, because the Good 5
Influence.
News that we brought came home to you, not merely as so
many words, but with a power and a fulness of conviction due
to the Holy Spirit. For you know the life that we lived among
you for your good. And you yourselves began to follow, not 6
only our example, but the Master's also; and, in spite of much
suffering, you welcomed the Message with a joy inspired by
the Holy Spirit, and so became a pattern to all who believed 7
in Christ throughout Macedonia and Greece. For it was 8
from you that the Lord's Message resounded throughout
Macedonia and Greece; and, more than that, your faith in
God has become known far and wide; so that there is no
need for us to say another word. Indeed, in speaking about 9
us, the people themselves tell of the reception you gave us,
and how, turning to God from your idols, you became servants
of the true and living God, and are now awaiting the return 10
from Heaven of his Son whom he raised from the dead—
Jesus, our deliverer from the Coming Wrath.

Yes, Brothers, you yourselves know that your   1
His Life reception of us was not without result. For,   2
among them. although we had experienced suffering and
ill-treatment, as you know, at Philippi, we had the
courage, by the help of our God, to tell you God's Good
News in spite of great opposition. Our appeal to you   3
was not based on a delusion, nor was it made from unworthy motives, or with any intention of misleading you.
But, having been found worthy by God to be entrusted with   4
the Good News, therefore we tell it ; with a view to please, not
men, but God who proves our hearts. Never at any time,   5
as you know, did we use the language of flattery, or make
false professions in order to hide selfish aims. God will bear
witness to that. Nor did we seek to win honour from men,   6
whether from you or from others, although, as Apostles of
Christ, we might have burdened you with our support. But   7
we lived among you with the simplicity of a child ; we were
like a woman nursing her own children. In our strong affec-   8
tion for you, that seemed to us the best way of sharing with you,
not only God's Good News, but our very lives as well—so dear
had you become to us. You will not have forgotten, Brothers,   9
our labour and toil. Night and day we used to work at our
trades, so as not to be a burden to any of you, while we proclaimed to you God's Good News. You will bear witness, and   10
God also, that our relations with you who believed in Christ
were pure, and upright, and beyond reproach. Indeed, you   11
know that, like a father with his own children, we used
to encourage and comfort every one of you, and solemnly
plead with you ; so that you should make your daily lives   12
worthy of God who is calling you into the glory of his Kingdom.

Their Persecu- This, too, is a reason why we, on our part, are   13
tion by their continually thanking God—because, in receiving
Fellow- the teaching that you had from us, you accepted
Citizens. it, not as the teaching of man, but as what it really
is—the teaching of God, which is even now doing its work
within you who believe in Christ. For you, Brothers, began   14
to follow the example of the Churches of God in Judaea which
are in union with Jesus Christ ; you, in your turn, suffering at
the hands of your fellow-citizens, in the same way as those
Churches did at the hands of the Jews—the men who killed   15
both the Lord Jesus and the Prophets, and persecuted us also.
They do not try to please God, and they are enemies to all mankind, for they would prevent us from speaking to the Gentiles   16
with a view to their Salvation, and thus are always ' filling up
the measure of their iniquity.' But the Wrath of God has come
upon them to the full !

Frustrated Plans. As for ourselves, Brothers, our having been 17 bereaved of you even for a short time—though in body only, and not in spirit—made us all the more eager to see your faces again ; and the longing to do so was strong upon us. That was why we made up our minds to 18 go to see you—at least I, Paul, did, more than once—but Satan put difficulties in our way. For what hope or joy will 19 be ours, or what crown shall we have to boast of, in the presence of our Lord Jesus, at his Coming, if it be not you ? You are our pride and our delight ! 20

Timothy's Mission. And so, as we could bear it no longer, we 1 **3** made up our minds to remain behind alone at Athens, and sent Timothy, our Brother and 2 God's Minister of the Good News of the Christ, to strengthen you, and to encourage you in your faith, so that none of you 3 should be shaken by the troubles through which you are passing. You yourselves know that we are destined to meet with such things. For, even while we were with you, 4 we warned you beforehand that we were certain to encounter trouble. And so it proved, as you know. Therefore, since I 5 could no longer endure the uncertainty, I sent to make inquiries about your faith, fearing that the Tempter had tempted you, and that our toil might prove to have been in vain. But, when Timothy recently returned to us from 6 you with good news of your faith and love, and told us how kindly you think of us—always longing, he said, to see us, just as we are longing to see you—on hearing this, we felt 7 encouraged about you, Brothers, in the midst of all our difficulties and troubles, by your faith. For it is new life to us to 8 know that you are holding fast to the Lord. How can we thank 9 God enough for all the happiness that you are giving us in the sight of our God ? Night and day we pray most earnestly 10 that we may see you face to face, and make good any deficiency in your faith.

The Apostle's Prayer for his Converts. May our God and Father himself, and Jesus, 11 our Lord, make the way plain for us to come to you. And for you, may the Lord fill you to 12 overflowing with love for one another and for every one, just as we are filled with love for you ; and so make 13 your hearts strong, and your lives pure beyond reproach, in the sight of our God and Father, at the Coming of our Lord Jesus, with all his Holy Ones.

III.—ADVICE UPON THE DAILY LIFE.

Further, Brothers, we beg and exhort you in the name of 1 **4** our Lord Jesus to carry out more fully than ever—as indeed you are already doing—all that you have heard from us as to

what your daily life must be, if it is to please God.   For you   2
have not forgotten the directions that we gave you on the
authority of our Lord Jesus.

For this is God's purpose—that you should be   3
Warning pure ; abstaining from all immorality ; each of   4
against you recognizing the duty of taking one woman
Immorality. for his wife, purely and honourably, and not for   5
the mere gratification of his passions, like the Gentiles who
know nothing of God; none of you over-reaching or taking   6
advantage of his Brother in such matters.   'The Lord takes
vengeance' upon all who do such things, as we have already
warned you and solemnly declared.   For God's Call to us does   7
not permit of an impure life, but demands purity.   Therefore   8
he who disregards this warning disregards, not man, but
God who gives you his Holy Spirit.

As to love for the Brethren there is no need to   9
Brotherly write to you ; for you have yourselves been taught
Love. by God to love one another ; and indeed you   10
do act in this spirit towards all the Brethren throughout
Macedonia.

Yet, Brothers, we urge you to still further
The Duty of efforts.   Make it your ambition to live quietly,
Work. and to attend to your own business, and to work   11
with your hands, as we directed you ; so that your conduct   12
may win respect from those outside the Church, and that you
may not want for anything.

IV.—THE DEAD IN CHRIST AT THE COMING OF THE LORD.

We do not wish you to remain in ignorance,   13
The Living Brothers, with regard to those who have passed
and the to their rest, that your grief may not be like that
Dead. of others, who have no hope.   For, as we believe   14
that Jesus died and rose again, so also we believe that God will
bring, with Jesus, those who through him have passed to their
rest.   This we tell you on the authority of the Lord—   15
that those of us who are still living at the Coming of the Lord will
not anticipate those who have passed to their rest.   For, with a   16
loud summons, with the shout of an archangel, and with the
trumpet-call of God, the Lord himself will come down from
Heaven.   Then those who died in union with Christ shall rise   17
first ; and afterwards we who are still living shall be caught
up in the clouds, with them, to meet the Lord in the air ; and
so we shall be for ever with the Lord.   Therefore, com-   18
fort one another with what I have told you.

5 Ps. 79. 6 ; Jer. 10. 25.   6 Ps. 94. 1.   8 Ezek. 37. 14.

The Time of the Lord's Coming. But as to the times and the moments, there is no need, Brothers, for any one to write to you. You yourselves know well that the Day of the Lord will come just as a thief comes in the night. When people are saying 'All is quiet and safe,' it is then that, like birth-pains upon a woman with child, Ruin comes suddenly upon them, and there will be no escape! You, however, Brothers, are not in darkness, that the daylight should take you by surprise as if you were thieves. For you all are 'Sons of Light' and 'Sons of the Day.'

The Necessity for Watchfulness. We have nothing to do with night, or darkness. Therefore let us not sleep as others do. No, let us be watchful and self-controlled. It is at night that men sleep, and at night that drunkards get drunk. But let us, who belong to the Day, control ourselves, and put on faith and love as a breastplate, and the hope of Salvation as a helmet. For God destined us, not for Wrath, but to win Salvation through our Lord Jesus Christ, who died for us, that, whether we are still watching or have fallen asleep, we may live with him. Therefore encourage one another, and try to build up one another's characters, as indeed you are doing.

1 **5**
2
3
4
5
6
7
8
9
10
11

V.—CONCLUSION.

Final Counsels. We beg you, Brothers, to value those who toil among you, and are your leaders in the Lord's service, and give you counsel. Hold them in the very greatest esteem and affection for the sake of their work. Live at peace with one another. We entreat you also, Brothers— warn the disorderly, comfort the faint-hearted, give a helping hand to the weak, and be patient with every one. Take care that none of you ever pays back wrong for wrong, but always follow the kindest course with one another and with every one. Always be joyful; never cease to pray; under all circumstances give thanks to God. For this is his will for you as made known in Christ Jesus. Do not quench the Spirit; do not make light of preaching. Bring everything to the test; cling to what is good; shun every form of evil. May God himself, the giver of peace, make you altogether holy; and may your spirits, souls, and bodies be kept altogether faultless until the Coming of our Lord Jesus Christ. He who calls you will not fail you; he will complete his work.

12
13
14
15
16, 17
18
19, 20
21
22, 23
24

8 Isa. 59. 17.   22 Job 1. 1 ; 2. 3.

Brothers, pray for us.   25

Farewell.   Greet all the Brothers with a sacred kiss.   I   26, 27
adjure you in the Lord's name to have this letter
read to all the Brethren.

May the blessing of our Lord Jesus Christ be with you.   28

TO THE THESSALONIANS.

II.

ST. PAUL'S SECOND LETTER TO THE THESSALONIANS.

WRITTEN PROBABLY DURING HIS STAY AT CORINTH, IN THE COURSE OF HIS SECOND MISSIONARY JOURNEY, ABOUT 53 A.D.

It is probable that about a year intervened between the Apostle's two Letters to this Macedonian Church. The Thessalonians had misunderstood what he had said in the first Letter as to the nearness of the time of Christ's Return to the earth ; a misunderstanding which led to the neglect of the ordinary duties of life, accompanied by unrestrained religious excitement. To correct this misapprehension, and to urge them to fortitude, calmness and industry, St. Paul wrote this second Letter.

TO THE
THESSALONIANS.
II.

I.—INTRODUCTION.

Greeting. To the Thessalonian Church in union with God
our Father and the Lord Jesus Christ,

FROM Paul, Silas, and Timothy.

May God, the Father, and the Lord Jesus Christ bless you and
give you peace.

II.—THE APOSTLE AND HIS CONVERTS.

His Thankfulness and Confidence. Brothers, it is our duty always to thank
God about you, as is but right, considering the
wonderful growth of your faith, and because,
without exception, your love for one another
is continually increasing. So much is this the case that
we ourselves speak with pride, before the Churches of God,
of the patience and faith which you have shown, in spite of all
the persecutions and troubles that you are enduring. These
persecutions will vindicate the justice of God's judgement, and
will result in your being reckoned worthy of God's Kingdom,
for the sake of which you are now afflicted; since God
deems it just to inflict suffering upon those who are now
inflicting suffering upon you, and to give relief to you who are
suffering, as well as to us, at the Appearing of the Lord Jesus
from Heaven with his mighty angels, 'in flaming fire.' Then he
will 'inflict punishment upon those who refuse to know God,
and upon those who turn a deaf ear' to the Good News of Jesus,
our Lord. These men will pay the penalty of unutterable
Ruin—banished 'from the presence of the Lord and from the
glorious manifestation of his might, when he comes to be
honoured in his People,' and to be revered in all who have learnt
to believe in him (for you also believed our testimony)—as he
will be on 'That Day.' With this in view, our constant

1

2

3

4

5

6

7

8

9

10

11

1

[8] Isa. 66. 14—15; Jer. 10. 25; Ps. 79. 6.   [9—10] Isa. 2. 10, 11, 19, 21; Ps. 80. 7;
68. 35 (Septuagint); Isa. 49. 3.

His Prayer for them. prayer for you is that our God may count you worthy of the Call that you have received, and by his power make perfect your delight in all goodness and the efforts that have resulted from your faith.   Then, in the loving- 12
kindness of our God and the Lord Jesus Christ, will the name of Jesus, our Lord, be honoured in you, and you in him.

III.—Events that must precede the Lord's Coming.

The 'Man of Sin,' and the 'Great Apostasy.' As to the Coming of our Lord Jesus Christ, and 1
our being gathered to meet him, we beg you,
Brothers, not lightly to let your minds become 2
unsettled, nor yet to be disturbed by any revelation, or by any message, or by any letter, purporting to come from us, to the effect that the Day of the Lord is come.   Do not let any 3
one deceive you, whatever he may do.   For it will not come until after the Great Apostasy, and the appearing of that Incarna-tion of Wickedness, that Lost Soul, who so opposes himself to 4
every one that is spoken of as a God or as an object of worship, and so exalts himself above them, that he seats himself in the Temple of God, and displays himself as God !   Do 5
not you remember how, when I was with you, I used to speak to you of all this ?   And you know now what the restraining 6
influence is which prevents his appearing before his appointed time.   Wickedness, indeed, is already at work in secret ; but 7
only until he who at present restrains it is removed out of the way.   Then will 'Wickedness Incarnate' appear, but the Lord 8
Jesus will destroy him with the breath of his lips, and annihilate him by the splendour of his Coming.   For at the Coming 9
of the Lord there will be great activity on the part of Satan, in the form of all kinds of deceptive miracles, signs, and marvels, as well as of wicked attempts to delude—to the ruin 10
of those who are on the path to destruction, because they have never received and loved the Truth to their own Salvation. That is why God places them under the influence of a delusion, 11
to cause them to believe a lie ; so that sentence may be passed 12
on all those who refuse to believe the Truth, but delight in wickedness.

The Need for Stedfastness. But, Brothers, whom the Lord loves, it is our 13
duty always to thank God about you, for,
from the first, God chose you for Salvation through the purifying influence of the Spirit, and your belief in the Truth.   To this you were called by the Good 14
News which we brought you, to attain to the glory of our Lord Jesus Christ.   Stand firm then, Brothers, and hold 15

¹² Isa. 66. 5.   ⁴ Dan. 11. 36—37 ; Ezek. 28. 2.   ⁸ Isa. 11. 4 ; Job 4. 9.
¹³ Deut. 33. 12.

fast to the truths that we taught you, whether by word or by letter.	And may our Lord Jesus Christ himself, and 16 God our Father, who loved us and, in his loving-kindness, gave us unfailing consolation and good ground for hope, console your hearts, and strengthen you to do and to say all 17 that is right.

IV.—CONCLUSION.

Mutual Prayer.	In conclusion, Brothers, pray for us—pray that 1 the Lord's Message may spread rapidly, and be received everywhere with honour, as it was among you; and that we may be preserved from wrong-headed and wicked 2 men—for it is not every one who believes in Christ.

But the Lord will not fail you; he will give you strength, 3 and guard you from Evil.	Yes, and the confidence that 4 our union with the Lord enables us to place in you leads us to believe that you are doing, and will do, what we direct you.	May the Lord bring you to the love of God, and 5 to the patience of the Christ.

The Duty of Work.	We urge you, Brothers, in the name of the 6 Lord Jesus Christ, to avoid any Brother who is living an ill-ordered life, which is not in agreement with the teaching that you received from us.	For you know well that 7 you ought to follow our example.	When we were with you, our life was not ill-ordered, nor did we eat any one's bread without 8 paying for it.	Night and day, labouring and toiling, we used to work at our trades, so as not to be a burden upon any of you.	This was not because we had not a right to receive 9 support, but our object was to give you a pattern for you to copy.	Indeed, when we were with you, what we urged 10 upon you was—'If a man does not choose to work, then he shall not eat.'	We hear that there are among you people who 11 are living ill-ordered lives, and who, instead of attending to their own business, are mere busy-bodies.	All such people 12 we urge, and entreat, in the name of the Lord Jesus Christ, to attend quietly to their business, and earn their own living.	You, Brothers, must not grow weary of doing 13 what is right.	If any one disregards what we have said in this 14 letter, mark that man and avoid his company, that he may feel ashamed.	Yet do not think of him as an enemy, but caution 15 him as you would a Brother.	May the Lord, from 16 whom all peace comes, himself give you his peace at all times and in all ways.	May he be with you all.

The Apostle's Autograph Farewell.	I, Paul, add this greeting in my own hand-writing. It is my signature to every letter.	This 17 is how I write.	May the blessing of our Lord 18 Jesus Christ be with you all.

3

TO THE GALATIANS.

ST. PAUL'S LETTER TO THE CHRISTIANS IN GALATIA.

WRITTEN PROBABLY DURING HIS STAY AT EPHESUS, ABOUT 54 A.D.

THE Roman province of 'Galatia,' in Asia Minor, included, not only the district which had previously borne that name, but also various adjacent districts subsequently included. Hence it is uncertain whether, in the New Testament, the name is used in its wider or in its narrower sense. Nor is it possible to fix with certainty the date of the Apostle's visits to 'Galatia,' or of this Letter to his converts there.

The Christian Churches in 'Galatia' appear to have been founded by St. Paul about the year 51 A.D., while he was on his second missionary journey (Acts 16. 6). Three years later he re-visited the district in the course of his third journey (Acts 18. 23). He appears to have been seriously ill on the first-mentioned occasion, but his impulsive converts gave him an eager welcome, and soon became devotedly attached to him (Gal. 4. 13—15). After he had left them, however, their enthusiasm for him and for his Message gradually cooled, and the present Letter was written as the result of information which reached him, that his converts were being led astray by teachers from Jerusalem, who impugned his apostolic authority and personal character, and insisted that all Christians ought to observe the Jewish Law and be circumcised.

St. Paul was now, for the first time, face to face with the question whether Christianity could stand alone as a new and universal religion, or could exist only as 'a modified and extended Judaism.' His reply takes the form, first, of a personal narrative in which he establishes the direct revelation to him of what he delights to call 'his Gospel' by the Christ himself, and its independence of Judaism; and, then, of a brief statement of the teaching (afterwards developed at length in his Letter to the Christians at Rome) that mere obedience to Law can never ensure a man's being 'pronounced righteous' by God; for this, the Apostle argues, can follow only upon faith in the Christ. The Law, intended only to be provisional, has been superseded by the Gospel.

TO THE

GALATIANS.

I.—INTRODUCTION.

Greeting. To the Churches in Galatia,   1
FROM Paul, an Apostle whose commission is not
from men and is given, not by man, but by Jesus Christ
and God the Father who raised him from the dead ;
AND FROM all the Brothers here.   2
May God, our Father, and the Lord Jesus Christ, bless you   3
and give you peace.   For Christ, to rescue us from this
present wicked age, gave himself for our sins, in accor-   4
dance with the will of our God and Father, to whom be   5
ascribed all glory for ever and ever.   Amen.

The Apostle's   I am astonished at your so soon deserting him,   6
Disappoint-   who called you through the love of Christ,
ment.   for a different 'Good News,' which is really no   7
Good News at all.   But then, I know that there are people
who are harassing you, and who want to pervert the Good
News of the Christ.   Yet even if we——or if an angel from   8
Heaven were to tell you any other 'Good News' than that
which we told you, may he be accursed !   We have said it   9
before, and I repeat it now——If any one tells you a 'Good
News' other than that which you received, may he be accursed !

Is this, I ask, trying to conciliate men, or God ?   Am I   10
seeking to please men ?   If I were still trying to please men,
I should not be a servant of Christ.

II.—THE INDEPENDENCE OF THE APOSTLE'S GOSPEL.

Its Special   I would remind you, Brothers, that the Good   11
Revelation.   News which I told is no mere human invention.
I, at least, did not receive it from man, nor was I taught it, but   12
it came to me through a revelation made by Jesus Christ.

L*

His Special Call. You heard, no doubt, of my conduct when I   13
was devoted to Judaism—how I persecuted the
Church of God to an extent beyond belief, and made havoc of it,
and how, in my devotion to Judaism, I surpassed many of my   14
contemporaries among my own people in my intense earnestness in upholding the traditions of my ancestors.   But   15
when God, who had set me apart even before my birth,
and who called me by his love, saw fit to reveal his Son   16
in me, so that I might tell the Good News of him among
the Gentiles, then at once, instead of consulting any human
being, or even going up to Jerusalem to see those who were   17
Apostles before me, I went into Arabia, and came back again
to Damascus.   Three years afterwards I went up to   18
Jerusalem to make the acquaintance of Peter, and I stayed
a fortnight with him.   I did not, however, see any other   19
Apostle, except James, the Master's brother. (As to what I   20
am now writing to you, I call God to witness that I am speaking
the truth).   Afterwards I went to the districts of Syria and   21
Cilicia. But I was still unknown even by sight to the Christian   22
Churches in Judaea; all that they had heard was—'The man who   23
once persecuted us is now telling the Good News of the very
Faith of which he once made havoc.' And they praised God   24
His on my account.   Fourteen years afterwards   1 **2**
independent I went up to Jerusalem again with Barnabas,
Action. and I took Titus also with me.   It was in   2
obedience to a revelation that I went ; and I laid before the
Apostles the Good News that I am proclaiming among the
Gentiles.   I did this privately before those who are thought
highly of, for fear that I might possibly be taking, or might have
already taken, a course which would prove useless.   Yet even   3
my companion, Titus, though a Greek, was not compelled to
be circumcised.   But, on account of the false Brothers who   4
had stolen in, the men who had crept in to spy upon the liberty
which we have through union with Christ Jesus, in order to
bring us back to slavery—why, we did not for a moment yield   5
submission to them, that the Truth of the Good News
might be yours always !   Of those who are thought some-   6
what highly of—what they once were makes no difference to
me ; God does not recognise human distinctions—those, I say,
who are thought highly of added nothing to my Message.
On the contrary, they saw that I had been entrusted with the   7
Good News for the Gentiles, just as Peter had been for the
Jews.   For he who gave Peter power for his mission to the   8
Jews gave me, also, power to go to the Gentiles. Recognizing   9
the charge entrusted to me, James, Peter, and John, who were
regarded as pillars of the Church, openly acknowledged
Barnabas and me as fellow-workers, agreeing that we should
go to the Gentiles, and they to the Jews.   Only we were to   10

[15] Isa. 49. 1.

remember the poor—the very thing I was myself anxious to
His Rebuke do.   But, when Peter came to Antioch, I   11
to Peter. opposed him to his face ; for he stood self-condemned.   Before certain persons came from James, he had   12
been in the habit of eating with the Gentile converts ; but,
when they came, he began to withdraw and hold aloof, for
fear of offending those who still held to circumcision.   The   13
rest of the Jewish converts were guilty of the same hypocrisy,
so that even Barnabas was led away by it.   But, when I saw   14
that they were not dealing straightforwardly with the Truth of
the Good News, I said to Peter, before them all, " If you, who
were born a Jew, adopt Gentile customs, instead of Jewish,
why are you trying to compel the Gentile converts to adopt
Jewish customs ? "

III.—The Law and the Gospel.

The Failure   We, though we are Jews by birth and not out-   15
of the Law. casts of Gentile origin, know that no one is   16
pronounced righteous as the result of obedience to Law, but
only through faith in Christ Jesus.   So we placed our faith in
Christ Jesus, in order that we might be pronounced righteous,
as the result of faith in Christ, and not of obedience to Law ;
for such obedience ' will not result in even one soul's being
pronounced righteous.'   If, while seeking to be pronounced   17
righteous through union with Christ, we were ourselves seen
to be outcasts, would that make Christ an agent of sin ?
Heaven forbid !   For, if I rebuild the very things that I pulled   18
down, I prove myself to have done wrong.   I, indeed,   19
through Law became dead to Law, in order to live for God.
I have been crucified with Christ.   So it is no longer I that   20
live, but it is Christ who lives in me ; and, as for my present
earthly life, I am living it by faith in the Son of God, who
loved me and gave himself for me.   I do not reject   21
the love of God.   If righteousness comes through Law, then
there was no need for Christ to die !

The Galatians   Foolish Galatians !   Who has been fascinating   1   **3**
misled as to you—you before whose very eyes Jesus Christ
the Law. was depicted upon the cross ?   Here is the one   2
thing that I want to find out from you—Did you receive the Spirit
as the result of obedience to Law, or of your having listened
with faith ?   Can you be so foolish ?   After beginning with   3
what is spiritual, do you now end with what is external ?
Did you go through so much to no purpose ?—if indeed it   4
really was to no purpose !   He who supplies you abundantly   5
with his Spirit and endows you with such powers—does he do

this as the result of obedience to Law? or as the result of
your having listened with faith? It is just as it was with 6
Abraham—

> 'He had faith in God, and his faith was regarded by God
> as righteousness.'

Faith, not Law, the Ground of Acceptance. You see, then, that those whose lives are based 7
on faith are the Sons of Abraham. And Scripture, 8
foreseeing that God would pronounce the Gentiles
righteous as the result of faith, foretold the Good
News to Abraham in the words—

> 'Through thee all the Gentiles shall be blessed.'

And, therefore, those whose lives are based on faith share the 9
blessings bestowed upon the faith of Abraham.

All who rely upon obedience to Law are under a curse, for 10
Scripture says—

> 'Cursed is every one who does not abide by all that is
> written in the Book of the Law, and do it.'

Again, it is evident that no one is pronounced righteous before 11
God through Law, for we read—

> 'Through faith the righteous man shall find Life.'

But the Law is not based on faith ; no, its words are— 12

> 'Those who practise these precepts will find Life through them.'

Christ ransomed us from the curse pronounced in the Law, by 13
taking the curse on himself for us, for Scripture says—

> 'Cursed is any one who is hanged on a tree.'

And this he did that the blessing given to Abraham might be 14
extended to the Gentiles through their union with Jesus Christ ;
that so, through our faith, we also might receive the promised
gift of the Spirit.

To take an illustration, Brothers, from daily life :—No one 15
sets aside even an agreement between two men, when
once it has been confirmed, nor does he add conditions to it.
Now it was to Abraham that the promises were made, 'and to 16
his offspring.' It was not said 'to his offsprings,' as if many
persons were meant, but the words were 'to thy offspring,'
showing that one person was meant—and that was Christ.
My point is this :—An agreement already confirmed by God 17
cannot be cancelled by the Law, which came four hundred
and thirty years later, so as to cause the promise to be set
aside. If our heritage is the result of Law, then it has ceased 18
to be the result of a promise. Yet God conferred it on
Abraham by a promise.

[6] Gen. 15. 6.   [8] Gen. 12. 3 ; 18. 18.   [10] Deut. 27. 26.   [11] Hab. 2. 4.   [12] Lev. 18. 5.
[13] Deut. 21. 23.   [16] Gen. 12. 7.

The Purpose of the Law. What, then, you ask, was the use of the Law? It was a later addition, to make men conscious of their wrong-doings, and intended to last only till the coming of that 'offspring' to whom the promise had been made; and it was delivered through angels by a mediator. Now mediation implies more than one person, but God is one only. Does that set the Law in opposition to God's promises? Heaven forbid! For, if a Law had been given capable of bestowing Life, then righteousness would have actually owed its existence to Law. But the words of Scripture represent the whole world as being in bondage to sin, so that the promised blessing, dependent, as it is, upon faith in Jesus Christ, may be given to those who have faith in him.

Before the coming of faith, we were kept under the guard of the Law, in bondage, awaiting the Faith that was destined to be revealed. Thus the Law has proved a guide to lead us to Christ, in order that we may be pronounced righteous as the result of faith. But now that faith has come we no longer need a guide. **The Effect of the Gospel.** For you are all Sons of God, through your faith in Christ Jesus. For all of you who were baptized into union with Christ clothed yourselves with Christ. All distinctions between Jew and Greek, slave and freeman, male and female, have vanished; for in union with Christ Jesus you are all one. And, since you belong to Christ, it follows that you are Abraham's offspring and, under the promise, sharers in the inheritance.

My point is this:—As long as the heir is under age, there is no difference between him and a slave, though he is master of the whole estate. He is subject to the control of guardians and stewards, during the period for which his father has power to appoint them. And so is it with us; when we were under age, as it were, we were slaves to the puerile teaching of this world; but, when the full time came, God sent his Son—born a woman's child, born subject to Law—to ransom those who were subject to Law, so that we might take our position as sons.

And it is because you are sons that God sent into our hearts the Spirit of his Son, with the cry—'Abba, our Father.' You, therefore, are no longer a slave, but a son; and, if a son, then an heir also, by God's appointment.

The retrograde Spirit of the Galatians. Yet formerly, in your ignorance of God, you became slaves to 'gods' which were no gods. But now that you have found God—or, rather, have been found by him—how is it that you are turning back to that poor and feeble puerile teaching, to which yet once again you are wanting to become slaves? You are scrupulous in keeping Days and Months and Seasons and

19

20

21

22

23

24

25

26

27

28

29

1 **4**

2

3

4
5

6

7

8

9

10

Years! You make me fear that the labour which I have spent   11
on you may have been wasted.

The Apostle and his Converts.   I entreat you, Brothers, to become like me, as   12
I became like you.   You have never done me any
wrong.   You remember that it was owing to   13
bodily infirmity that on the first occasion I told you the Good
News.   And as for what must have tried you in my condition, it   14
did not inspire you with scorn or disgust, but you welcomed me
as if I had been an angel of God—or Christ Jesus himself!
What has become, then, of your blessings?   For I can bear   15
witness that, had it been possible, you would have torn out
your eyes and given them to me!   Am I to think, then, that I   16
have become your enemy by telling you the truth?   Certain   17
people are seeking your favour, but with no honourable object.
No, indeed, they want to isolate you, so that you will have to
seek their favour.   It is always honourable to have your favour   18
sought in an honourable cause, and not only when I am with
you, my dear children—you for whom I am again enduring a   19
mother's pains, till a likeness to Christ shall have been formed
in you.   But I could wish to be with you now and speak in a   20
different tone, for I am perplexed about you.

An Allegory of the Law and the Gospel.   Tell me, you who want to be still subject to   21
Law—Why do not you listen to the Law?   Scrip-   22
ture says that Abraham had two sons, one the
child of the slave-woman and the other the child
of the free woman.   But the child of the slave-woman was   23
born in the course of nature, while the child of the free
woman was born in fulfilment of a promise.   This story may   24
be taken as an allegory.   The women stand for two Covenants.
One Covenant, given from Mount Sinai, produces a race of
slaves and is represented by Hagar (the word Hagar meaning   25
in Arabia Mount Sinai) and it ranks with the Jerusalem of to-
day, for she and her children are in slavery.   But the Jerusalem   26
above is free, and she it is who is our mother.   For Scripture   27
says—

> 'Rejoice, thou barren one, who dost never bear,
> Break into shouts, thou who art never in labour,
> For many are the children of her who is desolate—
> aye, more than of her who has a husband.'

As for ourselves, Brothers, we, like Isaac, are children born in   28
fulfilment of a promise.   Yet at that time the child born in the   29
course of nature persecuted the child born by the power of the
Spirit; and it is the same now.   But what does the passage   30
of Scripture say?

> 'Send away the slave-woman and her son; for the slave's
> son shall not be co-heir with the son of the free woman.'

[27] Isa. 54. 1.   [30] Gen. 21. 10.

And so, Brothers, we are not children of a slave, but of her 31
who is free.

IV.—The Gospel in the Daily Life.

Christian Freedom. It is for freedom that Christ set us free ; stand 1 **5**
firm therefore, and do not again be held under the
yoke of slavery.

Understand that I, Paul, myself tell you that if you allow 2
yourselves to be circumcised, Christ will avail you nothing.   I 3
again declare to every one who receives circumcision, that he
binds himself to obey the whole Law.   You have severed 4
yourselves from Christ—you who are seeking to be pronounced
righteous through Law ; you have fallen away from love.   For 5
we, by the help of the Spirit, are eagerly waiting for the fulfilment of our hope—that we may be pronounced righteous as
the result of faith.   If a man is in union with Christ Jesus, 6
neither is circumcision nor the omission of it anything, but
faith, working through love, is everything.
You were once making good progress !   Who has hindered 7
you from obeying the Truth ?   The persuasion brought to bear 8
on you does not come from him who calls you.   A little leaven 9
leavens all the dough.   I, through my union with the Lord, 10
am persuaded that you will learn to think with me.   But the
man who is disturbing your minds will have to bear his punishment, whoever he may be.   If I, Brothers, am still 11
proclaiming circumcision, why am I still persecuted ?   It seems
that the Cross has ceased to be an obstacle !   I could 12
even wish that the people who are unsettling you would go
further still and mutilate themselves.

The Limits of Christian Freedom. Remember, Brothers, to you the Call came to 13
give you freedom.   Only do not make your free-
dom an opportunity for self-indulgence, but serve
one another in a loving spirit.   Indeed, the whole Law has 14
been summed up in this one precept—

'Thou shalt love thy neighbour as thou dost thyself.'

But, if you are continually wounding and preying upon one 15
another, take care that you are not destroyed by one another.
The Guidance of the Spirit. This is what I have to say :—Let your steps be 16
guided by the Spirit, and then you will never gratify
the cravings of your earthly nature.   For these 17
cravings of our earthly nature conflict with the Spirit, and the
Spirit with our earthly nature—they are two contrary princi-
ples—so that you cannot do what you wish.   But, if you follow 18

14 Lev. 19. 18.

the guidance of the Spirit, you are not subject to Law. The sins of our earthly nature are unmistakeable. They are sins like these—unchastity, impurity, indecency, idolatry, sorcery, quarrels, strife, jealousy, outbursts of passion, rivalries, dissensions, divisions, feelings of envy, drunkenness, revelry, and the like. And I warn you, as I warned you before, that those who indulge in such things will have no place in the Kingdom of God. But the fruit produced by the Spirit is love, joy, peace, forbearance, kindliness, generosity, trustfulness, gentleness, self-control. Against such things there is no law! And those who belong to Jesus, the Christ, have already crucified their earthly nature, with its passions and its cravings. 19 20 21 22 23 24

Since our Life is due to the Spirit, let us rule our conduct also by the Spirit. Do not let us grow vain, and provoke or envy one another.   Brothers, even if a man should be caught committing a sin, you who are spiritually minded should, in a gentle spirit, help him to recover himself, taking care lest any one of you also should be tempted.   Bear one another's burdens, and so carry out the Law of the Christ. If a man imagines himself to be somebody, when he is really nobody, he deceives himself. Let every one test his own work, and then his cause for satisfaction will be in himself and not in a comparison of himself with his neighbour ; for every one must bear his own load.   He, however, who is being instructed in the Message ought always to share his blessings with the man who instructs him. 25 26 **6** 1 2 3 4 5 6

Do not be deceived. God cannot be mocked. What a man sows that he will reap. For he who sows the field of his earthly nature will from that earthly nature reap corruption ; while he who sows the field of the spirit will from that spirit reap Immortal Life. Let us never tire of doing right, for at the proper season we shall reap our harvest, if we do not grow weary.   Therefore, I say, as the opportunity occurs, let us treat every one with kindness, and especially members of the Household of the Faith. 7 8 9 10

V.—Conclusion in the Apostle's own Hand-writing.

See in what large letters I am writing with my own hand.   Those who wish to appear to advantage in regard to outward observances are the very people who are trying to compel you to be circumcised ; and they do it only to avoid being persecuted for the cross of Jesus, the Christ. Even these men who are circumcised do not themselves keep the Law ; yet they want you to be circumcised, so that they may boast of your observance of the rite. But, for my part, may I never boast of anything except the cross of Jesus Christ, 11 12 13 14 our Master, through whom the world has been crucified to me, and I to the world.   For neither is circumcision nor 15 the omission of it anything ; but a new nature is everything. May all who rule their conduct by this principle find peace 16 and mercy—they who are the Israel of God.

For the future let no one trouble me ; for I bear the marks 17 of Jesus branded on my body.

May the blessing of Jesus Christ, our Lord, rest on your 18 souls, Brothers.   Amen.

[16] Ps. 125. 5 ; 128. 6.

TO THE CORINTHIANS.

I.

ST. PAUL'S FIRST LETTER TO THE CORINTHIANS.

WRITTEN PROBABLY DURING HIS STAY AT EPHESUS, IN THE COURSE OF HIS THIRD MISSIONARY JOURNEY, ABOUT 54 A.D.

CORINTH was the capital of the Roman province of Achaia. It contained a large, mixed population of Greeks, Jews, and Italian freedmen. The community—famous for its trade, its festivals and games of world-wide renown, its wealth and its luxury—was highly cultured, but grossly immoral. The Christian Church at Corinth was founded by St. Paul during the year and a half that he stayed in that city in the course of his second missionary journey (Acts 18. 11); and this Letter to his Corinthian converts was probably written at Ephesus towards the close of St. Paul's stay there on his third missionary journey (Acts 19). News had been brought to the Apostle of dissensions and disorders which had arisen in the Church at Corinth (1 Cor. 1. 11); and about the same time he received a letter from that Church, asking guidance from him in several important matters (1 Cor. 7. 1). These were the circumstances under which he wrote the present Letter of rebuke and advice.

TO THE

CORINTHIANS.
I.

I.—INTRODUCTION.

Greeting. To the Church of God in Corinth, to those who **1-2 1** have been consecrated by union with Christ Jesus and called to become his People, and also to all, wherever they may be, who invoke the Name of our Lord Jesus Christ—their Master and ours,

FROM PAUL, who has been called to be an Apostle of Jesus Christ by the will of God,

AND FROM Sosthenes, our Brother.

May God, our Father, and the Lord Jesus Christ bless you and **3** give you peace.

The Apostle's Thankfulness and Confidence. I always thank God about you for the blessing **4** bestowed upon you in Christ Jesus. For through **5** union with him you were enriched in every way— in your power to preach, and in your knowledge of the Truth ; and so became yourselves a confirmation of my **6** testimony to the Christ. And thus there is no gift in which **7** you are deficient, while waiting for the Appearing of our Lord Jesus Christ. And God himself will strengthen you to the **8** end, so that at the Day of our Lord Jesus Christ you may be found blameless. God will not fail you, and it is he who **9** called you into communion with his Son, Jesus Christ, our Lord.

II.—THE STATE OF THE CHURCH AT CORINTH.

Prevalence of Party Spirit. But I appeal to you, Brothers, by the Name of **10** our Lord Jesus Christ, to agree in what you profess, and not to allow divisions to exist among you, but to be united—of one mind and of one opinion. For I have **11** been informed, my Brothers, by the members of Chloe's house-

hold, that party feeling exists among you. I mean this, 12
that every one of you says either 'I follow Paul,' or 'I Apollos,'
or 'I Kephas,' or 'I Christ.' You have rent the Christ in 13
pieces ! Was it Paul who was crucified for you ? or were
you baptized into the Faith of Paul ? I am thankful that I 14
did not baptize any of you except Crispus and Gaius, so that 15
no one can say that you were baptized into my Faith. I 16
baptized also the household of Stephanas. I do not know
that I baptized any one else. My mission from Christ was 17
not to baptize, but to tell the Good News ; not, however,
in the language of philosophy, lest the cross of the Christ
should be robbed of its meaning.

The Power of the Cross. The Message of the Cross is indeed mere folly 18
to those who are in the path to Ruin, but to us
who are in the path of Salvation it is the very
power of God. For Scripture says— 19

' I will bring the philosophy of the philosophers to nought,
And the shrewdness of the shrewd I will make of no account.'

Where is the Philosopher ? where the Teacher of the Law ? 20
where the Disputant of to-day ? Has not God shown the
world's philosophy to be folly ? For since the world, in God's 21
wisdom, did not by its philosophy learn to know God,
God saw fit, by the 'folly' of our proclamation, to save
those who believe in Christ ! While Jews ask for miraculous 22
signs, and Greeks study philosophy, we are proclaiming 23
Christ crucified !—to the Jews an obstacle, to the Gentiles
mere folly, but to those who have received the Call, whether 24
Jews or Greeks, Christ, the Power of God and the Wisdom of
God ! For God's ' folly ' is wiser than men, and God's ' weak- 25
ness ' is stronger than men.

'Weakness' and 'Strength.' Look at the facts of your Call, Brothers. There 26
are not many among you who are wise, as men
reckon wisdom, not many who are influential,
not many who are high-born ; but God chose what the world 27
counts foolish to put its wise men to shame, and God chose
what the world counts weak to put its strong things to shame,
and God chose what the world counts poor and insignificant— 28
things that to it are unreal—to bring its 'realities' to nothing,
so that in his presence no human being should boast. But 29,
you, by your union with Christ Jesus, belong to God ; and
Christ, by God's will, became not only our Wisdom, but
also our Righteousness, Holiness, and Deliverance, so that— 31
in the words of Scripture—

' Let him who boasts make his boast of the Lord ! '

[19] Isa. 29. 14.   [20] Isa. 19. 11—12 ; 33. 18.   [31] Jer. 9. 24.

Philosophy and Revelation.
For my own part, Brothers, when I came to 1 **2**
you, it was with no display of eloquence or
philosophy that I came to tell the hidden purpose
of God; for I had determined that, while with you, I would 2
know nothing but Jesus Christ—and him crucified! Indeed, 3
when I came among you, I was weak, and full of fears, and
in great anxiety. My Message and my Proclamation were not 4
delivered in the persuasive language of philosophy, but were
accompanied by the manifestation of spiritual power, so that 5
your faith should be based, not on the philosophy of man, but
on the power of God.

Yet there is a philosophy that we teach to those whose faith 6
is matured, but it is not the philosophy of to-day, nor that of
the leaders of to-day—men whose downfall is at hand. No, 7
it is a divine philosophy that we teach, one concerned with the
hidden purpose of God—that long-hidden philosophy which
God, before time began, destined for our glory. This philo- 8
sophy is not known to any of the leaders of to-day; for, had
they known it, they would not have crucified our glorified
Lord. It is what Scripture speaks of as— 9

'What eye never saw, nor ear ever heard,
What never entered the mind of man—
Even all that God has prepared for those who love him.'

Yet to us God revealed it through his Spirit; for the Spirit 10
fathoms all things, even the inmost depths of God's being.
For what man is there who knows what a man is, except 11
the man's own spirit within him? So, also, no one compre-
hends what God is, except the Spirit of God. And as for us, 12
it is not the Spirit of the World that we have received, but the
Spirit that comes from God, that we may realize the blessings
given to us by him. And we speak of these gifts, not in lan- 13
guage taught by human philosophy, but in language taught
by the Spirit, explaining spiritual things in spiritual words.
The merely intellectual man rejects the teaching of the Spirit 14
of God; for to him it is mere folly; he cannot grasp it,
because it is to be understood only by spiritual insight.
But the man with spiritual insight is able to understand 15
everything, although he himself is understood by no one.
For 'who has so comprehended the mind of the Lord as 16
to be able to instruct him?' We, however, have the very
mind of Christ.

But I, Brothers, could not speak to you as men with spiritual 1 **3**
insight, but only as worldly-minded—mere infants in the Faith
of Christ. I fed you with milk, not with solid food, for you 2
were not then able to take it.

9 Isa. 64. 4.   16 Isa. 40. 13.

No, and even now you are not able; you are 3
The true Position and Work of the Apostles. still worldly. While there exist among you jealousy and party feeling, is it not true that you are worldly, and are acting merely as other men do? When one says 'I follow Paul,' and another 'I 4 follow Apollos,' are not you like other men? What, I ask, is 5 Apollos? or what is Paul? Servants through whom you were led to accept the Faith; and that only as the Lord helped each of you. I planted, and Apollos watered, but it was God who 6 caused the growth. Therefore neither the man who plants, 7 nor the man who waters, is of any account, but only God who causes the growth. In this the man who plants and the 8 man who waters are one; yet each will receive his own reward in proportion to his own labour. For we are God's fellow 9 workers; you are God's harvest field, God's building.

In fulfilment of the charge which God had entrusted to me, 10 I laid the foundation like a skilful master-builder; but another man is now building upon it. Let every one take care how he builds; for no man can lay any other foundation than the 11 one already laid—Jesus Christ. Whatever is used by those 12 who build upon this foundation, whether gold, silver, costly stones, wood, hay, or straw, the quality of each man's work 13 will become known, for the Day will make it plain; because that Day is to be ushered in with fire, and the fire itself will test the quality of every man's work. If any man's work, 14 which he has built upon that foundation, still remains, he will gain a reward. If any man's work is burnt up, he will suffer 15 loss; though he himself will escape, but only as one who has passed through fire.

Do not you know that you are God's Temple, and that God's 16 Spirit has his home in you? If any one destroys the Temple 17 of God, God will destroy him; for the Temple of God is sacred, and so also are you.

Let no one deceive himself. If any one among you imagines 18 that, as regards this world, he is a wise man, let him become a 'fool,' that he may become wise. For in God's sight this 19 world's wisdom is folly. Scripture tells of—

'One who catches the wise in their own craftiness,'

and it says again— 20

'The Lord sees how fruitless are the deliberations of the wise.'

Therefore let no one boast about men; for all things are 21 yours—whether Paul, or Apollos, or Kephas, or the world, or 22 life, or death, or the present, or the future—all things are yours! But you are Christ's and Christ is God's. 23

Let men look upon us as Christ's servants, and as stewards 1 **4** of the hidden truths of God. Now what we look for in 2

stewards is that they should be trustworthy. But it weighs 3
very little with me that I am judged by you or by any human
tribunal. No, I do not even judge myself; for, though I am 4
conscious of nothing against myself, that does not prove me
innocent. It is the Lord who is my judge. Therefore do not 5
pass judgement before the time, but wait till the Lord comes.
He will throw light upon what is now dark and obscure, and
will reveal the motives in men's minds; and then every one
will receive due praise from God.

All this, Brothers, I have, for your sakes, applied to Apollos 6
and myself, so that, from our example, you may learn to
observe the precept—'Keep to what is written,' that none of
you may speak boastfully of one teacher to the disparagement
of another. For who makes any one of you superior to others? 7
And what have you that was not given you? But if you
received it as a gift, why do you boast as if you had not? Are 8
you all so soon satisfied? Are you so soon rich? Have you
begun to reign without us? Would indeed that you had, so
that we also might reign with you! For, as it seems to me, 9
God has exhibited us, the Apostles, last of all, as men doomed
to death. We are made a spectacle to the universe, both to
angels and to men! We, for Christ's sake, are 'fools,' but 10
you, by your union with Christ, are men of discernment. We
are weak, but you are strong. You are honoured, but we
are despised. To this very hour we go hungry, thirsty, and 11
naked; we are beaten; we are homeless; we work hard, 12
toiling with our own hands. We meet abuse with blessings,
we meet persecution with endurance, we meet slander with 13
gentle appeals. We have been treated as the scum of the
earth, the vilest of the vile, to this very hour.

It is with no wish to shame you that I am writing like this; 14
but to warn you as my own dear children. Though you 15
may have thousands of instructors in the Faith of Christ,
yet you have not many fathers. It was I who, through
union with Christ Jesus, became your father by means of
the Good News. Therefore I entreat you—Follow my 16
example. This is my reason for sending Timothy to 17
you. He is my own dear faithful child in the Master's service,
and he will remind you of my methods of teaching the Faith of
Christ Jesus—methods which I follow everywhere in every
Church.

Some, I hear, are puffed up with pride, thinking that I am 18
not coming to you. But come to you I will, and that soon, if it 19
please the Lord; and then I shall find out, not what words
these men use who are so puffed up, but what power they
possess; for the Kingdom of God is based, not on words, but 20
on power. What do you wish? Am I to come to you with a 21
rod, or in a loving and gentle spirit?

[20] Dan. 2. 44.

A flagrant Case of Immorality. There is a wide-spread report respecting a case 1 5 of immorality among you, and that, too, of a kind that does not occur even among the Gentiles—a man, I hear, is living with his father's wife! Instead 2 of grieving over it and taking steps for the expulsion of the man who has done this thing, is it possible that you are still puffed up?   For I myself, though absent in body, 3 have been present with you in spirit, and in the name of our Lord Jesus I have already passed judgement, just as if I had been present, upon the man who has acted in this way.   I have 4 decided—having been present in spirit at your meetings, when the power of the Lord Jesus was with us—to deliver such a man 5 as this over to Satan, that what is sensual in him may be destroyed, so that his spirit may be saved at the Day of the Lord.   Your boasting is unseemly.   Do not you know 6 that even a little leaven leavens all the dough?   Get rid en- 7 tirely of the old leaven, so that you may be like new dough— free from leaven, as in truth you are.   For our Passover Lamb is already sacrificed—Christ himself; therefore let us keep our 8 festival, not with the leaven of former days, nor with the leaven of vice and wickedness, but with the unleavened bread of sincerity and truth.

I told you, in my letter, not to associate with immoral 9 people—not, of course, meaning men of the world who are 10 immoral, or who are covetous and grasping, or who worship idols; for then you would have to leave the world altogether. But, as things are, I say that you are not to associate with any 11 one who, although a Brother in name, is immoral, or covetous, or an idolater, or abusive, or a drunkard, or grasping—no, not even to sit at table with such people.   What have I to do 12 with judging those outside the Church?   Is it not for you to judge those who are within the Church, while God 13 judges those who are outside?   'Put away the wicked man from among you.'

Lawsuits between Christians. Can it be that, when one of you has a dispute 1 6 with another, he dares to have his case tried before the heathen, instead of before Christ's People?   Do not you know that Christ's People will try the 2 world?   And if the world is to be tried by you, are you unfit to try the most trivial cases?   Do not you know that we are 3 to try angels—to say nothing of the affairs of this life?   Why, 4 then, if you have cases relating to the affairs of this life, do you set to try them men who carry no weight with the Church?   To your shame I ask it.   Can it be that there is 5 not one man among you wise enough to decide between two of his Brothers?   Must Brother go to law with Brother, and 6 that, too, before unbelievers?   To begin with, it is undoubtedly 7

7 Exod. 12. 21.   13 Deut. 22. 24.

a loss to you to have lawsuits with one another.   Why not
rather let yourselves be wronged?   Why not rather let
yourselves be cheated?   Instead of this, you wrong and   8
cheat others yourselves—yes, even your Brothers!   Do not   9
you know that wrong-doers will have no share in God's
Kingdom?   Do not be deceived.   No one who is
immoral, or an idolater, or an adulterer, or licentious, or a
sodomite, or a thief, or covetous, or a drunkard, or abusive, or   10
grasping, will have any share in God's Kingdom.   Such   11
some of you used to be; but you washed yourselves clean!
you became Christ's People! you were pronounced righteous
through the Name of our Lord Jesus Christ, and through the
Spirit of our God!

The Sacredness of the Body.   Everything is allowable for me! Yes, but every-   12
thing is not profitable.   Everything is allowable
for me!   Yes, but for my part, I will not let myself
be enslaved by anything.   Food exists for the stomach, and   13
the stomach for food; but God will put an end to both the
one and the other.   The body, however, exists, not for immorality, but for the Lord, and the Lord for the body; and, as   14
God has raised the Lord, so he will raise up us also by the
exercise of his power.   Do not you know that your bodies are   15
Christ's members?   Am I, then, to take the members that
belong to the Christ and make them the members of a prostitute?
Heaven forbid!   Or do not you know that a man who unites   16
himself with a prostitute is one with her in body (for 'the two,'
it is said, 'will become one'); while a man who is united with   17
the Lord is one with him in spirit?   Shun all immorality.   18
Every other sin that men commit is something outside the
body; but an immoral man sins against his own body.
Again, do not you know that your body is a shrine of the Holy   19
Spirit that is within you—the Spirit which you have from
God?   Moreover, you are not your own masters; you were   20
bought, and the price was paid.   Therefore, honour God in
your bodies.

III.—Answers to Questions asked by the Church at Corinth.

ON MARRIAGE. The Apostle's Views.   With reference to the subjects about which you   1 **7**
wrote to me:—It would be well for a man to
remain single.   But, owing to the prevalence of   2
immorality, I advise every man to have his own wife, and
every woman her husband.   A husband should give his wife   3
her due, and a wife her husband.   It is not the wife, but the   4

16 Gen. 2. 24.

husband, who exercises power over her body ; and so, too, it
is not the husband, but the wife, who exercises power over his
body.   Do not deprive each other of what is due—unless it is   5
only for a time and by mutual consent, so that your minds may
be free for prayer till you again live as man and wife—
lest Satan should take advantage of your want of self-control
and tempt you.   I say this, however, as a concession, not   6
as a command.   I should wish every one to be just what I am   7
myself.   But every one has his own gift from God—one in
one way, and one in another.

My advice, then, to those who are not married, and to   8
widows, is this :—It would be well for them to remain as I
am myself.   But, if they cannot control themselves, let them   9
marry, for it is better to marry than to be consumed with
passion.   To those who are married my direction is—   10
yet it is not mine, but the Master's—that a woman is not to
leave her husband (if she has done so, let her remain as she is,   11
or else be reconciled to her husband) and also that a man is not
Marriages   to divorce his wife.   To all others I say—I,   12
with   not the Master :—If a Brother is married to a
Unbelievers.   woman, who is an unbeliever but willing to live
with him, he should not divorce her ; and a woman who is   13
married to a man, who is an unbeliever but willing to live with
her, should not divorce her husband.   For, through his wife, the   14
husband who is an unbeliever has become associated with
Christ's People ; and the wife who is an unbeliever has
become associated with Christ's People through our Brother
whom she has married.   Otherwise your children would be
' defiled,' but, as it is, they belong to Christ's People.   How-   15
ever, if the unbeliever wishes to be separated, let him be so.
Under such circumstances neither the Brother nor the Sister
is bound ; God has called you to live in peace.   How can you   16
tell, wife, whether you may not save your husband ? and
how can you tell, husband, whether you may not save your
wife ?

Christianity   In any case, a man should continue to live in the   17
independent   condition which the Lord has allotted to him, and
of Conditions   in which he was when God called him.   This
of Life.   is the rule that I lay down in every Church.   Was   18
a man already circumcised when he was called ?   Then he
should not efface his circumcision.   Has a man been called
when uncircumcised ?   Then he should not be circumcised.
Circumcision is nothing ; the want of it is nothing ; but to   19
keep the commands of God is everything.   Let every one   20
remain in that condition of life in which he was when the
Call came to him.   Were you a slave when you were called ?   21
Do not let that trouble you.   No, even if you are able to gain
your freedom, still do your best.   For the man who was a   22

slave when he was called to the Master's service is the Master's freed-man ; so, too, the man who was free when called is Christ's slave. You were bought, and the price was paid. Do not let yourselves become slaves to men. Brothers, let every one remain in the condition in which he was when he was called, in close communion with God. 23 24

Difficulties connected with Marriage. With regard to unmarried women, I have no command from the Master to give you, but I tell you my opinion, and it is that of a man whom the Master in his mercy has made worthy to be trusted. 25

I think, then, that, in view of the time of suffering that has now come upon us, what I have already said is best—that a man should remain as he is. Are you married to a wife ? Then do not seek to be separated. Are you separated from a wife ? Then do not seek for a wife. Still, if you should marry, that is not wrong ; nor, if a young woman marries, is that wrong. But those who marry will have much trouble to bear, and my wish is to spare you.   What I mean, Brothers, is this :—The time is short. Meanwhile, let those who have wives live as if they had none, those who are weeping as if not weeping, those who are rejoicing as if not rejoicing, those who buy as if not possessing, and those who use the good things of the world as using them sparingly ; for this world as we see it is passing away. I want you to be free from anxiety. The unmarried man is anxious about the Master's Cause, desiring to please him ; while the married man is anxious about worldly matters, desiring to please his wife ; and so his interests are divided. Again, the unmarried woman, whether she is old or young, is anxious about the Master's Cause, striving to be pure both in body and in spirit, while the married woman is anxious about worldly matters, desiring to please her husband. I say this for your own benefit, not with any intention of putting a halter round your necks, but in order to secure for the Master seemly and constant devotion, free from all distraction. 26 27 28 29 30 31 32 33 34 35

If, however, a father thinks that he is not acting fairly by his unmarried daughter, when she is past her youth, and if under these circumstances her marriage ought to take place, let him act as he thinks right. He is doing nothing wrong—let the marriage take place. On the other hand, a father, who has definitely made up his mind, and is under no compulsion, but is free to carry out his own wishes, and who has come to the decision, in his own mind, to keep his unmarried daughter at home, will be doing right. In short, the one who consents to his daughter's marriage is doing right, and yet the other will be doing better. 36 37 38

A wife is bound to her husband as long as he lives ; but, if the husband should pass to his rest, the widow is free to marry any one she wishes, provided he is a believer. Yet 39 40 she will be happier if she remains as she is—in my opinion, for I think that I also have the Spirit of God.

ON HEATHEN FESTIVALS. A Question of Conscience. With reference to food that has been offered in sacrifice to idols—We are aware that all of us have knowledge ! Knowledge breeds conceit, while love builds up character. If a man thinks that he knows anything, he has not yet reached that knowledge which he ought to have reached. On the other hand, if a man loves God, he is known by God. With reference, then, to eating food that has been offered to idols—we are aware that an idol is nothing in the world, and that there is no God but one. Even supposing that there are so-called 'gods' either in Heaven or on earth—and there are many such 'gods' and 'lords'—yet for us there is only one God, the Father, from whom all things come (and for him we live), and one Lord, Jesus Christ, through whom all things come (and through him we live). Still, it is not eve y one that has this knowledge. Some people, because of their association with idols, continued down to the present time, eat the food as food offered to an idol ; and their consciences, while still weak, are dulled. What we eat, however, will not bring us nearer to God. We lose nothing by not eating this food, and we gain nothing by eating it. But take care that this right of yours does not become in any way a stumbling-block to the weak. For if some one should see you who possess this knowledge, feasting in an idol's temple, will not his conscience, if he is a weak man, become so hardened that he, too, will eat food offered to idols ? And so, through this knowledge of yours, the weak man is ruined—your Brother for whose sake Christ died ! In this way, by sinning against your Brothers and injuring their consciences, while still weak, you sin against Christ. Therefore, if what I eat makes my Brother fall, rather than make my Brother fall, I will never eat meat again.

The Apostle's Example. Am I not free ? Am I not an Apostle ? Have I not seen our Lord Jesus ? Are not you yourselves my work achieved in union with the Lord ? If I am not an Apostle to others, yet at least I am to you ; for you are the seal that stamps me as an Apostle in union with the Lord.

The defence that I make to my critics is this :—Have not we a right to food and drink ? Have not we a right to take a wife with us, if she is a Christian, as the other Apostles and the Master's brothers and Kephas all do ? Or is it only Barnabas and I who have no right to give up working for our bread ? Does any one ever serve as a soldier at his own expense ? Does any one plant a vineyard and not eat its produce ? Or does

any one look after a herd and not drink the milk ?   Am   8
I, in all this, speaking only from the human standpoint ?   Does
not the Law also say the same ?   For in the Law of Moses it is   9
said—

> 'Thou shalt not muzzle a bullock while it is treading out
> the grain.'

Is it the bullocks that God is thinking of ? or is not it said   10
entirely for our sakes ?   Surely it was written for our sakes,
for the ploughman ought not to plough, nor the thrasher to
thrash, without expecting a share of the grain.   Since   11
we, then, sowed spiritual seed for you, is it too much that we
should reap from you an earthly harvest ?   If others share in   12
this right over you, do not we even more ?   Still we did not avail
ourselves of this right.   No, we endure anything rather than
impede the progress of the Good News of the Christ.   Do not   13
you know that those who do the work of the Temple live on
what comes from the Temple, and that those who serve at the
altar share the offerings with the altar ?   So, too, the Master   14
has appointed that those who tell the Good News should get
their living from the Good News.   I, however, have not availed   15
myself of any of these rights.   I am not saying this to
secure such an arrangement for myself ; indeed, I would far
rather die——Nobody shall make my boast a vain one ! If I tell   16
the Good News, I have nothing to boast of, for I can but
do so.   Woe is me if I do not tell it !   If I do this work   17
willingly, I have a reward ; but, if unwillingly, I have been
charged to perform a duty.   What is my reward, then ?   To   18
present the Good News free of all cost, and so make but a
sparing use of the rights which it gives me.

Although I was entirely free, yet, to win as many converts as   19
possible, I made myself everyone's slave.   To the Jews I became   20
like a Jew, to win Jews.   To those who are subject to Law I became like a man subject to Law—though I was not myself subject to Law—to win those who are subject to Law.   To those   21
who have no Law I became like a man who has no Law—not that
I am free from God's Law ; no, for I am under Christ's Law—
to win those who have no Law.   To the weak I became weak,   22
to win the weak.   I have become all things to all men, so as
at all costs to save some.   And I do everything for the sake   23
of the Good News, that with them I may share n its blessings.

Do not you know that on a race-course, though all run,   24
yet only one wins the prize ?   Run in such a way that you
may win.   Every athlete exercises self-restraint in every-   25
thing ; they, indeed, for a crown that fades, we for one that
is unfading.   I, therefore, run with no uncertain aim.   I box—   26
not like a man hitting the air.   No, I bruise my body and   27

9 Deut. 25. 4.

make it my slave, lest I, who have called others to the contest, should myself be rejected.

A Warning from History. I want you to bear in mind, Brothers, that all ¹ **10** our ancestors were beneath the cloud, and all passed through the sea ; that in the cloud and in ² the sea they all underwent baptism as followers of Moses ; and ³ that they all ate the same supernatural food, and all drank the ⁴ same supernatural water, for they used to drink from a supernatural rock which followed them, and that rock was the Christ. Yet with most of them God was displeased ; for they were ⁵ ' struck down in the desert.'

Now these things happened as warnings to us, to teach us ⁶ not to long for evil things as our forefathers longed. Do not ⁷ become idolaters, as some of them became.   Scripture says—

' The people sat down to eat and drink, and stood up to dance.'

Nor let us act immorally, as some of them acted, with the result ⁸ that twenty-three thousand of them fell dead in a single day. Nor let us try the patience of the Lord too far, as some of them ⁹ tried it, with the result that they ' were, one after another, destroyed by the snakes.'   And do not murmur, as some of them ¹⁰ murmured, and so ' were destroyed by the Angel of Death.' These things happened to them by way of warning, and were ¹¹ recorded to serve as a caution to us, in whose days the close of the ages has come.

Therefore let the man who thinks that he stands take care ¹² that he does not fall.   No temptation has come upon you that is ¹³ not common to all mankind.   God will not fail you, and he will not allow you to be tempted beyond your strength ; but, when he sends the temptation, he will also provide the way of escape, so that you may have strength to endure.

The Apostle's Conclusions. Therefore, my dear friends, shun the worship ¹⁴ of idols.   I speak to you as men of discernment ; ¹⁵ form your own judgement about what I am saying.   In ¹⁶ the Cup of Blessing which we bless, is not there a sharing in the blood of the Christ ?   And in the Bread which we break, is not there a sharing in the Body of the Christ ?   The Bread is ¹⁷ one, and we, though many, are one body ; for we all partake of that one Bread.   Look at the people of Israel.   Do not those ¹⁸ who eat the sacrifices share with the altar ?   What do I mean ? ¹⁹ you ask.   That an offering made to an idol, or the idol itself, is anything ?   No ; what I say is that the sacrifices offered by ²⁰ the Gentiles ' are offered to demons and to a Being who is no God,' and I do not want you to share with demons.   You ²¹ cannot drink both the Cup of the Lord and the cup of demons.

⁵Num. 14. 16.   ⁶ Num. 11. 34.   ⁷ Exod. 32. 6.   ⁹ Num. 21. 6.   ¹⁰ 2 Sam. 24. 16.
²⁰ Deut. 32. 17.   ²¹ Mal. 1. 7.

You cannot partake at the Table of the Lord and at the table of demons. Or 'are we to rouse the jealousy of the Lord'? 22 Are we stronger than he?

Everything is allowable! Yes, but everything is not profit- 23 able. Everything is allowable! Yes, but everything does not build up character. A man must not study his own interests, 24 but the interests of others.

Eat anything that is sold in the market, without making 25 inquiries to satisfy your scruples; for 'the earth, with 26 all that is in it, belongs to the Lord.' If an unbeliever invites 27 you to his house and you consent to go, eat anything that is put before you, without making inquiries to satisfy your scruples. But, if any one should say to you 'This has been 28 offered in sacrifice to an idol,' then, for the sake of the speaker and his scruples, do not eat it. I do not say 'your' scruples, 29 but 'his.' For why should the freedom that I claim be con- demned by the scruples of another? If, for my part, I take 30 the food thankfully, why should I be abused for eating that for which I give thanks?

Whether, then, you eat or drink or whatever you do, do 31 everything to the honour of God. Do not cause offence either 32 to Jews or Greeks or to the Church of God; for I, also, 33 try to please everybody in everything, not seeking my own advantage, but that of men in general, that they may be saved. Imitate me, as I myself imitate Christ. 1 **11**

ON PUBLIC WORSHIP. As to Covering the Head. I praise you, indeed, because you never forget 2 me, and are keeping my injunctions in mind, exactly as I laid them upon you. But I 3 am anxious that you should understand that the Christ is the Head of every man, that man is the Head of woman, and that God is the Head of the Christ. Any man 4 who keeps his head covered, when praying or preaching in public, dishonours him who is his Head; while any woman, 5 who prays or preaches in public bare-headed, dishonours him who is her Head; for that is to make herself like one of the shameless women who shave their heads. Indeed, if a 6 woman does not keep her head covered, she may as well cut her hair short. But, since to cut her hair short, or shave it off, marks her as one of the shameless women, let her keep her head covered. A man ought not to have his head 7 covered, for he has been from the beginning 'the likeness of God' and the reflection of his glory, but woman is the reflection of man's glory. For it was not man who was taken from 8 woman, but woman who was taken from man. Besides, man 9 was not created for the sake of woman, but woman for the sake of man. And, therefore, a woman ought to wear on her head 10 a symbol of her subjection, because of the presence of the

22 Deut. 32. 21. 26 Ps. 24. 1. 7 Gen. 5. 1.

angels. Still, when in union with the Lord, woman is not   11
independent of man, or man of woman ; for just as woman   12
came from man, so man comes by means of woman ; and all
things come from God. Judge for yourselves. Is it fitting   13
that a woman should pray to God in public with her head
uncovered ? Does not nature herself teach us that, while for   14
a man to wear his hair long is degrading to him, a woman's   15
long hair is her glory ? Her hair has been given her to serve
as a covering.   If, however, any one still thinks it right   16
to contest the point—well, we have no such custom, nor have
the Churches of God.

**As to the
'Lord's
Supper.'**   In giving directions on the next subject, I   17
cannot praise you ; because your meetings do
more harm than good. To begin with, I hear   18
that, when you meet as a Church, divisions exist among
you, and, to some extent, I believe it. Indeed, there must   19
be actual parties among you, for so only will the men of real
worth become known.   When you meet together, as I   20
understand, it is not possible to eat the Lord's Supper ; for, as   21
you eat, each of you tries to secure his own supper first, with
the result that one has too little to eat, and another has too
much to drink ! Have you no houses in which you can   22
eat and drink ? Or are you trying to show your contempt for
the Church of God, and to humiliate the poor ? What can I
say to you ? Shall I praise you ? In this matter I cannot
praise you. For I myself received from the Lord the account   23
which I have in turn given to you—how the Lord Jesus,
on the very night of his betrayal, took some bread, and, after   24
saying the thanksgiving, broke it and said " This is my own
body given on your behalf. Do this in memory of me." And   25
in the same way with the cup, after supper, saying " This cup
is the new Covenant made by my blood. Do this, whenever
you drink it, in memory of me." For whenever you eat this   26
bread and drink the cup, you proclaim the Lord's death—till
he comes. Therefore, whoever eats the bread, or drinks the   27
Lord's cup, in an irreverent spirit, will have to answer for an
offence against the Lord's body and blood. Let each man   28
look into his own heart, and only then eat of the bread
and drink from the cup. For the man who eats and drinks   29
brings a judgement upon himself by his eating and drinking,
when he does not discern the body. That is why so many   30
among you are weak and ill, and why some are sleeping.
But, if we judged ourselves rightly, we should not be judged.   31
Yet, in being judged by the Lord, we are undergoing   32
discipline, so that we may not have judgement passed
upon us with the rest of the world. Therefore, my Brothers,   33
when you meet together to eat the Supper, wait for one

[25] Exod. 24. 8.

another. If a man is hungry, let him eat at home, so that your 34 meetings may not bring a judgement upon you. The other details I will settle when I come.

ON SPIRITUAL GIFTS. In the next place, Brothers, I do not want you 1 **12** to be ignorant about spiritual gifts. You 2 Their Variety and Unity. know that there was a time when you were Gentiles, going astray after idols that could not speak, just as you happened to be led. Therefore I tell you 3 plainly that no one who speaks under the influence of the Spirit of God says ' JESUS IS ACCURSED,' and that no one can say ' JESUS IS LORD,' except under the influence of the Holy Spirit.

Gifts differ, but the Spirit is the same ; ways of serving 4, 5 differ, yet the Master is the same ; results differ, yet the God 6 who brings about every result is in every case the same. To 7 each man there is given spiritual illumination for the general good. To one is given the power to speak with wisdom 8 through the Spirit ; to another the power to speak with knowledge, due to the same Spirit ; to another faith by the same 9 Spirit ; to another power to cure diseases by the one Spirit ; to another supernatural powers ; to another the gift of 10 preaching ; to another the gift of distinguishing between true and false inspiration ; to another varieties of the gift of ' tongues ' ; to another the power to interpret ' tongues.' All 11 these result from one and the same Spirit, who distributes his gifts to each individually as he wills.

For just as the human body is one whole, and yet has many 12 parts, and all its parts, many though they are, form but one body, so it is with the Christ ; for it was by one Spirit that we 13 were all baptized to form one Body, whether Jews or Greeks, slaves or free men, and were all imbued with one Spirit. The 14 human body, I repeat, consists not of one part, but of many. If the foot says ' Since I am not a hand, I do not belong to the 15 body,' it does not on that account cease to belong to the body. Or if the ear says ' Since I am not an eye, I do not belong to 16 the body,' it does not on that account cease to belong to the body. If all the body were an eye, where would the hearing 17 be ? If it were all hearing, where would the sense of smell be ? But in fact God has placed each individual part just where 18 he thought fit in the body. If, however, they all made up 19 only one part, where would the body be ? But in fact, although 20 it has many parts, there is only one body. The eye cannot say 21 to the hand ' I do not need you,' nor, again, the head to the feet ' I do not need you.' No ! Those parts of the body that 22 seem naturally the weaker are indispensable ; and those parts 23 which we deem less honourable we surround with special honour ; and our ungraceful parts receive a special grace which our graceful parts do not require. Yes, God has so 24 constructed the body—by giving a special honour to the part

that lacks it—as to secure that there should be no disunion in   25
the body, but that the parts should show the same care for one
another.   If one part suffers, all the others suffer with it, and   26
if one part has honour done it, all the others share its joy.
Together you are the Body of Christ, and individually its   27
parts.   In the Church God has appointed, first,   28
Apostles, secondly Preachers, thirdly Teachers; then he has
given supernatural powers, then power to cure diseases,
aptness for helping others, capacity to govern, varieties of the
gift of 'tongues.'   Can every one be an Apostle? can every   29
one be a Preacher? can every one be a Teacher? can every
one have supernatural powers? can every one have power to   30
cure diseases? can every one speak in 'tongues'? can
every one interpret them?   Strive for the greater gifts.   31

Love the   Yet I can still show you a way beyond all
greatest of comparison the best.   Though I speak in   1   **13**
all.   the 'tongues' of men, or even of angels, yet
have not Love, I have become mere echoing brass, or a
clanging cymbal!   Even though I have the gift of preaching,   2
and fathom all hidden truths and all the depths of knowledge; even though I have such faith as might move mountains, yet have not Love, I am nothing!   Even though I   3
dole my substance to the poor, even though I sacrifice my
body, that I may boast, yet have not Love, it avails me
nothing!   Love is long-suffering, and kind; Love is   4
never envious, never boastful, never conceited, never behaves   5
unbecomingly; Love is never self-seeking, never provoked,
never reckons up her wrongs; Love never rejoices at evil, but   6
rejoices in the triumph of Truth; Love bears with all things,   7
ever trustful, ever hopeful, ever patient.   Love never   8
fails. But, whether it be the gift of preaching, it will be done
with; whether it be the gift of 'tongues,' it will cease; whether
it be knowledge, it, too, will be done with.   For our knowledge   9
is incomplete, and our preaching is incomplete, but, when the   10
Perfect has come, that which is incomplete will be done with.
When I was a child, I talked as a child, I felt as a child, I   11
reasoned as a child; now that I am a man, I have done with
childish ways.   As yet we see, in a mirror, dimly, but then—   12
face to face!   As yet my knowledge is incomplete, but then I
shall know in full, as I have been fully known.   Meanwhile   13
Faith, Hope, and Love endure—these three, but the greatest
of these is Love.

The Gift of   Seek this Love earnestly, and strive for spiritual   1   **1**
the 'Tongues' gifts, above all for the gift of preaching.   He   2
and the Gift who, when speaking, uses the gift of 'tongues' is
of Preaching. speaking, not to men, but to God, for no one

6 Zech. 8. 17 (Septuagint).

understands him; yet in spirit he is speaking of hidden truths. But he who preaches is speaking to his fellow men 3 words that will build up faith, and give them comfort and encouragement. He who, when speaking, uses the gift of 4 'tongues' builds up his own faith, while he who preaches builds up the faith of the Church. Now I want you all to speak 5 in 'tongues,' but much more I wish that you should preach. A Preacher is of more account than he who speaks in 'tongues,' unless he interprets his words, so that the faith of the Church may be built up. This being so, Brothers, 6 what good shall I do you, if I come to you and speak in 'tongues,' unless my words convey some revelation, or know-ledge, or take the form of preaching or teaching? Even with in- 7 animate things, such as a flute or a harp, though they produce sounds, yet unless the notes are quite distinct, how can the tune played on the flute or the harp be recognized? If the bugle 8 sound a doubtful call, who will prepare for battle? And so with 9 you; unless, in using the gift of 'tongues,' you utter intelligible words, how can what you say be understood? You will be speaking to the winds! There is, for instance, a certain 10 number of different languages in the world, and not one of them fails to convey meaning. If, however, I do not hap- 11 pen to know the language, I shall be a foreigner to those who speak it, and they will be foreigners to me. And so 12 with you; since you are striving for spiritual gifts, be eager to excel in such as will build up the faith of the Church. Therefore let him who, when speaking, 13 uses the gift of 'tongues' pray for ability to interpret them. If, when praying, I use the gift of 'tongues,' my spirit 14 indeed prays, but my mind is a blank. What, then, is my con- 15 clusion? Simply this—I will pray with my spirit, but with my mind as well; I will sing with my spirit, but with my mind as well. If you bless God with your spirit only, how can the man 16 in the congregation who is without your gift say 'Amen' to your thanksgiving? He does not know what you are say-ing! Your thanksgiving may be excellent, but the other 17 is not helped by it. Thank God, I use the gift of 'tongues' 18 more than any of you. But at a meeting of the Church I 19 would rather speak five words with my mind, and so teach others, than ten thousand words when using the gift of 'tongues.'

Brothers, do not show yourselves children in understanding. 20 In wickedness be infants, but in understanding show your-selves men. It is said in the Law— 21

'In strange tongues and by the lips of strangers will I speak to this people, but even then they will not listen to me, says the Lord.'

Therefore the gift of the ' tongues ' is intended as a sign, not   22
for those who believe in Christ, but for those who do not, while
the gift of preaching is intended as a sign, not for those who
do not believe in Christ, but for those who do.   So,   23
when the whole Church meets, if all present use the gift of
' tongues,' and some men who are without the gift, or who
are unbelievers, come in, will not they say that you are mad ?
While, if all those present use the gift of preaching, and an   24
unbeliever, or a man without the gift, comes in, he is convinced of his sinfulness by them all, he is called to account by
them all ; the secrets of his heart are revealed, and then,   25
throwing himself on his face, he will worship God, and declare
" ' God is indeed among you ! ' "

What do I suggest, then, Brothers ? Whenever you meet for   26
worship, each of you comes, either with a hymn, or a lesson,
or a revelation, or the gift of ' tongues,' or the interpretation of them ; let everything be directed to the building up
of faith.   If any of you use the gift of ' tongues,' not more than   27
two, or at the most three, should do so—each speaking in his
turn—and some one should interpret them.   If there is no one   28
able to interpret what is said, they should remain silent at the
meeting of the Church, and speak to themselves and to
God.   Of preachers two or three should speak, and the rest   29
should weigh well what is said.   But, if some revelation is   30
made to another person as he sits there, the first speaker should
stop.   For you can all preach in turn, so that all may learn   31
some lesson and all receive encouragement.   (The spirit that   32
moves the preachers is within the preachers' control ; for God   33
is not a God of disorder, but of peace.)   This custom prevails
in all the Churches of Christ's People.

The Necessity   At the meetings of the Church married women   34
for Order.   should remain silent, for they are not allowed to
speak in public ; they should take a subordinate place, as
the Law itself directs.   If they want information on any   35
point, they should ask their husbands about it at home ;
for it is unbecoming for a married woman to speak at a
meeting of the Church.   What ! did God's Message   36
to the world originate with you ? or did it find its way to
none but you ?

If any one thinks that he has the gift of preaching or any   37
other spiritual gift, let him recognize that what I am now
saying to you is a command from the Lord.   Any one who   38
ignores it may be ignored.   Therefore, my Brothers, strive   39
for the gift of preaching, and yet do not forbid speaking in
' tongues.'   Let everything be done in a proper and orderly   40
manner.

25 Isa. 45. 14.

IV.—The Apostle's Teaching as to the Resurrection of the Dead.

Next, Brothers, I would remind you of the Good News 1 **15** which I told you, and which you received—the Good News on which you have taken your stand, and by means of which 2 you are being saved.   I would remind you of the very words that I used in telling it to you, since you are still holding fast to it, and since it was not in vain that you became believers in Christ.   For at the very beginning of my teaching I gave 3 you the account which I had myself received—that Christ died for our sins (as the Scriptures had foretold), that he was 4 buried, that on the third day he was raised (as the Scriptures had foretold), and that he appeared to Kephas, and then to the 5 Twelve.   After that, he appeared to more than five hundred 6 of our Brothers at one time, most of whom are still alive, though some have gone to their rest.   After that, he appeared 7 to James, and then to all the Apostles. Last of all, he appeared 8 even to me, who am, as it were, the abortion.   For I 9 am the meanest of the Apostles, I who am unworthy of the name of ' Apostle,' because I persecuted the Church of God. But it is through the love of God that I am what I am, and the 10 love that he showed me has not been wasted.   No, I have toiled harder than any of them, and yet it was not I, but the love of God working with me.   Whether, then, it was I or 11 whether it was they, this we proclaim, and this you believed.

Now, if it is proclaimed of Christ that he has been raised 12 from the dead, how is it that some of you say that there is no such thing as a resurrection of the dead ?   But, if there is no 13 such thing as a resurrection of the dead, then even Christ has not been raised ; and, if Christ has not been raised, then our 14 proclamation is without meaning, and our faith without meaning also !   Yes, and we are being proved to have borne false 15 testimony about God ; for we testified of God that he raised the Christ, whom he did not raise, if, indeed, the dead do not rise !   For, if the dead do not rise, then even Christ himself has 16 not been raised, and, if Christ has not been raised, your faith is 17 folly—your sins are on you still!   Yes, and they, who have 18 passed to their rest in union with Christ, perished ! If all that 19 we have done has been to place our hope in Christ for this life, then we of all men are the most to be pitied.

But, in truth, Christ has been raised from the dead, the first- 20 fruits of those who are at rest.   For, since through a man 21 there is death, so, too, through a man there is a resurrection of the dead.   For, as through union with Adam all men 22 die, so through union with the Christ will all be made

4 Hos. 6. 2.

to live.   But each in his proper order—Christ the   23
first-fruits ; afterwards, at his Coming, those who belong
to the Christ.   Then will come the end—when he surrenders   24
the Kingdom to his God and Father, having overthrown all
other rule and all other authority and power.   For he must   25
reign until God ' has put all his enemies under his feet.'   The   26
last enemy to be overthrown is death ; for God has placed all   27
things under Christ's feet. (But, when it is said that all things
have been placed under Christ, it is plain that God is excepted
who placed everything under him.) And, when everything has   28
been placed under him, the Son will place himself under God
who placed everything under him, that God may be all in all !

Again, what good will they be doing who are baptized on   29
behalf of the dead ?   If it is true that the dead do not rise, why
are people baptized on their behalf ?   Why, too, do we risk our   30
lives every hour ?   Daily I face death—I swear it, Brothers, by   31
the pride in you that I feel through my union with Christ Jesus,
our Lord.   If with only human hopes I had fought in the   32
arena at Ephesus, what should I have gained by it ?   If the
dead do not rise, then—' Let us eat and drink, for to-morrow
we shall die ' !   Do not be deceived.   33

' Good character is marred by evil company.'

Awake to a righteous life, and cease to sin.   There are some   34
who have no true knowledge of God.   I speak in this way to
shame you.

Some one, however, may ask ' How do the dead rise ? and   35
in what body will they come ? '   You foolish man !   The seed   36
you yourself sow does not come to life, unless it dies !   And   37
when you sow, you sow not the body that will be, but a mere
grain—perhaps of wheat, or something else.   God gives it   38
the body that he pleases—to each seed its special body.   All   39
forms of life are not the same ; there is one for men, another
for beasts, another for birds, and another for fishes.   There   40
are heavenly bodies, and earthly bodies ; but the beauty of the
heavenly bodies is not the beauty of the earthly.   There is a   41
beauty of the sun, and a beauty of the moon, and a beauty of
the stars ; for even star differs from star in beauty.   It is the   42
same with the resurrection of the dead.   Sown a mortal body,
it rises immortal ; sown disfigured, it rises beautiful ; sown   43
weak, it rises strong ; sown a human body, it rises a spiritual   44
body.   As surely as there is a human body, there is also
a spiritual body. That is what is meant by the words—' Adam,   45
the first man, became a human being ' ; the last Adam became
a Life-giving spirit.   That which comes first is not the   46
spiritual, but the human ; afterwards comes the spiritual ;

²⁵—²⁷ Ps. 110. 1 ; 8. 6.   ³² Isa. 22. 13.   ³³ Menander, Thais.   ⁴⁵ Gen. 2. 7

the first man was from the dust of the earth ; the second man 47
from Heaven. Those who are of the dust are like him 48
who came from the dust ; and those who are of Heaven
are like him who came from Heaven. And as we have borne 49
the likeness of him who came from the dust, so let us bear
the likeness of him who came from Heaven. This 50
I say, Brothers—Flesh and blood can have no share in the
Kingdom of God, nor can the perishable share the imperishable. Listen, I will tell you God's hidden purpose ! We 51
shall not all have passed to our rest, but we shall all be transformed—in a moment, in the twinkling of an eye, at the last 52
trumpet-call ; for the trumpet will sound, and the dead will
rise immortal, and we, also, shall be transformed. For this 53
perishable body of ours must put on an imperishable form, and
this dying body a deathless form. And, when this dying body 54
has put on its deathless form, then indeed will the words of
Scripture come true—

'Death has been swallowed up in victory ! Where, O 55
Death, is thy victory ? Where, O Death, is thy sting ?'

It is sin that gives death its sting, and it is the Law that 56
gives sin its power. But thanks be to God, who gives us the 57
victory, through Jesus Christ, our Lord. Therefore, 58
my dear Brothers, stand firm, unshaken, always diligent in the
Lord's work, for you know that, in union with him, your toil
is not in vain.

V.—CONCLUSION.

The Collection for the Poor at Jerusalem. With reference to the Collection for Christ's 1 **16**
People, I want you to follow the instructions that
I gave to the Churches in Galatia. On the first 2
day of every week each of you should put by
what he can afford, so that no collections need be made after
I have come. On my arrival, I will send any persons, whom 3
you may authorize by letter, to carry your gift to Jerusalem ;
and, if it appears to be worth while for me to go also, they 4
shall go with me.

The Apostle's Plans. I will come to you as soon as I have been 5
through Macedonia—for I am going through
Macedonia—and I shall probably make some stay with you or, 6
perhaps, remain for the winter, so that you may yourselves
send me on my way, wherever I may be going. I do not 7
propose to pay you a visit in passing now, for I hope to
stay with you for some time, if the Lord permits. I intend, 8
however, staying at Ephesus till the Festival at the close of
the Harvest ; for a great opening for active work has pre- 9
sented itself, and there are many opponents.

[47] Gen. 2. 7.   [54] Isa. 25. 8.   [55, 57] Hos. 13. 14.

Timothy. If Timothy comes, take care that he has no 10 cause for feeling anxious while he is with you. He is doing the Master's work no less than I am. No one, 11 therefore, should slight him. See him safely on his way to me, for I am expecting him with some of our Brothers.

Apollos. As for our Brother Apollos, I have often urged 12 him to go to you with the others. He has, however, been very unwilling to do so as yet; but he will go as soon as he finds a good opportunity.

Exhortations. Be watchful; stand firm in your faith; show 13 yourselves men; be strong. Let everything you 14 do be done in a loving spirit.

I have another request to make of you, Brothers. You 15 remember Stephanas and his household, and that they were the first-fruits gathered in from Greece, and set themselves to serve Christ's People. I want you, on your part, to 16 show deference to such men as these, as well as to every fellow labourer and earnest worker. I am glad Stephanas 17 and Fortunatus and Achaicus have come, for they have made up for your absence; they have cheered my heart, and your 18 hearts, also. Recognize the worth of such men as these.

Farewells. The Churches in Roman Asia send you their 19 greetings. Aquila and Prisca and the Church that meets at their house send you many Christian greetings. All our Brothers send you greetings.   Greet one another 20 with a sacred kiss.

The Apostle's own Farewell. I, Paul, add this greeting in my own hand- 21 writing. Accursed be any one who has no love 22 for the Lord. THE LORD IS COMING. May the 23 blessing of the Lord Jesus be with you. My love to all of 24 you who are in union with Christ Jesus.

TO THE CORINTHIANS.

II.

ST. PAUL'S 'SECOND LETTER' TO THE CORINTHIANS.

WRITTEN PROBABLY DURING HIS STAY IN MACEDONIA, IN THE COURSE OF HIS THIRD MISSIONARY JOURNEY, ABOUT 55 A.D.

In the brief period that seems to have intervened between the writing of St. Paul's two existing Letters to the Corinthians, the Apostle appears to have paid a second visit to Corinth, of which no account has come down to us (2 Cor. 12. 14; 13. 1.). Apparently that visit failed of its object, and the reception given to the Apostle was not such as he had the right to expect. It seems that St. Paul, returning to Ephesus, wrote a strongly-worded letter to his disloyal Corinthian converts, and that this letter effected, as he afterwards learned, the purpose which the visit had failed to effect. (That letter is generally thought to have been lost, but it has been suggested, with some proba-bility, that part of it forms the last four chapters of this so-called 'Second Letter' to the Corinthians). A few months later, a riot instigated by Demetrius, the silversmith, drove the Apostle from Ephesus (Acts 19. 20; 2 Cor. 1. 8). Travelling north-wards, the Apostle went to the Troad, in the hope of meeting Titus (who had been sent, possibly with the 'Lost Letter,' to Corinth), and of receiving from him some re-assuring news as to the position of matters in the Corinthian Church. But Titus had not yet arrived, and, after waiting for him for some time in vain, St. Paul, keenly disappointed (2 Cor. 2. 13), went on into Macedonia. There he met Titus at Philippi; and to the Apostle's great joy Titus was able to report that the Letter had been well received, and promptly acted upon, by the majority of the Corinthian Christians, and that they cherished a hearty affection for St. Paul himself. On the other hand the Apostle was greatly distressed to learn that there were members of the Church who still stubbornly refused to submit to his authority, and who attacked him with cruel and persistent slander. This news, brought by Titus, may have been the occasion of the present Letter. It is an outburst of passionate feeling, in which the Apostle expresses his gratitude for the kindness and obedience manifested towards him by the majority of the Church, and defends his own personal character and apostolic authority against the unscrupulous attacks of the minority.

TO THE
CORINTHIANS.
II.

I.—INTRODUCTION.

Greeting. To the Church of God in Corinth, and to all 1
Christ's People throughout Greece,
FROM Paul, an Apostle of Christ Jesus, by the will of God,
AND FROM Timothy, a Brother.
May God, our Father, and the Lord Jesus Christ bless you and 2
give you peace.

The Apostle's Thanksgiving for Encouragement. Blessed is the God and Father of Jesus Christ 3
our Lord, the all-merciful Father, the God ever
ready to console, who consoles us in all our 4
troubles, so that we may be able to console those
who are in any trouble with the consolation that
we ourselves receive from him. It is true that we have our full 5
share of the sufferings of the Christ, but through the Christ we
have also our full share of consolation. If we meet with 6
trouble, it is for the sake of your consolation and salvation ;
and, if we find consolation, it is for the sake of the consolation
that you will experience when you are called to endure the very
sufferings that we ourselves are enduring; and our hope for 7
you remains unshaken. We know that, as you are sharing our
sufferings, you will also share our consolation. We 8
want you, Brothers, to know that, in the troubles which befel
us in Roman Asia, we were burdened altogether beyond
our strength, so much so that we even despaired of life.
Indeed, we had the presentiment that we must die, so that we 9
might rely, not on ourselves, but on God who raises the dead.
And from so imminent a death God delivered us, and will 10
deliver us again ; for in him we have placed our hopes of future
deliverance while you, also, help us by your prayers. And 11
then many lips will give thanks on our behalf for the blessing
granted us in answer to many prayers.

II.—THE APOSTLE'S RELATIONS WITH HIS CONVERTS.

The Purity of his Motives. Indeed, our main ground for satisfaction is 12 this—Our conscience tells us that our conduct in the world, and still more in our relations with you, was marked by a purity of motive and a sincerity that were inspired by God, and was based, not on worldly policy, but on the help of God. We never write anything to you other than what you 13 read in public and acknowledge. And my hope is that you will acknowledge to the very end—and, indeed, you have 14 already partly acknowledged it about us—that you have a right to be proud of us, as we shall be proud of you, on the Day of our Lord Jesus.

The Postponement of his Visit. With this conviction in my mind, I planned to 15 come to see you first, so that your pleasure might be doubled—to visit you both on my way to 16 Macedonia, and to come to you again on my return from Macedonia, and then to get you to send me on my way into Judaea. As this was my plan, where, pray, did I show 17 any fickleness of purpose? Or do you think that my plans are formed on mere impulse, so that in the same breath I say 'Yes' and 'No'? As God is true, the Message that we brought you 18 does not waver between 'Yes' and 'No'! The Son of God, 19 Christ Jesus, whom we—Silas, Timothy, and I—proclaimed among you, never wavered between 'Yes' and 'No.' With him it has always been 'Yes.' For, many as were the promises of 20 God, in Christ is the 'Yes' that fulfils them. Therefore, through Christ again, let the 'Amen' rise, through us, to the glory of God. God who brings us, with you, into close union with 21 Christ, and who consecrated us, also set his seal upon us, and 22 gave us his Spirit in our hearts as a pledge of future blessings.

But, as my life shall answer for it, I call God to witness that 23 it was to spare you that I deferred my visit to Corinth. I do 24 not mean that we are to dictate to you with regard to your faith ; on the contrary, we work with you for your true happiness ; indeed, it is through your faith that you are standing firm. For my own sake, as well, I decided not to pay you 1 another painful visit. If it is I who cause you pain, why, who 2 is there to cheer me, except the very person whom I am paining? So I wrote as I did, for fear that, if I had come, I 3 should have been pained by those who ought to have made me glad ; for I felt sure that it was true of you all that my joy was in every case yours also. I wrote to you in sore trouble and 4 distress of heart and with many tears, not to give you pain, but to let you see how intense a love I have for you.

Now whoever has caused the pain has not so much pained 5 me, as he has, to some extent—not to be too severe—pained

every one of you. The man to whom I refer has been 6
sufficiently punished by the penalty inflicted by the majority
of you ; so that now you must take the opposite course, and 7
forgive and encourage him, or else he may be overwhelmed by
the intensity of his pain. So I entreat you to assure him of 8
your love. I had this further object, also, in what I wrote—9
to ascertain whether you might be relied upon to be obedient
in everything. When you forgive a man anything, I forgive 10
him, too. Indeed, for my part, whatever I have forgiven (if
I have had to forgive anything), I have forgiven for your sakes,
in the presence of Christ, so as to prevent Satan from taking 11
advantage of us ; for we are not ignorant of his devices.

When I went to the district round Troas to tell the Good 12
News of the Christ, even though there was an opening for
serving the Master, I could get no peace of mind because I 13
failed to find Titus, my Brother ; so I took leave of the people
there, and went on to Macedonia.   All thanks to God, 14
who, through our union with the Christ, leads us in one continual triumph, and uses us to spread the sweet odour of the
knowledge of him in every place. For we are the fragrance 15
of Christ ascending to God—both among those who are in the
path of Salvation and among those who are in the path to
Ruin. To the latter we are an odour which arises from death 16
and tells of Death ; to the former an odour which arises from
life and tells of Life. But who is equal to such a task ? Unlike 17
many people, we are not in the habit of making profit out of
God's Message ; but in all sincerity, and bearing God's commission, we speak before him in union with Christ.

His Converts the Vindication of his Ministry. Are we beginning to commend ourselves again ? 1 **3**
Or are we like some who need letters of com-
mendation to you, or from you ? You yourselves 2
are our letter—a letter written on our hearts, and
one which everybody can read and understand. All can 3
see that you are a letter from Christ delivered by us, a
letter written, not with ink, but with the Spirit of the Living
God, not on 'tablets of stone,' but on 'tablets of human
hearts.'

III.—THE MINISTRY OF THE APOSTLES.

The Glory of the Gospel contrasted with the Glory of the Law. This, then, is the confidence in regard to God 4
that we have gained through the Christ. I do not 5
mean that we are fit to form any judgement by
ourselves, as if on our own authority ; our fitness
comes from God, who himself made us fit to be 6
ministers of a New Covenant, of which the substance is, not a

³ Exod. 31. 18 ; 34. 1 ; Prov. 3. 3 ; Ezek. 11. 19 ; 36. 26.

written Law, but a Spirit.   For the written Law means Death, but the Spirit gives Life.

If the system of religion which involved Death, embodied 7 in a written Law and engraved on stones, began amid such glory, that the Israelites were unable to gaze at the face of Moses on account of its glory, though it was but a passing glory, will not the religion that confers the Spirit have still 8 greater glory?   For, if there was a glory in the religion that 9 involved condemnation, far greater is the glory of the religion that confers righteousness!   Indeed, that which then had glory 10 has lost its glory, because of the glory which surpasses it. And, 11 if that which was to pass away was attended with glory, far more will that which is to endure be surrounded with glory!

With such a hope as this, we speak with all plainness; 12 unlike Moses, who covered his face with a veil, to prevent 13 the Israelites from gazing at the disappearance of what was passing away.   But their minds were slow to learn.   14 Indeed, to this very day, at the public reading of the Old Covenant, the same veil remains unlifted; only for those who are in union with Christ does it pass away.   But, even to this 15 day, whenever Moses is read, a veil lies on their hearts. ' Yet, 16 whenever a man turns to the Lord, the veil is removed.'   And 17 the ' Lord ' is the Spirit, and, where the Spirit of the Lord is, there is freedom.   And all of us, with faces from which the veil 18 is lifted, seeing, as if reflected in a mirror, the glory of the Lord, are being transformed into his likeness, from glory to glory, as it is given by the Lord, the Spirit.

Therefore, since it is by God's mercy that we are engaged in 1   4. this ministry, we do not lose heart.   No, we have renounced the 2 secrecy prompted by shame, refusing to adopt crafty ways, or to tamper with God's Message, and commending ourselves to every man's conscience, in the sight of God, by our exhibition of the Truth.   And, even if the Good News that we bring is veiled, it is 3 · veiled only in the case of those who are on the path to Ruin— men whose minds have been blinded by the God of this Age, 4 unbelievers as they are, so that the light from the Good News of the glory of the Christ, who is the very incarnation of God, should not shine for them.   (For it is not ourselves that we 5 proclaim, but Christ Jesus, as Lord, and ourselves as your servants for Jesus' sake.)   Indeed, the same God who said 6 ' Out of darkness light shall shine,' has shone in upon our hearts, so that we should bring out into the light the knowledge of the glory of God, seen in the face of Christ.

The Weakness of the Apostles.   This treasure we have in these earthen vessels, 7 that its all-prevailing power may be seen to come from God, and not to be our own.   Though hard 8 pressed on every side, we are never hemmed in ; though per-

7—16 Exod. 34. 29, 30, 34, 35.   18 Exod. 24. 17.

plexed, never driven to despair ; though pursued, never aban-	9
doned ; though struck down, never killed ! We always bear	10
on our bodies the marks of the death that Jesus died, so that
the Life also of Jesus may be exhibited in our bodies. Indeed,	11
we who still live are continually being given over to death for
Jesus' sake, so that the Life also of Jesus may be exhibited
in our mortal nature. And so, while death is at work within us,	12
Life is at work within you. But, in the same spirit of faith as	13
that expressed in the words—'I believed, and therefore I spoke,'
we, also, believe, and therefore speak. For we know that he	14
who raised the Lord Jesus will raise us also with him, and
will bring us, with you, into his presence. For all this is for	15
your sakes, that the loving-kindness of God, spreading from
heart to heart, may cause yet more hearts to overflow with
thanksgiving, to his glory.

Therefore, as I said, we do not lose heart. No, even though	16
outwardly we are wasting away, yet inwardly we are being
renewed day by day. The light burden of our momentary	17
trouble is preparing for us, in measure transcending thought,
a weight of imperishable glory ; we, all the while, gazing not	18
on what is seen, but on what is unseen ; for what is seen is
transient, but what is unseen is imperishable. For we know	1 **5**
that if our tent—that earthly body which is now our home—is
taken down, we have a house of God's building, a home not
made by hands, imperishable, in Heaven. Even while in our	2
present body we sigh, longing to put over it our heavenly
dwelling, sure that, when we have put it on, we shall never be	3
found discarnate. For we who are in this 'tent' sigh under	4
our burden, unwilling to take it off, yet wishing to put our
heavenly body over it, so that all that is mortal may be
absorbed in Life. And he who has prepared us for this change	5
is God, who has also given us his Spirit as a pledge.

Therefore we are always confident, knowing that, while our	6
home is in the body, we are absent from our home with the
Lord. For we guide our lives by faith, and not by what we	7
see. And in this confidence we would gladly leave our home	8
in the body, and make our home with the Lord. Therefore,	9
whether in our home or absent from our home, our one ambi-
tion is to please him. For at the Bar of the Christ we must	10
all appear in our true characters, that each may reap the results
of the life which he has lived in the body, in accordance with
his actions—whether good or worthless.

Christ		Therefore, because we know the fear inspired	11
their Motive	by the Lord, it is true that we are trying to win
and Strength.	men, but our motives are plain to God ; and I
hope that in your inmost hearts they are plain to you also.

13 Ps. 116. 10.

We are not "commending ourselves" again to you, but rather 12 are giving you cause for pride in us, so that you may have an answer ready for those who pride themselves on appearances and not on character.   For, if we were "beside ourselves," it 13 was in God's service!   If we are now in our senses, it is in yours!   It is the love of the Christ which compels us, when we 14 reflect that, as one died for all, therefore all died ; and that he 15 died for all, so that the living should no longer live for themselves, but for him who died and rose for them.

For ourselves, then, from this time forward, we refuse to 16 regard any one from the world's standpoint.   Even if we once thought of Christ from the standpoint of the world, yet now we do so no longer.   Therefore, if any one is in union with 17 Christ, he is a new being !   His old life has passed away ; a new life has begun !   But all this is the work of God, who recon- 18 ciled us to himself through Christ, and gave us the Ministry of Reconciliation—to proclaim that God, in Christ, was recon- 19 ciling the world to himself, not reckoning men's offences against them, and that he had entrusted us with the Message of this reconciliation.

It is, then, on Christ's behalf that we are acting as 20 ambassadors, God, as it were, appealing to you through us. We implore you on Christ's behalf—Be reconciled to God. Him who never knew sin God made to be Sin, on our 21 behalf ; so that we, through union with him, might become the Righteousness of God.   Therefore, as God's fellow- 1 **6** workers, we also appeal to you not to receive his loving-kindness in vain.   For he says— 2

> ' At the time for acceptance I listened to thee,
>   And on the day of deliverance I helped thee.'

Now is the time for acceptance !   Now is the day of de-liverance !   Never do we put an obstacle in any one's way, 3 that no fault may be found with our ministry.   No, we are 4 trying to commend ourselves under all circumstances, as God's ministers should—in many an hour of endurance, in troubles, in hardships, in difficulties, in floggings, in imprisonments, in 5 riots, in toils, in sleepless nights, in fastings ; by purity, by 6 knowledge, by patience, by kindliness, by holiness of spirit, by unfeigned love ; by the Message of Truth, and by the 7 power of God ; by the weapons of righteousness in the right hand and in the left ; amid honour and disrepute, amid 8 slander and praise ; regarded as deceivers, yet proved to be true ; as unknown, yet well-known ; as at death's door, yet, 9 see, we are living ; as chastised, yet not killed ; as saddened, 10 yet always rejoicing ; as poor, yet enriching many ; as having nothing, and yet possessing all things !

[17] Isa. 43. 18, 19.   [2] Isa. 49. 8.   [9] Ps. 118. 17—18.

IV.—THE APOSTLE AND HIS CONVERTS.

His Appeal for their Love. We have been speaking freely to you, men of 11
Corinth ; we have opened our heart ; there is 12
room there for you, yet there is not room, in your love, for us.
Can you not in return—I appeal to you as I should to children— 13
open your hearts to us ?

His Warning against Heathen Influences. Do not enter into inconsistent relations with 14
those who reject the Faith. For what partnership
can there be between righteousness and lawless-
ness ? or what has light to do with darkness ?
What harmony can there be between Christ and Belial ? or 15
what can those who accept the Faith have in common with
those who reject it ? What agreement can there be between 16
a temple of God and idols ? And we are a temple of the
Living God. That is what God meant when he said—

' I will dwell among them, and walk among them ;
 And I will be their God, and they shall be my people.
Therefore " Come out from among the nations, 17
 And separate yourselves from them," says the Lord,
"And touch nothing impure ;
 And I will welcome you ;
And I will be a father to you, 18
And you shall be my sons and daughters,"
 Says the Lord, the Ruler of all.'

With these promises, dear friends, let us purify ourselves from 1 **7**
everything that pollutes either body or spirit, and, in deepest
reverence for God, aim at perfect holiness.

His Anxieties and Encouragements. Make room for us in your hearts. In no 2
instance have we ever wronged, or harmed, or
taken advantage of, any one. I am not saying 3
this to condemn you. Indeed, I have already
said that you are in our very heart, to live and die together. I 4
have the utmost confidence in you ; I am always boasting
about you. I am full of encouragement and, in spite of all our
troubles, my heart is overflowing with happiness.

Ever since we reached Macedonia, we have had no rest in 5
body or mind ; on every side there have been troubles—conflicts
without, anxieties within. But God, who encourages the 6
downcast, has encouraged us by the arrival of Titus. And it 7
is not only by his arrival that we are encouraged, but also by
the encouragement which he received from you ; for he tells
us of your strong affection, your penitence, and your zeal on
my behalf—so that I am happier still. For, though I caused 8
you sorrow by my letter, I do not regret it. Even if I were

11 Ps. 119. 32.   16—18 Lev. 26. 11, 12; Ezek. 37. 27; Isa. 52. 11; 2 Sam. 7. 14;
 Hos. 1. 10; Isa. 43. 6; Amos 4. 13 (Septuagint).

inclined to regret it—for I see that my letter did cause you sorrow though only for a time—I am glad now ; not because of the sorrow it caused you, but because your sorrow brought you to repentance. For it was God's will that you should feel sorrow, in order that you should not suffer loss in any way at our hands. For, when sorrow is in accordance with God's will, it results in a repentance leading to Salvation, and which will never be regretted. The sure result of the sorrow that the world knows is Death. For see what results that other sorrow—sorrow in accordance with God's will—has had in your case. What earnestness it produced ! what explanations ! what strong feeling ! what alarm ! what longing ! what eagerness ! what readiness to punish ! You have proved yourselves altogether free from guilt in that matter. So, then, even though I did write to you, it was not for the sake of the wrong-doer, or of the man who was wronged, but to make you conscious, in the sight of God, of your own earnest care for us. And it is this that has encouraged us.

In addition to the encouragement that this gave us, we were made far happier still by the happiness of Titus ; for his heart has been cheered by you all. Although I have been boasting a little to him about you, you did not put me to shame ; but, just as every thing we had said to you was true, so our boasting to Titus about you has also proved to be the truth. And his affection for you is all the greater, as he remembers the deference that you all showed him, and recalls how you received him with anxious care. I am glad that I can feel perfect confidence in you.

V.—THE PALESTINE FAMINE FUND.

The Example of the Macedonian Churches. We would remind you, Brothers, of the love that God has shown to the Churches in Macedonia —how, tried though they were by many a trouble, their overflowing happiness, and even their deep poverty, resulted in a flood of generosity. I can bear witness that to the full extent of their power, and even beyond their power, spontaneously, and with many an appeal to us for permission, they showed their love, and contributed their share towards the fund for their fellow-Christians. And that, not only in the way we had expected ; but first they gave themselves to the Lord, and to us also, in accordance with God's will. And this led us to urge upon Titus that, as he had started the work for you, he should also see to the completion of this expression of your love. And, remembering how you excel in everything —in faith, in teaching, in knowledge, in unfailing earnestness, and in the affection that we have awakened in you—I ask you to excel also in this expression of your love.

The Completion of the Collection at Corinth. I am not laying a command upon you, but I 8 am making use of the earnestness shown by others to test the genuineness of your affection. For you do not forget the loving-kindness of our 9 Lord Jesus Christ—how that for your sakes, although he was rich, he became poor, so that you also might become rich through his poverty. I am only making suggestions on this 10 matter; for this is the best course for you, since you were a year before others, not only in taking action, but also in showing your readiness to do so. And now I want you to 11 complete the work, so that its completion may correspond with your willing readiness—in proportion, of course, to your means. For, where there is willingness, a man's gift is valued by its 12 comparison with what he has, and not with what he has not. For our object is not to give relief to others and bring distress 13 on you, but, by equalizing matters, to secure that, on the present 14 occasion, what you can spare may supply their need, so that at another time what they can spare may supply your need, and thus matters may be equalized. As Scripture says— 15

' The man who had much had nothing over, and the man who had little did not lack ! '

Titus and others to assist. I thank God for inspiring Titus with the same 16 keen interest in your welfare that I have; for 17 Titus has responded to my appeals and, in his great earnestness, is starting to go to you of his own accord. We are sending with him the Brother whose fame in the 18 service of the Good News has spread through all the Churches ; and not only that, but he has been elected by the Churches to 19 accompany us on our journey, in connexion with this expression of your love, which we are personally administering to the honour of the Lord, and to show our deep interest. What we are 20 specially guarding against is that any fault should be found with us in regard to our administration of this charitable fund ; for we are trying to make arrangements which shall be right, 21 not only in the eyes of the Lord, but also in the eyes of men. We are also sending with them another of our Brothers, whose 22 earnestness we have many a time proved in many ways, and whom we now find made even more earnest by his great confidence in you. If I must say anything about Titus, he is 23 my intimate companion, and he shares my work for you ; if it is our Brothers, they are delegates of the Churches, an honour to Christ. Show them, therefore—so that the Churches 24 may see it—the proof of your affection, and the ground for our boasting to them about you.

With reference, indeed, to the Fund for your fellow- 1 **9** Christians, it is quite superfluous for me to say anything to you. I know, of course, your willingness to help, and I am 2

¹⁵ Exod. 16. 18. ²¹ Prov. 3. 4 (Septuagint).

always boasting of it to the Macedonians. I tell them that you in Greece have been ready for a year past; and it was really your zeal that stimulated most of them. So my 3 reason for sending our Brothers is to prevent what we said about you from proving, in this particular matter, an empty boast, and to enable you to be as well prepared as I have been saying that you are. Otherwise, if any Mace- 4 donians were to come with me, and find you unprepared, we—to say nothing of you—should feel ashamed of our present confidence. Therefore I think it necessary to urge 5 the Brothers to go to you in advance, and to complete the arrangements for the gift, which you have already promised, so that it may be ready, as a gift, before I come, and not look as if it were being given under pressure.

The Spirit in which to make the Collection. Remember the saying—'Scanty sowing, scanty 6 harvest; plentiful sowing, plentiful harvest.' Let 7 every one give as he has determined beforehand, not grudgingly or under compulsion; for God loves 'a cheerful giver.' God has power to shower all kinds of 8 blessings upon you, so that, having, under all circumstances and on all occasions, all that you can need, you may be able to shower all kinds of benefits upon others. (As Scripture says— 9

' He scattered broadcast, he gave to the poor ;
His righteousness continues for ever.'

And he who supplies 'seed to the sower, and bread for eating,' 10 will supply you with seed, and cause it to increase, and will multiply 'the fruits of your righteousness'). Rich in all 11 things yourselves, you will be able to show liberality to all, which, with our help, will cause thanksgiving to be offered to God. For the rendering of a public service such as this, not 12 only relieves the needs of your fellow-Christians, but also results in the offering to God of many a thanksgiving. Through the 13 evidence afforded by the service thus rendered, you cause men to praise God for your fidelity to your profession of faith in the Good News of the Christ, as well as for the liberality of your contributions for them and for all others. And they also, in their 14 prayers for you, express their longing to see you, because of the surpassing love of God displayed toward you.   All 15 thanks to God for his inestimable gift !

VI.—THE APOSTLE'S CLAIMS AND AUTHORITY.

The Assertion of his Authority. Now, I, Paul, make a personal appeal to you by 1 **10** the meekness and gentleness of the Christ—I who, "in your presence, am humble in my bearing towards you, but, when absent, am bold in my language to you"—I implore you not to drive me to "show 2

<hr>

7 Prov. 22. 8 (Septuagint). 9 Ps. 112. 9. 10 Hos. 10. 12 ; Isa. 55. 10.

my boldness," when I do come, by the confident tone which
I expect to have to adopt towards some of you, who are
expecting to find us influenced in our conduct by earthly
motives.   For, though we live an earthly life, we do not 3
wage an earthly war.   The weapons for our warfare are not 4
earthly, but, under God, are powerful enough to pull down
strongholds.   We are engaged in confuting arguments and 5
pulling down every barrier raised against the knowledge of
God.   We are taking captive every hostile thought, to bring
it into submission to the Christ, and are fully prepared to 6
punish every act of rebellion, when once your submission is complete.   You look at the outward appearance of things ! 7
Let any one, who is confident that he belongs to Christ, reflect,
for himself, again upon the fact—that we belong to Christ no
less than he does.   Even if I boast extravagantly about our 8
authority—which the Lord gave us for building up your faith
and not for overthrowing it—still I have no reason to be
ashamed.   I say this, that it may not seem as if I were trying 9
to overawe you by my letters.   For, people say " His letters are 10
impressive and vigorous, but his personal appearance is insignificant and his speaking contemptible."   Let such a man be 11
assured of this—that our words in our letters show us to be,
when absent, just what our deeds will show us to be, when
present.   We have not indeed the audacity to class or 12
compare ourselves with some of those who indulge in self-
commendation !   But, when such persons measure themselves
by themselves, and compare themselves with themselves, they
show a want of wisdom.   We, however, will not give way to 13
unlimited boasting, but will confine ourselves to the limits of
the sphere to which God limited us, when he permitted us to
come as far as Corinth.   For it is not the case, as it would be 14
if we were not in the habit of coming to you, that we are
exceeding our bounds !   Why, we were the very first to reach
you with the Good News of the Christ !   Our boasting, there- 15
fore, is not unlimited, nor does it extend to the labours of
others ; but our hope is that, as your faith grows, our influence
among you may be very greatly increased—though still confined
to our sphere—so that we shall be able to tell the Good News in 16
the districts beyond you, without trespassing on the sphere
assigned to others, or boasting of what has been already
done.   ' Let him who boasts make his boast of the 17
Lord.'   For it is not the man who commends himself that 18
stands the test, but the man who is commended by the
Lord.

**His Right
as an
Apostle.**   I could wish that you would tolerate a little folly 1 **11**
in me !   But indeed you do tolerate me.   I am 2
jealous over you with the jealousy of God.   For I
betrothed you to one husband, that I might present you to the

Christ a pure bride. Yet I fear that it may turn out that, just as **3**
the Serpent by his craftiness deceived Eve, so your minds may
have lost the loyalty and purity due from you to the Christ.
For, if some new-comer is proclaiming a Jesus other than him **4**
whom we proclaimed, or if you are receiving a Spirit different
from the Spirit which you received, or a Good News different
from that which you welcomed, then you are marvellously
tolerant! I do not regard myself as in any way inferior to the **5**
most eminent Apostles! Though I am no trained orator, yet **6**
I am not without knowledge; indeed we made this perfectly
clear to you in every way.

Perhaps you say that I did wrong in humbling myself that **7**
you might be exalted—I mean because I told you God's Good
News without payment. I robbed other churches by taking **8**
pay from them, so that I might serve you! And, when I was **9**
with you and in need, I did not become a burden to any of
you; for our Brothers, on coming from Macedonia, supplied
my needs. I kept myself, and will keep myself, from being
an expense to you in any way. As surely as I know anything **10**
of the Truth of Christ, this boast, as far as I am concerned,
shall not be stopped in any part of Greece. Why? Because **11**
I do not love you? God knows that I do!

What I am doing now I shall continue to do, that I may cut **12**
away the ground from under those who are wishing for some
ground for attacking me, so that as regards the thing of which
they boast they may appear in their true characters, just as we
do. Men of this stamp are false apostles, treacherous workers, **13**
disguising themselves as Apostles of Christ! And no wonder; **14**
for even Satan disguises himself as an angel of Light. It is not **15**
surprising, therefore, if his servants also disguise themselves as
servants of Righteousness. But their end will be in accordance
with their actions.

His Claims for Consideration; his Life and Work, I say again—Let no one think me a fool! Yet, **16**
if you do, at least welcome me as you would a
fool, that I, too, may indulge in a little boasting.
When I speak thus, I am not speaking as the **17**
Master would, but as a fool might, in boasting so
confidently. As so many are boasting of earthly things, I, **18**
too, will boast. For all your cleverness, you tolerate fools **19**
willingly enough! You tolerate a man even when he en- **20**
slaves you, when he plunders you, when he gets you into his
power, when he puts on airs of superiority, when he strikes
you in the face! I admit, to my shame, that we have been **21**
weak. But whatever the subject on which others are not
afraid to boast—though it is foolish to say so—I am not afraid
either! Are they Hebrews? So am I! Are they Israelites? **22**
So am I! Are they descendants of Abraham? So am I!

[17] Jer. 9. 24.   [3] Gen. 3. 13.

Are they 'Servants of Christ'? Though it is madness to 23
talk like this, I am more so than they! I have had more
of toil, more of imprisonment! I have been flogged times
without number. I have been often at death's door. Five 24
times I received at the hands of the Jews forty lashes, all
but one. Three times I was beaten with rods. Once I was 25
stoned. Three times I was shipwrecked. I have spent a 26
whole day and night in the deep. My journeys have been
many. I have been through dangers from rivers, dangers
from robbers, dangers from my own people, dangers from
the Gentiles, dangers in towns, dangers in the country,
dangers on the sea, dangers among false Brothers. I have 27
been through toil and hardship. I have passed many a sleepless night; I have endured hunger and thirst; I have often
been without food; I have known cold and nakedness. And, 28
not to speak of other things, there is my daily burden of
anxiety about all the Churches. Who is weak without my 29
being weak? Who is led astray without my burning with
indignation? If I must boast, I will boast of things which 30
show my weakness! The God and Father of the Lord Jesus— 31
he who is for ever blessed—knows that I am speaking the
truth. When I was in Damascus, the Governor under King 32
Aretas had the gates of that city guarded, so as to arrest me,
but I was let down in a basket through a window in the wall, 33
and so escaped his hands.

I must boast! It is unprofitable; but I will 1 **12**
his Visions. pass to visions and revelations given by the Lord.
I know a man in union with Christ, who, fourteen years ago— 2
whether in the body or out of the body I do not know; God
knows—was caught up (this man of whom I am speaking) to
the third Heaven. And I know that this man—whether in 3
the body or separated from the body I do not know; God
knows—was caught up into Paradise, and heard unspeakable 4
things of which no human being may tell. About such a 5
man I will boast, but about myself I will not boast except
as regards my weaknesses. Yet if I choose to boast, I shall 6
not be a fool; for I shall be speaking no more than the
truth. But I refrain, lest any one should credit me with
more than he can see in me or hear from me, and because
of the marvellous character of the revelations. It was for this 7
reason, and to prevent my thinking too highly of myself,
that a thorn was sent to pierce my flesh—an instrument of
Satan to discipline me—so that I should not think too highly
of myself. About this I three times entreated the Lord, praying 8
that it might leave me. But his reply has been—'My help is 9
enough for you; for my strength attains its perfection in the
midst of weakness.'

Most gladly, then, will I boast all the more of my weaknesses, so that the strength of the Christ may overshadow me.

That is why I delight in weakness, ill-treatment, hardships,   10
persecution, and difficulties, when borne for Christ. For, when
I am weak, then it is that I am strong !

VII.—CONCLUSION.

A Remonstrance.   I have been " playing the fool ! " It is you who   11
drove me to it.   For it is you who ought to have
been commending me ! Although I am nobody, in no respect
did I prove inferior to the most eminent Apostles. The marks   12
of the true Apostle were exhibited among you in constant
endurance, as well as by signs, by marvels, and by miracles.
In what respect, I ask, were you treated worse than the   13
other Churches, unless it was that, for my part, I refused to
become a burden to you? Forgive me the wrong I thus did
you !

A Defence.   Remember, this is the third time that I have   14
made every preparation to come to see you, and I
shall refuse to be a burden to you ; I want, not your money,
but you. It is not the duty of children to put by for their
parents, but of parents to put by for their children. For my   15
part, I will most gladly spend, and be spent, for your welfare.
Can it be that the more intensely I love you the less I am to
be loved ?   You will admit that I was not a burden to   16
you, but you say that I was " crafty " and caught you " by a
trick " ! Do you assert that I took advantage of you through   17
any of those whom I have sent to you ? I urged Titus to go,   18
and I sent our Brother with him. Did Titus take any advantage of you ? Did not we live in the same Spirit, and
tread in the same footsteps ?

A Warning.   Have you all this time been fancying that   19
it is to you that we are making our defence ? No,
it is in the sight of God, and in union with Christ, that we are
speaking. And all this, dear friends, is to build up your
characters ; for I am afraid that perhaps, when I come, I may   20
find that you are not what I want you to be, and, on the other
hand, that you may find that I am what you do not want me
to be. I am afraid that I may find quarrelling, jealousy, ill-
feeling, rivalry, slandering, back-biting, self-assertion, and
disorder. I am afraid lest, on my next visit, my God may   21
humble me in regard to you, and that I may have to mourn
over many who have long been sinning, and have not repented
of the impurity, immorality, and sensuality, in which they have
indulged.

1   For the third time I am coming to see you. ' By the word   1
of two or three witnesses each statement shall be established.'
I have said it, and I say it again before I come, just as if I   2

¹ Deut. 19. 15.

were with you on my second visit, though for the moment absent, I say to those who have been long sinning, as well as to all others—that if I come again, I shall spare no one. And that will be the proof, which you are looking for, that the Christ speaks through me. There is no weakness in his dealings with you. No, he shows his power among you. For though his crucifixion was due to weakness, his life is due to the power of God. And we, also, are weak in his weakness, but with him we shall live for you through the power of God.   Put yourselves to the proof, to see whether you are holding to the Faith. Test yourselves. Surely you recognize this fact about yourselves—that Jesus Christ is in you! Unless indeed you cannot stand the test! But I hope that you will recognize that we can stand the test. We pray God that you may do nothing wrong, not that we may be seen to stand the test, but that you may do what is right, even though we may seem not to stand the test. We have no power at all against the Truth, but we have power in the service of the Truth. We are glad when we are weak, if you are strong. And what we pray for is that you may become perfect.   This is my reason for writing as I am now doing, while I am away from you, so that, when I am with you, I may not act harshly in the exercise of the authority which the Lord gave me—and gave me for building up and not for pulling down.

Farewells.   And now, Brothers, good-bye. Aim at perfection; take courage; agree together; live in peace. And then God, the source of all love and peace, will be with you.   Greet one another with a sacred kiss.   All Christ's people here send you their greetings.

May the blessing of the Lord Jesus Christ, and the love of God, and the communion with the Holy Spirit, be with you all.

... with you in any sacred work, though for the moment ... should sometimes seem too long, bear long, shining as well as in all things; that I come again; I shall seem no less. And then will be the proof which you are looking for, that the Christ speaks through me. There is no weakness in his dealings with you. No; he shows his compassion too. For just as he was crucified on account of the life he did to the power of God. And we also are weak in these ways, but with him we shall live through the power of God ...

... The power which is meant is to set whether you are holding to the Faith, that you realize, each one among you. This fact about yourselves: that Jesus Christ is in you. Unless indeed you cannot stand the test. But I hope that you will recognize that we can stand the test. We pray God that you may do nothing wrong, not that we may be seen to stand the test, but that you to do what is right, even though we may seem unable to stand the test. We have no power at all against the Truth, but we have power to help the Truth. We are glad when we are weak, if you are strong. And what we pray for is that you may be made perfect. This is why, in my absence, I am writing as I am now doing, while I am away from you, so that I need not, when I am present, use any of the severity which the Lord gave me the authority to use, and gave me for building you up, and not for pulling down.

11 And now, Brothers, good-bye. Aim at per-

Exercise ... comfort, live together ... respect, live in peace; and our God, the source of all love and peace, will be with you. 12 Salute one another with a sacred 13 kiss. All Christ's people here send a loving greeting.

14 May the blessing of the Lord Jesus Christ and the love of God, and the communion with the Holy Spirit, be with you all.

TO THE ROMANS.

ST. PAUL'S LETTER TO THE CHRISTIANS IN ROME.

WRITTEN PROBABLY DURING HIS STAY AT CORINTH, IN THE COURSE OF HIS THIRD MISSIONARY JOURNEY, ABOUT 56 A.D.

St. Paul had often wished to visit Rome, but up to the time of writing this Letter he had been prevented by various causes from doing so (Rom. 1. 11, 13 ; Acts 19. 21). At last there seemed to be a prospect of the realization of his long-cherished desire. In the course of his third missionary journey he was in Corinth, and was about to go to Jerusalem to carry to the poorer Christians there the charitable contributions of several other Churches. It was his intention, upon leaving Jerusalem, to visit Spain, and he hoped on his way to spend a short time in Rome (Rom. 15. 24). He wrote the present Letter in anticipation of this journey to the West and for the purpose of putting in writing beforehand a full statement of certain important truths.

Philosophy, the Apostle teaches, had failed as a means of Salvation for the Gentile. The Law had failed as a means of Salvation for the Jew. In this Letter he establishes the doctrine that faith in Christ is the only ground of acceptance with God for all mankind.

The extent to which he develops his subject gives the Letter largely the aspect of a treatise.

TO THE
ROMANS.

I.—INTRODUCTION.

The Apostle's Greeting. To all in Rome who are dear to God and have 1-7 **1** been called to become Christ's People, FROM Paul, a servant of Jesus Christ, who has been called to become an Apostle, and has been set apart to tell God's Good News. This Good News God promised long ago through his Prophets in the sacred Scriptures, concerning his Son, Jesus Christ, our Lord ; who, as to his human nature, was descended from David, but, as to the spirit of holiness within him, was miraculously designated Son of God by his resurrection from the dead. Through him we received the gift of the Apostolic office, to win submission to the Faith among all nations for the glory of his Name. And among these nations are you—you who have been called to belong to Jesus Christ. May God, our Father, and the Lord Jesus Christ bless you and give you peace.

The Apostle's Thankfulness and Hope. First, I thank my God through Jesus Christ 8 about you all, because the report of your faith is spreading throughout the world. God, to whom 9 I offer the worship of my soul as I tell the Good News of his Son, is my witness how constantly I mention you when I pray, asking that, if he be willing, I may some day at 10 last find the way open to visit you. For I long to see you, 11 in order to impart to you some spiritual gift and so give you fresh strength—or rather that both you and I may find 12 encouragement in each other's faith. I want you to know, 13 Brothers, that I have many times intended coming to see you —but until now I have been prevented—that I might find among you some fruit of my labours, as I have already among the other nations.

II.—Faith the One Ground of Acceptance with God.

The Divine Ideal for Mankind.   I have a duty to both the Greek and the Barbarian, to both the cultured and the ignorant. And so, for my part, I am ready to tell the Good News to you also who are in Rome. For I am not ashamed of the Good News ; it is the power of God which brings Salvation to every one who believes in Christ, to the Jew first, but also to the Greek. For in it there is a revelation of the Divine Righteousness resulting from faith and leading on to faith ; as Scripture says— 14 15 16 17

    ' Through faith the righteous man shall find Life.'

Failure of the Gentile to reach this Ideal.   So, too, there is a revelation from Heaven of the Divine Wrath against every form of ungodliness and wickedness on the part of those men who, by their wicked lives, are stifling the Truth. This is so, because what can be known about God is plain to them ; for God himself has made it plain. For ever since the creation of the universe God's invisible attributes—his everlasting power and divinity—are to be seen and studied in his works, so that men have no excuse ; because, although they learnt to know God, yet they did not offer him as God either praise or thanksgiving. Their speculations about him proved futile, and their undiscerning minds were darkened. Professing to be wise, they showed themselves fools ; and they transformed the Glory of the immortal God into the likeness of mortal man, and of birds, and beasts, and reptiles. 18 19 20 21 22 23

Therefore God abandoned them to impurity, letting them follow the cravings of their hearts, till they dishonoured their own bodies ; for they had substituted a lie for the truth about God, and had reverenced and worshipped created things more than the Creator, who is to be praised for ever. Amen.   That, I say, is why God abandoned them to degrading passions. Even the women among them perverted the natural use of their bodies to the unnatural ; while the men, disregarding that for which women were intended by nature, were consumed with passion for one another. Men indulged in vile practices with men, and incurred in their own persons the inevitable penalty of their perverseness.   Then, as they would not keep God before their minds, God abandoned them to depraved thoughts, so that they did all kinds of shameful things. They revelled in every form of wickedness, evil, greed, vice. Their lives were full of envy, murder, quarrelling, treachery, malice. They became back-biters, 24 25 26 27 28 29 30

17 Hab. 2. 4.   23 Ps. 106. 20.

slanderers, impious, insolent, boastful. They devised new
sins. They disobeyed their parents. They were undiscerning,   31
untrustworthy, without natural affection or pity. Well aware   32
of God's decree, that those who do such things deserve to
die, not only are they guilty of them themselves, but they
even applaud those who do them.

Therefore you have nothing to say in your own defence,   1   **2**
whoever you are who set yourself up as a judge. In judging
others you condemn yourself, for you who set yourself up
as a judge do the very same things. And we know that   2
God's judgement falls unerringly upon those who do them.
You who judge those that do such things and yet are your-   3
self guilty of them—do you suppose that you of all men will
escape God's judgement? Or do you think lightly of his   4
abundant kindness, patience, and forbearance, not realizing
that his kindness is meant to lead you to repentance? Hard-   5
hearted and impenitent as you are, you are storing up for
yourself Wrath on the 'Day of Wrath,' when God's justice as
a judge will be revealed; for 'he will give to every man what 6
his actions deserve.' To those who, by perseverance in doing   7
good, aim at glory, honour, and all that is imperishable, he
will give Immortal Life; while as to those who are factious,   8
and disobedient to Truth but obedient to Evil, wrath and anger,
distress and despair, will fall upon every human being who   9
persists in wrong-doing—upon the Jew first, but also upon
the Greek. But there will be glory, honour, and peace for   10
every one who does right—for the Jew first, but also for the
Greek, since God shows no partiality.   11
All who, when they sin, are without Law will also perish   12
without Law; while all who, when they sin, are under Law,
will be judged as being under Law. It is not those who hear   13
the words of a Law that are righteous before God, but it is
those who obey it that will be pronounced righteous. When   14
Gentiles, who have no Law, do instinctively what the Law
requires, they, though they have no Law, are a Law to themselves; for they show the demands of the Law written upon   15
their hearts; their consciences corroborating it, while in their
thoughts they argue either in self-accusation or, it may be,
in self-defence——on the day when God passes judgement on   16
men's inmost lives, as the Good News that I tell declares that
he will do through Christ Jesus.

Failure of the   But, perhaps, you bear the name of 'Jew,' and   17
Jews   are relying upon Law, and boast of belonging to
to reach this   God, and understand his will, and, having been   18
Ideal.   carefully instructed from the Law, have learnt
to appreciate the finer moral distinctions. Perhaps you are   19
confident that you are a guide to the blind, a light to those

⁶ Ps. 62. 12; Prov. 24. 12.

N

who are in the dark, an instructor of the unintelligent, and 20
a teacher of the childish, because in the Law you possess the
outline of all Knowledge and Truth. Why, then, you teacher 21
of others, do not you teach yourself? Do you preach against
stealing, and yet steal? Do you forbid adultery, and yet com- 22
mit adultery? Do you loathe idols, and yet plunder temples?
Boasting, as you do, of your Law, do you dishonour God by 23
breaking the Law? For, as Scripture says— 24

'The name of God is reviled among the Gentiles because of
you'!

Circumcision has its value, if you are obeying the Law. But, 25
if you are a breaker of the Law, your circumcision is no better
than uncircumcision. If, then, an uncircumcised man pays 26
regard to the requirements of the Law, will not he, although
not circumcised, be regarded by God as if he were? Indeed, 27
the man who, owing to his birth, remains uncircumcised, and
yet scrupulously obeys the Law, will condemn you, who, for
all your written Law and your circumcision, are yet a breaker
of the Law. For a man who is only a Jew outwardly is not 28
a real Jew; nor is outward bodily circumcision real circumcision. The real Jew is the man who is a Jew in soul; and 29
the real circumcision is the circumcision of the heart, a
spiritual and not a literal thing. Such a man wins praise
from God, though not from men.

What is the advantage, then, of being a Jew? 1 **3**

**The One Hope
for Jew
and Gentile
alike.** or what is the good of circumcision? Great in 2
every way. First of all, because the Jews were
entrusted with God's utterances. What follows 3
then? Some, no doubt, showed a want of faith; but will their
want of faith make God break faith? Heaven forbid! God 4
must prove true, though every man prove a liar! As Scripture
says of God—

' That thou mayest be pronounced righteous in what thou sayest,
And gain thy cause when men would judge thee.'

But what if our wrong-doing makes God's righteousness all the 5
clearer? Will God be wrong in inflicting punishment? (I
can but speak as a man.) Heaven forbid! Otherwise how 6
can God judge the world? But, if my falsehood redounds to 7
the glory of God, by making his truthfulness more apparent,
why am I, like others, still condemned as a sinner? Why 8
should we not say—as some people slanderously assert
that we do say—' Let us do evil that good may come'? The
condemnation of such men is indeed just!

What follows, then? Are we Jews in any way superior to 9
others? Not at all. Our indictment against both Jews and
Greeks was that all alike were in subjection to sin.

²⁴ Isa. 52. 5. ⁴ Ps. 116. 11 ; 51. 4.

As Scripture says—   10

'There is not even one who is righteous,
  Not one who understands, not one who is searching for God !   11
They have all gone astray ; they have one and all become   12
    depraved ;
  There is no one who is doing good—no, not one !'
'Their throats are like opened graves ;   13
  They deceive with their tongues.'
'The venom of serpents lies behind their lips,'
  'And their mouths are full of bitter curses.'   14
'Swift are their feet to shed blood.   15
  Distress and trouble dog their steps,   16
  And the path of peace they do not know.'   17
        'The fear of God is not before their eyes.'   18

Now we know that everything said in the Law is addressed   19
to those who are under its authority, in order that every mouth
may be closed, and the whole world become liable to the judgement of God.   For ' no human being will be pronounced right-   20
eous before God' as the result of obedience to Law ; for it is Law
that shows what sin is.   But now, quite apart from Law, the   21
Divine Righteousness stands revealed, and to it the Law and
the Prophets bear witness—the Divine Righteousness which   22
is bestowed, through faith in Jesus Christ, upon all, without
distinction, who believe in him.   For all have sinned, and all   23
fall short of God's glorious ideal, but, in his loving-kindness,   24
are being freely pronounced righteous through the deliverance
found in Christ Jesus.   For God set him before the world, to   25
be, by the shedding of his blood, a means of reconciliation
through faith.   And this God did to prove his righteousness,
and because, in his forbearance, he had passed over the sins
that men had previously committed ; as a proof, I repeat, at   26
the present time, of his own righteousness, that he might be
righteous in our eyes, and might pronounce righteous the
man who takes his stand on faith in Jesus.
  What, then, becomes of our boasting?   It is excluded.   27
By what sort of Law ?   A Law requiring obedience ?   No,
a Law requiring faith.   For we conclude that a man is   28
pronounced righteous on the ground of faith, quite apart
from obedience to Law.   Or can it be that God is the God   29
only of the Jews ?   Is not he also the God of the Gentiles ?
Yes, of the Gentiles also, since there is only one God, and   30
he will pronounce those who are circumcised righteous as
the result of faith, and also those who are uncircumcised
on their showing the same faith.   Do we, then, use this   31
faith to abolish Law ?   Heaven forbid !   No, we establish
Law.

10--18 Ps. 14. 1, 3 ; 5. 9 ; 140. 3 ; 10. 7 ; 36. 1 ; Isa. 59. 7—8.
    20 Ps. 143. 2.

Faith the Ground of Acceptance before the Coming of the Law. What then, it may be asked, are we to say 1 about Abraham, the ancestor of our nation? If 2 he was pronounced righteous as the result of obedience, then he has something to boast of. Yes, but not before God. For what are the 3 words of Scripture?

'Abraham had faith in God, and his faith was regarded by God as righteousness.'

Now wages are regarded as due to the man who works, not 4 as a favour, but as a debt; while, as for the man who does 5 not rely upon his obedience, but has faith in him who can pronounce the godless righteous, his faith is regarded by God as righteousness. In precisely the same way David speaks of 6 the blessing pronounced upon the man who is regarded by God as righteous apart from actions—

'Blessed are those whose wrong-doings have been forgiven and 7 over whose sins a veil has been drawn! Blessed the man whom the Lord will never regard as sinful!' 8

Is this blessing, then, pronounced upon the circumcised only 9 or upon the uncircumcised as well? We say that—

'Abraham's faith was regarded by God as righteousness.'

Under what circumstances, then, did this take place? after 10 his circumcision or before it? Not after, but before. And it 11 was as a sign of this that he received the rite of circumcision —to attest the righteousness due to the faith of an uncircumcised man—in order that he might be the father of all who have faith in God even when uncircumcised, that they also may be regarded by God as righteous; as well as father of 12 the circumcised—to those who are not only circumcised, but who also follow our father Abraham in that faith which he had while still uncircumcised.

For the promise that he should inherit the world did not 13 come to Abraham or his descendants through Law, but through the righteousness due to faith. If those who take 14 their stand on Law are to inherit the world, then faith is robbed of its meaning and the promise comes to nothing! Law entails punishment; but, where no Law exists, no breach 15 of it is possible.

That is why all is made to depend upon faith, that all may 16 be God's gift, and in order that the fulfilment of the promise may be made certain for all Abraham's descendants—not only for those who take their stand on the Law, but also for those who take their stand on the faith of Abraham. (He is the Father of us all; as Scripture says—'I have made thee the 17

³ Gen. 15. 6.   7—8 Ps. 32. 1—2.   9 Gen. 15. 6.   11 Gen. 17. 11.   17 Gen. 17. 5.

Father of many nations.') And this they do in the sight of
that God in whom Abraham had faith, and who gives life to
the dead, and speaks of what does not yet exist as if it did.
With no ground for hope, Abraham, sustained by hope, put 18
faith in God ; in order that, in fulfilment of the words—'So
many shall thy descendants be,' he might become 'the Father
of many nations.' Though he was nearly a hundred years 19
old, yet his faith did not fail him, even when he thought of his
own body, then utterly worn out, and remembered that Sarah
was past bearing children. He was not led by want of faith 20
to doubt God's promise. On the contrary, his faith gave him 21
strength ; and he praised God, in the firm conviction that
what God has promised he is also able to carry out. And 22
therefore his faith 'was regarded as righteousness.'
Now these words—'it was regarded as righteousness'— 23
were not written with reference to Abraham only, but also 24
with reference to us. Our faith, too, will be regarded by
God in the same light, if we have faith in him who raised
Jesus, our Lord, from the dead ; for Jesus 'was given up to 25
death to atone for our offences,' and was raised to life that we
might be pronounced righteous.

**Results
of attaining
the Divine
Ideal.** Therefore, having been pronounced righteous 1 **5**
as the result of faith, let us enjoy peace with God
through Jesus Christ, our Lord. It is through 2
him that, by reason of our faith, we have obtained admission to that place in God's favour in which we now
stand. So let us exult in our hope of attaining God's glorious
ideal. And not only that, but let us also exult in our troubles ; 3
for we know that trouble develops endurance, and endurance 4
strength of character, and strength of character hope, and that 5
'hope never disappoints.' For the love of God has filled our
hearts through the Holy Spirit which was given us ; seeing 6
that, while we were still powerless, Christ, in God's good
time, died on behalf of the godless. Even for an upright man 7
scarcely any one will die. For a really good man perhaps
some one might even dare to die. But God puts his love for 8
us beyond all doubt by the fact that Christ died on our behalf
while we were still sinners. Much more, then, now that we 9
have been pronounced righteous by virtue of the shedding of
his blood, shall we be saved through him from the Wrath of
God. For if, when we were God's enemies, we were recon- 10
ciled to him through the death of his Son, much more, now
that we have become reconciled, shall we be saved by virtue
of Christ's Life. And not only that, but we exult in God, 11
through Jesus Christ, our Lord, through whom we have now
obtained this reconciliation.

[18] Gen. 15. 5; 17. 5.   [22—23] Gen. 15. 6.   [25] Isa. 53. 12 (Septuagint).
[5] Ps. 22. 5.

The
Divine Ideal Therefore, just as sin came into the world 12
recovered through one man, and through sin came death ;
in the Christ. so, also, death spread to all mankind, because all
men had sinned. Even before the time of the 13
Law there was sin in the world ; but sin cannot be charged
against a man where no Law exists. Yet, from Adam to 14
Moses, Death reigned even over those whose sin was not a
breach of a law, as Adam's was. And Adam foreshadows the
One to come. But there is a contrast between Adam's 15
Offence and God's gracious Gift. For, if by reason of the
offence of the one man the whole race died, far more were
the loving-kindness of God, and the gift given in the loving-
kindness of the one man, Jesus Christ, lavished upon the
whole race. There is a contrast, too, between the gift and the 16
results of the one man's sin. The judgement, which followed
upon the one man's sin, resulted in condemnation, but God's
gracious Gift, which followed upon many offences, resulted in
a decree of righteousness. For if, by reason of the offence of 17
the one man, Death reigned through that one man, far more
will those, upon whom God's loving-kindness and his gift
of righteousness are lavished, find Life, and reign through
the one man, Jesus Christ. Briefly then, just as a 18
single offence resulted for all mankind in condemnation, so,
too, a single decree of righteousness resulted for all mankind in that declaration of righteousness which brings Life.
For, as through the disobedience of the one man the whole 19
race was rendered sinful, so, too, through the obedience of
the one, the whole race will be rendered righteous. Law 20
was introduced in order that offences might be multiplied.
But, where sins were multiplied, the loving-kindness of God
was lavished the more, in order that, just as Sin had reigned 21
in the realm of Death, so, too, might Loving-kindness reign
through righteousness, and result in Immortal Life, through
Jesus Christ, our Lord.

III.—CONSIDERATION OF DIFFICULTIES ARISING FROM THIS TEACHING.

Is this Faith What are we to say, then ? Are we to continue 1 **6**
consistent to sin, in order that God's loving-kindness may
with a be multiplied ? Heaven forbid ! We became 2
Sinful Life? dead to sin, and how can we go on living in it ?
Or can it be that you do not know that all of us, who were 3
baptized into union with Christ Jesus, in our baptism shared
his death ? Consequently, through sharing his death in our 4
baptism, we were buried with him ; that, just as Christ was
raised from the dead by a manifestation of the Father's
power, so we also may live a new Life. If we have become 5

united with him by the act symbolic of his death, surely we
shall also become united with him by the act symbolic of his
resurrection. We recognize the truth that our old self was 6
crucified with Christ, in order that the body, the stronghold of
Sin, might be rendered powerless, so that we should no longer
be slaves to Sin. For the man who has so died has been pro- 7
nounced righteous and released from Sin. And our belief is, 8
that, as we have shared Christ's Death, we shall also share his
Life. We know, indeed, that Christ, having once risen from 9
the dead, will not die again. Death has power over him no
longer. For the death that he died was a death to sin, once 10
and for all. But the Life that he now lives, he lives for God.
So let it be with you—regard yourselves as dead to sin, but 11
as living for God, through union with Christ Jesus.

Therefore do not let Sin reign in your mortal bodies and 12
compel you to obey its cravings. Do not offer any part of 13
your bodies to Sin, in the cause of unrighteousness, but once
for all offer yourselves to God (as those who, though once
dead, now have Life), and devote every part of your bodies to
the cause of righteousness. For Sin shall not lord it over 14
you. You are living under the reign, not of Law, but of Love.

What follows, then? Are we to sin because we are living 15
under the reign of Love and not of Law? Heaven forbid!
Surely you know that, when you offer yourselves as servants, 16
to obey any one, you are the servants of the person whom you
obey, whether the service be that of Sin which leads to Death,
or that of Duty which leads to Righteousness. God be thanked 17
that, though you were once servants of Sin, yet you learnt to
give hearty obedience to that form of doctrine under which
you were placed. Set free from the control of Sin, you became 18
servants to Righteousness. I can but speak as men do 19
because of the weakness of your earthly nature. Once you
offered every part of your bodies to the service of impurity,
and of wickedness, which leads to further wickedness. Now,
in the same way, offer them to the service of Righteousness,
which leads to holiness. While you were still servants of 20
Sin, you were free as regards Righteousness. But what 21
were the fruits that you reaped from those things of which
you are now ashamed? For the end of such things is Death.
But now that you have been set free from the control of Sin, 22
and have become servants to God, the fruit that you reap is
an ever-increasing holiness, and the end Immortal Life. The 23
wages of Sin are Death, but the gift of God is Immortal Life,
through union with Christ Jesus, our Lord.

Can Law deliver from a Sinful Life? Surely, Brothers, you know (for I am speaking 1 **7**
to men who know what Law means) that Law
has power over a man only as long as he lives.
For example, by law a married woman is bound to her 2

husband while he is living ; but, if her husband dies, she is set free from the law that bound her to him. If, then, during 3 her husband's lifetime, she unites herself to another man, she will be called an adulteress ; but, if her husband dies, the law has no further hold on her, nor, if she unites herself to another man, is she an adulteress. And so with you, my 4 Brothers ; as far as the Law was concerned, you underwent death in the crucified body of the Christ, so that you might be united to another, to him who was raised from the dead, in order that our lives might bear fruit for God. When we were 5 living merely earthly lives, our sinful passions, aroused by the Law, were active in every part of our bodies, with the result that our lives bore fruit for Death. But now we are set free from the 6 Law, because we are dead to that which once kept us under restraint ; and so we serve under new, spiritual conditions, and not under old, written regulations.

What are we to say, then ? That Law and sin are the same 7 thing ? Heaven forbid ! On the contrary, I should not have learnt what sin is, had not it been for Law. If the Law did not say 'Thou shalt not covet,' I should not know what it is to covet. But sin took advantage of the Commandment to 8 arouse in me every form of covetousness, for where there is no consciousness of Law sin shows no sign of life. There was a 9 time when I myself, unconscious of Law, was alive ; but when the Commandment was brought home to me, sin sprang into life, while I—died ! The very Commandment that should 10 have meant Life I found to result in Death ! Sin took 11 advantage of the Commandment to deceive me, and used it to bring about my Death. And so the Law is holy, and 12 each Commandment is also holy, and just, and good.

Did, then, a thing, which in itself was good, involve Death in 13 my case ? Heaven forbid ! It was sin that involved Death ; so that, by its use of what I regarded as good to bring about my Death, its true nature might appear ; and in this way the Commandment showed how intensely sinful sin is. We know that 14 the Law is spiritual, but I am earthly—sold into slavery to Sin. I do not understand my own actions. For I am so far from 15 habitually doing what I want to do, that I find myself doing the very thing that I hate. But when I do what I want not 16 to do, I am admitting that the Law is right.   This 17 being so, the action is no longer my own, but that of Sin which is within me. I know that there is nothing good in me 18 —I mean in my earthly nature. For, although it is easy for me to want to do right, to act rightly is not easy. I fail to do the 19 good thing that I want to do, but the bad thing that I want not to do—that I habitually do. But, when I do the very thing 20 that I want not to do, the action is no longer my own, but

---

[7] Exod. 20. 14, 17 ; Deut. 5. 18, 21.

that of Sin which is within me.   This, then, is the   21
law that I find—When I want to do right, wrong presents
itself ! At heart I delight in the Law of God ; but throughout   22, 23
my body I see a different law, one which is in conflict with the
law accepted by my reason, and which endeavours to make
me a prisoner to that law of Sin which exists throughout my
body. Miserable man that I am ! Who will deliver me from   24
the body that is bringing me to this Death ? Thank God,   25
there is deliverance through Jesus Christ, our Lord ! Well
then, for myself, with my reason I serve the Law of God, but
with my earthly nature the Law of Sin.

God's   There is, therefore, now no condemnation for   1   **8**
Deliverance   those who are in union with Christ Jesus ; for   2
through the   through your union with Christ Jesus, the Law of
Christ
and the   the life-giving Spirit has set you free from the
Holy Spirit.   Law of Sin and Death. What Law could not do,   3
in so far as our earthly nature weakened its action, God did,
by sending his own Son, with a nature resembling our sinful
nature, to atone for sin. He condemned sin in that earthly
nature, so that the requirements of the Law might be satisfied   4
in us who live now in obedience, not to our earthly nature, but
to the Spirit. They who follow their earthly nature are earthly-   5
minded, while they who follow the Spirit are spiritually minded.
To be earthly-minded means Death, to be spiritually minded   6
means Life and Peace ; because to be earthly-minded is to be   7
an enemy to God, for such a mind does not submit to the Law
of God, nor indeed can it do so. They who are earthly can-   8
not please God.   You, however, are not earthly but   9
spiritual, since the Spirit of God lives within you. Unless a
man has the Spirit of Christ, he does not belong to Christ ;
but, if Christ is within you, then, though the body is dead as a   10
consequence of sin, the spirit is Life as a consequence of
righteousness. And, if the Spirit of him who raised Jesus from   11
the dead lives within you, he who raised Christ Jesus from the
dead will give Life even to your mortal bodies, through his
Spirit living within you.

So then, Brothers, we owe nothing to our earthly nature,   12
that we should live in obedience to it. If you live in obedience   13
to your earthly nature, you will inevitably die ; but if, by the
power of the Spirit, you put an end to the evil habits of the
body, you will live. All who are guided by the Spirit of God   14
are Sons of God.   For you did not receive the spirit of a   15
slave, to fill you once more with fear, but the spirit of a son
which leads us to cry 'Abba, Our Father.' The Spirit himself   16
unites with our spirits in bearing witness to our being God's
children, and if children, then heirs—heirs of God, and joint-   17
heirs with Christ, since we share Christ's sufferings in order
that we may also share his Glory.

N*

I do not count the sufferings of our present life worthy 18
of mention when compared with the Glory that is to be
revealed and bestowed upon us. All Nature awaits with 19
eager expectation the appearing of the Sons of God. For 20
Nature was made subject to imperfection—not by its own
choice, but owing to him who made it so—yet not without 21
the hope that some day Nature, also, will be set free from
enslavement to decay, and will attain to the freedom which
will mark the Glory of the Children of God. We know, indeed, 22
that all Nature alike has been groaning in the pains of labour
to this very hour. And not Nature only ; but we ourselves 23
also, though we have already a first gift of the Spirit—we
ourselves are inwardly groaning, while we eagerly await
our full adoption as Sons—the redemption of our bodies. By 24
our hope we were saved. But the thing hoped for is no longer
an object of hope when it is before our eyes ; for who hopes for
what is before his eyes ? But, when we hope for what is not 25
before our eyes, then we wait for it with patience.

So, also, the Spirit supports us in our weakness. We do 26
not even know how to pray as we should ; but the Spirit
himself pleads for us in sighs that can find no utterance.
Yet he who searches all our hearts knows what the Spirit's 27
meaning is, because the pleadings of the Spirit for Christ's
People are in accordance with his will. But we do know 28
that God causes all things to work together for the good
of those who love him—those who have received the Call in
accordance with his purpose. For those whom God chose 29
from the first he also destined from the first to be transformed
into likeness to his Son, so that his Son might be the eldest
among many Brothers. And those whom God destined for 30
this he also called ; and those whom he called he also pronounced righteous ; and those whom he pronounced righteous
he also brought to Glory.

What are we to say, then, in the light of all this ? If God 31
is on our side, who can there be against us ? God did not 32
withhold his own Son, but gave him up on behalf of us all ;
will he not, then, with him, freely give us all things ? Who 33
will bring a charge against any of God's People ? He who
pronounces them righteous is God ! Who is there to condemn 34
them ? He who died for us is Christ Jesus !—or, rather, it was
he who was raised from the dead, and who is now at God's
right hand and is even pleading on our behalf ! Who is there 35
to separate us from the love of the Christ ? Will trouble, or
difficulty, or persecution, or hunger, or nakedness, or danger,
or the sword ? Scripture says— 36

> ' For thy sake we are being killed all the day long,
>   We are regarded as sheep to be slaughtered.'

^{33—34} Isa. 50. 8—9 ; Ps. 110. 1.   ³⁶ Ps. 44. 22.

Yet amidst all these things we more than conquer through him   37
who loved us! For I am persuaded that neither Death, nor   38
Life, nor Angels, nor Archangels, nor the Present, nor the
Future, nor any Powers, nor Height, nor Depth, nor any
other created thing, will be able to separate us from the   39
love of God revealed in Christ Jesus, our Lord !

IV.—THE JEWS' REJECTION OF THE CHRIST.

The Apostle's Lament over Israel.   I am speaking the truth as one in union   1 **9**
with Christ ; it is no lie ; and my conscience,
enlightened by the Holy Spirit, bears me out
when I say that there is a great weight of sorrow upon me,   2
and that my heart is never free from pain. I could wish that   3
I were myself accursed and severed from the Christ, for the
sake of my Brothers—my own countrymen. For they are   4
Israelites, and theirs are the adoption as Sons, the visible
Presence, the Covenants, the revealed Law, the Temple worship, and the Promises. They are descended from the Patri-   5
archs ; and, as far as his human nature was concerned, from
them came the Christ—he who is supreme over all things, God
for ever blessed. Amen.   Not that God's Word has   6
The Justice of Israel's Rejection by God.   failed. For it is not all who are descended from
Israel who are true Israelites ; nor, because
they are Abraham's descendants, are they all his   7
Children ; but—

'It is Isaac's children who will be called thy descendants.'

This means that it is not the children born in the course   8
of nature who are God's Children, but it is the children
born in fulfilment of the Promise who are to be regarded as
Abraham's descendants. For these words are the words of a   9
promise—

'About this time I will come, and Sarah shall have a son.'

Nor is that all. There is also the case of Rebecca, when she   10
was about to bear children to our ancestor Isaac. For in order   11
that the purpose of God, working through selection, might not
fail—a selection depending, not on obedience, but on his Call—
Rebecca was told, before her children were born and before   12
they had done anything either right or wrong, that 'the elder
would be a servant to the younger.' The words of Scripture   13
are—

'I loved Jacob, but I hated Esau.'

7 Gen. 21. 12.   9 Gen. 18. 10.   12 Gen. 25. 23.   13 Mal. 1. 2—3.

What are we to say, then? Is God guilty of injustice? 14
Heaven forbid! For his words to Moses are— 15

> 'I will take pity on whom I take pity, and be merciful to
> whom I am merciful.'

So, then, all depends, not on human wishes or human efforts, 16
but on God's mercy. In Scripture, again, it is said to Pharaoh— 17

> 'It was for this very purpose that I raised thee to the throne,
> to show my power by my dealings with thee, and to make my
> name known throughout the world.'

So, then, where God wills, he takes pity, and where he wills, 18
he hardens the heart.

Perhaps you will say to me—'How can any one still be 19
blamed? For who withstands his purpose?' I might rather 20
ask 'Who are you who are arguing with God?' Does a thing
which a man has moulded say to him who has moulded it
'Why did you make me like this?' Has not the potter 21
absolute power over his clay, so that out of the same lump he
makes one thing for better, and another for common, use?
And what if God, intending to reveal his displeasure and make 22
his power known, bore most patiently with the objects of his
displeasure, though they were fit only to be destroyed, so as 23
to make known his surpassing glory in dealing with the
objects of his mercy, whom he prepared beforehand for glory,
and whom he called—even us—not only from among the Jews 24
but from among the Gentiles also! This, indeed, is what 25
he says in the Book of Hosea—

> 'I will call those my People who were not my People,
>   And her my beloved who was not beloved.
>   And in the very place where it was said to them— 26
>   "Ye are not my People",
>   They shall be called Sons of the Living God.'

And Isaiah cries aloud over Israel— 27

> 'Though the Sons of Israel are like the sand of the sea in
> number, only a remnant of them shall escape! For the Lord 28
> will execute his sentence upon the world, fully and without
> delay.'

It is as Isaiah foretold— 29

> 'Had not the Lord of Hosts spared some few of our race to us,
> We should have become like Sodom and been made to resemble
>   Gomorrah.'

The Cause of Israel's Rejection. What are we to say, then? Why, that Gentiles, 30
who were not in search of righteousness, secured it
—a righteousness which was the result of faith;
while Israel, which was in search of a Law which would ensure 31

15 Exod. 33. 19. 17 Exod. 9. 16. 18 Exod. 7. 3; 9. 12; 14. 4, 17. 20 Isa. 29. 16;
45. 9. 21 Jer. 18. 6; Isa. 29. 16; 45. 9; Wisd. of Sol. 15. 7. 22 Jer. 50. 25;
Isa. 13. 5, 6 (Hebrew); Isa. 54. 16. 25 Hos. 2. 23. 26—28 Hos. 1. 10;
Isa. 10. 22, 23. 29 Isa. 1. 9.

righteousness, failed to discover one. And why? Because they looked to obedience, and not to faith, to secure it. They stumbled over 'the Stumbling-block.' As Scripture says— 32 33

'See, I place a Stumbling-block in Zion—a Rock which shall prove a hindrance ;
And he who believes in him shall have no cause for shame.'

Brothers, my heart's desire and prayer to God for my People is for their Salvation. I can testify that they are zealous for the honour of God ; but they are not guided by true insight, for, in their ignorance of the Divine Righteousness, and in their eagerness to set up a righteousness of their own, they refused to accept with submission the Divine Righteousness. For Christ has brought Law to an end, so that righteousness may be obtained by every one who believes in him. For Moses writes that, as for the righteousness which results from Law, 'those who practise it will find Life through it.' But the righteousness which results from faith finds expression in these words—'Do not say to yourself "Who will go up into heaven?"'—which means to bring Christ down—'or "Who will go down into the depths below?"'—which means to bring Christ up from the dead. No, but what does it say? 'The Message is near thee ; it is on thy lips and in thy heart'—which means 'The Message of Faith' which we proclaim. For, if with your lips you acknowledge the truth of the Message that JESUS IS LORD, and believe in your heart that God raised him from the dead, you shall be saved. For with their hearts men believe and so attain to righteousness, while with their lips they make their Profession of Faith and so find Salvation. As the passage of Scripture says— 1 **10** 2 3 4 5 6 7 8 9 10 11

'No one who believes in him shall have any cause for shame.'

For no distinction is made between the Jew and the Greek, for all have the same Lord, and he is bountiful to all who invoke him. For 'every one who invokes the Name of the Lord shall be saved.' But how, it may be asked, are they to invoke one in whom they have not learnt to believe? And how are they to believe in one whose words they have not heard? And how are they to hear his words unless some one proclaims him? And how are men to proclaim him unless they are sent as his messengers? As Scripture says— 12 13 14 15

'How beautiful are the feet of those who bring good news!'

Still, it may be said, every one did not give heed to the Good News. No, for Isaiah asks— 16

'Lord, who has believed our teaching?'

32–33 Isa. 8. 14 ; 28. 16. 5 Lev. 18. 5. 6–9 Deut. 30. 12—14. 11 Isa. 28. 16. 13 Joel 2. 32. 15 Isa. 52. 7 (Hebrew). 16 Isa. 53. 1.

And so, we gather, faith is a result of teaching, and the 17
teaching comes in the Message of Christ. But I ask ' Is it 18
possible that men have never heard ? ' No, indeed, for—

> ' Their voices spread through all the earth,
> And their Message to the very ends of the world.'

But again I ask ' Did not the people of Israel understand ? ' 19
First there is Moses, who says—

> ' I, the Lord, will stir you to rivalry with a nation which
> is no nation ;
> Against an undiscerning nation I will arouse your anger.'

And Isaiah says boldly—   20

> ' I was found by those who were not seeking me ;
> I made myself known to those who were not inquiring of me.'

But of the people of Israel he says—   21

> ' All day long I have stretched out my hands to a people
> who disobey and contradict.'

The merciful   I ask, then, ' Has God rejected his People ? '   1 **11**
Purpose in   Heaven forbid ! For I myself am an Israelite, a
Israel's
Rejection.   descendant of Abraham, of the tribe of Benjamin.
God has not rejected his People, whom he chose from the 2
first. Have you forgotten the words of Scripture in the story
of Elijah—how he appeals to God against Israel ?

> ' Lord, they have killed thy Prophets, they have pulled 3
> down thy altars, and I only am left ; and now they are eager
> to take my life.'

But what was the divine response ?   4

> ' I have kept for myself seven thousand men who have
> never bowed the knee to Baal.'

And so in our own time, too, there is to be found a remnant of 5
our nation selected by God in love. But if in love, then no 6
longer as a result of obedience. Otherwise love would cease
to be love. What follows from this ? Why, that Israel as a 7
nation failed to secure what it was seeking, while those whom
God selected did secure it. The rest grew callous ; as 8
Scripture says—

> ' God has given them a deadness of mind—eyes that are
> not to see and ears that are not to hear—and it is so to this
> very day.'

David, too, says—   9

> ' May their feasts prove a snare and a trap to them—
> A hindrance and a retribution ;
> May their eyes be darkened, so that they cannot see ; 10
> And do thou always make their backs to bend.'

18 Ps. 19. 4.   19 Deut. 32. 21.   20—21 Isa. 65. 1—2.   1—2 Ps. 94. 14 ; 1 Sam. 12. 22.
3 1 Kings 19. 10.   4 1 Kings 19. 18.   8 Isa. 29. 10 ; Deut. 29. 4.   9—10 Ps. 69. 22, 23.

I ask then—'Was their stumbling to result in their fall?'   11
Heaven forbid! On the contrary, through their falling away
Salvation has reached the Gentiles, to stir the rivalry of Israel.
And, if their falling away has enriched the world, and their   12
failure has enriched the Gentiles, how much more will result
from their full restoration!

But I am speaking to you who were Gentiles. Being   13
myself an Apostle to the Gentiles, I exalt my office, in the hope   14
that I may stir my countrymen to rivalry, and so save some
of them. For, if their being cast aside has meant the reconcilia-   15
tion of the world, what will their reception mean, but Life
from the dead? If the first handful of dough is holy, so is the   16
whole mass; and if the root is holy, so are the branches.
Some, however, of the branches were broken off, and you,   17
who were only a wild olive, were grafted in among them, and
came to share with them the root which is the source of the
richness of the cultivated olive. Yet do not exult over the   18
other branches. But, if you do exult over them, remember
that you do not support the root, but that the root supports
you. But branches, you will say, were broken off, so that I   19
might be grafted in. True; it was because of their want of   20
faith that they were broken off, and it is because of your
faith that you are standing. Do not think too highly of
yourself, but beware. For, if God did not spare the natural   21
branches, neither will he spare you. See, then, both the   22
goodness and the severity of God—his severity towards those
who fell, and his goodness towards you, provided that you
continue to confide in that goodness; otherwise you, also, will
be cut off. And they, too, if they do not continue in their   23
unbelief, will be grafted in; for God has it in his power to
graft them in again. If you were cut off from your natural   24
stock—a wild olive—and were grafted, contrary to the course
of nature, upon a good olive, much more will they—the natural
branches—be grafted back into their parent tree.
Brothers, for fear that you should think too highly of your-   25
selves, I want you to recognize the truth, hitherto hidden, that
the callousness which has come over Israel is only partial, and
will continue only till the whole Gentile world has been
gathered in. And then all Israel shall be saved. As Scripture   26
says—
  'From Zion will come the Deliverer;
    He will banish ungodliness from Jacob.
  And they shall see the fulfilment of my Covenant,
    When I have taken away their sins.'   27

From the stand-point of the Good News, the Jews are God's   28
enemies on your account; but from the stand-point of God's
selection, they are dear to him on account of the Patriarchs.

  [11] Deut. 32. 21.   [26–27] Isa. 59. 20, 21; 27. 9.

For God never regrets his gifts or his Call. Just as you at one time were disobedient to him, but have now found mercy in the day of their disobedience; so, too, they have now become disobedient in your day of mercy, in order that they also in their turn may now find mercy. For God has given all alike over to disobedience, that to all alike he may show mercy. Oh! the unfathomable wisdom and knowledge of God! How inscrutable are his judgements, how untraceable his ways! Yes— 29, 31 32 33

'Who has ever comprehended the mind of the Lord? Who has ever become his counsellor? 34
Or who has first given to him, so that he may claim a recompense?' 35

For all things are from him, through him, and for him. And to him be all glory for ever and ever! Amen. 36

V.—Advice upon the Daily Life of Christians.

On Christian Sacrifice. I entreat you, then, Brothers, by the mercies of God, to offer your bodies as a living and holy sacrifice, acceptable to God, for this is your rational worship. Do not conform to the fashion of this world; but be transformed by the complete change that has come over your minds, so that you may discern what God's will is—all that is good, acceptable, and perfect. 1 12 2

On Christian Membership. In fulfilment of the charge with which I have been entrusted, I bid every one of you not to think more highly of himself than he ought to think, but to think till he learns to think soberly—in accordance with the measure of faith that God has allotted to each. For, just as in the human body there is a union of many parts, and each part has its own function, so we, by our union in Christ, many though we are, form but one body, and **On Christian Duties.** individually we are related one to another as its parts. Since our gifts differ in accordance with the particular charge entrusted to us, if our gift is to preach, let our preaching correspond to our faith; if it is to minister to others, let us devote ourselves to our ministry; the teacher to his teaching, the speaker to his exhortation. Let the man who gives in charity do so with a generous heart; let him who is in authority exercise due diligence; let him who shows kindness do so in a cheerful spirit. Let your love be sincere. Hate the wrong; cling to the right. In brotherly love, be affectionate to one another; in showing respect, set an example of deference to one another; never flagging in zeal; fervent in spirit; serving the Master; rejoicing in your hope; stedfast under persecution; per- 3 4 5 6 7 8 9 10 11 12

34—35 Isa. 40. 13, 14.

severing in prayer; relieving the wants of Christ's People; 13
devoted to hospitality. Bless your persecutors—bless and 14
never curse. Rejoice with those who are rejoicing, and weep 15
with those who are weeping. Let the same spirit of sympathy 16
animate you all, not a spirit of pride; be glad to associate
with the lowly. Do not think too highly of yourselves.
Never return injury for injury. Aim at doing what all men 17
will recognize as honourable. If it is possible, as far as 18
rests with you, live peaceably with every one. Never avenge 19
yourselves, dear friends, but make way for the Wrath of God;
for Scripture declares—

' " It is for me to avenge, I will requite," says the Lord.'

Rather— 20

' If your enemy is hungry, feed him; if he is thirsty, give
him to drink. By doing this you will heap coals of fire upon
his head.'

Never be conquered by evil, but conquer evil with good. 21

On Obedience to the Authorities. Let every one obey the supreme Authorities. 1 **13**
For no Authority exists except by the will of God,
and the existing Authorities have been appointed
by God. Therefore he who sets himself against the Authori- 2
ties is resisting God's appointment, and those who resist
will bring a judgement upon themselves. A good action 3
has nothing to fear from Rulers; a bad action has. Do you
want to have no reason to fear the Authorities? Then do
what is good, and you will win their praise. For they are 4
God's servants appointed for your good. But, if you do what
is wrong, you may well be afraid; for the sword they carry is
not without meaning! They are God's servants to inflict his
punishments on those who do wrong. You are bound, there- 5
fore, to obey, not only through fear of God's punishments, but
also as a matter of conscience. This, too, is the reason for your 6
paying taxes; for the officials are God's officers, devoting themselves to this special work. In all cases pay what is due from 7
you—tribute where tribute is due, taxes where taxes are due,
respect where respect is due, and honour where honour is due.

On Brotherly Love. Owe nothing to any one except brotherly love; 8
for he who loves his fellow men has satisfied
the Law. The commandments, ' Thou shalt not 9
commit adultery, Thou shalt not kill, Thou shalt not steal,
Thou shalt not covet,' and whatever other commandment
there is, are all summed up in the words—

' Thou shalt love thy neighbour as thou dost thyself.'

Love never wrongs a neighbour. Therefore Love fully satisfies 10
the Law.

16 Prov. 3. 7.   17 Prov. 3. 4 (Septuagint version).   19 Deut. 32. 35 (Hebrew).
20 Prov. 25. 21, 22.   9 Exod. 20. 13, 17; Deut. 5. 17, 21; Lev. 19. 18,

On the Approach of 'The Day.' This I say, because you know the crisis that 11 we have reached, for the time has already come for you to rouse yourselves from sleep ; our Salvation is nearer now than when we accepted the Faith. The night is almost gone ; the day is near. Therefore let us 12 have done with the deeds of Darkness, and arm ourselves with the weapons of Light. Being in the light of Day, let us 13 live becomingly, not in revelry and drunkenness, not in lust and licentiousness, not in quarrelling and jealousy. No ! 14 Arm yourselves with the spirit of the Lord Jesus Christ, and spend no thought on your earthly nature, to satisfy its cravings.

On Consideration for the Scrupulous. As for those whose faith is weak, always receive 1 **14** them as friends, but not for the purpose of passing judgement on their scruples. One man's 2 faith permits of his eating food of all kinds, while another whose faith is weak eats only vegetable food. The man 3 who eats meat must not despise the man who abstains from it ; nor must the man who abstains from eating meat pass judgement on the one who eats it, for God himself has received him. Who are you, that you should pass judgement on the 4 servant of another ? His standing or falling concerns his own master. And stand he will, for his Master can enable him to stand. Again, one man considers some days to be more sacred 5 than others, while another considers all days to be alike. Every one ought to be fully convinced in his own mind. He who 6 observes a day, observes it to the Master's honour. He, again, who eats meat eats it to the Master's honour, for he gives thanks to God ; while he who abstains from it abstains from it to the Master's honour, and also gives thanks to God. There is not one of us whose life concerns him- 7 self alone, and not one of us whose death concerns himself alone ; for, if we live, our life is for the Master, and, if we 8 die, our death is for the Master. Whether, then, we live or die we belong to the Master. The very purpose for which 9 Christ died and came back to life was this—that he might be Lord over both the dead and the living. I would ask 10 the one man ' Why do you judge your Brother ? ' And I would ask the other ' Why do you despise your Brother ? ' For we shall all stand before the Bar of God. For Scripture says— 11

' " As surely as I live," says the Lord, " every knee shall bend
before me ;
And every tongue shall make acknowledgement to God." '

So, then, each one of us will have to render account of himself 12 to God.

Let us, then, cease to judge one another. Rather let this 13 be your resolve—never to place a stumbling-block or an obstacle

11 Isa. 45. 23.

in a Brother's way. Through my union with the Lord Jesus, 14
I know and am persuaded that nothing is ' defiling in itself.'
A thing is ' defiling ' only to him who holds it to be so.
If, for the sake of what you eat, you wound your Brother's 15
feelings, your life has ceased to be ruled by love. Do not,
by what you eat, ruin a man for whom Christ died ! Do 16
not let what is right for you become a matter of reproach.
For the Kingdom of God does not consist of eating and drink- 17
ing, but of righteousness and peace and gladness through the
presence of the Holy Spirit. He who serves the Christ in 18
this way pleases God, and wins the approval of his fellow
men. Therefore our efforts should be directed towards all 19
that makes for peace and the mutual building up of character.
Do not undo God's work for the sake of what you eat. Though 20
everything is ' clean,' yet, if a man eats so as to put a stumbling-
block in the way of others, he does wrong. The right course 21
is to abstain from meat or wine or, indeed, anything that is a
stumbling-block to your Brother. As for yourself—keep this 22
faith of yours to yourself, as in the presence of God. Happy
is he who never has to condemn himself in regard to the very
thing which he thinks right ! He, however, who has mis- 23
givings stands condemned if he still eats, because his doing
so is not the result of faith. And anything not done as the
result of faith is a sin.

We, the strong, ought to take on our own shoulders the 1 **15**
weaknesses of those who are not strong, and not merely
to please ourselves. Let each of us please his neighbour 2
for his neighbour's good, to help in the building up of his
character. Even the Christ did not please himself ! On the 3
contrary, as Scripture says of him—

> ' The reproaches of those who were reproaching thee fell
> upon me.'

Whatever was written in the Scriptures in days gone by 4
was written for our instruction, so that, through patient endurance, and through the encouragement drawn from the
Scriptures, we might hold fast to our hope. And may God, 5
the giver of this patience and this encouragement, grant you
to be united in sympathy in Christ, so that with one heart and 6
one voice you may praise the God and Father of Jesus Christ,
our Lord.

Therefore always receive one another as friends, 7
On the Reception of the Gentiles. just as the Christ himself received us, to the glory
of God. For I tell you that Christ, in vindication 8
of God's truthfulness, has become a minister of
the Covenant of Circumcision, so that he may fulfil the promises

³ Ps. 69. 9.

made to our ancestors, and that the Gentiles also may praise **9**
God for his mercy. As Scripture says—

'Therefore will I make acknowledgement to thee
                                      among the Gentiles
  And sing in honour of thy Name.'

And again it says— **10**
'Rejoice, ye Gentiles, with God's People.'

And yet again— **11**
'Praise the Lord, all ye Gentiles,
  And let all Peoples sing his praises.'

Again, Isaiah says— **12**
'There shall be a Scion of the house of Jesse,
  One who is to arise to rule the Gentiles ;
  On him shall the Gentiles rest their hopes.'

May God, who inspires our hope, grant you perfect happiness **13**
and peace in your faith, till you are filled with this hope by the
power of the Holy Spirit.

I am persuaded, my Brothers—yes, I Paul, with regard to **14**
you—that you are yourselves full of kindness, furnished with
all Christian learning, and well able to give advice to one
another. But in parts of this letter I have expressed myself **15**
somewhat boldly—by way of refreshing your memories—
because of the charge with which God has entrusted me, that **16**
I should be a minister of Christ Jesus to go to the Gentiles—
that I should act as a priest of God's Good News, so that
the offering up of the Gentiles may be an acceptable sacrifice, consecrated by the Holy Spirit. It is, then, through my **17**
union with Christ Jesus that I have a proud confidence in my
work for God. For I will not dare to speak of anything but **18**
what Christ has done through me to win the obedience of
the Gentiles—by my words and actions, through the power **19**
displayed in signs and marvels, and through the power of the
Holy Spirit. And so, starting from Jerusalem and its neighbourhood, and going as far as Illyria, I have told in full the
Good News of the Christ ; yet always with the ambition to tell **20**
the Good News where Christ's name had not previously been
heard, so as to avoid building upon another man's foundations.
But as Scripture says— **21**

'They to whom he had never been proclaimed shall see ;
  And they who have never heard shall understand !'

VI.—CONCLUSION.

Personal   That is why I have so often been prevented from **22**
Plans.   coming to you. But now there are no further **23**
openings for me in these parts, and I have for several years been

9 Ps. 18. 49.   10 Deut. 32. 43.   11 Ps. 117. 1.   12 Isa. 11. 10.   21 Isa. 52. 15.

longing to come to you whenever I may be going to Spain. 24
For my hope is to visit you on my journey, and then to
be sent on my way by you, after I have first partly satisfied myself by seeing something of you. Just now, however, 25
I am on my way to Jerusalem, to take help to Christ's People
there.   For Macedonia and Greece have been glad to 26
make a collection for the poor among Christ's People at
Jerusalem. Yes, they were glad to do so ; and indeed it 27
is a duty which they owe to them. For the Gentile converts who have shared their spiritual blessings are in duty
bound to minister to them in the things of this world. When 28
I have settled this matter, and have secured to the poor at
Jerusalem the enjoyment of these benefits, I shall go, by way
of you, to Spain. And I know that, when I come to you, it 29
will be with a full measure of blessing from Christ.

I beg you, then, Brothers, by Jesus Christ, our Lord, and by 30
the love inspired by the Spirit, to join me in earnest prayer to
God on my behalf. Pray that I may be rescued from those in 31
Judaea who reject the Faith, and that the help which I am
taking to Jerusalem may prove acceptable to Christ's People ;
so that, God willing, I may be able to come to you with a joyful 32
heart, and enjoy some rest among you. May God, the giver of 33
peace, be with you all. Amen.

The Bearer
of the
Letter.   I commend to your care our Sister, Phoebe, who 1 **16**
helps in the work of the Church at Cenchreae ;
and I ask you to give her a Christian welcome— 2
one worthy of Christ's People—and to aid her in any matter in
which she may need your assistance. She has proved herself
a staunch friend to me and to many others.

Personal
Greetings.   Give my greeting to Prisca and Aquila, my 3
fellow-workers in the Cause of Christ Jesus,
who risked their own lives to save mine. It is not I 4
alone who thank them, but all the Churches among the
Gentiles thank them also. Give my greeting, also, to the 5
Church that meets at their house, as well as to my dear friend
Epaenetus, one of the first in Roman Asia to believe in
Christ ; to Mary, who worked hard for you ; to Andronicus 6, 7
and Junias, my countrymen and once my fellow-prisoners,
who are men of note among the Apostles, and who became
Christians before I did ; to my dear Christian friend Ampliatus ; 8
to Urban, our fellow-worker in the Cause of Christ, and to my 9
dear friend Stachys ; to that proved Christian Apelles ; to the 10
household of Aristobulus ; to my countryman Herodion ; to 11
the Christians in the household of Narcissus ; to Tryphaena 12
and Tryphosa, who have worked hard for the Master ; to my
dear friend Persis, for she has done much hard work for the
Master ; to that eminent Christian, Rufus, and to his mother, 13
who has been a mother to me also ; to Asyncritus, Phlegon, 14

Hermes, Patrobas, Hermas, and the Brothers with them ; also 15 to Philologus and Julia, Nereus and his sister, and Olympas, and to all Christ's People who are with them. Greet one 16 another with a sacred kiss. All the Churches of the Christ send you greetings.

I urge you, Brothers, to be on your guard against people 17 who, by disregarding the teaching which you received, cause divisions and create difficulties ; dissociate yourselves from them. For such persons are not serving Christ, our Master, 18 but are slaves to their own appetites ; and, by their smooth words and flattery, they deceive simple-minded people. Every 19 one has heard of your ready obedience. It is true that I am very happy about you, but I want you to be well versed in all that is good, and innocent of all that is bad. And God, the 20 giver of peace, will before long crush Satan under your feet.

May the blessing of Jesus, our Lord, be with you.

Timothy, my fellow-worker, sends you his greeting, and 21 Lucius, Jason, and Sosipater, my countrymen, send theirs. I, 22 Tertius, who am writing this letter, send you my Christian greeting. My host Gaius, who extends his hospitality to the 23 whole Church, sends you his greeting ; and Erastus, the City Treasurer, and Quartus, our Brother, add theirs.

A Doxology. Now to him who is able to strengthen you, as 25 promised in the Good News entrusted to me and in the proclamation of Jesus Christ, in accordance with the revelation of that hidden purpose, which in past ages was kept secret but now has been revealed and, in obedience to the 26 command of the Immortal God, made known through the writings of the Prophets to all nations, to secure submission to the Faith—to him, I say, the wise and only God, be ascribed, 27 through Jesus Christ, all glory for ever and ever. Amen.

TO THE COLOSSIANS.

ST. PAUL'S LETTER TO THE CHRISTIANS AT COLOSSAE.

WRITTEN PROBABLY DURING HIS IMPRISON-MENT AT ROME, ABOUT 61 A.D.

COLOSSAE was a town in Roman Asia, which had once been a place of considerable importance, but which, at the time of this Letter, had lost much of its former prosperity. It does not appear that St. Paul had had any close personal connexion with the Church at Colossae, but it is plain from the Letter itself that his authority was recognized over a wide area. The Apostle's attention had been drawn to the Church at Colossae by a visit which he had received from Epaphras, who had been closely associated with the Christians living there, and who had told St. Paul of a dangerous heresy which threatened to undermine the religious life of his fellow-Christians in that place.

This heresy consisted in a teaching, 'drawn from the atmosphere of mystical speculation,' and ' with no foundation in history,' which attempted to bridge the chasm between God and Man by the assumption that there were many angelic mediators. The necessity for this assumption lay in the prevalent error that all matter was evil and, therefore, in direct opposition to God.

Two obvious inferences from this heresy were the duty of the worship of angels, and the need for rigid asceticism.

Against such unsatisfying mediation, and its consequent dangers, St. Paul sets the Life, Work, and Person of the historical Christ—the one, all-sufficient mediator, the Head of all creation.

The obscurity of this Letter is due partly to the ruggedness and compression of the Apostle's style, and partly to the fact that the Letter combats a form of heretical teaching which is by no means familiar to the reader of to-day.

TO THE

COLOSSIANS.

=============

I.—INTRODUCTION.

Greeting. To Christ's People at Colossae—the Brothers who   1, 2 **1**
are faithful to him,
FROM Paul, an Apostle of Christ Jesus, by the will of God,
AND FROM Timothy, our Brother.
May God, our Father, bless you and give you peace.

The Apostle's Whenever we pray, we never fail to thank God,   3
Thankfulness the Father of our Lord, Jesus Christ, about you,
and Prayer. now that we have heard of your faith in Christ   4
Jesus and of the love that you have for all his People, on   5
account of the hope which awaits its fulfilment in Heaven. Of
this hope you heard long ago in the true Message of the Good
News which reached you—bearing fruit and growing, as it   6
does, through all the world, just as it did among you, from the
very day that you heard of God's loving-kindness, and understood what that loving-kindness really is.   It is just what you   7
learnt from Epaphras, our dear fellow-servant, who, as a
minister of the Christ, faithfully represents us, and who   8
told us of the love with which the Spirit has inspired
you.   And therefore we, from the very day that we   9
heard this, have never ceased praying for you, or asking that
you may possess that deeper knowledge of the will of God,
which comes through all true spiritual wisdom and insight.
Then you will live lives worthy of the Master, and so please   10
God in every way. Your lives will be fruitful in every kind of
good action, and your characters will grow through a fuller
knowledge of God ; you will be made strong at all points with a   11
strength worthy of the power manifested in his Glory—strong
to endure with patience, and even with gladness, whatever
may befall you ; and you will give thanks to the Father who   12
made you fit to share the lot which awaits Christ's People in
the realms of Light.

II.—THE PERSON AND WORK OF THE CHRIST.

His Deliverance. For God has rescued us from the tyranny of 13 Darkness, and has removed us into the Kingdom of his Son, who is the embodiment of his love, and through 14 whom we have found deliverance in the forgiveness of our sins.

His Pre-eminence. For Christ is the very incarnation of the invisible 15 God—First-born and Head of all creation ; for in 16 him was created all that is in Heaven and on earth, the visible and the invisible—Angels and Archangels and all the Powers of Heaven. All has been created through him and for him. He 17 was before all things, and all things unite in him ; and he 18 is the Head of the Church, which is his Body. The First-born from the dead, he is to the Church the Source of its Life, that he, in all things, may stand first. For it pleased 19 the Father that in him the divine nature in all its fulness **His Reconcilia- tion.** should dwell, and through him to reconcile all 20 things to himself (making peace by the shedding of Christ's blood offered upon the cross)—whether on earth or in Heaven. And it pleased God that you, once 21 estranged from him and hostile towards him in your thoughts, intent only on wickedness—but now he has reconciled you to 22 himself by the sacrifice of Christ's earthly body in death—it has pleased God that you should stand in his presence holy, pure, and blameless, if only you remain true to your Faith, firm 23 and immovable, never abandoning the hope held out in the Good News to which you listened, which has been proclaimed among all created things under Heaven, and of which I, Paul, was made a minister.

The Apostle's Share in this Work. Now at last I can rejoice in my sufferings on 24 your behalf, and in my own person I supplement the afflictions endured by the Christ, for the sake of his Body, the Church ; of which I myself became a minister 25 in virtue of the office with which God entrusted me for your benefit, to declare the Message of God in all its fulness—that 26 Truth which has been hidden from former ages and genera-tions. But now it has been revealed to God's People, to 27 whom it was his pleasure to make known the surpassing glory of that hidden Truth when proclaimed among the Gentiles —'Christ among you ! Your Hope of glory!' This is the 28 Christ whom we proclaim, warning every one, and instruct-ing every one, with all the wisdom that we possess, in the hope of bringing every one into God's presence perfected by union with Christ. It is for that I toil, struggling with all 29 the energy which he inspires and which works powerfully within me.

III.—CHRIST AND THE GNOSTIC TEACHING.

The Wisdom of God in Christ. I want you to know in how great a struggle 1 **2** I am engaged for you and for Christ's People at Laodicea, and for all who have not yet seen me ; in the hope that they, being bound to one another by 2 love, and keeping in view the full blessedness of a firm conviction, may be encouraged to strive for a perfect knowledge of God's hidden Truth, even Christ himself, in whom all treasures 3 of wisdom and knowledge lie hidden. I say this to 4 prevent any one from deceiving you by plausible arguments. It is true that I am not with you in person, but I am with you 5 in spirit, and am glad to see the good order and the unbroken front resulting from your faith in Christ.

Union with Christ. Since, therefore, you have received Jesus, the 6 Christ, as your Lord, live your lives in union with him—rooted in him, building up your characters through 7 union with him, growing stronger through your faith, as you were taught, overflowing with faith and thanksgiving.

Take care there is not some one who will carry you away 8 by his ' philosophy '—a hollow sham !—following, as it does, mere human traditions, and dealing with puerile questions of this world, and not with Christ. For in Christ the Godhead 9 in all its fulness dwells incarnate ; and, by your union with 10 him, you also are filled with it. He is the Head of all Archangels and Powers of Heaven. By your union with him you 11 received a circumcision that was not performed by human hands, when you threw off the tyranny of the earthly body, and received the circumcision of the Christ. For in baptism 12 you were buried with Christ ; and in baptism you were also raised to Life with him, through your faith in the omnipotence of God, who raised him from the dead. And to you, who 13 once were ' dead, ' by reason of your sins and your uncircumcised nature—to you God gave Life in giving life to Christ ! He pardoned all our sins ! He cancelled the bond which 14 stood against us—the bond that consisted of ordinances—and which was directly hostile to us ! He has taken it out of our way by nailing it to the cross ! He rid himself of all the 15 Powers of Evil, and held them up to open contempt, when he celebrated his triumph over them on the cross !

This Union obscured by Gnostic Teaching. Do not, then, allow any one to take you to task 16 on questions of eating or drinking, or in the matter of annual or monthly or weekly festivals. These things are only the shadow of what is to 17 come ; the substance is in the Christ. Do not let any one 18 defraud you of the reality by affecting delight in so-called

[3] Isa. 45. 3 ; Prov. 2. 3—4.

'humility' and angel-worship. Such a man busies himself
with his visions, and without reason is rendered conceited by
his merely human intellect. He fails to maintain union with
the Head, to whom it is due that the whole body, nourished
and knit together by the contact and connexion of every part,
grows with a divine growth. 19

Sharing Christ's Death. Since, with Christ, you became dead to the 20
puerile teaching of this world, why do you sub-
mit, as though your life were still that of the
world, to such ordinances as 'Do not handle, or taste, or 21
touch'? For all the things referred to in them cease to exist 22
when used. You are following mere human directions and
instructions. Such prohibitions appear reasonable where 23
there is a desire for self-imposed service, and so-called
'humility,' and harsh treatment of the body, but are of no
real value against the indulgence of our earthly nature.

Sharing Christ's Resurrection. Since, therefore, you were raised to Life with 1
the Christ, seek for the things that are above;
for it is there that the Christ is 'seated at the
right hand of God.' Fix your thoughts upon the things that 2
are above, not upon those that are on earth. For you died, 3
and your Life now lies hidden, with the Christ, in God. When 4
the Christ, who is our Life, appears, then you also will appear
with him in glory.

IV.—THE GOSPEL IN THE DAILY LIFE.

The Old Life and the New. Therefore destroy all that is earthly in you— 5
immorality, uncleanness, passions, evil desires,
and that greed which is idolatry. These are the things on 6
account of which the Wrath of God comes, and to which you, 7
like others, once devoted your lives, when you lived for them.
You, however, must now lay aside all such things—anger, 8
passion, malice, slander, abuse. Never lie to one another. 9
Get rid of your old self and its habits, and clothe yourselves 10
with that new self, which, as it gains in knowledge, is being
constantly renewed 'in resemblance to him who made it.' In 11
that new life there is no distinction between Greek and Jew,
circumcised and uncircumcised, barbarian, Scythian, slave,
freeman ; but Christ is all !—and in all !
Therefore, as God's People, consecrated and dear to him, 12
clothe yourselves with tenderness of heart, kindliness, humility,
gentleness, forbearance ; bearing with one another, and, when 13
there is any ground for complaint, forgiving one another
freely. As the Master freely forgave you, so you must forgive one another. Over all these virtues put on love ; for 14

²² Isa. 29. 13.   ¹ Ps. 110. 1.   ¹⁰ Gen. 1. 27.

that is the girdle which makes all complete. Let the 15
Peace that the Christ gives decide all doubts within your hearts;
for you also were called to the enjoyment of peace as members
of one Body. And show yourselves thankful. Let the Message 16
of the Christ dwell in your minds in all its wealth, bringing
all wisdom with it. Teach and admonish one another with
psalms, and hymns, and sacred songs, full of the loving-kindness of God, lifting your hearts in song to him. And, whatever 17
you say or do, do everything in the Name of the Lord Jesus;
and through him offer thanksgiving to God the Father.

Christian Family Life. Wives, submit to your husbands, as befits those 18
who belong to the Lord. Husbands, love 19
your wives, and never treat them harshly.
Children, always obey your parents; for that is pleasant to 20
see in those who belong to the Lord. Fathers, never 21
irritate your children, lest they should become disheartened.

Slaves, always obey your earthly masters, not only when 22
their eyes are on you, as if you had but to please men, but
giving them ungrudging service, in your reverence for the
Master. Whatever you do, do it with all your heart, as if 23
working for the Master and not for men, since you know that 24
it is from the Master that you will receive the inheritance
which will be your recompense. You are serving Christ, the
Master. Those who do wrong will reap the wrong they have 25
done; and there will be no partiality. Masters, do 1 **4**
what is right and fair by your slaves, for you know that you
also have a Master—in Heaven.

Rules for Christian Life. Devote yourselves to prayer. Give your whole 2
mind to it, and also offer thanksgiving; and at 3
the same time pray for us, that God may give us
an opening for our Message, so that we may speak of the
truths hidden in the Christ—the truths for which I am
in chains! Then I shall make them known, as I ought to 4
do. Show tact in your behaviour to the outside world, 5
making the most of every opportunity. Let your conversation 6
always be kindly, and seasoned, as it were, with salt; that
you may know in each case what answer you ought to give.

V.—CONCLUSION.

The Bearers of the Letter. Our dear Brother, Tychicus, will tell you all 7
about me. He is a faithful minister, and a fellow-
servant in the Master's cause. I send him to you 8
expressly that you may learn our circumstances, and that he
may give you encouragement. With him will be Onesimus, 9

our dear faithful Brother, who is one of yourselves. They will tell you all that is going on here.

Personal Greetings and Messages. My fellow-prisoner, Aristarchus, sends you his greeting, and Barnabas's cousin, Mark, sends his. (You have received directions about him. If he comes to you, make him welcome.) Joshua, who is called Justus, also sends his greeting. These are the only converts from Judaism who have worked with me for the Kingdom of God ; I have found them a great comfort. Epaphras, who is one of yourselves, sends you his greeting. He is a servant of Christ Jesus, and is always most earnest in your behalf in his prayers, praying that you may stand firm, with a matured faith and with a sure conviction of all that is in accordance with God's will. I can bear testimony to the deep interest he takes in you, as well as in the Brethren at Laodicea and at Hierapolis. Luke, our dear doctor, sends you his greeting, and Demas sends his. Give my greeting to the Brethren at Laodicea, and to Nymphe, and to the Church that meets at her house. And when this letter has been read to you, see that it is also read before the Church at Laodicea, and that you yourselves read the letter which will be forwarded from there. Give this message to Archippus—'Take care to discharge to the best of your ability the office to which you were appointed in the Master's Cause.'

The Apostle's own Farewell. I, Paul, add this greeting in my own hand-writing. Remember these chains of mine. God's blessing be with you.

TO PHILEMON.

ST. PAUL'S LETTER TO PHILEMON.

WRITTEN PROBABLY DURING HIS IMPRISON-MENT AT ROME, ABOUT 61 A.D.

ONESIMUS, who was the bearer of this Letter, had been a slave to Philemon. He had robbed his master and run away from him ; but, on reaching Rome, he had come under the influence of St. Paul, and had been converted to Christianity. Philemon, who lived probably at Laodicea in Asia Minor, was also one of the Apostle's converts; and St. Paul sent Onesimus back to him with this Letter, asking Philemon to forgive him, and to receive him as a Brother-Christian.

PHILEMON.

I.—Introduction.

To our dear friend and fellow-worker Philemon, to our sister   1, 2
Apphia, to our fellow-soldier Archippus ;
And to the Church that meets at Philemon's house ;
From Paul, now a prisoner for Christ Jesus,
And from Timothy, a Brother.
May God, our Father, and the Lord Jesus Christ bless you   3
and give you peace.

II.—The Apostle's Request concerning a run-away Slave.

I always mention you in my prayers and thank God   4
for you, because I hear of the love and the faith which   5
you show, not only to the Lord Jesus, but also to all his
People ; and I pray that your participation in the Faith   6
may result in action, as you come to a fuller realization
of everything that is good and Christlike in us. I have   7
indeed found great joy and encouragement in your love,
knowing, as I do, how the hearts of Christ's People have
been cheered, Brother, by you.

And so, though my union with Christ enables me, with all   8
confidence, to dictate the course that you should adopt, yet   9
the claims of love make me prefer to plead with you—yes,
even me, Paul, though I am an ambassador for Christ Jesus
and, now, a prisoner for him as well. I plead with you for   10
this Child of mine, Onesimus, to whom, in my prison, I have
become a Father. Once he was of little service to you, but   11
now he has become of great service, not only to you, but to
me as well ; and I am sending him back to you with this   12
letter—though it is like tearing out my very heart. For   13
my own sake I should like to keep him with me, so that,
while I am in prison for the Good News, he might attend
to my wants on your behalf. But I do not wish to do   14
anything without your consent, because I want your generosity

to be voluntary and not, as it were, compulsory. It may 15
be that he was separated from you for an hour, for this very
reason, that you might have him back for ever, no longer 16
as a slave, but as something better—a dearly loved Brother,
especially dear to me, and how much more so to you, not only
as your fellow man, but as your fellow Christian ! If, then, you 17
count me your friend, receive him as you would me. If he 18
has caused you any loss, or owes you anything, charge it to
me. I, Paul, put my own hand to it—I will repay you my- 19
self. I say nothing about your owing me your very self. Yes, 20
Brother, let me gain something from you because of your
union with the Lord. Cheer my heart by your Christlike
spirit.

Even as I write, I have such confidence in your compliance 21
with my wishes, that I am sure that you will do even more
than I am asking. Please also get a lodging ready for me, for 22
I hope that I shall be given back to you all in answer to your
prayers.

III.—MESSAGES AND BLESSING.

Epaphras, who is my fellow-prisoner for Christ Jesus, sends 23
you his greeting; and Marcus, Aristarchus Demas, and 24
Luke, my fellow-workers, send theirs.

May the blessing of the Lord Jesus Christ rest on your 25
souls.

TO THE EPHESIANS.

ST. PAUL'S LETTER TO THE CHRISTIANS AT EPHESUS.

WRITTEN POSSIBLY DURING HIS IMPRISONMENT AT ROME, ABOUT 61 A.D.

EPHESUS was a busy seaport and the chief city of Roman Asia. In it stood the famous temple of Diana. St. Paul's visit to Ephesus is recorded in the Acts (Chapter 19) and lasted for more than two years. His stay there was eventful; and, when it came to an end, the Apostle went to Greece, and then returned, by way of Miletus, to Jerusalem. Shortly afterwards he was arrested, on the complaint of the Jews, and taken to Caesarea (Acts 23. 23), and from there to Rome (Acts 28. 16). From one of these places—probably the latter—he may have written the present Letter.

The genuineness of this Letter has been frequently assailed, but it may, with some confidence, be attributed to the Apostle himself. It appears to have been a circular letter addressed, not merely to the Christians of Ephesus, but also to the other Churches in Roman Asia; indeed, it was also known as "The Letter to Laodicea," and may be the letter referred to in Colossians 4. 16. In it the Apostle is not so much replying to arguments hostile to Christianity, as developing, upon lines similar to those laid down in the Letter to the Colossians, his conception of the unity of all Christians in the Christ, the invisible Head of their one Society.

TO THE

EPHESIANS.

I.—INTRODUCTION.

Greeting. To Christ's People **[AT EPHESUS]** who are faith- 1 **1**
ful to him,
FROM Paul, an Apostle of Christ Jesus, by the will of God.
May God, our Father, and the Lord Jesus Christ bless you and 2
give you peace.

The Apostle's Blessed is the God and Father of Jesus Christ, 3
Ascription of our Lord, who has blessed us on high with every
Praise. spiritual blessing, in Christ.   For he chose us in 4
our union with Christ before the creation of the universe, that
we might be holy and blameless in his sight, living in the
spirit of love.   From the first he destined us, in his good- 5
will towards us, to be adopted as Sons through Jesus Christ,
and so to enhance that glorious manifestation of his loving- 6
kindness which he gave us in The Beloved ; for in him, and 7
through the shedding of his blood, we have found redemption in
the pardon of our offences.   All this accords with the loving- 8
kindness which God lavished upon us, accompanied by
countless gifts of wisdom and discernment, when he made 9
known to us his hidden purpose.   And it also accords with
the good-will which God purposed to exhibit in Christ, in 10
view of that Divine Order which was to mark the completion of the ages, when he should make everything, both
in Heaven and on earth, centre in him.   In him, I say, for by 11
our union with him we became God's Heritage, having from
the first been destined for this in the intention of him who,
in all that happens, is carrying out his own fixed purpose ;
that we should enhance his glory—we who have been the first 12
to rest our hopes on the Christ.   And you, too, by your union 13
with him, after you had heard the Message of the Truth, the
Good News of your Salvation—you believed in him and were
sealed as his by receiving the holy Spirit, which he had promised.   And the Spirit is a pledge of our future heritage, 14
fore-shadowing the full redemption of God's own People—to
enhance his Glory.

II.—THE POWER OF GOD DISPLAYED IN CHRIST, THE HEAD OF THE CHURCH.

Prayer for Knowledge of this Power. And therefore I, ever since I heard of the faith 15 in the Lord Jesus which prevails among you, and of your confidence in all Christ's People, have never omitted to thank God on your behalf, whenever I 16 make mention of you in my prayers. My prayer is that the 17 God of Jesus Christ our Lord, the all-glorious Father, may inspire you with wisdom and true insight through a fuller knowledge of himself; that your minds may be so enlightened that 18 you may realize the hope given by God's Call, the wealth of the glory of his heritage among Christ's People, and the transcen- 19 dant greatness of the power which he is able to exercise in dealing with us who believe in him. The same mighty 20 power was exerted upon the Christ, when he raised the Christ from the dead and 'caused him to sit at his right hand' on high, exalting him above all Angels and Archangels of every rank, and above every name 21 that can be named, whether in the present age, or in the age to come. And God placed 'all things under Christ's feet,' and 22 gave him to the Church as its supreme Head; for the Church 23 is Christ's Body, and is filled by him who fills all things everywhere with his presence. You yourselves were once dead be- 1 cause of your offences and sins. For at one time you lived in 2 sin, following the ways of the world, in subjection to the Ruler of the Powers of the air—the Spirit who is still at work among the disobedient. And it was among 3 them that we all once lived our lives, indulging the cravings of our earthly nature, and carrying out the desires prompted by that earthly nature and by our own thoughts. Our very nature exposed us to the Divine Wrath, like the rest of mankind. Yet God, in 4 his abundant compassion, and because of the great love with which he loved us, even though we were 'dead' because of our 5 offences, gave Life to us in giving Life to the Christ. (By God's loving-kindness you have been saved.) And, through our 6 union with Christ Jesus, God raised us with him, and caused us to sit with him on high, in order that, by his goodness to 7 us in Christ Jesus, he might display in the ages to come the boundless wealth of his loving-kindness. For it is by God's 8 loving-kindness that you have been saved, through your faith. It is not due to yourselves; the gift is God's. It is not due to 9 obedience to Law, lest any one should boast. For we are God's 10 handiwork, created, by our union with Christ Jesus, for the good actions in doing which God had pre-arranged that we should spend our lives.

This Power displayed in the Resurrection of Christ.

This Power displayed in the Conversion of the Gentiles.

[18] Deut. 33. 4. [20] Ps. 110. 1. [22] Ps. 8. 6.

This Power displayed in the Union of Jew and Gentile within the Church. Remember, therefore, that you were once Gentiles yourselves, as your bodies showed; you were called 'The Uncircumcised' by those who were called 'The Circumcised'—circumcised only by the hand of man! Remember that you were [11] [12] at that time far from Christ; you were shut out from the citizenship of Israel; you were strangers to the Covenants founded on God's Promise; you were in the world without hope and without God. But now, through your union with [13] Christ Jesus, you who once were 'far off' have, by the shedding of the blood of the Christ, been brought 'near.' He it [14] is who is our Peace. He made the two divisions of mankind one, broke down the barrier that separated them, and in his [15] human nature put an end to the cause of enmity between them—the Law with its injunctions and ordinances—in order to create, through union with himself, from Jew and Gentile, one New Man, and thus make peace. And when, upon the [16] cross, he had destroyed their mutual enmity, he sought by means of his cross to reconcile them both to God, united in one Body. He came with the Good News of peace for you who [17] were 'far off,' and of peace for those who were 'near'; for it [18] is through him that we, the Jews and the Gentiles, united in the one Spirit, are now able to approach the Father. It [19] follows, then, that you are no longer strangers and aliens, but are fellow-citizens with Christ's People and members of God's Household. You have been built up upon the foundation laid [20] by the Apostles and Prophets, Christ Jesus himself being 'the corner-stone.' United in him, every part of the building, closely [21] joined together, will grow into a Temple, consecrated by its union with the Lord. And, through union in him, you also are [22] being built up together, to be a dwelling-place for God through the Spirit.

III.—THE APOSTLE'S DIVINE COMMISSION TO THE GENTILES.

The Gospel made known to the Church through the Apostle. For this reason I, Paul, the prisoner of Jesus, [1] **3** the Christ, for the sake of you Gentiles——for you [2] have heard, I suppose, of the responsible charge with which God entrusted me for your benefit, and also that it was by direct revelation that [3] the hidden purpose of God was made known to me, as I have already briefly told you. And, by reading what I [4] have written, you will be able to judge how far I understand this hidden purpose of God in Christ. In former genera- [5] tions it was not made known to mankind, as fully as it has now been revealed by the Spirit to the Apostles and Prophets among Christ's People—that, by union with Christ Jesus and [6]

13—17 Isa. 57. 19; 52. 7.   20 Isa. 28. 16,

through the Good News, the Gentiles are co-heirs with us and members of one Body, and that they share with us in God's Promise. Of this Good News I became a minister, in virtue 7 of the charge with which God entrusted me in the exercise of his power—yes, to me, who am less than the least of all 8 Christ's People, was this charge entrusted!—to tell the Gentiles the Good News of the boundless wealth to be found in the Christ, and to make clear what is God's way of working 9 out that hidden purpose which from the first has been concealed in the mind of the Creator of all things; so 10

The Gospel made known to the Heavenly Powers through the Church. that now to the Archangels and to all the Powers on high should be made known, through the Church, the all-embracing wisdom of God, in 11 accordance with that purpose which runs through all the ages and which he has now accomplished in Jesus, the Christ, our Master. And in union 12 with him, and through our trust in him, we find courage to approach God with confidence.   Therefore I beg 13 you not to be disheartened at the sufferings that I am undergoing for your sakes; for they redound to your honour.

Prayer that the Church may comprehend this Gospel. For this reason, then, I kneel before the 14 Father—from whom all 'fatherhood' in Heaven 15 and on earth derives its name—and pray that, 16 in proportion to the wealth of his glory, he will strengthen you with his power by breathing his Spirit into your inmost soul, so that the Christ, through your 17 faith, may make his home within your hearts in love; and I pray that you, now firmly rooted and established, may, with 18 all Christ's People, have the power to comprehend in all its width and length and height and depth, and to understand— 19 though it surpasses all understanding—the love of the Christ; and so be filled to the full with God himself.

Doxology. To him who, through his power which is at 20 work within us, is able to do far more than anything that we can ask or conceive—to him be all glory through 21 the Church and through Christ Jesus, for all generations, age after age. Amen.

IV.—THE GOSPEL AND THE DAILY LIFE.

Unity in Christ. I urge you, then—I who am a prisoner in the 1   4 Master's cause—to live lives worthy of the Call that you have received; always humble and gentle, patient, 2 bearing lovingly with one another, and striving to maintain 3 in the bond of peace the unity given by the Spirit. There is 4 but one Body and one Spirit, just as there was but one hope

set before you when you received your Call.   There is but one   5
Lord, one Faith, one Baptism.   There is but one God and   6
Father of all—the God who is over all, pervades all, and is in
all.   Every one of us, however, has been entrusted with   7
some charge, each in accordance with the extent of the
gift of the Christ.   That is why it is said—   8

> ' When he went up on high, he led his captives into captivity,
>   And gave gifts to mankind.'

Now surely this 'going up' must imply that he had already   9
gone down into the world beneath.   He who went down is the   10
same as he who went up—up beyond the highest Heaven, that
he might fill all things with his presence.   And he it is who   11
gave to the Church Apostles, Prophets, Missionaries, Pastors,
and Teachers, to fit his People for the work of the ministry,   12
for the building up of the Body of the Christ.   And this shall   13
continue, until we all attain to that unity which is given by
faith and by a fuller knowledge of the Son of God ; until we
reach the ideal man—the full standard of the perfection of
the Christ.   Then we shall no longer be like infants, tossed   14
backward and forward, blown about by every breath of human
teaching, through the trickery and the craftiness of men,
towards the snares of error ; but holding the truth in a spirit   15
of love, we shall grow into complete union with him who is
our Head—Christ himself.   For from him the whole Body,   16
closely joined and knit together by the contact of every part
with the source of its life, derives its power to grow, in
proportion to the vigour of each individual part ; and so is
being built up in a spirit of love.

The New   This, then, as one in union with the Lord,   17
Life and the I say to you and urge upon you :—Do not con-
Old.   tinue to live such purposeless lives as the Gentiles live, with their powers of discernment darkened, cut off   18
from the Life of God, owing to the ignorance that prevails
among them and to the hardness of their hearts.   Lost to all   19
sense of shame, they have abandoned themselves to licentiousness, in order to practise every kind of impurity without
restraint.   But far different is the lesson you learnt   20
from the Christ—if, that is, you really listened to him, and   21
through union with him were taught the Truth, as it is to be
found in Jesus.   For you learnt with regard to your former   22
way of living that you must cast off your old nature, which,
yielding to deluding passions, grows corrupt ; that the very   23
spirit of your minds must be constantly renewed ; and that   24
you must clothe yourselves in that new nature which was
created to resemble God, with the righteousness and holiness
springing from the Truth.

8—11 Ps. 68. 18.

O*

Precepts for the Daily Life. Since, therefore, you have cast off what is 25 false, 'you must every one of you speak the truth to your neighbours.' For we are united to one another like the parts of a body. 'Be angry, yet do not 26 sin.' Do not let the sun go down upon your anger ; and give 27 no opportunity to the Devil. Let the man who steals steal 28 no longer, but rather let him toil with his hands at honest work, so that he may have something to share with any one in want. Never let any foul word pass your lips, but only such 29 good words as the occasion demands, that they may be a help to those who hear them. And do not grieve God's Holy Spirit ; 30 for it was through that Spirit that God sealed you as his, against the Day of Redemption. Let all bitterness, passion, anger, 31 brawling, and abusive language be banished from among you, as well as all malice. Be kind to one another, tender- 32 hearted, ready to forgive one another, just as God, in Christ, forgave you. Therefore imitate God, as his dear children, 1 **5** and live a life of love, following the example of the Christ, 2 who loved you and gave himself for you as 'an offering and a sacrifice to God, that should be fragrant and acceptable.'

As for unchastity and every kind of impurity, or greed, do 3 not let them even be mentioned among you, as befits Christ's People, nor shameful conduct, nor foolish talk or jesting, for 4 they are wholly out of place among you ; but rather thanks- giving. For of this you may be sure—that no one who is 5 unchaste or impure or greedy of gain (for to be greedy of gain is idolatry) has any place awaiting him in the Kingdom of the Christ and God.

Do not let any one deceive you with specious arguments. 6 Those are the sins that bring down the Wrath of God upon the disobedient. Therefore have nothing to do with such 7 people. For, although you were once in Darkness, now, by 8 your union with the Lord, you are in the Light. Live as 'Children of Light'—for the outcome of life in the Light 9 may be seen in every form of goodness, righteousness, and sincerity—always trying to find out what is pleasing to the 10 Lord. Take no part in deeds of Darkness, from which 11 no good can come ; on the contrary, expose them. It is 12 degrading even to speak of the things continually done by them in secret. All such actions, when exposed, have their 13 true character made manifest by the Light. For everything that has its true character made manifest is clear as light. And that is why it is said— 14

> 'Sleeper, awake !
> Arise from the dead,
> And the Christ shall give thee light !'

25 Zech. 8. 16.   26 Ps. 4. 4.   2 Ps. 40. 6 ; Ezek. 20. 41.

Take great care, then, how you live—not unwisely but 15
wisely, making the most of every opportunity ; for these are 16
evil days. Therefore do not grow thoughtless, but try to under- 17
stand what the Lord's will is.   Do not drink wine to excess, 18
for that leads to profligacy ; but seek to be filled with the
Spirit of God, and speak to one another in psalms and hymns
and sacred songs.   Sing and make music in your hearts to 19
the Lord.   Always give thanks for everything to our God and 20
Father, in the Name of our Lord Jesus Christ ; and submit to 21
one another from reverence for him.

Christian Family Life. Wives should submit to their husbands as sub- 22
mitting to the Lord.   For a man is the Head 23
of his wife, as the Christ is the Head of the Church—
being indeed himself the Saviour of his Body.   But as the 24
Church submits to the Christ, so also should wives submit to
their husbands in everything.   Husbands, love your 25
wives, just as the Christ loved the Church, and gave himself
for her, to make her holy, after purifying her by the Washing 26
with the Water, according to his promise ; so that he might 27
himself bring the Church, in all her beauty, into his own
presence, with no spot or wrinkle or blemish of any kind, but
that she might be holy and faultless.   That is how husbands 28
ought to love their wives—as if they were their own bodies.
A man who loves his wife is really loving himself ; for no one 29
ever yet hated his own body.   But every one feeds his body
and cares for it, just as the Christ for the Church ; for we are 30
members of his Body.

' For this cause a man shall leave his father and mother, and 31
be united to his wife ; and the man and his wife shall become
one.'

In this there is a profound truth—I am speaking of Christ 32
and his Church.   However, for you individually, let each love 33
his wife as if she were himself ; and the wife be careful to
respect her husband.

Children, obey your parents, as children of the Lord ; for 1 **6**
that is but right.   ' Honour thy father and mother '—this is the 2
first Commandment with a promise—' so that thou mayest 3
prosper and have a long life on earth.'   And fathers, do 4
not irritate your children, but bring them up with Christian
discipline and instruction.

Slaves, obey your earthly masters, with anxious care, giving 5
them ungrudging service, as if obeying the Christ ; not only 6
when their eyes are on you, as if you had merely to please men,
but as slaves of Christ, who are trying to carry out the will of
God.   Give your service heartily and cheerfully, as working for 7
the Master and not for men ; for you know that every one will 8

---

[18] Prov. 23. 31 (Septuagint).   [31] Gen. 2. 24.   [2—3] Exod. 20. 12 ; Deut. 5. 16.

be rewarded by the Master for any honest work that he has done, whether he is a slave or a freeman.   And masters, 9 treat your slaves in the same spirit. Give up threatening them ; for you know that he who is both their Master and yours is in Heaven, and that before him there is no distinction of rank.

The Christian's Armour. For the future, find strength in your union 10 with the Lord, and in the power which comes from his might. Put on the full armour of God, 11 so that you may be able to stand your ground against the strata- gems of the Devil. For ours is no struggle against enemies of 12 flesh and blood, but against all the various Powers of Evil that hold sway in the Darkness around us, against the Spirits of Wickedness on high. Therefore take up the full armour of 13 God, that, when the evil day comes, you may be able to with- stand the attack, and, having fought to the end, still to stand your ground. Stand your ground, then, 'with truth for your 14 belt,' and 'with righteousness for your breast-plate,' and with 15 the readiness to serve the Good News of Peace as shoes for your feet. At every onslaught take up faith for your shield ; 16 for with it you will be able to extinguish all the flaming darts of the Evil One. And receive 'the helmet of Salvation,' and 'the 17 sword of the Spirit'—which is the Message of God—always with prayer and supplication. Pray in spirit at all times. Be 18 intent upon this, with unwearying perseverance and sup- plication for all Christ's People—and on my behalf also, 19 that, when I begin to speak, words may be given me, so that I may fearlessly make known the inmost truth of the Good News, on behalf of which I am an Ambassador—in chains ! 20 Pray that, in telling it, I may speak fearlessly as I ought.

V.—CONCLUSION.

To enable you, as well as others, to know all that concerns 21 me and what I am doing, Tychicus, our dear Brother and faithful helper in the Master's Cause, will tell you everything. I am sending him to you on purpose that you may learn all 22 about us, and that he may cheer your hearts.

May God, the Father, and the Lord Jesus Christ give our 23 Brothers peace, and love linked with faith.   May God's 24 blessing be with all who love our Lord Jesus Christ with an undying love.

4 Isa. 11. 5; 59. 17.   15 Isa. 52. 7.   17 Isa. 59. 17; 11. 4; 49. 2 ; 51. 16 ; Hos. 6. 5.

TO THE PHILIPPIANS.

ST. PAUL'S LETTER TO THE CHRISTIANS AT PHILIPPI.

WRITTEN PROBABLY DURING HIS IMPRISON-MENT AT ROME, ABOUT 62 A.D.

PHILIPPI was a Roman military station in Macedonia, and the first place in Europe at which St. Paul is known to have preached (Acts 16. 12). The Apostle gained many converts there, but his stay was cut short by persecution. Subsequently he twice revisited the town (Acts 20. 2, 6). The Philippian Christians appear to have cherished a specially warm affection for the Apostle. Although their own means were but slender, they repeatedly contributed to his support with great generosity (Phil. 4. 15, 16). Upon hearing of his imprisonment at Rome, they sent Epaphroditus to carry their gifts to him, and to assure him of their heart-felt sympathy (Phil. 2. 25). While in Rome, Epaphroditus fell ill; upon his recovery St. Paul sent this Letter by him to Philippi, expressing to the members of the Church there his gratitude for their kindness, and urging them to unity and humility.

The Letter expresses warm personal affection, and contains counsel and warning to the Apostle's converts, mingled with kindly messages and encouragement. It was written at a time when his trial before the Emperor Nero was drawing to an end, and when St. Paul was daily awaiting the issue. His friends had deserted him, death stared him in the face, and yet the Letter sounds a note of confidence and joy.

TO THE

PHILIPPIANS.

I.—INTRODUCTION.

Greeting. To all Christ's People at Philippi, with the Pre-siding Officers and Assistants, **1** **1**

FROM Paul and Timothy, servants of Christ Jesus.

May God, our Father, and the Lord Jesus Christ bless you, and give you peace. **2**

The Apostle's Thankfulness and Prayer. Every recollection that I have of you is a cause of thankfulness to God, always, in every prayer that I offer for you all—and my prayers are full of joy—because of the share that you have had in spreading the Good News, from the first day that you received it until now. For of this I am confident, that he who began a good work in you will complete it in readiness for the Day of Jesus Christ. And, indeed, I am justified in feeling thus about you all; because you have a warm place in my heart—you who all, both in my imprisonment and in the work of defending and establishing the Good News, shared my privilege with me. God will bear me witness how I yearn over you all with the tenderness of Christ Jesus. And what I pray for is this—that your love may grow yet stronger and stronger, with increasing knowledge and all discernment, until you are able to appreciate all moral distinctions. And I pray, too, that you may be kept pure and blameless against the Day of Christ, bearing a rich harvest of that righteousness which comes through Jesus Christ, to the glory and praise of God. **3 4 5 6 7 8 9 10 11**

II.—THE APOSTLE IN PRISON AT ROME.

The Results of his Im-prisonment. Brothers, I want you to realize that what has happened to me has actually served to forward the Good News. It has even become evident, not only to all the Imperial Guard, but to every one else, that it is for **12 13**

Christ's sake that I am in chains. And besides this, most of our Brothers have gained confidence in the Lord through my chains, and now venture with far greater freedom to speak of God's Message fearlessly.

The Spread of the Gospel.   It is true that some do proclaim the Christ out of jealousy and opposition ; but there are others who proclaim him from good-will. The latter do it from love for me, knowing that I have been appointed to plead the cause of the Good News. The former spread the news of the Christ in a factious spirit, and not sincerely, thinking to add to the pain of my chains. But what of that? Only that in some way or other, either with assumed or with real earnestness, Christ is being made known ; and at that I rejoice. Yes, and I will rejoice, for I know that, through your prayers and through a rich supply of the Spirit of Jesus Christ, 'all this will make for my Salvation.' And this will fulfil my earnest expectation and hope that I shall have no cause for shame, but that, with unfailing courage, now as hitherto, Christ will be honoured in my body, whether by my life or by my death.

Life or Death.   For to me life is Christ, and death is gain. But what if the life here in the body—if this brings me fruit from my labours? Then which to choose I cannot tell! I am sorely perplexed either way! My own desire is to depart and be with Christ, for this would be far better. But, for your sakes, it may be more needful that I should still remain here in the body. Yes, I am confident that this is so, and therefore I am sure that I shall stay, and stay near you all, to promote your progress and joy in the Faith ; so that, when you once more have me among you, you, in your union with Christ Jesus, may find in me fresh cause for exultation.

III.—The Christian Life.

Unity.   Under all circumstances let your lives be worthy of the Good News of the Christ : so that, whether I come and see you, or whether I hear of your affairs at a distance, I may know that you are standing firm, animated by one spirit, and joining with one heart in a common struggle for the Faith taught by the Good News, without ever shrinking from your opponents. To them this will be a sign of their Destruction and of your Salvation—a sign from God. For, on behalf of Christ, you have had the privilege granted you, not only of trusting in him, but also of suffering on his behalf. You will be engaged in the same hard struggle as that which you once saw me waging, and which you hear that I am waging still.

19 Job 13. 16.

Humility. If, then, any encouragement comes through 1 union with Christ, if there is any persuasive power in love, if there is any communion with the Spirit, if there is any tenderness or pity, I entreat you to make my happiness 2 complete—Live together animated by the same spirit and in mutual love, one in heart, animated by one Spirit. Nothing 3 should be done in a factious spirit or from vanity, but each of you should with all humility regard others as of more account than himself, and one and all should consider, not only their 4 **The Great** own interests, but also the interests of others. Let 5 **Example.** the spirit of Christ Jesus be yours also. Though 6 the divine nature was his from the beginning, yet he did not look upon equality with God as above all things to be clung to, but 7 impoverished himself by taking the nature of a servant and becoming like men ; he appeared among us as a man, and 8 still further humbled himself by submitting even to death— to death on a cross ! And that is why God raised him to the 9 very highest place, and gave him the Name which stands above all other names, so that in adoration of the Name of 10 Jesus every knee should bend, in Heaven, on earth, and under the earth, and that every tongue should acknowledge JESUS 11 CHRIST as LORD—to the glory of God the Father.

Following Therefore, my dear friends, as you have always 12 **this Example.** been obedient in the past, so now work out your own Salvation with anxious care, not only when I am with you, but all the more now that I am absent. Remember it is God 13 who, in his kindness, is at work within you, enabling you both to will and to work. In all that you do, avoid murmuring and 14 dissension, so as to prove yourselves blameless and innocent— 15 ' faultless children of God, in the midst of an evil-disposed and perverse generation,' in which you are seen shining like stars in a dark world, offering to men the Message of Life ; and 16 then I shall be able at the Day of Christ to boast that I did not run my course for nothing, or toil for nothing. And 17 yet, even if, when your faith is offered as a sacrifice to God, my life-blood must be poured out in addition, still I shall rejoice and share the joy of you all ; and do you also rejoice and share 18 my joy.

IV.—PERSONAL PLANS.

Timothy. I hope, however, as one who trusts in the Lord 19 Jesus, to send Timothy to you before long, so that I may myself be cheered by receiving news of you. For 20 I have no one but him to send—no one of kindred spirit who would take the same genuine interest in your welfare. They 21 are all pursuing their own aims and not those of Christ Jesus.

10–11 Isa. 45. 2 .   15 Deut. 32. 5.   16 Isa. 49. 4.

But you know what Timothy has proved himself to be, and 22
how, like a child working for his father, he worked hard with
me in spreading the Good News.   It is Timothy, then, 23
whom I hope to send, as soon as ever I can foresee how it will
go with me.   And I am confident, as one who trusts in the 24
Lord Jesus, that before long I myself shall follow.   Still I think 25
Epaphroditus. it necessary to send Epaphroditus to you now,
for he is my brother, fellow-worker, and fellow-
soldier, and he was also your messenger to help me in my
need.   For he has been longing to see you all, and has been 26
distressed because you heard of his illness.   And I can assure 27
you that his illness very nearly proved fatal.   But God had
pity on him, and not on him only but also on me, that I might
not have sorrow upon sorrow.   I am all the more ready, there- 28
fore, to send him, so that the sight of him may revive your
spirits and my own sorrow be lightened.   Give him, then, 29
the heartiest of Christian welcomes, and hold such men
in great honour.   For it was owing to his devotion to the 30
Master's work that he was at the point of death, having risked
his own life in the effort to supply what was wanting in the
help that you sent me.

In conclusion, my Brothers, all joy be yours in your union 1 **3**
with the Lord.   To repeat what I have already written does
not weary me, and is the safe course for you.

V.—JUDAISM AND CHRISTIANITY.

The Apostle's Warning. Beware of those 'dogs'! Beware of those 2
mischievous workers!   Beware of the men who
mutilate themselves!   For it is we who are the 3
circumcised—we whose worship is prompted by the Spirit of
God, who exult in Christ Jesus, and who do not rely upon
external privileges ; though I, if any man, have cause to rely 4
even upon them.

The Apostle's Experience. If any one thinks he can rely upon external
privileges, far more can I !   I was circumcised 5
when eight days old ; I am an Israelite by race,
and of the tribe of Benjamin ; I am a Hebrew, and the child
of Hebrews.   As to the Law, I was a Pharisee ; as to zeal, I 6
was a persecutor of the Church ; as to such righteousness
as is due to Law, I proved myself blameless.   But 7
all the things which I once held to be gains I have now, for
the Christ's sake, come to count as loss.   More than that, I 8
count everything as loss, for the sake of the exceeding value of
the knowledge of Christ Jesus my Lord.   And for his sake
I have lost everything, and count it as refuse, if I may but

gain Christ and be found in union with him; any righteous- 9
ness that I have being, not the righteousness that results
from Law, but the righteousness which comes through faith
in Christ—the righteousness which is derived from God and
is founded on faith.   Then indeed I shall know Christ, and 10
the power of his resurrection, and all that it means to share
his sufferings, in the hope that, if I become like him in his
death, I may possibly attain to the resurrection from the dead. 11
Not that I have already laid hold of it, or that I am already made 12
perfect.   But I press on, in the hope of actually laying hold of
that for which indeed I was laid hold of by Christ Jesus.   For 13
I, Brothers, do not regard myself as having yet laid hold of it.
But this one thing I do—forgetting what lies behind, and
straining every nerve for that which lies in front, I press on to 14
the goal, to gain the prize of that heavenward Call which
God gave me through Christ Jesus.   Let all of us, 15
then, whose faith is mature, think thus.   Then, if on any
matter you think otherwise, God will make that also plain
to you.   Only we are bound to order our lives by what we have 16
already attained.

The Apostle's Example. Brothers, unite in following my example, and 17
fix your eyes on those who are living by the
pattern which we have set you.   For there are 18
many—of whom I have often told you, and now tell you even
with tears—who are living in enmity to the cross of the Christ.
The end of such men is Ruin; for their appetites are their 19
God, and they glory in their shame; their minds are given up
to earthly things.   But the State of which we are citizens is in 20
Heaven; and it is from Heaven that we are eagerly looking
for a Saviour, the Lord Jesus Christ, who, by the exercise of
his power to bring everything into subjection to himself, will 21
make this body that we have in our humiliation like to that
body which he has in his Glory.

VI.—Conclusion.

Exhortations. So then, my dear Brothers, whom I am long- 1 **4**
ing to see—you who are my joy and my crown,
stand fast in union with the Lord, dear friends.
I entreat Euodia, and I entreat Syntyche, to live in harmony, 2
in union with the Lord; yes, and I ask you, my true comrade, 3
to help them, remembering that they toiled by my side in
spreading the Good News; and so, too, did Clement and my
other fellow-workers, whose names are 'in the Book of Life.'
All joy be yours at all times in your union with the Lord. 4
Again I repeat—All joy be yours.   Let your forbearing spirit 5
be plain to every one.   The Lord is near.   Do not be anxious 6

³ Ps. 69. 28.

about anything ; but under all circumstances, by prayer and entreaty joined with thanksgiving, make your needs known to God. Then the Peace of God, which is beyond all human understanding, will stand guard over your hearts and thoughts, through your union with Christ Jesus. **7**

In conclusion, Brothers, wherever you find anything true or honourable, righteous or pure, lovable or praiseworthy, or if 'virtue' and 'honour' have any meaning, there let your thoughts dwell. All that you learnt and received and heard and saw in me put into practice continually ; and then God, the giver of peace, will be with you. **8** **9**

The Gift from Philippi. It was a matter of great joy to me, as one in union with the Lord, that at length your interest in me had revived. The interest indeed you had, but not the opportunity. Do not think that I am saying this under the pressure of want. For I, however I am placed, have learnt to be independent of circumstances. I know how to face humble circumstances, and I know how to face prosperity. Into all and every human experience I have been initiated— into plenty and hunger, into prosperity and want. I can do everything in the strength of him who makes me strong ! Yet you have acted nobly in sharing my troubles. And you at Philippi know, as well as I, that in the early days of the Good News—at the time when I had just left Macedonia—no Church, with the one exception of yourselves, had anything to do with me as far as giving and receiving are concerned. Indeed, even while I was still in Thessalonica, you sent more than once to relieve my wants. It is not that I am anxious for your gifts, but I am anxious to see the abundant return that will be placed to your account. I have enough of everything, and to spare. My wants are fully satisfied, now that I have received from Epaphroditus the gifts which you sent me—the sweet fragrance of a sacrifice acceptable and pleasing to God. And my God, out of the greatness of his wealth, will, in glory, fully satisfy your every need, through your union with Christ Jesus. To him, our God and Father, be ascribed all glory for ever and ever. Amen. **10 11 12 13 14, 15 16 17 18 19 20**

Farewell. Give my greeting to every one of the People of Christ Jesus.   The Brothers who are with me send you their greetings. All Christ's People here, and especially those who belong to the Emperor's household, send theirs. **21 22**

May the blessing of the Lord Jesus Christ rest on your souls. **23**

[18] Ezek. 20. 41.

TO TIMOTHY.

I.

THE FIRST LETTER TO TIMOTHY.

[DATE AND PLACE OF WRITING UNCERTAIN.]

NOTHING is known with any certainty as to the history either of this or of the other two 'Pastoral Letters.'

Timothy, to whom this and the next Letter are addressed, was the son of a Greek father and a Jewish mother, and was converted by St. Paul from Judaism to Christianity. He lived at Lystra in Asia Minor (Acts 16. 1—4), joined St. Paul on his second missionary journey, and, according to this Letter, was placed by the Apostle in charge of some Church. Tradition says that it was the Church in Ephesus.

The object of this Letter is to guide and encourage this young Officer of the Church in the discharge of his duties ; and it contains many general directions on the affairs of the Church.

TO
TIMOTHY.
I.

I.—INTRODUCTION.

Greeting. To Timothy, my true Child in the Faith,   1, 2 **1**
FROM Paul, an Apostle of Christ Jesus by the appointment of
   God, our Saviour, and Christ Jesus, our Hope.
May God, the Father, and Christ Jesus, our Lord, bless ycu,
   and be merciful to you, and give you peace.

Warning   I beg you, as I did when I was on my way into   3
against False Macedonia, to remain at Ephesus ; that you may
Teaching. instruct certain people there not to teach new and
strange doctrines, nor to devote their attention to legends and   4
interminable genealogies, which tend to give rise to argument
rather than to further that divine plan which is revealed in
the Faith. The object of all instruction is to call forth that love   5
which comes from a pure heart, a clear conscience, and a
sincere faith. And it is because they have not aimed at these   6
things that the attention of certain people has been diverted to
unprofitable subjects. They want to be Teachers of the Law,   7
and yet do not understand either the words they use, or the
subjects on which they speak so confidently. We know,   8
of course, that the Law is excellent, when used legitimately,
by one who recognizes that laws were not made for good men,   9
but for the lawless and disorderly, for irreligious and wicked
people, for those who are irreverent and profane, for those who
illtreat their fathers or mothers, for murderers, for the im-   10
moral, for people guilty of sodomy, for slave-dealers, for liars,
for perjurers, and for whatever else is opposed to sound
Christian teaching—as is taught in the glorious Good News   11
of the ever-blessed God, with which I was entrusted.

I am thankful to Christ Jesus, our Lord, who   12

The Apostle's Thankfulness for his Call to the Ministry. has been my strength, for showing that he thought me worthy of trust by appointing me to his ministry, though I once used to blaspheme, and to   13 persecute, and to insult. Yet mercy was shown me, because I acted in ignorance, while still an unbeliever ; and the loving-kindness of our Lord was boundless, and filled me   14 with that faith and love which come from union with Christ Jesus. How true the saying is, and worthy of the fullest accep-   15 tance, that 'Christ Jesus came into the world to save sinners'! And there is no greater sinner than I ! Yet mercy was shown   16 me for the express purpose that Christ Jesus might exhibit in my case, beyond all others, his exhaustless patience, as an example for those who were afterwards to believe on him and attain Immortal Life.   To the Immortal King, ever-   17 living, invisible, the one God, be ascribed honour and glory for ever and ever. Amen.

This, then, is the charge that I lay upon you,   18

His Charge to Timothy. Timothy, my Child, in accordance with what was predicted of you—Fight the good fight in the spirit of those predictions, with faith, and with a clear con-   19 science ; and it is because they have thrust this aside, that, as regards the Faith, some have wrecked their lives. Hymenaeus   20 and Alexander are instances—the men whom I delivered over to Satan, that they might be taught not to blaspheme.

II.—GENERAL DIRECTIONS ON CHURCH-MATTERS.

First of all, then, I urge that petitions, prayers,   1   2

Public Prayer. intercessions, and thanksgivings should be offered for every one, especially for kings and all who are in high positions, in order that we may lead a quiet   2 and peaceful life in a deeply religious and reverent spirit. This   3 will be good and acceptable in the eyes of God, our Saviour, whose will is that every one should be saved, and attain to a   4 full knowledge of the Truth.   There is but one God,   5 and one mediator between God and men—the man, Christ Jesus, who gave himself as a ransom on behalf of all men.   6 This must be our testimony, as opportunities

Public Testimony. present themselves ; and it was for this that I was   7 myself appointed a Herald and an Apostle (I am telling the simple truth and no lie)—a Teacher of the Gentiles in the Faith and Truth.

My desire, then, is that it should be the custom   8

Public Worship. everywhere for the men to lead the prayers, with hands reverently uplifted, avoiding heated con- troversy.   I also desire that women should adorn   9

themselves with appropriate dress, worn quietly and modestly, and not with wreaths or gold ornaments for the hair, or pearls, or costly clothing, but—as is proper for women who 10 profess to be religious—with good actions.   A woman 11 should listen silently to her teachers, and show them all deference.   I do not consent to a woman's becoming a teacher, 12 or exercising authority over a man ; she ought to be silent. Adam was formed first, not Eve.   And it was not Adam who 13, 14 was deceived ; it was the woman who was entirely deceived and fell into sin.   But women will find their salvation in mother- 15 hood, if they never abandon faith, love, or holiness, and behave with modesty.   How true is that saying !

3   When a man aspires to be a Presiding-Officer

Presiding Officers. in the Church, he is ambitious for a noble task. The Presiding-Officer should be a man of blame- 2 less character ; a faithful husband ; living a temperate, discreet, and well-ordered life ; hospitable, and a skilful teacher, not addicted to drink or brawling, but of a for- 3 bearing and peaceable disposition, and not a lover of money ; he should be a man who rules his own household well, 4 and whose children are kept under control and are well- behaved.   If a man does not know how to rule his own 5 household, how can he take charge of the Church of God ? The Presiding-Officer should not be a recent convert, that he 6 may not be blinded by pride and fall under the same con- demnation as the Devil.   He should also be well spoken of by 7 outsiders, that he may not incur censure and so fall into the snares of the Devil.   So, too, Assistant- 8

Assistant Officers. Officers should be serious and straightforward men, not given to taking much drink or to questionable money-making, but men who hold the deep 9 truths of the Faith and have a clear conscience.   They should 10 be tested first, and only appointed to their Office if no objection is raised against them.   It should be the same with the 11 women.   They should be serious, not gossips, sober, and trustworthy in all respects.   Assistant-Officers should be 12 faithful husbands, and men who rule their children and their households well.   Those who have filled that post with honour 13 gain for themselves an honourable position, as well as great confidence through the faith that they place in Christ Jesus.

III.—Special Directions to Timothy.

I am writing this to you, though I hope that I shall come to 14 see you before long ; but in case I should be delayed, I want 15 you to know what your conduct ought to be in the Household

of God, which is the Church of the Living God—the pillar and
stay of the Truth. Yes, and confessedly wonderful are the   16
deep truths of our religion ; for—

> ' He was revealed in our nature,
>   Pronounced righteous in spirit,
>   Seen by angels,
>   Proclaimed among the Gentiles,
>   Believed on in the world,
>   Taken up into glory.'

But the Spirit distinctly says that in later times   1 **4**
On Dealing there will be some who will fall away from the
with False Faith, and devote their attention to misleading
Teachers. spirits, and to the teaching of demons, who   2
will make use of the hypocrisy of lying teachers. These
men's consciences are seared, and they discourage marriage   3
and enjoin abstinence from certain kinds of food ; though God
created these foods to be enjoyed thankfully by those who hold
the Faith and have attained a full knowledge of the Truth.
Everything created by God is good, and there is nothing   4
that need be rejected — provided only that it is received
thankfully ; for it is consecrated by God's blessing and by   5
prayer.
Put all this before the Brethren, and you will be a good   6
servant of Christ Jesus, sustained by the precepts of the Faith
and of that Good Teaching by which you have guided your
life. As for profane legends and old wives' tales, leave them   7
alone. Train yourself to lead a religious life ; for while the   8
training of the body is of service in some respects, religion is
of service in all, carrying with it, as it does, a promise of Life
both here and hereafter. How true that saying is and worthy of   9
the fullest acceptance ! With that aim we toil and struggle,   10
for we have set our hopes on the Living God, who is the
Saviour of all men, and especially of those who hold the Faith.

Dwell upon these things in your teaching. Do   11, 1
On the not let any one look down on you because you
Development are young, but, by your conversation, your con-
of his Powers. duct, your love, your faith, and your purity, be
an example to those who hold the Faith. Till I come, apply   13
yourself to public reading, preaching, and teaching. Do not   14
neglect the divine gift within you, which was given you, amid
many a prediction, when the hands of the Officers of the
Church were laid on your head. Practise these things, devote   15
yourself to them, so that your progress may be plain to every
one. Look to yourself as well as to your teaching. Persevere   16
in this, for your doing so will mean Salvation for yourself as
well as for your hearers,

Do not reprimand an older man, but plead **1**
with him as if he were your father. Treat the
young men as brothers, the older women as **2**
mothers, and the younger women as sisters—
with all purity. Show consideration for **3**
widows—I mean those who are really widowed.
But, if a widow has children or grand-children, **4**
let them learn to show proper regard for the
members of their own family first, and to make some return to
their parents; for that is pleasing in God's sight. As for the **5**
woman who is really widowed and left quite alone, her hopes are
fixed on God, and she devotes herself to prayers and supplica-
tions night and day. But the life of a widow who is devoted **6**
to pleasure is a living death. Those are the points on which **7**
you should dwell, that there may be no call for your censure.
Any one who fails to provide for his own relations, and **8**
especially for those under his own roof, has disowned the
Faith, and is worse than an unbeliever. A widow, **9**
when her name is added to the list, should not be less
than sixty years old; she should have been a faithful wife,
and be well spoken of for her kind actions. She should have **10**
brought up children, have shown hospitality to strangers,
have washed the feet of her fellow Christians, have relieved
those who were in distress, and devoted herself to every
kind of good action. But you should exclude the younger **11**
widows from the list; for, when they grow restive under
the yoke of the Christ, they want to marry, and so they **12**
bring condemnation upon themselves for having broken their
previous promise. And not only that, but they learn to be idle **13**
as they go about from house to house. Nor are they merely
idle, but they also become gossips and busy-bodies, and talk
of what they ought not. Therefore I advise young widows **14**
to marry, bear children, and attend to their homes, and so
avoid giving the enemy an opportunity for scandal. There **15**
are some who have already left us, to follow Satan. Any **16**
Christian woman, who has relations who are widows, ought
to relieve them and not allow them to become a burden to the
Church, so that the Church may relieve those widows who are
really widowed.

On his Relations with those under his care.

On the Provision for Widows.

Those Officers of the Church who fill their **17**
office well should be held deserving of especial
consideration, particularly those whose work lies
in preaching and teaching. The words of Scripture are— **18**

As to the Officers of the Church.

'Thou shalt not muzzle the ox while it is treading out the
grain,'

and again—

'The worker is worth his wages.'

[18] Deut. 25. 4.

Do not receive a charge against an Officer of the Church, 19
unless it is supported by two or three witnesses; but rebuke 20
offenders publicly, so that others may take warning.   I   21

On various Subjects. charge you solemnly, before God and Christ Jesus and the Chosen Angels, to carry out these directions, unswayed by prejudice, never acting with partiality.   Never ordain any one hastily, 22
and take no part in the wrong-doing of others.   Keep your
life pure.   Do not continue to drink water only, but 23
take a little wine on account of the weakness of your
stomach, and your frequent ailments.   There are some 24
men whose sins are conspicuous and lead on to judgement,
while there are others whose sins dog their steps.   In the 25
same way noble deeds become conspicuous, and those which
are otherwise cannot be concealed.

As to Slaves. All who are in the position of slaves should 1 6
regard their masters as deserving of the greatest
respect, so that the Name of God, and our
Teaching, may not be maligned.   Those who have Christian 2
masters should not think less of them because they are their
Brothers, but on the contrary they should serve them all the
better, because those who are to benefit by their good work
are dear to them as their fellow Christians.

IV.—CONCLUSION.

False Teaching. Those are the things to insist upon in your
teaching.   Any one who teaches otherwise, and 3
refuses his assent to sound instruction—the instruction of our Lord Jesus Christ—and to the teaching
of religion, is puffed up with conceit, not really knowing 4
anything, but having a morbid craving for discussions and
arguments.   Such things only give rise to envy, quarrelling,
recriminations, base suspicions, and incessant wrangling on 5
the part of these corrupt-minded people who have lost all
hold on the Truth, and who think of religion only as a source
of gain.   And a great source of gain religion is, 6
True Wealth. when it brings contentment with it! For we 7
brought nothing into the world, because we cannot even carry anything out of it.   So, with food and shelter, 8
we will be content.   Those who want to be rich fall into the 9
snares of temptation, and become the prey of many foolish
and harmful ambitions, which plunge people into Destruction
and Ruin.   Love of money is a source of all kinds of evil; 10
and in their eagerness to be rich some have wandered away
from the Faith, and have been pierced to the heart by many a
regret.

19 Deut 19. 15.

But do you, Servant of God, avoid all this. 11
Personal Exhortations. Aim at righteousness, piety, faith, love, endurance, gentleness. Run the great race of the 12 Faith, and win the Immortal Life. It was for this that you received the Call, and, in the presence of many witnesses, made the great profession of Faith. I urge you, as in the 13 sight of God, the source of all life, and of Christ Jesus who before Pontius Pilate made the great profession of Faith—I 14 urge you to keep his Command free from stain or reproach, until the Appearing of our Lord Jesus Christ. This will be 15 brought about in his own time by the one ever-blessed Potentate, the King of all kings and Lord of all lords, who 16 alone is possessed of immortality and dwells in unapproachable light, whom no man has ever seen or ever can see—to whom be ascribed honour and power for ever. Amen.

Urge upon those who are wealthy in this life not to pride 17 themselves, or fix their hopes, on so uncertain a thing as wealth, but on God, who gives us a wealth of enjoyment on every side. Urge upon them to show kindness, to exhibit a 18 wealth of good actions, to be open-handed and generous, storing up for themselves what in the future will prove to be 19 a good foundation, that they may gain the only true Life.

Timothy, guard what has been entrusted to you. Avoid the 20 profane prattle and contradictions of what some miscall 'theology,' for there are those who, while asserting their pro- 21 ficiency in it, have yet, as regards the Faith, gone altogether astray.

Blessing.   God bless you all.

TO TIMOTHY.

II.

THE SECOND LETTER TO TIMOTHY.

[DATE AND PLACE OF WRITING UNCERTAIN.]

WHAT has been said as to the history of the first of these two " Letters to Timothy" applies equally to the second.

This Letter contains warnings against false Teachers, and exhortations to an earnest discharge of duty. It has been supposed to be the last extant letter written by St. Paul.

TO

TIMOTHY.

II.

I.—INTRODUCTION.

Greeting. To Timothy, my dear Child,   1-2 **1**

FROM Paul who, by the will of God, is an Apostle of Christ
   Jesus, charged to proclaim the Life that comes from
   union with Christ Jesus.

May God, the Father, and Christ Jesus, our Lord, bless
   you, and be merciful to you, and give you peace.

An Appeal to   I am thankful to God, whom I serve, as my   3
Timothy. ancestors did, with a clear conscience, when I
remember you, as I never fail to do, in my prayers—night and
day alike, as I think of your tears, longing to see you, that my   4
happiness may be completed, now that I have been reminded   5
of the sincere faith that you have shown.   That faith was seen
first in your grandmother Lois and your mother Eunice, and
is now, I am convinced, in you also.   And that is my reason   6
for reminding you to stir into flame that gift of God, which is
yours through your ordination at my hands.   For the Spirit   7
which God gave us was not a spirit of cowardice, but a spirit
of power, love, and self-control.   Do not, therefore, be ashamed   8
of the testimony which we have to bear to our Lord, nor yet of
me who am a prisoner for him ; but join with me in suffering
for the Good News, as far as God enables you.   It was God   9
who saved us, and from him we received our solemn Call—
not as a reward for anything that we had done, but in fulfilment of his own loving purpose.   For that love was extended
to us, through Christ Jesus, before time began, and has now   10
been made apparent through the Appearing of our Saviour,
Christ Jesus ; who has made an end of Death, and has
brought Life and Immortality to light by that Good News, of   11
which I was myself appointed a Herald and Apostle, and

P

Teacher. That is why I am undergoing these sufferings; yet I feel no shame, for I know in whom I have put my faith, and am convinced that he is able to guard what I have entrusted to him until 'That Day.' Keep before you, as an example of sound teaching, all that you learnt from me as you listened with that faith and love which come from union with Christ Jesus. Guard by the help of the Holy Spirit, who is within us, the glorious trust that has been committed to you. **Onesiphorus.** You know, of course, that all our friends in Roman Asia turned their backs on me, and among them Phygellus and Hermogenes. May the Lord show mercy to the household of Onesiphorus; for he often cheered me and was not ashamed of my chains. On the contrary, when he arrived in Rome, he sought eagerly for me till he found me. The Lord grant that he may find mercy at the hands of the Lord on 'That Day.' The many services that he rendered at Ephesus you have the best means of knowing.

II.—INJUNCTIONS TO TIMOTHY.

The Service of the Good News. Do you, then, my Child, find strength in the help which comes from union with Christ Jesus; and what you learnt from me, in the presence of many listeners, entrust to reliable men, who will be able in their turn to teach others. Share hardships with me, as a true soldier of Christ Jesus. A soldier on active service, to please his superior officer, always avoids entangling himself in the affairs of ordinary life. No athlete is ever awarded the wreath of victory unless he has kept the rules. The labourer who does the work should be the first to receive a share of the fruits of the earth. Reflect upon what I say; the Lord will always help you to understand. Keep before your mind Jesus Christ, raised from the dead, a descendant of David, as told in the Good News entrusted to me; in the service of which I am suffering hardships, even to being put in fetters as a criminal. But the Message of God is not fettered; and that is why I submit to anything for the sake of God's People, that they also may obtain the Salvation which comes from union with Christ Jesus, and imperishable glory. How true this saying is— 'If we have shared his death, we shall also share his life. If we continue to endure, we shall also share his throne. If we should ever disown him, he, too, will disown us. If we lose our trust, he is still to be trusted, for he cannot be false to himself!'

The Danger of Controversy. Remind people of all this; urge them solemnly, as in the sight of God, to avoid controversy, a useless thing and the ruin of those who listen to it. Do your

12
13
14
15
16
17
18

1 2
2
3 4
5 6
7 8
9
10
11
12
13
14
15

12—18 Isa. 2. 11.

utmost to show yourself true to God, a workman with no reason to be ashamed, accurate in delivering the Message of the Truth. Avoid profane prattle. Those who indulge in it 16 only get deeper into irreligious ways, and their teaching will 17 spread like a cancer. Hymenaeus and Philetus are instances of this. They have gone completely astray as regards the 18 Truth ; they say that a resurrection has already taken place, and so upset some people's faith. Yet God's firm foundation 19 still stands unmoved, and it bears this inscription—

'THE LORD KNOWS THOSE WHO ARE HIS';
and this—

'LET ALL THOSE WHO USE THE NAME OF THE LORD TURN AWAY FROM WICKEDNESS.'

Now in a large house there are not only things of gold and 20 silver, but also others of wood and earthenware, some for better and some for common use. If, then, a man has escaped from 21 the pollution of such errors as I have mentioned, he will be like a thing kept for better use, set apart, serviceable to its owner, ready for any good purpose. Flee from the passions 22 of youth, but pursue righteousness, faith, love, and peace, in the company of those who, with a pure heart, invoke the Lord. Shun foolish and ignorant discussions, for you know that they 23 only breed quarrels ; and a Servant of the Lord should never 24 quarrel. He ought, on the contrary, to be courteous to every one, a skilful teacher, and forbearing. He should instruct 25 his opponents in a gentle spirit ; for, possibly, God may give them a repentance that will lead to a fuller knowledge of Truth, and they may yet come to a sober mind, and escape 26 from the snares of the Devil, when captured by the Lord's Servant to do the will of God.

Be sure of this, that in the last days difficult 1 **3**
Impending times will come. Men will be selfish, mercenary, 2
Evils. boastful, haughty, and blasphemous ; disobedient to their parents, ungrateful, impure, incapable of affection, 3 merciless, slanderous, wanting in self-control, brutal, careless of the right, treacherous, reckless, and puffed up with pride ; 4 they will love pleasure more than they love God ; and while 5 they retain the outward form of religion, they will not allow it to influence them. Turn your back on such men as these. For among them are to be found those who creep into homes 6 and captivate weak women—women who, loaded with sins, and slaves to all kinds of passions, are always learning, and 7 yet never able to attain to a real knowledge of the Truth. Just as Jannes and Jambres opposed Moses, so do these 8 people, in their turn, oppose the Truth. Their minds are corrupted, and, as regards the Faith, they are utterly worth-

¹⁹ Num. 16. 5 ; Isa. 26. 13.

less. They will not, however, make further progress; for their wicked folly will be plain to every one, just as that of Jannes and Jambres was.   But you, Timothy, were a close observer of my teaching, my conduct, my purposes, my faith, my forbearance, my love, and my patient endurance, as well as of my persecutions, and of the sufferings which I met with at Antioch, Iconium, and Lystra. You know what persecutions I underwent; and yet the Lord brought me safe out of all! Yes, and all who aim at living a religious life in union with Christ Jesus will have to suffer persecution; but wicked people and impostors will go from bad to worse, deceiving others and deceived themselves. You, however, must stand by what you learnt and accepted as true. You know who they were from whom you learnt it; and that, from your childhood, you have known the Sacred Writings, which can give you the wisdom that, through belief in Christ Jesus, leads to Salvation. Everything that is written under divine inspiration is helpful for teaching, for refuting error, for giving guidance, and for training others in righteousness; so that the Servant of God may be perfect himself, and perfectly equipped for every good action.

I solemnly charge you, in the sight of God and of Christ Jesus, who will one day judge the living and the dead—I charge you by his Appearing and by his Kingdom :—Proclaim the Message, be ready in season and out of season, convince, rebuke, encourage, never failing to instruct with forbearance. For a time will come when people will not tolerate sound teaching. They will follow their own wishes, and, in their itching for novelty, procure themselves a crowd of teachers. They will turn a deaf ear to the Truth, and give their attention to legends instead. But you, Timothy, must always be temperate. Face hardships; do the work of a Missionary; discharge all the duties of your Office.

As for me, my life blood is already being poured out; the time of my departure is close at hand. I have run the great Race; I have finished the Course; I have kept the Faith. And now the crown of righteousness awaits me, which the Lord, the just Judge, will give me on 'That Day'—and not only to me, but to all who have loved his Appearing.

III.—Conclusion.

Do your utmost to come to me soon; for Demas, **Personal Messages.** in his love for the world, has deserted me. He has gone to Thessalonica, Crescens to Galatia, and Titus to Dalmatia. There is no one but Luke with me. Pick up Mark on your way, and bring him with you, for he is

[8] Isa. 2. 11.

useful to me in my work. I have sent Tychicus to Ephesus. 12
Bring with you, when you come, the cloak which I left at 13
Troas with Carpus, and the books, especially the parch-
ments.   Alexander, the coppersmith, showed much ill- 14
feeling towards me. 'The Lord will give him what his actions
deserve.' Do you also, be on your guard against him, for he 15
is strongly opposed to our teaching.   At my first trial 16
no one stood by me. They all deserted me. May it never be
counted against them ! But the Lord came to my help and 17
strengthened me, in order that, through me, the proclamation
should be made so widely that all the Gentiles should hear it ;
and I was rescued ' out of the Lion's mouth.' The Lord will 18
rescue me from all evil, and bring me safe into his Heavenly
Kingdom. All glory to him for ever and ever ! Amen.

Give my greeting to Prisca and Aquila, and to 19
Farewells and the household of Onesiphorus.
Blessing.   Erastus remained at Corinth, and I left 20
Trophimus ill at Miletus.   Do your utmost to come 21
before winter.
   Eubulus, Pudens, Linus and Claudia send you their greet-
ings, and so do all our Brothers.

May the Lord be with your soul. God bless you all. 22

14 Ps. 62. 12 ; Prov. 24. 12.   17 Ps. 22. 21.

TO TITUS.

THE LETTER TO TITUS.

[DATE AND PLACE OF WRITING UNCERTAIN.]

NOTHING is known as to the history of this Letter.

Titus, to whom it is addressed, was a Gentile by birth, but, after his conversion, became a companion of St. Paul on his Missionary Journeys, and often served as his Messenger (2 Cor. 8. 23 ; 12. 18). According to this Letter, he was placed by the Apostle in charge of the Church in the island of Crete.

TO
TITUS.

I.—INTRODUCTION.

Greeting. To Titus, my true Child in our one Faith, 1-4 **1**
From Paul, a servant of God, and an Apostle of
Jesus Christ, charged to strengthen the faith of God's
Chosen People, and their knowledge of that Truth which
makes for godliness and is based on the hope of Immortal
Life, which God, who never lies, promised before the
ages began, and has revealed at his own time in his
Message, with the proclamation of which I was entrusted
by the command of God our Saviour.
May God, the Father, and Christ Jesus, our Saviour, bless
you and give you peace.

II.—THE MISSION OF TITUS IN CRETE.

My reason for leaving you in Crete was that **5**
The you might put in order what had been left un-
Appointment settled, and appoint Officers of the Church in the
of Officers
of the Church. various towns, as I myself directed you. They **6**
are to be men of irreproachable character, who
are faithful husbands, whose children are Christians and have
never been charged with dissolute conduct or have been unruly.
For a Presiding-Officer, as God's steward, ought to be a man **7**
of irreproachable character; not self-willed or quick-tempered,
nor addicted to drink or to brawling or to questionable
money-making. On the contrary, he should be hospitable, **8**
eager for the right, discreet, upright, a man of holy life and
capable of self-restraint, who holds doctrine that can be relied **9**
on as being in accordance with the accepted Teaching ; so
that he may be able to encourage others by sound teaching, as
well as to refute our opponents.

p*

all wickedness, and to purify for himself a People who should be peculiarly his own and eager to do good.

DIRECTIONS as to his Teaching. — Speak of all this, and encourage and rebuke with all authority. Do not let any one despise you.

Remind your hearers to respect and obey the Powers that be, to be ready for every kind of good work, to speak ill of no one, to avoid quarrelling, to be forbearing, and under all circumstances to show a gentle spirit in dealing with others, whoever they may be. There was, you remember, a time when we ourselves were foolish, disobedient, misled, slaves to all kinds of passions and vices, living in a spirit of malice and envy, detested ourselves and hating one another. But, when the kindness of God our Saviour and his love for man were revealed, he saved us, not as the result of any righteous actions that we had done, but in fulfilment of his merciful purposes. He saved us by that Washing which was a new birth to us, and by the renewing power of the Holy Spirit, which he poured out upon us abundantly through Jesus Christ our Saviour ; that, having been pronounced righteous through his loving-kindness, we might enter on our inheritance with the hope of Immortal Life. How true that saying is ! And it is on these subjects that I desire you to speak special stress, so that those who have a firm faith to trust in God may be careful to devote themselves to doing good. Such subjects are excellent in themselves, and of real use to mankind. But have nothing to do with foolish discussions, or with genealogies, or with controversy, or disputes about the Law. They are useless and futile. If a man disobeying you, after warning him once or twice, have nothing more to say to him. You may be sure that such a man has forsaken the Truth and is in the wrong ; he stands self-condemned.

CLOSING MESSAGE AND GREETING. — As soon as I send Artemas or Tychicus to you, join me as quickly as possible at Nicopolis, for I have arranged to spend the winter there. Do your best to help Zenas, the Teacher of the Law, and Apollos on their way, and see that they want for nothing. Let all our People learn to devote themselves to doing good, so as to meet the most pressing needs, and that their lives may not be unfruitful.

All who are with me here send you their greeting. Give my greeting to our friends in the Faith.

God bless you all.

TO HEBREWS.

A LETTER TO JEWISH CHRISTIANS.

[DATE AND PLACE OF WRITING UNCERTAIN.]

THE Traditions concerning the authorship of this Letter are unreliable. From the Letter itself it may be safely inferred that the writer was a man of intellectual power, that he was familiar with the modes of thought prevalent in Alexandria, that his home and work lay among Jewish Christians, and that he was in some way connected with those teachers who looked to St. Paul as their leader. It is certain that the Apostle Paul was not the author. The Letter has been attributed with some show of probability to several writers, in particular to Barnabas (Acts 11. 22—24; 13. 1—5) and to Apollos (Acts 18. 24—28).

The Jewish Christians to whom the Letter is addressed were a community living, possibly, in Palestine, but more probably in Alexandria or in Rome; and the primary object of the Letter was to explain, to those who were well acquainted with the ritual of the old Covenant, the fulfilment of its types in the heavenly realities of the Christian Faith.

From certain passages in the Letter it has been inferred that, at the time when it was written, the worship of the Temple had not been entirely swept away, as it was by the fall of Jerusalem in 70 A.D.

TO
HEBREWS.

I.—THE PARAMOUNT POSITION OF THE CHRIST AS THE MEDIATOR OF THE NEW REVELATION.

His Superiority to Angels. God, who, of old, at many times and in many ways, spoke to our ancestors, by the Prophets, has in these latter days spoken to us by the Son, whom he appointed the heir of all things, and through whom he made the universe. For he is the radiance of the Glory of God and the very expression of his Being, upholding all creation by the power of his word ; and, when he had made an expiation for the sins of men, he 'took his seat at the right hand' of God's Majesty on high, having shown himself as much greater than the angels as the Name that he has inherited surpasses theirs.

For to which of the angels did God ever say—

'Thou art my Son ; this day I have become thy Father'?

or again—

'I will be to him a Father, and he shall be to me a Son'?

And again, when God brought the First-born into the world, he said—

'Let all the angels of God bow down before him.'

Speaking of the angels, he said—

'He makes the winds his angels
And the fiery flames his servants';

while of the Son he said—

'God is thy throne for ever and ever ;
The sceptre of his Kingdom is the sceptre of Justice ;
Thou lovest righteousness and hatest iniquity ;
Therefore God, thy God, has anointed thee with the festal oil
more abundantly than thy peers.'

---

3 Ps. 110. 1. 5 Ps. 2. 7 ; 2 Sam. 7. 14. 6 Deut. 32. 43 (Septuagint) ; Ps. 97. 7.
7 Ps. 104. 4. 8—9 Ps. 45. 6—7.

Again—   10

' Thou, Lord, in the beginning didst lay the foundation of the
          earth,
    And the heavens are the work of thy hands.
        They shall perish, but thou remainest ;   11
    As a garment they shall all grow old ;
    As a mantle thou wilt fold them up,   12
    And as a garment they shall be changed,
        But thou art the same, and thy years shall know no end.'

To which of the angels has God ever said—   13

          ' Sit thou at my right hand
          Until I put thy enemies as a stool for thy feet ' ?

Are not all the angels spirits in the service of God, sent out to   14
minister for the sake of those who are destined to obtain
Salvation ?

    Therefore we must give still more heed to what we were   1   **2**
taught, for fear we should drift away. For, if the Message   2
which was delivered by angels had its authority confirmed, so
that every offence against it, or neglect of it, met with a
fitting requital, how can we, of all people, expect to escape, if   3
we disregard so great a Salvation ? It was the Master who
at the outset spoke of this Salvation, and its authority
was confirmed for us by those who heard him, while God   4
himself added his testimony to it by signs, and marvels, and
many different miracles, as well as by imparting the Holy
Spirit as he saw fit.

    God has not given to angels the control of that Future   5
World of which we are speaking ! No ; a writer has declared   6
somewhere—

    ' What is Man that thou should'st remember him ?
      Or a Son of Man that thou should'st regard him ?
    Thou hast made him, for a while, lower than angels ;   7
      With glory and honour thou hast crowned him ;
    Thou hast set him over all that thy hands have made ;
      Thou hast placed all things beneath his feet.'   8

This ' placing of everything ' under man means that there was
nothing which was not placed under him. As yet, however,
we do not see everything placed under man. What our eyes   9
do see is Jesus, who was made for a while lower than angels,
now, because of his sufferings and death, crowned with
glory and honour ; so that his tasting the bitterness of
death should, in God's loving-kindness, be on behalf of all
mankind.   It was, indeed, fitting that God, for whom   10
and through whom all things exist, should, when leading
many sons to glory, make the author of their Salvation perfect

10—12 Ps. 102. 25—27.   13 Ps. 110. 1.   6—9 Ps. 8. 4—6.

through suffering. For he who purifies, and those whom he 11
purifies, all spring from One ; and therefore he is not ashamed
to call them ' Brothers.' He says— 12

> ' I will tell of thy Name to my Brothers,
> In the midst of the congregation I will sing thy praise.'

And again— 13

> 'As for me, I will put my trust in God.'

And yet again—

> ' See, here am I and the children whom God gave me.'

Therefore, since human nature is the common heritage of 14
' the Children,' Jesus also shared it, in order that by death he
might render powerless him whose power lies in death—that
is, the Devil—and so might deliver all those who, from 15
fear of death, had all their lives been living in slavery. It 16
was not, surely, to the help of the angels that Jesus came,
but ' to the help of the descendants of Abraham.' And 17
consequently it was necessary that he should in all points be
made like ' his Brothers,' in order that he might prove a
merciful as well as a faithful High Priest in man's relations
with God, for the purpose of expiating the sins of his People.
The fact that he himself suffered under temptation enables 18
him to help those who are tempted.

Therefore, Christian Brothers, you who, all 1 **3**
His Superiority to Moses and Joshua. alike, have received the Call from Heaven, fix
your attention on Jesus, the Apostle and High
Priest of our Religion. See how faithful he was 2
to the God who appointed him, as Moses was in the whole
House of God. He has been deemed worthy of far higher 3
honour than Moses, just as the founder of the House is
held in greater regard than the House itself. For every 4
House has its founder, and the founder of the universe is
God. While the faithful service of Moses in the whole 5
House of God was that of a servant, whose duty was to bear
testimony to a Message still to come, the faithfulness of 6
Christ was that of a Son set over the House of God. And we
are his House—if only we retain, unshaken to the end, the
courage and confidence inspired by our hope.

Therefore, as the Holy Spirit says— 7

> ' If to-day you hear God's voice,
> Harden not your hearts, as when Israel provoked me 8
>   On the day when they tried my patience in the desert,
> Where your ancestors tried my forbearance, 9
>   And saw my mighty deeds for forty years.

11–12 Ps. 22. 22,   13–14 Isa. 8. 17–18.   16 Isa. 41. 8–9.   17 Ps. 22. 22.
2–5 Num. 12. 7,

Therefore I was sorely vexed with that generation,   10
And I said—" Their hearts are always straying ;
    They have never learnt my ways " ;
While in my wrath I swore—   11
    " They shall never enter upon my Rest." '

Be careful, Brothers, that there is never found in any one of   12
you a wicked and faithless heart, shown by his separating
himself from the Living God.   Rather encourage one another   13
daily— while there is a ' To-day '—to prevent any one among
you from being hardened by the deceitfulness of Sin.   For   14
we now all share in the Christ, if indeed we retain, unshaken
to the end, the confidence that we had at the first.   To use the   15
words of Scripture—

    ' If to-day you hear God's voice,
    Harden not your hearts, as when Israel provoked me.'

Who were they who heard God speak and yet provoked him ?   16
Were not they all those who left Egypt under the leadership
of Moses ?   And with whom was it that God was sorely vexed   17
for forty years ?   Was not it with those who had sinned, and
who fell dead in the desert ?   And who were they to whom   18
God swore that they should not enter upon his rest, if not
those who had proved faithless ?   We see, then, that they   19
failed to enter upon it because of their want of faith.   We   1   **4**
must, therefore, be very careful, though there is a promise
still standing that we shall enter upon God's Rest, that none
of you even appear to have missed it.   For we have had the   2
Good News told us just as they had.   But the Message which
they heard did them no good, since they did not share the
faith of those who were attentive to it.   Upon that Rest   3
we who have believed are now entering.   As God has said—

    ' In my wrath I swore—
    " They shall never enter upon my Rest ; " '

Although God's work was finished at the creation of the world ;
for, in a passage referring to the seventh day, you will find   4
these words—

    ' God rested upon the seventh day after all his work.'

On the other hand, we read in that passage—   5

    ' They shall never enter upon my Rest.'

Since, then, there is still a promise that some shall enter   6
upon this Rest, and since those who were first told the
Good News did not enter upon it, because of their disbelief,
again God fixed a day.   ' To-day,' he said, speaking after a   7

7—19 Ps. 95. 7—11.   17 Num. 14. 29.   1—3 Ps. 95. 11.   3—4 Gen. 2, 2,
                   5—7 Ps. 95. 11, 7—8,

long interval through the mouth of David, in the passage
already quoted—

> ' If to-day you hear God's voice
> Harden not your hearts.'

Now if Joshua had given 'Rest' to the people, God would 8
not have spoken of another and later day. There is, then, a 9
Sabbath-Rest still awaiting God's People. For he who 10
enters upon God's Rest does himself rest after his work,
just as God did. Let us, therefore, make every effort 11
to enter upon that Rest, so that none of us fall through such
disbelief as that of which we have had an example. God's 12
Message is a living and active power, sharper than any two-
edged sword, piercing its way till it penetrates soul and
spirit—not the joints only but the very marrow—and detecting
the inmost thoughts and purposes of the mind. There is no 13
created thing that can hide itself from the sight of God.
Everything is exposed and laid bare before the eyes of him
to whom we have to give account.

We have, then, in Jesus, the Son of God, a great High 14
Priest who has passed into the highest Heaven; let us, therefore, hold fast to the Faith which we have professed. Our 15
High Priest is not one unable to sympathize with our weaknesses, but one who has in every way been tempted, exactly as
we have been, but without sinning. Therefore, let us draw 16
near boldly to the Throne of Love, to find pity and love for
the hour of need.

His Superiority to Aaron. Every High Priest, taken from among men, is 1 **5**
appointed as a representative of his fellow-men in
their relations with God, to offer both gifts and
sacrifices in expiation of sins. And he is able to sympathize 2
with the ignorant and deluded, since he is himself subject to
weakness, and is therefore bound to offer sacrifices for sins, not 3
only for the People, but equally so for himself. Nor does any 4
one take that high office upon himself, till he has been called
to do so by God, as Aaron was. In the same way, even 5
the Christ did not take the honour of the High Priesthood upon
himself, but he was appointed by him who said to him—

> ' Thou art my Son; this day I have become thy Father';

and on another occasion also— 6

> ' Thou art a priest for all time of the order of Melchizedek.'

Jesus, in the days of his earthly life, offered prayers and supplica- 7
tions, with earnest cries and with tears, to him who was able
to save him from death; and he was heard because of his

devout submission. Son though he was, he learnt obedience 8
from his sufferings; and, being made perfect, he became to all 9
those who obey him the source of eternal Salvation, while
God himself pronounced him a High Priest of the order of 10
Melchizedek.

The Superiority of the Christian's Position. Now on this subject I have much to say, but it 11
is difficult to explain it to you, because you have
shown yourselves so slow to learn. For whereas, 12
considering the time that has elapsed, you
ought to be teaching others, you still need
some one to teach you the very alphabet of the Divine Revelation, and need again to be fed with 'milk' instead of with
'solid food.' For every one who still has to take 'milk' 13
knows nothing of the Teaching of Righteousness; he is a
mere infant. But 'solid food' is for Christians of mature 14
faith—those whose faculties have been trained by practice to
distinguish right from wrong. Therefore, let us leave 1 **6**
behind the elementary teaching about the Christ and press on
to perfection, not always laying over again a foundation of
repentance for a lifeless formality, of faith in God—teaching 2
concerning baptisms and the laying on of hands, the resurrection of the dead and a final judgement. Yes and, with God's 3
help, we will. For if those who were once for all 4
brought into the Light, and learnt to appreciate the gift from
Heaven, and came to share in the Holy Spirit, and learnt 5
to appreciate the beauty of the Divine Message, and the
new powers of the Coming Age—if those, I say, fell away, it 6
would be impossible to bring them again to repentance; they
would be crucifying the Son of God over again for themselves,
and exposing him to open contempt. Ground that drinks in 7
the showers that from time to time fall upon it, and produces
vegetation useful to those for whom it is tilled, receives a
blessing from God; but, if it 'bears thorns and thistles,' it is 8
regarded as worthless, it is in danger of being 'cursed,' and its
end will be the fire.

But about you, dear friends, even though we speak in this 9
way, we are confident of better things—of things that point to
your Salvation. For God is not unjust; he will not forget the 10
work that you did, and the love that you showed for his Name,
in sending help to your fellow Christians—as you are still doing.
But our great desire is that every one of you should be equally 11
earnest to attain to a full conviction that our hope will be
fulfilled, and that you should keep that hope to the end. Then 12
you will not show yourselves slow to learn, but you will copy
those who, through faith and patience, are now entering upon
the enjoyment of God's promises.

9 Isa. 43. 17.   10 Ps. 110. 4.   7 Gen. 1. 11—12.   8 Gen. 3. 17—18.

When God gave his promise to Abraham, since there was no   13
one greater by whom he could swear, he swore by himself.
His words were—   14

    ' I will assuredly bless thee and increase thy numbers.'

And so, after patiently waiting, Abraham obtained the fulfil-   15
ment of God's promise. Men, of course, swear by what is   16
greater than themselves, and with them an oath is accepted as
putting a matter beyond all dispute. And therefore God, in his   17
desire to show, with unmistakeable plainness, to those who
were to enter on the enjoyment of what he had promised, the
unchangeableness of his purpose, bound himself with an oath.
For he intended us to find great encouragement in these two   18
unchangeable things, which make it impossible for God to
prove false—we, I mean, who fled for safety where we might
lay hold on the hope set before us. This hope is a very anchor   19
for our souls, secure and strong, and it ' reaches into the
Sanctuary that lies behind the Curtain,' where Jesus, our Fore-   20
runner, has entered on our behalf, after being made for all
time a High Priest of the order of Melchizedek.

II.—THE PARAMOUNT PRIESTHOOD OF THE CHRIST.

Parallel with the Priesthood of Melchizedek.
It was this Melchizedek, King of Salem and   1   **7**
Priest of the Most High God, who met Abraham
returning from the slaughter of the kings, and
gave him his blessing; and it was to him that   2
Abraham allotted a tithe of all the spoil. The meaning of his
name is ' King of Righteousness,' and besides that, he was
also King of Salem, which means ' King of Peace.' There is   3
no record of his father, or mother, or lineage, nor again of
any beginning of his days, or end of his life. In this he
resembles the Son of God, and stands before us as a priest
whose priesthood is continuous.

Consider, then, the importance of this Melchizedek, to whom   4
even the Patriarch Abraham himself gave a tithe of the choicest
spoils. Those descendants of Levi, who are from time to   5
time appointed to the priesthood, are directed to collect tithes
from the people in accordance with the Law—that is from
their own Brothers, although they also are descended from
Abraham. But Melchizedek, although not of this lineage,   6
received tithes from Abraham, and gave his blessing to the
very man who had God's promises. Now no one can dispute   7
that it is the superior who blesses the inferior. In the one case   8
the tithes are received by mortal men ; in the other case by one
about whom there is the statement that his life still continues.

13—14 Gen. 22. 16—17.   19 Lev. 16. 2—12.   20 Ps. 110. 4.   1—3 Gen. 14. 17—19;
Ps. 110. 4.   4—10 Gen. 14. 17—20.

Moreover, in a sense, even Levi, who is the receiver of the 9
tithes, has, through Abraham, paid tithes; for Levi was still 10
in the body of his ancestor when Melchizedek met Abraham.

If, then, Perfection had been attainable through the 11
Levitical priesthood—and it was under this priesthood that
the people received the Law—why was it still necessary that a
priest of a different order should appear, a priest of the order
of Melchizedek and not of the order of Aaron? With the 12
change of the priesthood a change of the Law became a
necessity.   And he of whom all this is said belonged to quite a 13
different tribe, no member of which has ever served at the altar.
For it is plain that our Lord has sprung from the tribe of 14
Judah, though of that tribe Moses said nothing about their
being priests.   All this becomes even yet plainer when 15
we remember that a new priest has appeared, resembling
Melchizedek, and that he was appointed, not under a Law 16
regulating only earthly matters, but by virtue of a life beyond
the reach of death; for that is the meaning of the declaration— 17

'Thou art for all time a priest of the order of Melchizedek.'

On the one hand, we have the abolition of a previous regulation 18
as being both inefficient and useless (for the Law never brought 19
anything to perfection); and, on the other hand, we have the
introduction of a better hope, which enables us to draw near
to God.   Then again, the appointment of this new priest 20
was ratified by an oath, which is not so with the Levitical
priests, but his appointment was ratified by an oath, when God 21
said to him—

'The Lord has sworn, and will not change, "Thou art a
priest for all time."'

And the oath shows the corresponding superiority of the Coven- 22
ant of which Jesus is appointed the surety.   Again, new 23
Levitical priests are continually being appointed, because death
prevents their remaining in office; but Jesus remains for all 24
time, and therefore the priesthood that he holds is never liable
to pass to another.   And that is why he is able to save 25
perfectly those who come to God through him, living for ever,
as he does, to intercede on their behalf.

This was the High Priest that we needed—holy, innocent, 26
spotless, withdrawn from sinners, exalted above the highest
Heaven, one who has no need to offer sacrifices daily as those 27
High Priests have, first for their own sins, and then for those
of the People.   For this he did once and for all, when he
offered himself as the sacrifice.   The Law appoints as High 28
Priests men who are liable to infirmity; but the words of God's
oath, which was later than the Law, name the Son as, for all
time, the perfect Priest.

Superior to the Levitical Priesthood. To sum up what I have been saying:—Such is **1 8** the High Priest that we have, one who 'has taken his seat at the right hand' of the throne of God's Majesty in Heaven, where he ministers in the **2** Sanctuary, in that true Tabernacle set up by the Lord and not by man. Every High Priest is appointed for the purpose of **3** offering gifts and sacrifices to God; it follows, therefore, that this High Priest must have some offering to make. If he **4** were, however, still upon earth, he would not even be a priest, since there are already priests who offer the gifts as the Law directs. (These priests, it is true, are engaged in a **5** service which is only a copy and shadow of the heavenly realities, as is shown by the directions given to Moses when he was about to construct the Tabernacle. 'Look to it,' are the words, 'that thou make every part in accordance with the pattern shown thee on the mountain.') But Jesus, **6** as we see, has obtained a ministry as far excelling theirs, as the Covenant of which he is the intermediary, based, as it is, on better promises, excels the former Covenant. If that first Covenant had been faultless, there would have **7** been no occasion for a second. But, finding fault with the **8** people, God says—

'"Behold, a time is coming," says the Lord,
"When I will ratify a new Covenant with the People of
Israel and with the People of Judah—
Not such a Covenant as I made with their ancestors **9**
On the day when I took them by the hand to lead them out
of the land of Egypt.
For they did not abide by their Covenant with me,
And therefore I disregarded them," says the Lord.
"This is the Covenant that I will make with the People of Israel **10**
After those days," says the Lord.
"I will impress my laws on their minds,
And will inscribe them on their hearts;
And I will be their God,
And they shall be my People.
There shall be no need for every man to instruct his fellow- **11**
citizen,
Or for a man to say to his Brother 'Learn to know the
Lord';
For every one will know me,
From the lowest to the highest.
For I will be merciful to their wrong-doings, **12**
And I will no longer remember their sins."'

By speaking of a 'new' Covenant, God at once renders the **13** former Covenant obsolete; and whatever becomes obsolete and loses its force is virtually annulled.

---

¹ Ps. 110. 1.   ² Num. 24. 6.   ⁵ Exod. 25. 40.   ⁸⁻¹³ Jer. 31. 31—34.

III.—The Superiority of the New Revelation to the Old.

It is true that even the first Covenant had its regulations for divine worship, and its Sanctuary—though only a material one. For a Tabernacle was constructed, with an outer part which contained the stand for the lamps, and the table, and the consecrated bread. This is called the Sanctuary. The part of the Tabernacle behind the second Curtain is called the Inner Sanctuary. In it is the gold incense-altar, and the Ark containing the Covenant, completely covered with gold. In the Ark is a gold casket containing the manna, Aaron's rod that budded, and the tablets on which the Covenant was written ; while above it, and overshadowing the Cover on which atonement was made, are the Cherubim of the Presence. But I must not now dwell on these things in detail. Such, then, was the arrangement of the Tabernacle. Into the outer part priests are constantly going, in the discharge of their sacred duties ; but into the inner only the High Priest goes, and that but once a year, and never without taking the blood of a victim, which he offers on his own behalf, and on behalf of the errors of the People. By this the Holy Spirit is teaching that the way into the Sanctuary was hidden, as long as the outer part of the Tabernacle still remained. For that was only a type, to continue down to the present time ; and, in keeping with it, both gifts and sacrifices are offered, though incapable of satisfying the conscience of the worshipper ; the whole system being concerned only with food and drink and various ablutions—external ceremonials imposed until the coming of the New Order.

But, when Christ came, he appeared as High Priest of that Better System which was established ; and he entered through that nobler and more perfect ' Tabernacle,' not made by human hands—that is to say, not a part of this present creation. Nor was it with the blood of goats and calves, but with his own blood, that he entered, once and for all, into the Sanctuary, and obtained our eternal deliverance. For, if the blood of goats and bulls, and the sprinkling of the ashes of a heifer, purify those who have been defiled (as far as ceremonial purification goes), how much more will the blood of the Christ, who, through his eternal Spirit, offered himself up to God as a victim without blemish, purify our consciences from a lifeless formality, and fit us for the service of the Living God ! And that is why he is the intermediary of a new Covenant : in order that, as a death has taken place to effect a

As regards its Sanctuary.

As regards its Power to purify.

1
2
3
4
5
6
7
8
9
10
11
12
13
14
15

9

deliverance from the offences committed under the first Covenant, those who have received the Call may obtain the eternal
inheritance promised to them. Whenever such a Covenant as a   16
will is in question, the death of the testator must of necessity
be alleged.   For such a Covenant takes effect only upon   17
death ; it does not come into force as long as the testator is
alive.   This explains why even the first Covenant was   18
not ratified without the shedding of blood. For, when every   19
command had been announced to all the people by Moses in
accordance with the Law, he took the blood of the calves and
of the goats, with water, scarlet wool, and a bunch of hyssop,
and sprinkled even the Book of the Law, as well as all the
people, saying, as he did so—"This is the blood that renders   20
valid the Covenant which God has commanded to be made
with you." And in the same way he also sprinkled with the   21
blood the Tabernacle and all the things that were used in
public worship. Indeed, under the Law, almost everything is   22
purified with blood ; and, unless blood is shed, no forgiveness
is to be obtained.

            While, then, it was necessary for the copies of   23
As regards the heavenly realities to be purified by such
its High means as these, the heavenly realities themselves
Priest. required better sacrifices. For it was not into a   24
Sanctuary made by human hands, which merely foreshadowed
the true one, that Christ entered, but into Heaven itself, that
he might now appear in the presence of God on our behalf.
Nor yet was it to offer himself many times, as year after year   25
the High Priest entered the Sanctuary with an offering of
blood—but not his own blood ; for then Christ would have had   26
to undergo death many times since the creation of the world.
But now, once and for all, at the close of the age, he has
appeared, in order to abolish sin by the sacrifice of himself.
And, as it is ordained for men to die but once (death being   27
followed by judgement), so it is with the Christ. He was   28
offered up once and for all, to 'bear away the sins of many';
and the second time he will appear—but without any burden
of sin—to those who are waiting for him, to bring Salvation.

            The Law, though able to foreshadow the Better   1 **10**
As regards System which was coming, never had its actual
its substance. Its priests, with those sacrifices
Sacrifices. which they offer continuously year after year, can
never make those who come to worship perfect. Otherwise,   2
would not the offering of these sacrifices have been abandoned,
as the worshippers, having been once purified, would
have had their consciences clear from sins ? But, on the   3
contrary, these sacrifices recall their sins to mind year after
year.   For the blood of bulls and goats is powerless to remove 4

[20] Exod. 24. 8.   [28] Isa. 53. 12.

sins.   That is why, when he was coming into the world,   5
the Christ declared—

> ' Sacrifice and offering thou dost not desire, but thou dost pro-
> vide for me a body ;
>   Thou dost take no pleasure in burnt offerings and sacrifices   6
>   for sin.
>   So I said, "See, I have come" (as is written of me in the pages   7
>   of the Book),
>   "To do thy will, O God." '

First come the words—'Thou dost not desire, nor dost   8
thou take pleasure in, sacrifices, offerings, burnt offerings,
and sacrifices for sin' (offerings regularly made under the
Law), and then there is added—'See, I have come to do thy   9
will.' The former sacrifices are set aside to be replaced by
the latter. And it is in the fulfilment of the will of God that   10
we have been purified by the sacrifice, once and for all, of
the body of Jesus Christ.   Every other priest stands day   11
after day at his ministrations, and offers the same sacrifices
over and over again—sacrifices that can never take sins away.
But this priest, after he had offered one sacrifice for sins,   12
which should serve for all time, 'took his seat at the right
hand of God,' and has since then been waiting 'for his enemies   13
to be put as a stool for his feet.' By a single offering he   14
has made perfect for all time those who are being purified.   We have also the testimony of the Holy Spirit.   15
For, after saying—

> ' " This is the Covenant that I will make with them   16
>   After those days," says the Lord ;
> " I will impress my laws on their hearts,
>   And will inscribe them on their minds," '

then we have—

> ' And their sins and their iniquities I will no longer remember.'   17

And, when these are forgiven, there is no further need of an   18
offering for sin.

IV.—Encouragement and Warning based on the previous Teaching.

Therefore, Brothers, since we may enter the Sanctuary with   19
confidence, in virtue of the blood of Jesus, by the way which
he inaugurated for us—a new and living way, a way through   20
the Sanctuary Curtain (that is, his human nature) ; and, since   21
we have in him 'a great priest set over the House of God,' let   22

5—10 Ps. 40. 6—8.   12—13 Ps. 110. 1.   16—17 Jer. 31. 33—34.   21 Zech. 6. 11—13 ;
Num. 12. 7.

us draw near to God in all sincerity of heart and in perfect faith, with our hearts purified by the sprinkled blood from all consciousness of wrong, and with our bodies washed with pure water. Let us maintain the confession of our hope unshaken, for he who has given us his promise will not fail us. 23 Let us vie with one another in a rivalry of love and noble 24 actions. And let us not, as some do, cease to meet together ; 25 but, on the contrary, let us encourage one another, and all the more, now that you see the Day drawing near.

Remember, if we sin willfully after we have gained a full 26 knowledge of the Truth, there can be no further sacrifice for sin ; there is only a fearful anticipation of judgement, and a 27 burning indignation which will destroy all opponents. When 28 a man disregarded the Law of Moses, he was, on the evidence of two or three witnesses, put to death without pity. How 29 much worse then, think you, will be the punishment deserved by those who have trampled underfoot the Son of God, who have treated the blood that rendered the Covenant valid— the very blood by which they were purified—as of no account, and who have outraged the Spirit of Love ? We know who it 30 was that said—

> ' It is for me to avenge, I will requite ' ;

and again—
> ' The Lord will judge his people.'

It is a fearful thing to fall into the hands of the Living God. 31

Call to mind those early days in which, after you had 32 received the Light, you patiently underwent a long and painful conflict. Sometimes, in consequence of the taunts 33 and injuries heaped upon you, you became a public spectacle ; and sometimes you suffered through having shown yourselves to be the friends of men who were in the very position in which you had been. For you not only sympathised with 34 those who were in prison, but you even took the confiscation of your possessions joyfully, knowing, as you did, that you had in yourselves a greater possession and a lasting one. Do 35 not, therefore, abandon the confidence that you have gained, for it has a great reward awaiting it. You still have need of 36 patient endurance, in order that, when you have done God's will, you may obtain the fulfilment of his promise.

> ' For there is indeed but a very little while 37
> Ere He who is Coming will have come, without delay ;
> And through faith the Righteous man shall find his Life, 38
> But, if a man draws back, my heart can find no pleasure in him.'

But we do not belong to those who draw back, to their Ruin, 39 but to those who have faith, to the saving of their souls.

[27] Isa. 26. 11 (Septuagint). [28] Deut. 17. 6. [29] Exod. 24. 8. [30] Deut. 32. 35—36.
[37-39] Isa. 26. 20 ; Hab. 2. 3. 4.

V.—HEROES OF FAITH.

The Power of Faith. Faith is the realization of things hoped for—the proof of things not seen. And it was for faith that the men of old were renowned. 1 2

Faith enables us to perceive that the universe was created at the bidding of God—so that we know that what we see was not made out of visible things. Faith made the sacrifice which Abel offered to God a better sacrifice than Cain's, and won him renown as a righteous man, God himself establishing his renown by accepting his gifts; and it is by the example of his faith that Abel, though dead, still speaks. Faith led to Enoch's removal from earth, that he might not experience death. 'He could not be found because God had removed him.' For, before his removal, he was renowned as having pleased God; but without faith it is impossible to please him, for he who comes to God must believe that God exists, and that he rewards those who seek for him. It was faith that enabled Noah, after he had received the divine warning about what could not then be foreseen, to build, in reverent obedience, an ark in which to save his family. By his faith he condemned the world, and became possessed of that righteousness which follows upon faith. It was faith that enabled Abraham to obey the Call that he received, and to set out for the place which he was afterwards to obtain as his own; and he set out not knowing where he was going. It was faith that made him go to live as an emigrant in the Promised Land—as in a strange country—living there in tents with Isaac and Jacob, who shared the promise with him. For he was looking for the City with the sure foundations, whose architect and builder is God. Again, it was faith that enabled Sarah to conceive (though she was past the age for child-bearing), because she felt sure that he who had given her the promise would not fail her. And so from one man—and that when his powers were dead—there sprang a people as numerous 'as the stars in the heavens or the countless grains of sand upon the shore.' 3 4 5 6 7 8 9 10 11 12

All these died sustained by faith. They did not obtain the promised blessings, but they saw them from a distance and welcomed the sight, and they acknowledged themselves to be only aliens and strangers on the earth. Those who speak thus show plainly that they are seeking their fatherland. If they had been thinking of the land that they had left, they could have found opportunities to return. But no, they were longing for a better, a heavenly, land! And therefore God was not ashamed to be called their God; indeed he had already prepared them a city. 13 14 15 16

---

4 Gen. 4. 4.   5-6 Gen. 5. 24.   8 Gen. 12, 1.   12 Gen. 22. 17; 32. 12.
13 1 Chron. 29. 15; Ps. 39. 12; Gen. 23. 4.

It was faith that enabled Abraham, when put to the test, to   17
offer Isaac as a sacrifice—he who had received the promises
offering up his only son, of whom it had been said—   18

> ' It is through Isaac that there shall be descendants to bear
> thy name.'

For he argued that God was able even to raise a man from   19
the dead—and indeed, figuratively speaking, Abraham did
receive Isaac back from the dead.   It was faith that   20
enabled Isaac to bless Jacob and Esau, even with regard to
the future.   Faith enabled Jacob, when dying, to give   21
his blessing to each of the sons of Joseph, and ' to bow himself
in worship as he leant upon the top of his staff.'   Faith   22
caused Joseph, when his end was near, to speak of the future
migration of the Israelites, and to give instructions with regard
to his bones.   Faith caused the parents of Moses to hide   23
the child for three months after his birth, for they saw that he
was a beautiful child ; and they would not respect the King's
order.   It was faith that caused Moses, when he was   24
grown up, to refuse the title of ' Son of a Daughter of
Pharaoh.' He preferred sharing the hardships of God's People   25
to enjoying the short-lived pleasures of sin. For he counted   26
' the reproaches that are heaped upon the Christ' of greater
value than the treasures of Egypt, looking forward, as he did,
to the reward awaiting him.   Faith caused him to leave   27
Egypt, though undaunted by the King's anger, for he was
strengthened in his endurance by the vision of the invisible
God.   Faith led him to institute the Passover and the   28
Sprinkling of the Blood, so that the Destroyer might not
touch the eldest children of the Israelites.   Faith enabled   29
the people to cross the Red Sea, as if it had been dry land,
while the Egyptians, when they attempted to do so, were
drowned.   Faith caused the walls of Jericho to fall after   30
being encircled for seven days.   Faith saved Rahab,   31
the prostitute, from perishing with the unbelievers, after she
had entertained the spies with friendliness.

Need I add anything more ? Time would fail me if I   32
attempted to relate the stories of Gideon, Barak, Samson, and
Jephthah, and those of David, Samuel, and the Prophets.
By their faith they subdued kingdoms, ruled righteously,   33
gained the fulfilment of God's promises, ' shut the mouths of
lions,' quelled the fury of the flames, escaped the edge of the   34
sword, found strength in the hour of weakness, displayed
their prowess in war, and routed hostile armies. Women   35
received back their dead raised to life. Some were tortured
on the wheel, and refused release in order that they might
rise to a better life. Others had to face taunts and blows,   36

17 Gen. 22. 1, 2, 6.   18 Gen. 21. 12.   21 Gen. 47. 31.   23 Exod. 2. 2.   24 Exod. 2. 11.
     26 Ps. 89. 50, 51 ; 69. 9.   28 Exod. 12. 21—23.   33 Dan. 6. 22.

and even chains and imprisonment. They were stoned to 37
death, they were tortured, they were sawn asunder, they were
put to the sword ; they wandered about clothed in the skins
of sheep or goats, destitute, persecuted, ill-used—men of 38
whom the world was not worthy—roaming in lonely places,
and on the mountains, and in caves and holes in the ground.

Yet, though they all won renown by their faith, they did 39
not obtain the final fulfilment of God's promise ; since God 40
had in view some better thing for us, that they, apart from us,
should not attain perfection.

The Encourage-   Seeing, therefore, that there is on every side 1
ment of their of us such a throng of witnesses, let us also lay
Endurance. aside everything that hinders us, and the sin
that clings about us, and run with patient endurance the race
that lies before us, our eyes fixed upon Jesus, the Leader and 2
perfect Example of our faith, who, for the joy that lay before
him, endured the cross, heedless of its shame, and now ' has
taken his seat at the right hand' of the throne of God. Weigh 3
well the example of him who had to endure such opposition
The Purpose from 'men who were sinning against themselves,'
of Discipline. so that you should not grow weary or faint-
hearted.   You have not yet, in your struggle 4
with sin, resisted to the death ; and you have forgotten the 5
encouraging words which are addressed to you as God's
Children—

> ' My child, think not lightly of the Lord's discipline,
>   Do not despond when he rebukes you ;
> For it is him whom he loves that he disciplines,
>   And he chastises every child whom he acknowledges.' 6

It is for your discipline that you have to endure all this. God 7
is dealing with you as his Children. For where is there a
child whom his father does not discipline ? If you are left 8
without that discipline, in which all children share, it shows
that you are bastards, and not true Children. Further, when 9
our earthly fathers disciplined us, we respected them. Shall
we not, then, much rather yield submission to the Father of
souls, and live ? Our fathers disciplined us for only a short 10
time and as seemed best to them ; but God disciplines us
for our true good, to enable us to share his holiness. No 11
discipline is pleasant at the time ; on the contrary, it is
painful. But afterwards its fruit is seen in the peacefulness
of a righteous life which is the lot of those who have been
trained under it.   Therefore ' lift again the down- 12
dropped hands, and straighten the weakened knees ; make 13
straight paths for your feet,' so that the lame limb may not
be put out of joint, but rather be cured.

2 Ps. 110. 1.   3 Num. 16. 38.   5—8 Prov. 3. 11—12.   12 Isa. 35. 3 (Hebrew).
13 Prov. 4. 26 (Septuagint).

VI.—CONCLUSION.

Exhortations. Try earnestly to live at peace with every one, 14
and to attain to that purity without which no one
will see the Lord. Take care that no one fails to use the 15
loving help of God, 'that no bitterness is allowed to take root
and spring up, and cause trouble,' and so poison the whole
community. Take care that no one becomes immoral, or 16
irreligious like Esau, who sold his birthright for a single
meal. For you know that even afterwards, when he wished 17
to claim his father's blessing, he was rejected—for he never
found an opportunity to repair his error—though he begged
for the blessing with tears.

Warnings. It is not to tangible 'flaming fire' that you 18
have drawn near, nor to 'gloom, and darkness,
and storm, and the blast of a trumpet, and an audible voice.' 19
Those who heard that voice entreated that they might hear
no more, for they could not bear to think of the command— 20
'If even an animal touches the mountain, it is to be stoned
to death;' and so fearful was the sight that Moses said— 21
'I tremble with fear.' No, but it is to Mount Zion that 22
you have drawn near, the City of the Living God, the
heavenly Jerusalem, to countless hosts of angels, to the festal
gathering and assemblage of God's Eldest Sons whose 23
names are enrolled in Heaven, to God the Judge of all
men, to the spirits of the righteous who have attained
perfection, to Jesus, the intermediary of a new Covenant, 24
and to the Sprinkled Blood that tells of better things than
the blood of Abel. Beware how you refuse to hear 25
him who is speaking. For, if the Israelites did not escape
punishment, when they refused to listen to him who taught
them on earth the divine will, far worse will it be for
us, if we turn away from him who is teaching us from
Heaven. Then his voice shook the earth, but now his 26
declaration is—

'Still once more I will cause not only the earth to tremble,
but also the heavens.'

And those words 'still once more' indicate the passing away 27
of all that is shaken—that is, of all created things—in order
that only what is unshaken may remain. Therefore, let 28
us, who have received a kingdom that cannot be shaken, be
thankful, and so offer acceptable worship to God, with awe
and reverence. For our God is 'a consuming fire.' 29

14 Ps. 34. 14. 15 Deut. 29. 18 (Septuagint). 16 Gen. 25. 33. 18—19 Deut. 4. 11—12;
Exod. 19. 16; Deut. 5. 23, 25, 26. 20 Exod. 19. 12—13. 21 Deut. 9. 19.
26—27 Hag. 2. 6. 29 Deut. 4. 24.

Certain Christian Virtues. Let your love for the Brethren continue. Do not neglect to show hospitality; for, through being hospitable, men have all unawares entertained angels.   Remember the prisoners, as if you were their fellow-prisoners, and the oppressed, not forgetting that you also are still in the body.   Let marriage be honoured by all and the married life be pure; for God will judge those who are immoral and those who commit adultery.   Do not let your conduct be ruled by the love of money.   Be content with what you have, for God himself has said— 1, 2

3

4

5

' I will never forsake you, nor will I ever abandon you.'

Therefore we may say with confidence— 6

' The Lord is my helper, I will not be afraid.
What can man do to me?'

Loyalty to Christ and the Leaders in the Church. Do not forget your Leaders, the men who told you God's Message.   Recall the close of their lives, and imitate their faith.   Jesus Christ is the same yesterday and to-day —yes, and for ever!   Do not let yourselves be carried away by the various novel forms of teaching.   It is better to rely for spiritual strength upon the divine help, than upon regulations regarding food; for those whose lives are guided by such regulations have not found them of service.   We are not without an altar; but it is one at which those who still worship in the Tabernacle have no right to eat.   The bodies of those animals whose blood is brought by the High Priest into the Sanctuary, as an offering for sin, are burnt outside the camp.   And so Jesus, also, to purify the People by his own blood, suffered outside the gate.   Therefore let us go out to him 'outside the camp,' bearing the same reproaches as he; for here we have no permanent city, but are looking for the City that is to be.   Through him let us offer, as our sacrifice, continual praise to God—an offering from lips that glorify his Name.   Never forget to do kindly acts and to share what you have with others, for such sacrifices are acceptable to God. 7

8

9

10

11

12
13

14
15

16

Obey your Leaders, and submit to their control, for they are watching over your souls, as men who will have to render an account, so that they may do it with joy, and not in sorrow. That would not be to your advantage. 17

Final Requests, Messages, and Blessing. Pray for us, for we are sure that our consciences are clear, since our wish is to be occupied with what is good.   And I the more earnestly ask for your prayers, that I may be restored to you the sooner. 18

19

---

5 Deut. 31. 6, 8; Jos. 1. 5.   6 Ps. 118. 6.   11–13 Lev. 16. 27.   15 Ps. 50. 14; Lev. 7. 12; 2 Chron. 29. 31; Isa. 57. 19 (Hebrew); Hos. 14. 2.

May God, the source of all peace, who brought back from 20
the dead him who, ' by virtue of the blood that rendered valid
the unchangeable Covenant, is the Great Shepherd of God's
Sheep,' Jesus, our Lord—may God make you perfect in every- 21
thing that is good, so that you may be able to do his will.
May he bring out in us all that is pleasing in his sight, through
Jesus Christ, to whom be all glory for ever and ever. Amen.

I beg you, Brothers, to bear with these words of advice. 22
For I have written only very briefly to you.

You will be glad to hear that our Brother, Timothy, has 23
been set free. If he comes here soon, we will visit you
together.

Give our greeting to all your Leaders, and to all Christ's 24
People.   Our friends from Italy send their greetings to
you.

May God bless you all. 25

[20] Isa. 63. 11 ; Zech. 9. 11 ; Isa. 55. 3 ; Ezek. 37. 26.

Q

FROM PETER.

I.

A LETTER TO THE CHRISTIANS OF ASIA MINOR.

(KNOWN AS 'THE FIRST LETTER OF ST. PETER').

WRITTEN PROBABLY BETWEEN 65 AND 68 A.D.

THIS Letter was written evidently at a time when the Christians throughout Asia Minor were suffering from calumny and threatened with persecution. Such hints of their sufferings as we get from the Letter (2. 12 ; 3. 16 ; 4. 4, 14 and 1. 6, 7 ; 3. 14—17 ; 4. 12—19) fit in well with the accounts, derived from other sources, of the persecution of Christians that broke out under the Emperor Nero in 64 A.D., and spread to Roman Asia. The object of the Letter is to give encouragement in the face of impending persecution, and to convey the advice needed as to the conduct of Christians at an important crisis in the early history of the Church. Those to whom it is addressed probably included Christians of Gentile, as well as of Jewish, birth (1. 21 ; 2. 10 ; 3. 6).

FROM PETER.

I.

I.—INTRODUCTION.

Greeting. To the People of God who are living abroad, dis- 1
persed throughout Pontus, Galatia, Cappa-
docia, Roman Asia, and Bithynia, and who were chosen 2
in accordance with the foreknowledge of God the Father,
through the consecration of the Spirit, to learn obedience,
and to be purified by the sprinkling of the Blood of Jesus
Christ,

FROM Peter, an Apostle of Jesus Christ.

May blessing and peace be yours in ever-increasing measure.

II.—THE CHRISTIAN'S HOPE OF SALVATION.

Blessed is the God and Father of our Lord Jesus Christ, who 3
has, in his great mercy, through the resurrection of Jesus Christ
from the dead, given us the new Life of undying hope, that pro- 4
mises an inheritance, imperishable, stainless, unfading, which
has been reserved for you in Heaven—for you who, through faith, 5
are being guarded by the power of God, awaiting a Salvation
that is ready to be revealed in the last days. At the thought 6
of this you are full of exultation, though (if it has been
necessary) you have suffered for the moment somewhat from
various trials; that the genuineness of your faith—a thing far 7
more precious than gold, which is perishable, yet has to be
tested by fire—may win praise and glory and honour at the
Appearing of Jesus Christ. Though you have never seen him, 8
yet you love him; though you do not even now see him, yet
you believe in him, and exult with a triumphant happiness
too great for words, as you receive the reward of your faith in 9
the Salvation of your souls! It was this Salvation that 10
the Prophets, who spoke long ago of the blessing intended for

you, sought, and strove to comprehend ; as they strove to discern what that time could be, to which the Spirit of Christ within them was pointing, when foretelling the sufferings that would befall Christ, and the glories that would follow. And it was revealed to them that it was not for themselves, but for you, that they were acting as Ministers of the truths which have now been told to you, by those who, with the help of the Holy Spirit sent from Heaven, have brought you the Good News—truths into which even angels long to look. 11 12

III.—The Christian's Character.

Therefore concentrate your minds, with the 13 strictest self-control, and fix your hopes on the blessing that is coming for you at the Appearing of Jesus Christ. Be like obedient children ; do 14 not let your lives be shaped by the passions which once swayed you in the days of your ignorance, but in your whole life show 15 yourselves to be holy, after the pattern of the Holy One from whom you received your Call. For Scripture says— 16

Holiness of Life.

' You shall be holy, because I am holy.'

And since you call upon him as ' Father,' who judges every 17 one impartially by what he has done, let reverence be the spirit of your lives during the time of your stay upon earth. For 18 you know that it was not by perishable things, such as silver and gold, that you were ransomed from the aimless way of living which was handed down to you from your ancestors, but 19 by precious blood, as it were of a lamb, unblemished and spotless, the Blood of Christ. Destined for this before the beginning 20 of the world, he has been revealed in these last days for your sakes, who, through him, are faithful to God who raised him 21 from the dead and gave him honour, so that your faith and hope are now in God.

Brotherly Love.

Now that, by your obedience to the Truth, you 22 have purified your lives, so that there is growing up among you a genuine brotherly affection, love one another earnestly with all your hearts ; since your 23 new Life has come, not from perishable, but imperishable, seed, through the Message of the Everliving God. For— 24

' All earthly life is but as grass,
And all its splendour as the flower of grass.
The grass fades,
Its flower falls,
But the Teaching of the Lord remains for ever.' 25

16 Lev. 11. 44 ; 19. 2 ; 20. 7. ¹⁷ Jer. 3. 19. ¹⁸ Isa. 52. 3. ²³ Dan. 6. 26. 24—25 Isa. 40. 6—9.

And that is the Teaching of the Good News which has been
told to you.   Now that you have done with all malice, **1 2**
Innocence. all deceitfulness, insincerity, jealous feelings, and
all back-biting, like newly born infants, crave **2**
pure spiritual milk, so that you may be enabled by it to grow
till you attain Salvation—since 'you have found by experience **3**
Consecration. that the Lord is kind.' Come to Him, then, as to **4**
a living stone, rejected, indeed, by men, but in
God's eyes choice and precious ; and, as living stones, form **5**
yourselves into a spiritual House, to be a consecrated Priesthood, for the offering of spiritual sacrifices that will be
acceptable to God through Jesus Christ.   For there is a **6**
passage of Scripture that runs—

'See, I am placing in Zion a choice and precious corner-stone ;
    And he who believes in him shall have no cause for shame.'

It is to you, then, who believe in him that he is precious, but to **7**
those who do not believe he is 'a stone which, though rejected
by the builders, has now itself become the corner-stone,' and **8**
'a stumbling-block, and a rock which shall prove a hindrance.'
They stumble because they do not accept the Message.   This
was the fate destined for them.   But you are 'a chosen race, **9**
a royal priesthood, a consecrated nation, God's own People,'
entrusted with the proclamation of the goodness of him who
called you out of Darkness into his wonderful Light.   Once **10**
you were 'not a people,' but now you are 'God's People'; once
you 'had not found mercy,' but now you 'have found mercy.'

IV.—Practical Exhortations in view of the Dangers of the Times.

The
Necessity of Dear friends, I urge you, as pilgrims and **11**
setting a good strangers upon earth, to refrain from indulging
Example. the cravings of your earthly nature, for they
make war upon the soul.   Let your daily life **12**
among the Gentiles be so upright, that, whenever they malign
you as evil-doers, they may learn, as they watch, from the
uprightness of your conduct, to praise God 'at the time when
he shall visit them.'

Submission Submit to all human institutions for the Lord's **13**
to the Civil sake, alike to the emperor as the supreme
Authorities. authority, and to governors as the men sent by him **14**
to punish evil-doers and to commend those who do
right.   For God's will is this—that you should silence the **15**
ignorance of foolish people by doing what is right.   Act as free **16**
men, yet not using your freedom as those do who make it a

3 Ps. 34. 8.   **4—7** Ps. 118. 22 ; Isa. 28. 16.   **8** Isa. 8. 14, 15.   **9** Isa. 43. 20—21 ;
Exod. 19. 5—6.   **10** Hos. 1. 6—9 ; 2. 1, 23.   **11** Ps. 39. 12.   **12** Isa. 10. 3.

cloak for wickedness, but as Servants of God.   Show honour   17
to every one.   Love the Brotherhood, 'revere God, honour
the emperor.'

Those of you who are domestic servants should   18
The Duty of always be submissive and respectful to their
Servants. masters, not only to those who are good and
considerate, but also to those who are arbitrary.   For this   19
wins God's approval when, because conscious of God's presence, a man who is suffering unjustly bears his troubles
patiently.   What credit can you claim when, after doing   20
wrong, you take your punishment for it patiently?   But, on
the other hand, if, after doing right, you take your sufferings
patiently, that does win the approval of God.   For it was to   21
this that you were called!   For Christ, too, suffered—on your
behalf—and left you an example, that you should follow in
his steps.   He 'never sinned, nor was anything deceitful   22
ever heard from his lips.'   He was abused, but he did not   23
answer with abuse; he suffered, but he did not threaten; he
entrusted himself to him whose judgements are just.   And he   24
'himself carried our sins' in his own body to the cross, so
that we might die to our sins, and live for righteousness.
'His bruising was your healing.'   Once you were straying   25
like sheep, but now you have returned to the Shepherd and
Guardian of your souls.

Again, you married women should submit to   1   **3**
The Relations your husbands, so that if any of them reject the
between
Husbands and Message, they may, apart from the Message, be
Wives. won over, by the conduct of their wives, as   2
they watch your submissive and blameless conduct.   Yours   3
should be, not the external adornment of the arrangement of the hair, the wearing of jewelry, or the putting on of dresses, but the inner life with the imperishable   4
beauty of a quiet and gentle spirit; for this is very precious
in God's sight.   It was by this that the holy women of old,   5
who rested their hopes on God, adorned themselves; submitting to their husbands, as Sarah did, who obeyed Abraham,   6
and called him master.   And you are her true children, as long
as you live good lives, and let nothing terrify you.

Again, those of you who are married men should live   7
considerately with their wives, showing due regard to their
sex, as weaker than their own, and not forgetting that they
share with you in the gift of Life.   Then you will be able to
pray without hindrance.

Lastly, you should all be united, sympathetic,   8
Christian full of brotherly love, kind-hearted, humble-
Sympathy and
Forbearance. minded; never returning evil for evil, or abuse   9
for abuse, but, on the contrary, blessing.   It was
to this that you were called—to obtain a blessing!

17 Prov. 24. 21.   22—25 Isa. 53. 5—12.   6 Gen. 18. 12; Prov. 3. 25.

' He who would enjoy life 10
    And see happy days—
Let him keep his tongue from evil
    And his lips from deceitful words,
Let him turn from evil and do good, 11
    Let him seek for peace and follow after it ;
For the eyes of the Lord are on the righteous, 12
    And his ears are attentive to their prayers,
        But the face of the Lord is set against those who do wrong.'

Endurance after the Example of Christ. Who, indeed, is there to harm you, if you prove 13 yourselves to be eager for what is good ? Even if 14 you should suffer for righteousness, count yourselves blessed ! 'Do not let men terrify you, or allow yourselves to be dismayed.' Revere the Christ as Lord in 15 your hearts ; always ready to give an answer to any one who asks your reason for the hope that you cherish, but giving it humbly and in all reverence, and keeping your consciences 16 clear, so that, whenever you are maligned, those who vilify your good and Christian conduct may be put to shame. It is 17 better that you should suffer, if that should be God's will, for doing right, than for doing wrong. For Christ himself died 18 to atone for sins once for all—the good on behalf of the bad— that he might bring you to God ; his body being put to death, but his spirit entering upon new Life. And it was then that 19 he went and preached to the imprisoned spirits, who once were 20 disobedient, at the time when God patiently waited, in the days of Noah, while the ark was being prepared ; in which some few lives, eight in all, were saved by means of water. And baptism, which this foreshadowed, now saves you—not 21 the mere cleansing of the body, but the search of a clear conscience after God—through the resurrection of Jesus Christ, who has gone into Heaven, and is at God's right hand, where 22 Angels and Archangels and the Powers of Heaven now yield submission to him.

Renunciation of the Heathen Life. Since, then, Christ suffered in body, arm your- 1 **4** selves with the same resolve as he ; for he who has suffered in body has ceased to sin, and so will 2 live the rest of his earthly life guided, not by human passions, but by the will of God. Surely in the past 3 you have spent time enough living as the Gentiles delight to live. For your path has lain among scenes of debauchery, licentiousness, drunkenness, revelry, hard-drinking, and profane idolatry. And, because you do not run to the same 4 extremes of profligacy as others, they are astonished, and malign you. But they will have to answer for their conduct 5 to him who is ready to judge both the living and the dead. For that was why the Good News was told to the dead also— 6

10—12 Ps. 34. 12—16. 14—15 Isa. 8. 12—13. 22 Ps. 110. 1.

that, after they have been judged in the body, as men are judged, they might live in the spirit, as God lives.

But the end of all things is near.   Therefore   7
Self-control, exercise self-restraint and be calm, that you may
Love, and be able to pray.   Above all things, let your love   8
Service. for one another be earnest, for ' Love throws a
veil over countless sins.'   Never grudge hospitality to one   9
another.   Whatever the gift that each has received, use it in   10
the service of others, as good stewards of the varied bounty of
God.   When any one speaks, let him speak as one who is   11
delivering the oracles of God.   When any one is endeavouring
to serve others, let him do so in reliance on the strength which
God supplies ; so that in everything God may be honoured
through Jesus Christ—to whom be ascribed all honour and
might for ever and ever.   Amen.

Dear friends, do not be astonished at the fiery   12
The Ordeal of trials that you are passing through, to test you,
Suffering. as though something strange were happening to
you.   No, the more you share the sufferings of the Christ,   13
the more may you rejoice, that, when the time comes for
the manifestation of his Glory, you may rejoice and exult.
If you are reviled for bearing the name of Christ, count your-   14
selves blessed ; because the divine Glory and the Spirit of
God are resting upon you.   I need hardly say that no one   15
among you must suffer as a murderer, or a thief, or a criminal,
or for interfering in matters which do not concern Christians.
But, if a man suffers as a Christian, do not let him be   16
ashamed of it ; let him bring honour to God even though he
bears that name.   For the time has come for judgement to begin   17
with the House of God ; and, if it begins with us, what will be
the end of those who reject God's Good News ?   If 'a good   18
man is saved only with difficulty, what will become of the
godless and the sinful ?'   Therefore, I say, let those who   19
suffer, because God wills it so, commit their lives into the
hands of a faithful Creator, and persevere in doing right.

V.—CONCLUSION.

As for the older men among you, who bear   1
Special office in the Church, I, their fellow-Officer, and a
Exhortations. witness to the sufferings of the Christ, who shall
also share in the glory that is to be revealed—I urge you to   2
be true shepherds of the flock of God among you, not because

8 Prov. 10. 12 (Hebrew).   14 Ps. 89. 50—51 ; Isa. 11. 2.   17 Ezek. 9. 6.
18 Prov. 11. 31.

you are compelled, but of your own free will ; not from a base love of gain, but with a ready spirit ; not as lords of your charges, but as examples to your flock. Then, when the Chief Shepherd appears, you will win the crown of glory that never fades.   Again, you younger men should show deference to the older.   And all of you should put on the badge of humility in mutual service, for 'God is opposed to the proud, but gives his help to the humble.'

General Exhortations. Humble yourselves, therefore, under the mighty hand of God, so that he may exalt you in his good time, laying all your anxieties upon him, for he makes you his care.   Exercise self-control, be watchful. Your adversary, the Devil, like a roaring lion, is prowling about, eager to devour you. Stand firm against him, strong in your faith ; knowing, as you do, that the very sufferings which you are undergoing are being endured to the full by your Brotherhood throughout the world. God, from whom all help comes, and who called you, by your union with Christ, into his eternal glory, will, when you have suffered for a little while, himself perfect, establish, strengthen you. To him be ascribed dominion for ever. Amen.

Messages and Blessing. I have been writing to you briefly by the hand of Silas, our true-hearted Brother (for so I regard him), to urge upon you, and to bear my testimony, that in what I have written is to be found the true love of God. On that take your stand.   Your sister-Church in 'Babylon' sends you greeting, and so does Mark, who is as a son to me.   Greet one another with the kiss of love.

May God give his peace to you all in your union with Christ.

5 Prov. 3. 34.   7 Ps. 55. 22.

FROM PETER.

II.

A LETTER TO CHRISTIAN PEOPLE.

(KNOWN AS 'THE SECOND LETTER OF ST. PETER').

DATE AND PLACE OF WRITING UNCERTAIN.

———

THIS Letter is addressed to Christians in general, and is mainly directed against the separation of Christianity from a holy life. It also contains an assertion of the certainty of the 'Second Coming' of the Christ, though at a time which might still be far off according to human reckoning. The resemblances of this Letter to the 'Letter of St. Jude,' and to the writings of the Jewish historian Josephus, are most remarkable; and so, too, are the apparent references to passages in the writings of the Alexandrian Philosopher, Philo. Both Philo and Josephus wrote in the First Century of the Christian Era.

FROM PETER.

II.

I.—INTRODUCTION.

Greeting.

To those to whom, through the justice of our 1
God and Saviour Jesus Christ, there has
been granted faith equally privileged with
our own,

FROM Simon Peter, a servant and an Apostle of Jesus Christ.

May blessing and peace be yours in ever-increasing measure, 2
as you advance in the knowledge of God and of Jesus,
our Lord.

Christian Privileges and Christian Life.

For his divine power has given us everything 3
that is needful for a life of piety, as we advance
in the knowledge of him who called us by a
glorious manifestation of his goodness. For it 4
was through this that he gave us what we prize
as the greatest of his promises, that through them you might
participate in the divine nature, now that you have fled from
the corruption in the world, resulting from human passions.
Yes, and for this very reason do your best to supplement your 5
faith by goodness, goodness by knowledge, knowledge by 6
self-control, self-control by endurance, endurance by piety,
piety by brotherly affection, and brotherly affection by love. 7
For, when these virtues are yours, in increasing measure, they 8
prevent your being indifferent to, or destitute of, a fuller
knowledge of our Lord Jesus Christ. Surely the man who 9
has not these virtues is shortsighted even to blindness, and
has chosen to forget that he has been purified from his sins of
the past ! Therefore, Brothers, do your best to put God's Call 10
and Selection of you beyond all doubt; for, if you do this, you
will never fall. For thus you will be given a triumphant 11
admission into the eternal Kingdom of our Lord and Saviour,
Jesus Christ.

II.—The Transfiguration and the 'Second Coming' of the Christ.

I shall, therefore, always be ready to remind you of all this,   12
even though you know it and are firmly established in the
Truth that you now hold.   But I think it my duty, as long as   13
I live in this 'tent,' to rouse you by awakening memories of
the past ; for I know that the time for this 'tent' of mine to   14
be put away is soon coming, as our Lord Jesus Christ himself
assured me.   So I will do my best to enable you, at any   15
time after my departure, to call these truths to mind.
For we were not following cleverly devised stories when we   16
told you of the Coming in power of our Lord Jesus Christ,
but we had been eye-witnesses of his majesty.   For he received   17
honour and glory from God the Father, when from the Glory
of the Divine Majesty there were borne to his ears words
such as these—'This is my Son, my Beloved, in whom I
delight.'   These were the words that we heard, borne to our   18
ears from Heaven, when we were with him on that Sacred
Mountain.   And still stronger is the assurance that we have   19
in the teaching of the Prophets ; to which you will do well to
pay attention (as if it were a lamp shining in a gloomy place),
until the Day dawns and the Morning Star rises in your
hearts.   But first be assured of this :—There is no prophetic   20
teaching found in Scripture that can be interpreted by man's
unaided reason ; for no prophetic teaching ever came in the   21
old days at the mere wish of man, but men, moved by the
Holy Spirit, spoke direct from God.

III.—Warning against separating Christianity from a Holy Life.

But there were false prophets also in the nation, just as there   1   **2**
will be false teachers among you, men who will secretly intro-
duce ruinous divisions, disowning even the Lord who bought
them, and bringing speedy Ruin upon themselves.   There will   2
be many, too, who will follow their licentious courses, and
cause the Way of the Truth to be maligned.   In their covetous-   3
ness they will try to make you a source of profit by their
fabrications ; but for a long time past their Sentence has not
been standing idle, nor their Ruin slumbering.   Remember,   4
God did not spare angels when they sinned, but sent them
down to Tartarus, and committed them to caverns of darkness, to be kept under guard for judgement.   Nor did he spare   5
the·world of old ; though he preserved Noah, the Preacher of
Righteousness and seven others, when he brought a flood

2 Isa. 52. 5.   4 Enoch 10. 6, 13.

upon the godless world.   He condemned the cities of Sodom 6
and Gomorrah and reduced them to ashes, holding them up as
a warning to the godless of what was in store for them ; but he 7
rescued righteous Lot, whose heart was vexed by the wanton
licentiousness of his neighbours ; for, seeing and hearing what 8
he did, as he lived his righteous life among them, day after day,
Lot's righteous soul was tortured by their wicked doings.   The 9
Lord, therefore, knows how to deliver the pious from temptation, and to keep the wicked, who are even now suffering
punishment, in readiness for 'the Day of Judgement'—
especially those who, following the promptings of their lower 10
nature, indulge their polluting passions and despise all control.
Audacious and self-willed, they feel no awe of the Mighty,
maligning them, even where angels, though excelling them 11
in strength and power, do not bring against them a malignant
charge before the Lord.   These men, however, like animals 12
without reason, intended by nature to be caught and killed—
these men, I say, malign those of whom they know nothing,
and will assuredly perish through their own corruption,
suffering themselves, as the penalty for the suffering that 13
they have inflicted.   They think that pleasure consists in the
self-indulgence of the moment.   They are a stain and a disgrace, indulging, as they do, in their wanton revelry, even
while joining you at your feasts.   They have eyes only for 14
adulteresses, eyes never tired of sin ; they entice weak souls ;
their minds are trained to covet ; they live under a curse.
Leaving the straight road, they have gone astray and followed 15
in the steps of Balaam, the son of Beor, who set his heart on
the reward for wrong-doing, but was rebuked for his offence. 16
A dumb animal spoke with the voice of a man, and checked the
prophet's madness.   These men are like springs without water, 17
or mists driven before a gale ; and for them the blackest darkness has been reserved.   With boastful and foolish talk, they 18
appeal to the passions of man's lower nature, and, by their
profligacy, entice those who are just escaping from the men
who live such misguided lives.   They promise them freedom, 19
while they themselves are slaves to corrupt habits ; for a man
is the slave of anything to which he gives way.   If, after 20
having escaped the polluting influences of the world, through
knowing our Lord and Saviour, Jesus Christ, men are again
entangled in them, and give way to them, their last state has
become worse than their first.   It would, indeed, have been 21
better for them not to have known the Way of Righteousness,
than, after knowing it, to turn away from the holy Command
delivered to them.   In their case is seen the truth of the pro- 22
verb—'A dog returns to what he has vomited' and 'A sow
after washing to her wallowing-place in the mud.'

⁹ Enoch 10. 6.   ²² Prov. 26. 11.

IV.—A RE-ASSERTION OF THE 'SECOND COMING' OF THE CHRIST.

Long-delayed but certain. This, dear friends, is my second letter to you. 1 In both of them I have tried, by appealing to your remembrance, to arouse your better feelings. I want you to 2 recall what was foretold by the holy Prophets, as well as the Command of our Lord and Saviour given to you through your Apostles. First be assured of this, that, as the age draws to 3 an end, scoffers, led by their own passions, will come and ask 4 scoffingly—'Where is his promised Coming? Ever since our fathers passed to their rest, everything remains just as it was when the world was first created!' For they wilfully shut their 5 eyes to the fact that long ago the heavens existed; and the earth, also—formed out of water and by the action of water, by the fiat of God; and that by the same means the world which 6 then existed was destroyed in a deluge of water. But the 7 present heavens and earth, by the same fiat, have been reserved for fire, and are being kept for the day of the judgement and destruction of the godless.

'The Day of the Lord.' But you, dear friends, must never shut your eyes 8 to the fact that, to the Lord, one day is the same as a thousand years, and a thousand years as one day. The Lord is not slow to fulfil his promise, as some count 9 slowness; but he is forbearing with you, as it is not his will that any of you should perish, but that all should be brought to repentance. The Day of the Lord will come like a 10 thief; and on that day the heavens will pass away with a crash, the elements will be burnt up and dissolved, and the earth and all that is in it will be disclosed. Now, since 11 all these things are in the process of dissolution, think what you yourselves ought to be—what holy and pious lives you ought to lead, while you await and hasten the coming of the 12 Day of God. At its coming the heavens will be dissolved in fire, and the elements melted by heat, but we look for 'new 13 heavens and a new earth,' where righteousness shall have its home, in fulfilment of the promise of God.

The needful Preparation. Therefore, dear friends, in expectation of these 14 things, make every effort to be found by him spotless, blameless, and at peace. Regard our Lord's 15 forbearance as your one hope of Salvation. This is what our dear Brother Paul wrote to you, with the wisdom that God gave him. It is the same in all his letters, when he speaks in 16 them about these subjects. There are some things in them difficult to understand, which untaught and weak people

[8] Ps. 90. 4.   [12—13] Isa. 33. 4; 65. 17; 66. 22.

distort, just as they do all other writings, to their own Ruin. Do you, therefore, dear friends, now that you 17 know this beforehand, be on your guard against being led away by the errors of reckless people, and so lapsing from your present stedfastness; and advance in the love and 18 knowledge of our Lord and Saviour, Jesus Christ. All glory be to him now and for ever.

THE LETTER OF JUDE.

FROM JUDE.

A LETTER TO CHRISTIAN PEOPLE.

(KNOWN AS 'THE LETTER OF ST. JUDE').

[DATE AND PLACE OF WRITING UNCERTAIN.]

THIS Letter was written apparently by the Jude (or Judas) who was a "brother of James," and so a brother of Jesus. Neither this Judas, nor his brother James, was an Apostle. The Letter may have been written in Palestine; and the historical allusions in it make it possible that it was addressed to Christians of Jewish origin. It is full of resemblances to 'The Second Letter of St. Peter,' and consists of a stern denunciation of those nominal Christians who were using their Christianity as a cover for an evil life.

FROM

JUDE.

I.—INTRODUCTION.

Greeting. To those who, having received the Call, have been loved by God the Father and protected by Jesus Christ, 1

FROM Jude, a servant of Jesus Christ, and the brother of James.

May mercy, peace, and love be yours in ever-increasing measure. 2

II.—WARNINGS AGAINST THE MORAL CORRUPTION INTRODUCED BY FALSE TEACHERS.

The Object of the Letter. Dear friends, while I was making every effort to write to you about our common Salvation, I felt that I must write to you at once to urge you to fight in defence of the Faith that has once for all been entrusted to the keeping of Christ's People. For there have crept in among you certain godless people, whose sentence has long since been pronounced, and who make the mercy of God an excuse for profligacy, and disown our only lord and master, Jesus Christ. 3

4

The false Teachers and their certain Doom. Now I want to remind you—but you already know it all—that, though the Lord delivered the People from Egypt, yet he afterwards destroyed those who refused to believe in him ; and that even those angels, who did not keep to their appointed spheres, but left their proper homes, have been kept by him for the judgement of the Great Day in everlasting chains and black darkness. Like Sodom and Gomorrah and the towns near them, which gave themselves up to fornication, and fell into unnatural vice, these angels now stand out as a 5

6

7

---

⁴ Enoch 48. 11.   ⁶ Enoch 10, 6, 9.

warning, undergoing, as they are, the punishment of aeonian fire.

Yet in the very same way these men, too, cherishing vain   8
dreams, pollute our human nature, reject control, and malign
the Mighty.   Yet even Michael, the Archangel, when,   9
in his dispute with the Devil, he was arguing about the body
of Moses, did not venture to charge him with maligning,
but said merely 'The Lord rebuke you!'   But these   10
men malign whatever they do not understand; while they
use such things as they know by instinct (like the animals
that have no reason) for their own corruption.   Alas for them!   11
They walk in the steps of Cain; led astray by Balaam's love
of gain, they plunge into sin, and meet their ruin through
rebellion like that of Korah.   These are the men who are   12
blots upon your 'Love-feasts,' when they feast together and
provide without scruple for themselves alone.   They are clouds
without rain, driven before the winds; they are leafless trees
without a vestige of fruit, dead through and through, torn up
by the roots; they are wild sea waves, foaming with their   13
own shame; they are 'wandering stars,' for which the
blackest darkness has been reserved for ever.

To these men, as to others, Enoch, the seventh in descent   14
from Adam, declared—'See! the Lord has come with his
hosts of holy ones around him, to execute judgement upon all   15
men, and to convict all godless people of all their godless acts,
which in their ungodliness they have committed, and of all
the harsh words which they have spoken against him, godless
sinners that they are!'

These men are always murmuring, and complaining of their   16
lot; they follow where their passions lead them; they have
arrogant words upon their lips; and they flatter men for the
sake of what they can get from them.

                   But do you, dear friends, recall what was fore-   17
A Christian's   told by the Apostles of our Lord Jesus Christ; how   18
Attitude   they used to say to you—'As time draws to an end,
towards   there will be scoffers, who will be led by their
these   godless passions.'   These are the people—   19
Teachers.
animal and unspiritual—who cause divisions.   But do   20
you, dear friends, build up your characters on the foundation
of your most holy Faith, pray under the guidance of the Holy
Spirit, and keep within the love of God, while waiting for the   21
mercy of our Lord Jesus Christ, to bring you to Immortal
Life.   To some show pity, because they are in doubt.   22
'Drag them out of the fire,' and save them.   To others show   23
pity, but with caution, hating the very clothing polluted by
their touch.

9 Dan. 12. 1; Zech. 3. 2.   12 Ezek. 34. 8.   13 Enoch 18. 16.   14—15 Enoch 59. 8;
        Deut. 33. 2; Zech. 14. 5.   23 Zech. 3. 2—4.

III.—Ascription.

To him who is able to guard you from falling, and to bring 24
you into his glorious presence, blameless and rejoicing—to
the one God, our Saviour, be ascribed, through Jesus Christ,
our Lord, glory, majesty, power, and dominion, as it was
before time began, is now, and shall be for all time to come.
Amen.

FROM JOHN.

I.

'THE FIRST LETTER OF ST. JOHN.'

WRITTEN PROBABLY AT EPHESUS AFTER 70 A.D

THIS Letter was apparently written by the author of 'The Good News according to John,' with which book, both in language and thought, it has a close connexion. It deals with errors that were rife in the Church in the writer's day, by re-asserting the revelation in the incarnate Christ of the Life, and Light, and Love of God.

It is a Homily rather than a Letter, and was possibly intended to circulate among the Churches of Asia Minor. It seems to have been written after the fall of Jerusalem, and at a time when the Second Coming of the Christ appeared to be imminent (2. 18).

FROM JOHN.

I.

I.—THE IMMORTAL LIFE.

Manifested in Christ. It is of what has been in existence from the Beginning, of what we have heard, of what we have seen with our eyes, of what we watched reverently and touched with our hands—it is about the Word who is the Life that we are now writing. That Life was made visible, and we have seen it, and now bear our testimony to it, and tell you of that Immortal Life, which was with the Father and was made visible to us. It is of what we have seen and heard that we now tell you, so that you may have communion with us. And our communion is with the Father and with his Son, Jesus Christ. And we are writing all this to you that our joy may be complete.

Lived in the Light. These, then, are the Tidings that we have heard from him and now tell you—'God is Light, and Darkness has no place at all in him.' If we say that we have communion with him, and yet continue to live in the Darkness, we lie, and are not living the Truth. But, if our lives are lived in the Light, as God himself is in the Light, we have communion with one another, and the Blood of Jesus, his Son, purifies us from all sin. If we say that there is no sin in us, we are deceiving ourselves, and the Truth has no place in us. If we confess our sins, God may be trusted, in his righteousness, to forgive us our sins and purify us from all wickedness. If we say that we have not sinned, we are making God a liar, and his Message has no place in us.

My Children, I am writing to you to keep you from sinning; but if any one should sin, we have one who can plead for us with the Father—Jesus Christ, the Righteous—and he is the atoning sacrifice for our sins, and not for ours only, but for

those of the whole world besides.   And by this we   3
know that we have learnt to know him—by our laying his
commands to heart.   The man who says ' I know Jesus,' but   4
does not lay his commands to heart, is a liar, and the Truth
has no place in him ; but, whenever a man lays his Message   5
to heart, in that man the love of God has indeed reached its
perfection.   By this we know that we are in union with
God—He who professes to maintain union with God is himself   6
bound to live as Christ lived.

Dear friends, it is no new command that I am writing to   7
you, but an old command, which you have had from the first.
That old command is the Message to which you listened.
Yet, again, it is a new Command that I am writing to you—   8
manifest in Christ's life and in your own—for the Darkness is
passing away and the true Light is already shining.

He who says that he is in the Light, and yet hates his   9
Brother, is in the Darkness even now.   He who loves his   10
Brother is always in the Light, and there is nothing within
him to cause him to stumble ; while he who hates his Brother   11
is in the Darkness, and is living in the Darkness, and does
not know where he is going, because the Darkness prevents
his seeing.

I am writing, Children, to you, because your sins have been   12
forgiven you for Christ's sake.   I am writing, Fathers, to you,   13
because you have learnt to know him who has been from the
Beginning.   I am writing, Young Men, to you, because you
have conquered the Evil One.   I write, Children, to you, because you have learnt to know the Father.   I write, Fathers, to   14
you, because you have learnt to know him who has been from
the Beginning.   I write, Young Men, to you, because you
are strong, and God's Message is always in your hearts, and
you have conquered the Evil One.   Do not love the   15
world or what the world can offer.   When any one loves the
world, there is no love for the Father in him ; for all that the   16
world can offer—the gratification of the earthly nature, the
gratification of the eye, the pretentious life—belongs, not to
the Father, but to the world.   And the world, and all that it   17
gratifies, is passing away, but he who does God's will remains
for ever.

II.—Warnings against Anti-Christ.

My Children, these are the last days.   You   18
The Anti-Christs. were told that an Anti-Christ was coming ; and
many Anti-Christs have already arisen.   By that
we know that these are the last days.   From us, it is true,   19

they went out, but they had never belonged to us ; for, if they had belonged to us, they would have remained among us. They left us that it might be made clear that they do not, any of them, belong to us.   You, however, have received conse- 20
cration from the Holy One.   You all know——But I am not 21
writing to you because you do not know the Truth, but because you do know it, and because nothing false can come from the Truth.

Who is a liar, if not the man who rejects the truth that 22
Jesus is the Christ ?   He is the Anti-Christ—the man who rejects the Father and the Son.   No one who rejects the Son 23
has found the Father ; he who acknowledges the Son has found the Father also.   As for you, let what you were 24
told at the first be always in your thoughts.   If, then, what you were told from the first is always in your thoughts, you yourselves will maintain your union both with the Son and with the Father.   And this is what he himself promised us— 25
The Immortal Life !

In writing thus to you, I have in mind those 26
The Christian's Consecration. who are trying to mislead you.   But you—you 27
still retain in your hearts that consecration which you received from the Christ, and are not in need of any one to teach you ; but, since his consecration of you teaches you about everything, and since it is a real consecra-tion, and no lie, then, as it has taught you, maintain your union with him.   Yes, my Children, maintain your union with 28
Christ, so that, whenever he appears, our confidence may not fail us, and we may not be ashamed to meet him at his coming.   Knowing him to be righteous, you realize that 29
every one who lives righteously has received the new Life from him.

III.—The Privileges and Duties of God's Children.

The Father's Love. Think what love the Father has shown us in 1 **3**
allowing us to be called ' Children of God ' ; as indeed we are.   The reason why the world does not know us is that it has not learnt to know him.   Dear 2
friends, we are God's Children now ; what we shall be has not yet been revealed.   What we do know is that, when it is revealed, we shall be like Christ ; because we shall see him as he is.   And every one who has this hope with regard to Christ 3
tries to make himself pure—as Christ is pure.

The Children's Lives. Every one who lives sinfully is living in vio- 4
lation of Law.   Sin is violation of Law.   And 5
you know that Christ appeared to take away our sins ; and in him Sin has no place.   No one who maintains 6

union with him lives in sin ; no one who lives in sin has ever really seen him or learnt to know him.   My Children, 7 do not let any one mislead you. He who lives righteously is righteous—as Christ is righteous. He who lives sinfully 8 belongs to the Devil, for the Devil has sinned from the first. It was for this that the Son of God appeared, that he might undo the Devil's work.

No one who has received the new Life from God lives 9 sinfully, because the very nature of God dwells within him ; and he cannot live in sin, because he has received the new Life from God. By this the Children of God are dis- 10 tinguished from the Children of the Devil—No one who lives unrighteously comes from God, and especially the man who does not love his Brother. For these are the Tidings 11 that we heard from the first—that we are to love one another. We must not be like Cain, who belonged to the 12 Evil One and killed his brother. And why did he kill him ? It was because his life was bad while his brother's was good.

Love of 'The Brethren.' Do not wonder, Brothers, if the world hates 13 you. We know that we have passed out of 14 Death into Life, because we love our Brothers. The man who does not love remains in a state of Death. Every one who hates his Brother is a murderer ; and 15 you know that no murderer has Immortal Life within him.

We have learnt to know what love is from this—that 16 Christ laid down his life on our behalf. Therefore we also ought to lay down our lives on behalf of our Brothers. But, if 17 any one has worldly possessions, and yet looks on while his Brother is in want, and steels his heart against him, how can it be said that the love of God is within him ?   My 18 Children, do not let our love be mere words, or end in talk ; let it be true and show itself in acts.

By that we shall know that we are on the side of the Truth ; 19 and we shall satisfy ourselves in God's sight, that if our 20 conscience condemns us, yet God is greater than our con- science and knows everything.   Dear friends, if our 21 conscience does not condemn us, then we approach God with confidence, and we receive from him whatever we ask, because 22 we are laying his commands to heart, and are doing what is pleasing in his sight. His Command is this—that we should 23 put our trust in the Name of his Son, Jesus Christ, and love one another, in accordance with the Command that he gave us. And he who lays his commands to heart maintains union 24 with Christ, and Christ with him. And by this we know that Christ maintains union with us—by our possession of the Spirit which he gave us.

IV.—True and False Inspiration.

Dear friends, do not trust every inspiration,   1 **4**
The Test of Inspiration. but test each inspiration, to see whether it proceeds from God ; because many false Prophets have gone out into the world.

This is the way by which to know the inspiration of God—   2
All inspiration that acknowledges Jesus Christ as come in our human nature is from God ; while all inspiration that   3 does not acknowledge Jesus is not inspiration from God.   It is the inspiration of the Anti-Christ ; you have heard that it was to come, and it is now already in the world.

You, my Children, come from God, and you have success-   4 fully resisted such men as these, because he who is in you is greater than he who is in the world.   Those men belong to   5 the world ; and therefore they speak as the world speaks, and the world listens to them.   We come from God.   He who   6 knows God listens to us ; the man who does not come from God does not listen to us.   By that we may know the true inspiration from the false.

V.—Love of God and Love of Man.

Dear friends, let us love one another, because Love comes   7 from God ; and every one who loves has received the new Life from God and knows God.   He who does not love has   8 not learnt to know God ; for God is Love.   The love of God   9 was revealed to us by his sending his only Son into the world, that we might find Life through him.   His love is seen in   10 this—not in our having loved God, but in his loving us and sending his Son to be an atoning sacrifice for our sins.

Dear friends, since God loved us thus, we, surely, ought to   11 love one another.   No human eyes have ever seen God ; yet,   12 if we love one another, God remains in union with us, and his love attains its perfection in us.   We know that we remain   13 in union with him, and he with us, by this—by his having given us some measure of his Spirit.   Moreover, our   14 eyes have seen—and we are testifying to the fact—that the Father has sent the Son to be the Saviour of the world.   Who-   15 ever acknowledges that Jesus Christ is the Son of God—God remains in union with that man, and he with God.   And,   16 moreover, we have learnt to know, and have accepted as a fact, the love which God has for us.

God is Love ; and he who lives in love lives in God, and God in him.   It is through this that love has attained   17 its perfection in us, so that we may have confidence on the Day of Judgement, because what Christ is that we also are in this

R

world.   There is no fear in love.   No ! Love, when perfect, 18
drives out fear, for fear implies punishment, and the man who
feels fear has not attained to perfect love.   We love, 19
because God first loved us.   If a man says ' I love God,' and 20
yet hates his Brother, he is a liar ; for the man who does not
love his Brother, whom he has seen, cannot love God, whom
he has not seen.   Indeed, we have this Command from God— 21
' He who loves God must also love his Brother.'

VI.—A Christian's Faith and Confidence.

Faith. Every one who believes that Jesus is the Christ 1 **5**
has received the new Life from God ; and every one
who loves him who gave that Life loves him who has received
it.   By this we know that we love God's Children—when we 2
love God and carry out his commands.   For to love God is to 3
lay his commands to heart ; and his commands are not burden-
some, because all that has received the new Life from God 4
conquers the world.   And this is the power that has conquered
the world—our faith ! Who is he that conquers the world but 5
the man who believes that Jesus is the Son of God ?   He 6
The Three-fold it is whose Coming was attested by means of
Testimony. Water and Blood—Jesus Christ himself ; not
by Water only, but by Water and by Blood.   And
there is the Spirit also to bear testimony, and the Spirit is
Truth itself.   It is a three-fold testimony—that of the Spirit, 8
the Water, and the Blood—and these three are at one.   We 9
accept the testimony of men, but God's testimony is still
stronger ; and there is the testimony of God—the fact that he
has already borne testimony about his Son.   He who believes 10
in the Son of God has that testimony within him.   He who
does not believe God has made God a liar, by refusing to
believe in that testimony which he has borne about his Son.
And that testimony is that God gave us Immortal Life, 11
and that this Life is in his Son.   He who finds the Son 12
finds Life ; he who does not find the Son of God does not find
Life.

Confidence. I write this to you, that you may realize that 13
you have found Immortal Life—you who believe
in the Name of the Son of God.   And this is the confidence 14
with which we approach him, that whenever we ask anything
that is in accordance with his will, he listens to us.   And if 15
we realize that he listens to us—whatever we ask—we realize
that we have what we have asked from him.   If any 16
one sees his Brother committing some sin that is not a deadly
sin, he will ask, and so be the means of giving Life to him—
to any whose sin is not deadly.   There is such a thing as
deadly sin ; about that I do not say that a man should pray.

Every wrong action is sin, and there is sin that is not   17
deadly.

We know that no one who has received the new Life from   18
God lives in sin.   No, he who has received the new Life from
God keeps the thought of God in his heart, and then the Evil
One does not touch him.   We realize that we come from God,   19
while all the world is under the influence of the Evil One.
We realize, too, that the Son of God has come among us, and   20
has given us the discernment to know the True God ; and we
are in union with the True God by our union with his Son,
Jesus Christ.   He is the True God and he is Immortal
Life.   My Children, guard yourselves against false ideas   21
of God.

FROM JOHN.

II.

THE LETTER TO A CHRISTIAN LADY.

(KNOWN AS 'THE SECOND LETTER FROM JOHN').

[PLACE AND DATE OF WRITING UNKNOWN.]

THIS Letter may be either a letter addressed to a Church which stands pre-eminent in the writer's affections, or a private letter addressed to a Christian lady and her family. In the latter case the lady's name may possibly be Kyria, or may have been intentionally suppressed on account of the dangers to which Christians were frequently exposed. The writer also veils his own identity under the vague designation 'the Officer of the Church.' The Letter contains an appeal for the exhibition of Christian love, and a warning against false Teachers.

FROM JOHN.
II.

To an eminent Christian Lady,   1
AND TO her Children,
FROM the Officer of the Church.
I sincerely love you all, and not I only, but also all those who
have learnt to know the Truth. We love you for the sake   2
of that Truth which is always in our hearts; yes, and it
will be ours for ever.
Blessing, mercy, and peace will be ours—the gift of God, the   3
Father, and of Jesus Christ, the Father's Son—in a life of
truth and love.

It was a great joy to me to find the lives of some of your   4
children guided by the Truth, in obedience to the command
that we received from the Father. And now, I pray you,   5
Lady—not as though I were writing a new command for you;
no, it is the command which we had from the first—Let us
love one another. And this is love—to live in obedience to the   6
Father's commands. This is the Command as you learnt from
the first, to live in a spirit of love. I say this because many   7
impostors have left us to go into the world—men who do not
acknowledge Jesus as Christ come in our human nature. It
is that which marks a man as an impostor and an anti-Christ.
Take care that you do not lose the fruit of all our work; rather,   8
reap the benefit of it in full. Every one who goes beyond the   9
limits of the Teaching of the Christ has failed to find God; the
man who keeps to that Teaching—he has found both the
Father and the Son. If any one comes to you and does not   10
bring this Teaching, do not receive him into your house or
welcome him; for the man who welcomes him is sharing with   11
him in his wicked work.

Though I have a great deal to say to you, I would rather   12
not trust it to paper and ink, but I am hoping to come and see
you, and to speak with you face to face, so that your joy may be
complete. The children of your eminent sister send   13
you their greetings.

FROM JOHN.

III.

THE LETTER TO GAIUS.

(KNOWN AS 'THE THIRD LETTER FROM JOHN').

[PLACE AND DATE OF WRITING UNKNOWN.]

THIS is a private Letter, addressed by a writer, who, as in the previous Letter, describes himself as 'the Officer of the Church,' to a friend of the name of Gaius. It contains the writer's thanks for hospitality shown to certain missionaries—a hospitality which, under the conditions of travel in those early days, was an important Christian duty.

FROM JOHN.
III.

To his dear friend Gaius, whom he sincerely loves,   1
FROM the Officer of the Church.

Dear friend, I pray that all may be well with you and that   2
you may have good health—I know that all is well with your
soul. For it was a great joy to me, when some Brothers   3
came and testified to your fidelity to the Truth—I know that
your own life is guided by the Truth. Nothing gives me   4
greater pleasure than to hear from time to time that the lives
of my Children are guided by the Truth.

Dear friend, whatever you do for our Brothers is done in a   5
Christian spirit—even when they are strangers to you. They   6
themselves have testified before the Church to your love ; and
you will do well to help them on their way in a manner
worthy of the service of God. For it was on behalf of the   7
Name that they left their homes, and refused to take anything
from the Gentiles. We, therefore, ought to give such people   8
a hearty welcome, and so take our share in their work for
the Truth.

I wrote a few lines to the Church ; but Diotrephes, who   9
loves to be first among them, declines to recognize us. There-   10
fore, when I come, I shall not forget his conduct in ridiculing
us with his wicked tongue. Not content with that, he not
only declines to recognize our Brothers himself, but actually
prevents those who would, and expels them from the Church.

Dear friend, take what is good for your example, not what   11
is bad. The man who does what is good is from God ; the
man who does what is bad has never seen God. Every one   12
has always had a good word for Demetrius, and the Truth
itself speaks for him. Yes, and we also add our good word,
and you know that what we say about him is true.

I have a great deal to say to you, but I do not care to trust   13
it to pen and ink in a letter. I hope, however, it will not   14
be long before I see you, and then we will speak face to
face.   Peace be with you.   Our friends here send you
their greetings.   Greet each one of our friends.

AN APOCALYPSE.

THE REVELATION OF JOHN.

THE REVELATION.

THE REVELATION.

WRITTEN IN ASIA MINOR, AFTER 68 A.D.

IN the later days of Jewish History the place of prophecy was taken by that form of revelation by visions which was known as an 'Apocalypse.'

'The Revelation of John' is the only example of an Apocalypse in the New Testament. Like all books of the kind, Jewish as well as Christian, its purpose is to encourage its readers in the belief that the ultimate triumph of their Faith is assured. In such writings the historical crisis of the day is taken as the model from which a picture is drawn of a great final catastrophe. This Apocalypse is no exception. The Persecutions of 64 A.D. and onwards, and the events of the reign of the Emperor Nero, afforded abundant material for a picture of the horrors wrought by the enemies of the Christ, and of their impending final judgement.

The events of contemporaneous history are here, as in all Apocalypses, half-hidden by the mystical shape in which they are presented. This is accounted for, partly by the fact that their authors saw that the solemnity of their revelations was enhanced by their mystery, and partly by the fact that it was not safe to indicate with too great clearness the hostile Authorities of the day. (Thus, for example, in this Book, the name of the Emperor Nero is apparently veiled under the symbolical number 666, the numerical value of which is represented by the Hebrew letters which spell that title). In spite of their obscure presentation, many events of this writer's time can be detected in the mystical scenes and figures here described.

The strange idioms in which this Book abounds show that, though the author wrote in Greek, he thought in Hebrew. There is at present no certain clue to his identity.

THE
REVELATION OF JOHN.

The Revelation of Jesus Christ, which God gave to him to make known to his servants, concerning what must shortly take place, and which he sent and revealed by his angel to his servant John, who testified to the Message of God and to the testimony to Jesus Christ, omitting nothing of what he had seen. Blessed is he who reads, and blessed are they who listen to, the words of this prophecy, and lay to heart what is here written; for The Time is near. 1 2 3

I.—MESSAGES TO THE SEVEN CHURCHES.

From John, to the seven Churches which are in Roman Asia. Blessing and peace be yours from him who is, and who was, and who shall be, and from the seven Spirits that are before his throne, and from Jesus Christ, 'the faithful Witness, the First-born from the dead, and the Ruler of all the Kings of the earth.' To him who loves us and freed us from our sins by his own blood—and he made us 'a Kingdom of Priests in the service of God,' his Father!—to him be ascribed glory and dominion for ever. Amen. 'He is coming among the clouds!' Every eye shall see him, even those who pierced nim; 'and all the nations of the earth shall wail for fear of him.' So shall it be. Amen. 4 5 6 7

'I am the Alpha and the Omega,' says the Lord, the God who is, and who was, and who shall be, the Almighty. 8

I, John, who am your Brother, and who share with you in the suffering and kingship and endurance of Jesus, found myself on the island called Patmos, for the sake of the Message of God and the testimony to Jesus. I fell into a trance on the Lord's Day, and I heard behind me a loud voice, like the blast of a trumpet. It said—'Write what you see in a book and send it to the seven Churches, to Ephesus, 9 10 11

---

1 Dan. 2. 28. 4 Exod. 3. 14; Isa. 41. 4; Ps. 89. 37, 27; 130. 8; Isa. 40. 2.
6 Exod. 19. 6. 7 Dan. 7. 13; Zech. 12. 10—14. 8 Exod. 3. 14; Isa. 41. 4;
Amos 4. 13 (Septuagint),

Smyrna, Pergamus, Thyatira, Sardis, Philadelphia, and
Laodicaea.'   I turned to see what voice it was that   12
spoke to me ; and when I turned, I saw seven golden lamps,
and in the midst of the lamps one 'like a man, in a robe   13
reaching to his feet,' and with a golden girdle across his
breast.   'The hair of his head was as white as wool, as white   14
as snow ; his eyes were like flaming fire ; and his feet   15
were like brass' as when molten in a furnace ; 'his voice
was like the sound of many streams,' in his right hand he   16
held seven stars, from his mouth came a sharp two-edged
sword, and his face was like 'the sun in the fulness of its
power.'   And, when I saw him, I fell at his feet like one   17
dead. He laid his hand on me and said—
   'Do not be afraid. I am the First and the Last, the Ever-   18
living. I died, and I am alive for ever and ever. And I hold
the keys of the Grave and of the Place of the Dead. Therefore   19
write of what you have seen and of what is happening now
and of what is about to take place—the mystic meaning of   20
the seven stars which you saw in my right hand, and the
seven golden lamps. The seven stars are the Angels of the
seven Churches, and the seven lamps are the seven Churches.

To the Angel of the Church in Ephesus write :—   I   **2**

   " These are the words of him who holds the seven stars in
his right hand, and walks among the seven golden lamps :—I   2
know your life, your toil and endurance, and I know that you
cannot tolerate evil-doers. I know, too, how you tested those
who declare that they are Apostles, though they are not, and
how you proved them false. You possess endurance, and   3
have borne much for my Name, and have never grown weary.
But this I have against you—You have abandoned your first   4
love. Therefore remember from what you have fallen, and   5
repent, and live the life that you lived before ; or else,
I will come and remove your Lamp from its place, unless you
repent. But this is in your favour—You hate the life lived by   6
the Nikolaïtans, and I also hate it.   Let him who has   7
ears hear what the Spirit is saying to the Churches.   To
him who conquers—to him I will give the right 'to eat the
fruit of the Tree of Life, which stands in the Paradise of God.'"

To the Angel of the Church in Smyrna write :—   8

   " These are the words of him who is the First and the Last,
who died, but is restored to life :—I know your persecution   9

    13 Dan. 7. 13 ; Ezek. 1. 26 ; 8. 2 ; 9. 2, 3 (Septuagint), 11 (Septuagint) ; Dan. 10. 5
(Chaldaean).   14 Dan. 7. 9.   14—15 Dan. 10. 6.   15 Ezek. 1. 24 ; 43. 2 (Hebrew).
16 Judges 5. 31.   17 Dan. 10. 12, 19 ; Isa. 44. 6 (Hebrew) ; 48. 12 (Hebrew).
19 Isa. 48. 6 ; Dan. 2. 29 (Chaldaean).   20 Dan. 2. 20,   7 Gen. 2. 9 ; 3. 22 ; Ezek. 31. 8,
8 Isa. 44. 6 (Hebrew) ; 48. 12 (Hebrew).

and your poverty—yet you are rich ! I know, too, the slanders that come from those who declare that they are Jews, though they are not, but are a Congregation of Satan. Do not be afraid of what you are about to suffer. The Devil is about to throw some of you into prison, that you may be tempted, and may undergo persecution for ten days. Be faithful even to death, and I will give you the Crown of Life. Let him who has ears hear what the Spirit is saying to the Churches. He who conquers shall suffer no hurt from the Second Death."

To the Angel of the Church in Pergamus write :—

" These are the words of him who holds the sharp two-edged sword :—I know where you dwell, where the Throne of Satan stands. And yet you hold to my Name, and you did not disown my Faith even in the days of Antipas, my faithful witness, who was put to death among you where Satan dwells. Yet I have a few things against you—You have among you those who hold to the Teaching of Balaam, who taught Balak to put temptations in the way of the Israelites, so that they should eat idol-offerings and commit licentious acts. Again you have among you those who hold in the same way to the Teaching of the Nikolaïtans. Therefore repent, or else, I will come quickly and contend with such men with words that will cut like a sword. Let him who has ears hear what the Spirit is saying to the Churches. To him who conquers—to him I will give a share of the mystic manna, and I will give him a white stone ; and on the stone shall be inscribed a new name, which no one knows except him who receives it."

To the Angel of the Church in Thyatira write :—

" These are the words of the Son of God, ' whose eyes are like flaming fire, and whose feet are like brass ' :—I know your life, your love, faith, service, and endurance ; and I know that your life of late has been better than it was at first. Yet I have this against you—You tolerate the woman Jezebel, who declares that she is a Prophetess, and misleads my servants by her teaching, till they commit licentious acts and eat idol-offerings. I gave her time to repent, but she is determined not to turn from her licentiousness. Therefore I am laying her upon a bed of sickness, and bringing great suffering upon those who are unfaithful with her, unless they repent and turn from a life like hers. I will also put her children to death ; and all the Churches shall learn that I am he who

10 Dan. 1. 12, 14.   14 Num. 31. 16 ;   25. 1, 2.   17 Ps. 78. 24 ; Isa. 62. 2 ; 65. 15.   18 Dan. 10, 6.   20 Num. 25. 1, 2.   23 Jer. 17. 10 ; Ps. 7. 9 ; 62. 12,

'looks into the hearts and souls of men'; and I will give to each one of you what his life deserves.   But I say to the rest of 24 you at Thyatira—all who do not accept such teaching, those who did not learn 'the secrets of Satan,' as men call them— I am not laying on you any further burden; only hold fast to 25 what you have received, until I come.   To him who 26 conquers and is careful to live my life to the end—to him I will give authority over the nations, and 'he shall rule them with an 27 iron rod, as when earthen vessels are broken in pieces' (as I myself have received from my Father) and I will give him 28 the Morning Star.   Let him who has ears hear what 29 the Spirit is saying to the Churches."

To the Angel of the Church in Sardis write :—   1 **3**

" These are the words of him who has the seven Spirits of God and the seven stars :—I know your life, and that men say of you that you are living, though you are dead.   Be on 2 the watch, and strengthen what still survives, though once it was all but dead ; for I have not found your life perfect in the eyes of my God.   Therefore remember what you have received 3 and heard, and lay it to heart and repent.   Unless you are on the watch, I shall come like a thief, and you will not know at what hour I am coming to you.   Yet there are some few 4 among you at Sardis who did not soil their robes ; they shall walk with me, robed in white, for they are worthy.   He 5 who conquers shall be clothed in these white robes, and I will not 'strike his name out of the Book of Life'; but I will own him before my Father, and before his angels.   Let him 6 who has ears hear what the Spirit is saying to the Churches."

To the Angel of the Church in Philadelphia write :—   7

" These are the words of him who is holy and true, who holds 'the Key of David, who opens and no one shall shut, and shuts and no one opens':—I know your life (see, I have 8 set a door open before you which no one is able to shut), I know that, though you have but little strength, you kept my teaching in mind, and did not disown my Name.   Listen, I 9 give some of the Congregation of Satan, the men who declare that they are Jews, though they are not, but are lying——I will make them 'come and bow down at your feet,' and they shall learn that I loved you.   Because you kept in mind the 10 story of my endurance, I will keep you in the hour of trial that is about to come upon the whole world, the hour that will test all who are living upon earth.   I will come quickly.   Hold 11 to what you have received, that no one may take your

---

26—27 Ps. 2. 8, 9.   5 Exod. 32. 33 ; Ps. 69. 28.   7 Isa. 22. 22.   9 Isa. 45. 14 ; 49. 23 ; 60. 14 (Hebrew) ; 66. 23 ; 43. 4.

crown.   He who conquers—I will make him a pillar in 12
the Temple of my God ; and never more shall he leave it ; and
I will write on him the name of my God and the name of the
City of my God, the New Jerusalem, which is coming down
out of Heaven from my God, and I will write on him my new
name.   Let him who has ears hear what the Spirit is 13
saying to the Churches."

To the Angel of the Church in Laodicaea write :— 14

" These are the words of the Unchanging One, 'the Witness
faithful and true, the Beginning of the Creation of God ' :—I 15
know your life ; I know that you are neither cold nor hot.
Would that you were either cold or hot ! But now, because 16
you are lukewarm, neither hot nor cold, I am about to spit
you out of my mouth. You say ' I am rich and have grown 17
rich, and I want for nothing,' and you do not know that you
are wretched, miserable, poor, blind, naked ! Therefore I 18
counsel you to buy from me gold which has been refined by
fire, that you may grow rich ; and white robes, that you may
be clothed and your shameful nakedness be hidden ; and
ointment to anoint your eyes, that you may see. ' All whom 19
I love I rebuke and discipline.' Therefore be in earnest and
repent.   I am standing at the door and knocking ! If 20
any one hears my voice and opens the door, I will go in, and
will feast with him, and he shall feast with me.   To him 21
who conquers—to him I will give the right to sit beside me on
my throne, as I, when I conquered, took my seat beside my
Father on his throne.   Let him who has ears hear what 22
the Spirit is saying to the Churches."

II.—THE VISION OF THE SEVEN SEALS.

After this, in my vision, I saw an open door in the heavens, 1 **4**
and the first voice that I heard was like the blast of a trumpet
speaking to me. It said—' Come up here and I will show you
what must take place.' Immediately after this I fell into 2
a trance. There stood a throne in Heaven, and on the
throne was One seated. He who was seated on it was in 3
appearance like a jasper and a sardius ; and ' round the throne
there was a rainbow ' of the colour of an emerald. And round 4
the throne were twenty-four other thrones, and on these I saw
twenty-four Councillors sitting, clothed in white robes ; and
on their heads they had crowns of gold. Out from the throne 5
' come flashes of lightning, cries, and peals of thunder' !

---

[12] Ezek. 48. 35 ; Isa. 62. 2 ; 65. 15.   [14] Ps. 89. 37 ; Prov. 8. 22.   [17] Hos. 12. 8.
[19] Prov 3. 12 (Septuagint).   [1] Exod. 19. 16, 24 ; Dan. 2. 29.   [2] Isa. 6. 1 ; Ps. 47. 8.
[3] Ezek. 1. 26—28. [5] Ezek. 1. 13 ; Exod. 19. 16 (Hebrew and Septuagint).

S*

There are seven torches burning in front of the throne, which
are the seven spirits of God ; and in front of the throne is   6
what seemed to be a sea of glass, 'resembling crystal, while
within the space before the throne and round the throne are
four Creatures full of eyes' in front and behind.   The first   7
Creature is like a lion, the second Creature like a calf, the
third Creature has a face like a man's, and the fourth Creature
is like an eagle on the wing.   These four Creatures have each   8
of them six wings, and all round, and within, they are full of
eyes ; and day and night they never cease to say—

> 'Holy, holy, holy is the Lord, our God, the
> Almighty, who was, and who is, and who shall be.'

And, whenever these Creatures give praise and honour and   9
thanks to him who is 'seated on the throne, to him who lives
for ever and ever,' the twenty-four Councillors prostrate them-   10
selves before him who is seated on the throne, and worship
him who lives for ever and ever, and throw down their crowns
before the throne, saying—

> 'Worthy art thou, our Lord and God, to receive   11
> all praise, and honour, and power, for thou didst
> create all things, and at thy bidding they came into
> being and were created.'

Then I saw at the right hand of him who was 'seated on   1   **5**
the throne a book, with writing inside and out, and sealed'
with seven seals ; and I saw a mighty angel who was pro-   2
claiming in a loud voice—'Who is worthy to open the book
and break its seals ?'   But no one either in Heaven or   3
on earth or under the earth was able to open the book
or look within it.   At this I wept long, because no one   4
could be found who was worthy to open the book or look
within it.   But one of the Councillors said to me—'Do not   5
weep.   The Lion conquered—the Lion of the tribe of Judah,
the Scion of David—and can therefore open the book with
its seven seals.'

Then, within the space between the throne and the four   6
Creatures, and in the midst of the Councillors, I saw, standing,
a Lamb, which seemed to have been sacrificed.   It had seven
horns and seven eyes.   (These eyes are the seven Spirits of
God, and they are sent into all the world.)   The Lamb came   7
forward ; and he has taken the book from the right hand of
him who was seated on the throne.   And, when he had   8

6 Ezek. 1   5, 18, 22, 26; 10. 1 ; Isa. 6. 1—2.   7 Ezek. 1. 10 ; 10. 14.   8 Isa. 6. 2, 3 ;
Ezek. 1. 18; 10. 12 ; Amos 4. 13 (Septuagint) ; Exod. 3. 14 ; Isa. 41. 4.
9—10 Isa. 6. 1 ; Ps. 47. 8 ; Dan. 4. 34 ; 6. 26 ; 12. 7.   1 Isa. 6. 1 ; Ps. 47. 8 ;
Ezek. 2. 9—10 ; Isa. 29. 11.   5 Gen. 49. 9 ; Isa. 11. 10.   6 Isa. 53. 7 ; Zech. 4. 10.
7 Isa 6, 1 ; Ps. 47. 8,   8 Ps. 141. 2.

taken the book, the four Creatures and the twenty-four
Councillors prostrated themselves before the Lamb, each of
them holding a harp and golden bowls full of incense. (These
are the prayers of Christ's People.) And they are singing a 9
new song—

> 'Thou art worthy to take the book and break its
> seals, for thou wast sacrificed, and with thy blood
> thou didst buy for God men of every tribe, and
> language, and people, and nation, and didst make 10
> them a Kingdom of Priests in the service of our God,
> and they are reigning upon the earth.'

Then, in my vision, I heard the voices of many angels 11
round the throne, and of the Creatures, and of the Councillors.
In number they were 'ten thousand times ten thousand and
thousands of thousands,' and they cried in a loud voice— 12

> 'Worthy is the Lamb that was sacrificed to re-
> ceive all power, and wealth, and wisdom, and might,
> and honour, and praise, and blessing.'

And I heard every created thing in the air, and on the earth, 13
and under the earth, and on the sea, and all that is in them
crying—

> 'To him who is seated on the throne and to the
> Lamb be ascribed all blessing, and honour, and
> praise, and dominion for ever and ever.'

And the four Creatures said 'Amen,' and the Councillors 14
prostrated themselves and worshipped.

Then I saw the Lamb break one of the seven seals, and I 1 **6**
heard one of the four Creatures crying with a voice like
thunder—'Come.' And in my vision I saw 'a white horse.' 2
Its rider held a bow, and he was given a crown, and he went
out conquering and to conquer.

When the Lamb broke the second seal, I heard the second 3
Creature crying—'Come.' Then there went out another 4
horse, 'a red horse,' and to its rider was given the power to
deprive the earth of peace, so that men should kill one
another ; and he was given a great sword.

When the Lamb broke the third seal, I heard the third 5
Creature crying—'Come.' And in my vision I saw 'a black
horse.' Its rider held scales in his hand. And I heard what 6
seemed to be a voice, coming from among the four Creatures,

9 Ps. 144. 9. 10 Exod. 19. 6. 11 Dan. 7. 10. 12 Isa. 53. 7. 13 Isa. 6. 1 ; Ps. 47. 8.
2—5 Zech. 1. 8 ; 6. 2—3, 6.

crying—' A quart of wheat for a florin, and three quarts of barley for a florin !   But do not harm the oil and the wine.'

When the Lamb broke the fourth seal, I heard the voice of   7
the fourth Creature crying—' Come.'   And in my vision I saw   8
a grey horse.   His rider's name was Death, and the Lord of the Place of Death rode behind him ; and power was given them over the fourth part of the earth, so that they might ' destroy with sword and famine and death, and by means of the wild beasts of the earth.'

When the Lamb opened the fifth seal, I saw under the altar   9
the souls of those who had been killed for the sake of God's Message and for the testimony which they had borne.   They   10
cried in a loud voice—' How long, O Sovereign Lord, holy and true, before thou wilt give judgement and avenge our blood upon all who are living upon the earth ? '   Then to each   11
of them was given a white robe, and they were told to rest yet a little longer, till the number of their fellow-servants and of their Brothers who were about to be put to death, as they had been, should be complete.

And I saw the Lamb break the sixth seal, and then there   12
was a great earthquake.   The sun became black, like sack-cloth, and the moon, which was at its full, like blood.   ' The   13
stars of the heavens fell ' to the earth, as when a fig-tree, shaken by a strong wind, drops its unripe fruit.   The heavens   14
disappeared like a scroll when it is rolled up, and every moun-tain and island was moved from its place.   Then all the   15
kings of the earth, and the princes, and the generals, and the rich, and the powerful, and every slave and free man, ' hid themselves in the caves and under the rocks ' of the mountains ; and they are crying to the mountains and the rocks—' Fall   16
upon us, and hide us from the eyes of him who is seated on the throne, and from the Wrath of the Lamb, for the great   17
Day of their Wrath is come, and who can stand to meet it ? '

After this, I saw four angels standing ' upon the four   1   **7**
corners of the earth,' restraining the four winds of the earth, that no wind should blow over the earth, or over the sea, or against any tree.   And, in the east, I saw another angel,   2
ascending, holding the seal of the Living God ; and he cried in a loud voice to the four angels, to whom there had been given power to harm the earth and the sea—' Do not harm the   3
earth, or the sea, or the trees, until we have sealed the servants of our God upon their foreheads.'   I heard,   4
too, the number of those who had been sealed.   It was one hundred and forty-four thousand ; and they were from every tribe of the Israelites.

8 Hos. 13. 14; Ezek. 33. 27 ; 14. 21 ; 5. 12 ; 29. 5 ; 34. 28.   10 Zech. 1. 12; Deut. 32. 43 ; 2 Kings 9. 7 ; Hos. 4. 1.   12 Joel 2. 31.   13–14 Isa. 34. 4 ; 13. 10. 15 Ps. 48. 4 (Septuagint); 2. 2 ; Isa. 24. 21 ; 34. 12 ; Jer. 4. 29 ; Isa. 2. 10. 16 Hos. 10. 8 ; Isa. 6. 1 ; Ps. 47. 8.   17 Joel 2. 11 ; Zeph. 1. 14—15, 18 ; Mal. 3. 2. 1 Ezek. 7. 2 ; 37. 9 ; Zech. 6. 5.   3 Ezek. 9. 4.

From the tribe of Judah twelve thousand were sealed,   5
from the tribe of Reuben twelve thousand,
from the tribe of Gad twelve thousand,
from the tribe of Asher twelve thousand,   6
from the tribe of Napthali twelve thousand,
from the tribe of Manasseh twelve thousand,
from the tribe of Simeon twelve thousand,   7
from the tribe of Levi twelve thousand,
from the tribe of Issachar twelve thousand,
from the tribe of Zebulon twelve thousand,   8
from the tribe of Joseph twelve thousand,
from the tribe of Benjamin twelve thousand were sealed.

After this, in my vision, I saw a vast throng which no man   9
could number, of men from every nation and of all tribes, and
peoples, and languages. They stood in front of the throne
and in front of the Lamb, robed in white, holding palm
branches in their hands. And they are crying in a loud   10
voice—

   'Salvation be ascribed to our God who is seated
on his throne and to the Lamb.'

And all the angels were standing round the throne and the   11
Councillors and the four Creatures, and they prostrated them-
selves on their faces in front of the throne and worshipped
God, saying—   12

   'Amen. Blessing, and praise, and wisdom, and
thanksgiving, and honour, and power, and might be
ascribed to our God for ever and ever. Amen.'

Then one of the Councillors turned to me and said 'Who   13
are these who are robed in white? and whence did they
come?'

   'My Lord,' I answered, 'it is you who know.'   14
   'These,' he said, 'are they who come through the Great
Persecution; they washed their robes white in the blood
of the Lamb. And therefore it is that they are before the   15
throne of God, and are serving him day and night in his
Temple; and he who is seated on the throne will shelter
them. Never again shall they be hungry, never again shall   16
they be thirsty, nor shall the sun smite upon them, nor any
scorching heat; for the Lamb that stands in the space before   17
the throne will be their shepherd, and will lead them to life-
giving springs of water; and God will wipe away all tears
from their eyes.'

---

10 Isa. 6. 1; Ps. 47. 8.   14 Dan. 12. 1; Gen. 49. 11.   15 Isa. 6. 1; Ps. 47. 8.
16–17 Isa. 49. 10.   17 Ezek. 34. 23; Jer. 2. 13; Isa. 25. 8; Jer. 31. 16.

As soon as the Lamb had broken the seventh seal, there   1   **8**
was silence in Heaven for, it might be, half-an-hour.

III.—THE VISION OF THE SEVEN TRUMPET-BLASTS.

Then I saw the seven angels who stand before God, and   2
seven trumpets were given to them.

Next, another angel came and stood at the altar with a   3
golden censer in his hand ; and a great quantity of incense
was given to him, to mingle with the prayers of all Christ's
People upon the golden altar before the throne.   The smoke   4
of the incense ascended, with the prayers of Christ's People,
from the hand of the angel before God.   Then the angel took   5
the censer, and filled it with fire from the altar, and threw it
down upon the earth ; and there followed ' peals of thunder,
cries, flashes of lightning,' and an earthquake.

Then the seven angels holding the seven trumpets prepared   6
to blow their blasts.

The first blew ; and there came hail and fire mixed with   7
blood, and it fell upon the earth.   A third part of the earth
was burnt up, and a third of the trees, and every blade of
grass.

Then the second angel blew ; and what appeared to be a   8
great mountain, burning, was hurled into the sea.   A third of
the sea became blood, and a third part of all created things   9
that are in the sea—that is, of all living things—died, and a
third of the ships was destroyed.

Then the third angel blew ; and there fell from the heavens   10
a great star, burning like a torch.   It fell upon a third of the
rivers and upon the springs.   (The star is called ' Worm-   11
wood.')   A third of the water became bitter as wormwood,
and so bitter was the water that many died from drinking it.

Then the fourth angel blew ; and a third of the sun and a   12
third of the moon and a third of the stars were blasted, so
that a third of them was eclipsed, and for a third part of the
day there was no light, and at night it was the same.

And, in my vision, I heard an eagle flying in mid-heaven   13
and crying in a loud voice—' Woe, woe, woe for all who live
on the earth, at the other trumpet-blasts of the three angels
who have yet to blow.'

Then the fifth angel blew ; and I saw a Star that had fallen   1   **9**
upon the earth from the heavens, and to him was given the
key of the bottomless pit.   He opened the bottomless pit, and   2

---

[3] Amos 9. 1.   [3–4] Ps. 141. 2.   [5] Lev. 16. 12 ; Exod. 19. 16 (Hebrew and Septuagint).   [7] Exod. 9. 24 ; Ezek. 38. 22 ; Joel 2. 30.   [8] Jer. 51. 25 ; Exod. 7. 19.
[10] Isa. 14. 12.   [2] Gen. 19. 28 (Hebrew) ; Exod. 19. 18 ; Joel 2. 10.

from the pit rose a smoke like the smoke of a great furnace. The sun and the air grew dark because of the smoke from the pit. Out of the smoke locusts descended upon the earth, and 3 they received the same power as that possessed by scorpions. They were told not to harm the grass, or any plant, or any 4 tree, but only those who have not ' the seal of God upon their foreheads.' Yet they were not allowed to kill them, but it 5 was ordered that those men should be tortured for five months. Their torture was like the torture caused by a scorpion when it stings a man. In those days men ' will seek Death and 6 will not find it '; they will long to die, but Death flees from them. In appearance the locusts were like horses equipped 7 for battle. On their heads there were what appeared to be crowns that shone like gold, their faces resembled human faces, and they had hair like the hair of a woman, their teeth 8 were like lions' teeth, and they had what seemed to be iron 9 breastplates, while the noise of their wings was like the noise of chariots drawn by many horses, galloping into battle. They 10 have tails like scorpions, and stings, and in their tails lies their power to harm men for five months. They have as their 11 king the Angel of the bottomless pit, whose name, in Hebrew, is ' Abaddon,' while, in Greek, his name is ' Apollyon ' (the Destroyer).

The first Woe has passed ; and still there are two Woes to 12 follow !

Then the sixth angel blew ; and I heard a voice proceeding 13 from the corners of the golden altar that stood before God. It spoke to the sixth angel—the angel with the trumpet—and 14 said ' Let loose the four angels that are in chains at the great river Euphrates.' Then the four angels, that were held in 15 readiness for that hour and day and month and year, were let loose, to destroy a third of mankind. The number of the 16 hosts of horsemen was ten thousand times ten thousand, twice told ; I heard their number. And this is what the horses and 17 their riders appeared to be like in my vision :—They had breastplates of fire, blood-red and sulphurous, and the heads of the horses were like lions' heads, while out of their mouths issue fire, and smoke, and sulphur. Through these three 18 Curses a third of mankind perished—because of the fire, and the smoke, and the sulphur that issued from their mouths ; for the power of the horses lies in their mouths and in their 19 tails. For their tails are like snakes, with heads, and it is with them that they do harm. But those who were left of mankind, 20 who had not perished through these Curses, did not repent and turn away from what their own hands had made ; they would

---

3—4 Exod. 10. 12, 15.   4 Ezek. 9. 4.   6 Job 3. 21.   7 Joel 2. 4, 5.   8 Joel 1. 6.
9 Joel 2. 5.   14 Gen. 15. 18; Deut. 1. 7; Josh. 1. 4.   20 Isa. 17. 8; Dan. 5. 3, 23 (Septuagint); Dan. 5. 4, 23 (Chaldaean); Deut. 32. 17; Ps. 115. 7.

not abandon the worship of 'demons, and of idols made of gold or silver or brass or stone or wood, which can neither see, nor hear, nor walk'; and they did not repent of their murders, or their sorceries, or their licentiousness, or their thefts.   21

Then I saw another mighty angel, descending from Heaven.   1 **10**
His robe was a cloud; over his head was the rainbow; his face was like the sun, and his feet like pillars of fire; in his   2
hand he held a little book open. He set his right foot on the sea, and his left on the land; and he cried in a loud voice like   3
the roaring of a lion. At his cry the seven peals of thunder spoke, each with its own voice.   And, when they spoke,   4
I was about to write; but I heard a voice from Heaven say— 'Keep secret what the seven peals of thunder said, and do not write it down.'   Then the angel, whom I had seen   5
standing on the sea and on the land, 'raised his right hand to the heavens, and swore by him who lives for ever and ever,   6
who created the heavens and all that is in them, and the earth and all that is in it, and the sea and all that is in it,' that time should cease to be. Moreover at the time when the seventh   7
angel shall speak, when he is ready to blow his blast, then the hidden purposes of God, of which he told the good news to his servants, the Prophets, are at once fulfilled.   Then   8
came the voice which I had heard from Heaven. It spoke to me again, and said—' Go and take the book that is open in the hand of the angel who stands on the sea and on the land.'
So I went to the angel and asked him to give me the little   9
book. And he said 'Take it, and eat it. It will be bitter to your stomach, but in your mouth it will be as sweet as honey.'
I took the little book out of the angel's hand 'and ate it, and,   10
while in my mouth, it was like the sweetest honey'; but, when I had eaten it, it was bitter to my stomach. And I was   11
told—' You must prophesy again about men of many peoples, and nations, and languages, and about many kings.'

Then I was given a measure like a rod, and a voice said to   1 **11**
me—' Go and measure the Temple of God and the altar, and count the worshippers there. But omit the court outside the   2
Temple, and do not measure that, for it has been given up to the nations; and the holy City will be under their heel for forty-two months. Then I will give permission to my Two Witnesses,   3
and for those twelve hundred and sixty days they will continue teaching, clothed in sackcloth.'   These men are repre-   4
sented by ' the two olive trees and the two lamps that stand before the Lord of the earth.' When any one wishes to harm   5
them, 'fire comes from their mouths and consumes their enemies'; and whoever wishes to harm them will, in this way,

---

[21] 2 Kings 9. 22.   [4] Dan. 8. 26; 12. 4.   [5—6] Dan. 12. 7; Gen. 14. 19, 22; Neh. 9. 6; Exod. 20. 11; Ps. 146. 6.   [7] Amos 3. 7 (Hebrew); Dan. 9. 6, 10; Zech. 1. 6.   [9—10] Ezek. 3. 1—3.   [11] Jer. 1. 10; 25. 30; Dan. 3. 4; 7. 14.
[1] Ezek. 40. 3.   [2] Zech. 12. 3 (Septuagint); Isa. 63. 18; Ps. 79. 1; Dan. 8. 10.
[4] Zech. 4. 2—3, 11, 14.   [5] 2 Kings 1. 10; 2 Sam. 22. 9; Jer. 5. 14; Ps. 97. 3.

inevitably perish. These men have the power to close the 6
heavens, that 'no rain may fall' during the time that they are
teaching ; and they have power 'to turn the streams into
blood, and to smite the land with any Curse,' whenever they
will. As soon as they have completed their testimony, 'the 7
wild Beast that ascends from the bottomless pit will make
war upon them and conquer' and kill them. Their dead 8
bodies will lie in the streets of the great City, which is mysti-
cally spoken of as 'Sodom' and 'Egypt,' where their Master
was crucified. Men of all peoples, and tribes, and languages, 9
and nations look at their dead bodies for three days and a half,
and do not allow them to be laid in a grave. Those who live 10
on the earth rejoice over them and are merry, and they will
send presents to one another, because these two Prophets
brought torments upon those who live on the earth. After three 11
days and a half 'the life-giving breath of God entered these
men, and they stood up upon their feet,' and a great terror
took possession of those who were watching them. The two 12
men heard a loud voice from Heaven which said to them—
'Come up here,' and they went up to Heaven in the cloud,
while their enemies watched them.   At that very time a 13
great earthquake occurred. A tenth part of the city fell, and
seven thousand people perished in the earthquake. Those who
escaped were much terrified, and praised the God of Heaven.

The second Woe has passed ; and there is a third Woe soon 14
to follow !

Then the seventh angel blew ; and loud voices were heard 15
in Heaven saying—

> 'The Kingdom of the World has become the
> Kingdom of our Lord and of his Christ, and he will
> reign for ever and ever.'

At this the twenty-four Councillors, who were seated on their 16
thrones before God, prostrated themselves on their faces and
worshipped Him, saying—   17

> 'We thank thee, O Lord, our God, the Almighty,
> who art and who wast, that thou hast assumed thy
> great power and reigned. The nations were enraged, 18
> and thy Wrath fell upon them ; the time came for the
> dead to be judged, and for thee to give the reward to
> thy servants the Prophets, and to the People of
> Christ, and to those who reverence thy Name—the
> high and the low alike—and to destroy those who are
> destroying the earth.'

6 1 Kings 17. 1 ; Exod. 7. 17, 19 ; 1 Sam. 4. 8.   7 Dan. 7. 3, 7—8 (Septuagint), 21.
8 Isa. 1. 10.   10—11 Ps. 105. 38.   11 Ezek. 37. 5, 10.   12 2 Kings 2. 11.
13 Ezek. 38. 19—20 ; Dan. 2. 19 (Chaldaean). 15 Obad. 21 ; Ps. 22. 28 ; Exod. 15. 18 ;
Ps. 10. 16 ; Dan. 2. 44 ; 7. 14 ; Ps. 2. 2.   17 Amos. 4. 13 (Septuagint) ; Exod. 3. 14 ;
Isa. 41. 4.   17—18 Ps. 99. 1.   18 Ps. 2. 1 (Hebrew), 5 ; 46. 6 (Hebrew) ; 115. 13 ;
Amos 3. 7 ; Dan. 9. 6, 10 ; Zech. 1. 6.

Then the Temple of God in Heaven was opened, and the Ark   19
containing his Covenant was seen in his Temple; and there
followed 'flashes of lightning, cries, peals of thunder,' an
earthquake, and 'a great storm of hail.'

IV.—THE VISION OF SEVEN SYMBOLICAL FIGURES.

Then a great portent was seen in the heavens—a woman   1   **12**
whose robe was the sun, and who had the moon under her
feet, and on her head a crown of twelve stars. She was with   2
child; and 'she is crying out in the pain and agony of child-
birth.' Another portent also was seen in the heavens. There   3
was a great red Dragon, with seven heads and ten horns,
and on his heads were seven diadems. His tail draws after   4
it a third of the stars in the heavens, and it hurled them down
on the earth. The Dragon is standing in front of the woman
who is about to give birth to the child, so that he may devour
it as soon as it is born. The woman gave birth to a son, a   5
male child, who is destined to rule all the nations with an iron
rod; and her child was at once caught up to God upon his
throne. But the woman fled into the wilderness, where there is   6
a place prepared for her by God, to be tended there for twelve
hundred and sixty days.

Then a battle took place in the heavens. Michael and his   7
angels fought with the Dragon. But though the Dragon,
with his angels, fought, he did not prevail; and there was   8
no place left for them any longer in the heavens. Then the   9
great Dragon, the primeval Serpent, known as the 'Devil'
and 'Satan,' who deceives all the world, was hurled down to
the earth, and his angels were hurled down with him. And   10
I heard a loud voice in Heaven which said—

> 'Now has begun the day of the Salvation, and
> Power, and Dominion of our God, and the Rule of
> his Christ; for the Accuser of our Brothers has been
> hurled down, he who has been accusing them before
> our God day and night. Their victory was due to   11
> the Blood of the Lamb, and to the Message to which
> they bore their testimony. In their love of life they
> shrank not from death. Therefore, be glad, O   12
> Heaven, and all who live in Heaven! Alas for the
> earth and for the sea, for the Devil has gone down to
> you in great fury, knowing that he has but little
> time.'

19 1 Kings 8. 1, 6; 2 Chron. 5. 7; Exod. 19. 16 (Hebrew and Septuagint);
Exod. 9. 24. 2 Isa. 66. 6—7. 3 Dan. 7. 7. 4 Dan. 8. 10. 5 Isa. 66. 7; Ps. 2. 8—9.
7 Dan. 10. 13—20. 9 Gen. 3. 1; Zech. 3. 1—2 (Hebrew and Septuagint).
12 Isa. 44. 23; 49. 13.

When the Dragon saw that he was hurled down to the 13
earth, he pursued the woman who had given birth to the male
child.   But to the woman were given the two wings of the 14
great eagle, so that she might fly to her place in the wilderness,
where she is being tended for ' one year, and for two years,
and for half a year,' in safety from the Serpent.   Then the 15
Serpent poured water from its mouth after the woman, like a
river, so that it might sweep her away.   But Earth came to 16
her help, and opened her mouth and drank up the river which
the Dragon had poured out of its mouth.   The Dragon was 17
enraged at the woman, and went to fight with the rest of her offspring—those who lay to heart the commands of God and bear
their testimony to Jesus; and he took his stand on the sea-shore.

Then I saw, 'rising out of the sea, a wild Beast with ten 1 **13**
horns' and seven heads.   On its horns were ten diadems, and
on its heads were blasphemous names.   The Beast that I saw 2
was like a leopard; but its feet were like a bear's, and its
mouth like the mouth of a lion.   The Dragon gave it his
power and his throne, and wide dominion.   One of its heads 3
seemed to me to have been mortally wounded, but its deadly
wound had been healed.   The whole earth followed the Beast,
wondering; and men worshipped the Dragon, because he had 4
given his dominion to the Beast; while, as they worshipped
the Beast, they said—'Who can compare with the Beast?
and who can fight with it?'   The Beast was given 'a mouth 5
that spoke proudly' and blasphemously, and it was empowered
to work its will for forty-two months.   It opened its mouth 6
only to blaspheme God, to blaspheme his Name and his
Tabernacle—those who dwell in his Tabernacle in Heaven.
It had been permitted to fight with Christ's People and to 7
conquer them, and it had received power over men of every
tribe, and people, and language, and nation.   All who are 8
living on earth will worship it—all whose names have not
been written in the Lamb's Book of Life, the Lamb that has
been sacrificed from the foundation of the world.   Let 9
him who has ears hear.   'Whoever is destined for captivity 10
goes into captivity.'   Whoever shall kill with the sword must
inevitably be killed with the sword.   (Here there is
need for endurance and faith on the part of Christ's People.)

Then I saw, rising out of the earth, another wild Beast.   It 11
had two horns like those of a lamb, and its voice was like a
dragon's.   It exercises all the authority of the first Beast 12
under its very eyes; and it makes the earth and all who are
living on it worship that first Beast, whose mortal wound was
healed.   It performs great marvels, even causing fire to fall 13
from the heavens to the earth, before men's eyes; and in con- 14

---

[14] Dan. 7. 25; 12. 7.   [1] Dan. 7. 3, 7.   [2] Dan. 7. 4–6, 8.   [5] Dan. 8. 12, 24.
[7] Dan. 7. 8 (Septuagint), 21.   [8] Dan. 12. 1; Ps. 69. 28; Isa. 53. 7.   [10] Jer. 15. 2.

sequence of the marvels which it was allowed to perform under the eyes of the Beast, it is able to deceive all who are living on the earth. It bids those who live on the earth to make a statue in honour of the Beast, who, despite the wound from the sword, yet lived. It was permitted to breathe life into the 15 image of the Beast, so that the image of the Beast might speak ; and it was also permitted to cause all who refused to worship the image of the Beast to be put to death. High 16 and low, rich and poor, freemen and slaves—it causes a brand to be put on the right hand or on the forehead of every one of them, so that no one is able to buy or sell, except those that 17 bear this brand—either the name of the Beast or the number indicated by the letters of his name.   (Here there is need 18 for discernment.) Let him who has the ability compute the number of the Beast ; for the number indicates a man's name. Its number is six hundred and sixty-six.

Then, in my vision, I saw the Lamb standing on Mount 1 **14** Zion. With him were a hundred and forty-four thousand men, with his name and the name of his Father written on their foreheads. And I heard a sound from Heaven, 'like the 2 sound of many waters,' and like the sound of a loud peal of thunder ; the sound that I heard was like the music of harpers playing on their harps. They are singing what seems to be a 3 new song, before the throne, and before the four Creatures and the Councillors ; and no one was able to learn that song except the hundred and forty-four thousand who had been re-deemed from earth. These are the men who never defiled 4 themselves in their intercourse with women ; they are as pure as virgins. These are the men who follow the Lamb wherever he goes. They were redeemed as the first-fruits of mankind for God and for the Lamb. 'No lie was ever heard upon 5 their lips.' They are beyond reach of blame.

Then I saw another angel, flying in mid-heaven. He had 6 the Good News, decreed from eternity, to announce to those who dwell on the earth—to men of every nation, and tribe, and language, and people ; and he cried in a loud voice— 'Reverence God, and give him praise (for the hour of his 7 Judgement has come) and worship him who made the heaven and the earth and the sea and all springs of water.'

Then a second angel followed, crying—'She has fallen ! 8 She has fallen—Babylon the Great, who has made all the nations drink the maddening wine of her licentiousness !'

Then a third angel followed them, crying in a loud voice— 9 'Whoever worships the Beast and its image, and receives its

[15] Dan. 3. 5—6. [1] Ezek. 9. 4. [2] Ezek. 1. 24 ; 43. 2 (Hebrew) ; Dan. 10 6. [3] Ps. 144. 9. [5] Isa. 53. 9 ; Zeph. 3. 13. [7] Exod. 20. 11 ; Ps. 146. 6. [8] Isa. 21. 9 ; Dan. 4. 30 ; Jer. 51. 7—8.

brand on his forehead or on his hand, that man shall drink 10 the maddening wine of God that has been poured unmixed into the cup of his Wrath, and he shall be tortured with fire and sulphur before the eyes of the holy angels and before the eyes of the Lamb. The smoke from their torture rises for ever 11 and ever, and they have no rest day nor night—those who worship the Beast and its image, and all who are branded with its name.' (Here there is need for endurance on 12 the part of Christ's People—those who lay to heart the commands of God and the Faith of Jesus.)

Then I heard a voice from Heaven saying 'Write—" Blessed 13 are the dead who from this hour die in union with the Lord." " Yes," answers the Spirit, "that they may rest from their toil. Their good deeds go with them."'

Then, in my vision, I saw a white cloud, and on the cloud 14 there was sitting one 'like a man.' On his head he had a crown of gold, and in his hand a sharp sickle.

Then another angel came out from the Temple, crying in a 15 loud voice to him who was sitting on the cloud—' Take your sickle and reap, for the time to reap has come ; the Harvest of Earth is ready.' He who was sitting on the cloud brought 16 his sickle down upon the earth, and the Harvest of Earth was reaped.

Then another angel came out of the Temple in Heaven ; he, 17 also, had a sharp sickle.

Then another angel came out of the altar ; he had power 18 over fire, and he called in a loud voice to the angel that had the sharp sickle—' Take your sharp sickle, and gather the bunches from the Vine of Earth, for its grapes are ripe.' The 19 angel brought his sickle down on the earth and gathered the fruit of the Vine of Earth, and threw it into the great winepress of the Wrath of God. The 'grapes were trodden in 20 the press' outside the city ; and blood came out of the press, rising as high as the bridles of the horses for a distance of two hundred miles.

V.—The Vision of the Seven Curses.

Then I saw another portent in the heavens—a great and 1 **15** marvellous portent—seven angels with the seven last Curses ; because with them the Wrath of God is ended.

Then I saw what appeared to be a sea of glass mixed 2 with fire ; and, standing by this sea of glass, holding the harps of God, I saw those who had come victorious out of the conflict with the Beast and its image and the number that

10 Isa. 51. 17 ; Ps. 75. 8 ; Gen. 19. 24 ; Ezek. 38. 22.   11 Isa. 34. 10.
14 Dan. 7. 13 ; 10. 16.   15–20 Joel 3. 13.   1 Lev. 26. 21.

formed its name. They are singing the song of Moses, the **3** Servant of God, and the song of the Lamb—

'Great and marvellous are thy deeds, O Lord,
our God, the Almighty. Righteous and true are thy
ways, Eternal King. Who will not reverence and
praise thy Name, O Lord? Thou alone art holy! All **4**
nations will come and worship before thee, for thy
judgements have become manifest.'

After this I saw that the inmost shrine of the Tabernacle of **5**
Revelation in Heaven was opened, and out of it came the **6**
seven angels with the seven Curses. They were adorned with
precious stones, pure and bright, and had golden girdles
round their breasts. One of the four Creatures gave the seven **7**
angels seven golden bowls, filled with the Wrath of God
who lives for ever and ever. 'The Temple was filled with **8**
smoke from the Glory' and Majesty of God; and no one
could enter the Temple, until the seven Curses inflicted by the
seven angels were at an end. Then I heard a loud **1** **16**
voice, which came from the Temple, saying to the seven
angels—'Go and empty the seven bowls of the Wrath of God
upon the earth.'

The first angel went and emptied his bowl upon the **2**
earth; and it turned to loathsome and painful sores upon all
who bore the brand of the Beast and who worshipped its
image.

Then the second angel emptied his bowl upon the sea; and **3**
it turned to blood like the blood of a corpse, and every living
thing died—everything in the sea.

Then the third angel emptied his bowl upon the rivers and **4**
springs of water; and it turned to blood. And I heard **5**
the Angel of the Waters saying—'Righteous art thou, thou
who art and who wast, the Holy One, in inflicting this judgement; for men shed the blood of Christ's People and of the **6**
Prophets, and thou hast given them blood to drink. It is
what they deserve.' And I heard the response from the **7**
altar—'Yes, O Lord, our God, the Almighty, true and
righteous are thy judgements.'

Then the fourth angel emptied his bowl upon the sun; and **8**
he was permitted to scorch men with fire; and men were **9**
scorched by the intense heat. They blasphemed the Name of
God who controlled these Curses, yet they did not repent and
give him praise.

Then the fifth angel emptied his bowl upon the throne of the **10**

---

³ Exod. 15. 1; Josh. 14. 7; Ps. 111. 2; Exod. 34. 10; Ps. 139. 14; Amos 4. 13
(Septuagint); Deut. 32. 4; Jer. 10. 10 (Hebrew). ⁴ Jer. 10. 7 (Hebrew);
Ps. 86. 9; Mal. 1. 11; Deut. 32. 4; Ps. 145. 17. ⁵ Exod. 40. 34. ⁶ Lev. 26. 21;
Ezek. 28. 13. ⁸ Isa. 6. 4; Exod. 40. 34—35; Lev. 26. 21. ¹ Isa. 66. 6; Ps. 69. 24;
Jer. 10. 25; Zeph. 3. 8. ² Exod. 9. 9—1͡; Deut. 28. 35. ³ Exod. 7. 20 (Hebrew), 21.
⁴ Ps. 78. 44; Exod. 7. 20 (Hebrew). ⁵ Ps. 119. 137; Exod. 3. 14; Isa. 41. 4;
Deut. 32. 4; Ps. 145. 17. ⁶ Ps. 79. 3 Isa. 49. 26. ⁷ Amos 4. 13 (Septuagint);
Ps. 19. 9; 119. 137. ¹⁰ Exod. 10. 22.

Beast; and darkness fell upon its Kingdom. Men gnawed their tongues for pain, and blasphemed the God of Heaven, because of their pains and because of their sores; yet they did not repent of what they had done. 11

Then the sixth angel emptied his bowl upon the great river Euphrates; and the water in the river was dried up, so that the road for the Kings of the East might be made ready.   And I saw three foul spirits, like frogs, come from the mouth of the Dragon and from the mouth of the Beast and from the mouth of the false Prophet. They are the spirits of demons, and perform marvels; they go to kings all over the world, to collect them for the battle on the Great Day of Almighty God.   ('I am coming like a thief! Happy will he be who is on the watch, and keeps his clothing at hand, so that he will not have to walk about unclothed and let men see his nakedness.')   And the spirits collected the kings at the place called in Hebrew ' Har-Magedon.' 12 13 14 15 16

Then the seventh Angel emptied his bowl upon the air.   (A loud voice came from the throne in the Temple; it said ' All is over.')   There followed 'flashes of lightning, cries, and peals of thunder'; and there was a great earth-quake, such as had not occurred since man began to be upon the earth—none so great; and the great City was torn in three, and the cities of the nations fell, and God remembered Babylon the Great, and gave her the maddening wine-cup of his Wrath; and every island vanished, and the mountains disappeared. Great hailstones, a pound in weight, are falling upon men from the heavens. And men blasphemed God because of the Curse of the hail, for it was a very terrible Curse. 17 18 19 20 21

VI.—THE DOOM OF THE ENEMIES OF THE CHRIST.

Then one of the seven angels who held the seven bowls came and spoke to me. ' Come here,' he said, 'and I will show you the sentence passed upon that Great Harlot who is seated at the meeting of many waters, and with whom all the kings of the earth have had licentious intercourse; while all who live upon the earth have been made drunk by the wine of her licentiousness.' And he bore me away in a trance to a lonely place, and I saw a woman seated upon a scarlet Beast, which was covered with blasphemous names; it had seven heads and ten horns. The woman was clothed in purple and scarlet, and glittering with gold ornaments, precious stones, and pearls. In her hand she held a gold cup, full of idolatrous **17** 1 2 3 4

11 Dan. 2. 19 (Chaldaean).   12 Isa. 44. 27; Jer. 50. 38 (Hebrew); Gen. 15. 18; Deut. 1. 7; Josh. 1. 4; Isa. 41. 2, 25.   13 Exod. 8. 3.   14 Amos 4. 13 (Septuagint). 16 Zech. 12. 11 (Hebrew).   17 Isa. 66. 6.   18 Exod. 19. 16 (Hebrew and Septuagint); Dan. 12. 1.   19 Dan. 4. 30; Isa. 51. 17; Jer. 25. 15.   21 Exod. 9. 24. 1–2 Jer. 51. 13 (Hebrew), 7.   2 Isa. 23. 17 (Hebrew).   3 Dan. 7. 7.   4 Jer. 51. 7.

abominations, and the unclean fruits of her licentiousness; while on her forehead there was written this mystic name— 'BABYLON THE GREAT, THE MOTHER OF HARLOTS AND OF ALL IDOLATROUS ABOMINATIONS UPON EARTH.' And I saw the woman drunk with the blood of Christ's People and with the blood of the martyrs for Jesus.   When I saw her, I was amazed beyond measure; but the angel said to me—'Why were you amazed? I will tell you the mystic meaning of the vision of this woman, and of the Beast, with the seven heads and ten horns, that carries her. The Beast that you saw was, but is not, and is about to rise out of the bottomless pit, and is on its way to destruction. Those who are living on earth will be amazed—those whose names have not been written in the Book of Life from the foundation of the world—when they see that the Beast was, but is not, and yet will come.'   (Here there is need for the discerning mind.) The seven heads are seven mountains upon which the woman is seated. They are also seven kings; of whom five have fallen and one remains, while one is not yet come. When he comes, he must stay for a little while. So must the Beast that was, but is not. He counts as an eighth king, although he is one of the seven, and is on his way to destruction. The ten horns that you saw are ten kings, who have not yet received their kingdoms, but for an hour they receive the authority of kings, together with the Beast. These kings are of one mind in surrendering their power and authority to the Beast. They will fight with the Lamb, but the Lamb will conquer them, for he is Lord of lords and King of kings; so, too, will those with him who have received the Call and are chosen and faithful.   And the angel said to me—'The waters that you saw, where the Harlot is seated, are throngs of people and men of all nations and languages. The ten horns that you saw, and the Beast—they will hate the Harlot, and cause her to become deserted and strip her bare; they will eat her very flesh and utterly consume her with fire. For God has put it into their minds to carry out his purpose, in carrying out their common purpose and surrendering their kingdoms to the Beast, until God's decrees shall be executed. As for the woman whom you saw, she is the great city that holds sway over all the kings of the earth.'

After this I saw another angel, descending from Heaven, invested with great authority; and the earth was illuminated by his splendour. With a mighty voice he cried—'She has fallen! She has fallen—Babylon the Great! She has become an abode of demons, a stronghold of every wicked spirit, a stronghold of every foul and hateful bird. For, after drinking

⁵ Dan. 4. 30.   ⁸ Dan. 7. 3; 12. 1; Ps. 69. 28.   ¹² Dan. 7. 24.   ¹⁴ Deut. 10. 17; Dan. 2. 47. ¹⁵ Jer. 51. 13 (Hebrew). ¹⁸ Ps. 2. 2; 89. 27. ² Isa. 21. 9; Dan. 4. 30; Jer. 9. 11; Isa. 13. 21; 34. 14. ³ Jer. 51. 7; 25. 16, 27; Isa. 23. 17.

the maddening wine of her licentiousness, all the nations have fallen ; while all the kings of the earth have had licentious intercourse with her, and the merchants of the earth have grown rich through the excess of her luxury.'   Then I 4 heard another voice from Heaven saying—'Come out of her, my People, that you may not participate in her sins, and that you may not suffer from the Curses inflicted upon her. For 5 her sins are heaped up to the heavens, and God has not forgotten her misdeeds. Pay her back the treatment with which 6 she has treated you ; yes, repay twice over what her actions deserve ; in the cup which she mixed for you, mix for her as much again ; for her self-glorification and her luxury, give her 7 now an equal measure of torture and misery. In her heart she says ' I sit here a queen ; no widow am I ; I shall never know misery.' Therefore in one day shall these Curses befall 8 her—death, misery, and famine, and she shall be utterly consumed by fire ; for mighty is the Lord God who condemned her. All the kings of the earth who had licentious intercourse 9 with her and shared her luxury will weep and lament over her, when they see the smoke from the burning city, while they 10 stand at a distance, horrified at her torture, and cry—' Alas ! Alas ! Great City ! O mighty City of Babylon ! In a single hour your judgement fell. And the merchants of the earth 11 weep and wail over her, because no longer does any one buy their cargoes—their cargoes of gold, or silver, or precious 12 stones, or pearls, or fine linen, or purple robes, or silk, or scarlet cloth ; nor their many scented woods ; nor their many articles of ivory ; nor their many articles of choicest wood, or brass, or iron, or marble ; nor their cinnamon, or spice, or incense, 13 or perfumes, or frankincense, or wine, or oil, or fine flour, or wheat, or cattle, or sheep ; nor their horses, or chariots, or slaves ; nor the bodies and souls of men. The fruit 14 that your soul craved is no longer within your reach, and all dainties and luxuries are lost to you, never to be found again.' The merchants who sold these things, and grew rich 15 by her, will stand at a distance weeping and wailing, horrified at her torture, and crying—' Alas ! Alas ! Great City ! O City 16 clothed in fine linen, and purple, and scarlet cloth ! O City adorned with gold ornaments, and precious stones, and pearls ! In a single hour your vast wealth vanished.' Every ship's 17 captain and all who sail to any port, and sailors, and all who get their living from the sea, stood at a distance, and seeing 18 the smoke from the burning city, cried—' What city can compare with the Great City ?' They threw dust on their heads, 19 and, as they wept and wailed, they cried—' Alas ! Alas ! Great

4–5 Jer. 51. 6, 9, 45.   6 Ps. 137. 8 ; Jer. 50. 29 ;   7–8 Isa. 47. 7—9.   8 Jer. 50. 34. 9 Ezek. 26. 16—17 ;   27. 30, 33 ; Ps. 48. 4 (Septuagint) ; Ezek. 27. 35 ; Isa. 23. 17. 10 Dan. 4. 30 ; Ezek. 26. 17.   11 Ezek. 27. 36, 31.   13 Ezek. 27. 13.   15 Ezek. 27. 36, 31. 17 Ezek. 27. 28—29.   18 Ezek. 27. 32.   19 Ezek. 27. 30—31, 36, 33, 9 ; 26. 19.

City! All who have ships on the sea grew rich through her magnificence. In a single hour it has vanished.' Rejoice over her, O Heaven, and People of Christ, and Apostles, and Prophets, for God has avenged you on her! 20

Then a mighty angel took up a stone like a great millstone, and threw it into the sea, crying—'So shall Babylon, the Great City, be violently overthrown, never more to be seen. No more shall the music of harpers, or minstrels, or fluteplayers, or trumpeters be heard in you; no more shall any worker, skilled in any art, be found in you; no more shall the sound of a mill be heard in you; no more shall the light of a lamp shine in you; no more shall the voices of bridegroom and bride be heard in you. Your merchants were the great men of the earth, for all the nations were deceived by your magical charms. Yes, and in her was to be found the blood of the Prophets and of Christ's People, and of all who have been put to death upon the earth.' 21 22 23 24

After this, I heard what seemed to be a great shout from a vast throng in Heaven, crying— 1 **19**

'Hallelujah! To our God belong Salvation, and Glory, and Power, for true and righteous are his judgements. For he has passed judgement upon the Great Harlot who was corrupting the earth by her licentiousness, and he has taken vengeance upon her for the blood of his servants.' 2

Again they cried—'Hallelujah!' And the smoke from her ruins rises for ever and ever. Then the twenty-four Councillors and the four Creatures prostrated themselves and worshipped God who was seated upon the throne, crying—'Amen, Hallelujah!'; and from the throne there came a voice which said— 3 4 5

'Praise our God all you who serve him,
You who reverence him, both high and low.'

Then I heard 'what seemed to be the shout of a vast throng, like the sound of many waters,' and like the sound of loud peals of thunder, crying— 6

'Hallelujah! For the Lord is King, our God, the Almighty. Let us rejoice and exult; and we will pay him honour, for the hour for the Marriage of the Lamb has come, and his Bride has made herself ready. And to her it has been granted to robe herself in fine linen, white and pure, for that linen is the good deeds of the People of Christ.' 7 8

20 Deut. 32. 43.   21 Jer. 51. 63—64; Ezek. 26. 21; Dan. 4. 30.   22 Ezek. 26. 13.
22—23 Jer. 25. 10 (Hebrew).   23 Isa. 23. 8; 47. 9.   24 Jer. 51. 49.   1 Ps. 104. 35.
2 Ps. 19. 9; 119. 137; Deut. 32. 43; 2 Kings 9. 7.   3 Isa. 34. 10.   3—4 Ps. 104. 35.
4 Isa. 6. 1; Ps. 47. 8.   5 Ps. 134. 1; 135. 1; 22. 23; 115. 13.   6 Dan. 10. 6;
Ezek. 1. 24; 43. 2 (Hebrew); Ps. 104. 35; 93. 1; 99. 1; Amos 4. 13 (Septuagint);
6—7 Ps. 97. 1.

Then a voice said to me 'Write—" Blessed are those who 9
have been summoned to the marriage feast of the Lamb."'
And the voice said—' These words of God are true.' I 10
prostrated myself at the feet of him who spoke to worship him,
but he said to me—' Forbear ; I am your fellow-servant, and
the fellow-servant of your Brothers who bear their testimony
to Jesus. Worship God. For to bear testimony to Jesus
needs the inspiration of the Prophets.'

Then I saw that Heaven lay open. There appears a white 11
horse ; its rider is called ' Faithful ' and ' True ' ; righteously
does he judge and make war. His eyes are flaming fires ; on 12
his head there are many diadems, and he bears a name, written, which no one knows but himself ; he has been clothed in 13
a garment sprinkled with blood ; and the name by which he
is called is ' The Word of God.' The armies of Heaven 14
followed him, mounted on white horses and clothed in fine
linen, white and pure. From his mouth comes a sharp sword, 15
with which ' to smite the nations ; and he will rule them with
an iron rod.' He ' treads the grapes in the press ' of the
maddening wine of the Wrath of Almighty God ; and on his 16
robe and on his thigh he has this name written— ' KING OF
KINGS AND LORD OF LORDS.'

Then I saw an angel standing on the sun. He cried in a 17
loud voice to all the birds that fly in mid-heaven—' Gather
and come to the great feast of God, to eat the flesh of kings, 18
and the flesh of commanders, and the flesh of mighty men,
and the flesh of horses and their riders, and the flesh of all
freemen and slaves, and of high and low.'

Then I saw the Beast and the kings of the earth and their 19
armies, gathered together to fight with him who sat on the
horse and with his army. The Beast was captured, and with 20
him was taken the false Prophet, who performed the marvels
before the eyes of the Beast, with which he deceived those
who had received the brand of the Beast and those who
worshipped his image. Alive, they were thrown, both of
them, into the fiery lake ' of burning sulphur.' The rest were 21
killed by the sword which came out of the mouth of him who
rode upon the horse ; and all the birds fed upon their flesh.

Then I saw an angel coming down from Heaven, with the 1 **20**
key of the bottomless pit and a great chain in his hand. He 2
seized the Dragon, the primeval Serpent (who is the ' Devil '
or ' Satan '), and bound him in chains for a thousand years.
He flung him into the bottomless pit and locked it, and set 3
his seal upon it ; that he should not deceive the nations any

[11] Ezek. 1. 1 ; Ps. 96. 13. [12] Dan. 10. 6. [15] Isa. 11. 4 ; Ps. 2. 8—9 ; Joel 3. 13 ;
Amos 4. 13 (Septuagint). [16] Deut. 10. 17 ; Dan. 2. 47. [17—18] Ezek. 39. 17—18, 20.
[19] Ps. 2. 2. [20] Gen. 19. 24 ; Isa. 30. 33 ; Ezek. 38. 22. [21] Ezek. 39. 17—18, 20,
[2] Gen. 3. 1 ; Zech. 3. 1—2 (Septuagint and Hebrew).

more, until the thousand years were ended. After that he must be let loose for a while.

Then I saw thrones, and to those who took their seats 4
upon them authority was given to act as judges. And I saw the souls of those who had been beheaded because of the testimony to Jesus and because of the Message of God, for they had refused to worship the Beast or its image, and had not received the brand on their foreheads and on their hands. They were restored to life, and they reigned with the Christ for a thousand years. (The rest of the dead were not 5
restored to life till the thousand years were ended.) This is the First Resurrection. Blessed and holy will he be who 6
shares in that First Resurrection. The second Death has no power over them ; but they will be priests of God and the Christ, and they will reign with him for the thousand years.

When the thousand years are ended, Satan will be let loose 7
from his prison, and he will come out to deceive the nations 8
that live in 'the four corners of the earth—Gog and Magog.' He will come to gather them together for battle ; and their number will be as great as the sand on the sea-shore. They 9
went up over the breadth of the whole earth, and surrounded the camp of Christ's People and the beloved city. Then fire fell from the heavens and consumed them ; and the Devil, 10
their deceiver, was hurled into the lake of fire and sulphur, where the Beast and the false Prophet already were, and they will be tortured day and night for ever and ever.

Then I saw a great white throne, and him who was seated 11
on it. 'The earth and the heavens fled from his presence ; no place was left for them.' And I saw the dead, high and 12
low, standing before the throne ; and books were opened. Then another book was opened, the Book of Life ; and the dead were judged, according to their actions, by what was written in the books. The sea gave up its dead, and Death 13
and the Lord of the Place of Death gave up their dead ; and they were judged, one by one, each according to his actions. Then Death and the Lord of the Place of Death were hurled 14
into the lake of fire. This is the Second Death—the lake of fire ; and all whose names 'were not found written in the 15
Book of Life' were hurled into the lake of fire.

VII.—The New Creation.

Then I saw new heavens and a new earth. The former 1   **21**
heavens and the former earth had passed away ; and the sea has ceased to be. And I saw the Holy City, Jerusalem, 2

[4] Dan. 7. 9—10, 22. [6] Isa. 61. 6. [8] Ezek. 7. 2 ; 38. 2. [9] Hab. 1. 6; Ecclus. 24. 11 ; 2 Kings 1. 10. [10] Gen. 19. 24 ; Ezek. 38. 22. [11] Isa. 6. 1 ; Dan. 7. 9; Ps. 114. 7, 3 ; Dan. 2. 35 (Chaldaean). [12] Dan. 7. 10 ; Ps. 69. 28. [12—13] Ps. 28. 4 ; 62. 12 ; Jer. 17. 10. [15] Dan. 12, 1 ; Ps. 69. 28. [1] Isa. 65. 17 ; 66. 22. [2] Isa. 52. 1 ; 61. 10.

descending new out of Heaven from God, like a bride adorned in readiness for her husband. And I heard a loud voice from 3 the throne, which said—'See! the Tabernacle of God is set up among men. God will dwell among them, and they will 4 be his Peoples, and God himself will be among them, and he will wipe away all tears from their eyes. There will be no more death, nor will there be any more grief or crying or pain. The old order has passed away.' And he who was seated on the 5 throne said—'See, I make all things new!' And he said— 'Write this, for these words may be trusted and are true.' And he said to me—'They are fulfilled. I am the Alpha and 6 the Omega, the Beginning and the End. To him who thirsts I will give of the spring of the Water of Life, freely. He who 7 conquers shall enter into possession of these things, and I will be his God, and he shall be my Son. But as for cowards, un- 8 believers, the degraded, murderers, the impure, sorcerers, idolaters, and all liars—their place will be in the burning lake of fire and sulphur. That is the Second Death.'

Then one of the seven angels who had the seven bowls, and 9 were laden with the seven last Curses, came and spoke to me. 'Come here,' he said, 'and I will show you the Bride, the Wife of the Lamb.' He carried me away in a trance to a great 10 high mountain, and showed me Jerusalem, the Holy City, descending out of Heaven from God, filled with the glory of 11 God. Its brilliance was like that of some very precious stone, like a jasper, transparent as crystal. It had a great high 12 wall, in which were twelve gates; and at these gates there were twelve angels, and there were names inscribed on the gates, the names of the twelve tribes of the Israelites. 'There 13 were three gates on the east, three gates on the north, three gates on the south, and three gates on the west.' The wall of 14 the City had twelve foundation stones, on which were the twelve names of the twelve Apostles of the Lamb. And the 15 angel who was speaking to me had as a measure a gold rod, with which to measure the City and its gates and its wall. The City is square; the length and the breadth are the 16 same. The angel measured with his rod; it was twelve hun- dred miles; its length, and breadth, and height are equal. Then he measured the wall; it was two hundred and eighty- 17 eight feet, as men measure, that is as the angel measured. The material of the wall of the City was jasper, and the City 18 was built of pure gold, which shone like clear glass. The 19 foundations of the wall of the City were ornamented with every kind of precious stone. The first foundation stone was

3 Ezek. 37. 27; Zech. 2. 10—11; Isa. 8. 8. 4 Isa. 25. 8; Jer. 31. 16; Isa. 65. 19, 17. 5 Isa. 6. 1; Ps. 47. 8; Isa. 43. 19. 6 Isa. 55. 1; Zech. 14. 8. 7 2 Sam. 7. 14; Ps. 89. 26. 8 Gen. 19. 24; Isa. 30. 33; Ezek. 38. 22. 9 Lev. 26. 21. 10 Ezek. 40. 1—2; Isa. 52. 1. 11 Isa. 58. 8; 60. 1—2, 19. 12—13 Ezek. 48. 31—34 (Hebrew). 15—17 Ezek. 40. 3, 5. 16 Ezek. 43. 16. 18—19 Isa. 54. 11—12.

a jasper; the second a sapphire; the third a chalcedony; the
fourth an emerald; the fifth a sardonyx; the sixth a carnelian;   20
the seventh a chrysolite; the eighth a beryl; the ninth a topaz;
the tenth a chrysoprase; the eleventh a hyacinth; and the
twelfth an amethyst.   The twelve gates were made of twelve   21
pearls, each gate of one pearl.   The street of the City was of
pure gold, transparent as glass.   And I saw no Temple   22
there, for the Lord, our God, the Almighty, and the Lamb are
its Temple.   The City has no need of 'the sun or the moon to   23
shine upon it, for the Glory of God illuminated it,' and its
Lamp was the Lamb.   'The nations walk by the light of it;   24
and the kings of the earth bring their glory into it.   Its gates   25
will never be shut by day,' and there will be no night there.
And men will bring the glory and honour of the nations into   26
it.   'Never shall any unhallowed thing enter it,' nor he whose   27
life is shameful and false, but only 'those whose names have
been written in the Lamb's Book of Life.'   And the angel   1   **22**
showed me 'a river of the Water of Life,' as clear as crystal,
issuing from the throne of God and of the Lamb, in the middle   2
of the street of the City.   On each side of the river was a Tree
of Life which bore twelve kinds of fruit, yielding its fruit
each month; and the leaves of the tree were for the healing
of the nations.   'Every thing that is accursed will cease to   3
be.'   The throne of God and of the Lamb will be within it,
and his servants will worship him; they will see his face, and   4
his name will be on their foreheads.   Night will cease to be.   5
They have no need of the light of a lamp, nor have they the
light of the sun; for the 'Lord God will be their light, and
they will reign for ever and ever.'

VIII.—Conclusion.

Then the angel said to me—'These words may be trusted   6
and are true.   The Lord, the God that inspires the Prophets,
sent his angel to show his servants what must quickly take
place; and he said "I will come quickly."   Blessed will he   7
be who lays to heart the words of the prophecy contained in
this book.'

It was I, John, who heard and saw these things; and, when   8
I heard and saw them, I prostrated myself in worship at the
feet of the angel that showed them to me.   But he said to   9
me—'Forbear; I am your fellow-servant, and the fellow-
servant of your Brothers, the Prophets, and of all who lay to
heart the words in this book.   Worship God.'

Then the angel said to me—'Do not keep secret the words   10

22 Amos 4. 13 (Septuagint).   23–26 Isa. 60. 1–3, 6, 10–11, 13, 19.   24 Ps. 89. 27.
27 Isa. 52. 1; Dan. 12. 1; Ps. 69. 28.   1 Zech. 14. 8.   1–2 Gen. 2. 9–10; 3. 22;
Ezek. 47. 1, 7, 12.   3 Zech. 14. 11.   4 Ps. 17. 15.   5 Isa. 60. 19; Dan. 7. 18.
6 Dan. 2. 28.   7 Isa. 40. 10.   10 Dan. 12. 4.

of the prophecy contained in this book; for The Time is
near. Let the wrong-doer continue to do wrong; the filthy-
minded man continue to be filthy; the righteous man continue
to act righteously; and the holy-minded man continue to
be holy.' ('I will come quickly. I bring my rewards
with me, to give to each man what his actions deserve. I am
the Alpha and the Omega, the First and the Last, the Beginning and the End.') Blessed will they be who wash
their robes, that they may have the right to approach the Tree
of Life, and may enter the City by the gates. Outside will
be the filthy, the sorcerers, the impure, the murderers, the
idolaters, and all who love the false and live it.'

'I, Jesus, sent my angel to bear testimony to you about
these things before the Churches. I am the Scion and the
Offspring of David, the bright Star of the Morning.'

'Come,' say the Spirit and the Bride; and let him who
hears say 'Come.' Let him who thirsts come; let him who
will take the Water of Life freely.

I declare to all who hear the words of the prophecy contained in this book—'If anyone adds to it, God will add to his
troubles the Curses described in this book; and if any one
takes away any of the words in the book containing this
prophecy, God will take away his share in the Tree of Life,
and in the Holy City—as described in this book.'

He whose testimony this is says—'Assuredly I will come
quickly.' 'Amen, come, Lord Jesus.'

May the blessing of the Lord Jesus Christ, be with his
People.

¹² Isa. 40. 10; Ps. 28. 4; 62. 12; Jer. 17. 10. ¹³ Isa. 44. 6 (Hebrew); 48. 12
(Hebrew). ¹⁴ Gen. 49. 11; 2. 9; 3. 22. ¹⁶ Isa. 11. 10. ¹⁷ Isa. 55. 1; Zech. 14. 8.
¹⁸⁻¹⁹ Deut. 4. 2; 12. 32; 29. 20. ¹⁹ Gen. 2. 9; 3. 22.

CHATHAM:
W. & J. MACKAY & CO., LTD.